THE CHARTIST MOVEMENT IN BRITAIN
1838–1850
Volume 4

THE CHARTIST MOVEMENT
IN BRITAIN
1838–1850

Volume 4

Edited by
Gregory Claeys

LONDON
PICKERING & CHATTO
2001

Published by Pickering & Chatto (Publishers) Limited
21 Bloomsbury Way, London, WC1A 2TH

Old Post Road, Brookfield, Vermont 05036, USA

www.pickeringchatto.com

BRITISH LIBRARY CATALOGUING IN PUBLICATION DATA
The Chartist Movement in Britain, 1838–1850
    1. Chartism. 2. Labor movement – Great Britain – History – 19th century.
I. Claeys, Gregory.
322.4'4'0941

ISBN 1851963308

LIBRARY OF CONGRESS CATALOGING-IN-PUBLICATION DATA
The Chartist movement in Britain, 1838–1850 / edited by Gregory Claeys.
    p. cm.
    A collection of pamphlets by Chartist writers.
    ISBN 1-85196-330-8 (alk. paper)
    1. Chartism. 1. Claeys, Gregory.

HD8396.C536 2001
322'.2'094109034–dc21   00-053031

Typeset by P&C

Printed and bound by
Bookcraft (Bath) Ltd,
Midsomer Norton

CONTENTS

RIGHTS OF LABOUR.

WITH PROPOSALS FOR A NEW BASIS
FOR THE NATIONAL SUFFRAGE.[1]
By Thomas Bailey.[2]

LONDON: G. & J. DYER, PATERNOSTER-ROW;
NOTTINGHAM: E. RENALS, SOUTH-PARADE;
MANCHESTER: BOWLER, WHEELER, AND HAYWOOD;
STOCKPORT: LOMAN AND SONS; ADVERTISER OFFICE;
ASHTON-UNDER-LYNE: CUNNINGHAM; AND ALL BOOKSELLERS.
1844.

---

1 One edn, Nottingham, 1844, 60 pp.

2 Thomas Bailey (1785–1856), Nottingham silk hosier, then wine merchant, member of Nottingham town council 1835–43, editor of the *Nottingham Mercury* 1846–52, author of *Annals of Nottinghamshire* (4 vols, 1852–5), *Records of Longevity* (1857), *The Advent of Charity, and Other Poems* (1851), *A Discourse on the Causes of Political Revolutions* (c. 1831), *A Letter to Earl Grey, on the Necessity of Fixing a Principle of Representation in the Constitution* (1831), *Village Reform* (1854).

DEDICATION.

To the labouring population of the United Kingdom – the toiling millions in whose persevering industry, and unrivalled skill, is laid the foundations of Britain's commercial and political greatness – these pages are respectfully dedicated by their sincere friend and well-wisher,

THE AUTHOR.

Basford, near Nottingham,
November 21, 1844.

RIGHTS OF LABOUR.

If it be true that the study of the laws and institutions by which any given society is governed, and the bearing they have upon the happiness and well-being of such community generally, constitute one of the most interesting and important inquiries to which the mind of the politician and moralist of such country can be directed, then is the present existing excitement in the public mind of Britain, on the subject and tendencies of her gigantic manufacturing establishments, which have produced, by their operation, during the last seventy years, so important a change in the social habits and moral condition of the millions of its population, and is, in a greater or lesser degree, working a similar change in the state and condition of the people of every region of the civilized world, nor only fully justified, and accounted for, but every attempt made, however humble, to solve the important problems which these new social relations of mankind present to the reflecting mind, ought not only to be tolerated, but encouraged.

This plea, I scruple not to avow, I am induced to put forward as my apology with the public, for attempting to grapple with the difficult subject of providing a remedy for a portion of the evils which have flowed, and are still flowing, to the laboring classes, from the want of proper legislative protection of their interests; – from which want of proper legislative protection, the enormous wealth accumulated in the hands of a portion of the community, by means of the matchless skill and untiring industry of our laboring population, has been made but the means of rendering that skill and industry, now, to a considerable extent, unavailing to the procurement for themselves and families, even the ordinary comforts of civilized life.

Never has there been, in the history of the world, such opportunity for the generous, philosophic mind of man to indulge in high and refined theories on the elevating destinies of the species, as in this country during the last fifty years, and more especially during the latter half of that period. All that the moralist, the patriot, the philanthropist could desire, as a fair field in which to try the noble experiment of the steady advancement of a nation in a career of public prosperity and private happiness, has been, in appearance at least, conceded to him, by the course of events connected with the history of this country during the present century. War suspended, except upon a very limited scale, and in the most remote parts of the world, during the lives of a generation – commerce extended to every region of the habitable globe – the useful and ornamental arts of life encouraged both by the Government and individual members of the community beyond any former period – knowledge diffused through all ranks of society, and religion patronized and promulgated with a zeal and a liberality which are unparalleled in the history of Christendom – while agriculture, manufactures, navigation, and science, fostered and encouraged by the most ample remuneration and boundless munificence, have all joined their mighty streams, and poured through a thousand channels the countless riches derived by the skill, and industry, and enterprise of those engaged in the prosecution of their stupendous undertakings, into the national treasury; presenting, in the aggregate of benefits bestowed on the community, a spectacle of moral and political grandeur, unknown to any other country, in any region of the world, or period of its history.

To the mind of a speculative political economist, living at a distance from the scene, in such a community as that of Britain, not an element of social prosperity – not an ingredient of individual happiness would appear to be wanting: every one would seem to have been cared for – every evil thing to have been guarded against. Yet what is the *real* state of British society, after half a century thus passed in the enjoyment of the fruits of these splendid achievements in the useful arts? – after the most extraordinary developement and application of industrial power among our humbler classes of citizens, and the realization of the most comprehensive and curiously elaborated plans and schemes for the advancement of trade, and the perfection of manufactures, which the world has ever beheld? Distress, privation, and consequent dissatisfaction among the labouring classes, to an extent never before witnessed!

The late commotions in the manufacturing districts, and the outrages on property still more recently perpetrated in the agricultural counties, have aroused, in every reflecting mind, a deep consideration of the dangers of the future. We all feel that we have been within a stage of an universal 'servile war,' if it can even yet be said that we are freed from the danger. When the GIANT LABOUR, in a fit of gloomy resentment from the injuries he had sustained, and the privations he was enduring, flung down the implements of his drudgery, and raised himself, in an attitude of bold defiance against those lords to whose service, and for whose aggrandisement, principally, he had so long and so patiently endured those wrongs and insults, who did not tremble for the consequences which every hour might bring forth? And though the mighty one has again returned, with seeming complacency, to his servile tasks, no one but must feel apprehensive that the sense of injuries endured, and still unabated, which awakened that awful, though momentary phrenzy through his frame, may still throb in the pulses of the millions, and lead them, under some event of national adversity, to that most awful of all convulsions in the body politic, an indiscriminate war of labour against property.

The manufacturing labourers of the country are now again, apparently, quietly engaged in the prosecution of their ordinary industrial pursuits; but are they, because quiet, contented with their condition? for, without this feeling predominates among them, there can be no security for society. The terrors of the law may have restrained the expression of their violence, but the terrors of the law cannot convey to their bosoms the feeling of contentment, whilst smarting under a sense of wrong and injustice inflicted on them by their employers, under security of that law, which is only powerless when their interests are required to be promoted, and their labour protected. The punishments of law, or the terrors of military execution, may keep vast masses of discontented men for a while in subjection; but they can only be rendered contented and trustworthy by the exercise of justice and humanity.

An hundred considerations have rushed upon the public mind of Britain, in consequence of the outbreaks of 1842, in the manufacturing districts, to which, it appears, previously, to have been an almost entire stranger. Every one is now inquiring what is to be done to avert the possibly future mischief? Can an extension of foreign commerce, through the operation of what is termed the Free Trade system, meet the difficulties of the case, and avert the dangers to which we are exposed? Can restrictions on the creations of the mechanician, or the removal of the fiscal restraints at present imposed on the importation of food, raise the condition of the manufacturing and agricultural labourer to that permanent condition of comfort, when there shall be, at all times, something like a just equilibrium between their wants, and their means of supplying them – between their power to consume, and their ability to purchase? I shall not attempt to enter at length into a discussion of any of these nostrums, or of their efficacy to meet the disease at present preying on the vitals of British society: but shall, as briefly as possible, assign the reasons which lead me to entertain the opinion, that none of these proposed remedies are sufficiently direct and powerful in their operation, to meet the exigencies of the case at issue.

If the further extension of foreign commerce, through the exportation of the manufactures of this country, was a sure and certain *panacea* for the removal of the miseries inflicted on the manufacturing operatives of Lancashire and Yorkshire, and the agricultural labourers of Suffolk and Essex, by excessive toil and low wages, their condition ought to be so much the better as the present amount of goods exported exceeds that exported twenty, thirty, or forty years ago. But if no such benefit has arisen to the labourers of these important districts, from the vast increase which has already taken place in the exportation to foreign countries of the products of our looms and factories, but, on the contrary, their condition has progressively deteriorated, through a number of years, then I cannot perceive how any given additional amount to what is *now* exported, shall necessarily produce a result the opposite of what has already been obtained by the exports being doubled, triplicated or quadrupled, beyond what they were in time past.

My opinion is, that no material increase can take place in the amount of manufactured goods sent from this country to foreign parts, but what must result in a further deterioration in the remuneration paid for labour here; and from this cause, that you will have to enter still poorer markets than those you have hitherto supplied, and compete with labourers still worse paid than those with whom you have hitherto engaged in competition. To render useless and unemployed the native looms which at present supply the hundreds of millions of Hindoostan, and China, and Japan, with the simple habiliments in which they are clothed, you must furnish them with fabrics in their own markets, after importing the raw material from them, and transmitting it, wrought into cloth, back again ten thousand miles by sea, and from one hundred to four or five thousand by inland

conveyance, at a less price than they have been accustomed to pay for such articles; and this you can accomplish only by such a diminution in the cost of
production, by one means or another, as shall be equivalent to all the charges
incurred, and the difference added of the cost of living to your operatives, arising
from taxation and national habits, as compared with the labourers against whom
they are competing.

When you have accomplished all this, and made sure that such countries will
demand a continually increasing supply of goods, proportionate to your continually increasing power of production, and that they can furnish you with an
amount of raw manufacturing material, or articles of subsistence or luxury,
needed by you, in exchange for the goods so exported – and invoiced to you at a
less price, or, at most, no greater than you could obtain the same description of
articles for in markets several thousand miles nearer home – you have to encounter the additional disadvantage that the price at which you must henceforth
supply all the richer markets, and even the wealthiest of your customers at home
– must be on the same reduced scale of remuneration as that which you have
been enabled to realize in the poorest markets of the world. There is no fact connected with manufacturing, better established than this – that you cannot, at
your option, give a higher and a lower price for making the same article, according to the different markets to which it may be intended the goods shall be sent.
A higher price may be, and undoubtedly is, occasionally obtained by the merchant in one market than is realized in another, according to the circumstances
of his transaction; but this does not affect the rate of wages, nor the general cost
of production, in the producing country, which must be always, in the long run,
regulated by the price which can be obtained in the poorest market to which the
manufacturer sends his goods. How it shall possibly be, then, that a wider diffusion of British manufactures amongst still poorer markets, and in the face of still
lower paid labour than those you have previously been in possession of, or hitherto had to compete against, shall enrich the British operative, I confess myself
at loss to comprehend.

Providence, it would seem, has, for beneficent purposes, set bounds to national
as well as individual concupiscence. The man who attempts to sweep all the
world into his net, commonly finds that its meshes break with their load. And
the same fatality, ordinarily, awaits the greedy ambition of empires to monopolize
the political or commercial power of the world. Much more might be said on this
subject, but I hasten on to the consideration of the subject of restriction on the
employment of machinery, as a cure for the privations and cruel drudgery at
present so extensively inflicted on the working classes of this country. That the
application of mechanical power to the multiplication of manufactured products
requires regulation, and some interference of the Legislature where it inflicts even
only temporary loss and privation on any portion of the industrious classes, I am
fully convinced: that you can safely attempt to restrict its use or employment
within given limits, I hold to be impossible. Mechanical power applied to the uses
of social life, is not one of the things to which you can wisely say, 'hitherto shalt

thou come, but no further.' So to act would be to drive man back again, by rapid stages, to the condition of barbarism.

It is the glory and triumph of mind to make inert matter subservient to its lofty will, and the advancement of its daring purposes. Legislation ought not to prevent, if it could, the erection of a factory, or even an individual machine, which, singly, might be able to produce as much yarn or calico as is at present produced by the united power of all the machinery in operation throughout the whole Lancashire district, could the genius of man enable him to perfect such a wonderful agent of production. But it ought to take care – and if the affairs of the nation were continually under the supervision of an enlightened and paternal Government, care would be taken – that one or two individuals did not derive the sole, or principal, benefit from such a splendid discovery as this would be; but that all the population of Lancashire at present employed in the manufacture of yarn or calico, as well as their descendants, were enabled to derive a joint benefit from its operations. Not a single labourer, or his child, ought to be the worse off for such a signal triumph of the genius of the mechanician as this would be; but, on the contrary, all ought to be better provided for: when all would have cause to rejoice, and all would really participate in the exultation which civilized man everywhere would indulge in at such a splendid triumph of mind over matter. And this principle ought, in its degree, to apply to all improvements in machinery.

The people, universally, would then have an interest, direct and personal, in the advance of mechanical improvement. Nor would there, or could there, be a single wish in their minds to retard or limit the application of such power to the furtherance of all the useful or ornamental arts of life. But the evil of the present system of things is, that the industrious operative is being continually forced into more severe competition with new and more rapid methods of producing the fabrics on which he has been accustomed to employ his labour, or is altogether superseded in the manufacture, without any measures being taken by the Legislature of his country, that the vested interest which he has in his peculiar property, his labour – an interest as valid, and in truth much more sacred, than the interest which can be holden in any other property or privilege – is, in the least degree, provided for, either permanently or temporarily. I do not want to withhold from capital or talent its fair share of the benefit sought to be derived from such improvements – I would even grant to both a large reward, or at least allow them the most ample opportunities of remunerating themselves for all the toils and risks they have run, in perfecting, or maturing, a scheme which shall have had the effect of cheapening any of the comforts or necessaries of life, and thus, it may be, virtually, of adding to the property of every man in society, by increasing his power to purchase other needed articles for himself and family.

In thus giving scope and verge to capital, however, to add to its stores, and to talent to acquire wealth, as the reward of industry and ingenuity, I would not forget the interests of the thousands of sentient labourers to whom this inanimate producer may have become a formidable and dreaded rival: nor the tens of thousands who are continually pressing forward into existence as their successors in increasing numbers.

I have now only a few words to say on the other proposed remedy for the bettering of the condition of the labouring classes, by the repeal, or extensive modification, of the laws which regulate the importation of corn and other necessaries of life into these kingdoms. For a Legislature to pass laws which should absolutely restrict the supply of food to be furnished to a continually-increasing population, to such an amount as should, by reason of its price, allow but a *minimum* means of subsistence to millions, would be an act at once of the greatest folly and the most crying injustice; and, if it can be clearly shown that the Corn and Provision Laws of this country have such an effect, there cannot be a doubt but they ought forthwith to be totally repealed. Again, if it be true, as I have stated above, that whatever tends to cheapen or reduce the money-value of any of the necessaries of life in the same ratio, increases the value of the property of every man in society, by adding to his power to purchase other articles needed for the comfort of himself and family, then, with a due regard to temporary and existing interests, there can likewise be no doubt that these laws ought forthwith to be put into a state for total abrogation. My own opinion, however, is, (and I shall not shrink from avowing it here, as on other occasions) that the greatest amount of delusion is in existence in the public mind of Britain on this subject, which ever pervaded it at any period, or on any other matter or thing. Nor is that delusion, I apprehend, confined either to the pro-Corn Law, or anti-Corn Law party, but attaches to both: the one, I believe, as much overrates the benefit to be derived by the people at large from the repeal of these laws, as the other overstates the mischiefs which would flow upon the agricultural body, and by reaction upon the nation generally, from the removal of the enactments at present in force for the protection against unlimited importation.

If at full supply of the necessaries of life, derived from the labours of the native agriculturalist, can be obtained, and at as reasonable a price, through a series of years, as they *would be furnished to our markets by the foreigner, were we to have recourse to him for a large amount of produce raised expressly to meet our wants*, then it is clear, that no benefit would arise to the population generally from a repeal of the laws not in force to regulate such importation, either by reason of a diminution in price, or an increased demand for exchanges in the shape of manufactured goods; for, if we now take 10,000,000 quarters of grain from the agriculturalists of this country, for the supply of the general manufacturing and non-agricultural population, and were, in case of a repeal of the Corn Law, to take the same amount from foreigners, it is clear that this could create no additional stimulus to the corn market of this country. Whatever the manufacturing population purchases of the agricultural, for the supply of their wants, or the carrying on of their processes, whether it be food, fuel, metals, or timber, it can only be paid for in the products of their industry – that is, in manufactured goods of some kind or other. The whole of commercial transactions is but an elaborate system of barter; and this barter, or exchange, as certainly and fully takes place between the manufacturer and the agriculturalist at home, through the medium of the domestic shopkeeper, for whatever the former purchases of the products of the latter, as it does between the foreign cultivator of the soil, through the medium of the wholesale or shipping merchant. But there is this advantage arises to the non-agricultural population, from expending fifty millions, or any other given sum, annually, in their domestic markets, in the purchase of the necessaries of life, over what would arise to them from purchasing the same amount in value of such necessaries in foreign and distant markets; that, whereas, foreigners chiefly purchase but those articles on which, comparatively, little manual labour has been bestowed, such as cotton and woollen goods, the produce of our power-looms and spinning jennies, the native or domestic land proprietor and cultivator takes in payment, for the use of his capital, and the employment of his strength and skill in the cultivation of the soil, most of the elegancies of life in which he is enabled to indulge himself – those articles on which the greatest amount of manual labour is bestowed – as well as his necessaries, thus furnishing a vastly-increased demand for better, and higher paid, labour, than would, or could, by possibility, be created, were the bread and meat, and other agricultural products which we consume, purchased of foreign land proprietors and cultivators, instead of native. My own opinion is, that from the operation of one cause or another, no important reduction in the price of bread, in this country, would take place, on an average of years, from any modification of the present laws for regulating the importation of corn, as such importation would not, materially, exceed in amount what now takes place. Should that amount even be doubled, and it was to come in steadily and regularly, it would be gradually absorbed as not to be felt upon the market. If it occasioned a small or temporary glut, at any time, in consequence of an extraordinary home production, it would soon be excluded by the decline in price; and if, under no circumstances, it occasioned such glut, it would prove that such importation was needed, for the supply of the wants of the people, and would, therefore, afford *prima facie* evidence of its necessity and general advantage to the community. On the whole review of the matter, then, I am led to the conclusion, that no such benefit would arise to the working classes of this country from any modification, or even a total repeal of the Corn Law, as would be efficient to afford them any sensible relief from the evils under which they are now labouring. At the same time I do not say, nor do I mean to insinuate, that they derive any advantage from the laws at present in force for regulating the importation of corn and other provisions into this country; nor do I believe that any class derives any sensible, permanent benefit from them. I am, therefore, perfectly indifferent as to which side the working-classes take on the vexatious question at present agitating the country through the machinations of the cotton-lords and the land-lords, but would advise them not to enlist themselves under either banner, as they may rely upon it they will, eventually, be victimized by whatever party is enabled to gain the advantage through their means, unless they can, by such co-operation, secure the assistance of the finally dominant party, in enabling them to secure some more certain share of the national wealth derived from their skill and industry, than what is to be made contingent upon an uncertain addition to the foreign trade of the country, in consequence of the repeal of these laws; or some equally uncertain increased demand for labour, which is predicted to be the result of the present system of protection being continued.

Reduction in the remuneration for labour is, at present, the plague-spot of advancing civilization everywhere. In England – in France – in Germany – in the United States of America – under every form of government – in every country where the arts of life are in an advanced state, we hear murmurings of a gathering storm among the elements of society, on account of the ill-requited labour of the industrial classes. How can this be? From what poisoned source can this root of bitterness arise? Can no remedy be found, at once safe and practicable, for this great social malady, which threatens to render abortive all attempts made by political sagacity, and enlightened philanthropy, for the permanent happiness and improvement of mankind? Shall that which has been the *desideratum* of philosophy in every age – the subjection of the laws of matter to the control of mind – the substitution of skill for the application of animal drudgery in the performance of the necessary labours of life, (and which objects have attained a realization of purpose, and a perfection of applicability, in our day, never even anticipated by the most sanguine mind of antiquity) become, after all, but a blight upon our land, and a splendid curse to our population? It cannot be! The tree of knowledge, it may be, is at present yielding but deadly fruit; but this can only arise from its culture not being properly understood.

There is a phrase current, in our day, among capitalists, and manufacturers, and statesmen, and writers on political economy, and which is banded about in their political discussions, from mouth to mouth, with all the indifference of a common household word, to which our ancestors were utter strangers – a phrase, nevertheless, of most fearful import, in regard to those to whom it more immediately refers, and calculated to awaken most serious consideration even in those who employ it, though frequently used without either feelings or anxiety:

'THE LABOUR MARKET IS OVERSTOCKED!'

'*The labour market is overstocked*!' Let us pause for a few moments, and examine and weigh over, with the seriousness it deserves, this terrible exclamation. 'The labour market is overstocked,' that is, in plain language, the man, and woman, and child market – the market where gaunt poverty, with his now unfleshed, yet sinewy arm, and hollow cheek, and haggard eye – the market where famine-stricken mothers, with milkless breasts, and attenuated forms, and hungry, naked children, born but to toil and suffer, assemble to offer to inordinate wealth, and greedy concupiscence, the remainder of their enfeebled powers, on the lowest terms which can enable them to obtain a morsel of bread to satisfy the demon of hunger gnawing at their vitals – is glutted with applicants. 'The labour-market is over-stocked!' Oh! what a fearful announcement is that to the hundreds of thousands of despair-stricken, phrenzied men, and women, and children, who are continually pressing, in increasing numbers, into its arena – an arena which, by the cruel regulations of a selfish and unfeeling community, whose laws, and the regulations for whose foreign and domestic policy, are entirely enacted by capitalists and economists, is continually contracting the limits allowed to them for the employment of those exertions, upon the full exercise of which, nevertheless, their very existence is made to depend. Need I ask any considerate mind, ought this state of things to exist any longer in its present unmitigated form of horror and deformity? Ought it ever so to have existed in a nation like this? – a nation which, in its aggregation, contains more riches, more external resources, and more internal appliances for the advancement of the comfort and permanent well-being of its labouring millions, than any other people which exist on the face of the earth? Surely not! But 'the labour-market is over-stocked!' and the fearful record of this afflicting truth meets us in ghastly characters, wherever we turn our eyes! And, by a strange infatuation, we seem almost universally to acquiesce in the dogma of the economists, that this revolting and dangerous condition of society is inseparable from a high condition of civilization, and a large developement of mechanical power employed in the production of the necessaries of life. But we must arouse ourselves from this condition of political lethargy, and, breaking through the trammels of party subserviency and political dependence, vigorously set about to inquire, whether the rights of labour cannot be as well protected by a code of enlightened legislative enactments, as the property of the capitalist in his houses, or lands, or merchandize?

If, indeed, the fearful announcement be made by those in authority, that LAW, the rule of civil society, is only efficient for the protection of the material property of the wealthy from invasion by the selfish, the dishonest, and the powerful, but is wholly incapable, and cannot be rendered by political sagacity, honestly bent upon the purpose, equal to the task of protecting the property of the labourer in his skill and industry, from the cupidity and oppression of the rich and the mighty – if it be proclaimed by legislators, that their boasted system of law-making is only inefficient when applied to the work of protecting the most helpless portion of the community, (helpless solely by the hourly recurrence of the imperious calls of nature in themselves and their families, for that support without which the agent must perish) but is all-powerful for the protection of every description of material property, then is the social compact, so far as the labourer is concerned, who owns little besides the immaterial property which he possesses in his strength, and skill, and industry, virtually dissolved; and he is morally liberated from any obligation to respect the material property of others: such obligation to respect the rights of other members of the body politic, being founded on the assumed original compact of society, that its civil institutions should, for ever, be maintained on the principle of affording protection alike to all, in the enjoyment of their inalienable right to live, and partake freely of the fruits which their own labour or skill might produce, and not to afford to the few a more secure opportunity for trampling on the rights of the many. If, however, the labouring classes, joined by the intelligent and philanthropic members of the other classes of society, even though at first few in number, be but true to themselves, there is no need, at present, if at any future time, to act upon this frightful alternative.

It is only justifiable to implead social oppression at the tribunal of nature, when we have exhausted, without success, every means to obtain a redress of wrong, which the constitution and forms of society have placed at our disposal.

This, I contend, we have not yet done; nay, we have not even entered, in all our schemes for the amelioration of the condition of the suffering labourers of this country, upon any direct and practical means for the accomplishment of this desirable and necessary object: this can only be done by *making them immediate partakers with the wealthier classes of those pecuniary benefits which their toil has conferred upon their employers*. All that has, at present, been projected, or attempted, for the improvement of the condition of the millions of men, and women, and children, who crowd the labour-market of this great and wealthy country, and ask of the capitalist, in supplicating strains, that they may be allowed to toil in his service, is, to devise, through some legislative scheme, the means whereby the population of these countries may, the more readily, bring their cheap labour, aided by the productive powers of the creatures which the subtle genius of our mechanicians are continually bringing into existence, into more ready competition with the industry of the other families of mankind, and thus establish a monopoly of ill-paid labour for the population of Britain, on the ruins of the independent labour of the rest of the world – a process by which, no doubt, great wealth would be derived by many classes, as has been the case already by the operation of this principle, but the success of which would be productive of no more advantage to the labourer than what has already taken place.

How far the multiplication of the powers of production in this country, during the last fifty years, and the consequent great increase in the amount of the trade and commerce of the nation, has served its legitimate purpose of improving the condition of the labouring class, along with those of the upper classes of the community, I will now endeavour to examine, as likewise to demonstrate the immense addition which has been made to the capital stock of the nation during that period, and the consequent vast increase of wealth in the hands of the employers of labour.

In the year 1791, Mr Pitt,[1] in bringing forward his budget for the parliamentary year, stated, in a tone of triumphant exultation at the then prosperous condition of the nation, that the aggregate of the national wealth was equivalent to *one thousand three hundred million* of pounds sterling. At that time, the population of Great Britain and Ireland was about fourteen million of souls. In 1841, (fifty years afterwards) the national wealth is estimated to have reached the enormous amount of six thousand millions of pounds and upwards, the population, in the meantime, having advanced to twenty-seven million of souls.

In 1797, the total amount of personal property conveyed by will, which came under the inspection of the legacy duty office, was *one million one hundred and sixteen thousand* pounds sterling. In the year 1837, (forty years after that time) the same description of property passing by will to legatees, and on which duty was paid, amounted to more than *forty million* of pounds sterling; and there is every reason to believe, that the amount for the last year, (1843) cannot have been less than *forty-five million*: indicating an increase in the amount of wealth possessed by

---

1 William Pitt (1759–1806), Chancellor of the Exchequer and Prime Minister 1783–1801, 1804–6.

the middle classes of our community – for it is unquestionable that it is the property of that class which is principally affected by the legacy duties – so enormous as to exceed belief, were it not for a test like this to verify its amount.

Real property, not being subject to legacy duty, it is difficult, if not impossible, to arrive at any satisfactory calculation as to the amount which passes annually into fresh hands by legacy and inheritance, so as to judge of its progressive increasing value with anything like the certainty which appertains to personal property; but, in all probability, it cannot be less than twice the amount of the personal property. This would give us ninety million of pounds sterling as the value of the real property which passes annually by death into fresh hands. The increase in the amount of such bequests and inheritances, at the present time, as compared with what they were in the year 1797, cannot be less, from the enormous additions which have been made to the rentals of the country, in every way, of from fifty to sixty million. This vast increase in the value of the real property of the country, may be said to be principally in favour of the upper classes, as the increased amount of personal property transmitted is, in the most degree, in favour of the middle classes.

It may as well, then, be here asked, what is the present condition of the lower, or working-classes of the community, as contrasted with *their* condition forty-five or fifty years ago? Whilst those for whom they weave and spin, plough and dig, toil and labour, amidst summer's heats and winter's snows – in the fetid atmosphere of factories, and the chilling damps and dreary darkness of pits and mines – have advanced so much, and so rapidly, in the acquisition of wealth, and the consequent ample enjoyment of the comforts and delights of civilized life, how have the sons and daughters of industry themselves fared? Has their social condition undergone a corresponding degree of improvement with that of the upper and middle classes?

The incomes of ministers of religion of all denominations, as likewise the incomes of the other learned professions, and those of public and private instructors, with official functionaries, and agents, and *employees* of every degree, have undergone considerable augmentation during the last fifty years, so that *they* likewise are enabled to enjoy more of the comforts and elegancies of life, and are better qualified to provide for the education and settlement of their children, than the same class of persons were enabled to accomplish fifty years ago. Nor does even the ample list which includes within its category the nobility, the gentry, the clergy, and professional men – the capital agriculturalist, the merchant, the trader, and the manufacturer, comprise all of British society whose condition have undergone improvement during the last half century. Soldiers and sailors, by an advance of pay or wages, and greater attention paid to the quality and quantity of their provision, and the nature of their clothing and lodging, have had *their* comfort promoted, and their social and pecuniary interests advanced: even the prisoners in our jails – the lunatics in our asylums – the dissolute in our bridewells and penitentiaries – the convicts at our hulks, and penal settlements, are all better fed, better clothed, better lodged, and more carefully instructed, (especially the young, in all those duties, a right knowledge of which may tend to improve their future moral and social condition) than they were at any previous period, or than they are, I apprehend, in any other country in the world. Over every one of these dependent classes has the law, or the regulations of the peculiar service to which they belong, extended the hand of protection and assistance.

They who encounter danger, and undergo privation, for the security of our persons and properties, or for the advancement of the public interests, it is justly contended, ought to partake freely of the benefits which their toils and dangers confer upon others; ought to have their comfort promoted, their health cared for, their pecuniary interests attended to, their wives and children, to a considerable degree, at least, provided for by the public whom they serve, whilst engaged in active service, and to have a comfortable provision made for them by the nation, when age, or the casualties attendant upon their service, disqualifies them for longer active or laborious exertion. And who can deny the justice of this claim? Who will be bold enough to say, that whilst the soldier and the sailor are spending the strength of their manhood in the service of their country – devoting their energies, ceaselessly, to the upholding of its honour, and the advancement of its highest and most important interests, among the nations of the earth, it ought to be, or might safely, be left to the option of greedy or selfish superiors, whether they should be well or ill-fed – well or ill-clothed – well or ill-lodged – or well or ill-provided for, when the period of life arrives when they could no more, with comfort to themselves, or advantage to the community, discharge the active duties in which they were once engaged?

The humanity of British society, it is seen, will not even allow the criminal to rot in gaol as he once rotted, the victim of cold, and famine, and disease – will not permit that the idle and dissolute pauper, even when known to be such, shall lack something like a sufficiency of food, and warm clothing, and comfortable lodging. The consciousness, by society, of the fact, that they have men and women to deal with, in each of these unfortunate, though culpable classes – sentient beings, with wants and feelings like their own, and who, after all, are but erring brothers and sisters, frail, perhaps principally, through the want of that instruction which it was their duty to have communicated; and now the most helpless, because the most profligate, members of the community, leads it to take care, that even these wretched creatures shall not be left to live and die, unpitied and unprotected, in damp cellars or cheerless attics, without food, or destitute of necessary clothing. What, then, I again ask, amidst all this humane and patriotic provision for soldiers, and sailors, and criminals, and paupers, is the condition of the free labourers of England? – the men, and women, and children, whose long enduring, and patient toil, has enabled every other class to advance so rapidly, and so mightily, in the acquisition of wealth, and conferred the power on society to reward so liberally its naval and military heroes, and to provide so efficiently, and benevolently, for every unfortunate class of their fellow-subjects at home and abroad? For, to the endurance in toil, of these classes of our humble citizens, it is unquestionably owing, that, not only the princely landowner, and the princely merchant, of these realms, are indebted for their stupendous wealth, but, to them likewise, the West India slave owes his costly manumission, and the African and the Hindoo, and the inhabitants of the hundred islands of the great South Sea, their civilization and instruction in the truths of the Gospel. To say that a population like that of this country, so enduring, so industrious, so enterprising and skilful, should have derived *little* permanent advantage themselves, from the toils which have conferred so many benefits on others, would be uttering a reproach on the upper classes of society, and impeaching the value of the institutions under which they had lived. To have it shown, by indubitable evidence, that the labourers of this country, manufacturing and agricultural, are no better fed, no better clothed, no better housed, than were their forefathers half a century ago – nor possess any more facilities for providing against seasons of sickness and decrepitude, than did those whose more imperfect skill and industry conferred so much less of benefit on their country and the world at large, than their own, would be a disgrace – a lasting, indelible disgrace, on all those classes, in whose hands is placed the power to establish such laws and institutions, as may be necessary to protect the weak and dependent portion of society, against the selfishness and oppression of the powerful and the wealthy. What then shall we say of them? In what bitter terms of reproach and indignation shall we hold them up to the scorn and contempt of this and future generations, when compelled to make known the truth, that, whilst riches have increased during that period amongst the wealthy orders of society, and the employers of labour in Britain, to an extent never before known, or even dreamed of amidst the wildest speculations of the most enthusiastic political economist, the condition of the labourer and the artizan, with a few favoured exceptions, is felt by himself to be more grievous, is known by those around him, wallowing in the superfluity of their riches, to be more wretched, all circumstances considered, than was, perhaps, the lot of any other labouring population which ever before existed upon earth?

It may be said, with the strictest propriety of language, that tens of thousands of the adult labouring population of Britain, in the manufacturing districts, have never experienced the delights and benefits of the season of childhood and youth. Forced, whilst as yet in a comparative state of infancy, into the whirl of drudgery in factories and workshops, they were reduced in early life, to the rank of mere animal machines – to the condition of breathing automata – and thus became expert labourers at a period of life before they ought to have known, in their own persons, what continuous labour, for any lengthened period, meant; and, if we may credit the statements latterly put forth from high authority, during the late debates in Parliament on the 'bill for limiting the hours of working by young persons in factories,' the whole fabric of British manufacturing and commercial greatness depends upon this costly offering of the blood and tears of the innocents, on the altar of our modern Moloch, being continued!

The consequence of this premature application of the powers of the body, and the limitation of the energies of the mind, to routine labour, is, that at a period of life when, according to the course of years, the labourer ought only to be in the vigour of manhood, they become old men, and are proclaimed by their former employers, to be regularly 'used up,' and totally disqualified to keep pace with the increased velocity of movement continually demanded from those who are employed in their monster establishments, and are, in consequence, discharged.

At forty years of age, the females employed in many of the finer branches of our manufactures, are considered as old women: their eyes become dim, and their bodies enfeebled, by reason of their close application, from infancy, to the destructive sedentary employment in which they are engaged, and, unable to keep pace with their juniors in the dispatch of work – if compelled to depend solely upon their unaided exertions for support, as widows or single women – are reduced to a condition of the greatest wretchedness, or eventually necessitated to take refuge in the union workhouse.

Many painful instances of the truth of these remarks, calculated to harrow up the humane feelings of the country in the most intense degree, could be easily adduced from the history of several branches of manufacture, but I shall refrain from so doing on the present occasion. Can any scene in human society, however, I venture to ask, be more pitiable, than the spectacle of a man, or woman, whose life has been devoted, from the early period of seven or eight years, up to fifty, or threescore, to incessant toil, from which others have derived comforts innumerable, and the nation, in its aggregate capacity, the most important benefits, condemned to spend the remnant of their days of toil and usefulness, after such periods, in the vain struggle to compete with youthful rivals, for a morsel of bread to sustain their sinking nature, or to be reduced, after the period of their activity is gone by, to the miserable condition of being dependents on the stinted bounty of a parish, either within the walls of a workhouse, or on a paltry out-door allowance, for the means of perpetuating their existence.

But, stinted as is the bounty of the parish, or the poor-law guardians generally, to the worn-out labourer, when at last compelled, by the circumstances of his age and infirmities, to afford him regular assistance, this boon is uniformly denied so long as ever his ebbing strength can be taxed to the performance of a day's labour of any description, the remuneration for which is not, strictly, in agreement with the value of the labour performed, according to the rate prevailing in the general labour market of the district, but, in conformity with some arbitrary rule laid down by the overseers of the poor, or surveyors of highways, as to how much is needful for the support of an old man, and how much aid he can obtain from children who, themselves, are always struggling on the brink of starvation.

When the soldier has served twenty, or twenty-five years, even though he may not have seen any very severe service, or been exposed to much danger, or have become, in the least degree, maimed or mutilated, he is entitled, by the laws of the service to which he belongs, to a discharge from his toils, and a pension from the nation, which is paid him ungrudgingly, at regular stated periods, during the whole course of his future life, whatever may be the amount of his previous accumulations, or the subsequent improvement in his circumstances.

But how fares the poor, old, worn-out hero of industry, who has spent, not merely twenty, but forty, perhaps fifty years of his life, in the dreary damp and gloom of a mine, or a coal-pit, or a slate or stone-quarry, exposed, through every year of that period, to toils, and dangers, and privations, infinitely more oppressive to the animal spirits, and tending more to the wasting of health, and the destruction of life, than all which vast numbers of military men encounter through the whole period of their service? Why, if he has become so cramped, and crooked, and disabled by years of toil, in the uneasy posture in which he has been compelled to carry on his dangerous employment, as to be utterly unable, longer, to use a mattock or a shovel, in any servile task, he is either condemned to be imprisoned through the remainder of his life within the precincts of a union workhouse, or allowed, as a special act of grace and favour, by the 'guardians' of that said union, some two shillings and sixpence, or three shillings a week, to maintain himself, and perhaps an aged wife. Should, however, the poor, toil-worn veteran of industry, have so far escaped mutilation, or blindness, or general debility, until sixty, or sixty-five years of age, as to be able still to wield some implement of drudgery, though so far worked-up, as to be cast off from the employment to which he has been accustomed, he is refused any gratuitous support by the community to whose wealth and comforts, his toils, through so long a period, have contributed, but is thence condemned by his unfeeling taskmasters, barely fed, and poorly clothed, to break stones, or riddle gravel, for the repair of the highways, or stand almost up to the ankles, amidst the cold and sleet of a winter's day, raking mud from the public roads, for the paltry remuneration of sixpence or eightpence a day, until he reaches seventy or seventy-five years – sometimes, should his strength hold out, to even a more advanced period than this.

Bad, however, as is the case of the classes above alluded to, theirs is not the worst which is to be found in the annals of the aged poor. The agricultural labourer, the miner, the collier, the quarryman, and many others of a similar class, from their exposure to cold and wet, through every period of their previous lives, suffer, comparatively, but little, when set by boards of highways, and overseers of the poor, to such labours as those described, compared with what is endured by worn-out mechanical and manufacturing labourers and handicraftsmen, who, after being blinded and debilitated by their sedentary and enfeebling occupations, find themselves, in tens of thousands of instances, at sixty years of age, or earlier, cast out of the factories and workshops in which they have been accustomed to the employed, as useless human lumber, and condemned, in order to save themselves and aged partners from being immured in the workhouse, to undertake, at the offer of some official of the parish to which they belong, the performance of labours utterly at variance with all their previous habits, and the performance of which tends, by subjecting them to exposure to wet and cold, to which they have been previously entirely unaccustomed, to abridge the extent of their remaining days, or superadd, to the natural infirmities of age, and the maladies engendered in their constitutions by many years of severe application to labour, in close and heated workshops and factories, a load of painful and distressing diseases, which embitter the few years afforded to them by Providence, before the workhouse, and the grave, closes upon them forever.

Yet these are the men whose unrivalled skill and untiring industry have built up the proud edifice of Britain's commercial and manufacturing glory – who have made of her merchants, princes – of her manufacturers, *millionaires* – of her sovereigns, the arbiters of the fate of nations, and the virtual rulers of the world.

Ought, then, the hero of industry to be thus cast off in his declining years, as an offal and an incumbrance on society? Ought the men and women who have spent their strength – who have exhausted the powers of their bodies, and weakened the energies of their minds, by half a century of continuous, wearisome labours, to be allowed no respite between the end of their toils, and being deposited in their graves, but what they may chance to find within the prison walls of a workhouse? – and that, whilst they have, by those very labours, quintupled the aggregate wealth of the nation, and enabled their employers to transmit annually, by legacy, to their successors, in personal property alone, instead of one and a half million of pounds, the enormous amount of forty-five million of pounds sterling! Justice to the individual himself, no less than the honour and safety of the community to which he belongs, demand that opportunity shall be afforded to every labourer who reaches the advanced age of sixty years, at furthest, of retiring from his toils on something like a comfortable provision for the remainder of his days. The state of the 'labour market' in these kingdoms, I am aware, is such, that to do complete justice to the labourer, the proposed pensions should take place at fifty, instead of sixty years of age, and be of considerably larger amount than what I shall now venture to propose as the retiring allowance; and such, I have no doubt, will, in the course of a few years, be the case, should the nation continue to progress in wealth during the next half century, as it has during the last, and the principle of the 'Labour Fund' become once established among us, as a part of our national domestic policy.

By such means alone, as it appears to me, can the labour market be continually kept in that healthy, active state, in which the skilful and industrious labourer, male or female, shall be ensured to live in the possession of regular employment, at fair remunerating wages, and free and full scope be afforded to mechanical inventions for the abridgement of manual labour, without entailing, as is now, too frequently the case, misery upon the ejected labourer and his family.

The substitution of mechanical for manual labour, in the various operations of manufactures, is an evil in society only so far as it may tend to make the condition of the sentient agent worse than it was before he had a rival raised up to him in the 'labour market,' by the creative power of that great sorcerer of our age, the inventive mechanician. To render these agents of the skill and genius of man an unqualified blessing to all classes of the community, instead of a very dubious one to the largest and most necessitous, it is only necessary to make such legal provision for the operative, as shall place him in a correspondingly improved condition, with that in which his employer, and all the upper classes, are placed in, and he will have much cause to rejoice in their adoption as those classes now have. And this is the natural course which affairs would have taken, in reference to subjects of this kind, and the certain result which would have arisen from the astonishing developement of the power of mechanical production in this country, during the last seventy years, in furnishing the elegancies and comforts of life so cheaply, and in such abundance, if the welfare of the labourer had been as much studied by statesmen as has been the welfare of the upper classes, and a tithe of the laws and regulations framed for the protection of his property – his labour – which have been passed for the preservation and security of the material property of the capitalist. Nothing is left unprotected by legislative enactment, in this great country, but LABOUR – now undefended from the aggression of the knavish and the powerful, but the LABOURER!

Let but the labouring population, as is their just due, partake, in their full proportion, of the benefits thus accruing from the introduction of improved machinery into all the departments of manufacturing and agricultural labour, and the now discontented, because ill-used, operative, will rejoice as much as the capitalist, in every invention which tends, by cheapening products, to facilitate their introduction into every market of the world, and thus to add to the sum of individual and national wealth.

If the principle, that the men who gain all the world, shall be legally compelled to maintain, in comfort, all the people, (and nothing can be more equitable, and consonant to nature, than such a regulation) be in future embodied in the laws and institutions of society, then may the people see without grudging or repining, the *millionaire* capitalist continually enlarging the sphere of his operations, and the mechanician continually increasing the productive powers of the creatures of his plastic hand; feeling assured, that the triumphs of mind over the *inertia* of matter, shall lead but to the increase of their ease and comfort, and the more perfect establishment of the benefits of civilization and knowledge among themselves and their children.

It will thus be seen, that I am no enemy to machinery, nor one who is desirous of restricting its most extensive application to the purposes of society.

The superseding of human labour, by mechanical contrivances, in the performance of the heavy and irksome drudgeries of social life, I hold to be the very triumph of intelligence – the crown and glory of advancing civilization; but its benefits have, hitherto, been shamefully misapplied – its uses have been cruelly and awfully perverted. It is high time that this stigma on the capitalist and the mechanician should be obliterated, not by doing away with machinery, and thus raising the cost of products to the consumer – (a mode of procedure which, though it might confer some benefit on the comparatively few persons employed in carrying on the processes of manufacture by manual labour, for the use of those who could afford to purchase them, would, I feel persuaded, occasion a vastly greater amount of mischief among the infinitely greater number of consumers, by diminishing their means of procuring the other necessaries and comforts of life, which their circumstances might require) – but, by giving to the labouring millions a fair share of the benefits derived from the employment of machinery and the extension of markets with the capitalist, who, as things stand at present, has contrived, under the artificial and oppressive regulations of society, to monopolize almost the whole benefits to himself, leaving to the industrious labourer, as his share of the concern, little besides the life of a slave, and the death of a pauper.

When it is considered, that though the mass of British manufacturing labourers, male and female, are set down to regular employment from nine hours to twelve hours a day, at so early an age as eight or nine years, and in many branches of trade when no more than five or six years old, they never can justly be said to enjoy the opportunity, owing to the average low rate of wages, of making any substantive provision for the period of age and decrepitude, whilst their employers, generally speaking, are enabled to amass great fortunes, and the nation, in its aggregate character, has increased in wealth and power, through their labours and privations, to an amount which it is dazzling to the mind to contemplate: it surely cannot be too much to demand, on the part of this highly-useful and important class of society, that, not only shall some restrictions be legally imposed on the period at which, in infancy, they shall be placed out to regular employment, but, that likewise, in advancing life, an honorable and independent provision shall be made, to some extent, at least, for their future maintenance, and to which they shall possess as valid, and legally-recognized a claim, as the capitalist to the possession of his houses or lands, or public or private securities. Unless some direct and positive provision be made for the labourers of Britain in their declining years, and under the pressure of those casualties which are, now, of such constant occurrence, in every department of industry, from the use of so much powerful, and in many cases, hazardous machinery, in carrying forward their operation, so that the labour market may be kept constantly relieved from the burthen of that portion of the population which are always found to press most heavily upon it; and unless the pension of the retired labourer – his share of the national prize money, won by skill and industry, from a subject world – be as certainly guaranteed to him, under the sanction of law, as is the pension and prize-money of the soldier and sailor, I am fully convinced, that not only cannot the future peace and tranquillity of the country be preserved, and an universal war of labour against property, at some time, be prevented, but likewise, that no possibly conceived extension of the foreign commerce of the country – no reduction in the cost of provisions to the labourer – no diminution in the amount of national taxation – can be made available, in any sensible degree, to the bettering of his condition, or procuring for him a more ample share of those vast revenues derived by the employers of his labour, from the application of his skill and industry, than he has hitherto derived.

During the last forty years, the quantity of cotton wool taken for consumption in the mills and factories of this country, has risen from little more than fifty million pounds weight, to five hundred and fifty million; and the official value of the fabrics wrought therefrom, and exported to foreign countries, has advanced from seven million pounds sterling, to nearly sixty million pounds sterling: whilst, during the same period, by a striking coincidence, the amount of personal property passed by will, by the employers of labour in the country, has increased in a similar ratio, having swelled from *five million* of pounds, its amount in the first year of the series, to *forty-five million* of pounds sterling in the last. In the same interval of time, too, not less than two thousand bills were passed by Parliament, for the inclosing of what were termed, the waste lands of the country, by which means alone, an addition has been made to the capital stock of the owners of the soil of the country, amounting, at the least, to two hundred millions of money, besides all the enormous amount which has been added to its value from other causes. It is necessary, then, here again to pause, and inquire how much of all this augmentation of the wealth of the country, during the last half century, has been shared by the labouring classes themselves – the men, and women, and children, through whose enduring toil this enormous addition to the amount of personal property, and this increase in the value of the real property possessed by their employers, has been accomplished? To how much greater extent can the working classes indulge in the luxuries or comforts of civilized life, now, by the exercise of their skill and industry, than could their fathers half a century ago? Will any man venture to say that the material property possessed by ten thousand, or a million, of British labourers, in the year 1844, has undergone any sensible increase in value over that held by an equal number of the same class of our fellow-citizens fifty years ago?

It is my opinion, founded on some extensive observation, and constant inter-course with the working-classes during the whole of that period, that the gross value of the material property, clothes, furniture, money, and general household stuff, possessed at the present time by such a number of labourers as that above quoted, (say a million) would fall short in value by several million of pounds ster-ling, of what was the value of the same descriptions of property held by an equal number of the operatives of the country of the preceding generation. But, ought this discrepancy between the condition of the labourer, and the employer of labour, to have arisen? – or, having arisen, ought it longer to be allowed to exist? Must not the social system of that community be radically bad – its political institutions be grossly imperfect in their adaptation to promote the happiness and prosperity of the industrious classes, (if not wickedly partial, and oppressively unjust, by design) where such an anomalous condition of things has grown up, and continues to be maintained under the sanction of law, as prevails in this coun-try, in the relations of the employers of labour and the employed? Nothing, then, can be clearer than this fact, that whilst the holders of capital, in every degree – the employers of labour throughout these realms – have been enabled, during the last forty years, to augment their personal property thirty-fold, and increase the value of their real property by at least a thousand million of pounds sterling, in consequence of the extension of commerce and manufactures during that period, the labourers of the nation – the men and women in whose skill and industry the foundations of this mighty fabric of social grandeur and political power has been laid, and by whose quiet submission to the laws and institutions of their country, it is still enabled to be maintained in its integrity – have not, as a class, derived one single tittle of benefit from its creation! – have not been allowed, by circum-stances, to partake, in the smallest degree, in any of the advantages which their toils and endurances have conferred upon the superior classes. Their hours of working are no fewer – the remuneration for their labour during the hours of toil is no greater – their means of making provision against age and sickness is no more ample – their capability to feed, and clothe, and educate their children, is no better – but, on the contrary, astounding as the statement may appear, and disgraceful as is the fact proved, against all those orders of their fellow citizens, whose rank, and station, and influence, placed them in a position to prevent this perversion of the benefits which industry and order are calculated to confer upon a people – they are, in all respects, as regards their domestic condition, worse off than when their employers could bequeath only one and a half million of pounds sterling of personal property annually to their successors, instead of forty-five million; and then the real aggregate wealth of the general proprietary of the empire, at home and abroad, was less in value by two thousand million of pounds sterling, than it is at the present time.

Up to this period, then, all that the labouring classes of Great Britain can see, as the result of their indomitable spirit of industry, and their steady perseverance in habits of order and submission to the laws, through which the commerce and manufacturing products of the country have been so enormously increased as to have quadrupled the aggregate amount of the national wealth, in the short space of fifty years, and, consequently, added to the political power and influence of the state among the nations of the earth in a similar ratio, is, that whilst landlords, and cotton-lords, and all the upper classes of society, including bankers, and merchants, and manufacturers – fundholders, annuitants, and pensioners – placemen, lawyers, and ministers of religion, of all denominations – have had their incomes virtually increased, to a considerable degree, by the reductions which have taken place in taxation, and in the cost price to them of all the necessaries, and many of the luxuries, of life, so that they are enabled to enjoy more themselves, and, at the same time, make more ample provision for their children, than the same classes were enabled to do thirty, forty, or fifty years ago – their own condition in life, so far from having been bettered by the reduction in the money-value of articles of consumption, the produce of their industry, which has taken place during that period, has actually deteriorated to a ruinous and frightful extent.

Need it now be asked of any philanthropic or patriotic mind, whether such a shockingly perverted order of things ought longer to be perpetuated in a country possessing such ample means for redressing the evils complained of as does this? and, at the same time, where such loud pretensions to a love of justice, and a desire to advance the interests of religion and civilization among the various families of the earth, are made, as we continually witness in England? Need it be asked of the politician – of the political economist – of any man who has attentively studied the aspect of society, and marked the working of the principles which are, at the present time, silently, but, nevertheless, violently agitating its bosom – whether such gross injustice to the toiling, yet innately brave and high-spirited millions, who constitute the labouring population of these realms – whether the systematic violation of the rights of the labourer, springing out of the existing imperfect relations recognized as subsisting between the employer and the employed; the oppression of his youth in denying to him that ample opportunity, in the day-spring of life, for the recreation of his body, and the cultivation of his mind, which are essential to his future well-being as a physico-moral agent, and subjecting him, instead, from his infancy, to an almost ceaseless routine of drudgery; whether, that withholding from him, in manhood, such a remuneration for his toils, as is necessary to enable him to discharge, satisfactorily to himself, and advantageously to those connected with him, the duties of a husband, a parent, a citizen; whether the denying to him, during the season of old age and decrepitude, after a life spent in a course of patient and untiring industry, those comforts and consolations that his period of life and infirmities require, which has so long been the course pursued by the employers of labour in this country, towards those dependent upon them, can much longer be persevered in, and a universal servile war not be the result? Men will suffer much, and suffer patiently, from an oppression with which long habit has made them familiar, and hardly hope for a release from its bondage – they will endure for years, and toil on, almost without a murmur, under a weight of ills, from an accustomed source, the bare contemplation of which would, at one time, have worked them up into a phrenzy of despair, rather than venture, so long as its weight is bearable, to seek a remedy for their affliction through the hazards and dangers of encountering 'ills they know not of;' but it is not in human nature to suffer injustice for always, with quiet resignation – to endure for ever the burden and degradation of accumulated wrongs, with unresisting submission.

I do not, however, profess to hold out the language of threatening, neither do I propose, in these pages, to address myself to the fears of Englishmen of rank, and station, and influence in the state, in pleading 'the rights of labour,' and urging on their attention the present sunken and stretched condition of the labouring population; but would rather appeal to their humanity – to their sense of justice – to their conscientious regard to the obligations imposed on them by a common brotherhood with the humbler classes – men to whom they owe so much, and from whose severe toils, and extreme privations, has been, in a principal degree, extracted, that wealth which has purchased to themselves and their families, the ample store of enjoyments and benefits with which they are enabled constantly to solace themselves: though I have not attempted, nor will I attempt, to conceal my opinion, that there is cause for fear to all men of property, if more effectual means be not taken to promote the comfort and well-being of the labouring population, and protect them from that grinding oppression to which they have been so extensively subjected, than have hitherto been adopted by statesmen and the wealthy proprietary of the land.

The agreeable lull which at present overspreads the face of British society, may be taken, and no doubt is, by many, taken as an indication of contentedness among the labouring millions with their condition and future prospects; from whence a feeling of security springs up in the minds of such persons, and a self-gratulation at the success of their plans, and the brilliancy of their future prospects, and they are apt to denounce, as highly improper, and most inopportune, remarks such as those which have been here indulged in. But let them not deceive themselves: IT IS NOT SO. The sense of wrong inflicted, of oppression endured, is as keenly felt – is as deeply fixed in the heart of the labouring population, at this moment of apparent repose, as it was two years ago, when they raised the arm of menace in the face of authority, and gave vent to the long-smothered wrath of their hearts, in words of fearful, and never-to-be-forgotten, import.

We are, at best, but living in a state of *fancied* security – in a house of combustibles, where an accidental spark, struck by the hoof even of some petty despot, in his career of self-seeking aggrandizement, amidst the ruin and wretchedness of the sons and daughters of toil, may explode the whole magazine of accumulated discontent throughout the realm, and hurl the whole citadel of oppression, which now frowns, with gloomy austerity, over the homes of patient, lowly industry, into certain and irretrievable destruction.

Having now briefly, but earnestly, set forth the wrongs under which, I conceive, the labouring population of the United Kingdom are suffering, with some of the causes which have led to their present debased condition, as likewise glanced at the insufficiency of the principal remedies proposed for the alleviation of their distresses, I shall proceed to detail the plan I have in view, for effecting, to some extent, at least, and as the beginning of a better system, an improvement in their condition.

In the earlier part of this essay, I have ventured to say, that the desired amelioration, in the circumstances of the labouring classes, can only be effected, by making them, in their degree, direct participators with their employers, and capitalists in general, in those extensive pecuniary benefits, which have flowed in upon the other classes, from the application of their skill and industry to the cultivation of the soil of the country, and the carrying forward of its great manufacturing and commercial operations. No effort of any number of individuals, can, I am convinced, at present, accomplish this desirable object, to the full extent to which strict justice to the working-man would demand that it should be carried. Still, I am of opinion, that much more of good is attainable for the labourer, in this respect, by the active, united exertions of a few persons, than has ever yet been realized by him, or attempted to be accomplished by the philanthropy of others; and that, too, without disturbing, in the most remote degree, the settled order of society in these countries. I ask for no confiscations of property belonging to any class, to aid my plans for improving the condition of the working-classes – no agrarian laws – no diminution in the value of any 'securities,' public or private – no interruption of the regular pursuits of merchants, manufacturers, bankers, or traders; but would leave to every man, as at present, the quiet prosecution of the duties of his profession or calling, according to his own peculiar way of acting, neither limiting his power of accumulation, nor interfering with the application of his capital for the advancement of his interests.

Nothing, I am aware, is so sensitive of approaching danger, as money; nobody so embarrassed by restraint, or alarmed by governmental interference with his projects, as your money-getting man. Those Reformers, therefore, who attempt to better the condition of the working-classes, by plans designed to control the operations of the capitalist, in the application of his means to purposes of further aggrandizement, or which are calculated to alarm the holders of property generally, as to the future security of their possessions, adopt, certainly, the most direct method to defeat their object, of any which could be proposed.

I only seek, on the part of the labourers of this country, by the plan I am about to recommend, a small, but certain and direct participation in the accumulating wealth of the nation – which, it cannot be denied, they are principally instrumental, by their skill and industry, and quiet obedience to the laws, in creating – by recognized means, such as the government of the country regularly employs, when it demands from the executors of the last wills of deceased persons, and before the remainder passes into the hands of the legatees, a portion of the accumulated wealth of the deceased, towards defraying the current expenses of the state.

I propose, then, upon the plan of the 'Legacy Duties,' but only on a different scale of charge, to establish a 'NATIONAL LABOUR FUND,' *to the support of which fund, all descriptions of property, real and personal, passing to heirs or legatees, by inheritance, or testamentary devise, shall be made liable*: the present legacy duties to be entirely abolished, and their amount supplied by Parliament from some other source. No mode of raising and supplying a large fund, such as that I aim at establishing, and for such a purpose as that contemplated, can be attended with less disadvantage, or inconvenience, to any one, than taking it at the time of the decease of the owner, and before it has, strictly, become the property of another. In this way, a man is left in the most complete enjoyment of his property, so long as he can enjoy it at all. Neither the feeling of self-love, or self-complacency, with which he has been accustomed to solace himself, in the contemplation of his hoarded wealth, for all the toil and anxieties to which he has exposed himself in the accumulation of this oftentimes, nevertheless, superfluous store; nor the selfishness which has led him to refuse to share, voluntarily, with others, that which has, for so many years, been the idol of his heart, is at all interfered with. Most men, in our day, and in our country, in particular, seem to doat on dying rich. I would not interfere with this apparently universal weakness of our nature: the rich man should, for me, or for aught that I would do, be allowed the satisfaction of dying rich; but, having died rich, I would endeavour to take care that, when dead, a portion of his riches should be secured, by the hand of law, for the benefit of those from whose toils and privations, he mainly derived them. And this, it must be apparent, would answer to the purpose fully as well, and keep the fund as regularly supplied with the means of effecting its object, whilst it would be much less offensive and objectionable in form, as if the amount was drawn from the pocket of the capitalist by direct taxation, or levied, like the present poor-rate, by a constantly-recurring assessment on property.

Nor could devisees of any class, I conceive, have just cause for complaint against such a demand, for such a purpose, on the property of their devisor. Wealth, coming to a man by legacy from another, even to the children of the testator, is, to use a common phrase, 'all found money.' The legatee could not, therefore, with any show of reason, begrudge an amount taken by law from a property which was not, in truth, his at all, in possession, and, at most, only in expectancy, to improve the present condition, or to render more comfortable, the future days of dependants, to whom devisor and devisee alike owed so much of all the blessings of life the one had enjoyed from past possession, and the other hoped to derive from the large share which would still descend to him.

I would, then, propose, that a fund be created by Act of Parliament, to be called 'The National Labour Fund,' *supported, principally, by a duty of ten per cent. charged on all devised or inherited property*, whether real or personal – under the direction and management of a Board of Commissioners, similarly constructed with the present board for the management of the ordinary legacy duties. Such fund to be devoted to the furnishing of pensions to all persons, male and female, at a rate to be hereafter specified, who would accept it on the proposed conditions, namely, that *they should, so long as they were in receipt of the same, refrain from following any description of employment, for hire or profit*. No one should be restrained from following regular or occasional employment, in consequence of having attained the age of threescore years, every one being left at liberty to shape his course according to his own views of what would best conduce to the promotion of his individual advantage; but simply, *if they availed themselves of the benefit of the fund, they should not continue to labour for hire*. Nor should any impediments to the enjoyment of the pension be created by consideration of the circumstance, should such an one arise, that the individual receiving it could very well do without this addition to his income. A fund created by the capital of all the united product of the skill, and industry, and property of all, should be for the benefit of all, restricted by no other limitation than that the recipient of its benefits should not employ the additional means furnished by those benefits, to the injury of any one other member of the community, which might possibly be the case, were the pensioners, whilst in the receipt of their annuities, allowed to interfere with the labour of those debarred by age from partaking of its assistance: as, with the help of five, six, or seven shillings a week, derived from another source, they would be enabled, were they so disposed, to work for so much less than the labourer who enjoyed no such advantage, as seriously to interfere with his well-being as a workman. It must, therefore, be made an absolute condition of title to the allowance from the 'Labour Fund,' in addition to the individual, male or female, being sixty years of age, that they should entirely refrain from labour for hire. This, of course, would not be construed into an interference with them in the performance of any duty for themselves, and referable entirely to their own immediate personal comfort, such as washing or mending their own clothes, repairing an article of furniture, or cultivating, for their own benefit, a little garden plot.

I shall now proceed to the details of the fund I propose to raise, stating its probable amount, the sources from which I would raise the supplies, and the application I would make of them for the accomplishment of the objects alluded to.

The gross sum necessary to constitute an efficient 'National Labour Fund,' adequate to meet anything like the wants of the labouring classes, and to discharge, fairly, the obligations due to them from the higher orders of society, cannot possibly be less than FIFTEEN MILLION OF POUNDS STERLING PER ANNUM.

This amount, I propose, should be raised from two sources: a legacy duty, and a tax on the possession of the elective franchise. From these two sources alone, I am fully persuaded, the whole sum, and even a much larger one, might be raised without any sensible burden being felt by any one.

Not having said anything before on the latter branch of supply to the 'Labour Fund,' I beg leave, before proceeding further, to state a few of the reasons which induce me to recommend its adoption, and which, I flatter myself, will be found sufficiently cogent to carry the assent of most persons to the value of the principle, though I am fully sensible, at the same time, that the extension of the suffrage to which it would lead, will, at first sight, constitute a ground of objection to one class of persons: whilst the consideration, that a limit of any kind is to be imposed on this principle of citizenship, will awaken the jealousy, if not the open hostility, of another part, to the plan proposed.

I will say a few words, first, in defence of the new basis for the elective franchise, in answer to those who object to such an extension of the suffrage as it might, and I have no doubt would, occasion. There can be no valid ground for refusal to extend the privileges of the national franchise to the utmost possible limits to which the adult male population of the empire might, at any time, extend, but that derived from the possible circumstance, that the majority of electors might thus become of too poor, or too vicious, a class, to have the property of the country, over which they would then possess, through their representatives, the entire control, placed at their disposal; or, else, that they might be too ignorant of the great and established truths of political science, even when not intentionally bent on mischievous legislation against the interests of their richer fellow-citizens, to feel the value of property to a nation, or to appreciate the importance of a community of freemen sustaining a high character for honour and integrity among the nations of the earth, and thus be led, on the recommendation of short-sighted, or unprincipled politicians, for some temporary advantage, to sanction measures which, by weakening the credit, or sacrificing the honour of the country, would plunge all orders of the community into difficulties and disgrace, and finally into irremediable ruin.

For these reasons it is, that tests and qualifications for the exercise of this, the highest privilege of citizenship, have, ostensibly, at least, been created. Now, I will concede to you, that since men quitted the woods and the mountain side, and formed themselves into communities for mutual support and protection – laws, and institutions, and conventionalties, must supply the place of abstract rights and individual self-government, in order that the peace of such societies may be preserved, and the due security of person and property be obtained. But, I submit, that in the present moral and intellectual condition of the population of this empire, your precautionary conventionalities overshoot themselves. In your alleged anxiety to maintain obedience to the laws and institutions of the country amongst that portion of your fellow-citizens from whom you profess to apprehend danger, if granting to them co-ordinate powers in the constitution with yourselves, you are continually exciting feelings of ill will to your persons, and hatred of your political institutions, from which cause they are at all times exposed to become ready and willing instruments in the hands of bold and designing men, who may be aiming at the subversion of your power and authority in the realm; and thus you are endangering, by your own short-sightedness or prejudice, the stability of that mighty, though complicated, fabric of political power, of which you boast yourselves to be the firmest and truest guardians.

The working-man who will deny himself, if necessary, some customary indulgence, or, to his already protracted hours of labour, add an additional hour or half-hour daily, in order, by the punctual discharge of his franchise-tax, to secure to himself the exercise of that honourable function of citizenship, which is involved in being one of the constituency from which the popular branch of the great deliberative council of the nation shall proceed, presents you with the most indubitable testimony, alike to his intelligence, his public spirit, and private worth, which can, by possibility, be adduced by any one. How insignificant is the forty-shilling annual freehold test, or even the ten pounds rental qualification, as a guarantee for fitness to exercise aright the electoral franchise, compared with what would be afforded by the sacrifice of twenty shillings a year, by a working-man, for the possession of the suffrage!

A man may possess forty shillings a year in the rent of a cottage, or half an acre of garden plot; or, from the circumstance of living in a city or borough where house-rent is expensive, he may possess a ten pounds a year rental qualification, yet be, after all, a poor, mean-spirited, and ignorant being, with neither intelligence sufficient to discern the value of the function with which he is entrusted by the state, nor virtue adequate to the task of exercising it patriotically and independently, if discerned.

Such men as these, with the idle, the dissolute, the grovelling, and the selfish of every class, would exclude themselves from the list of voters soon as ever the franchise had to be paid for, by the cost of a little extra labour, an increased amount of self-denial, or as little of that sordid pelf, upon which their hearts are exclusively set. And who will say that they ought not to be excluded from the exercise of a privilege which they are too much debased to know the value of, or too sordid to care about the exercise of, in an honorable manner? And who will doubt the propriety of allowing the idle, the dissolute, and the sordid, thus to exclude themselves from the electoral roll of their country, as a precaution against the alleged chances of a base, or ignorant majority, obtaining predominancy in the affairs of the nation, over a virtuous, intelligent minority, rather than excluding, by the enactment of arbitrary qualifications, along with them, multitudes of humble, but trustworthy citizens, who could give to the state all the assurances of fitness for the discharge of the duties involved in the possession of the franchise, which it ought fairly to require of them, in order to guard against the possibility of an evil arising.

To impose legal qualifications for the discharge of any privilege of citizenship, which you know cannot be fulfilled by the majority of intelligent, industrious citizens, in the humble walks of life, is, in effect, as certainly to exclude them from its possession, as though you drew a line of exclusion by positive enactment: a proceeding which all men would characterize as an act of the greatest folly, and which would only be saved from their contempt, by the horror which they would feel at its injustice.

Instead of the qualification for the exercise of the elective franchise, amongst a population like to ours, being reduced to some simple, tangible form, which shall make its possession honorable, and its attainment easy, it is placed upon such a footing as to keep up, in the body politic, a constantly-dangerous state of irritation amongst its various members, by which the energy of its powers is continually weakened, and its natural tendency towards improvement greatly retarded.

I would remove all these sources of irritation – these galling, invidious distinctions, which now prevail amongst the body of our humbler citizens, from the partial, capricious disposal of the franchise, tending to render one portion of them corrupt and profligate, and destroying, or at least diminishing, in the bosom of another portion, those feelings of self-respect, which it is at all times so important to foster in the hearts of men who, from their position in society, can exercise but little influence over it, except through the medium of their virtues and intelligence.

No honest, industrious man, even of the humblest class, should be exposed to feel, that by the laws and institutions of his country, whose burdens he had always helped cheerfully to bear, and whose advancement in civilization and wealth he had contributed to promote, he was excluded from the possession of that honourable privilege which those same institutions had capriciously conferred upon others, with, perhaps, far less just title to the regard and esteem of society than himself, and whose only claim to the distinction was, that they were born, or resided, in some peculiar locality, or had become possessed of a certain amount in value of material property, but which, after all, was utterly insignificant in its power to promote the well-being of its proprietor, or advance the general interests of the community, compared with that property, though immaterial in its nature, which he possessed in his skill and industry.

Whatever test is created – whatever qualification may be demanded by the state, as the guarantee for the moral worth and social fitness of those citizens, to whom she delegates the important trust of choosing the representatives of the people to the great council of the nation, and all those other subordinate councils and boards of management, for conducing the affairs of the realm – it ought to be simple in its character – uniform in the principle of its operation – and of easy attainment by every worthy member of the community.

Such advantages, I respectfully submit to the sense of my fellow-countrymen, would attach to the test here proposed, and accompany the adoption of a qualification, created by the payment of a tax for the exercise of the electoral suffrage.

I shall now say a few words in vindication of the proposed new basis for the elective franchise, in reply to possible objections made by those who advocate the 'universal,' or 'complete suffrage' theory.

Whilst agreeing with you in the justness and reasonableness of the abstract principle, that all citizens have an equal claim to a voice in the election of the men to whom is delegated the power to make the laws by which all shall be governed, and to which all shall yield a cheerful and loyal obedience, I am obliged, after a moment's reflection, to acknowledge with you, that no more than yourselves, can I practically realize all that such a principle involves, without, in some degree at least, creating a political Babel, and compromising, to a considerable degree, the well-being of the community.

The 'universal suffragist' fixes upon a particular period in the life of the citizen – the completion of his twenty-first year – before which day, the young man, whatever his fitness in other respects, by natural endowments, or acquired attainments, to form a correct judgment upon any matter or thing submitted to his understanding, shall not be permitted to exercise the elective franchise. He excludes women of every age and degree, however independent their social condition as wealthy widows or spinsters may be, of whatever their acknowledged powers of mind, or extent of attainment in political science – and that at a period when some of the finest intellects of the age, and some of the most useful public writers of our country, are found among the sex upon whom this barbarous brand of moral and intellectual inferiority is fixed; and more especially whilst he is living under the sway of a woman who manifests, in the exercise of the office of sovereign of this great country, a wisdom, a discretion, and a punctual discharge of the onerous duties of her important station, which puts to shame the conduct of many sovereigns of his own sex in this and foreign countries. He likewise denies the possession of the suffrage to the poor man whom, it may be, the force of circumstances alone, over which he could exercise no control, have necessitated to become temporarily dependant on the property and industry of others, for the bread which he breaks among his famishing children, instead of providing it by his own labour; a duty he would readily and willingly perform, were the means as much at his command as the inclination: thus punishing his oftentimes involuntary poverty, as a positive and wilful offence against society. The 'complete suffragist' likewise refuses to recognise the man 'tainted with crime' as a citizen, or to allow his name to continue, or to appear, upon the electoral roll of his country, whose deviation from rectitude may have been, after all, but the result of some new or peculiar form of temptation, which his moral sense had not been sufficiently well trained to grapple with, and which he may have sincerely repented of as soon as committed, but which, nevertheless, this theorist in political institutions, continues to visit, through the whole course of the offender's life, with perpetual exclusion from the honours of citizenship; thus contributing, as far as in him lies, to bar up the way of the man's return to virtuous habits, by striking down, in his heart, at one fell blow, every feeling of self-respect, and making him, in the eyes of his children, and, it may be, of living parents, a ghastly monument of undying social pollution.

Here, then, is settled at once, the possible controversy between myself and the 'complete,' or 'universal suffragist,' as to whether the possession of the elective franchise may be lawfully, or reasonably, made the subject of conventional regulations. They decide that it may be so treated; and I acknowledge the propriety of the decision, without, however, binding myself, by this concession, to the admission, that all the conventionalities introduced by the 'complete suffragist,' into his plan for reforming the institutions of the country, are necessary to the well-being of that society, on whose behalf, and for whose safety, we are alleged to be required, nor yet of the justice of them to the individuals against whom they are directed. I have no wish, or design, by the plan for the franchise here laid down, to narrow the limits of the elective franchise to the population of the country, any more than the class of reformers to whom I have alluded; but rather, to widen the door of entrance into the pale of the constitution: and all I ask for, of them, is to allow me to substitute a new, and what, in my conscience, I believe to be a safer – a more honourable and beneficial conventionality, or qualification, for the exercise of the national suffrage, both to the state and the individual, than any which has hitherto been recognized, or recommended, by the reformers of our political institutions.

It will, perhaps, be urged by some, that the payment of a sum annually – say twenty shillings – would operate as an insurmountable impediment, in the way of many deserving citizens of the humbler class, participating in the elective franchise. Such is not my opinion. That it might operate, in some small degree, to produce such a result, I will not attempt to gainsay. All conventionalities have the unavoidable effect of excluding some one or other from a participation in the privileges of the institution whose interests they are designed to advance or protect; but I am fully persuaded, that the instances would be of extremely rare occurrence, if they were to be found at all, wherein a virtuous, intelligent citizen – a good father, a faithful servant, or an esteemed neighbour – would be found to be deprived of his franchise, for the sake of the payment of this fourpence-half-penny per week.

The payment of this sum might, possibly, require a little extra exertion on the part of some, and make a demand upon the self-denial of others, in accustomed indulgences; and in these things would consist its value, as a test of property and intelligence. If the labourer, of whatever class, could, after discharging the other and more important obligations imposed upon him by his natural and social relations in life, by extra exertion, or the practice of a little restraint in the use of allowed indulgences, spare so much as would enable him punctually to pay his franchise tax, it would prove incontestibly, that he was a valuable member of society: one that might justly, and safely, be entrusted by the state, with the most ample privileges of citizenship.

When it is further taken into consideration, to what purpose the required payment for the exercise of the franchise would be devoted – the honour derived to each individual of the working-classes from the possession of the franchise, under arrangements which would place them upon a level, in this respect, with the wealthiest of the land who should exercise the privilege, and the advantages likely to accrue to him as a labourer and his family, from having such a heavy burden removed from the labour-market, as now presses upon it by the half-million of ill-paid, but hard-worked, aged labourers, male and female, from whom it would, in all probability, be relieved – the diminution of the poor's-rate, in consequence of so many old and infirm persons being otherwise provided for – the consciousness that he was immediately rescuing his aged parents from the imprisonment of a union workhouse, or closing a life of toil in penury out of it, which it was not in his power, in any material degree, to alleviate, and prospectively providing a shelter for himself, in old age, against the storm of life, should he, by the pressure of circumstances, a large family, or the afflictive dispensations of Providence, have been unable, by his independent exertions, to provide a better – I cannot believe that many, if any instances, would occur, where the virtuous, intelligent, industrious citizens, even in the humblest walk of life, would either repine against the payment of the franchise tax, or allow it to operate as an exclusion to him from the possession of the suffrage.

But it may possibly be objected here by some one, that it is unjust to the labouring classes, to fix the payment of the same sum by them for the exercise of the elective franchise, as is required from persons of independent or large fortunes – that there ought to be a considerable difference made between the amount paid by the man who derives five thousand pounds a year from real property, and him who obtains only fifty pounds a year by the result of his labour. My answer to such objections is, that the introduction of a regulation into the proposed new basis for the franchise, which went to recognize the principle, that all the citizens of a state are not equal in the eyes of the law, which, it appears to me, would result from charging one man twenty pounds for the exercise of a privilege for which another paid only twenty shillings, would be productive of incalculable mischief, by interfering with the simplicity of the proposed plan, and thus destroying, to a considerable extent, its efficiency. In granting the franchise, we are only dealing with men as citizens who have lives, and liberties, and properties valuable to each of them, to be kept by the institutions of the country from violence, irrespective of the station they may occupy in society, or the nominal value of the stake they may have in its property. It is to the interest of the working-man, I feel persuaded, no less than to his honour, that he should enter the polling-booth by the same avenue as admits his wealthier neighbour. If he asks for favours here, he must return them when at the hustings. If he requires that a larger fee shall be paid by the rich man, than is demanded for his own admission, he must concede to him the plurality of votes when he is admitted: a regulation which would neutralize at once all the benefits to be derived from the order to which he belongs, being more extensively invested with the franchise.

I, therefore, venture to recommend, that this part of the proposed plan be preserved intact, and that one uniform sum be paid by all persons, from the peer to the peasant, for being placed on the electoral roll of the country; and that every qualification at present required for the exercise of the suffrage, in the choice of Members of Parliament, Municipal Councils, or Parochial Boards of Management, be thenceforward completely and entirely abolished: by which means a fruitful source of irritation, and ill-will, and party spleen, which now keeps the country in an almost continued state of excitement, would be effectually dried-up, and a vast amount of expense be saved to individuals and the nation; which is now expended in litigating disputed claims to the suffrage.

There is, again, another class of persons who will affirm, that such a provision as that I propose shall be made, through the means of a 'National Labour Fund,' for the aged and infirm labourers of the country, will tend to render them improvident, if not profligate and wasteful, during the earlier and more active period of their lives, when they might, it is asserted, be laying up for themselves a store out of their earnings, against the contingencies of age and decrepitude; and that their interests will best be promoted, by leaving them to trust, through every period of their lives, to their own exertions to provide resources against age, or want and sickness: only providing, agreeably with the regulations of the poor-law, that the more delicate nerves of the wealthy shall not be shocked by the spectacle of the poor and the aged perishing through absolute destitution on the thresholds of their doors.

And these same persons will be apt to rail at the injustice, as they will term it, of having their children *robbed* of a tenth part of their patrimony, after the decease of their father, in order to supply the wants of those who may have been rendered improvident, and thus morally prevented from making a more ample provision for themselves, in consequence of having this small patrimony provided for them by the state; and they will, in all probability, tell gravely, that to hold out a prospect to the labourer advancing towards old age, and to whom, perhaps, they have never paid more than from seven to ten shillings a week for his severe drudgery on their behalf, even when in full employment, that if he lives until sixty years of age, and can no longer help himself, he shall be entitled, as of right, to six shillings a week, and his wife to four shillings a week out of a national fund, drawn from the superfluous wealth of former employers, you are rendering him improvident, and inducing him not to take the necessary steps to save four or five hundred pounds for himself; which amount of capital, they well know, it would require, to enable him to realise such an income as should be sufficient to render him independently comfortable in his circumstances; and which amount, they equally well know, none save a comparatively favoured few among the working classes can realize, by any extent of industry and frugality.

That there would be a class of improvident persons who would trust to this fund entirely for a subsistence in their declining years, who might have made some provision for such a contingency, by their labour in the active period of their lives, I make no doubt; but these same persons would have trusted to something else, if they had not the Labour Fund to depend on: the private benevolence of individuals – an asylum in some alms-house – the parish, or any other source of eleemosynary aid, rather than apply themselves vigorously to the task of making a provision for themselves against a season of sickness or decrepitude. But such persons, I assert, do not, and never will, constitute the rule of the class to which they belong; they are but the exceptions, and their conduct cannot support the argument attempted to be founded upon it, without establishing a precedent which would disorganize the whole system of social and parental duties at present recognized among men.

If there be any truth or reason in the objection made against providing a fund for the relief of the wants of the labourer in his old age, on the ground that you will thereby weaken, or destroy, the wholesome stimulus to industry, and the exercise of skill, which now exists from his being left to his own resources for the supply of his future as well as his present wants, and thus render him improvident, at least, if not profligate, we ought not, by a parity of reasoning, as it appears to me, to make any provision for our children or dependant relatives, or, at furthest, not after the period of childhood, lest we weaken the general tone of their moral feelings, and render them improvident and profligate, through the knowledge, that there is laid up for them, after our decease, a store of good things, which they, consequently, have no need to exert themselves to procure. And might not the law, therefore, which took away from the children of the capitalist a portion of their father's accumulations – often much beyond what their natural, or even artificial wants require, to render them comfortable – be considered as having a beneficial aspect, rather than a malignant one, upon the well-being of such families, by stimulating them to greater exertions to supply its place, or by inducing for awhile, at least, a healthy habit of self-denial, in the enjoyment of some customary, though perhaps injurious luxury. To both cases, I conceive, the argument employed to show, that making a known provision for others, against possible and contingent wants, must be injurious to the true interests of the recipient parties – must equally apply, or to neither. If providing a large fund before the eyes of our children, to be by them enjoyed after our decease, be not productive to them generally of any moral or social disadvantage, by inducing immoral or improvident habits, then I cannot see how creating a small fund, for the relief of our dependants during the period of nature's decay, and when the sorrows and weaknesses of age press sore upon their sinking frames, can, by possibility, have any injurious effect upon their habits and principles during the earlier and more active periods of life, even though it be with the knowledge, on their part, that such a provision is making for them.

I believe, on the contrary, that the establishment of a National Labour Fund, such as that I have been advocating, and for such a purpose, would have the certain and immediate effect of elevating the moral tone, both of feeling and acting, among the working-classes generally, and inducing more provident and orderly habits among them, more especially if accompanied by a more liberal and enlightened system of education during their youth, than what has ever prevailed, or ever can prevail, under the present wretched and debasing system, of providing for their necessities. The operative of our manufacturing towns and villages, no less than the rustic labourer, feels that it is of no use, on his part, making any attempt to provide a fund against old age, scarcely even to obtain a little good and substantial furniture, as he well knows from the painful experience of those around him, if not in his own or that of his aged parents, that should any season of dearth of employment arise, or a period of sickness come on, much more when old age arrives, and he is necessitated to make application to his parish for relief, the officer of the union to which he belongs, or in which he may reside, almost uniformly refuses to recommend his case for relief – and consequently the Board of Guardians object to make an order to that effect – so long as he possesses either known funds of his own, however small, or any decent furniture, which he can convert, at whatever sacrifice of value, or old associations, into money. And, consequently, since the labourer knows that he cannot save sufficient to procure himself, in age, even a moderate independent maintenance – and whatever he does save, by extraordinary industry, and the practice of a more rigid economy than those around him – will eventually only contribute to save the purses of those employers in whose service he has spent his health and strength from a little earlier draught upon them, than though he had not made such exertions to effect his trifling savings, and not permanently to advance his individual comfort and well-being. All stimulus to save anything is destroyed, and a fatal habit of 'living from day to day' – the fruitful source of improvidence and waste – becomes habitual to him.

Now this injurious propensity of the labouring classes would, I firmly believe, be more effectually eradicated from among them, by the establishment of the National Labour Fund, accompanied, I again say, by a sound moral education in youth, than by any other means. The love of accumulation, in some form or other so natural to the human breast, might then be indulged in by such of the labouring population as at all enjoyed the opportunity, with a prospect of safety; and we should have the satisfaction of seeing the cottages of our agricultural and manufacturing labourers, presenting the cheering spectacle of a good oaken table, and an elbow chair, and

'A modest clock which clicks behind the door,'

and a good bed on which to rest their weary limbs, when they entertained no alarming apprehension, that if they were enabled to procure a few such useful, and to them interesting, articles, during the vigorous period of their lives, by the exercise of a more persevering industry, or the practice of a greater degree of self-denial in the use of unnecessary enjoyments, than some of their less provident neighbours, they should not have them taken away by the parish, or be compelled to sacrifice them to the supply of their own wants, and thus be reduced to the same condition of destitution as them, before they could, in the season of age and decrepitude, receive any permanent assistance from those, to the building up of whose fortunes, the strength and activity of their youth and manhood had been devoted.

But it will be said, perhaps, that the present flourishing condition of the savings' banks, with the large and constantly-increasing amount of deposits made therein, is conclusive evidence against the statements put forward in these pages, as to the low and wretched condition of the labouring classes. I answer, so it would, if it could be shown, by the returns of those establishments, that their funds were the accumulations of the class on whose behalf I am pleading: but such is well known not to be the case. It is from the ranks of the twelve hundred thousand domestic servants, male and female, of the United Kingdom – the lower grade of excise and revenue officers – from the warehouse, and shopmen and women of our large manufacturing and trading establishments – from the list of county shopkeepers, milliners, dress-makers, and small traders of every description, and their children – from the gardeners, gamekeepers, and bailiffs, on the estates of gentlemen and noblemen – with a goodly number of the members of benefit societies, under one denomination or another, but whose

individual contributions are very small – with a sprinkling of artificers, and manufacturing and agricultural labourers of the better class, who are either living in
a state of celibacy, or are peculiarly advantageously situated, as to employment,
or the smallness of their families – that the eight hundred thousand depositors in
the savings' banks are drawn, and not from the mass of country labourers in general, nor yet from the body of manufacturing operatives of our populous districts.
But, indeed, it would be but a waste of time to show that it were impossible for
any considerable number of these depositors to be obtained from the handloom
weavers – the stocking and lacemakers – the agricultural labourers, and colliers,
and quarrymen, of England, and Ireland, and Scotland, whose weekly earnings
average from 5s. to 12s. each. No, it is not from these classes; nor is it from the
savings of the persons who generally come under the denomination of labourers,
whether agricultural or manufacturing, that the twenty-seven millions of money
now constituting the capital stock of the savings' banks is derived; and it is a
gross delusion on that portion of the community who do not pause to investigate
reports like those put forward by the commissioners for the management of savings' banks, to have it supposed that these returns afford any substantial evidence
of the real condition of the toiling millions of this country.

I shall now say a few words on the scheme for permanently bettering the condition of the working-classes, and relieving the labour market from the weight
of that severe pressure which is constantly resting upon it, by means of an extensive emigration of the labourers to foreign countries: a plan, than which, I can
conceive nothing more futile or unfeeling. For, in the first place, to be in any way
effectual to the accomplishment of its proposed end, it would incur a cost, annually, nearly as great as that which would arise from the establishment of the
proposed National Labour Fund, without giving anything like the contentment
to the population, or being in any degree productive of equal advantages to the
community, by the expenditure of so large a sum. Then it would require powers
to be taken by law, to compel emigration; for certainly, so large a number of the
population as would be required to relieve the labour market from its present
pressure, would not be induced, voluntarily, to leave their native homes, for a
promised better residence amidst the wilds of Canada, or on the plains of Australia: when a storm of popular indignation and resentment would have to be
encountered, that no Government would be strong enough to stand against.
Instead of this emigration scheme, compulsory or voluntary, as a means of promoting the general well-being of the working-classes of the United Kingdom, I
propose to render the people contented and happy at home – attached to the
Government of the country, because they will feel that it is acting towards them
a kind and paternal part – and earnestly devoted to the maintenance of its institutions, because, whether considering themselves, in relation to the upper classes,
simply as men and brothers, or socially as members of the same body politic, they
will know that they are participators with them in like privileges and benefits:
that if national wealth increases, they shall certainly, in a humble degree at least,
partake with the wealthy of the blessings it is calculated to confer: that if political
privileges are to be enjoyed honourably, and exercised freely for the good of all,

they will be allowed the opportunity of possessing them, upon the same free and honourable conditions as the rest of their fellow-citizens.

Having now endeavoured to reply briefly to most of the important objections which I can anticipate being made to the principles of the proposed National Labour Fund, I shall proceed to detail a little more at length, the objects I have in view, and the means I would take for their accomplishment.

There are, I believe, about six million of male persons in the United Kingdom, twenty-one years of age and upwards. Of this number, about three million two hundred thousand will be found in England, eight hundred thousand in Scotland and Wales, and nearly two million in Ireland. Of these, it may well be imagined, that nearly one-third would not make the necessary sacrifice to obtain the elective franchise. I should be extremely happy, on the proposed plan being adopted, to find by the result, that the number of defaulters had been overstated, but am not inclined, at present, to base my revenue calculations on a less number than that above quoted.

This would give four million as the amount of the electoral body, and as contributors to the Labour Fund.

Though the contribution of Ireland, both from the legacy duty and the franchise tax, would, in all probability, be much less in proportion to its population, than any other branch of the Great British family, I would not, on that account, at all diminish the superannuation allowance to their aged labourers, but would pay them back, in this manner, out of the superfluous riches of England, a portion of that wealth which it may be justly said to lose by the present system of absenteeism by its landed proprietors; and thus unite the masses, by the bonds of interest, more firmly to England than they are at present bound.

I have previously estimated the amount of property, real and personal, which annually passes by devise or inheritance to new possessors, at

135,000,000 pounds sterling:
10 per cent. on this sum would realise   £13,500,000
4,000,000 electors, paying a tax of one pound per annum each   4,000,000
                                                      £17,500,000

It appears from the census tables, that out of a population of twenty-seven million, there are something beyond two million of persons living, of sixty years of age and upwards. To avoid factional parts in our calculation, we will take them at even two millions. All these persons I propose, so far, at least, as they are disposed to accept of the conditions under which they can avail themselves of its benefits, to place on the National Labour Fund. As I apprehend, however, that there would be little short of eight hundred thousand of these persons who, from superior condition in life, and other causes, would not avail themselves of its assistance on the terms proposed, the actual number to be provided for would not exceed *twelve hundred thousand*. Again, supposing, for the more readily estimating the results of the division of this sum among the claimants, that we take the sexes at equal numbers, this would give six hundred thousand males, to whom I propose that fourteen pounds five shillings per annum, or five shillings and sixpence weekly, shall be granted as a pension for life; and to an equal number of aged females, nine pounds two shillings per annum, or three shillings and sixpence weekly, payable under the superintendence of District Boards of Management, but which Boards should possess no power to refuse claimants, properly certified, nor to diminish the allowance on account of the pecuniary circumstances of the applicant; their duties being strictly ministerial in their character, and confined to the superintendence of the disbursement of the monies received from the general treasury, auditing accounts, verifying the claims of new applicants, and certifying to the decease of old pensioners, so that their names might be duly removed from the roll.

But there is another class of persons to whom I would extend the benefits of the National Labour Fund, besides the aged. Persons who become maimed, or in any way sustain serious bodily injury in carrying on the operations of the great agricultural, manufacturing, and mining concerns of this opulent empire, including the fisheries, and the general commercial marine of the country; and the widows and orphans of men who lose their lives whilst so employed.

Various casualties are of constant occurrence, some of them of a very extensive and distressing character, in the different departments of the peaceable public service of the nation, by which men lose their lives, whilst yet in the strength of their days, and sustaining all the touching relations of husband and father, in their tenderest and most extensive amplitude; and before they have been able, by their exertions, to make any provision beyond the passing day, for the supply of the wants of those they loved. In which case, the widow and orphans of the man, who was, perhaps, an ornament to the walk of life to which he belonged – bold, skilful, industrious and enterprising – sink rapidly down into a condition of the most pitiable misery: or, where death does not immediately ensue, the late honest, robust labourer, who, up to the period of the accident occurring, which may have deprived him of his eyesight, or the use of some one of his limbs, or have otherwise incapacitated him from labour, had been accustomed to support himself and family in comfort and independence, becomes compelled, with that family, or such portion of it, at least, as are immediately dependant upon him for support, to take refuge from starvation within the walls of a workhouse; or, if allowed to enjoy a freedom from this restraint, but on condition that he takes up with an allowance from his parish, cut down to the lowest possible amount, generally, on which life can be sustained.

Now, I contend, that justice and humanity alike demand, on the part of these unfortunates, that the society in whose service the husband and father has been maimed, or injured, should make at least decent provision for his wants, and the necessities of those who have no resources but that they have been accustomed to derive from his labour: much more ought it to make provision for the widows and orphans of the men who have perished in their service.

To leave such a family to be dealt with, after the loss of their head, as troublesome and burthensome paupers, who may be confined within the narrow limits, and subjected to the insulting degradation of an union workhouse; or be half-starved out of it, according to the option, or caprice, of some inconsiderate or unfeeling parochial official, whilst you make an ample and honourable provision for your wounded and disabled soldiers and sailors; or, even where not wounded nor disabled, after a specified number of years spent in the service of their country, by large annual grants of the public money, which they enjoy in honour and independence – is the maximum of cruelty and injustice.

I propose to entirely do away with this invidious distinction, by the nation, in its treatment of the sons of war, and the children of peaceful industry, considering that, of the two classes, the latter has the greater claim upon the gratitude and generosity of their country; by giving to the labourer or mechanic, the merchant's seaman, the miner, or artificer, who becomes maimed, mutilated, or rendered, in any way, incapable of obtaining a supply for his wants and that of his family, whilst engaged in carrying on the operations of industry, or assisting in the preservation of life and property from the ravages of flood or fire, an independent pension for life, similar in amount to those enjoyed by the pensioners of the royal naval and military colleges: as, likewise, to make a suitable provision for the widows and orphans of such men as lose their lives in the performance of the duties of their station.

It is somewhat difficult, perhaps, to make anything like a correct estimate, in the absence of all statistical information on the subject, of the number of claimants which this provision would bring upon the Labour Fund; but they would not, in all probability, be less than *two hundred and fifty thousand*, which, on an average allowance of eight pounds annually to each person, to be apportioned according to the circumstances of each individual case, by the different district boards before alluded to, would amount, in the gross, to two million pounds.

The total amount of the various items which, it is proposed, shall constitute the great National Labour Fund, it will have been seen, are estimated to amount to seventeen million five hundred thousand pounds. After having made this statement, I shall now proceed to detail the probable amount of the claims likely to be made upon it.

Income of fund, say		£17,500,000
Six hundred thousand male persons, at		
£14 5s. per annum each	8,550,000	
Six hundred thousand females, at £9 2s.		
per annum each	5,460,000	
Two hundred and fifty thousand persons, of		
all ages, widows, orphans, and disabled		
men, at £8 per annum each	2,000,000	
		15,900,000
Balance in favour of fund		£1,590,000[1]

It will thus be seen, that with the allowance I have proposed to make to the aged and infirm labouring population of the empire – and which would place half a million, at least, of persons now suffering under undeserved privation and degradation, in a condition of independence and comparative affluence – there

---

1 N. B. Error in original.

remains a million and a half pounds sterling, to cover arrears of calculation and unavoidable expenses attendant upon working the system laid down, or to be added to the amount of the pensions, as at present fixed, or extending the benefits of the fund to other claimants, as circumstances might require.

When it is further considered, that all the mass of wretchedness at present endured by the classes above alluded to, might be redressed, and a long train of positive and direct benefits be conferred upon the labouring classes in general, from the diminished action upon the labour market of the country, by reason of so many hands being withdrawn from it through the operation of the fund, more especially in the agricultural districts, thereby causing labour to become more abundant for the young and active of both sexes, and thus again operating indirectly to enhance the value of labour in the manufacturing districts, by inducing the rural population to remain at home, instead of flowing, with a constant stream, into the towns, as is at present the case – I think the plan proposed cannot but commend itself to the consideration of every humane and patriotic mind in the community.

The farmer is not called upon, by the scheme of social improvement here recommended, as by some philanthropic plans now advocated through the press, to employ labourers that he cannot find sufficient work for, and at wages which he cannot afford, in order to save his person from the vengeance of an infuriated multitude, or his property from the torch of the incendiary. A fund, created by the aggregate wealth of the empire – collected in a way, too, which gives no just cause of complaint to any individual, on the ground of his being deprived, by fiscal exaction, of the fruits of his industry, for the maintenance of others – relieves him, at once, from a great proportion of his superfluous labour, and converts those who remain into cheerful and obedient servants, instead of being sullen and revengeful serfs, as is their present character, very extensively.

Take, for example, the county of Suffolk, at present the scene of so much calamitous disorders. Out of the three hundred and fifteen thousand population which it numbers, there are about twenty-six thousand five hundred persons sixty years of age and upwards, and, of course, eligible candidates for the benefits of the proposed National Labour Fund. Of this number we may venture to strike off eight thousand five hundred, agreeably with the rule formerly laid down, who would not accept the aid of the fund from one cause or another: this would leave eighteen thousand as the number to be provided for by the Labour Fund, the whole of which mass of persons are now, as paupers, or half superannuated labourers, either a dead weight upon the labour market, or a direct and oppressive burthen upon the already impoverished tenantry of the soil, preventing, at once, the active younger labourer from obtaining full employment, and debarring the enterprising, but poverty-stricken agriculturalist, from undertaking those improvements on his land, from which himself would derive immediate benefit, and the community ultimately lasting advantage.

Did Suffolk alone derive pecuniary advantages from the labours of its toiling masses, it might be right that to the proprietary of Suffolk alone should be left the duty of providing for the wants of the eighteen thousand aged labourers which are found among its population: but it is not so. The labourer of Suffolk, as well as of every other district, is less the labourer of a particular locality than he is the labourer of the nation; and the *millionaire* of Threadneedle-street or Grosvenor-square is not less indebted to his sturdy and persevering labours for a portion of the enormous wealth he possesses, than is the lord of the soil on which he was bred. It then is as impolitic as it is unjust, to fling upon the struggling industry of a district, that charge which ought to be paid out of the accumulated wealth of the nation. Till this be done, the working-classes never can derive any certain advantages from the improvement of machinery, the extension of foreign commerce, or a reduction in the cost of the necessaries of life. Give them this boon – secure to them a certain, though even but a small share in that vast and continually-accumulating store of national wealth, which their skill and industry mainly contribute to create, and you will remove the barrier to the improvement of their moral and physical condition, which at present stops the advance of civilization among them, and renders them, by reason of their sufferings and degradation, an easy prey to the designs of evil-minded and designing men.

Many other advantages arising from the adoption of the principle of a National Labour Fund, and its application to the objects contemplated in these pages, I humbly think, cannot but suggest themselves to every unprejudiced reflecting mind, which will condescend to entertain the subject. I have studiously avoided, in treating on the important questions before me, any attempt to go into minute details as to the management of the proposed fund – the various methods by which evasion of the payment of the legacy duty might be checked – the way in which the franchise tax should be collected, or any other matter not appearing to me as absolutely called for in the present state of the question, lest I should distract the attention of my readers from the consideration of the leading subjects.

If I am but so fortunate as to be enabled, by these pages, to convince any considerable number of my countrymen, that there is great danger to the peace and ultimate well-being of British society, in the continuance of the present ill-regulated relations between the producers of wealth and its possessors, I shall, for the present, be satisfied. I am now contending but for *principles* – principles which I believe to be sound and practicable, and the adoption of which I hold to be essential to the present prosperity and future security of these realms. The recognition of them by the Government and leading men of the empire, would tranquillize the now irritated labourers of the country – would allay, to a considerable extent, if not entirely, the discontent of the non-privileged class, at being excluded from the elective franchise – would soothe the wounds of Ireland, and render England happy, glorious, and secure, the pride of her own children, and the admiration of the population of every other country under Heaven.

'All Men are Brethren.'

AN ADDRESS TO THE
FRIENDS OF HUMANITY & JUSTICE
AMONG ALL NATIONS,

BY THE
DEMOCRATIC FRIENDS OF ALL NATIONS.[1]

London:
PUBLISHED BY J. CLEAVE, 1, SHOE LANE, FLEET STREET;
SOLD BY H. HETHERINGTON, 40, HOLYWELL STREET, STRAND;
J. WATSON, 5, PAUL'S ALLEY, PATERNOSTER ROW;
C.H. ELT, 18, HIGH STREET, ISLINGTON;
AND ALL BOOKSELLERS.
1845.

---

1 One edn, 1845, 8 pp. Probably written by William Lovett.

ADDRESS.

BRETHREN,

We who presume to address you are a few persons belonging to different countries, who, recognizing 'THE UNIVERSAL BROTHERHOOD OF MAN,' are desirous of seeing some efforts made towards the carrying out of a principle so often acknowledged, so seldom practised, and so frequently violated.

All men being *'brethren'* should surely seek to promote each others happiness, whatever may be their individual country, creed or colour. All being brethren, should evidently stand on an equality to determine what political and social arrangements are best necessary to promote the welfare of all. All being brethren, possessing various powers and capacities of mind and body, have surely equal claims to have those powers developed and cultivated, so as to cause them to become good and useful members of society. All being brethren, whose lot is cast in various climes and countries, but whose labour is more or less required in all, should, in justice, stand on an equality to perform some useful labour or employment, and have the fruits of their industry and frugality secured to them. All men of all countries, being connected by their wants and necessities, should surely live in amity and peace, freely exchanging their productions, and benefiting and improving *all* by the labours and fruits of *each*.

These few propositions we believe are true and just deductions from the great principle of *human brotherhood*; and were we competent to lay them before the minds and consciences of universal humanity, we are assured that they would readily respond to their justice.

But in what way is this righteous principle recognized in what are called 'the civilized nations of the world'? Is it not for the most part a mere lip response of momentary feeling, a hollow sentiment of sympathy or charity, rather than a practical principle of humanity and justice? Is it regarded in our social or political arrangements? is it practised in our trade or commerce? is it thought of in our wars and devastations? is it recognized by our rulers, governors, or teachers? The almost universal reign of oppression and injustice throughout the world will answer, 'No!'

First let us look to those of *our brethren*, by whose incessant labours this earth has been redeemed from marsh and forest, and made to teem with every production necessary for human enjoyment. Do we not find millions of them yet condemned to perpetual bondage? mere human property, to be scourged, lacerated and condemned to mental darkness at their masters' will? Are not millions of them mere toiling serfs, compelled to labour out existence for the coarsest of food and clothing? and are not millions toiling, *yet starving while they toil?* Those beings, naturally endowed with capacities of mind for high and noble purposes, are either left a prey to the vices of ignorance, or if awakened to reason, only to feel their fate with a keener pang.

Turn we next to the millions of *our brethren* by whose skill and labour our cities have been raised, our habitations built and furnished with every necessary for convenience and comfort – to those whose ingenuity and industry have converted almost every production of nature to the uses and arts of life – to those who have constructed and have manned our fleets, and by their enterprize converted the seas into highways of commerce – turn we to view the skill and industry evinced in every department of life; in field, factory and workshop; and what condition in the social scale shall we find the majority to be in *who have contributed so largely to human enjoyment?*

Are they treated politically or socially as *brethren of the same human family?* Do we not find millions of them daily dependant, and supplicating for leave to toil? – braving all hardships, from birth till death, for the scantiest pittance – their families often rendered desolate by a fluctuation in trade or a whim of fashion – the fruits of their industry monopolized, taxed, tithed and extorted to the life-sustaining point – their prayers for justice disregarded, their petitions sneered at, their claims to all rights despised.

Is the principle of *human brotherhood* practised in our trade and commerce? After all the exertions of humanity, are not millions annually sacrificed by the execrable traffic in human beings? A republican government upholds it; men called civilized consider it just; the power of wealth sustains it; monopoly pleads its policy; and statesmen connive at its monstrous injustice.

Where, too, is the *justice* of the host of monopolies, foreign and domestic, which in all countries still paralize the hands of industry, and poison the fountain head of commerce? severing nation from nation, and depopulating, starving and oppressive in their effects.

Have rulers or statesmen ever regarded *humanity* or *justice* towards their *brethren* in their cruel warfare against each other? In their forcing by proscription or stratagem the helpless and ignorant portion of them to take up weapons of destruction against those they had not seen nor had just cause for resentment? What pyramids of bones! what rivers of blood! has earth concealed, of the brutal victories and savage trophies of those pests to human happiness and human kind!

Have those who are considered our teachers been mindful of their duties on behalf of *the great brotherhood of man?* Have they been true to their professions in condemning the injustice and corruption of rulers? in denouncing war, cruelty and oppression? – in labouring to call up the mental powers of man on behalf of suffering humanity? – have they sought to unite *individuals* in harmony and *nations* in fraternity and peace? So far from honestly performing their duties in these respects, they have (with few noble exceptions) sought their own personal interests, by flattery, by silence, or by perverting the truth.

Perceiving, therefore, that selfishness, force and fraud are every where allied against the just interests of the many, and that this alliance is productive of misery so extensive, of injustice so universal, and of humanity every where so trodden down and degraded; we appeal to you, *men and women of all nations*, whose natures have been quickened by the essence of humanity, whose minds have been awakened to justice, to join heart to heart and mind to mind, in an earnest resolution to IMPROVE, EXALT, INSTRUCT AND REFORM SOCIETY, IN ALL COUNTRIES, AMONG ALL NATIONS.

It is not to your *charitable* feelings we appeal, but to your sense of *justice* towards those you regard as *brethren*. The deep-rooted evils of society need other specifics than alms-giving, charitable institutions, or pauper aid; they need the *causes* to be removed which have placed the industrious many at the mercy of the few. Those causes we believe you will find in *exclusive political power, class legislation, defective knowledge, corrupt rulers, bad laws, unjust privileges, and monopolies of various kinds;* and we have the experience of the past, with its black train of evils, to convince us that so long as exclusive power prevail, so long will such fruits follow and humanity suffer.

We would implore you then to make common cause with the oppressed – to blend your voices with theirs in a demand for justice – to devote your talents and energies in quickening and directing the mental and moral energies of society to the establishing of free and equal institutions throughout the world, under which intelligence, peace and happiness may be universally established, in place of injustice, oppression, cruelty and wrong.

Not that we would incite you to outbreaks or violence; for we have faith in the mental and moral combinations of men being able to achieve victories for humanity beyond the force of armies to accomplish. What is wanting are men armed in all the moral daring of a just cause, and resolved at all risks to pursue and achieve their righteous object. Let but the same daring, mind and resources which have so often warred with tyranny, and so often been worsted in the conflict, be once *morally applied and directed*, and citadels, armies and dungeons will soon lose their power for evil.

A cheering prospect to encourage you to espouse the cause of humanity is seen in the extent of mental light which is so rapidly being diffused among the productive classes. They are gradually awakening to a sense of the wrongs inflicted on them by exclusive institutions and privileged orders, and are beginning to declare that they too *are brethren of the same common family*. Many of them may have mistaken the *forms* for the *principles* of true democracy; may have had too much faith that others would accomplish that freedom for which each individual must strive, and may still have too much confidence in arms and sinews, and too little reliance on mental and moral effort. But the spark of mind once kindled is inextinguishable; it will spread silently and surely, to the destruction of old errors, time-worn institutions and gothic privileges; till the mind-illumined ranks of labour shall rise up in all their moral grandeur, to declare them vain and puerile, and that henceforth *the brotherhood of man shall be their rule and motto*, and that the heroes of their veneration shall be the wise, the good, the true, and useful, who have laboured to redeem the world from slavery, oppression, ignorance and crime.

Convinced that the subjects upon which we have addressed you are above all national, sectarian or party views, and that good men of all opinions and of all countries should be united in the good work, we have for some time past laboured to effect a better understanding between reformers of all nations. We possess neither rank, wealth nor station, considered so necessary in this age to command success; but we believe we have espoused the cause of *right*, we desire to do something to aid it, and think we deserve the alliance of all those who believe that our object is good.

We remain your brothers in the struggle of humanity, 'The Democratic Friends of all Nations.'

Signed on their behalf,
L. OBORSKI, Chairman.[1]
CHARLES SCHAPPER,[2] Hon. Sec.
24, King-street, Soho.

20 January 1845.

---

1 Ludwig Oborski (1787–1873), Polish ex-military officer.
2 Karl Schapper (1812–70), German socialist exile, teacher.

AN ADDRESS TO THE CHARTISTS
OF THE UNITED KINGDOM,

BY THE NATIONAL ASSOCIATION FOR PROMOTING THE POLITICAL AND SOCIAL IMPROVEMENT OF THE PEOPLE.[1]

London:
PUBLISHED BY J. CLEAVE, 1, SHOE LANE, FLEET STREET;
SOLD BY H. HETHERINGTON, 40, HOLYWELL STREET, STRAND;
J. WATSON, 5, PAUL'S ALLEY, PATERNOSTER ROW;
C. H. ELT, 18, HIGH STREET, ISLINGTON;
AND ALL BOOKSELLERS.
1845.

---

1 One edn, 1845, 8 pp. Probably by William Lovett.

ADDRESS.

FELLOW COUNTRYMEN,

It is now nearly seven years since those principles which we deem essential for securing the *just* representation of the people, were embodied by the Working Mens' Association in the document called the PEOPLE'S CHARTER; and we think the time has arrived when it will be well to review the past, and consider of the future prospects of our righteous cause.

The principles of democracy, of mental and moral progress, put forth about that period by the Association referred to, and reciprocated by a great number of similar societies in different parts of the country, were fast calling up friends and advocates among all classes; were uniting the scattered elements of radicalism so as to infuse new hopes in the minds of all genuine reformers; were gradually undermining prejudices and inspiring confidence in the working millions of our country, when a few active emissaries, under the guise of reformers, commenced their career to undo, by violence and folly, what good had been thus effected.

That you may judge how far they were *friends* to our cause; – they began by ridiculing all mental and moral reformation, and boasted of their victories over all those who sought the attainment of their political rights by *moral means*. They industriously sought to break up the Associations formed, and maligned, calumniated and denounced all who disapproved of their projects. They showed what was *their* democratic spirit, by seeking to inspire the working classes with feelings of hate and deadly hostility against the middle classes of society. They exhibited *their* spirit of toleration, in endeavouring to put down by conspiracy, force and clamour, all individual opinion, all free discussion, and all public meetings, except such as administered to their sinister interests. In short, no despotism (wanting the power of life and death) could have evinced a more persecuting, intolerant and revengeful spirit, than that shown by those *professed friends* of popular rights.

By such conduct they immediately scared back all who refused to be participators in folly and intolerance – by their falsehoods, and misrepresentations through their own corrupt organs, they soon spread distrust, alarm and division among us; and thus opening a breach for the enemy, they brought persecution, incarceration, banishment and death into our ranks; and the consequent contentions which have weakened us, and strengthened our oppressors.

All subsequent attempts to promote an effectual union of the people have been marred by the same anti-democratic spirit; intolerance and bitterness have been nursed and panegyrised by those marplots of our cause, to the disgust of all true reformers, the disspiriting of all sincere Chartists.

Of those who first sowed the seeds of disunion among us, some have since appeared in their true *tory* colours; but others are now as sedulous as ever in preventing all union, save such as can be made subservient to their purposes. Their dupes and tools are weekly hounded on to bark down all independency of mind, and to mar every reform effort which does not square with their master's interest. Such, too, is their inconsistency, that those who approach the nearer to their professed principles, are marked out as especial objects of their hatred and persecution. Yet while they boast of their *'whole hog'* principles, the have suffered themselves to be dragged through the mire of *Toryism* – to be spurned at for their fawnings after *Repeal* popularity – and to be used for purposes and crotchets as foreign to Chartist principles as they have proved themselves to be from true reformers. By such conduct they have disgraced our principles and rendered our name odious; so much so, that great numbers who admire the justice of the Charter, have been constrained to plead the cause of equal rights under a name less objectionable. The vast numbers of our countrymen once banded in Chartist brotherhood, have either shrunk back in disgust from Chartist intolerance, have gradually been persecuted from our ranks by Chartist despotism, or are silently waiting the result of time and events to awaken their unhappy countrymen to a sense of their degradation.

Such is the condition to which our cause has been reduced by bad men and pernicious council; in the meantime all the evils of class legislation are perpetuated, and the enemy, secure by our divisions, sneers at all proposals for redress.

Amid this state of disunion and despondency we deem it our duty to address you, for *we cannot be brought to believe that you would knowingly consent to be the instruments of your own slavery*. We are persuaded that numbers of you have been deceived by sophistry, and led by falsehood to injure the cause you have so warmly espoused. We seek to call you back to reason; we have no interests apart from yours, we may honestly differ from you regarding the best mode of effecting our object, but we are equally agreed on the necessity for its attainment.

For amid the present distracted state of our cause we have the strongest faith *in the justice of Chartist principles* – still believe that those who have once espoused them will always cherish them, and still hope, that you, the Chartists of the United Kingdom, will yet arise *in your mental and moral might*, purified from past errors, and will unitedly and ardently strive for the attainment of those rights, proclaimed by the Charter, by conduct which shall win the esteem of the wise and good of all classes, so that ere long government will be powerless in opposing your claims.

We would ask you then, in all sincerity, whether the conduct we have referred to is in accordance with your professions of democracy? *Democracy*, in its just and most extensive sense, *means the power of the people, mentally, morally, and politically directed, in promoting* THE HAPPINESS OF THE WHOLE HUMAN FAMILY, *irrespective of their country, creed or colour*. In its limited sense, as regards OUR OWN COUNTRY, it must evidently embrace *the political power of all classes and conditions of men*, directed in the same wise manner, *for the benefit of all*. In a more circumscribed sense, as regards INDIVIDUALS, the principle of *democracy* accords to every individual *the right* of freely putting forth his opinion on all subjects affecting the general welfare – the right of publicly assembling his fellow-men to consider any project *he may conceive* to be of public benefit, and the right of being heard patiently and treated courteously, however his opinion may differ from others.

We regret to say, fellow-countrymen, that, in almost all these particulars the principle of democracy has been violated by a great number of professing Chartists. What would *you* think of your arguments and resolutions *in favour of the Charter*, being continually met by speeches and amendments in favour of any one political measure? of every public meeting you got up being invaded by them, and your proceedings drowned by clamour? Would you not justly denounce them as despots, thus to assail and obstruct your right of public meeting, by constantly introducing a subject foreign to the object for which you had assembled? And is it just, we would ask, to do that to others which you would condemn in their conduct?

Be assured, fellow-men, that such proceedings can never serve our righteous cause; and the proof is afforded in seeing that those who have indulged in it are only powerful for mischief, the disgust of all reflecting Chartists, dupes of the enemy, blind to their best interests; not only disgusting their friends, but affording their enemies plausible arguments of their unfitness for the suffrage. We can readily believe that some persons may find their interests promoted by such insane proceedings; but surely you who desire to see the Charter the law of England, can never suppose it can be realized by such disgraceful means. We would ask the thoughtful and considerate among you, whether such conduct has not driven from our ranks hundreds of intelligent and active individuals, who, in different localities, once formed the stay and strength of our cause? Nay, are not hundreds to be found, who lament the loss of parents and friends sacrificed by violence and folly, instigated by those same individuals, who are still the fomentors of strife and disunion?

Judging from their conduct towards the middle, the trading and commercial classes, persons might be led to suppose that the Charter was some exclusive working-class measure, giving license for abuse, threats, and violence, instead of a measure of justice for uniting all classes in holy brotherhood, for promoting the common good of all. That the working classes too often experience wrong and injustice from persons in all those classes, as well as from those who possess the political power of the State, is admitted; but surely those evils can never be redressed by such conduct! No, friends! There is a principle of goodness, of right and justice, pervading universal humanity! to that principle we must appeal, that we must cultivate, that combine, if ever we hope to see political justice established.

Be assured that those who flatter your prejudices, commend your ignorance, and administer to your vices, are not your friends. 'Unwashed faces, unshorn chins,' and dirty habits, will in nowise prepare you for political or social equality with the decent portion of your brethren; nor will the ridiculous title of 'imperial Chartists,' prepare you for the far better one of 'honest democrat.' Empty boastings, abusive language, and contempt for all mental and moral qualifications, will rather retard than promote your freedom; nay, if even you possessed political power, would still keep you the slaves and puppets of those who flourish by popular ignorance.

But it is for you, *the reflecting portion of the Chartist body*, to determine whether renewed efforts shall be made to redeem our cause from its present position; whether the enemy shall continue to avail himself of those means hitherto so successfully applied to divide us; whether we shall continue to be pitied by the good, feared by the timid, and despised by all those who fatten on the fruits of our industry; or whether we shall purge and purify our ranks of those who now disgrace it, and by a combination of the wise and good, once more rise into vitality and strength.

About three years ago we addressed you on the same subject. We then especially told you that 'YOU MUST BECOME YOUR OWN SOCIAL AND POLITICAL REGENERATORS OR YOU WOULD NEVER ENJOY FREEDOM.' That while you were contending for the Charter you should apply your means to develope the mental and moral energies of your brethren, so that they might the sooner obtain the suffrage, and use it wisely when obtained, instead of being, as they then were, the dupes of those who lived by their credulity. We also pointed out the means by which this desirable object might be effected. Instead of us receiving that courtesy due to all proposals of public benefit, we were assailed with the grossest abuse and vilest persecution; week after week the most unblushing falsehoods were put forth against us, till great numbers of you were induced to believe that we had abandoned the Charter and the people's cause.

Fellow-countrymen, we have advanced our cause despite of this conduct; we have since proved what combined and prudent efforts can achieve, in one locality, which, if our plan had been carried out at the period referred to, might now be realized in about two hundred and fifty different districts of the kingdom; we having now a spacious Hall, Reading Room, Library, and Sunday School; and our past success gives us the most auspicious prospects for the future.

Having so far succeeded, we once more invite you to make similar exertions in your respective localities; and be assured that if you evince a disposition to politically instruct and morally improve yourselves, you will not want assistance from the well-disposed of other classes who interest themselves in your welfare. However few you may begin with, however humble may be your means, if you direct your attention to your own moral and political elevation, if you are sober in your habits, and prudent in your conduct, you will gradually win the respect and confidence of all good men, and will be making the best preparations for freedom.

If you desire your Associations to be confined to your own locality, and under your own management, there is nothing in the plan of our Association to prevent this from being effected; it having been so constructed as to render this practicable, and at the same time in accordance with the laws of the land. We may act individually in our own localities, and yet be all legally united in the bonds of fellowship for the advancement of our great object, *the Political and Social Improvement of the People*.

But whether you adopt the plan of our Association or that of some other which you may deem more efficient for the effecting of this great object, we would implore you to discountenance the intolerant and anti-democratic conduct which has brought odium on our name, still rationally and peacefully to pursue your agitation for the People's Charter, as the foundation of your political rights, *and prove that you deserve it* by conduct superior to that of those who now exercise the exclusive power of legislation.

We remain your friends in the struggle for political rights, the Members of the National Association.

Signed on their behalf,
W. LOVETT, Sec.

National Hall, 242, Holborn, Feb. 12, 1845.

AN ADDRESS
FROM THE NATIONAL ASSOCIATION FOR PROMOTING THE POLITICAL AND SOCIAL IMPROVEMENT OF THE PEOPLE

TO THE WORKING CLASSES OF AMERICA,
ON THE WAR SPIRIT
THAT IS SOUGHT TO BE EXCITED BETWEEN
THE TWO COUNTRIES.[1]

London:
J. CLEAVE, 1, SHOE-LANE, FLEET STREET;
SOLD BY H. HETHERINGTON, 40, HOLYWELL STREET, STRAND;
J. WATSON, 5, PAUL'S ALLEY, PATERNOSTER ROW;
C.H. ELT, 18, HIGH STREET, ISLINGTON;
AND ALL BOOKSELLERS.
1846.

---

1 One edn, 1846, 8 pp. Probably by William Lovett.

ADDRESS, &c.

WORKING MEN OF AMERICA,

By our alliance of blood, of language, and religion, as well as by every aspiration we feel for the mutual freedom, peace, prosperity and happiness of our respective countries, we would address you as *brethren*; in the assurance that, as brethren, our interests are identified, and in the hope that no other spirit than that of brotherhood may long continue to exist between us.

But the hostile threats and warlike preparations, the jealousies and prejudices now sought to be fomented by the interested, thoughtless, and immoral of your country and our own, have awakened us to a deep sense of the dangers which threaten the peace and welfare of the *Working Classes of all Countries*; – evils which we believe our mutual understanding and wise and determined resolutions may timely avert.

You, fortunately, possessing political power to restrain the unjust acts of your rulers, are, we fear, too apt to believe that the persecutions, encroachments, and insolence which for ages past have characterised the Aristocracy of England towards most nations of the earth, have been shared in by the great body of the industrious classes; who, unhappily, for the most part, have hitherto had *neither voice nor vote* in the matter.

That the power and influence of our Aristocracy over the minds and consciences of men, their perversion of every principle of morality and precept of religion to uphold their power and monopolies, have often enabled them to enlist great numbers of our unreflecting brethren to fight their battles, and espouse their cause, we readily admit; but those, we conceive, should be pitied, rather than blamed, as the deluded victims of selfish and hypocritical men; persons who have perverted justice and truth for gain, and the religion of peace and good-will for the purposes of war, contention, and strife.

Within the last few years, however, knowledge has been rapidly extending its influence among the industrious millions of England – universal right is now asserted, and is progressing, despite persecutions and sufferings – anomalies, corruptions, and vices in Church and State, are being exposed – unjust privileges and monopolies decried; and mental and moral worth fast allying itself to the cause of humanity and justice. Thus knowledge, extending and combining, is fast calling forth mental light and political power, tending to the good of our country, such as our State Church can no longer mislead, standing armies restrain, nor aristocratic influence avert.

This progressive improvement towards a higher state of civilization and happiness, to which all good men are looking forward with delight, our aristocratic rulers would gladly mar, and nothing but war and national commotion would favour the accomplishment of their wishes. With the high-swelling cant of 'individual glory' and 'national honour!' the din and dazzle of warlike preparation, they would speedily intoxicate the unreflecting. They would then be enabled to turn the national mind from all social and political improvement to the prospects of foreign battles, and brilliant (though expensive) victories. Our present moral and intellectual progress, the advance of trade, commerce, and the peaceful arts of life, would then be stayed and obstructed by the unholy scourge of war, and thousands of our brethren, having their worst passions loosened and excited, would be transformed into savage demons, thirsting for blood.

We beseech you, working men of America, do not permit yourselves to be drawn or seduced into war, and thus afford the enemies of our liberties and the haters of yours, a pretext and opportunity to produce those lamentable results; nay, it may be, to jeopardize the rights and liberties which you now enjoy. Your country has long been an asylum for persecuted freedom throughout the world, and your democratic institutions inspire the hopeful and struggling among all nations; but while your Republic offers a beacon to cheer and animate the friends of human rights and equal laws, it at the same time sends forth a light that despotism would fain extinguish. For, be assured, the Despots of Europe would gladly cast aside their petty contentions to form another unholy alliance against the growing Republic of America; and though their combined power might fail to crush your liberties, they would not fail in desolating your shores, and in destroying great numbers of your people.

What, too, has prevented the further developement of *your* national resources? – the cultivation of your fertile soil? – the increase of your capital? – the progress of your commerce? – and the further prosperity of your people? What, but the same power that has retarded *our* liberties, paralized our manufactures, crippled our commerce, and pauperised and impoverished our country? What, but the selfish monopolising aristocracy of England? who, by their prohibitory laws, their imposts and burthens, have raised up barriers of injustice and enmity, to prevent the prosperity of both countries.

Despite their maddened efforts, however, those barriers are fast yielding to the progress of thought; the knell of monopoly and injustice is sounding, and the prospect of political righteousness and social happiness is lighting up with hope the cheeks of our famished and pauperised population. Working men of America, do not, we pray you, by any unwise proceedings on you part, retard or prevent the consummation of such prospective happiness, the fruits of which you will not eventually fail to share.

We fain hoped that Republican America was free from that mania of Kings and Princes, the grasping after territory and dominion. They think that any amount of *real power or advantage*, either to you or to us, could be gained by the possession of such an inhospitable and savage region as that now disputed by your rulers and ours? Think you that the *strength* of England is augmented by her dominion over her colonies, most of which she must keep bristling with bayonets, to keep down her half-rebellious progeny? It is true, they may form objects of solicitude to the scions and offshoots of our aristocracy, enabling them to eat the bread of idleness, but to the mass of the English people they are far more burthensome than profitable. Surely the disputed question, regarding the territory of Oregon,[1] might be amicably settled by arbitration, the peaceful and just mode of arranging all such matters, without plunging our two countries into war, and, it might be, the whole of Europe also; and, with such an unfortunate event, all its destructive consequences – a state of desolation and misery it would take centuries to repair.

And surely you, the Working Classes of America, cannot so readily have forgotten the lessons of your greatest statesmen and profoundest philosophers respecting the evils and consequences of war; nor can we suppose that you have less regard for those great principles of morality and religion which unitedly condemn it as one of the monster evils that afflict our race.

Working Men, this military and warlike spirit must be curbed and kept in subjection, if ever we desire the civilization and happiness of our race. Men, indeed, cannot be called civilized who will consent to be made the tools and playthings of statesmen, or who delight in the playing of soldiers on their own account. The constant appeals to the individual vanity and mere animal propensity of the soldier, and the narrow spirit of nationality sought to be engendered, are antagonist to the mental and moral developement of our nature, and the broad and ennobling principles of universal brotherhood and peace.

How much longer will the labouring population of the world submit that that wealth which is accumulated by their incessant toils, anxieties, and privations, shall be applied to the keeping of thousands in idlenesss and vice, with no other object in view than that of still making them toil for the drones of society, or the going forth at the bidding of their rulers to murder and destroy. For, in our desire for human progress, we could wish that what is called '*honorable warfare*' and '*glorious victories*' were properly designated NATIONAL CRIMES! For were they for the most part stripped of their gloss and glory, *and tried by our moral or Christian code*, one of them would exhibit an aggregate of crime, comprising murder, robbery and devastation, more black and atrocious than could be found in the collected annals of a century.

The war spirit already excited between our two countries has prepared the way and given a pretext to our rulers to inflict additional burthens on our working-class population. Already they have announced their intention of adding, under the name of a militia, upwards of 40,000 soldiers to our present army; to take our brethren from their homes and avocations; and while, on the one hand, they cause us to pay upwards of *ten millions annually* for our Clergy, to preach to them

---

1 Disagreements between Britain and the United States over the western boundary of Canada in the region between the Columbus River and the 49th Parallel were finally settled by the Oregon Treaty in 1846.

the religion of *peace and brotherhood*, to impose additional taxes, on the other hand, for the purpose of imbuing their minds with the spirit of *war and vengeance*.

This additional number of human beings, who by their skill and labour could raise food, clothing and habitations to bless the half-starved millions of our country, are to be taken, many of them from their wives and children, *for three years*, to be drilled and disciplined in the arts of destruction; and, it is said, to be kept apart from their fellow-citizens in *military barracks*, doubtless lest sympathy and interchange of thought should disqualify them for their brutal profession.

This burthen too will, in all probability, as usual, fall upon *the Working Classes* for the most part; for, should they seek, *by fine or substitute*, to avoid being taken from their homes and families, the poorest labourer on his shilling per day will have to pay equally with the wealthiest person in the kingdom; the consequence will be, that wealth will in most cases procure exemption, and the sons of poverty be left to their fate.

Such, friends, are the first fruits of this warlike excitement here, about a portion of territory of little use to either country, and which perhaps, in strict justice, belongs to neither. But why should we, the industrious classes, year after year, and age after age, thus submit to injustice? We, whose interest is in the peaceful cultivation of our respective countries – in the production of the conveniences and arts of life – in the peaceful interchange of our commodities, – and in the intellectual and moral developement of ourselves and children – why should we, who have no quarrels or disputes with one another, be thus continually made the *victims or tools* of those who delight in contention and profit by war?

Fellow-men! deeply impressed with the wickedness, injustice and misery that always flow from such contentions, we would call upon *all good men*, but more especially on you, *the Working Classes of England and America*, to use every intellectual, moral, and political means you possess, to extinguish that spark of national animosity which is now sought to be fanned into a flame, and to be prepared to make any personal sacrifice to prevent the direful calamity of war between the two countries. On this subject we have morality, Christianity, and justice on our side; and if our firm and peaceful conduct should call forth the power of the law or the strength of the oppressor, *we had better be martyrs in the cause of right, than suffer ourselves to be coerced into the shedding of human blood, and the retarding of the civilization of our race*.

We trust, however, that this dispute of our rulers may be speedily settled by arbitration; and earnestly hope that the growing intelligence of the age may lead men to perceive *the demoralizing and deteriorating effects of soldiers and armies*, and to perceive that *war is more fatal in its moral and physical effects, than the plagues, earthquakes, and tornadoes of nature*. That so impressed, they will speedily *free themselves from the evils and expences of standing armies, garrisons, and ships of war* – that they will soon seek amicably to settle their national disputes by a CONGRESS OF NATIONS, freely chosen by the people of their respective countries – and that through such instrumentality universal peace and human brotherhood may be established, freedom extended, commerce promoted, and the arts, industry, and civilisation of *each*, be made to contribute to the welfare of *all*.

In the ardent desire for fellowship and peace, and in the hope that both our countries may advance in knowledge and happiness, and seek to promote the happiness of all others, we remain, your brethren, the MEMBERS of the NATIONAL ASSOCIATION.

Signed on their behalf,
W. LOVETT, SEC.

National Hall, 242, Holborn,
January 20th, 1846.

AN ADDRESS FROM
THE NATIONAL ASSOCIATION
FOR PROMOTING THE
POLITICAL AND SOCIAL IMPROVEMENT
OF THE PEOPLE

TO THE WORKING CLASSES OF THE UNITED KINGDOM,
ON THE SUBJECT OF THE MILITIA.[1]
ADOPTED BY A PUBLIC MEETING AT THE NATIONAL HALL,
FEBRUARY 11, 1846.

London:
J. CLEAVE, 1, SHOE-LANE, FLEET STREET;
SOLD BY H. HETHERINGTON, 40, HOLYWELL STREET, STRAND;
J. WATSON, QUEEN'S HEAD PASSAGE, PATERNOSTER ROW;
C.H. ELT, 18, HIGH STREET, ISLINGTON;
AND ALL BOOKSELLERS.
1846.

---

1 One edn, 1846, 8 pp. Probably by William Lovett.

ADDRESS.

FELLOW COUNTRYMEN,

Our hopes and interests being identified with yours, in the *freedom, peace, prosperity* and *happiness* of our country; and, entertaining the most ardent desire that we may all *rapidly progress onwards towards the realization of those blessings*, we believe it to be the duty of each and all of us to be ever watchful of all movements likely to counteract the good which our oppressed countrymen are so much in need of.

And believing that the movement now making towards re-organizing of the Militia force, calls for the watchful attention of all those interested in the welfare of their brethren, we are thus induced to address you; so as to lay before you such information as we have obtained on the subject, such reasons as we conceive should be urged against such a mischievous and uncalled for measure, and at the same time to express our belief that if it is not timely frustrated by the combined sense and moral determination of the people, it will inevitably produce an extensive amount of social and individual wrong.

Our information regarding this movement is as follows: –

On the 25th of December last a circular appeared in the public papers addressed by Sir James Graham,[1] to the Lord Lieutenants of Counties, requesting them to fill up vacancies of officers in the various regiments of Militia *before the spring.*[2] At the same time, suggesting that those officers who had been reported as unfit for active duty might still be competent to perform local duties connected with the *billeting, enrolment, and training of the Militia.*

On the 27th of the same month there appeared in the Times and Chronicle, articles referring to the above circulars, in which they inform their readers that the subject ought not to be lightly treated, as *no one above the age of twenty-one need flatter himself that he could avoid the ballot* – that out of the number enrolled in a district, *one-third of them were to be called on for duty for three years*, and that they would be continually required *at the barracks* for that period, after which they would have the option of volunteering into the line.

By the tenor of those documents, by the increase of men in different regiments, by the orders for arms and accoutrements, as well as by the active recruiting that has been recently going on, both for army and navy, there can be little doubt of the spirit and intention of this warlike movement. And though explanations have been given by those in authority tending to lull the unreflecting into apathy and indifference, yet they are all, in our opinion, far from

---

1 Sir James Graham (1792–1861), Home Secretary under Peel, 1841–6.
2 See *The Times*, 1 December 1845, p. 5.

satisfactory; for they all go to inform us that the Militia Acts are to be altered, '*so as to afford greater facilities for the calling out and training of the Militia force*,' though a less onerous system than the ballot is to be introduced. That, though 'government has no power under the present law to embody the Militia, yet *it hath the power to call them out for training*, and *beyond that it was not intended to go*.'

But, fellow-countrymen, it behoves us to tell those by whose acts we shall be the principal sufferers, that the question is not the mere distinction between embodying or training – between *embodying* additional thousands of our brethren, by some new process, or *the calling out and training* of upwards of forty thousand of them who were embodied under the old – but the question is, *whether there is any necessity for any addition to our present warlike establishment or not?*

That there is *no necessity for any additional force*, but that the force we already possess is detrimental to the best interests of society, we submit the following reasons: which we solemnly give as our *protest against the whole debasing machinery*, by the aid of which the toiling millions have ever been made the slaves of the few.

1st. Because, as the Industrious Working-Class population of the United Kingdom are debarred of *all political right*, they ought not to be made either the *tools* or the *victims* of political wrong-doers – and inasmuch as an exclusive few have hitherto abrogated to themselves all power of law and government, of peace and war, they alone ought to be made responsible for their own acts, by being obliged to settle their own disputes.

2nd. Because an addition of 42,000 *Militiamen* to our present *Standing Army* would be an uncalled-for aggravation of our national evils; burthensome and demoralizing to the people of this country, *and would cause other nations to believe that we were more desirous of war than of an amicable settlement of our disputes*.

3rd. Because our present monstrous War Establishment of 220,009 *fighting men! costing nearly fifty millions annually!* is a disgrace to a civilised country, and the more so to a country professing the religion of 'peace and good-will to all mankind;' producing no other results than those of burthening, pauperising, and enslaving the people of this country, and, by exciting the apprehensions and jealousies of others, causing them to inflict similar evils on their people.

4th. Because the warlike establishment of most of the countries of the world are fostered and promoted by the *few* for the purpose of keeping the *many* in subjection – and in this country in particular have been used for the purpose of restraining freedom at home and abroad, and for maintaining the exclusive power, privileges, and monopolies of a corrupt and grasping aristocracy.

5th. Because, through the instrumentality of this system of force, fraud, and injustice, millions of our countrymen have perished by battle, famine, fire, and shipwreck – millions their hard-earned wealth have been vilely wasted, and our country at present kept poor and pauperised *by her war debts of eight hundred millions*.

6th. Because the spirit nurtured by soldiers, armies, and war, has hitherto been *the great perverter of morality*, as it has created two opinions on this vital subject the most opposite and inconsistent; the one teaching that it is *right and moral for nations and governments* to murder, plunder, and destroy the lives and property of their fellow-men, and the other that it is wrong and *highly immoral for individual members* of the same nation or government to do so; thus perverting the eternal principles of right and justice in favour of the vices of the powerful, and wreaking vengeance on the weak for having followed such pernicious examples.

7th. Because the spirit of war, being that of vengeance, is opposed to 'peace, forgiveness and charity,' and must tend therefore to *corrupt or nullify the religious feelings of the community*; for the preacher or expounder of those humanizing precepts who is constrained by his rulers to consecrate the colours of a regiment, to offer up prayers for victory, or thanksgiving for the reeking triumphs of war, must appear before an enlightened people as a hypocrite or a perverter of the truth.

8th. Because the spirit of war, by more or less imbuing the *literature* of a country, *poisons the fount of education and learning*; for the false lustre cast on warlike achievements, on savage battle and human carnage, perverts the moral sympathies, and gives ambition a stimulus to evil; and the false notions of *greatness* so generally stamped on the men-destroying heroes of society, must cause great numbers to be more emulous of being earth's tyrants than man's deliverers.

9th. Because the war spirit of a country, combined with aristocratic wealth and power, prevents *the efforts of genius and achievements of art* from being made more efficient means of human refinement and moral elevation; those being oftener employed in pourtraying the destructive prowess of kings, princes, and warriors, and in transmitting their forms and vices to posterity, than of those whose acts and deeds have dignified our nature, and shed blessings on their country.

10th. Because *the industrious classes of all countries have in reality but one great brotherly interest*, that of living in friendly and peaceful intercourse, enjoying the fruits of their industry, and causing the blessings of each country to contribute to the welfare of all; and as soldiers and armies are instruments in the hands of the few by which nations are divided, impoverished, and enslaved, it is the paramount duty of every man desirous of improving society or blessing his race, not only to refuse to be made such an instrument of oppression and cruelty himself, but to warn all others of becoming such.

These, fellow-countrymen, are a few of the *reasons* we would urge, not merely against the present *Militia movement* (because that may individually affect us), but for the purpose of directing your serious attention to the deepest foundation and remotest consequences of *the whole destructive machinery of war and warriors*. For so long as you, the industrious classes, can be induced to believe that standing armies are necessary for our country's safety – that bayonets and bullets are the best instruments for settling the disputes of nations, and that it is 'honourable' *to murder* by the process of war; so long, we fear, are you likely to be enamoured with drums, ribbons, and the false glare of military glory! and will those who maintain their power and ascendancy by brute force, be enabled to raise their *fighting tools*, and always find fresh disputes to keep them in exercise.

But when *you* are taught to perceive that the *safety* of our country is more likely to be secured by the freedom, prosperity, and happiness of our people, by our strict love of justice in all our foreign relations, and by our seeking to cultivate a free and friendly intercourse with all nations, than by trusting its safety to ambitious statesmen or warlike adventurers, with thoughtless soldiers at their command – when *you* are taught to perceive, that by our country exhibiting such a just and benevolent example to other nations, that mutual interests and fraternal obligations would speedily spring up so as to *prevent disputes from arising*, or if occasioned, to be peacefully settled – when *you* are convinced that war is man's greatest curse, and soldiers the chief instruments by which he is enslaved, then *will your knowledge give you power* to commence a new era in the history of nations.

Then will you refuse not only to become soldiers yourselves, but will seek to show your brethren throughout the world, of the individual and national evils they everywhere inflict – then will princes and statesmen, wanting their instruments of *coercion*, be obliged to listen to the *reasonable* demands of their subjects – then shall we witness the peaceful triumphs of human industry, of intellectual and moral elevation, and will men be more anxious to blot out from remembrance such tales of human carnage as have recently assailed our ears, than to laud their perpetrators as heroes, or to erect statues to their memory.

To the accomplishment of this desirable end all good men should direct their energies, and though power and privilege, church and state, are at present allied against them, yet right, justice and humanity are destined to prevail.

But, working men, do not, we pray you, regard the present movement in the mere spirit of selfishness, conceiving that you are only interested so far as your person or property may be individually affected, the inconveniences of which you may hope to avoid, by getting your more needy brother to risk his liberty and life for some paltry consideration.

If you think, with us, that *soldiers are instruments of human oppression and individual degradation, the chief means of generating national disputes, war and misery,* – if you thus think, you will be prepared with us to make any sacrifice, rather than *directly* or *indirectly* aid in fostering so monstrous an evil.

This conduct may possibly involve our personal safety or individual liberty, but you should remember that no great object has yet been accomplished without sacrifice, and be assured that our individual sacrifices will be diminished in proportion as we are united in the support and countenance of one another, and as our conduct is firm, peaceful, and determined.

Trusting that you will not permit your interests to be betrayed by your apathy – that you will be watchful of all warlike measures introduced by your rulers, and that your voices may be raised throughout the land against the whole debasing machinery by which we are impoverished and politically enslaved, is the sincere wish of your fellow-countrymen.

Signed on their behalf,
WM. LOVETT, Sec.

[James Leach.][1]

AN ADDRESS TO THE PEOPLE OF GREAT BRITAIN ON THE PROTECTION OF NATIVE INDUSTRY,[2]

BY A
CONFERENCE
OF THE UNDERSIGNED FRIENDS OF THE PEOPLE,
ASSEMBLED IN THE PEOPLE'S HALL,
BIRMINGHAM,
JUNE 22ND, 1846.

PRINTED BY JAMES LEACH, 40, OAK-STREET.

---

1 Ascribed to James Leach.
2 One edn, Manchester, 1846, 12 pp.

Fellow Countrymen, – The present important crisis is pregnant with the most serious events, and involves consequences, on the direction of which depends the future welfare or misery of millions of our fellow-beings. Though there is no country in the world which displays such an abundance of wealth as England, through the skill and industry of her people, combined with the productive power of chemical and mechanical science, yet there is not a nation at this moment where the industrious classes so essentially require a comprehensive and just legislative protection to insure a righteous distribution of the produce of labour – such a distribution as would render and secure happiness to the great body of labourers and artisans.

As labour is the source of all wealth, so is the fair distribution of its produce the true foundation of all national greatness. 'To live and let live,' is an old & valuable maxim, and the nation or people that disregards it lays the foundation of social ruin, paves the way to anarchy and confusion, and but too often leads to rapine and bloodshed in moments of excitement, and to bitter tears of sorrow in the hours of reflection.

The principle of buying cheap and selling dear, which is sought to be established as the basis of our legislation, is not only opposed to the permanent welfare of society, but its advocates forget, or seem rather to disregard, the great fact, that to make labour cheap, *which is the foundation of all other cheapness*, is to make everything which is produced relatively dearer to the labourer, when it exhibits to every enlightened and humane mind that anomalous state of social derangement existing in this country of the industrious millions starving amidst the abundance of wealth which their own industry created. The end of all legislation is to protect the weak against the strong, and to accomplish this object is the great purpose of national combination and the only source of human justice; hence the injustice and impolicy of those laws and institutions, whatever might have been the motives that induced their formation, which tend to increase the disproportion of means between the various classes of society; rendering the wealth and resources of the country the elements of class aggrandisement, instead of securing a wise and just distribution amongst all ranks whose services contribute to the riches and strength of the Commonwealth, and whose interests are inseparable from its welfare and prosperity. Those laws and institutions which defeat this order of things, frustrate the very blessing this government is instituted to dispence, every enjoyment which art and industry could confer, and makes legislation the supreme instrument of public wrong and oppression, instead of the source of protective justice and the foundation of social advancement. The laws of nature teach man to produce the necessaries of life, the arts and sciences enable him to acquire its comforts. A wise and just system of legislation would insure an equitable distribution, and all would possess that

happiness, security, and rational enjoyment ordained by the wisdom of a beneficent Providence.

Let us then review the calamitous consequences which have resulted from the
principles upon which the commercial policy of the league is based, and which
has now been carried into the legislation of the country by the force of that
immense wealth which has been accumulated at the expence of human life, degradation, and misfortune; to such an extent that we feel assured, when known to
the people, will call forth such a demonstration of moral combination and power
as must command equally the attention of the Government and the respect of
the enlightened of every rank of British society. To deprive labour of all legislative
protection – to expose the British artisan and labourer to the unlimited competition of all nations, to leave the toiling millions without either representatives in
the Legislature or protection for their labour by law, is so repugnant to the immutable principles of justice and reason, and so fraught with popular adversity and
oppression, that no man who can foresee the dredful results, or contemplate the
eventual insecurity and misery of the people, performs his duty to his country if
he remains unmoved a mere idle observer. The utter hopelessness of the people
of any substantial act of national justice, to guarantee to them for their assiduous
industry a just and ample reward, has made the labouring classes utterly regardless of the progress of these mischievous and fatal doctrines promulgated by the
advocates of Free Trade.

Public ignorance is the real source of public wrong, and hence those classes
whose interests and personal aggrandisement is advanced by the sacrifice of the
general welfare ever seek to engage the public confidence and to excite by mis-
tatements the most extravagant hopes the people may become the instruments
of their own degradation, and the means of accomplishing the oppressive measures of their avaricious and unprincipled advisers. The progress of science and
national wealth, which ought to have contributed to the moral elevation and
social comforts of the industrious, have, on the contrary, been usurped by a section at the State, and however anomalous it may appear, it is an incontrovertable
fact that, in the proportion as science has been developed, labour has been depre-
ciated; that as commerce has been extended, the reward of skill and industry has
been abridged; that as the riches and resources of the nation have increased, the
happiness and security of the people has been diminished; that as the general
abundance of wealth has been augmented, in the same proportion has crime, disease, poverty, and premature death increased amongst the labouring population;
that as mechanical power has been applied to the produce of manufacture and to
substitute human labour, the hours of toil have extended, and even infant labour
been used to supersede, nay, to annihilate the labour of the British artisan. In evidence of this we insert the following table:–

Lbs of Cotton Manufactured.

In 1797	23,000,000	M'Culloch's Statistics of the British Empire.
1804	61,364,158	
1811	90,309,668	
1818	162,122,705	Porter's Progress of the
1825	202,546,869	Nation, Vol. 1, p. 205.
1835	333,043,464	
1840	460,000,000	Parliamentary Papers.

In the same years the wages in weaving and spinning departments decreased as follows: –

The wages of the hand-loom weavers were per week,

In 1797	£1	6	8	
1804	1	0	0	
1811	0	14	0	
1818	0	8	9	John Fielden, Esq., MP
1825	0	6	4	
1835	0	5	6	
1840	0	3	6	

Since 1840 the manufacturers of cotton have proportionally increased, while wages have not advanced; but, on the contrary, have either decreased or the amount of labour has been augmented.

From this we find, that in two branches of our important manufactures the trade has increased no less than two thousand per cent within 43 years, during which period wages have been reduced in a progressive ratio to one-seventh of what was formerly paid. It is impossible to conceive, from the table above cited, the privations and domestic misery which inevitably must have been entailed upon this class of operatives; and to establish the correctness of the calculations just made, we here insert an extract from a pamphlet issued by the Anti-Corn-Law League in 1842: –

'In addition to the enormous reductions in the virtual wages, and the purchasing power of the operative classes, it has been calculated that the total amount of money wages paid to the operatives engaged in the cotton manufactures throughout the kingdom is seven millions less per annum than it was 5 years ago.'

This deteriorated condition of the operatives engaged in manufactures has been the result of that unlicensed competition which now pervades British society, and which is carrying before it every vestige of social right and domestic security formerly enjoyed by the working classes, rendering human life and happiness mere merchandise in the hands of the overgrown capitalists; for, while the wages of labour, which constitute the only means of existence of the operative, has undergone so fearful a depreciation we find that the accumulations of wealth

by the manufacturers is without parallel in the history of trade, yet these manufacturers league together – contribute enormous sums of money – for what
purpose? Surely humanity would suggest, to restrict this fatal and destructive
progress of social misery and disorganization. Alas! it is but to extend the system
which has produced this state of things – to widen the field of competition which
has already involved society in one universal struggle for existence – manufacturer against manufacturer, tradesman against tradesman, and operative against
operative; the worst passions of all classes are thus brought into conflict. The
large capitalist pursues his scheme of accumulations – competition, to him, is
increased wealth. The mechanic organises his trades unions, contributes a portion
of his declining wages to arrest its progress; for every stride competition makes,
while it increases the riches of the manufacturers or employers, it makes further
encroachments upon the life of the working man, on his comfort, or the welfare
of his family, and dooms him to the fate of thousands which he beholds around
him perishing amidst the wealth which they have laboured to produce!

The various trades which, by extraordinary efforts of combination, or from
peculiar social advantages, have been enabled to sustain their wages, will no
longer find combination an available means of protecting wages. Competition,
however ruinous, however disastrous, even confined internally to Great Britain,
is but the index of the consequences which must ensue from a universal competition with every nation on the continents of Europe and America. Let this table
demonstrate how far we are enabled to compete with foreign countries: –

Taxation per head per annum in the different countries of Europe.

	£	s	d
Tuscany	0	8	4
Naples	0	9	2
Rome	0	10	0
Sweden	0	10	0
Prussia	0	11	8
Portugal	0	13	4
Austria	0	12	6
Spain	0	15	0
Russia	0	17	6
Denmark	0	18	4
Netherlands	1	7	6
France	1	8	4
England	3	13	4

Names of Countries	*Wages paid on the continent of Europe*			
Odessa	Mechanic	1s.	2d.	per day
	Labourer	0s.	4d.	
Russia and Poland	Mechanic	1s.	3d.	
	Labourer	0s.	5d.	
Spain and Portugal	Mechanic	1s.	3d.	
	Agriculturist	0s.	7d.	
Denmark and Germany	Mechanic	1s.	4d.	
	Labourer	0s.	9d.	

Names of Countries	Wages paid on the continent of Europe		
France	Mechanic	2s.	7d.
	Labourer	1s.	2d.
England	Mechanic	3s.	4d.
	Labourer	1s.	6d.

Leaving the above tables to speak for themselves, we turn to another part of the subject, still more serious.

It has also been industriously circulated 'that increase of commerce has ever been accompanied with proportionate beneficial effects on the social condition of the working classes.' That such is not the fact we have amply proved, so far as wages have been concerned; but let us pursue the investigation further, that we may ascertain the general extention of our trade compared with the health and morality of our increasing population. The official value of exports in 1805 amounted to, 25,003,308*l.*; 1815, 41,712,002*l.*; 1825, 46,468,282*l.*; 1835, 78,376,732*l.*; 1841, 102,180,517*l.* Committals for crime during the same period: – In 1805, 4,605; 1815, 7,898; 1825, 14,437; 1835, 20,731; 1841, 27,760.

However lamentably the above table illustrates the demoralisation of the people, and establish the great fact, that our commercial regulations are based upon the moral and social degradation of the working men, we find that even the numerous advantages which wealth places in the hands of our employers has not in any manner been employed to mitigate those evils, by improving the condition, or otherwise alleviating the domestic privations of their suffering operatives. We find, by returns to Parliament, that in twenty parishes, examined by her Majesty's Commissioners, in Gloucestershire, that one in thirteen were educated, whilst in seventeen manufacturing towns, the numbers were one in twenty-four, in Manchester, one in thirty-five, and in Leeds, one in forty-one!

From the same authority we take the following table, exhibiting the contrast of the durations of life in manufacture and agriculture. The proportions of deaths in children under three years of age, out of one thousand, are in

Dorsetshire	281
Devonshire	296
Westmoreland and Cumberland	253
Manchester	496
Leeds	447
England and Wales	334

The rate of mortality, therefore, is greater in Manchester than in England and Wales by forty-four per cent., and that in Westmoreland and Cumberland by ninety-six per cent.

The proportion of deaths in persons of seventy years of age, out of every thousand, is as follows: –

Agricultural part of Durham	202
Devonshire	208
The Metropolis	99

The whole of England and Wales 140
Manchester 53
Liverpool 60
Leeds 68

To contemplate the amount of human misery to which the working population of our manufacturing districts is subjected, we have only to reflect upon the fearful fact, that in Manchester and Leeds one-half of the children born die before they attain the age of three years. Would the removal of all protection to native industry put an end to this horrible system of human sacrifice, seeing that the removal of Protection is only sought for the purpose of accelerating the progress of that unrestrained competition which produces those very results? A change is required, a great and comprehensive reform is inevitable. But, is the League the moral instrument for this great work? Have its members any interest in putting a termination to the oppressions by which they have acquired their enormous riches? No. Justice must be the fruit of our own public efforts. If we have not intelligence, moral integrity, and energy, aided by the enlightened and humane of all classes, then our lives, our skill, and industry must remain the mere property of our oppressors. But we have those elements of political power in our own ranks – we can produce advocates in defence of native industry, who, sustained by the consciousness of a just cause, will cult forth an expression of public opinion, to which the Legislature must listen.

What, however, can we think of the opponents of Protection to labour – the rich manufacturers, who comprise the League – labouring to attribute the whole evils from which we suffer to the effect of the Corn Laws and our commercial Tariff? Their conduct, however, has not simply been confined to the force of arguments, but they have adopted means, as discreditable to their honour as gentlemen as their principles are detrimental to the country, to arouse hatred between the different classes of society and to throw the sole responsibility of public oppression on the aristocracy alone, who, whatever may have been their policy as legislatures (and God forbid we should palliate wrong!) however culpable of neglecting the interests of the masses of agricultural labourers engaged in the cultivation of the soil, however much they have failed by judicious measures of legislation to restrain the tyranny of capital, or to promote as far as laws could properly advance the means of all classes, whether employed on the land or in manufactures, procuring an ample reward for their labour.

We nevertheless have evidence far beyond what the limits of our present space will admit, to prove that there exists a system of oppression, in the manufacturing districts, without parallel in the history of civilisation although the League, as if poverty afforded the members composing that body the only subject of ridicule, manufactured beds which were exhibited in the bazaar at Covent Garden Theatre, London, to be given away in charity to the agricultural labourers of Dorsetshire, whilst the Rev. Daniel Hearne,[1] Roman Catholic Priest, of St Patrick's Chapel, Manchester, stated in the 'League Conference,' held in Manchester, 'that

---

1 Daniel Hearne (d. c. 1852).

in one district of that town, there were two thousand families without a bed amongst them.'

In conclusion, we solemnly protest against the measures brought forward by her Majesty's Ministers, as utterly destructive of our interests as workmen, and this protest is still further strengthened by the fact, that the working classes are not represented in the Legislature; and hence the introduction and success of extensive measures of commercial change through both Houses of Parliament, without consulting the judgment of the people, is equally opposed to justice, and to the spirit of the British institutions. If the industrious millions are to be excluded from legislation – if their interests are to be invaded, the remaining fraction of their comforts to be further abridged, every element of social and national security is to be abrogated to gratify the avarice or ambition of political faction – then that period is not far distant when the people, betrayed by the professions of statesmen, by the artifice of popular agitators, and legislation made the instrument of national wrong, will cease to rely on either the wisdom or justice of those who exercise the functions of supreme government. And who that desires the welfare of his country would not come forward at this crisis to avert the calamities of national convulsions which ever accompany the defection and despair of oppressed humanity.

To the enlightened of all ranks we now make an appeal, to co-operate with the people in the great national undertaking of establishing an efficient protection for national industry. The rights of labour cannot be held sacred in the legislature of the state, and the labourer will reciprocate his respects to the law. With those who hold the land and wealth of the country rests the responsibility of peaceably and legally accomplishing this essential improvement of the working classes.

It will not be the work of a day, but its success is as certain as its justice. It will not be consummated by isolated efforts, but we have the capabilities of sustaining a national struggle, and the safety, prosperity, and future greatness of the country now demand both our energy and perseverance.

With prudence, decision, and peaceful agitation we must triumph; but we must have an efficient organisation, embracing men of all classes favourable to our welfare – an organisation extending from the metropolis to every village throughout the country.

The objects and rules of the National Association for the Protection of British Industry are now in the course of preparation, and will be ready in a few days. We will then, relying on the approval of providence, and engaged in the cause of justice, proceed, with an enthusiasm worthy of our great undertaking.

JAMES LEACH, Printer, Manchester.
C. S. DEVANPORT, Japanner, Manchester.
WM. JONES, Operative Bootcloser, Liverpool.
JOHN MASON, Operative Bootmaker, Birmingham.
JOHN LEACH, Operative Tailor, Hyde.
R. G. GAMMAGE, Cordwainer, Stoney Stratford.
WM. BELL, Fustian Cutter, Heywood.

P. M. BROPHY, Wood Turner, Manchester.
JOHN WEST, Silkweaver, Macclesfield.
E. WILLIAMS, Ropemaker, London.

THE FRATERNAL DEMOCRATS.

ADDRESS OF THE FRATERNAL DEMOCRATS
ASSEMBLING IN LONDON
TO THE WORKING CLASSES OF GREAT BRITAIN
AND THE UNITED STATES.[1]

1846.

The usual weekly meeting of this society took place on Monday evening, July 6th, at the White Hart, Drury Lane. Joseph Moll[2] in the chair.

Some new members were elected, and a considerable number of candidates were nominated for election.

JULIAN HARNEY[3] then moved the adoption of an 'Address to the Working Classes of Great Britain and the United States' on the settlement of the Oregon question. The 'address' had been prepared by the secretaries on the 4th of July, the anniversary of the Declaration of American Independence.

Carl SCHAPPER[4] seconded the motion, and briefly addressed the meeting.

DAVID ROSS[5] supported the motion.

The address was unanimously adopted.

JULIAN HARNEY moved that a copy of the address be forwarded to the Editor of *Young America*, with a letter of thanks to the National Reformers of New York for the course pursued by them in relation to the Oregon question and the Mexican war. Agreed to.

---

1 One edn, 1846, broadsheet.
2 Joseph Moll (1813–49), Cologne tailor.
3 George Julian Harney (1817–97), Chartist leader.
4 Karl Schapper (1812–70), German revolutionary.
5 David Ross, elocution lecturer, O'Brienite.

ADDRESS OF THE FRATERNAL DEMOCRATS ASSEMBLING IN LONDON TO THE WORKING CLASSES OF GREAT BRITAIN AND THE UNITED STATES.

'All men are brethen!'

Friends and brothers, – On the fourth of March last – four months past – we addressed to you a lengthy and earnest appeal on the then hostile attitude of the two nations, occasioned by the unsettled state of 'the Oregon question.'

In that 'appeal' we protested against the then threatened 'war' between the two countries, and endeavoured to show the barbarity, inhumanity, and folly of a physical contest, and the ruinous consequences to both nations, which could not fail to result from such a struggle.

Happily our fears have been dispelled, and our best hopes realised, by the amicable adjustment of the differences between the two governments.

It is our pleasing task to congratulate you on the peaceful and honourable settlement of 'the Oregon question' – a settlement which testifies to the progress of those principles of international justice and universal brotherhood, which it is the object of our organisation to promote and extend.

Working men of the United States, – It is with pain we accompany these congratulations with a notice of the war now raging between you and the people of Mexico. We will not too closely scrutinise the merits of the question at issue between the two Republics; but we may at least be permitted to doubt the necessity for this contest, when we find it condemned by bodies of your own countrymen. The National Reformers of New York have, in a series of resolutions, denounced this war as unjust to Mexico, and disgraceful to the United States. The people of Massachusetts, or at least that portion of them who are devoted to the Anti-Slavery Cause – forming, we believe, the majority of the people of that State – have gone further, and denounced this war as 'a war for the extension of slavery' – pledged themselves not to support the war – asserted that there is an end to the constitution of the United States – and, finally, have *summoned the people of that state to take the initiative in establishing a new compact, 'which shall be a union of freemen, and freemen only.'* With these facts before us we must at least question the justice of your cause in this unhappy war. As to its policy, there can be no doubt that it is a policy exceedingly short-sighted and anti-republican.

In our former address we endeavoured to show what would be the evils which would necessarily result to you from a war with Great Britain. We were then speaking of a great and mighty war – a war which would have shook the world. Of course, equally serious results are not likely to flow from the 'little war' with Mexico, but some of those results will undoubtedly be seen.

In the first place, the United States' 'regular army' – that pre-eminent curse of modern nations – is to be doubled; fifty thousand volunteers are to be enrolled and provided for; and your government is empowered to greatly increase the navy. At the commencement of the war your President had ten millions of dollars at his disposal, to meet the cost of the contest; but if the war continues for even a short time, he will require five, perhaps ten, times that sum.

Increase of taxation, the derangement of trade and commerce, with the loss of life, and the usual horrors of war; – all these are but minor evils compared with those against which we warned you in our former address: –

'Increase of territory will bring with it a permanent increase of your navy and "standing army," an increase of naval and military officers, an increase of tax-gatherers, and other locusts, who, having a disrelish for honest labour, will strive to permanently quarter themselves upon you – first by prolonging the war, and afterwards by voting the continuance of "war establishments" in time of peace, to retain your force-won possessions. The result cannot fail to be the corruption of public morals, and the ultimate destruction of your Republican institutions.'

Already some of these evils are seen. Your military men already assume a position inimical to the safety of the republic. Thus you have seen General Scott[1] intriguing for his own nomination as the future President, instead of attending to his military duties. On the other hand, you have seen General Gaines[2] issue an edict for raising, not merely the militia, but a regular army of twelve thousand men, without a vote of Congress, without the warrant of the President, without any warrant indeed save the General's own idea of the necessity of raising the force. A monstrous stretch of power, which, no matter what may have been the intentions of the General, no matter how honourable and patriotic his motives, was nevertheless practical *treason* to your institutions, and must excite the anxious fears of all who wish well to your republic.

Much as we abhor slavery, and strongly as we question the justice of your course towards Mexico, still we should regard the division of your republic as suggested by the Massachusetts 'abolitionists' to be one of the greatest calamities that could befall the human race. Besides, the Massachusetts 'abolitionists' only see half the evil. In their own state, and throughout the 'free' states, a system of slavery exists, practically destructive of the theoretical equality guaranteed by your institutions; the slavery we allude to is the 'slavery of wages,' a system which has already reduced the 'free-born' men of your order almost to a level with the degraded state of the industrious orders of Europe. The land, which should be the property of the state, is becoming rapidly monopolised by private landlords, speculators, and traffickers, while the working class, hived up in huge cities, are competing with each other for a bare subsistence, the prey of the profitocracy who, with their brother plunderers of the landlord class, are fast acquiring all the substantialities of aristocracy, and even now rival in luxury, arrogance, and tyranny the Molochs of rank and money in the old world. To give mere personal liberty to the slave of the South, without at the same time guaranteeing him the

---

1 General Winfield Scott (1786–1866).
2 General Edmund Pendleton Gaines (1777–1849), who commanded the department of the southwest during the Mexican War.

means of subsistence by endowing him with a portion of the soil, would be conferring upon him only a nominal emancipation. On the other hand, experience has proved that the 'equality' which gives men votes but leaves them the social slaves of wealth, and subjected to the demoralising influences of great cities is but an illusory equality. This last section of workers are, however, not altogether helpless; they have franchises, the proper exercise of which would save them; and if you, working men of America, suffer from the evils which afflict European society, you have in a great measure yourselves to blame for your own misfortunes.

People of the United States, in addressing you on this day – the anniversary of the immortal Declaration of Independence, which your heroic fathers sealed with their blood, we shall best perform our duty, not by an indiscriminate use of complimentary epithets, but by reminding you of the duties which you owe to yourselves and to mankind. We shall do so in the briefest terms by again quoting from our former address, – plain truths will bear reiteration: –

> 'Working men of America, you are, or should be, the pioneers of freedom; such was the mission bequeathed to you by WASHINGTON and his great brother patriots. That mission you will best fulfil by perfecting your institutions – by abolishing the slavery of white and black – wages and the whip – by driving from your legislatures landlords, usurers, lawyers, soldiers, and other idlers and swindlers; by making the veritable people, the wealth-producers, really "sovereign," and thus establishing a real, instead of a nominal, Republic. War will not aid, but will prevent you accomplishing these reforms. Achieve these reforms, and everywhere the people will demand your institutions, and your triumph will be complete.'

Working men of Great Britain and America, in concluding this address, we desire to offer a few words on a proposition lately advanced and much insisted on by the 'friends of peace.' We allude to the proposition for holding a Congress of Nations, to which Congress shall be referred all national disputes for amicable adjustment. This idea, excellent in the abstract, would, we fear, be found exceedingly objectionable in the present state of the world. Under present circumstances, such a Congress – at least so far as Europe was concerned – would be a Congress not of nations, but of governments, which governments do not represent the rights and interests of the nations they rule over. Such Congress it is to be feared would be anti-progressive and anti-democratic – a new 'Holy Alliance' with which it would be impossible for the United States to co-operate.

As regards 'war' we are not of those who cry 'peace at any cost!' We too ardently admire the American heroes of '76 to adopt so inane a creed. We fear the time has not yet arrived for 'permanent and universal peace.' There are nations so tightly fettered that we can see no prospect of their chains being broken without the aid of the sword. Poland and Italy are striking examples of this state of things. Our doctrine is, that not only are nations justified in releasing themselves from slavery and misery 'by any means,' but also that it is the duty of a strong people to aid a weaker. Did not a cowardly, and selfish, yet stupid policy guide the councils of the Courts of St. James and the Tuilleries – or was national right and national justice enthroned in Great Britain and France, the tyrants of Eastern and Southern Europe would be made to comprehend this doctrine.

While the friends of man set their faces against war arising out of mere national disputes, not involving the existence and freedom of nations, let them be wary that they do not fall into the error of peacefully acquiescing in 'things as they are' and thus strengthen the oppressor, and consign the oppressed to despair.

When the nations are free; when the people of Great Britain have acquired those rights which will assuredly be theirs; when Frenchmen shall reap the fruits of their fifty years of heroic sacrifice, by putting an end to *bourgeoise* rule and establishing the veritable sovereignty of the people; when thirty-five millions of Germans shall form a people free and indivisible; when Italy shall be emancipated; when Poland shall be Poland once more; when millions of fettered Slavons shall burst their chains; when Greece shall retain her ancient limits and more than her ancient freedom; when Spain shall be redeemed; when, in short, Europe shall be what Europe must and will be, *then* a Congress of Nations will be the crowning glory of European progress. *Then* may the representatives of free nations, assembling alternately in the old and in the new world, unite the interests of both, and then may war finally cease and peace permanently reign.

In the meantime much may be done towards promoting both objects of our mission – freedom and peace – by the friends of progress in all nations communicating and co-operating with each other. So that if wars do come, they shall be wars unavoidable and indispensable, in defence of the sacred rights of man, and not wars to gratify the brutal instincts of kingly rapacity or national vanity.

Working men of Great Britain and America, working men of all countries, freedom and justice, and ultimately peace and happiness, are before you if you will learn to repudiate national antipathies and national prejudices. You may do for yourselves what governments will not do for you: –

> 'Rise! form yourselves the Holiest Alliance,
> Nations join heart and hand!'

JOSEPH MOLL, (native of Germany,) *Chairman*.
G. JULIAN HARNEY (native of Great Britain),
CARL SCHAPPER (native of Germany),
JEAN A. MICHELOT[1] (native of France),   } *Secretaries*
PETER HOLM (native of Scandinavia),
A. NEMETH (native of Hungary),
HENRY HUBERT (native of Switzerland),
   July 4th, 1846.

---

1 Jean Michelot (b. 1792), French exile.

A PRACTICAL WORK
ON THE MANAGEMENT OF SMALL FARMS.[1]

BY FEARGUS O'CONNOR, ESQ.[2]
BARRISTER-AT-LAW.
THIRD EDITION.

MANCHESTER:
ABEL HEYWOOD, 58, OLDHAM STREET.
SOLD BY ALL BOOKSELLERS AND NEWSVENDERS.
1846

---

1 First edn, 1843; second edn, 1845; third edn, Manchester, 1846, 192 pp.
2 Feargus O'Connor (1794–1855), Chartist leader.

PREFACE.

I had originally intended to devote the first number of this work to a devel-opement of the means by which the working classes might, by a concentration of their own powers, acquire a sufficiency of land whereby the plan which I pro-pose for their amelioration would be practically carried out upon a large scale. Upon re-consideration however (as many, very many, abuses of which the work-ing classes are ignorant, and upon which other writers will not instruct them, and which stand in the way of all improvement), I have thought it best to commence my work with an exposure of those several abuses, lest I should be taunted with my inability to prove the existence of any practical grievances under the present system. For these reasons, then, I shall postpone the publication of the plan to which I look for the fulfilment of my object till a future number, when I shall have exposed those abuses which stand in the way of agricultural improvement. The task that I have undertaken not being a very easy one, no less in fact than that of giving a wholly new direction to the public mind upon the question of social improvement, the reader will see, that to have left my work half done or badly done, would have had the effect of marring that object, which I have so much at heart, and he will, therefore, at once acquiesce in the propriety of antici-pating what may be urged in favour of the present system, and in opposition to that which I propose as a substitute. It has been the practice of all those writers who have preceded me upon this subject to mix up the question of agriculture with our commercial, manufacturing and monetary arrangements, not that I see how they can be well separated, if agriculture was made the main spring, instead of a mere stream flowing from those other sources. They, however, have reversed the natural order of things, by treating the question of agriculture as one merely of finance, and as a medium of investment for surplus capital when it can be spared from the artificial market. I, upon the contrary, while I admit the minute and indissoluble connection which exists between those several interests, would make agriculture the source, and all others tributary streams flowing from it. Indeed, if I would rest satisfied with basing the argument upon a mere sweeping assertion, I could establish my position from this one fact: that although under even the present limited and vicious system, agriculture is treated as a mere sec-ondary consideration, and although the difference between the value of a good and a middling harvest is, in point of amount, comparatively insignificant, and positively so when compared with the year's produce of machinery, yet do we find that the prospect of a good or a bad harvest has a much more powerful effect upon the other three interests unitedly than any other consideration could possi-bly have. It gives the standard value to real money, because artificial money cannot be successfully used in the natural market. Thus, if twenty millions sterling worth of British goods were sunk to the bottom of the sea, it would be a great advantage to 999 in every thousand, whereas if the difference between a good and a bad harvest required five millions sterling to supply the deficiency, the necessity for such a drag would paralyze all other interests which are regulated by the artificial standard. If, then, our present artificial system merely opens a narrow market for speculation in human labour to the great injury of a vast majority of society, and, if this injustice can be only checked by opening the natural market so wide that all may be enabled 'to buy in the cheapest and sell in the dearest market,' I think the working classes are justly entitled to demand the fulfilment of this principle of political economy, the justice of which is admitted by all, and the immediate necessity for acting upon which is so loudly advocated by those who demand 'high wages, cheap bread, and plenty to do for the working classes.'

INTRODUCTION.

The object which I have in view in submitting a practical work upon the management of small farms to the working men of this country is, that each man who is willing to work may be independent of every other man in the world for his daily bread; so that the prosperity of the country shall consist in an aggregate of happy individuals, rather than in a community of a few owners of all its aggregate wealth; and upon whose speculation, whim, and caprice, the poor man must now depend for his bread. If I was to allow myself to enter upon a political discussion, I think I should be enabled to convince all those who boast of a love of country, that, upon the cultivation of their own domestic resources alone must the wealth, the stability, and the happiness of a people depend: – that in all our commercial transactions foreign countries can interfere so as materially to disarrange those rules and regulations by which trade and traffic are governed, and that such interference materially affects the condition of the working classes; while our land, and that alone, is a branch of the national wealth with which no foreign state can by possibility interfere. England has long been the work-shop of the world; and, while her sons were employed in the manufacture of that machinery by which their own labour has now become a drug, they had not the foresight to discover that they were violating even the Malthusian rule,[1] by creating the very worst description of over-population, a surplus which had no power of resistance, no rights to contend for, and consumed nothing: a surplus of machinery. The political economists assert, that when one channel of industry is closed another channel is opened. It is, then, because the whole course of industry is now choaked up, that I seek to open a field so wide that for centuries to come the people of this country would not be an overstock for the pasture. In short, to repeat it once more, my desire is to open a free labour market, wherein the value of labour in the artificial market can be established by a fixed rule, whereby, in

---

1 That population always outstrips the means of subsistence.

all future manufacturing operations, demand and supply shall be regulated by some definable standard. I have upon many occasions expressed my disapproval of limiting the uses of machinery by any legal enactment, and of correcting its abuses simply by driving its owners into the free labour market, for the employment of those hands by whom it is to be worked. In a word, if the man, whose labour when expended for himself be worth 2s., 3s., 5s., or 10s. a day, wishes to hire himself to work for another for 1s. a day, he is a willing slave and has no right to complain; while, upon the other hand, the prices established in the free labour market would compel the English manufacturer to abandon that thimble-rigging system of speculation, by which that body, formerly respected throughout the world, and honoured and beloved at home, are now looked upon as smugglers of bad goods abroad, and as tyrant slave masters at home. I, in conjunction with all my friends, have ever honestly contended for a repeal of the Corn Laws, while those who call themselves *the real anti-monopolists*, would merely make such changes as would open a wider market for their productions created by artificial labour. We say that the Corn Laws must be repealed, and that the only way of doing so is by enabling the English workman, by growing his own corn, to be independent of all the foreign corn growers in the world, whether the value of his free labour production be 20s. or a 100s. the quarter. Such then are the motives with which I submit the following work for your perusal and consideration; in the anxious hope that, should the plan meet with your approval, you will join with me in seeing it carried into practical operation.

PRELIMINARY OBSERVATIONS.

A good excuse and a patron may be looked upon as two things essential to an author. An excuse for having undertaken to write upon a subject already exhausted by others, and a patron whose countenance may be profitable. In my present undertaking, however, I look for neither the one nor the other. I need no excuse, as the subject upon which I am about to write has not only not been exhausted, but, as regards the interest of that class whose condition I wish to improve, it may be said to be wholly untouched; and, as to a profitable patron, I much doubt that any work of mine would be likely to receive the countenance, the favour, or support of individuals, whose obstinacy, perverseness and monopoly, I charge as the causes of every existing evil which by this publication I hope to destroy.

On the anniversary of the battle of Waterloo[1] I sit down to consider whether man may not in the nineteenth century have assigned to him a better, a more pleasing, more profitable, more civilized, and more Christian occupation than that of human butcher. In the middle of summer, when every man should be able to make some calculation as to his prospects for the ensuing year, I am led to enquire why it is that none, save money-brokers and speculators in human

---

1 18 June 1815.

misery, appear to be interested in that scarcity or abundance by which the Creator of the world may please to curse or bless his people. When I read of the
progress of civilization through the diffusion of the Scriptures, while the eye daily
dwells upon the reprobation of slavery, I am led to enquire by what means the
theory of those professing philanthropists can be best carried into practice; and
in my research I have come to the conclusion, that the emancipation of the working classes of this and of every other country can never be achieved except by
placing the working population, or so many of them as may choose to embrace
the offer, upon so much land as each can conveniently cultivate for his own sole
use, behoof, and benefit.

It would but ill serve that purpose which I have so deeply at heart to compile
a mass of theories upon the subject of agriculture without first having assigned
good and sufficient reasons for leading me to the conclusion that it is within the
power of the people to achieve the means of carrying those theories into practice.
It may be said that the subject of agriculture is not a new one. I admit it; but
then it has only been discussed as a question between landlord and tenant,
between monopolists and anti-monopolists. In the discussion of this all-embrac-
ing subject, the immediate interest of the working classes has been left wholly
out of view; nay, guardedly so, lest a proper explication of the subject as regards
their interest should deprive the landlords of that monopoly of legislation which
the mal-appropriation of their estates confers upon them, and lest it should
deprive the capitalist of that slave-labour by which he is enabled to hoard riches
– the restrictions and conditions of the one class creating an artificial surplus population in the labour market for the other class. I think I may lay it down as an
indisputable, or at least as an incontrovertible, fact, that England, according to
her system of government, is over-populated; and it must be further admitted
that, while ten millions may constitute an over-population under unwholesome
restrictions and a bad system, forty millions may prosper in the same country
under a good system. The greatest difficulty against which I shall have to contend in my present undertaking will be, not so much the ignorance of the
working classes upon the subject of agriculture, as the difficulty of leading the
mind trained up in an artificial life to a belief in the advantages to be derived from
my system, and the practicability of availing themselves of those advantages. It
is not enough that I feel convinced of the feasibility of my plan and the power of
the working people to carry it into effect; it will be necessary, for the achievement
of this great national object, to enlist in its support the attention and the co-operation of the working classes themselves, and then it is done.

Much that I have written in newspapers upon this subject has had its weight
with the factory slaves, and, as I intend this work to form a complete compen-
dium, I shall here condense from those publications the social and political
bearings of the landed question. Socially, then, it will be admitted, that of late
years the bulk of the population have been starving in the midst of a surplus capital created by their industry, and so reduced in value by the substitution of
machinery for their labour; and whereby they have ceased to be wholesome or
profitable consumers, as not to be worth more than one per cent. Remedy after

remedy has been proposed for this great national disease, as power has passed from the hands of one party to the other: the landlords arraigning the savage tyranny of the manufacturers without having the courage or the honesty to place the people in a condition successfully to contend against their atrocities; the manufacturers, upon the other hand, contending for an extension of that trade, the overstock of which has already brought ruin upon the country, and each extension of which will but add new misfortunes, until at length, should they be powerful enough to succeed, they would become bankrupt in the midst of an artificial abundance.

While I contend that machinery under the present system is the greatest enemy of the working classes, of knowledge, of civilization, of morality and freedom, I would not wish to see its progress restrained by law. I complain not of the use, but of the abuse, of machinery, and the wholesome restriction which I would lay upon it would be that of fair competition for its working in the free labour market. I would not say to the capitalist, whether cotton spinner, iron master, or mine owner, you shall not use machinery in your several trades; nor would I lay a tax upon that machinery, because the capitalist always has it in his power to hold himself harmless and of even making profit of taxes. The change therefore that I would suggest would be just this, instead of allowing the capitalist to send his slave master to the market-place or cellar for the purpose of bidding for the labour of an impoverished set of unwilling idlers, whose very necessities compel them not only to underbid each other, but to look upon each other with jealousy, as a farmer looks upon the rival stock of his neighbour – instead, I say, of sending him to such a market to purchase slaves, I would let him go for a supply to the free labour market, where man would at least have that protection which would give him a choice in the selection of work. I would allow him to say to a man, earning by his own labour upon the land a sufficiency to maintain himself and his family in a state of independence and comfort, to educate them, to clothe them, and, after all, to lay up annually wherewith the old couple in the winter of life may live cheerfully without being indebted to the hospitality of an Almshouse. I would let him say to a man in that state, if you are dissatisfied with responsibility, if you would prefer house labour to field labour, the town fog to the country air, and the gin palace to the lecture room, come with me and you shall have precisely the same rate of wages that you have been able to earn by your labour on your farm. If that man went, he would have gone of his own free will, and to oppose him would be tyranny, while the necessity imposed upon the capitalist to measure his wages by the standard of the free labour market, would of itself impose a sufficient and a wholesome restriction upon machinery. Such a hiring would at once restore to English manufacturers that character which they gained for themselves, when the wages for labour was satisfactory to the workmen and remunerating to them, and which they lost as the rate of wages declined. While discussing the subject under this head, I think I may without ostentation direct attention to the fact, that, for twenty years, I have been strenuously advocating the small-farm system, and the necessity that existed for the improvement of the land, without receiving support, from any quarter, until the tariff of Sir Robert Peel[1] opened the eyes of the landlords of England; and since then there is no subject treated of in the press or the literature of the day, discussed in the House of Commons, or talked of in society, into which the land is not introduced as the leading feature.

Socially, then, I declare it as my opinion that no Minister, that no party, that no combination of interests, can long withhold the land from its legitimate, most just, and most profitable uses. Politically, every man who has been in the habit of taking part at elections, as an elector or non-elector, must have discovered that the present franchise differs but in amount, and not at all in principle, from the forty-shilling franchise that existed in Ireland previous to 1829. In fact, the dependence of a tenant who holds 100 acres upon a short lease, or fifty pounds' worth of land at will, is much greater than that of the forty-shilling freeholder; and therefore is the present constituency more subservient than even the old forty-shilling constituency of Ireland, who were looked upon as a portion of the live-stock on his honour's estate. It is almost an insult to the understanding of a working man to remind him, that, as long as the vast estates of the present proprietors best serve the purposes of their owners by so leasing them in such large and unprofitable allotments as will give to the tenant an interest in the holding greater than as a free man he will have in his vote, and so long as the use of that vote by the landlord gives to him political patronage to a much larger amount than he has sacrificed by the mal-appropriation of his land, so long will the land be used by him as a mere political machine, and so long will the people, disinherited from the land, be looked upon as slaves living upon sufferance.

The question may here arise then, as to which of the changes that I contend for should have the priority: – the establishment of the small farm principle – or the enactment of the People's Charter, by which the land would be stripped of its political qualification. I was engaged for some years with the working classes in their struggle for political emancipation, before I ventured to introduce the subject of the land for their consideration, well knowing that a time of artificial commercial prosperity was not the most fitting for the entertainment of so large a question. Perhaps, therefore, I may be pardoned, if in the course of the remarks that I am about to make, I shall be guilty of a usual error, that of estimating the forwardness of the public mind upon this subject, by the amount of thought which I have given to it myself. In answer, therefore, to the question that I have propounded, I should say, that without political power the system never could be made so general as to be of national benefit; while, upon the other hand, I do not believe that any other inducement, save that of the practical result of the plan of small farms, ever will be sufficiently strong to produce such a public feeling as will bring into moral action such an amount of mind in favour of both changes, as neither minister or party would dare to resist. Therefore, from this reasoning I incline to think that the possession of political power is indispensable as a means for making the plan of free labour a national benefit; while I am further of opin-

---

1 Sir Robert Peel (1788–1850), second Baronet; MP for Tamworth from 1833; Conservative Prime Minister 1834, 1841–6.

ion, that no writing, no talking, no reasoning, no declamation, no exaggeration, can have the check of enlisting, in support of the small farm plan, the one hundredth part of that thought and mind which the *practice*, if seen to a considerable extent, would produce. So powerful has been the reliance of intolerant faction upon the ignorance and prejudice of the people, that they have not unfrequently had recourse to a mere perversion of terms as a means of upholding their own superiority. Thus the term 'social,' which means neither more nor less than 'fit for society,' is invariably thwarted into a declaration of infidelism.[1] Allow me then, for your protection, and in justice to myself, here for the first time in my life to state my own religious feelings, without being so unchristian or intolerant as to make them a justification for harshly judging those of others. I am a Socialist in the true sense of the word by desiring to fit all things for society, while I am, I trust, a Christian in the purest sense of the word, having a thorough conviction that I was created by an all-wise God for some more profitable purpose than that of waddling through the world as a selfish being looking only to my own ease and comfort in my passage through life. I believe that I, in common with all others, was sent here for some better purpose, and that purpose was to be a cog in the great social wheel, by the working of which that fitness of things to society is to be brought about. I do not believe in the wicked doctrine of death-bed repentance, nor in the damnable doctrine that good works are of no avail. If I could bring my mind to that state of obtuse bigotry, I should at once abandon the holy work of attempting to serve God's creatures, and fit myself for holy orders. I believe that I shall have one day, when it pleases God to call upon me, to give an account of my life, and while I do not expect to be able to establish its entire purity, I shall guard myself against the severest of all judgments, that of being judged for harshly judging others. For this reason, while I thus declare my own religious feelings, I abstain from pronouncing an anathema upon those who have the honesty to confess their inability to arrive at the same conclusions. I do not feel myself lessened by being thus compelled in a work of this kind to declare my religious creed, while I hold the obligation to do so to be a censure upon those prejudices which demand it.

In conformity then with the terms of my belief, I am about to present to the industrious of all classes the means whereby social happiness, political freedom, and the pure spirit of religion, may be introduced into this country, as a substitute for the misery, the discomfort, and the immorality at present prevailing, and all of which are consequences of that inequality created by class legislation, and upheld for no better purpose than that of distinguishing society, by making one portion so wealthy that all consideration of duty, of morality and religion, is lost in the enjoyment of too easily acquired luxuries, and another class so poor that all the finer feelings (which if properly cultivated would lead to an honourable distinction,) are sacrificed, as the exercise of them in our present state of *commercial civilization* would but render a poor man an object of ridicule, laughter, and contempt.

---

1 Because of its association with Robert Owen's brand of 'socialism'.

It has been a mystery to some of our muddle-pated writers upon first princi-ples – men whom I call intellectual miners, how any system could at the same time benefit the whole of society: some contending that what is beneficial to the landlord would be prejudicial to the manufacturer: others, that what is meat for the tenant would be poison to the Landlord. Every man, however, who takes the trouble to analyse the whole subject, must come to the conclusion, that the most profitable cultivation of our national resources would open a field for industry so large, that the security of the landlord, the capitalist, and the speculator, would be considerably increased, and their profits enlarged by a judicious employment of the labour of the country.

What now obliges us to attach so much importance to a repeal of the Corn Laws, and the importation of foreign grain? What is it that has reduced the prof-its of the landlord, the capital of the tenant, and the profit of the manufacturer? Surely not that with an increased population land at home has become cheaper, manufactured goods less in use, and capital of less value; but simply because the one great natural labour market has been closed against the population by polit-ical speculators, while the whole population of the world could not consume in three years the amount of English goods produced in the artificial market in one year, to the great disadvantage of 999 in every 1,000 of the community.

Political Economy is in the mouth of all your large manufacturers and their interested supporters, whereas, their practice is diametrically opposed to the true principles of that science. If the term means, as I take it to mean, the most prof-itable and just application of the industrial powers to the productive means of a country, then I hold that a system which has directly an opposite tendency cannot be considered political economy. Let us see what the result of a large competitive trade in artificial production must inevitably be, and let us then see whether or no the present anomalous state of society has been produced by this system. We know that the only profits which masters can now rely upon, are those derived from low wages, fines, batings and stoppages, and that, therefore, the traffic of the present race of manufacturers is in the labour of the poor man. For instance, let us suppose a master employing two thousand hands, and let us take our pic-ture fairly from this community of two thousand and one persons. Supposing machinery to be so improved that a portion of the operative class which in June was scanty as compared with the requirements for working the old machinery, in July becomes a surplus population, made so by the improvements – Now in such case the employer makes no calculation as to the relative value of produce in June and July, for even supposing the article to have risen, it is not upon that, so much as upon the labour reduced by this overplus, that he speculates. He will very nat-urally go to his hands and say, there is a large stock of unemployed labour in the market and you must either consent to have yours reduced, or else I will go into the market and purchase it at a cheaper rate. Under these circumstances what alternative has the poor slave other than to consent either to a reduction or dis-missal, and consequent starvation. Let us, then, suppose that the master, placed in this advantageous situation, reduces the wages of his hands even 4d. a day, that, upon 2,000, would amount to £10,400 per annum. Let us, then, see in how far this gentleman's system of political economy is beneficial to the landlord class and the shop-keeping class, having already shown its effects upon the producing class. You will see that I am compelled to take this course, in order to meet the prejudices and to check the insanity of those of the middle classes who bawl out for a repeal of the corn laws, in the hope that an extension of trade would give them some share in the profits. What I want to do is this; I want to show them that the power of the masters to speculate upon labour, and that alone, will always have the effect of keeping wages down to that point at which it ceases to be of any benefit to the shopkeeping class, and that the only effect of what is called free trade, would be to magnify the present frightful difference between the one and the 2,000 of that community whose relative positions I am now con-trasting. The effect of this arrangement is to enable one man to rob 2,000 of £10,400 a year; and, let me ask, or, rather, let me draw a picture of what must be the state of the shop-keeping class, whose lot it is to serve such a community. In the present case, where the master unjustly takes £10,400 a year, and mind, independent of stoppages, fines, and batings, the shopkeepers not only lose their entire profit upon that amount, but the very capital invested in the hope of better trade, and which has been thus sacrificed to the power of the manufacturer, becomes deteriorated: whereas, had that sum circulated through the legitimate channel, every farthing of it, and more, would have gone into the tills of the shop-keepers. But I will follow the portrait up, as from the miniature that I am now painting I mean to represent the full-length picture of misery which the state of this country at present presents. Herein, then, lies the error; not only do the monies belonging to 2,000 find their way into the pocket of the one, to the injury of those over whom he has power, but it indirectly operates against the interest of those over whom he does not appear to have any influence. And not only that, but every new injustice successfully practised enables him to extend his pecula-tion, while it leaves those directly and indirectly dependent upon him still more at his mercy and disposal. To speak very familiarly to all classes, let me now ask whether it would be more beneficial to society generally if one man was possessed of an enormous income, or the whole community of which he was a member were comparative participients in the amount. Then let us ask what the individual benefits and the national losses are which are created by this arrangement. The one usurper looks for some national security or bubble investment, wherefrom he may derive profit for his £10,400, while the landlords and the shopkeepers are compelled to submit to taxation for the relief of the poor, a rural police to keep them in subjection in their poverty, law proceedings to persecute them if they complain, and assessments for dispensaries and hospitals when diseased from want; while the eye is shocked and the feelings fretted by the constant exhibition of those objects produced by this system of tyranny and oppression.

The reader who may have purchased this work from the notice in the announcement of it to the public, may very naturally ask what connection these varied subjects have with the consideration of the best mode of cultivating small farms? To such I would reply, that, unless I am enabled, by a fair exposure of existing fallacies, to enlist a sufficient support for that which I propose as a substitute, I can have but little hope of success; while I have a strong reliance upon the prudence and good sense of the middling classes, when fairly instructed upon this subject, that they will aid and assist, by all the legitimate means at their disposal, in the accomplishment of my plan. If we now take the monstrous disparity existing between the one and the two thousand of a community which I have described, I think we may adopt the standard as a fair representation of the whole of society. That is, that at present there is, out of all comparison, in the hands of a small number of individuals, more money and money's worth than ever was known to be in the possession of the whole population before, while at the same time there is more distress simultaneously existing. Now, what is the cause of this but the usurpation by one of what belongs to two thousand and one; and which, if legitimately distributed among the whole, would also add to the profit and comfort of those who have no other means of support or existence than that which springs from their traffic as shopkeepers. Suppose the £10,400, extorted as I have described, to be consolidated into a fund, for the general benefit of the 2,000, that, at five per cent., would amount to £520 a year for ever; while its proper administration, for the benefit of the indigent of that body, would be a good substitute for a rural police, poor laws, legal persecution, hospital and dispensaries, and the cost of maintaining which now falls, as I have described, upon the middle classes and landlords. But the evil does not even end here, for independently of the gross injustice thus directly inflicted upon the two thousand, they are further injured by the necessity imposed upon them of subscribing out of their reduced means to those several clubs, unions, and societies to which they are obliged to look as a substitute for that wages of which they have been robbed, and for the existence of which there would be no necessity but for the plunder of the ONE. As labour is admitted to be the source of all wealth, I hope to establish, on behalf of the labourer, his fair claim to that protection, the withholding of which has originated every grievance of which all classes of society justly complain; and the restoration of which can alone save the empire from the convulsion which no other power on earth can long retard. I have supposed, then, the improvement in machinery, itself, without reference to any decline in the price of its produce, to enable the one proprietor to make profit of the labour of two thousand. I am therefore justified in considering this an act of outrageous injustice, and one which, if not resisted and put down, would justify me in designating the ministers that would uphold it as a rebel administration. There is no feeling which so sweetens the bread of life, or which so reconciles the slave to his daily toil, as the fond hope that he is laying up in youth a store whereon he may live in quiet in his old age. And if all other classes are induced by such anticipation to live sparingly, and spend grudgingly, in the hope of one day retiring from the scene of busy life, why, I should ask, is the industrious man, by whose labour this anticipation is to be realized, to be the only one who can have no chance of realizing it for himself.

I will now suppose this £10,400 per annum to be spent in the purchase of that quality of land which would require no other capital than that of labour for bringing it to the very highest state of cultivation; and from that calculation I shall be enabled to show how soon the really industrious, if 'THROWN UPON THEIR OWN RESOURCES,' would be enabled to work out their own salvation. I shall value such land then at fifteen shillings per acre, and at the usual price such land would be worth twenty-five years' purchase. That is, each acre would be worth £18 15s., if bought for ever, and the whole sum of £10,400 per annum, that is the sum stolen by the one from the two thousand, if laid out in the purchase of land, would buy five hundred acres and leave a surplus of one thousand and twenty-five pounds. Let us now have recourse to a bit of real political economy, and let us see how the producing power could be best applied to the producing means. Five hundred acres would divide into one hundred and twenty-five farms, of four acres each. Each farm would support, upon the labour of one man, a family of seven, and leave a large overplus for his own use. If we multiply a hundred and twenty-five, the number of families that that quantity of ground would maintain, by seven, the number in each family, we have eight hundred and seventy-five of the two thousand located for life upon land purchased out of a fund which is now appropriated by the one usurper. Moreover, the surplus of one thousand and twenty-five pounds would allow to each a sum of eight pounds to begin with, while the freehold of four acres would be good security upon which to raise sixty pounds wherewith to erect a suitable habitation, and from which no tyrant could eject him. I think I am entitled to ask any political economist, which of my assertions, or which of my calculations, he objects to, or can refute. I will make them clear in a short summary, so that none shall misunderstand or can pervert them. What I assert then is, that master manufacturers have the power of reducing wages by being enabled to fall back upon a system-made over-population, and that they do reduce wages in the same ratio in which that over stock is augmented by the new improvements of machinery, and without any reference to the rise or fall in the production of that machinery. No doubt the answer to this assertion will be, that the manufacturers themselves have of late years sustained considerable losses. This, however, I deny as furnishing any answer to my assertion. But, on the contrary, I assert that the very system of accumulation by the heads of trades, and which I have before pointed out, applies as well to that of manufacturers as to any other. The cause of complaint then, as regards the falling off in profits, has been made an unjust use of by the fortunate in that trade. Thus, while I am ready to admit the stoppage of many mills with old machinery, and the failure of many masters with small capitals; yet I assert that there is in the hands of the remaining portion, more money and more trade than ever there was before in the possession of the larger community of speculators. It is all very well for gentlemen who made millions in 'the good times' to grumble now at losing hundreds in bad times, brought about by their own reckless gambling. However, as I am quarrelling with the system which has produced this general despondency and sorrow, I have a perfect right not only to object to the accumulation of monies in the hands of the survivors, but I have also a right to take into my calculation the injury done to the labouring classes, and through them to society in general by those very failures which seem to excite sympathy for the unfortunate. Indeed, it is one of the things I complain of, that the imprudence, the neglect, or the speculations of one should bring destruction upon the remaining two thousand of the community, whereas, had justice been done to the whole body, either the one would not have failed, or, if he had, his failure would have only injured himself, had he while in business dealt justly with those in his employ. That forms one of my assertions: the next is, that four-pence a day is a very small amount for masters to reduce upon the improvement of machinery and the consequent glut of the labour market. The next is, that good land can be had for fifteen shillings an acre, and can be bought at twenty-five years' purchase. My calculation as to the capabilities of that land, and its power of supporting the numbers that I have assigned to it, together with the overplus of production, I shall establish beyond refutation in its proper place. Thus then, I assert, let who can deny it, that two thousand men, whose wages are reduced by four-pence a day, would be enabled but for that reduction, and if that amount was applied to the purchase of land, to provide annually for eight hundred and seventy-five, or nearly one half of the whole body, while the labour of one hundred and twenty-five of that number, would, after supplying the eight hundred and seventy-five with a sufficiency of every thing, leave more than enough of surplus production for the remaining eleven hundred and twenty-five of the community of two thousand, while, according to the present system, they would be compelled to go on slaving through the longest life, for the mere means of preserving a miserable existence for another hour of misery, and always furnishing auxiliaries to the plunderers and demagogues in their attacks and crusades upon the little that yet remains valuable of the institutions of the country. I now ask you, working man, who has read, or who has heard this calculation read to you, whether or not I have established the truth of the saying that 'labour is the source of all wealth.' I further ask you what hope you can have that those who are thus enabled to live upon you will ever join in any plan calculated in the slightest degree to relieve you from their aggressions, or to make you independent of their will and controul. Perhaps one great reason to be assigned for the middling classes not having sooner turned their attention to the improvement capable of being made in their own condition by bettering that of the working classes, has been the very brisk and fascinating agitation kept up by the anti-corn-law league, with professedly the same object, and which they are persuaded would be more easily achieved by a repeal of the corn-laws than by the small farm system. Many of the working classes themselves, unused to sophistry, incapable of deceiving, and disinclined to doubt others, were really inspired with hope through a repeal of the corn-laws. All anticipations from that measure, however, have now failed; not more in consequence of the information that has been spread amongst them by their own lecturers, than by the practices resorted to by some of the loudest advocates of free trade. And as one fact is worth a thousand arguments, I shall here faithfully narrate a circumstance which has this moment come to my knowledge. The leading advocate of free-trade principles in Spitalfields has recently reduced the wages of his hands by 4d. a-day, at a time when the price of their produce has considerably risen, and at a time when the masters find it difficult to procure a sufficiency of workmen. Now this gentleman was one of those who succeeded in leading the Spitalfields weavers to the belief that a repeal of the corn-laws would have the effect of raising the price of wages from the competition which the increased demand for labour would create; and yet this very man, upon the first appearance of briskness in his own trade, reduces the wages of his hands as I have stated; and the consequence is, that the Spitalfields weavers have, since that occurrence took place, driven the anti-corn-law lecturers out of their district as treacherous deceivers.

Having thus established the fact that labour, when confined to the artificial market, must be sold at whatever price the capitalist pleases to give for it, I shall now proceed shortly to contrast the difference between the life of an operative selling his labour in the artificial market, and that of a farming labourer, working for himself in the natural market. Socially, then, if that term means the fitting of things to society, the man who hires his labour must, under any circumstances, be a slave, if the act is not a voluntary one, inasmuch as he loses all self-controul, and becomes a machine at the disposal of another, and under no conceivable system could this state of dependency be pushed to greater lengths than it has been by the present race of master manufacturers. I shall therefore draw a picture of the unnatural state in which the present class of operatives are compelled to live, and contrast it with that of a free labourer. In some cases women only are employed, and in such cases the house loses its greatest ornament, and the family its greatest support, the children being deprived of their natural and most interested protector and adviser just at that time when they stand most in need of a mother's care. This system of hiring women to the rejection of men must naturally debase the character of both, by reversing their natural positions and making the husband a dependant upon the labour of his wife, while his creditable support of her and the family should constitute his greatest pride. But beyond those now prevalent disagreements between husband and wife, which we daily read of with so much sorrow, and which are wholly attributable to these unnatural causes, we may add the general disorganization of the whole family circle. The more nearly we can conform to nature's rules without trenching upon the rights of others the better, and where they are deviated from, it can only be tolerated upon the plea that that deviation is of general advantage. But where all those rules by which the human family should be governed are hourly violated to the disadvantage of thousands for the advantage of individuals, then does it become the duty of every philanthropist to lend his aid in their destruction. What can be more unnatural than that a father should be compelled to walk in idleness while his wife is constrained to absent herself from her home and her family every day in the year to labour like a slave for their maintenance. What can be more at variance with the ordinances of nature than that a whole family, old and young, male and female, weakly and robust, sick and healthy, should be constrained to rise at the same hour, to eat at the same time, to work almost the same number of hours, and to retire to rest together. What can be more degrading than the task imposed upon the father of taking the babe to the charnel house at stated periods, to be suckled by its toiling mother? Or what can be more fretting to the feelings of the mother than to be compelled to consign her babe to the care of a hired nurse, in order that she may be the sooner fitted for her toil? Such are the outrages to which this system subjects those who are compelled to sell their labour in the artificial market. Alas! what a striking contrast the life of a free labourer, working for himself, presents to that sorrowful picture that I have just drawn. It is his pride to rise betimes, according to his strength, rejoicing in the reflection that upon his industry the whole family must depend; while, in return, he looks for that contentment which a happy home alone can bestow. He is a Socialist in the true acceptation of the word, fitting things to that small society of which he is the head. If he should be overworked, or even drowsy, he dreads not the awful sound of the morning toll of the factory bell. He is not deprived of the comfort of the society of his wife; he is not degraded by living as a prostitute upon her and his children's labour. He is not reduced to the humiliating necessity of shaking his slumbering babe into a kind of artificial life, in order that she may obey the capitalist's morning summons. He sees no cripple at his board, no dwarf in his family. All are straight, erect, and healthy, because each has been trained according to their strength. There is no obligation imposed upon him of estrang- ing his child from its mother's breast. He is master of himself and of his time, and is answerable to society for the disposal of both. He seeks no refuge for wounded feelings in the beer shop or the gin palace. His every hour of recreation is too short for the enjoyment of the society of that family, the proper bringing up of which is his greatest pride; and the neglect of which, as a free agent, would entail upon him the highest censure. The system which I propose would at once deve- lope all the virtues of our nature, while I defy the devil himself to invent one so well calculated to foster and encourage all those vices to which man is heir, as that which I labour to destroy. Never lose sight of this one irrefutable fact, that man is born with propensities which may be nourished into virtues, or thwarted into vices, according to his training. That the system which I propose would nourish those propensities into virtues, which would constitute the characteristic of Eng- lishmen, while the slave system now in operation, thwarts those propensities into vices, and gives to our code of laws the appearance of enactments made upon a general scale of prison discipline, rather than laws for the proper government of society. Before I commence my work upon Practical Farming, which I trust will, before I die, be carried into general effect, allow me here to observe that passing events fully prove that I saw many years ago the destruction and danger which the monopoly of landlords and the conditions upon which land was leased would bring upon society: I then sought to remedy those evils by Act of Parliament, but was laughed at by the very parties who are now contending for the very altera- tions which I then endeavoured to bring about. Early in 1835 I placed a notice of the following motion upon the order book of the House of Commons, 'To move for leave to bring in a bill to compel landlords to make leases for ever at a corn rent, and in all cases of existing contracts under which lands were held at too high a rate, to establish the real value by the decision of a jury, in like manner as the crown and corporate bodies have the power of assessing the value of private property when required for public purposes.' If we look to Ireland, a purely agri- cultural country, at the present moment, what are the changes which are now sought for? Is not the general principle contended for, 'fixity of tenure,' not, I admit, as comprehensive as that which I proposed to establish, while, at the same time we hear of the valuation of a jury being demanded as a means of doing justice to the occupying tenant. This altered tone inspires me with great confidence as far as the acknowledgment of the principle goes, while I fear that its recognition, like all other changes under our present representative system, and the awful dependancy of the working classes upon capitalists, would only affect the interest of large farmers, while it would not in the slightest degree tend to create a class of farming labourers: in short the law being made by one class would be confined to the advantage of that class alone.

I shall now proceed with a work, which, however it may be read by the jaundiced eye of living prejudice, will, when I am no more, and when that prejudice is destroyed, constitute a part of the property of many a free man yet unborn, and will be cherished as one of the sources from whence his freedom has sprung, and the means by which his independence may be preserved. If I can accomplish so desirable an object, or if I can be the means of inducing others to do so, then may the hired scribe, the slanderer, the self tormentor, and hypocrite, call me devil, Jew, or infidel, while I can take my morning walk and evening stroll, and rejoicing in the contentment, the prosperity and comfort by which, at every step, my eye is gladdened, exclaim, in the language of the proud Peruvian, 'THIS, THIS IS MY WORK.'

ON PRACTICAL FARMING.

'A true labourer earns that he eats; gets that he wears; owes no man hate; envies no man's happiness; glad of other men's good; content under his own privations; and his chief pride is in the modest comforts of his condition.' – *Shakspeare.*[1]

WASTE LANDS.

Although in the present scanty state of the population of England, as compared with the amount of partially-reclaimed land, I do not mean to dwell upon waste lands as a means of opening a field for the most profitable application of free labour, yet, as many works have been written upon the subject, and as writers upon agriculture do in general, as I have before stated, direct the attention of the readers principally, if not entirely, to a consideration of those means whereby surplus capital, as it is called, may be most beneficially expended in agricultural

---

1   William Shakespeare, *As You Like It*, III. ii. 73.

pursuits, I feel myself called upon to combat such notions. Those who attach so much importance to the cultivation of waste lands, are, for the most part, if not altogether, advocates of the large farm system. Taking, then, this double approval of the cultivation of waste lands and of large farms, we must consider such writers merely in the light of inventors of new securities for accumulated wealth, without any reference whatever to the improvement of the working classes. I never have contended for the bringing in, as it is called, and the cultivation of, waste lands as a means of affording relief to the working classes. This is a branch of agriculture well worthy the consideration of those who would expend capital in the hope of a fair, nay, of a very large return. But, inasmuch as it requires an amount of money-capital beyond the reach of the working classes, as far as their interest is concerned I leave it out of the question as a means of bettering them, until such time as an amount of money sufficiently large to assign to each enough to carry on the necessary operations shall be raised by a Government loan, and appropriated for that purpose. Nothing could more damp the ardour of those who are now anxious about the small farm system, than to see it attempted to be carried out upon a cold, swampy moor, or barren heath; while, upon the other hand, nothing could so wed them to the system as the rapid improvement that would be observable in the condition of the occupiers of land of an average quality. If I was again to make agriculture my pursuit, and if the value of land could be ascertained by an unerring, or by even a probably correct standard, I would much prefer giving £5 an acre for land valued at £4, to giving 30s. an acre for land valued at 40s., and I would prefer giving £3 an acre for land valued at 20s. to taking £2 an acre as a bonus upon land worth but 1s. an acre. Now the reason of this must be obvious to every practical farmer, and must be made intelligible to those who are to become such. My reason, then, for the preference, is because where land is held for ever, or even upon a long lease, rent is comparatively an insignificant item in the farmer's general account, while, as I shall show under the head of 'Large Farms,' it is the item of greatest importance. Now, if I paid a higher rent, say by a pound an acre, than the land was worth, for four acres of ground I would have the following disadvantages and advantages. The disadvantage would be the payment of £4 extra rent. The advantages would be that less seed is required for ground in proportion to its excellence, less labour is required in its cultivation, and less damage is to be apprehended to the crops from adverse seasons; while the extra value of the total produce upon the four dearer acres, as compared with the total value of the four cheaper acres produced by the same amount of labour, would far exceed the amount of the whole rent of the good land. Upon the other hand, place the best labourer upon the four acres worth a shilling per acre, and give him £2 per annum, that is £8, as a reward for cultivating it, and in less than three years his heart would break from disappointment. What a miserable picture he would present as contrasted with a neighbour paying £20 a year for four acres, upon which every delve would tell and every ray of sunshine would have its due effect, while every seed set would return its multiplied abundance. The improvement of waste lands, then, is a speculation in which capitalists may with the greatest safety invest their spare monies and with a certainty of good interest, while for the poor man it is of all others the most hopeless source from whence to expect any return for the expenditure of his labour. Moreover, under a good system and the abandonment of horse labour, we have in cultivation a sufficient amount of good and improvable land, quite capable of supporting more than four times our population in contentment, comfort and happiness, while a just appropriation would even add to the wealth, the comforts and security of the already too rich but comfortless and insecure. Waste lands are merely to be quibbled at, a bit here, and a bit there occasionally brought into cultivation, or, may be, improved in large portions by dint of capital and with a rapidity of action neither of which are within the reach of the poor man. The several writers upon the cultivation of waste lands all write in the same strain. Draining, paring, burning, adding to surface soil and recommending their favorite manures, all of which are expensive operations in themselves, and which, when quickly done, may leave a fair remuneration for the expenditure of capital, but without which they would be a great gullet swallowing up without a return the slow labour of one individual. As I really write with a view to instruct all classes and to bring all within the pale of profitable cultivation, I shall now, having instructed you upon the question of waste lands, give directions for their proper cultivation to those who have capital to invest in that process.

The first thing to be done then is to make as many main drains as are necessary to cut across the several springs that may be discovered, striking at the source or head as nearly as possible. The drains should be made in this form V taking care so to bevel the sides that the earth shall not crumble and thereby stop the course of the water. The next process should be that of rolling with a heavy roller. When the surface appears to be well dried, it should be pared, that is, cut into sods of about two inches thick, this should be done upon the first appearance of dry weather in spring, and the sods should be turned until they are sufficiently dry to be cocked, or placed in the form of a cocked hat, three placed on the end, resting against each other, with space for the wind to pass through. When sufficiently long in that position they should be turn-cocked, so that the part which had formerly been resting on the ground should be placed uppermost to give it the benefit of the wind. When the sods are sufficiently dry they should be made into small heaps, something larger than a wheelbarrow, and set on fire. When burnt to ashes, and after the fire is completely extinguished, the heaps should be spread before clotted by rain, and the calmest time should be selected for the operation to prevent the wind blowing the ashes about. The crops most suited to the ground in its then state, are potatoes, which make the very best seed for upland, black or Tartary oats, or rape, the latter of which I would much prefer.

The great difficulty, however, of the bringing in of waste lands consists in hitting upon the most congenial manure and in giving a surface to the peat soil. It has frequently been my lot to see an ignorant capitalist burying his money in bogs and swamps, while just at hand there was a mine of gold. I will explain what

I mean. This spewey ground requires a greater weight of surface than from its nature it can afford for the pressure of that surface water which in such soils no drains can reach. It retains the water like a sponge, and requires surface pressure to keep it out of harm's way. Well then, this object can only be effected by the addition of some artificial surface, no manure of any sort will be of the slightest benefit until this grand object is firstly achieved, and to the means of attaining which I now beg leave to direct the attention of the waste-land-improving capitalist.

Suppose, then, one person to set about reclaiming one hundred acres of moorland. His first object must be to look for the means of adding a heavy artificial surface. This can only be effected by the following process: I must naturally suppose that he has land of a better quality in the immediate neighbourhood of his waste. I will suppose a small hill or mound of earth covering a quarter of an acre of ground, this, if his own, or if purchased at twenty times its value and mixed with lime after being dug, will enable him to give from time to time an artificial surface of three inches in depth and of the very best description to his one hundred acres. By proper management an inch and a half of the sub-soil, that immediately under the artificial surface, may be added to it every year, and thus in the fourth year he would have a good surface of nine inches. The proximity of this artificial surface to that immediately under it of itself considerably enriches its neighbour, while it is admitted that this artificial surface is of all things necessary to complete the process of bringing in waste lands. Perhaps I may be told that the hill for effecting the object is not always at hand: I don't say that it is, I merely say, that, if it is there, it should be applied as I describe as being the cheapest mode, while the want of it, if not there, must be supplied by other means, and the thing then is to consider those means. We may naturally presume that in the neighbourhood of this moor, either the proprietor himself will have six acres of land worth a pound an acre, or one hundred and twenty pounds; or, if he has not got it himself, he may be able to purchase it even at an exorbitant rate in the neighbourhood. Being possessed either of the hill or of the six acres of ground then, what I would recommend him to do to his 100 acres of land is this – or rather, for the more easy illustration of my plan, let us take sixteen acres, or nearly one sixth of the whole, and apply one acre of ground for its reclamation. One acre, then, stripped of four feet of the surface mixed with lime and turned until ready to be put out, should give somewhat more than three inches of surface to the sixteen acres, while the land thus stripped of four feet of surface would be far from valueless, as, even after that loss it would be in a better state to yield a most beneficial crop, (and which in all agricultural works I am astonished to find wholly unnoticed,) than it was before. I mean French furze, and of which I shall treat in its proper place, merely observing for the present that wild earth is the soil in which this plant best flourishes; while one acre will support more cattle of any description than three acres of the very best meadow. However, dismissing all consideration of the after purposes to which this land strip of its surface might be applied, I shall content myself now with merely entering upon a consideration of the relative value of the swamp before and after the application of the artificial surface.*

Before its application it was worth nothing, and all the labour which I have described as necessary for producing a bad crop of potatoes, oats, or rape, must have been expended upon it, and, therefore, I am justified in starting from that point when it was rendered capable of receiving the artificial surface. The acre of sacrificed land I estimate at £25, that is a pound an acre at twenty-five years' purchase. The lime, which, independently of the earth, would have been applied but not so beneficially, I leave altogether out of the calculation. The labour expended upon preparing the compost would have been fruitlessly expended, or perhaps five times the amount, in the vain endeavour to produce the same result. The capitalist then has expended £25 in the one operation indispensable to ensure the success of his undertaking. And what is the result? From the first year his land, which previously was not worth a shilling an acre, and which, without the addition of an artificial surface never would have been worth 5s. an acre, increases from year number one from 10s. an acre to year number four, when it will be richly worth a pound an acre or more. If then we estimate its value after the present mode of cultivating moors at 5s. an acre, and estimate its value after the addition of the artificial surface at 20s. an acre, we find that the capitalist has £12 a year for ever for his expenditure of £25. Now, for all these reasons I have come to the conclusion that the cultivation of waste lands may be a profitable investment for the spare money of capitalists, while it furnishes no field for the exercise of individual labour.

LARGE FARMS.

A vast number of ignorant landlords have been induced by as ignorant writers to adopt the large farm system very extensively, from the idea that the country was over populated and that the small cotter tenants were so many drones living upon the industry of the large farmer. When the demand for operative labour to work the now exploded machinery increased, the manufacturers worked heaven

---

* I had three acres and a quarter of this description of swamp adjoining one of my lawns of about forty acres which fronts the house, and which was a great eye-sore. In my brother's life-time he lost many cows and a horse in this spot, added to which many more cows slipped their calves, and were rendered useless for the season, from sticking in the swamp. He took the round-about way of guarding against the evil, by making an immense ditch round the swamp, and which became a greater eye-sore than the original blemish. When I came into possession, I drained the swamp as I have described, pared it and burned it, and sacrificed about half an acre of the best ground in forming an artificial surface as I have described. In its original state it was not worth a shilling an acre; in fact it was convicted and imprisoned, as I have stated, for a nuisance; while you may now drive a waggon with a four-horse load over any part of it, and it is about the most valuable three acres and a quarter of ground that I have. I sowed French furze in the part I stript, and it has, from the second year, been worth any three acres of meadow; while the stuff procured from making the drains in the swamp, when mixed with lime, afforded me the very best top-dressing for upland.

and earth to seduce the agricultural population from the natural to the artificial market, which had the effect of increasing this great national malady. The reform bill had a further tendency both in England and Ireland to multiply this grievance. The £50 tenants-at-will clause in the English reform bill induced landlords to throw three £20 farms into one £60 vote, while the desire of the protestant landlords of Ireland to withhold the franchise from the Catholic population induced them to knock several of those small holdings into one overgrown farm to suit the scanty protestant population, and which might be safely entrusted as a qualification to some good Protestant, and which he had not capital sufficient to cultivate. This is the mere political evil. I shall now show the evil tendency of this system generally.

Under the head 'Waste Lands,' I have stated that, under the small farm system, rent is a comparatively insignificant item, while to the large farmer it becomes one of importance passing all others. If a man holds four acres of land at a rent of £4 above its real value, he may, by a very little additional labour and attention, overcome the difficulty, whereas, if a large farmer pays £1 an acre over and above the real value for 1,000 acres of land, he could not, by any possibility, according to the established rule for treating large farms, bear up against the overcharge. To him, every additional 1s. per acre becomes an additional rent of £50 a-year, and the difference between £1 an acre and 25s. an acre would amount to £250 a-year, and which increase if saddled upon the actual producing part, say 200 acres, or one-fifth, would impose an additional rent of £1 5s. per acre upon that quantity. Now I will explain it to you. I have allowed that a man holding 1,000 acres of land in his own hands will cultivate 200 acres of that quantity well, whereas he will only cultivate it comparatively well; that is, well as compared to the treatment of the remaining 800 acres. It is impossible, however, even though he should be inclined to spend the required amount of labour upon it, for him to make it as productive as the same quantity of land would be in the possession of fifty husbandmen, occupying four acres each. The distance to which he is obliged to carry his manure, and the distance which he is obliged to draw his produce are ruinous, while neither of those difficulties stand in the way of the small farmer, whose humble cot stands in the centre of his little holding, not more than forty perches distant from the extremity of his allotment. I am quite aware that your large farm gentry will point to the Lothians, to Fife, to Norfolk, to Sussex, to Kent, and other agricultural counties, exclaiming, 'Oh, you Goth! where have you been, not to have heard of our system of encamping our cattle, of thrashing upon the spot, of feeding upon the field, and of making our beasts carriers and depositors of their own manure?' To all this I answer, I have heard of it all; I have seen it all; I have canvassed it all. I have calculated all as a whole, and have come to the conclusion that it is all but the best mode of carrying out a bad system, while, as compared to that which I offer as a substitute, it cannot for one moment be upheld. The amount of capital expended in the maintenance of a sufficient number of horses to make this system perfect, must, of itself, without any other drawback, disadvantage, failure, or casualty, bring ruin upon the farmer, independently of each acre cultivated well, cultivated ill, or not cultivated at all, being liable to the same amount of rent. The capital disadvantageously expended for the carrying out of this system is enormous, and all, or nearly so, expended in a wrong direction. Sheep and black cattle are kept rather as substitutes for labour than as a source of profit. Horses supported where spade husbandry might be beneficially substituted, and responsibility undertaken in the mere hope of being able to live and secure an interest of 4 or 5 per cent. upon capital, after payment of rent and other liabilities.

As I shall devote a chapter to a consideration of the present extensive employment of horse labour, I shall here merely make a calculation of the additional rent that horse tax imposes upon the farmer who occupies 1,000 acres of land. I am below the average when I set his stud down at twenty horses, and assign a man to each pair. This allows that the horses are either engaged in ploughing with long reins, or in drawing a double horse cart. Now, if we estimate the man's wages at 12s. per week, it amounts to £31 4s. per annum; and which, multiplied by 10 makes £312 a-year. Then, if we allow £25 for the keep of each horse, it produces £500. If we add to this £5 a horse for wear and tear, for smiths' work, wheelwrights' work, and harness makers' work, and other incidental expenses, we find that this amount imposes an additional tax of £100. If we, then, estimate the value of his stud, his ploughs, his carts, his harrows, and other horse instruments, tackling, &c., at £1,000, and allow him 10 per cent. upon this description of property, which is much lower than it is usually valued at, being perishable and to be insured, we have £100 additional. Now those four amounts consequent upon the keeping of twenty horses, make £1,012 per annum, and which sum imposes an additional rent of more than £1 an acre upon the 1,000 acres. These are the circumstances which are now leading to the very nice calculations as to the value of land; 2s. or 3s., or even 1s. an acre, upon large engagements, making a serious item in the large farmer's account, and being taken into calculation by him when estimating profit and loss upon the amount of capital he may have engaged. Thus, suppose he loses 3s. an acre and has £3,000 capital invested, that amounts to £150, or a loss of 5 per cent upon the entire. We are, then, to suppose that all manure made in the straw-yard, in the stables, and about the farm-yard, is to be carried, say to the distance of one-third of the extreme. The very cost per acre of putting out the manure at that distance will amount to more than double the rent, while I pity the poor clodpole who relies upon the system of penning, of folding, and encamping cattle for the purpose of cheap manuring. I pity him, because he must imagine that a sheep can apply its manure more equally and more profitably than he can; I pity him when I see a crop of half-scooped turnips after a thaw or wet weather, filled up with sheep's dung and earth, and which are obliged to be drawn as refuse or part waste, and certainly not as profitably applied as if wheeled in a barrow a distance of some forty yards, and measured out in sufficient feeds for the animals for whose support they are designed. Of course, in my advocacy of the small farm system I shall be compelled to enter hereafter into the further consideration of the disadvantages of the large farm system to the landlord, to the tenant, and to the working classes, while for the

present I have thrown out such suggestions as, I trust, will lead those for whom
I write to sound conclusions upon the subject.

RENTS.

This is a difficult head under which anything new can be said. But as, in all
other works on agriculture, the question of rent has been treated as a mercantile
speculation, and as part of the erroneous system in existence, merely taking into
consideration the value of land from a calculation of the current price of produce,
and as not a word has been written on this subject with reference to the real value
of the raw material in the retail or small farm market, this question, like all others, has been left untouched by those who have preceded me, as far as the interest
of the labouring classes is concerned. Where I can admit the principle laid down
by other writers, I am quite willing to do so, while I hope to draw very different
conclusions from their premises. Rent is the return which the tenant undertakes
to make to the landlord for whatever amount of land he holds under him, and I
shall now proceed to canvass the present system of undertaking those engagements. There is an old saying that 'a landlord of straw can break a tenant of steel.'
This superiority of the landlord class over the tenant class is occasioned by the
great power which the landlords of this country possessed exclusively, prior to the
introduction of manufactures, and from the fact of the landlords in those earlier
times being law makers. Hence we find upon the statute book thousands and
tens of thousands of the most repugnant laws, all framed for the purpose of protecting the privileges of the landlords to the great disadvantage of the tenant,
and to the great discouragement of improvement. Their rights, known or
unknown, are protected, whether recognized in things existing and developed,
or in things existing but undiscovered. Under the title 'Royalties,' all that which
lies hid in the bowels of the earth, and which may, if industriously sought for and
advantageously used, become a source of individual remuneration and national
wealth, is preserved for the use, not of the industrious seeker but of the idle
owner; while, under the game laws and fishing restrictions, the birds of the air,
the beasts of the field, and the fishes of the stream, contrary to God's ordinance,
are preserved to the use of the landlord, so that, in due time, he may enjoy them.
Add to these great powers, they have availed themselves of their position as population pressed hardly upon the available means of subsistence, so to hem in and
enclose millions of acres of land belonging to the people as to set an increased
value upon their monopoly in the same ratio in which population increased. It is
not wonderful, then, having filled the statute book with laws protective of their
own interest, that *a landlord of law should be able to break a tenant out-lawed*. As I
have observed above, I am quite ready to admit the existence of any injustice
which does exist, and which other writers complain of, while, at the same time, I
cannot allow myself merely to paddle in the shallow waters as they have done.
On the contrary, I shall plunge at once into the very vortex, and dive to the bottom. I admit, then, the perfect right of other writers to take advantage of low

prices and high rents as a means of exposing the fallacies of the present system, while at the same time I am justified in asking wherefore they have abstained from proposing a remedy. And the answer must either be that they were ignorant of any means of correcting it, or that in the only real mode they saw the dread of elevating the working classes. What avails it that a declaimer shall tell a farmer that there exists a condition on parchment that he shall pay forty shillings an acre for land, which, when he took it, produced wheat worth eighty shillings a quarter, while the same conditions are still in force and the fulfilment of which may be extracted out of his capital, though wheat may only be worth forty or fifty shillings the quarter. The tenant knows all this as well as the declaimer, and the very fact of reminding him of it without proposing a remedy is an insult to the feeling and the understanding of the injured party. What then is the remedy? The remedy consists in substituting a corn for a money rent, and in that alone, and now I shall proceed to establish the truth of this assertion. Let me first surround myself with precedents of the very highest nature, and I shall afterwards go into a minute calculation as to the advantages that society would gain by the change. Firstly, then, we find that the title of the church to the tenth part of the produce of the land, and after labour has been expended upon bringing it to maturity, is superior to the title of the landlord, and that this superiority is acknowledged by the law; that is, that, if a farm worth a thousand pounds fails to produce more than enough to satisfy the demand of the church, the tithe lord steps in and takes the all in satisfaction of his demand and in the honour of God, and leaves the difference, which is nothing, to be divided between the landlord and the tenant. Here, then, we have the principal of a yearly render, according to the value of the produce established by law, and although a composition and rent charge has been established as a substitute for a render of one tenth of the produce, yet it is but a law, and the very fact of making the law, which interfered with a title superior to that of the landlord, is at once an answer to those Legislative protectors of the rents of the latter, when they declare the incompetency of the House of Commons to interfere with the existing arrangements between landlord and tenant. They have done so, as regards the church, and why stop short when the necessities of the state demand their interference as legislators between landlord and tenant. The answer to this is, because, as landlords and politicians, they hoped by an undue exercise of political power to preserve their own rights by trenching upon those of the church. Again, if the government enters into a contract for a supply of anything produced from the land, they will do so but for a year, lest the change of prices from one year to another should have a prejudicial effect upon the bargain. If then we take the church and the government as a fair representation of church and state, we find that both parties scrupulously guard themselves against unintelligible contracts – so much for precedent of the very highest order – and now let us ask what a manufacturer would say if a buyer went into the market and said 'I will make a contract with you to supply me for the next seven, fourteen, or twenty-one years, or during the lives of myself and two of my children, with cloth at such a fixed price, with calico at such a fixed price, or with hard ware at such a fixed price?' Why, as a matter of course the manufacturer would treat the offer as the ravings of a maniac, while the present system of leasing land for the like terms does not evince less insanity than the offer for the supply of manufactured goods for any of the same periods. Three very foolish notions have been circulated with respect to a corn rent; the one is the supposition that the whole render should be made in corn; another is the difficulty of establishing the value of grass land, or of light soils not calculated for producing wheat, and the other is the disinclination that farmers have to be deprived of the advantages to be derived from high prices and low fixed rent. The first objection is nonsense, inasmuch as the establishment of a corn rent would not imply the necessity of the payment of any portion of that rent throughout the Empire in one bushel of corn. A corn rent simply means, that if land is taken at forty shillings an acre when wheat is worth eighty shillings a quarter, the rent that shall be paid for the same land when the wheat is sixty shillings, fifty shillings, or forty shillings, shall vary in a like proportion as the price of produce. That is, that the rent assumed at forty shillings shall fall to thirty shillings when wheat sells at sixty shillings a quarter, and to twenty shillings when wheat sells at forty shillings a quarter, always taking into calculation a further reduction in favour of declining prices, because the same amount of labour should be expended upon the production of a quarter of wheat worth forty shillings, as upon the same wheat worth eighty shillings a quarter. The next absurdity is the supposed difficulty of establishing the price of grass land, or light soils. This, however, is a monstrous absurdity, inasmuch as the price of wheat land in general regulates the prices of other lands, while upon the other hand, if there are three, four, fifty or a hundred different classes of land, and if the relative value, according to current prices, of the produce of one class cannot be applied as a just standard for ascertaining the value of others, let each class in such case be valued by its own proper standard. The third assertion, that farmers prefer the chances of high prices and low fixed rent, would equally apply to those zealous and enthusiastic speculators, who imagined that they were ruined by the extinction of state Lotteries. Moreover, the question has never been fairly propounded to this class of farmers, while those, especially in Scotland, who pay a corn rent, are far more comfortable and better satisfied than their neighbours who pay in money. And for this reason, when prices are low they have the advantage and only pay in proportion, while, if prices are high, they have a four-fold increase, while the landlords are confined to the single advantage. Thus, suppose the price of wheat to be eighty shillings and the rent to be forty shillings, and the produce to be four quarters to the acre, in such case the landlord would receive £2 out of £16, leaving £14 to the tenant. Upon the other hand, suppose the price to be forty shillings a quarter and the rent £1 – in such case the landlord would receive £1 out of the £8, while the tenant would receive only £7. It may be said that the whole of the land not under wheat would be liable to the same high rent when wheat was dear. So it would, and it would be worth it for two reasons. Firstly, because all other produce is in general regulated by the price of wheat, and secondly, the larger profit upon wheat when the price is high would enable the wheat land to bear a portion of the higher rent of the remainder.

I shall now proceed to a consideration of the justice, the necessity, and the advantages to be derived from the substitution of a corn for a money rent. Firstly, then, it is a step indispensable to the establishment of the *'fixity of tenure,'* principle; a principle which means the holding of land in perpetuity, that is, for ever, so long as the tenant is satisfied to pay (for he will always be able to pay) that relative amount of rent annually which the price of his produce would impose upon him. I never have been able to assign any good reason why landlords should object to receiving their rents according to the prices of the produce of their land. It is, however, because it would be impossible, as well as unjust to both parties, to act upon the principle of 'fixity of tenure' without first establishing the principle of corn-rent, that I advocate the system. It is always a hardship upon a rising generation to find their comforts restricted and their rights interfered with, from the disinclination of our legislators and comfortable classes to interfere with things as they are, while it is not only an act of barbarism, but of cowardice, to allow existing abuses to remain from an apprehension of danger which might arise from their correction. The whole landed question, and indeed the whole commercial, manufacturing, labour, and money question, are so entrammelled and mystified by the laws of primogeniture, of settlement, and of entail, that he who attempts to write upon any one of those questions without embracing all, must either leave his subject incomplete or so complicated as to make his part-explanation unintelligible. For these reasons I shall abstain, until I have first made my readers acquainted with the principles of agriculture from any comment upon these several nuisances and shall proceed simply to a consideration of the justice, the convenience and necessity of substituting a 'corn rent' for a 'money rent.' I have already explained how foolish it would be for a buyer to contract with a manufacturer for a certain amount of goods for a long period, and, *'vice versa,'* how equally foolish it would be for the manufacturer to be tempted by a high offer to furnish the supply. Suppose, for instance, such a contract had been entered into previously to the introduction of machinery, and suppose the buyer had conditioned to give for thirty-one years the then prices for such articles as he should require, and that those articles should fall in price, as many articles have, to one-third or one-fourth of the then value. In such case would not the bargain be ruinous to him who contracted for the supply, and an injustice to the whole community. Well, then, what possible difference can be discovered between his position and that of a tenant, who, during the last war, when lands were raised to full double their value – say, when wheat was 120*s.* the quarter – contracted to pay an amount of rent, estimated by the then high price of wheat every year for twenty-one years, thirty-one years, forty-one years, or three lives, and without reference to the existing price of wheat during any single year of the whole period with the exception of the first. Suppose, as was frequently the case, that a tenant deposited a large sum of money with his landlord as security, and for which he was to receive the interest by deductions from his rent. Suppose for instance that he took one hundred acres of land at £2 an acre, and that he deposited £2,000 as security for twenty-one years. Suppose then, that from the fall of prices, the value of the land fell to thirty shillings an acre. In such case, the landlord would hold the tenant to his bargain, deducting any deficiency in his rent from the capital placed in his hands, so that in twenty years he would have appropriated to himself £1,000 or £50 a year over and above the value of his land.

But let us now consider the justice of a corn-rent as regards the interest of all parties. Every bargain between man and man should be made so clear, so intelligible, and so defined that neither should be able to take any advantage of the other, and perhaps nothing has so led to the complication of law, and the prostration of the English character, as those advantages which the existing system affords to the wily to traffic in the necessities of the ignorant and less cunning portion of society. It is therefore of all things necessary that those abuses should be destroyed, and as the present system of leasing land for a long term at a fixed rent, stands prominently forward in the catalogue of abuses, I am thus pains-taking in making it clear to the most obtuse understanding. If a man buys a bale of cotton, he estimates its value by the price that the produce when manufactured will bring in the market; so with the shoemaker who buys a hide, so with the cutler who buys steel, with the carpenter who buys wood, and the tailor who buys cloth, and why not so then with the husbandman who buys land, for taking for a term of years is a buying for each year. I must explain to you one great stumbling block in the way of adopting a corn rent. It is this, the laws of settlement and entail have so hampered, clogged and embarrassed the owners of large estates, that they look to a *fixity of rent* as necessary to a fixity of payment of debts. With them a certainty for themselves and a certainty of that amount which shall remain as their fixed income after paying their fixed debts, is the one all-absorbing thought. Thus fixity for them, means unfixing all those interests by which the rest of the community suffers so much injury and injustice.

Suppose we were to commence anew, would the system which now prevails be adopted? And if not, is its long continuance a sufficient or justifiable cause for still adhering to it? What can be more fair than that the owner of land should be satisfied with his fair annual proportion of its produce. His necessities, if not regulated by money contracts and barbarous engagements which can only be fulfilled by inflicting a great injustice upon society at large, would be met annually. If produce was dear, and as the price of produce would regulate all his household arrangements, if his establishment, in consequence of high prices, became more expensive, he would receive a high rent commensurate with those necessities, and his living would be as good, and his savings as great, though his expenses would be increased. Upon the other hand, if the price of produce is low, the expence of his household becomes comparatively diminished, while his mode of living is the same, and his savings relatively to the value of money in proportion. He pays his bills half yearly or yearly according to his contract with his trades-people, and at prices regulated by the then value of produce. But then, while the Jew, the mortgagee, the simple contract creditor, the mother, the brother, the sister, all stand in the way and demand a fixity of amount every half-year or quarter-day, he is not a free agent, and society suffers in consequence. Before the tithe composition bill was substituted for the payment in kind, the church lord participated with the tenant in every calamity, casualty, and disadvantage. Suppose, for instance, that all his corn was damaged so as to render it valueless, in fact, he had the power, if dissatisfied with the proctor's valuation, to serve the parson with notice to draw every tenth sheaf for his share. So with hay, if damaged or a bad crop, so with potatoes, and flax, and all other things. As I have shewn, then, that the title of the church to the 'first fruits' of the land is superior to the title of the landlord, and as for centuries this system of paying the parson a corn rent prevailed, surely it cannot be considered unfair that the landlord, with an inferior title, should be bound by the same rule.

Perhaps the querulous may say – True, but this system of paying the church in kind has been abolished, and a fixed amount has been commuted for in lieu of it. To such I answer: – Firstly, that the change was made against the consent of the church. Secondly, that the change was made not so much with the view of altering the mode of payment, as for the purpose of making tithes an equable tax upon land, rather than upon any description of produce. I am now speaking of Mr Goulburn's[1] Irish Composition Bill, first established upon the voluntary system, requiring the sanction of the payers themselves before it could be adopted, subsequently made compulsory and which only applied to Ireland, and which has been further commuted for a rent charge chargeable upon the estate and payable by the landlord. Sir Robert Peel's tithe bill for England had a similar tendency, but then we must always bear in mind, that the church was opposed to those several alterations, and merely yielded to the necessity of the times, a convenient term used by landlords when they want to commit an injustice upon any other body. Well then, the necessity of the times now imperatively demands that alteration of the agricultural system which I contend for, and the whole people now require the landlords to disgorge some of that plunder stolen from the church and appropriated to their own uses, together with such a new arrangement as will restore to the people their fair share of that inheritance with which it has pleased Almighty God to endow them, but of which rapacious man has deprived them. The 'fixity of tenure' contended for on behalf of the people of Ireland just now, does not mean 'fixity of tenure' at all, it simply means a contract between landlord and tenant, that the latter shall receive from the former compensation at the expiration of his term for monies expended in improvements. It leaves the whole question of duration of time, and of annual value, wholly untouched. Indeed, I will explain to you the folly of persons attempting to handle subjects of which they are wholly ignorant. From my thorough knowledge of the love of justice entertained by the working classes, I have come to the pleasing conclusion that they would not, if they had the power, violate the rights of others, and it is because I write for justice for all, as well protection for the rich under a good system as protection for the poor, that I feel myself called upon to expose the injustice which the bastard fixity of tenure principle now contended for would be likely to inflict upon the rights of others.

---

1 Henry Goulburn (1784–1856), MP for Horsham 1808, St Germans, West Looe, Armagh city and Cambridge University 1831–56; Chief Secretary for Ireland 1821–7.

Suppose, for instance, that a wealthy capitalist took twenty, thirty, or fifty acres of land from a widow or a poor man for twenty-one years, upon the condition, that at the expiration of that term the out-going tenant, that is, the rich capitalist, should be allowed compensation money for his improvements. Suppose also, that he had expended an amount in those improvements which the poor man could not pay, in such case, he, the poor man, though bearing the dignified title of landlord, is wholly at the mercy of the wealthy capitalist. Now, just suppose a very possible case – suppose a dying father to have one hundred acres of land, which he wishes an infant son to take possession of and to cultivate upon attaining his majority, and that during his minority it shall be leased to a good and solvent tenant; well, it might just happen as I have stated above, that the father's desire, the mother's wish to carry it into effect, and the son's inclination to follow it, may all be frustrated by this new-fangled principle of 'fixity of tenure,' which allows one man to speculate to the disadvantage of another. I may probably be told that this new principle would have such details fixed for carrying it out that none of those objections could arise. Now it is to those complicated details which are always required for carrying out a bad principle that I object, while I the more zealously contend for the establishment of my principle, because it would be impossible for the most wily, the most artful or cunning, to entangle it in the meshes of the law, or to thwart it by quibbling and nonsensical details. For all these reasons then I lay it down as an irrefutable conclusion that 'fixity of tenure' is indispensable to the interest of all classes of society; while, without the substitution of a corn for a money-rent, it would be an injustice against which neither of the contracting parties could protect themselves. Besides being an injustice to the landlord and to the tenant, it is a great injustice to the working-classes, inasmuch as doubtful tenure and fixed rents considerably interfere with their wages and employment, while the whole body of consumers are much injured by the limitation which the present system imposes upon production.

'A fair day's wages for a fair day's work' is a favourite maxim of mine, and one the justice of which is acquiesced in by all. Let us then have a fair amount of rent for the amount of land held; a maxim which, in principle, is as just and fair as that of a fair day's wage for a fair day's work.

HORSES APPLIED TO AGRICULTURE.

It would really appear as if that noble animal, the horse, had been sent into the world as a curse to mankind. There is no portion of society so depraved as that which is engaged in speculations respecting the powers of this noble animal. The horse appears to be the rallying point for every description of barbarity, depravity, obscenity, drunkenness, debauchery, and villany; and it is a melancholy reflection to think, that as civilization progresses, the barbarism to which this animal gives rise, increases. The daily practices resorted to in the betting world go far to make society depraved; while if we look for drunkards, cheats, and blackguards of the very highest order, we shall find them pre-eminent among the leading frequenters of the turf, associating with horse-dealers, horse-keepers, slang-jockeys, racing-grooms, and horse-butchers. So much I am obliged to say of this noble animal, who has been the innocent means of ruining thousands, and of bringing sorrow upon whole families; while the uses to which he is put as an agricultural beast, make him a competitor for manual labour to the great disadvantage of his owner. A horse, if kept for agricultural purposes, can be only valuable when constantly employed according to its strength, and when only employed at such work as man cannot, or should not, perform. The first breaking up of tough grass-land, the carrying of produce to market, the carting of manure, being tackled for draining purposes, and to work the thrashing-machine, are the only agricultural uses to which a horse should be applied. The difference between horse labour and manual labour is this – a farmer is always sure to have more horses than he requires, and they must be idle a great portion of the year, while he can suit himself with the exact number of hands he requires. The greatest objection that I have, however, to the use of the horse is, that man can do its work more profitably. The large farm-system makes horse-labour necessary; while in the small farm-system it might be dispensed with nearly altogether, and, when it was required, the exact amount of work to be performed would be paid for without the necessity of keeping him for the year being imposed upon the husbandman. Add to these objections the amount of capital vested in these animals, and the alarming amount of produce that they consume, imposes a heavy tax upon the owner, and a great injustice upon the working classes. As, however, I shall have frequent opportunities of contrasting the relative value of horse and spade labour, I shall conclude my present observations under this head, and proceed to that which is minutely connected with it.

SPADE HUSBANDRY.

'When Adam delved and Eve span
Who was then the gentleman?'[1]

The spade and the spinning wheel are two of man's oldest and best friends, and he has derived but a poor benefit from the substitution of the plough and the 'rattle-box.' The great disparity which all modern inventions and improvements have created in the human family, have each and all tended to the centralization of wealth and power, and to the prostration of industry and character, while those who would re-harmonize by destroying those unholy distinctions, are designated by the foul names of 'levellers' and 'destructives.' There is no sight, however, which can be presented to my eyes so beautiful, so cheering, so natural and becoming, as that of the husbandman tilling the ground for his own and his family's sole use, behoof and benefit. When I see a man with his foot upon his spade, I think I recognize the image of his God, and see him in that character which even the

---

1 The text preached by the radical peasants' minister John Ball (d. 1381).

Malthusian deigns to assign him – A MAN STANDING ON HIS OWN RESOURCES. He honours himself, respects the laws that protect him, and loves the God who has been so bountiful as to create the means for yielding him subsistence. He looks upon his parish church as a sanctuary, and pants for that day of rest, when, after six days' toil, he may offer up thanksgivings in it for the blessings that he enjoys. To him every day is a laughing holiday. In his own little holding he recognizes the miniature of nature. When he leaves his castle in peace, it is ever in his sight as the repository of all that is dear to him, and when he returns at noon, his eyes are gladdened, his feelings are excited, and his heart bounds, while receiving the welcome, the attentions, and caresses of his wife and darling children. What cares he for that splendour that is beyond his reach, those luxuries for which he feels not the want, or the enjoyments of those whose vices he would not imitate. If he is a leveller, he would take virtue for his standard instead of vice. He at once becomes a civilized being, panting for knowledge, in order that he may stand distinguished in that community of which he is a free member. He is happy because he is contented, he is contented because he is free, and satisfied with that freedom which does not trench upon the rights or liberties of others. Such a being do I pant to see, and such a one are the resources of his country capable of making him, and shall we not then continue to struggle even to the death for so desirable an object? His vices are consequences of oppression and mis-rule, and not characteristics of his nature or voluntary acts of free-will. Let us then, in the name of all that is holy, endeavour to place man in his right position.

Before I begin to discuss the relative merits of the plough and the spade, I shall, according to a promise made in one of my letters upon agriculture, relate an experiment that I made upon large scale. It was this: – There is a very handsome field adjoining my house and containing about fifteen acres of land: this field, from its proximity to the house, was kept for many years in meadow, until, in fact, it became high bound, tough, and almost barren. I was one day walking through the field with Dr. Longfield,[1] who was then professor of Political Economy as well as a fellow of Trinity College, a man with a mind far surpassing anything I have ever met in my life, one, in fact, who would know everything that could be known, and who, though not a practical farmer, was thoroughly acquainted with the theory of the science. In our walk he kicked two or three times at the surface, and said 'Now, what can you do with this field for the next five years? Its run out?' I replied, 'You shall see.' Upon the following morning I put a pair of ploughs to work and turned it up. As soon as the sod was rotted, I employed a great number of men and dug it well; I allowed it to remain in ridges during the winter, and upon the first fine weather in March I employed about a hundred hands. I set them to dig as you would dig a kitchen garden, making the mould as fine as that used in flower pots, while women followed the spades with baskets, picking up every root and fibre. When the whole surface was as level as a carpet, I laid the field out in beds of twelve feet wide, and furrows eighteen

---

1   Mountifort Longfield (1802–84), Irish judge.

inches wide, with garden lines. I then gave the whole a mere sprinkling of compost, that is, of old earth and lime mixed. I then sowed the seed myself (barley) and set the men, two to each furrow, one digging and the other shovelling and covering the seed. It would have taken a plough with one horse and a man to sow an acre, while four men, two with spades and two with shovels, performed the work, that is, sixty men completed the sowing of the field. When the farmers in the neighbourhood heard that I was going to sow barley in such a field, one in which barley never grew before, they declared unanimously that I was stark staring mad. Spring advanced, however, and all those who came far and near for legal advice, as well as the neighbours in passing, gazed in astonishment. Summer arrived and my field presented more the appearance of a large yellow carpet than of a corn field. The weeds which lay smothered for years had all come to life and I was well laughed at. I set all hands to work however, and did not leave one yellow spot in the whole fifteen acres. In harvest time the crop was literally a show, which people came from various parts to see. Every grain being sown upon a level surface, and each having exactly the same amount of coverings, all grew to pretty nearly an equal height. The harvest, as is very usual in the south of Ireland, was wet, what the farmers call 'catching weather.' As soon as the crop was ripe, I took advantage of one thoroughly fine day, in which I reaped, bound and stacked the barley all within it; a thing which I believe never was attempted before, because barley in general requires two or three days on the swarth before it is bound, and two or three days more to season its 'stooks' before it can be safely stacked. The harvest weather broke, and nearly all the barley in the country was lost from the tedious process in saving that crop. The result was that I got 1s.4d. per stone, the very highest price, for my barley, whilst others either lost the crop altogether or sold it for half price. Of that crop I made £12 10s. an acre. As soon as the crop was off I dug a furrow a foot wide and a foot deep in every alternate bed, and carted the earth to the farmyard. Even the success of the barley did not save me from the reiteration that I must be mad now for 'taking the field away.' I then prepared the whole for potatoes, and again I outraged their feelings by selecting the very largest potatoes that I could buy for seed, and planting them whole. I made my drills more than a yard asunder, opened them very shallow and put the potatoes in, leaving three feet between each. I then covered the drills up, and in proper season earthed them with the spade instead of with the plough, not allowing the horse to tread down and break every second plant. At the time that I was digging those potatoes, Mr Waller,[1] who was then as a barrister engaged by the Liberal interests to assist in the registration of votes, was on a visit with me. He resides in the very richest part of the county of Limerick, the land of which is not surpassed by any in the three kingdoms for richness. My steward, being proud of the crop, requested the Limerick gentleman to go and take a look at what we could do with light soil. He did come, and confessed that in all his life he never saw any produce at all approaching it. The process could not be called digging, it rather resembled that of shovelling potatoes out of the heap; many plants

---

1 Probably John Francis Waller (1810–94).

yielding a large basket of the largest potatoes, while each man could dig more in the day than six could dig of an ordinary crop. That crop of potatoes, at three-pence a stone, was valued at £40 an acre, and it was below the mark. The manure that I used was principally what had been taken out of the barley stubble after having been put into the cow-houses, sheep houses, and working horse stables for a certain time. I then gave the ground twenty barrels of lime to the acre, each barrel costing two shillings, and sowed it with wheat. I sold ten bags of wheat of twenty stone to the bag off each acre, and for which I got the very highest price, £1 10s. per bag, that is one shilling and sixpence a stone. In the spring, when the weather was dry, I sowed clover with the wheat, and during the two following years it produced two as fine crops as could be seen, leaving the field, after 'taking it away,' worth double the rent that it was when I commenced.

Let us now see what was the profit and loss upon this speculation. I sold the barley for £12 10s. an acre; the potatoes were worth £40 an acre. I sold the wheat for £15 an acre, and the two years' clover was richly worth £10 the acre, making in all £77 10s.; and if we deduct the value of the straw, and allow £27 10s. for the rent, labour and seed for the three years when it was in tillage, it will leave £50 per acre, or, at six per cent., the usual interest of money in Ireland, it would yield £3 per acre for ever, even if the field was 'carried away;' while, in fact, it was worth twice as much after the process that I have stated as it was before. I do not think that I could furnish a better illustration of the respective value of rent and labour. Indeed, I feel convinced that the man who occupies just as much ground as he can possibly till by his own labour, would be able in three years to purchase the fee simple of that quantity, no matter what the amount of rent might be.

The superiority of spade culture over all other modes is clearly established by the perfection to which market gardens are brought, as compared with the same quality of land under the very best system of plough husbandry. The following are some of the advantages which the spade has over the plough. A spade can be had for a few shillings, while a plough and a pair of horses, besides the cost of purchase, will stand the farmer in fully one hundred pounds a year. The spade will find its way any where, up hills and between rocks, where a plough cannot be used. It can be used at times when a plough cannot; but even these advantages are insignificant when their relative effects upon the soil are compared. For instance, I have stated that I was enabled to save my barley cultivated by spade labour in one day, whereas it would have been impossible to do so, had it been produced by plough cultivation. And here I will consider an advantage to be derived from spade cultivation which I have not seen treated of in any other work. It is this, and by which I was enabled to save my crop all in one day. If you prepare your field ever so well for the seed, if you make the surface as level as a carpet, yet will it be impossible with the plough, or even by a drilling machine, to give it that equal covering which you can with the spade, some of the grains will receive six inches of covering, some five, and so on, whilst some are left close to the surface. Now it is this circumstance which leads to the loss of a great por-tion of the crop and to the necessity of allowing the corn when reaped to remain in swarth at the mercy of the weather. Those grains nearest the surface will come up first and so on, those with the heaviest amount of covering making their way up last. This inequality of growth is always visible in a field sown with the harrow or under a plough. In harvest every man must have observed the uneven manner in which crops generally ripen, a large portion remaining green and unripe while the major part is, as they term it, 'falling off the head;' and to which the backward crop must be sacrificed. Now, if the farmer attempted to stack or draw such a crop before the green part had been sufficiently seasoned, the consequence would be, that the whole would take fire. Upon the other hand, when the surface is made even, the seed sown even, and all equally covered, and the seed not disturbed or buried by the horses' feet, the whole will come up even as I have described and come simultaneously to perfection. It is true that many writers dwell upon the necessity of pulverising the earth well, but how can this be so effectually done as by giving a clod a slap with the back of a spade. They also attach much importance to ploughing in fallow lands, when weeds begin to shew themselves, but how can they be so successfully destroyed by a plough as they can by a spade? The plough will leave them near the surface, and its imperfect mode of administering the proper cure imposes the necessity for its frequent use, while a spade will turn them upside down, burying them to rise no more; and, for this reason, one good digging is worth three ploughings and as many harrowings. I am aware that the almost impossibility of large farmers employing a sufficient number of hands to carry out the principle of spade husbandry will be urged as a reason against its adoption, but it must be borne in mind that that is my very greatest objection to the large farm system – viz. that it compels a man to act upon an erroneous plan in compliance with an erroneous system, while upon the other hand it is a great injustice to those who are told that they must either starve or clamor for the right to receive their breakfast, dinner and supper from some foreign country.

I have directed attention to the condition of market gardens, and perhaps I may be fancifully asked if I would make market gardens of all England; and if I was asked my answer should be – Why not! and would to God that we had a sufficient amount of population to drive us to the holy necessity. When we speak of market gardens we must always bear in mind, that altho' vegetables only appear to be produced there, that yet every root grown is capable of being manufactured into beef, mutton, pork, leather, fur, cloth, wool, milk, butter, eggs, and even horse flesh, and that, after all, a market garden is but the most perfect system of cultivation. In fact, our best cultivated farms now are, to what the land might be brought to, just what the raw and undressed flax is to the finest cambric that can be manufactured from it. A landlord has no objection to receive £30 an acre for market garden ground, which, if a great distance from town, may not be worth a pound an acre, while its distance from the metropolis would not at all stand in the way of a labouring man making it just as profitable to himself. It is true that ten tons' weight of cabbages, of potatoes, parsnips or carrots, may not fetch as much as beef as they would as vegetables, and that it would be difficult for a man in Leicestershire to send the vegetables to the London market, but then, according to the Norfolk plan, he might make the sheep or the ox carry them there in beef or mutton. When a town or city is to be built the founders and projectors do not attach so much importance to the quality of land in the neighbourhood of the site, as they do to water, and especially a navigable river, and yet we find that without the assistance of the plough the most barren soils in the neighbourhood of a new congregation are very speedily converted into fertile gardens by spade cultivation. – In fact a man with a spade and a hut to cover him, and as much land as he can cultivate by his own industry, is a capitalist, capable of discounting his health and strength as a means of independence.

I have very frequently directed the attention of slovenly farmers to the lumpy condition of their land, and they have told me that the clods, when rolled or bush-harrowed in spring, would afford great nutriment to the growing crop. This is all folly. The earth contained in those clods never reaches the plant at all, whereas, had it been used as nutriment in proper time by applying it to the seed, it would have had a beneficial effect. Indeed, so ignorant are some farmers, that they would endeavour to convince you that too much pulverization was injurious to ground. I wish that some of those clod-poles would go to some of my gardening neighbours and tell them so. I have very often taken up a clod as large as a goose's egg, and asked the farmer in whose field I happened to be, of what use that clod was? The answer has invariably been, it would be broke in spring, and when I have crumbled it between my hands, rubbing it well, he has been struck with astonishment at the quantity of fine mould that he allowed to remain inactive.

For all these reasons, then, I am a great advocate for adopting the system of spade cultivation. I advocate it because it is within the reach of every man, and can be used by all men. I advocate it in preference to the plough, because the plough with its necessary accompaniments, is a thing out of the reach of 9,999 in every 10,000 of the working classes. I advocate it because it is wholesome labour, natural labour, and profitable labour. I advocate it because so long as the land is placed out of the reach of the poorest man, so long will that class-inequality, so destructive of human happiness, continue to exist. I advocate it because I feel firmly convinced that, by the adoption of the small farm system, to which it is applicable, and by that alone, can the poor of this country be saved from the force of tyrants and the fraud of cheats. I advocate it because I feel that there is a point beyond which human endurance cannot go, and because I believe we have arrived nearly at that point. I advocate it as a means of turning all the vast inventions and improvements in the arts and sciences of latter years to general instead of to class purposes. I advocate it as the now only means remaining of arresting a civil war, and of sparing human blood.

MANURES.

How very minutely these apparently different subjects are mingled with the grand question of labour. We are actually inundated with theories upon chemical processes for producing manures, while labour, if unshackled, would be an admirable substitute for all, or, if required, they would be a great auxiliary. I have always asserted, that the richest of all manures was that to be found in the arms of a man, and I shall proceed in the outset, to prove the truth of my assertion. It has been a mystery for many years how the poor of Ireland, without a spot of land or without work, can contrive to live, and yet it is a problem very easily solved: they live upon their own labour, without renting land or being hired. The process is as follows: they gather together as much wild earth as they can come at; or, perhaps, buy an old ditch or a lump of wild soil; or, if they are partially employed with a small farmer, they receive those advantages which are called privileges: that is, they are allowed to take a quantity of wild earth, earth which if put out upon land in the state in which they get it, would sterilize it for three or four years. It is as yellow as a guinea, and all its fertilizing qualities have been destroyed by secretion from atmospheric influence for God knows how long. In this wild state, they draw it into their little yard about October or November, and there they keep digging it, and digging it at every spare moment, until, by dint of labour, they bring it to be excellent manure, and for which they get a sufficiency of ground from a neighbouring farmer to put it out for potatoes. And after it has produced a right good crop of potatoes for the labourer, it will produce a crop of wheat and a crop of oats for the farmer. The wheat produced upon such lands is always the best upon the farm, and for this reason: because, while the farmer uses his own sparingly, he will see that his poorer neighbour's is profusely administered. If a poor man has good chances, he will make by this means as much manure as will grow an acre of potatoes. Indeed, if his whole time was devoted to it, and if he could get a sufficient quantity of wild earth, he would make enough for five acres. Allowing him, however, to make enough for one acre, and that acre to be worth £10 10s., let us see how he stands.

The Irish labourer who can earn eight-pence a day for a constancy becomes a rich man, and in ten years, is able to over-bid his neighbour for twenty or thirty acres of ground and to stock it, always procuring an old horse to begin with. Allowing a man, then, to be in constant employment at eight-pence a day, and to work every working day in the year, say 300, he can earn but £10, whereas the poor man, snatching an hour now and then to turn wild earth into manure by his labour, can earn ten guineas in the year. So far, then, we may accept it as a truism, that artificial manures are for the most part but the best substitute for labour, whereas, I contend, that every acre of usable ground has within itself the means of producing a sufficiency of the very best description of manure. I shall here speak generally of the system of making manure that I practised myself, and I shall enter more minutely into the subject, when I come to lay down rules for the management of small farms.

The plan that I adopted, then, was this. Before I broke up a stubble-field, I took trenches, say twenty feet asunder, out of the field, and, as I required it, I drew it into the houses in the following manner: – Say, on the first of the month, I wheeled with a wheelbarrow into the cow-houses, sheep-houses, and working-horse stables, a foot thick of earth, which was littered over with straw for the cows and horses – the sheep preferring earth to any other bed – on that day week these floors of earth in the cow-houses and stables were turned upside down with the spade, while that in the sheep-house was scratched over every morning to keep it dry, as the wet would give the sheep the foot rot and injure their wool; on the following week, that is, when the first floor had been in for a fortnight, I covered it, after taking off the litter, with another floor of equal thickness. After that had remained there for a week I turned it up, and during the following week, that is when all had been there for a month, I wheeled it out, and made it into a heap, shaped in the best way to keep the rain off as much as possible.

An old ditch not worth a farthing the thousand loads, except for this purpose, was just as good as any other. As, then, it is most likely that several gentlemen in my neighbourhood, and those of the farming class, will see this account, I think I may appeal to them with confidence whether or no they ever saw so large a quantity of such good manure ever produced by ten farmers. I have some years manured as much as thirty acres with this description of manure, and it invariably happened that it produced better potatoes, wheat, barley, vetches, rape, and grass than any other description of manure whatever, while it gave the advantage over all others of adding to the surface and producing a larger effect upon the ground. The potatoes produced from this manure were larger, heavier in proportion to size, and much drier, than those produced by any other manure, while the grain of the wheat was larger, brighter, heavier and thinner skinned. In short, I discovered that, however horse-dung or cow-dung may, during the time of fermentation, have a quicker effect upon the growing crop, yet, when in its ripening state it began to suck hard and to require more nutriment, then the fermented manures failed, and the superiority of the solid was discovered. If you take an acre of ground as nearly equal in quality as possible, and top-dress one half with the best stable-dung and the other half with manure made as I have described, its superiority will be then discovered. That top-dressed with horse dung will spring up in the commencement and grow longer, but when you come to the scale you will then find the difference, as that produced by the manure made in houses will weigh at least one-third more than that produced by the horse-dung, while the after-grass will be worth three times as much. Now this is all practical knowledge after frequent experiments, and is the best answer that I can give to those wild and unmanageable theorists who are always contending against the possibility of procuring manure enough to grow corn enough for our own people.

When I come to lay down my rules for the practical management of small farms, I shall state to the wheel-barrowful the exact amount of manure required for each crop, and the mode by which it is to be procured. I am not to be supposed to be an enemy to any description of manure that can be made serviceable for agricultural purposes; but what I contend is, that all chemical preparations are but substitutes, and bad ones too, for labour, which, if free and properly apportioned, would always command more than a sufficiency of food for the land, which is manure, without being obliged to have recourse to the chemical processes, which are physic. Let any man vary those new inventions as he may for five or six years, and at the end he will discover that they are but so many alternatives, annually losing their effect, until, at length, he will be compelled to give up the system of dosing and quacking, and of returning to the solids. I know that your large farm gentry will say, 'Pooh! who could manage 1,000, 2,000, 3,000, or 7,000 acres of land, not at all an unusual undertaking, without having recourse to those stimulants?' I would wish those gentlemen to understand that that is another of my great objections to large farms; the very evil of being compelled to have recourse to the ruinous system of physicking land that they are not able to feed; whereas, again I say, if the 1,000 acres were divided into 250 farms of four acres each, the occupant of one of those allotments would not give you two-pence for all the chemical manures that you could bestow upon him, having a good substitute in his labour. Another very great difficulty which stands in the way of large farmers making a sufficient quantity of manure is, the want of a sufficient number of outhouses for that purpose, and the necessity consequently imposed upon them of exposing their manures to the rain; whereas, if there is one object which should more arrest the attention of the farmer than another it is that of keeping his manure as dry as possible.

When I commenced farming, I was myself strongly possessed with this difficulty of manuring mania, and was obliged to have recourse to fallowing, and paring and burning, because I had not thought of the practice of making manure in the houses as I have described; and, indeed, if I had thought of it, the knowledge would have been of little value, as I had not then a sufficient quantity of out-offices to put it into practice. At that time I held nearly 100 acres of land on my father's estate, rent free, and, finding the want of manure, and the great expense of drawing sea-sand sixteen or eighteen miles, and which merely gives a colour to the grain of one crop, I set about some new invention, and, after a little thought, I decided upon trying my hand at ashes. I commenced a fire on the 24th of June, and kept it burning till the latter end of October. I paid one man, Richard Donovan, six shillings a week, being two shillings over the usual rate of wages, to attend to the fire late and early. The summer happened to be the finest that we had had for many years, and the result of my experiment was that at the end of October I had more ashes than I knew what to do with; but which, however, were very valuable. I refused £70 for one heap, and £25 for another, from two neighbouring farmers. The process that I pursued was this: I selected a swamp of very deep soil, with a peat surface, and a kind of yellow clay substratum. I dug a large number of sods, and a quantity of the undersoil, and exposed it to the weather to be dried before I commenced my fire, as the great art of succeeding in such an undertaking is to have a sufficient quantity of earth and sods well dried to insure you against failure, till the heap arrives at that size and strength that you may defy bad weather. When I was thus prepared, I lighted my fire, and fed it as it required for the first week, by placing a row of dried sods around the base, and covering it with dried earth to the top. When the fire was about three weeks old the process of drying became unnecessary, as it was impossible to quench it. I have seen it covered of a wet evening with sods, and undersoil thrown up as they were dug, with the water dripping from them, and all was ashes in the morning. As I never was, and never shall be, a great friend to turnips, I put the greater part of the ashes out for wheat and potatoes, and some upon grass, and I never saw finer crops than it produced. The wages paid for making the ashes were six shillings a-week, for about seventeen weeks, or £5 2s., and the value of the ground consumed would never have been worth more than £1 an acre per annum, and I did not use more than the sixteenth part of an acre, which, if purchased at twenty-five years' purchase, would amount to £1 11s. 3d., making the whole expense £6 13s. 3d., while the ashes were richly worth £200; the difference being all labour.

Much ignorance prevails upon the subject of manures. Stable dung, whether good or bad, has always assigned to it a like property. The farmer who feeds his horse upon vetches, grass or hay, supposes that his stable dung, because made in a stable, is just as good as his neighbour's whose horse is fed upon hay and oats; whereas there is as much difference as there is between the light of a bude-light and that of a halfpenny candle. So with those graziers who feed cattle upon turnips, they suppose that the manure produced is as good as manure produced by cattle fed on potatoes; but never was there a greater mistake, the latter being very far superior. I have thought it necessary to enter largely upon this subject, in consequence of the writers upon political economy in agriculture having recently mixed up the subject of manuring land with the question of free-trade; their argument being, that an extensive system of grazing is indispensable as a means of keeping up the wheat crop of this country to something about its present deficiency, and that the encouragement given to the importation of live stock will materially tend to diminish the quantity of manure necessary for producing even the deficient supply, and thereby increasing that deficiency every year. This, however, is but an additional blunder of the blundering political economists, and is an evil consequent upon the system of large farms, and can be only remedied by substituting that of small farms. I never can let slip an opportunity of exposing the fallacies of the free-traders, if, indeed, their blunders deserve so mild a name. The reason, then, why those gentlemen contend so loudly for the necessity of large farms and extensive grazing as a means of producing a large quantity of manure, is, because they know that large farms are managed by horse-labour, while the expense of a grazing farm is insignificant when compared with the same amount kept in tillage, and from these facts they come to the conclusion, that large farms and grazing throw the agricultural labourers out of employment, and drive them into their slave-market as competitors with the already surplus pauper population.

DAIRIES.

Having now disposed of my subject as far as relates to waste lands, large farms, rents, horse labour, spade husbandry and manures, I shall proceed to discuss the question of farming, treating of each branch under its own proper head; firstly, in order to lead my readers to a knowledge of the most profitable application of the several crops; and I shall then treat of the mode of producing those several crops, and compare their relative returns for the amount of labour expended in their production.

The cow, then, being an indispensable to a mother in labour, to a child in arms, to the infant growing, to the adult in process of formation, to the labourer at work, and to the aged in declining life, I treat of this domestic animal firstly. I pity the man who has not a cow, and who is obliged to wait till driven by sickness to the necessity of sending to a neighbour for a half-penny or pennyworth of the most wholesome, the most nutritious, and the most grateful beverage. It is a melancholy thing to see an able and willing workman reduced to the necessity of feeding his little children upon unwholesome slops, as a substitute for that, of which, had he fair play, he could have an abundance. No labouring man can say that he is as he ought to be if he is not possessed of a cow; and it is because I propose that a sufficient stock of that useful animal should constitute the staple of the small farmer's reliance, that I make the cow my first consideration. I propose, that every man occupying four acres of ground shall be possessed of four cows as the main stock of his establishment. As, however, I shall enter minutely into the mode of treating the cow, as well as into a minute calculation as to the return to be expected from that treatment, I shall now proceed, under my present head, to treat the subject generally.

I have derived my knowledge upon this subject from practical experience, having not only had a dairy myself, but, from the circumstance of living close to a near relation, who, for many years has made a large dairy of from thirty to fifty cows a great hobby, to the process of managing which I paid the very greatest attention, and which he has brought to greater perfection than any other person that I know of. Indeed, as any digression which will serve my purpose will be pardoned by the reader, I may here state, while speaking of that gentleman, the fact that he has gone farther in establishing the value of a plot of ground to the working man, than all the landlords and practical writers in existence. He is an immensely large landed proprietor, and the best landlord in the country. In every one of his leases he inserts a condition, that the farmer shall allow every labourer he employs so much land rent free, a house of stipulated dimensions, and always kept in proper repair; and the result of this plan is, that the labourers of his tenants and their families are as comfortable as the tenants themselves.

In order to make profit of a dairy, the farmer must always have a sufficient number of cows to make a certain quantity of butter, say, a firkin, or about sixty pounds as nearly as possible, at one churning, and this is one of the reasons why I have thought proper to assign four cows to each small farmer. It is impossible that all could carry on the trade of selling new milk and fresh butter, and, therefore, in speaking of a dairy, it must always be treated as a manufactory for the wholesale market, rather than as a means of supplying the retail demand. In many parts of Ireland, the system of large farms is carried on by the same farmer cultivating extensively, and also keeping a dairy. This system is practised in many parts of England as well, to a most ruinous extent, and, from calculations made from such sources, no fair conclusions as to the profits of a dairy can be arrived at. From twenty to thirty cows, according to the size of the farm, in general constitute the dairy. These animals are kept upon the lands, let out to rest, not half fed, and, being perished and starved in winter, just when they require attention and care, the cost of renewing the stock is excessive, while their produce, besides being poor in quality, does not amount to one-half the quantity which the same number of cows, if properly fed and attended to, would produce. And yet a dairy of this kind is the principal reliance of the farmers for paying their May rent. An Irish farmer generally pays his November rent from the sale of his harvest, and he pays his May rent by raising money upon the supposed produce of his dairy for the coming half year, by obtaining money at the rate of forty, fifty, sixty, and even seventy-two per cent. from the butter merchant, to whom he is in the habit of selling his produce. It would not, then, be fair to make wholesale calculations upon so imperfect a system, while, there being no retail market for milk and butter in the country districts in Ireland, those who can not afford to keep a sufficient number of cows to make the quantity required for the wholesale market at once, must be ruined. Let me explain this to you familiarly. If a poor man has two or three cows badly fed, he will expect to make somewhere about ninety-six pounds weight of butter 'under each cow' in the season. He attempts to make a firkin, or sixty pounds, for the wholesale market, and which, if made at once, would sell as first quality, and fetch, say £2 5s. or at the rate of £4 10s. per cwt; whereas, it will take him six or seven weeks to make the required amount, adding seven or eight pounds at a churning to the stock, which, when ready for sale, has as many colours as a rainbow, and as many different smells as a farm yard, and, when he takes it to market, instead of getting first quality price, or £4 10s. the cwt, it is bored, smelt, and tasted, and branded as a 'bishop,' a title given to butter which does not merit that of 1st, 2nd, 3rd, 4th or 5th quality, and which are the several classes that that article is sold under. For this he will receive about fifteen shillings, or at the rate of £1 10s. the cwt instead of £2 5s., or at the rate of £4 10s. per cwt, the price of first quality; thus for want of a retail market, and not having a sufficient number of cows to make the required quantity for the wholesale market, he loses two-thirds of the price of the article.

I shall now lay down some practical rules for the management of a dairy. The cow being the first requisite in the establishment, I shall describe what she ought to be, and how she should be treated. There are as many opinions as to the cow most preferable as there are different breeds. I shall, therefore, state the qualities for which they are respectively preferred, and leave the reader to his choice.

The Ayrshire is now coming into very extensive use in all descriptions of farms, whether light or heavy; their recommendation being their beauty, and that they thrive better than most other breeds upon light soil and scanty fodder; their milk, however, is not to be compared to many others, either for quantity or quality; to the Hereford for quantity, or to the Devon or Alderney for quality, or to the common Irish or English cow for either one or the other. This breed has been pushed of late years amongst some farmers who would be better without them, especially by the Duke of Devonshire and his friends, more I presume, from the state of perfection that they have been brought to by those gentlemen upon their rich domains, than from the intrinsic merit of the animal. The Ayrshire, however, is a good cow for a large dairyman, as she has that property much prized by them, viz., if she misses for milk, she will turn out well for the butcher, a consideration, however, which never should weigh with a man having three or four cows.

The white-faced Hereford, is, perhaps, generally speaking the most milchy, and has the property of fatting at an earlier age than any other breed. I may be allowed to state my own preference, and I certainly give it to the Hereford, above all others. I have had a dairy exclusively of Hereford cows, and they averaged over twenty-four quarts a-day, three or four of them giving as much as sixteen quarts at a meal, and of average richness; richer, I think, than the Ayrshire, but not so rich as the Devon or Alderney, or the common Irish or English. They require good keep, and will give good produce in return, and I have found them of all breeds the most gentle. There is one peculiarity, however, belonging to the Hereford, and from want of a knowledge of which I lost three of the very best of my cows when I first got them. It is this, if they make a very large show about three weeks or a month before calving, they should be moderately milked, otherwise the teat becomes diseased and it is impossible to bring them to their milk after calving, in fact, they can't give a drop, as the pipe is stopped up, I presume from the milk which ought to have been drawn first corrupting, and then turning to a hard lump. I have tried to recover this neglect by putting the calf to them, but all to no purpose.

The Devon surpasses all others in the richness of her milk, but is far inferior to almost any other in quantity.

The common Irish cow can scarcely be surpassed in value. Some of them will give from twelve to fifteen quarts at a meal, upon keep far inferior to what any other breed requires, while for richness her milk is much beyond the average quality.

The short-horned is a breed coming into extensive use, and I am sure I can't tell why, if it is not that their size renders them valuable to the grazier, after they shall have served their time at the dairy.

There is another breed which deserves notice, the thorough bred Scotch, generally of a black and white colour, large, of beautiful symmetry, with head resembling a buck, flat in the forehead, and very pretty small horns. I know of no cow superior to a thorough bred Scotch cow, but I regret to say that they have become very scarce of late years, the Ayrshire having supplied their place.

There is another breed also that deserves mention, I mean the little black Galloways that are to be found in the southern counties of Scotland. I have a great fancy for this breed, which I would distinguish by the name of the poor man's cow; they are very small, of beautiful symmetry, and have no horns, which, in my opinion, is an advantage not to be overlooked. The owners tell you that they would live upon the road, which is a mere figurative mode of telling you that they will live upon the most spare keep. They give very good milk, in some cases as much as ten quarts at a meal, or twenty quarts a-day, are easily fatted when dry, and will live certainly upon one-half of what a Hereford, Ayrshire, or short horned cow would consume.

The common English, like the common Irish, when good, in my opinion surpasses most others in this climate, and as a native of the soil is, perhaps, the best suited to the country.

The next direction, then, that I shall give to the farmer is, how to choose his cow at a fair. He should look well about him, and make up his mind not to be captivated by the first that takes his fancy, always bearing in mind that, if taken in, his first loss is the least, as a bad cow will entail a daily injury upon him. The head, then, should be well looked at; it should be fine and rather flat than round in the forehead, the countenance mild and gentle, the horn small and of a rich creamy colour, well set, and not cocking; the neck fine, thin at the mane, and a fall of loose flesh underneath running towards the breast; the tail and limbs should be fine, the hind quarter wide, with a good space between the hind legs, and the udder spreading up towards the chest rather than hanging down between the legs; the teats, instead of hanging down, should project, pointing as it were towards the fore-legs, great attention being paid to the size of the two back teats which are never milked, a cow usually having six teats. I have seldom seen a cow of this form that had not the two back teats unusually large.

I have now spoken of a cow ready for milking, and with the presumption that no man would be mad enough to buy a cow that has been stocked for sale, that is, a cow which has not been milked for, perhaps, twenty-four hours; a system as foolish as it is cruel, and the practice of which has destroyed many a fine animal, and has injured many an ignorant man. It will be a long time before a cow that has been driven some distance with a bursting udder can be brought to herself, while she seldom thoroughly recovers for the season, and, therefore, none but the hopelessly ignorant can be injured by this cruel practice. I have frequently felt inclined to punish the owner of a cow that I have seen in the situation that I describe; I believe that under Mr Martin's act[1] I should succeed, while, I am sure, the ruffian would deserve the punishment.

If the farmer is wise, he will prefer a three year old heifer springing, that is, about to calve, to any other, and for this reason, because she could not have been previously injured or sold for any fault, and in 999 instances in every 1,000, a cow, if properly treated from the commencement, will turn out well. The same directions that I have laid down for regulating the choice of a cow will also apply to the heifer. If, however, the farmer should prefer a cow that has calved, I would recommend him to observe the following directions. Suppose he fancies a cow, for which he is asked £12, let him then ask what milk she gives, and if the owner says twelve quarts at a meal with good feed, let the purchaser say, then I'll place the whole amount in the hands of a mutual friend, I'll put the cow on good keep, and you shall name any day within eight as the trial day to come and see her milked, and if she gives the promised quantity you shall have the money. This is what is called 'engaging a cow,' a practice invariably acted upon by dairymen in Ireland, and found very beneficial. If the seller refuses this offer, let the farmer

---

1 The Cattle Cruelty Act of 1822, the work of Thomas Barnewall Martin (d. 1847).

turn upon his heel and leave him, as the cow is sure to have some defect. So much for the purchase of a dairy cow.

Let us now consider her treatment, which, for the present, I shall confine to her management, as hereafter I shall lay down rules for feeding her, supposing merely for the present that she is to be as well fed as she possibly can be; in such case, then, a very middling cow, if well chosen, will give twenty-four quarts of milk a-day. Care should be taken not to allow her to calve much before the beginning of May, in order that she may be brought to a full flow of milk by an abundance of food given immediately after calving. She should be turned into an open place when about to calve. As soon as she drops the calf, the calf should be sprinkled over with about two table spoonsful of common salt, which will induce the cow to lick it over more greedily, and will have the effect of making her 'clean' more speedily. As soon as she 'cleans,' that is, as soon as she throws off the calf bag, it should be instantly taken from her, and buried, as otherwise she will be sure to eat it, and probably suffer great injury. I am aware that a difference of opinion exists upon this point, many believing that the 'cleansing,' if eaten by the cow, operates as a medicine. It is so asserted in the second volume of an admirable work entitled 'British Husbandry,'[1] published under the superintendence of the Society for the Diffusion of Useful Knowledge, a book unequalled, in my humble opinion, by any other that has ever been written upon the subject of Agriculture, one indeed which should constitute an indispensable portion of the property of every man possessed of any quantity of ground from a rood to any amount, and to its extensive circulation I attach the greatest importance. I should feel extreme delicacy in expressing any difference of opinion with the writer of this work; but as, upon the point in question, there is a variance between the text and a note upon the same subject, I incline to that of the note. In the text it is recommended to allow the cleansing to remain with the cow, as the eating of it will 'amuse' her; but in the note the writer gives directions as to the proper medicine to be administered in the event of this amusement making the cow sick. It is, therefore, because I consider prevention better than cure, and because the amusement may be purchased at the expense of the cow's life, that I recommend the cleansing to be taken away as soon as she relieves herself of it. The calf should then be taken from her, and never, under any circumstances, should it be allowed to suck her, as, in such case, she will frequently refuse to give her milk to the hand, while there would always be much trouble in inducing her in the outset after the calf has been let to her. The cow should get warm drinks, bran and water, or meal and water, with the cold just taken off and a little salt mixed in it, for three or four days after calving, and if the calf is to be reared or vealed, it should be kept out of hearing. In about nine days the cow will come to her full milk. And now I will lay down rules for milking which never should be departed from.

The usual practice is to milk cows twice a-day, whereas I would strongly recommend the plan of milking three times a-day, at five in the morning, one at

---

1 *British Husbandry; Exhibiting the Farming Practice in Various Parts of the United Kingdom*, 3 vols (1834–40).

noon, and nine in the evening; thus leaving eight hours between each meal. By following this plan, I will venture to say that a cow will give one-fourth more milk than if only milked twice a-day. If a good cow is well fed, she will begin to drop her milk at least two hours before the time when she is usually milked. If the milk is taken from her by the calf, he will keep tugging at her nine or ten times a-day, and, therefore, it appears contrary to the rules of nature that she should be allowed to go twelve hours without milking. I assign a lapse of eight hours between each milking because I feel convinced that in that period she would gather a full meal of milk. It is of all things necessary that a cow should be treated with the greatest gentleness, as much depends upon temper, and which can be made for the animal by those entrusted with her management. Speak kindly to a cow, pat her, and scratch her, before you sit under her, and she will give every drop of her milk freely: on the other hand, scold her, and kick her about the hind legs – a very usual practice of milkmen to bring other men's cows into a convenient position – and the odds are, either that she upsets the milk, or refuses to give it all. For these reasons I would recommend the small farmer always to allow his wife or daughter to perform the operation of milking. Cows, when properly treated, are very gentle animals, and always prefer being milked by those to whom they are accustomed. Before the woman begins to milk, she should wash the whole udder and teats well over with cold spring water, and then dry it. From constant habit she will soon learn how much milk the cow gives, and when she has taken within a pint of the whole, she should milk that last pint into a separate vessel; it is called the strippings, and is twice as rich as any other portion of the milk, and perhaps three times as rich as the first pint drawn from the cow: that is, the pint of strippings will yield more cream or butter than the three pints first drawn from the cow. Great care should be taken to milk the cow as clean as possible, in fact not leaving a drop with her, and immediately after she is milked she should be fed.

If the milk is to be used for making butter, the greatest attention must be paid to the cleanliness of the vessels in the first instance, and to the mode of keeping the cream and making the butter. The vessels should be all of wood, and well scoured with hay and fine sand, or gravel and hot water, and afterwards well rinsed out with cold water, and placed in the air to dry, before the milk is strained into them. The milk may be set in summer for twenty-four hours, and then skimmed, and the cream thrown into a clean crock, which is preferable to wood for keeping cream; while wood is preferable to earthenware for making the milk yield its cream. The strippings taken from the cows may be thrown at once into the cream-crock, and great care should be taken to stir the cream upon each addition made to it; a peeled willow-stick being preferred by old hands for this purpose, while I would much prefer the clean hand and arm of a dairymaid, which can sweep round the edges better than any stick. In winter the cream may stand for forty-eight hours, all the same rules being observed that I have laid down for summer treatment. In summer the cream should be churned twice a-week; in winter once a-week. And, now, in order that all the trouble should not go for nothing, I will lay down rules for making butter.

As soon as your butter is thoroughly churned, all the butter-milk must be let off; after which the barrel-churn should be whisked round rapidly, a little cold water having been poured in; this will purge the butter of a great portion of the butter-milk. The butter should then be taken out of the churn, and taken up in large lumps, and well clapped against the bottom of a large wooden keeler, placed in a sloping position. As soon as that process has been performed, it should then be placed in the keeler, and, being well opened with the fingers, the keeler should be filled with spring water, and the dairymaid should knead the butter just as a baker kneads his dough, changing the water as long as it has any tinge of milk, and when the water comes off clean, then the butter, when thoroughly discharged of the water by another good clapping is ready for the salt, which may be added in the proportion of about an ounce and-a-half to the pound of butter. The salt should be common marine salt, and, should be well pounded, and made as fine as possible, and, when thoroughly worked, the butter may be placed in the firkin, packing it as firmly as possible, care being taken to select your vessel, if for the wholesale market, of the size most suitable to the means of filling it as speedily as possible; that is, the man who has four cows should prefer the keg which will hold 30 lbs. to the firkin that contains 60 lbs. A good cow, such as I have described, well fed and properly managed, will yield 2 cwt of butter in the season, which may be said to last from May to December, both inclusive; of course she will begin to fall off after she has been served in August, but I will take that time as an average. Four cows, then, will make 8 cwt of butter in the season, or 1 cwt in each month; a firkin, or half a cwt in each fortnight; or a keg, or quarter of a cwt in each week. If the farmer, having four cows, churns twice a-week, then he will fill a keg at two churnings, and will always be sure of first-quality price for his butter. As butter, however, is a very ticklish thing, the butter-taster and the butter-smeller discovering the slightest imperfection, great care must be taken in preparing it for his inspection. I will suppose a woman to have churned fifteen pounds weight of butter, or half a keg, on Wednesday, and the butter to have been packed in the bottom of the keg as before recommended. When she churns again on Saturday, and after that day's produce has been salted, I would recommend her to take the fifteen pounds made on the Wednesday, and mix the produce of both churnings right well up together, and then pack all up in a clean keg, when it will be just as good, and of equal quality, as if made at one churning. The butter should be then kept in a cool place, a little fine salt being shaken over the top, and, if the weather is very hot, the keg may be placed standing in a keeler of water. I have thought it necessary to be very explicit under this head for the reasons that I stated in the outset, namely, that I propose making the small farmer's dairy of four cows the staple of his establishment, and his greatest source of emolument, and, therefore, the want of knowledge, or the want of management, would considerably injure him in this most vital point; while the acquirement of the one, and the observance of the other, would constitute his greatest pleasure, and greatest profit. I must make one observation in concluding under this head, it is this, that the cow is to be fed in the house throughout every day in the year, and never to be pastured on the field, while I must also observe that she should be driven morning and evening each day into a yard or enclosed place where she could stretch her legs, and receive some fresh air. The house should be well ventilated, and she should never be tied by the head, or otherwise restrained, for good and sufficient reasons which I shall state hereafter. In winter a cow likes warmth, and can have it better in the house than under a hedge. In summer she dislikes the sun and the gadfly, and can be defended against both better in the house than in the field. I dare say there are few who have not seen a set of heavy milch cows with ten hours' stock of milk in their udders, galloping with cocked tails over the country, to the great injury of the animal itself, and to the still greater injury of her milk. A cow should, in all cases, be kept as cool and free from excitement as possible, and her milk will always be in the best possible state. Moreover, when a cow is housed, you have the advantage of all the manure that she makes, and which can be more profitably disposed of at the discretion of the farmer than, by the encampment and folding system, it can be applied by the animal itself. All the rules that I have laid down under this head equally apply to the management of large as to that of small dairies.

WHEAT.

If I was bound to classify the produce of the land according to the relative value of the several crops, I certainly should not have given the preference to wheat, inasmuch as, in my opinion, it is less profitable than many other crops. However, the notoriety that it has obtained as an article of importance in the money-market in consequence of our artificial mode of life, as well as the necessity for its general use as an article of food, and which latter necessity arises merely from the fact that wheat can be preserved for many years, while the working classes generally would not be so dependent upon it for support if they had a sufficiency of land whereby their food might be diversified, and good substitutes found in many, very many things, which, however, being for the most part perishable, cannot be brought into the wholesale market as competitors against wheat, which will keep for many years in stack if well made and well thatched, and for many more if kiln-dried and well managed in the warehouse. For these reasons then I place it at the head of the list of produce, and shall treat of the mode of producing it.

The old system which generally prevailed was that of fallowing for wheat, the process of which was as follows: – A piece of ground, generally a stubble or some exhausted field, was broken up with a plough in the months of October or November, and allowed to remain in that state until spring, when it was back-ploughed, that is, the position of the sods was reversed. In about six weeks after it had remained in that condition, it was cross-ploughed across the sods. When the weeds began to grow it was then drag-harrowed, a very heavy process performed by a large double harrow with long teeth, drawn by five, six, or seven horses. It then went through the process of ploughing and harrowing as often as the weeds made their appearance. In June the surface was rendered very fine, and all the couch-grass gathered in rows with pitchforks, made heaps of, and burned on the spot. When the ashes were spread the field underwent the last process, which is called gorrowing. This consisted of a very deep ploughing, by which somewhat about two inches of wild earth was thrown up to the surface as a means of adding strength to it after it had received the atmospheric influence. So it remained until about the end of August, when it received a fine harrowing, and was then ready, about the latter end of September for the seed, which was sown in narrow ridges about four feet wide, under the plough, and allowed to remain in this rough state until the first dry weather in spring, when sheep and lambs were turned in to eat it down, and, by trampling it, to make it plant, or throw out more shoots. It was then bush-harrowed and rolled, but not made very fine, as the farmers are very deeply impressed with the value of a fool's adage, held in high respect by their order, 'sow wheat with a clod;' which, however, means no more than that stiff clay-land is better suited for wheat than for any other grain. Thus it will be seen that the land was two years producing one crop, simply because the plough was substituted for the spade; whereas, under a good system of spade-husbandry, the same land would have produced four or five crops within the same period.

As I shall assign to this crop its proper place when I come to lay down rules for the management of small farms, I shall here merely describe the system which has now been substituted for that of fallowing, which latter is almost exploded. Wheat is now sown either upon a clover-ley which has been fed by sheep, or after a crop of white turnips, fed off late in autumn, or early in winter, or in spring after a crop of Swedish turnips, or after a crop of potatoes, dug out in October. There are various descriptions of seed, which the farmer must be guided in the use of, according to the description of his land, according to the season at which he sows, whether spring or winter, and of which I shall treat hereafter. I very much prefer a crop of spring to winter wheat. The amount of seed required is about ten stone to the acre; but I think that the man who sows his wheat under the shovel, as I shall describe, instead of under the plough, will find eight stone, of good seed, ample for an acre. The time that I shall recommend for sowing this crop will be, from the last week in March to the second week in April. The following is the way to sow wheat, and to prepare the seed. However clean the wheat may appear to be, the farmer should pick the weeds out of the sheaf before they are threshed. A child will pick five hundred sheaves in the day, and five hundred sheaves will produce somewhat more, if of ordinary size and quality, than 100 stone of wheat; therefore, one child would pick in one day a sufficiency to sow more than twelve acres of wheat: whereas, if the weeds are thrashed and sown with the corn, it may take the same child six days to weed an acre. I am not supposing that there are to be any weeds, for the farmer who had half-a-dozen weeds upon his four acres would be a very dirty fellow. But, as I am laying down rules for the dirty large farmer, as well as for the clean small farmer, I think it necessary to suppose the existence of weeds. Not only the weeds, but the small dead and unripe ears, should also be picked out. When this is done, the wheat intended for seed should be threshed as nearly as possible to the time when it is required for use, and upon a very clean floor; the farmer always taking care to renew his seed constantly; preferring that grown on light soils, if his is of a clayey nature, and *vice versa*. When the seed is threshed, it should be laid upon a flag-floor and well 'clogged,' that is, dashed over with a strong limewash with a brush. When the lime is thoroughly dried upon it, it should then be sown with an even and careful hand; and its white colour, contrasted with the dark colour of the ground, will be a very good guide for the seedsman. When the seed is sown, it should be instantly covered up with a shovel, giving all about two inches and a half of earth, making the beds eight feet wide, and the furrows, from whence the earth to cover them is taken, about fifteen inches wide. If weeds should grow up, the bed can be weeded from the furrow, without trampling the wheat. As good depth of soil is matter of primary importance to the farmer; I recommend the following process to be performed after the wheat has been sown. It is this: – The furrows should be dug to the depth of at least one foot, and the earth should be dug and re-dug at every spare hour that is available throughout the summer. By this means the farmer will have made a foot deep of manure in nearly one-sixth of his whole field, and by observing the same rule with regard to the furrows when his potatoes are planted, the whole field will have acquired an additional surface in the course of three years; or rather the same land will have received this addition after a succession of three potato-crops and three wheat-crops. When once dug and broken, one man will re-dig the furrows of an acre in two days with great ease. And if the process is repeated six times, from seed-time to harvest, he will have expended about fourteen days' labour, being four days for the first digging, and two for every subsequent one, and for which he will have acquired good remuneration, in a large supply of the best manure made upon the spot.

Wheat, although a very hardy plant, is liable to many diseases, such as smut, which means the ear, just as the grains are formed, turning into a kind of sooty substance. The red-gum, which is like a smut, but of a red colour. Blight, blast and mildew are also diseases to which wheat is subject, and now I will explain the most probable cause of these many diseases. In the beginning of summer the wheat begins to flower, and while in that state the head or flowering part is lapped over with the leaf of the straw. As soon as the ear shoots from the boot, as it is called, it requires dry weather to allow the grains to form, and to come to maturity. If, however, the weather is wet, or even damp, and calm or foggy at the period when the ear is being formed in the boot, there is a strong probability that the crop will be damaged; and for this reason the boot is like a cup, or, to describe it more perfectly, it resembles a pistol, and the ear the ramrod. If the pistol is filled full of water, the ramrod will be sure to be wet; so, if the boot is filled full of water, the ear, before it has shot from it, will be wet; and if the weather is so calm that the water must remain in the boot, the flower is perished, and, instead of grains of wheat, you have the substances that I have before described. There is only one way of meeting this calamity, which is this, whenever the weather is wet, or muggy, and no breeze to shake the water out of the boot, the small farmer and his wife should take a line, about the substance of a common Jack-line, nine or ten feet long, and walking at a brisk pace in the furrows, should draw the line right along the wheat, shaking it well night and morning, or after rain or fog. I will undertake to say that in few instances will a crop of wheat fail if this practice is observed, while the process of shaking an acre would not take more than ten minutes. I am aware that the several diseases to which wheat is liable, are attributed by the ablest writers to various other causes than those to which I have ascribed them. One of the most generally received notions as to the cause of several of those diseases is, that at particular seasons the wheat, as well as the turnip-crop, is liable to the visitation of swarms of flies of one description or another, who deposit their eggs in the boot, and thus cause the ruin of the crop. Another cause that has been assigned is, from infection communicated to the seed by its being threshed on a floor where damaged wheat has been threshed, or by being put into sacks in which damaged wheat has been before. Others ascribe them to a want of proper management in preparing the seed; some recommending the use of one description of pickle, and others recommending the use of other descriptions; while all appear to agree as to the necessity for the use of lime, and which, in my opinion, is a good substitute for all others, if the practice of shaking the growing crop, as I have described, is observed. I cannot possibly understand how any imperfection in the seed can be assigned as the cause of disease after the straw shall have shot to that height when shooting from the boot may be expected to commence. The two great points to be observed then, after a proper selection of seed, is, the preservation of the grain from insects, and the preservation of the crop from those subsequent calamities to which it is liable through the various stages of its growth. The use of lime will, in my opinion, best effect the first object, while, admitting the fly to be the cause of any of those diseases which I attribute to the weather and bad sowing, I think that the eggs deposited in the boot may be effectually got rid of by the shaking system. The process of 'steeping' is relied upon rather as a means of discovering and getting rid of the light grains that float to the surface, than for any other purpose, and this, in my opinion, can be as well accomplished by a cautious picking of the shrivelled and damaged ears while the wheat is in the sheaf. Another general cause to which I would attribute many diseases to which wheat is liable is, that of uneven sowing, and too deep sowing. I can very well understand how it is that a grain of wheat, having made its way through seven or eight inches of various descriptions of soil, may grow to a certain point, and then fail. For instance, it will go through the several stages of vegetation, tillering, and flowering, while it may lack the strength to bring the ear to perfection. I can also very well understand why it is that one portion of a field, all sown perhaps upon the same day, and with seed taken from the same heap, may be diseased, while other portions have wholly escaped all calamities. I would ascribe this apparent anomaly to the following causes: – When you sow wheat with a very unequal covering, those grains which have a sufficiency over them, and a good bed under them, will come to perfection; while those that have to struggle through too deep a covering, with a hard glazed and wild bed under them, will be sure to suffer. As regards diseases, then, and the several precautions against them, I would recommend good seed, the use of lime, equal covering, and never too deep, and shaking the crop, as I have described, in suspicious seasons.

A great fault with farmers is, allowing their wheat to get too ripe, waiting till the neck turns, and the ear drops before they reap it; whereas they should judge by the knee or knot which separates the head from the straw, instead of by the ear. When that knot becomes black, all communication between the earth and the ear then ceases, and all that can be done by allowing it to stand after that time can be as well accomplished, and indeed better, after than before reaping. In speaking of this knot, I should observe, that one of the greatest calamities to which the wheat-crop is liable, is the premature closing the communication between the earth and the ear, and which may be always observed from the appearance of the knot, which, upon its first formation, assumes a pale green, then a darker green, then a transparent yellow, then a harder appearance and a darker yellow, and so on, becoming darker and darker until at length it becomes black, hard, and impenetrable, stopping the communication altogether. This disease is most likely to occur when the seed is sown too deep, or too near the wild earth, or in bad soils; as in such cases the earth will yield a sufficient amount of nutriment to ripen the straw, but not to ripen the ear. But I will venture to assert that such a calamity will not occur once in forty years when the wheat is sown upon the surface with a good bed under it, and from two to three inches of good mould over it, which daily becomes richer from its exposure to the atmosphere. Let the farmer beware then of giving his seed too much covering, and of sowing it in ground incapable of nursing it, supporting it, and maturing it, with the chances of the required nutriment being prematurely withdrawn, or altogether wanting.

By observing these rules the grain will be brighter and plumper, while, by giving the seed an equal covering with the shovel, instead of an uneven one with the plough, the whole crop will ripen together, and the unripe or growing portion will not have to be sacrificed to the riper portion, nor will the process of saving be as tedious or expensive. If the crop is properly managed, six quarters an acre would be by no means a large produce, while I would consider the man unfortunate who had no more than four, and which, according to the present system, is very much beyond an average crop. The straw of wheat is better bedding for cattle than any other description of straw, while, in my opinion, if used fresh and chopped, it makes better fodder and certainly much better manure, while it is not so tender or so hard to be saved in bad weather as either oats or barley. And, in conclusion, wheat may be made much more beneficial to the working classes if it ceased to be an article of such extensive traffic in the hands of speculators, and which never can be accomplished until either every man becomes a grower of as much as he will require himself, or until there are so many growers, that the monopoly of a corporation of speculators in human misery shall be broken down.

POTATOES.

The misery which the exclusive use of the potatoe as an article of food has brought upon my own country, would rather lead me to discourage, than to recommend, its propagation. As it arises, however, more from necessity than choice, I will not allow such a consideration to weigh with me, neither shall I be led to under-value its uses in consequence of its abuses. Scores of volumes have been written upon the subject of Agriculture, and in not one of which has the potatoe had its proper value assigned to it, whereas I think, without over-straining or exaggerating its merits, I shall be enabled to show, that the potatoe is, for every reason, the most profitable crop that that land can be brought to produce as an article of general use.

The turnip being for the most part the farmer's grand crop, and potatoes being the best substitute for turnips, it has been the practice of writers to contrast the relative value and merit of the two crops. One great preference that all agree upon giving to the turnip crop is, that turnip ground must be kept clear and free from weeds, while the necessary mode of cultivation is the best preparation for a wheat crop. To the first proposition, I reply, that if the turnip ground 'must' be kept clear, the potatoe ground *ought* to be kept clear, and *might* be kept clear at as little expense as the turnip ground. To the second, I reply, that those writers have given the preference to cultivation of turnips of the most approved description, while in general they contrast it with the rudest mode of cultivating the potatoe, while I further contend, that the land, if properly cultivated for potatoes, both from its preparatory and subsequent treatment, that is, before they are planted, and when they are dug, is in a better state for a wheat crop than it is after the most approved method of cultivating it for turnips. Here, again, we find the evils of the large farm system brought in aid of the cultivation of turnips, in consequence of the facilities afforded for consuming the crop upon the ground, whereas, as I have before explained under the head 'large farms,' much of the crop is lost by this slovenly practice. The advantages, then, that the potatoe has over the turnip are these: –

Firstly. – The potatoe has the double advantage of being good food for all sorts of animals, while it is also a favourite root for man's use.

Secondly. – The chances of success in favour of the potatoe against the turnip in all seasons are as twenty to one.

Thirdly. – The potatoe can be planted at seasons when the turnip cannot be sown.

Fourthly. – The potatoe crop can be taken out in time for a crop of winter wheat, and the produce can be safely stored.

Fifthly. – A crop of the best potatoes will fat nearly double the quantity of cattle that the best acre of turnips would fat.

Sixthly. – The farmer can bring his beast to market in little more than one-half the time upon potatoes than he can upon turnips, thus giving him the advantage, and a great one it is, of feeding off a double stock in the one winter season, and of disposing of a cow in the most profitable condition if she shall fall off in her milk unexpectedly in winter or even in spring.

Seventhly. – The manure made by cattle fed on potatoes is far superior to the manure of cattle fed upon turnips.

Eighthly. – Potatoes are good food for horses, cows, sheep, oxen, pigs, poultry, dogs, and man, while turnips are only fit for black cattle and sheep, or windy stuffing for horses and pigs, and a very indigestible vegetable for man.

I shall now state the mode of cultivating the potatoe, and the reasons why the crop sometimes fails. The best season for planting potatoes for a general crop is in the first fine weather in March, and the reasons why it has been deferred of late years till late in April, May, and in some instances June, are in consequence of numberless failures which have taken place arising out of the unseasonable weather we have had at the earlier period of the year for the last few seasons. I am perfectly aware that March is six weeks earlier than can safely be relied upon according to the usual method of cultivation. But I will state what this arises from, and how it may be counter-acted. Potatoes are thus prepared for planting. The middling size are selected for seed and are cut into settings, leaving one or two eyes in each cut. The farmer, apprehensive of losing his seed by being too long cut before the season will admit of using them, is disinclined to commence that operation until the very season arrives for planting. This apprehension, in the first place, prevents him from cutting them in March, while the immediate use which he is compelled to make of the seed before the wound is healed, frequently leads to a failure of the whole crop. If settings are to be used, they should be kept until they just begin to sprout and should be then planted, but if they are used fresh from the knife, and if the weather comes wet before they have shot out, the seed rots and the whole crop is consequently lost. I have seen scores upon scores of acres of potatoes lost from this practice.

Perhaps the advocate for turnips may ask me how I would obviate this danger, and say, that the loss from the failure of an acre of potatoes is very much greater than the loss occasioned by the failure of an acre of turnips. I admit this at once, but, upon the other hand, I contend, that there is no necessity for running the most remote chance of failure upon the score of seed, while he cannot defend himself from the fly, the worm, bad seed, bad season, 'fingers and toes,' and the thousand and one chances of failure to which the turnip is liable. I once lost a very fine field of eight acres by a failure of the seed, which was cut as I have described, and I learned my practical experience from one small corner of that field, for which I had not a sufficiency of seed. I was short for the seed of about six perches, and I told my steward to go into one of the potatoe houses, and to sweep it up and bring out the produce, he brought out a hamper of stalks, earth, and some small potatoes, varying from the size of a small marble to that of a large gooseberry. We made holes and dropped two of those small potatoes into each. The season turned out very wet, there was a general failure, most fields had to be renewed, while not one single one of the small potatoes planted whole failed, and from that day to the present I have never planted any other seed than the largest whole potatoes I could procure, and plant them where I would, wet or dry, cold or warm, I have never had the failure of a single stalk. I was determined that all the farmers in my neighbourhood should have the benefit of the knowledge that I had acquired, and as an Irish farmer will require anything new that he hears to 'have a face upon it,' as he terms it, I hit upon the happy expedient of illustrating my assertion in favour of the whole potatoe, by referring them to the potatoes growing amongst their wheat, and the seed of which had remained whole in the ground from the time when the potatoe crop was dug in the previous November, and which must consequently have remained out during the whole winter. This is what I mean: – When a farmer digs his potatoes he will not be able to find all. Those that remain in the ground grow up amongst the wheat, and, upon examining their wheat fields, they discovered throughout the whole neighbourhood, that there was rather more than an average crop from the whole potatoes that had remained from the previous year, while the crop generally had failed from the cut seed having rotted. As, however, they consider it a great waste of ground to plant whole potatoes at the required distance asunder, and as planting whole ones as thick as they are accustomed to plant the seed (four perhaps cut from each potatoe), they imagine that they should use four times as much seed, which is expensive, (the seed of an acre in ordinary times costing a pound, besides 2s. 8d. for cutting it) if they substituted the whole potatoe for cuttings.

Before I lay down general rules for the cultivation of the potatoe, the uses to be made of it, and the manner in which the crop is to be saved, I shall make a few general observations to guide the small farmer in his choice of seed, as well as to direct him in the mode of procuring it. There is an immense variety of the potatoe, and to enumerate each according either to its local or general name, would be impossible; the same potatoe being known in different localities by different names. As I am very anxious that those who produce luxuries should be partakers of them, and as I am most desirous to inculcate a spirit of rivalry amongst the peasantry of this country, I shall treat the potatoe as an article of luxury, as well as being an indispensable ingredient for the general uses of both large and small farmers.

Passing over, then, the enumeration of the several sorts of potatoes, I shall content myself with merely recommending those of different kinds which should constitute the farmer's stock. These may be classed under three heads; – the early potatoe, the harvest potatoe, and the late potatoe. The different sorts which, in my opinion, the farmer will do well to confine himself to, are, the ash-leafed kidney, the copper kidney, or the red-nosed kidney in his garden for an early dish; the pink eye, the white eye, or the white American, or quarry potatoe, for his harvest crop; and the black or red apple, the cup or minion, and champion, for a late crop. In all cases, but more especially as regards the early potatoe, which must be planted in unsettled weather, the seed should be planted whole, and although it is difficult to drive an old system out of the heads of those who have been trained up in it, yet I incline to think that the practice of substituting the whole potatoe for cuttings will, upon the whole, be found rather a saving, than a useless expenditure, even of the seed. But of this hereafter.

Whatever sort of potatoe is selected as an early crop, should be planted as soon as the weather breaks after Christmas, and in the following manner: – The ground, being level, should be laid out in beds of about three feet wide; the potatoe should be then dibbled in whole, and not too deep, say two inches at the most; three rows will be ample, one row in the centre, and another within a foot of each side of it, thus leaving a foot between each row, and six inches between the two outside rows and the breast of the bed. As soon as the potatoes are planted, and without stopping the holes, a sufficient quantity of manure should be laid over the whole surface of the bed, and about two inches of earth should then be cast over the manure, from furrows of a foot wide. Though I am by no means friendly to the frequent use of stable dung, and especially in an unfermented state, yet I am of opinion that half-made stable dung, or that made by cattle fed in the houses, would be best suited for the early potatoe, for the two following reasons: – firstly, because it furnishes an excellent barrier between the two earths against frost; and, secondly, because it possesses the property of communicating nutriment more speedily, and at seasons when colder kinds cannot be got to act. I have seen most excellent crops of early potatoes produced by substituting a good covering of hay, taken from under the mangers, for manure.

The harvest crop may be planted as early as possible in March; the mode not varying from that which I have recommended for the cultivation of the earlier kind, with the single exception that, in the latter case, the beds may be four feet wide, and have four rows of seed; and, perhaps, as it requires a shorter time for arriving at maturity than the later sort, and consequently taking more out of the ground, it may require somewhat less manure than the early sort, and somewhat more than the later. The late, or general crop, may be planted precisely at the same time and in the same manner as the second, or the harvest crop.

The kind selected for early use should be covered with ferns or dry straw at night, until it has passed over all danger from frost. This process will require but a few minutes night and morning, and must not be neglected. If care be taken of the crop, the farmer may calculate, in the southern districts, upon having a good dish of well-grown early potatoes on, or a little before, the first of June, and, in a northern district, from the 10th to the 15th of the same month. I have set thirty men into a ten-acre field of white Americans, to supply four neighbouring markets with full-grown, dry, and well-flavoured potatoes on the 24th of June, and have not stopped until the field was dug out.

The harvest potatoe will be fit for use about the first week in August, and may be dug as required until the second week in October, when the late crop will be ready for general use, and may be dug. In passing, I may here make one general observation which I find has escaped the notice of other writers; it is this: – the early potatoe and the harvest potatoe may be considered in a more perfect state for use before they have arrived at maturity than the late crop will be during its similar stage; that is, supposing the harvest crop to be perfectly ripe on the first of September, it will be more fit for use on the first of August than the late crop which may be ripe on the tenth of October will be on the tenth of September, and for this reason, if for no other, should the farmer be careful in having a succession of crops, and never allow a spade to go into his late crop until it is ready for storing. I have no hesitation in saying that fully one third of the late crop of potatoes is annually lost in Ireland from this system of 'rooting' at it before the potatoes are ripe.

I shall now proceed to give directions to the old system-men, who will continue to use cut seed in order to render the error as harmless as possible. Firstly, then, – in all cases a good sized potatoe should be selected, and those that have grown in peat-ground burned, or in moist land, should be preferred for upland and dry soils. A good judge will at once discern any bastard or spurious kinds, and should never cut them. The eye, nearest the top, where in most kinds there are a cluster of four or five, is the prime cut of the potatoe, and the dint, or large dimple at the bottom, from which the stalk has shot, should be invariably rejected, as in fact it has no power of growing at all, though it is often mistaken for an eye. Those eyes nearest the heel of the potatoe, as I will call it, are not so good, or as much to be relied upon, as those near the nose. The mode that I recommend then, in cases where moderate sized seed, say somewhat larger than an egg, has been selected, is this; – the heel or bottom part should be sliced off, and thrown on one side for pigs or cattle; – the top or nose should then be cut off, leaving a sufficient amount of pulp, and the remainder of the potatoe may then be cut in two. When the seed is cut, it should be laid upon a dry earthen floor, say three cuts thick, and at night may be covered over with straw as a protection against frost. When the wounds have healed, and the eyes have begun to shoot, the seed will then be ready for use; the farmer taking care not to plant any that have not shown symptoms of budding.

If the season between cutting and planting should prove unpropitious, the cuts, by admitting a proper current of air over them, and keeping them stirred, and not allowing them to heat, may be preserved for five or six weeks, and by proper treatment, will be in as good a condition as if they had been used when originally intended. When the farmer bears the fact in mind, that his very existence depends upon the seed in all cases, it is astonishing that more pains have not been devoted to its selection, treatment, and use.

I shall suppose a late crop of potatoes to be planted in drills at a distance of three feet from centre to centre, and the farmer to use whole potatoes that, if cut, would give four sets each. If he plants whole potatoes, he may safely trust to a yard apart in the drills for a full crop, whereas if he plants cuts he will use the four in that space, planting them usually about nine inches asunder. He saves then all the expense of cutting, all the chances of blind eyes or bad seed, while he provides against general failure from bad weather, or a hasty use of cut seed; and, above all, he guards himself against that most fatal of all errors, namely, that of thinking that he may cut his seed upon the head-land, while the plough is opening the drill. As soon as the early potatoe peeps above the ground it should be earthed over, or what is called second earthed, by casting about two inches more of the earth from the furrow over the ridge. The crop should then be kept free from a single weed. Harvest potatoes may be allowed to spread their first leaves over the ground before they are second earthed, say when they have grown to three inches high, they should then be second earthed, leaving the leader, or top of the stalk, just above ground. The late crop may be allowed to attain a still greater height before it is second earthed, because at that late season there is not so much danger to be apprehended from frost, and as the later kinds, for the most part, rise to the surface, this crop may get a heavier covering than either the early or the harvest potatoe, say three inches, making in the whole about seven inches of covering besides the manure; dibbled in two inches, first earthing two inches, and second earthing three inches.

I shall now explain several causes from which failure in the potatoe crop arise. The first is, as I have already stated, from the rotting of the seed; the second arises from the error of treating all sorts similarly, giving an equal amount of covering to those sorts that grow down even below the root and the seed, and to those that shoot up and grow out laterally from side sprouts. There are a great variety of potatoes, and especially those in most general use for cattle, which grow down, and which, being planted upon a glazed hard substance, get flat, dinged, and stunted at a very early period, while the seed itself not unfrequently decays before it has communicated full vigour to the plant. To provide against this calamity I have recommended that the potatoe should in all cases be planted within two inches of the surface, with the manure placed over it, which gives to the down-growing potatoe a substratum of ten inches of good soil to grow in, while it affords seven inches, besides the manure, of covering for those sorts that shoot upwards.

Farmers, then, who will continue to grow 'horse-potatoes,' 'beldrums,' 'lump-ers,' and 'cluster-potatoes,' and various other sorts which present fascination from the quantity that may be produced, will do well to observe the following rules in the exercise of their folly. They should take care not to put too much covering over those sorts that grow down, and to put plenty of covering over those sorts, which are principally of the later kind, that shoot upwards and grow from the knees of the lateral sprouts. If the sceptic will not be convinced by my reasoning, I would recommend him to get up at four or five o'clock of a harvest morning, and visit his late crop of potatoes, and there he will find that whether in drills or in beds the crows have been up before him, and have laid claim to that portion of the crop that had grown to the surface, and which he justly forfeited by his neglect. The necessity of guarding against this calamity would reconcile me to the drill-system, if it could not be otherwise overcome, but only for the cultiva-tion of late potatoes, as the depth at which drills are opened is injurious to the propagation of the earlier kinds. Much controversy has arisen between writers upon Agriculture as to the proper use and most beneficial disposal of manure in the cultivation of potatoes. I have tried it in all ways, as well under the potatoe as over the potatoe, and, after many experiments, reason and common sense have led me to give the preference to the latter practice, namely, that of placing it over the seed, and at some distance too, for the following reasons. If the cut potatoe is placed in manure in a state of fermentation, it will be very apt to rot: again, as the nutritive property of the manure keeps continually descending, it communi-cates a strength to the seed below, which it cannot communicate to that above

it. Even where potatoes are planted that grow downwards, they derive more benefit from the manure when spread over them, provided they have a sufficiency of
subsoil made loose, and prepared as it ought to be.

The usual modes of planting potatoes in those parts of Ireland where the crop
is best understood, are as follows: – The manure made, as I have described under
the head 'Manures,' is spread upon the ground in the first fine weather after
Christmas, and, when the grass grows well through it, it is then ploughed in six-
sod ridges, leaving about eighteen inches of the centre of the ridge uncovered and
unploughed – the sod from the furrow being cast half to the ridge on either side.
It is then what is called 'hacked,' with an instrument stronger than but resembling, a carpenter's adze without the pole. This process is performed by dragging
the inner sods over the unploughed centre, and breaking the whole surface very
fine. The seed is then dibbled into about the depth of the sod; the holes are then
closed, and the furrows are shovelled over the ridge. Another mode is that of
ploughing the field before the manure has been put out, and of spreading it over
the earth after the potatoes have been dibbled in, and I have invariably observed
that the best crops have been produced by the latter mode, from the fact, I presume, of the manure communicating its strength downwards.

It must be evident, however, that in either case the ground, treated as I have
described, is not in a fit state to yield a good crop, because the subsoil is not only
not properly prepared, but it is further rendered unfit by the glazed condition in
which the sole of the plough leaves it. One great advantage is derived from those
modes of planting potatoes, it is this – they allow the farmer to get over his other
spring work before he earths his potatoes, for when dibbled in, and the manure
is spread over them, they are allowed to remain for some time in that state, the
farmer never remembering that his manure is daily losing its strength from exposure. When the latter mode is adopted, then I would recommend him not to put
out his manure until he is prepared to cover it immediately after its being spread.

Some altercation has taken place as to whether potatoes should be allowed to
remain in the ground until they are quite ripe, or whether they should be dug a
little before they are ripe. I was once bitter with this anti-ripe mania myself, and
tried it, and the result was that I lost a large quantity of very fine potatoes, which,
from fermentation, all rotted, whereas I have never lost one if the crop has been
allowed to ripen fully; and, perhaps, it may be laid down as a safe principle, that
the potatoe, above any other root, may even be allowed, without the slightest
damage, to remain in the ground a considerable time after it is ripe. I do not recommend the practice, however.

I shall now describe the mode of saving the crop. They should be dug with
four-pronged forks, the prongs being about three quarters of an inch wide, and
blunt at the top, with a space of an inch to an inch and-a-half wide between the
prongs. Great care should be taken in placing the fork about midway between
the stalks to avoid cutting the potatoes. Women should follow with the basket,
picking up all those of a size for keeping, making heaps of the small ones on the
ridge, which may be gathered in the evening, and kept together for the immediate use of pigs and poultry. Many a fine crop of potatoes has been lost by mixing

all sizes up together; the small potatoes acting as a kind of grouting, filling up the spaces which should be allowed for ventilation. The large potatoes should then be stored in the following manner: — A potatoe-pit of the required dimensions should be dug to a depth not exceeding four or six inches. The space should be then filled with strong dry wheaten straw, and upon that bed the potatoes may be laid to any length, and from three to four feet wide, and to the same height; with a batta from base to top in the form of a wedge. If the weather answers, they may be left in that state for some days, and then covered with a good layer of wheaten straw placed all over them, and covered like a grave, with about six inches of mould well clapped and made glazed with the back of the spade after it is laid on. A drain to the depth of a foot and a half should then be made round the pit, communicating by the fall of ground with some other drain which will carry off the water. Potatoes stored in this way, and dug in proper season, will keep without the slightest damage till the following April. In fact they will keep in this way better than in any other way, while the end of the pit may be opened at any time for the purpose of taking from it a week or a fortnight's supply for immediate use.

I am aware that many recommend the practice of nipping off the blossom from the stalk. I have never tried the plan myself, but I must in fairness say that I think it has a face upon it, and is one, as to the adoption of which every farmer may come to a rational conclusion by trying the experiment upon a small scale. I think that removing the blossom from those kinds which bear apples or potatoe-seed, would be found beneficial, and for this reason, because in case of their removal, all that nutriment necessary for their support would be communicated to the root itself. However, these are all matters upon which very rational conclusions can be arrived at, and therefore I leave the solution of them to those who wish to try the experiment.

The following is the mode of acquiring a variety of new seed. When the apples are ripe, they should be plucked from the stalk and put, in quantities of from four to six pounds, in bags made of strong brown paper, which should be tied up and hung in a dry place. When thoroughly dry they may be crushed open, when the seed will fall out, and it, too, should be put into bags of the same description, but in smaller quantities. The seed so procured may be sown in the first fine weather in spring, as onions are sown, and it may happen that the seed of an apple-potatoe will yield from forty to fifty different varieties of potatoes. The farmer must watch them in their growth, selecting the most healthy, and those which give best promise for seed for the next year. He should then plant them whole in the spring of the following year, always making the best selections, and at the end of three years he may have made some wonderful discovery.

I have already compared the potatoe with the turnip as a general crop, and I must now state some of those causes which have led to the preference given to the turnip. A potatoe is a potatoe, so is a turnip a turnip; but while there are scores of varieties of the potatoe, all varying in the amount of the solid nutriment they contain, the root has never been cultivated with reference to this essential consideration, the farmer supposing that a stone weight of 'lumpers,' and a stone weight of 'cups,' 'apples,' or 'champions,' is one and the same thing; while, upon the other hand, although the variety of the turnip kind is comparatively insignif- icant; yet the relative property of the few varieties has been made matter of important consideration. For instance, I believe that an acre of the best Swedish turnips will turn out more fat, and make greater profit, than an acre of lumpers; while, upon the other hand, I am convinced that the best acre of 'cups, apples, or champions,' will turn out more fat than two acres of the best Swedes, and as much as any three acres of the best 'globe,' 'stone,' or 'white Norfolk.'

Another fallacy upon which the potatoe has been condemned has arisen from the improper use made of it, many farmers giving it to cattle, pigs, and horses, in a raw state, or unripe, or after the season for giving it with advantage has passed. The potatoe never should be given in a raw state to any animal or any thing, with the exception of a sheep or a goose. A goose will thrive better, and have a better flavour, upon raw potatoes sliced than if fed upon any other food; while the sheep will thrive more rapidly upon it in a raw state than upon any other food. Upon the other hand, raw potatoes, and especially in the commence- ment, will scour cattle and horses, and not unfrequently cause death; while there is no danger from steamed potatoes to either the one or the other. Pigs will not always eat, and never can be fatted upon, raw potatoes; while boiled potatoes will bring them to the greatest weight that they are capable of acquiring, and to greater perfection than any other food which can be continuously used with safety, admitting always, that from three weeks to a month's feeding upon oats or barley is necessary, if not indeed indispensable, to make the bacon firm and to give it a flavour.

I have already, in the commencement of this chapter, given my reasons so fully for preferring the potatoe to the turnip, and especially for the small farmer, that I shall now close under this head with one or two general observations, and one or two particular ones which I have made myself. In point of value, then, I con- tend that the best acre of potatoes is, for any use, worth four times as much as the best acre of turnips, while the manure produced from the former is much preferable to that produced from the latter; and that a careless use is made of the turnip which is not made of the potatoe in consequence of its greater value.

The particular observations that I made respecting the relative value of steamed and raw potatoes are as follows. – I took two thorough-bred colts up from grass in November, both rising four years old. From their then appearance, I had reason to fear that they would not be 'weight carriers.' After they had gone through their regular course of physic, I gave them a small feed of boiled pota- toes, with bran, night and morning, and a sufficient quantity of hay. As they got used to the food, I increased it to a small bucket for each nearly full, night and morning. In a short time I found that they had altogether rejected the hay, and for the four last months they never tasted any other food than potatoes and bran, nor did they taste water. Their eyes shone like diamonds; their skins were like satin; their growth was so improved that they gave every promise of becoming first-rate hunters, and which they subsequently did. The same year I had about thirty head of cattle fattening upon potatoes. I gave them, in the first instance, raw, and found that all, or nearly all, were seized with violent scouring, while one of the best died. I then changed the food of some to a sufficient quantity of the best hay, and of a few others to boiled potatoes, and the result was such a change in the animals as astonished me and every body else. One most important circumstance in the feeding of all sorts of cattle should not be omitted, and is well worthy the consideration of the farmer; it is this: – At the time that I speak of, I had eleven head of cattle 'bailed up' in a cow-house, and all the rest loose, each having a single house to itself. While in the cow-house I frequently witnessed the great difficulty that the animals experienced in lying down and getting up. I also found that those that were loose lay down in an entirely different position. This induced me to change them, and I put six of the most backward and of the worst thriving into the cowhouse into the single houses, and put those that had been in the single houses into their places, and the result was that those in the single houses began to thrive rapidly, while those that had been changed to the bail as rapidly fell off. The reason of this will be at once seen: rest is as necessary for an animal as food itself, and, by observing the natural posture of a cow while sleeping in the field, it will be seen that she usually lies with her head inclined to the flank across the fore-shoulder, a position which she never can acquire when bailed up or tied by the head amongst other beasts. For these reasons I have not for many years allowed a beast of mine to be tied up, or a collar to be put upon one of my horses.

I have thought it necessary to enter fully upon the relative value of potatoes and turnips, because the preference for the latter has gone far to induce landlords to adopt the large farm system; while the proper cultivation of the latter is indispensable to the complete working of the small farm system, and is peculiarly adapted to spade husbandry.

TURNIPS.

If many writers have attributed the poverty of the Irish people to the facility with which they can procure an almost unlimited supply of potatoes, I think I may attribute much of the poverty and degradation of the English working classes, as well as the growing contentions between landlord and tenant, to the extensive propagation of the turnip. I am aware that it will be considered heterodox, to attempt any disparagement of this now favoured and fashionable root. It is, however, to the agricultural labourer what machinery is to the factory operative, and it is, in the hands of the landlord, what the factory itself is in the hands of the cotton lord, each enabling their respective owners to dispense with manual labour to a considerable extent. Was it not for the encouragement of the turnip, it would be impossible for the landlords of this country to have so allotted their estates as to render a supply of any description of food from foreign countries necessary. The rage for turnips is always in proportion to the size of the farm, and may be considered as the very main spring of the large farm system.

Before I proceed to a consideration of the value of this crop, I shall treat of the different descriptions most in use; the soil most genial to its growth; the mode of culture; treatment while growing; diseases to which it is liable; mode of saving the crop; and its application.

The descriptions of turnip most in use for a succession of food are, the globe or white Norfolk, the Aberdeen or red-topped yellow, and the Swedish turnip. There are some others which, however, with the exception of the stone turnip, vary but little from those that I have mentioned.

The soil in which turnips of all descriptions thrive best, is that of a deep, loose, mellow, friable nature; dry and free from clay. The turnip thrives best in a cool temperate climate, and although it requires a dry bed, it delights in a moist atmosphere. Hence we find the turnip cultivated to much greater perfection in Scotland, and in the northern counties, than in the southern counties of England. I am not quite sure, however, that much of the preference given to those districts does not arise out of the fact, that the land in the southern districts can be turned to better account. However, I am ready to yield the superiority to Scotland and the northern districts.

The usual mode of preparing for a crop of turnips after corn is as follows: – the stubble should be broke up as soon as possible after harvest, and allowed to remain rough in ridgelets till the first dry weather in spring, when it is cross ploughed and well harrowed, and from that time to the time of sowing the crop it should be ploughed and harrowed whenever weeds show themselves. The ground for the turnip should be ploughed deeper than for any other crop with the exception of mangul wurtzel and carrots, all of which grow from a tap root and to a great depth. Before the seed is sown, the usual practice is to make the surface as fine as possible, drills are then opened at rather better than two feet from centre to centre; the manure, which must be of the very best and richest quality, at the rate of full twenty tons an acre, should be then liberally spread in the drill, which is closed up just as if planted with potatoes. The seed is then sown by some one of the various implements now in use for that purpose, and to all of which there is a roller attached, which flattens the top of the drill, leaving it from six to eight inches wide.

Another system in very general use is that of sowing in broad cast, or sowing the whole field in the same manner as clover is sown. If the latter method is adopted the manure should be ploughed in with the second last ploughing, so as to admit of its being thoroughly incorporated with the soil previous to the seed being sown. If lime is used, the too frequent use of which should be discouraged, it should be laid upon the stubble before the field is broke up, as its effect upon the soil is more durable than any other description of manure, while its use imme-diately before sowing fails of producing that effect which an earlier application would produce. After the lime is laid on, its vigour is increased by every subse-quent stirring. If bone dust is used the seed should be sown as speedily as possible after its application. I incline, however, to a union of those two plans.

I approve decidedly of the system of sowing in drills, while I am greatly in favour of an early application of the manure in order that it may be well incorporated with the soil to aid in the early growth of the plants. I approve of the drill, because by that means the earth can be most profitably arranged, so as to insure that depth of soil which the broad cast will not admit of, whereas the space between turnips sown in broad cast is wholly lost and of no earthly value. The principal objection to the drill system is, that the crop cannot be safely fed off by sheep, as they are very apt to lie down in the furrows, to turn upon the back and die, before they are discovered. One rule as regards turnips must be observed, that is, that the ground must be as fine as it can be possibly made before the seed is sown. If sown in drills, the turnip will generally shoot up in about ten or twelve days and will very shortly throw out what is called the rough leaf, or present a miniature of the plant. At this stage the earth should be taken away from the breast of the drill, as well for the purpose of cutting off the weeds, as of preparing it in the valley for its subsequent application to the crop. Shortly after this process, a pretty fair guess can be made of the prospect, and the farmer may then proceed with the operation of thinning the crop with a hand hoe, leaving the plants ten or eleven inches asunder, and cutting up the weeds. When the plants get a-head after this process, which they will do very speedily, the farmer should again go over the drills, cutting out any fresh plants that have sprouted up and clearing off the weeds.

The principal advantage of the Swedes over other descriptions is, that if unhealthy plants, or plants that have started into head, shall appear, or if any failures should take place, their places may be supplied by transplanting from parts which will admit of being thinned. After this process has been performed, the plants should be carefully earthed by applying the mould in the valleys with a hand hoe. The crop will then speedily cover the ground, which will go far to prevent the growth of weeds; should any appear, however, neither time nor pains should be spared in eradicating them, and should the weather turn out very dry and the ground become hard, the space between the plants may be poked with a sharp crow-bar, which, being prised, will loosen the soil and thus afford fresh nutriment to the plants, while it will be the means of enabling the loosened soil to retain the moisture of the night dews. Great damage frequently occurs to the turnip crop by the ground becoming caked and hard from long drought.

The diseases to which the turnip crop is liable have been before stated, the principal of which are, destruction by the fly, and the fingers and toes. The use of quick lime, sulphur, and other nostrums have been recommended as means of protection against the ravages of the fly, but I have not heard of any plan which can be relied upon with certainty as a means of prevention. Very wet weather, bad cultivation, poor ground, or insufficiency of manure, may, I think, account for the disease of fingers and toes, while, in my opinion, as many failures take place from negligence in the selection of seed, as from any other cause.

The best season for sowing Swedes may be considered to be from the second week in April to the first week in May; for the Aberdeen from the first week in May to the middle of that month; and for the while globe or Norfolk from the second week in May to the first week in June.

Turnips are either fed off on the ground by sheep; drawn as they are required for the use of store or stall fed cattle; or stored, if the ground is either wet or required for a winter crop. If stored, they are drawn about the latter end of October or the beginning of November; the heads and tails are then chopped off, and they are piled in the same manner and shape in which the potatoes are placed in the pit, and are then well covered with dry ferns or wheaten straw. A deep drain should be dug round the heap, as I have described in treating of the potatoe pit. They may be then taken from the heap as required for use, the globes being first used, the Aberdeens second, and the Swedes kept for spring feeding, as they will last the longest.

There is one curious fact that ought not to be forgotten as regards the relative value of the several descriptions. It is this: – The Swede increases in its nutritive quality in proportion to its size, that is, there will be more nutriment in one Swede of twenty pounds weight, than in two Swedes of ten pounds each, while there will be more nourishment in four white Norfolks of five pounds each, than in one of the same description weighing twenty pounds; and, for this reason, I think more space should be allowed between the Swedes in the drills than to any other description of turnip.

Turnips are given to sheep, store and stall fed cattle; Swedes are very frequently steamed and given to working horses and pigs, but for neither are they sufficient food. I shall now state my general objection to the extensive propagation of the turnip. In the first place, then, they encourage landlords to compel their tenants to keep a large quantity of ground in grass; as the turnip can only be considered as valuable from its capability of keeping up the grass fed cattle in the condition to which the pasture has brought them, so that they may be marketable in all seasons. Thus, a beast weighing eight hundred weight in the month of November, when the grass begins to fall off, can be kept in the same condition throughout the winter by turnips, and the value, therefore, that can be assigned to the crop, is the difference of price occasioned by the difference of season; for instance, a beast in the same condition will be worth more in March, April, or May, than in September, October, or November.

I believe, however, it will be admitted that turnips do not possess the property of fatting cattle, but merely that of keeping up their condition. This, I admit, is a very great advantage, but by no means equal to that possessed by the potatoe, which is capable of fatting a beast from the very lowest state to the highest perfection to which it can be brought. I have seen many beasts fall off upon turnips, while I have never known potatoes to fail in bringing the very poorest to the highest state of perfection. The reason, then, that I prefer the potatoe to the turnip is, because it affords the means which the turnip lacks of finishing a beast; because the cultivation of potatoes would induce landlords to bring more land under spade cultivation, while the extensive use of the turnip induces them to keep it either in grass, or if in tillage, to be cultivated by the plough.

Machinery for sowing and cultivating turnips has been brought to great perfection of late years. I am not to be understood as objecting to the use of machinery, even for the purposes of agriculture, on the contrary, I should look to great benefit for the small farmer from the threshing machine, and also, if he chose to cultivate turnips, from those machines which are used for that purpose, and, in the event of the system which I advocate being carried into effect, I will venture to say that every small farmer would derive his full share of benefit from every improvement that was made in machinery, and that each district would be stocked with a sufficiency of the very best description, which might be hired as wanted by those who required it; for instance, in district A, containing a thousand acres of land, and in which somewhere about 1,200 quarters of wheat would be produced annually, it would be very well worth the while of one individual to have a thrashing machine for hire, which would perform the amount of labour required, while it would be a very useless expenditure for a man who had only five quarters of wheat to thrash, to go to the expence of buying a threshing machine. So with the man who had half an acre of turnips, he could hire all the most improved machinery as he required it, while to purchase it would be absolute madness. Perhaps I could not have hit upon a more happy illustration whereby to explain how machinery has become man's curse, and how it could be made man's holiday. I should much rather see the horse hoe, the grubber, the roller, and the drilling machine, performing the required work, while the man who paid for it was otherwise spending his labour to much greater advantage, than see him expending his strength upon work which might be more profitably performed by machinery.

As it is my intention to enter fully into the questions of the quantity, the different descriptions of food, the time for applying it, the seasons at which it should be grown, and the succession of crops required by the small farmer, when I come to lay down rules for the Management of Small Farms, I have abstained from entering as much into detail under the several heads as I otherwise should have done, and I have confined myself more to general observations than to minute directions.

REMARKS.

Having now disposed of what may be considered the three grand crops, I shall only treat, in the present number, of such other crops as I consider necessary for the small farmer, as I am anxious to commence my next number with a clear developement of the mode by which I hope to see the small farm system brought into immediate practical operation. My remarks, therefore, will be brief with regard to the remaining produce, giving sufficient information as to the mode of producing them; the purposes to which they may be applied; and their relative value.

If I should hereafter deem it necessary to publish a complete agricultural dictionary, the trouble that such a work will impose upon me shall not deter me from the undertaking, and, in truth, the time is fast approaching when there will be a much greater demand for works upon Agriculture than ever there has been, for good guesses, upon commerce and manufactures. It so happens that almost every work upon farming consists either of a compilation from the writings of the most popular theorists, or of a collection of mere isolated experiments communicated to the author either by the steward of some squire, or the manager of some agricultural society. Upon the other hand, if my little work should bear the appearance of presumption or arrogance from the absence of reference to other writers, my only apology is, that, as I write for those who cannot afford to experimentalize to any great extent, I prefer starting them upon the straight road of simple practice, allowing them to diverge into experiment when they have established their footing; never for a moment denying, or even doubting, that the science of agriculture, in this country, is merely in its infancy, while I look to its improvement as an easy means of establishing for England a position which may enable her people to bid defiance to the foreign invader, and make them independent of the foreign producer.

MANGEL WURTZEL.

There are two descriptions of this root, both as to colour and manner of growing, the one of a flesh colour, the other white. Another difference is supposed to exist between these two species, namely, that while the one strikes its roots deep in the soil, the other grows partly above it. I incline to think, however, that this is an error into which writers have been led by persons who have sown the root in soil not fitted to its growth, and that both species will strike down and grow down, and grow under ground, if the soil is of sufficient depth.

The soil best suited to this valuable root is a deep, heavy, rich loam, and in order to bring the crop to the highest state of perfection, it should be sown in ridgelets, after a liberal quantity of manure has been well worked up with the soil. It being a great object to bring the roots to their full size before the frost sets in, and not to sow the seed so early as to run the risk of damage from frost, every attention should be paid to bring it to maturity within the season which may be relied upon. For this purpose I am friendly to the system of transplanting for two reasons, firstly, because you can take better care of your plants in the seed bed until they are fit for removal, and, secondly, it affords the farmer more time for preparing the ground. Besides these advantages, as the after culture of mangel wurtzel is more tedious and precarious than that required by the turnip, these difficulties will be overcome by transplanting, instead of sowing the seed.

The seed may be sown in a small bed in the garden about the middle of May, and will be fit for removal about the middle of June, when they should be carefully taken up and planted in drills of two and a half feet apart, from centre to centre, and within fifteen inches of each other in the drill. Perhaps it may be as well to mention here, that all those processes which may be said to belong to gardening rather than to farming, should be performed by persons for whom, in each district, there would be sufficient demand to ensure a proper supply. For instance, I should by all means recommend the four acre farmer to have recourse to the practical gardener whenever he required his services, and that not being more than a portion of three or four days in the year, a district of a thousand acres would furnish ample employment for a number of scientific gardeners. About the latter end of August the under leaves of the mangel wurtzel may be taken off and given to cattle. Milch cows especially like this food, and it increases their milk considerably.

During the first fine weather in October, and before the crop becomes frost-bitten, the root should be drawn, and may be stored in the same manner as turnips, and will furnish a large supply of the most favourite, most wholesome, and nutritive food, while care should be taken to give a portion of some other more binding food with it, chopped straw, hay, or boiled potatoes, for instance. If proper care is bestowed upon mangel wurtzel by selecting the most healthy plants from the seed bed, and preserving a sufficient quantity to replace any failures that may take place in the drills, from fifty to sixty tons weight will be found to be by no means an unusual produce for an acre of good ground. The after culture for mangel wurtzel in no way differs from that of the turnip after the first hand-hoeing.

VETCHES.

There are two descriptions of vetch, but I believe that we ourselves have created the distinction, merely by sowing the seed at different seasons of the year. They are now known by the spring and winter vetch.

The winter vetch should be sown about two bushels of seed to the acre, precisely as I have described the method of sowing wheat. The ground should be made very fine, a rather moist soil is that which it thrives best in, but well drained, which the furrow on either side will accomplish. The seed may be sown any time in September, the earlier the better. In a southern climate I have cut vetches two feet high on the 17th of March, but I think about the 20th of April is the earliest period at which a crop may be generally relied upon. Care should be taken to sow either black oats or beans liberally with the vetch crop, as they serve as standards for the vetch and keep the crop from lodging upon the ground.

Spring vetches may be sown in the first fine weather in March, and will be fit for use by the middle of June. They may be sown rather thicker than the winter crop, say two bushels and a half, and the covering may be lighter than that of the winter vetch, say an inch and a half. Vetches are in the best state for milch cows and young cattle and pigs, when the pod has acquired nearly its full size, and care should be taken to give them sparingly in the first instance, although no other danger is to be apprehended from a liberal use of them than that of creating a temporary weakness, especially in milch cows, as they give an almost incredible quantity of milk when fed upon them.

The vetch does not require a deep soil, and, if cut before ripe, does little or no injury to the land. In fact, it is rather an improving crop, and may be safely taken between a crop of potatoes and barley, cabbages, mangel wurtzel, or white turnips.

RAPE.

I am not sure that rape has ever been sufficiently esteemed for general purposes, it being usually confined to the feeding of sheep. I sowed sixteen acres of rape broad cast, after a crop of early potatoes, in the last week in August, and from December till March I fed six score hoggets upon it with the greatest success; the milch cows also devoured it greedily; while I found a great increase both in the richness and quantity of their milk, and the same field gave a luxuriant crop of barley, sown in the second week of April. The stalk of the rape is the richest part, and for that reason great pains should be taken in its management. In broad cast it will grow to leaf; while in drills the stalk will attain an immense thickness. The practice, then, which I recommend for the cultivation of rape, is as follows: –

This crop thrives best in a rich moist soil, and the land does not require so much working as for turnips, mangel-wurtzel, or carrots. The rape seed may be sown like mangel-wurtzel, in a bed in the garden, and may be planted out in drills, twenty inches from centre to centre, and nine inches asunder in the drills. If the plants are taken from a seed-bed, the seed may be sown the latter end of June, and transplanted from the middle to the latter end of August. The crop does not require much after culture, but will be the better for being steadied in the ground during the first dry weather in October, by casting a little earth round each plant with the hand-hoe. Rape seldom or never fails, and is so hardy, that it has been found very difficult to eradicate it from the ground when the crop has been allowed to ripen; indeed there are instances of fields that have been twenty years in grass after rape, throwing up a considerable crop after the first ploughing.

Rape, managed as I have described, would be fit for use in December, and will furnish an abundance of the very best description of food until the ground is required for a succeeding crop; while, like vetches, it has the property of not exhausting the land, if not allowed to run to seed.

CARROTS.

There is no food to which all kinds of animals are more partial than the carrot, especially horses. I have seen four teams of working-horses, eight carriage-horses, and several saddle-horses, fed from November to March upon carrots, with a small quantity, of about half a peck a-day, of vetches, that had heated in the stack and were unfit for seed, given to each, and I never saw horses in finer condition; while, at the same time, I doubt that they were capable of doing as much work as if they had been fed upon hay and corn. However, they were in top condition, with coats like satin, and very healthy. Milch cows eat carrots greedily; and, while fed upon them, both the quantity and the quality of the milk is considerably improved. The great objection to the carrot as a general crop is, the difficulty of procuring land with a sufficient depth of mould, and which the carrot, above all other roots, requires, not less than two feet at least of loose friable mould being necessary to insure a full crop. I have already given directions as to the mode by which, in about three years, almost any amount of good soil may be insured by digging the furrows, when the earth has been shovelled out of them. I have been led to recommend this practice for the purpose of insuring a sufficient amount of soil for growing mangle-wurtzel and carrots, to both of which I attach great value. Supposing then the farmer to have a piece of ground capable of producing carrots, the following is the mode of culture which I recommend.

In November the field should be liberally covered with the compost made under the cattle, as I have described under the head 'Manure'. It should be then dug in and allowed to remain rough in ridgelets until the first fine weather in spring, when it should receive a thoroughly good digging, care being taken to mix the manure well with the soil; the land may remain so till the middle of April when it should be laid out in beds of four feet wide and furrows a foot wide and eighteen inches deep, this will give an addition of four inches and a half to the depth of the bed, while as carrots require immense attention lest they may be smothered with weeds, the furrow will furnish good standing room, from which each bed to the centre may be weeded without the labourer being compelled to stoop; the ground should be made as fine as possible, not only on the surface, but to the extreme depth to which it can be effected. The seed being of an adhesive, or rather tangling, nature, should be mixed with coarse sand, and sown liberally, say seven pounds to the acre, and covered in with about an inch and a half of the bottom half foot of the furrow. The plants are very slow in making their appearance, and care should be taken to pull up the weeds with the hand should any appear. The crop will not make its appearance until the beginning of June, when it should be thinned, leaving the plants in the bed fully fifteen inches asunder, and it requires no further care than that of weeding and poking and stirring the earth with a crowbar between the plants should the weather prove dry.

The crop may be drawn about the latter end of October, and the tops may be cut off any time from the middle of September until they begin to decay and given to cattle; a food which they devour greedily. The carrots may then be laid in a bed of dry sand, and built up to any height with alternate layers of sand and carrots, and in this way they may be preserved perfectly fresh and fit for use till the following spring. One great advantage that the carrot has over most other roots is, that, I never knew a beast to surfeit upon them, to refuse them, or to tire of them, while they possess more nutritive matter than any other, with the single exception of the potatoe. Pigs relish carrots and will thrive rapidly upon them, while cows and horses may be more safely fed upon them as their sole food with the single exception of the potatoe. – Carrots are not an impoverishing crop if the ground is properly treated, neither do they require so much a rich as a deep loose soil.

CABBAGES.

There are many varieties of the cabbage tribe; those most generally cultivated as field crops are the ox-head, the drum-head, and York, all of which grow to an immense size. As with potatoes so it is with cabbages: however, those who grow the latter looking more to size than to the quantity of nutriment. Upon the contrary, as a beast will generally prefer that which is most nutritious, as it is also in general most palatable, I prefer the sugar loaf, although not considered a field cabbage, to any that I have named. The cabbage requires better soil and more manure than any other root. The ground most fitted for producing cabbages is a warm clayey deep soil, as rich as possible.

The ground in which spring cabbages are to be grown should be well covered with manure and trenched up before Christmas. It should be again dug to a considerable depth in the first fine weather in spring, and, previous to the plants being put out, another good covering of manure should be applied and immediately covered in; the ground may be then allowed to remain level until the operation of planting commences, when it should be stirred to the depth of about six or eight inches, refreshing the surface for the young plants. The seed should be sown in a well sheltered spot in the garden, about the middle of September, and may be planted out early in April. The crop will be fit for use about the middle of September, and furnishes an abundance of the very best description of food for milch or stall fed cattle, while hogs and sheep prefer it to almost any other.

Great attention must be paid to drawing the young plants from the bed, and also to setting them in the rows. I recommend the gardener of the district to be employed for this job, and I would advise him, his line being set and his plants ready, to furnish himself with a tub of strong tank water, which he may apply liberally with a watering pot without the rose to a dozen plants according as he sets that number. It is of all things necessary that the cabbage plant should be well steadied in the ground, and that the soil should be as well prepared as possible for its reception. The rows may be planted, if for sugar loaf, at a distance of three feet from centre to centre, and the plants may be of an equal distance in the row. Those of the larger kind, however, should be allowed a yard space every way, as they grow to a much greater size.

Cabbages intended for winter use should be sown in the bed about the middle of April, and may be planted out any time from the middle of June to the middle of July, the ground being well prepared and well manured. Cabbages planted at this season will furnish an abundance of the very best food for cattle from the middle of October to the following spring; care being taken to pull up the stalk instead of cutting off the head, as I fear cabbages, like potatoes, have got a bad name in consequence of mismanagement, it being a generally received opinion that cabbage is a very exhausting crop, a charge arising, I apprehend, out of the slovenly practice of cutting off the heads and allowing the stalk to remain, exhausting the ground to a greater extent than before the head had been cut off. Moreover, there is no better manure than a heap of cabbage stumps will make, if covered while fresh with a little good dung, and then turned and chopped and mixed with a small quantity of compost.

Field cabbages will attain as much as fifty pounds weight, sugar loaves from six to nine pounds, and the crop has the great advantage of standing the winter well, and of being wholesome food, and easily managed for all sorts of stock. In the after culture care must be taken to land the plants well with a hand hoe, to pick off snails and slugs when they make their appearance, or, what is still better, to shake a little quick lime on the surface after each landing, immediately around the plant. The farmer who wishes to have an abundant crop of this excellent food, will find his advantage in occasionally applying a middling sized watering pot full of tank water to every twenty plants.

Should any of the plants become starters, that is, run up prematurely to seed, or should any fail, they should be replaced from the seed bed. The notion that cabbage gives a disagreeable taste to milk or butter is an erroneous one, and has been derived from the damage done to both by the practice of giving decayed stinking outside cabbage leaves to milch cows, whereas, a good sugar loaf in autumn, or a winter cabbage that has been touched with frost, is as sweet, as wholesome, and as nutritious food as a milch cow can eat. A great advantage that the cabbage has over the turnip is, that it stands the frost better, while it can be better got at in snow.

FLAX.

A certain quantity of flax being indispensable, as well as for the purpose of giving the family employment during the winter nights as of supplying them with a good stock of linen, I consider it necessary to lay down rules for its culture and management. Flax may be sown in any ground of moderate richness, and does not require so rich a soil as most other crops. However, I do not mean to assert that the crop will not be in proportion to the ground in which it is sown; good ground, if not too rich, producing the best crop.

The ground should be made very fine, and the seed should be sown as early as possible in March, at the rate of between two and three bushels per acre. Great care must be taken in the selection of the seed, as much depends upon its freshness and soundness. The seed should be covered either with a garden rake, or with a bush harrow, carefully made, and cautiously used. When the crop makes its appearance, the ground should be kept well weeded. When the flax is about six inches high, clover seed may be sown at the rate of about eighteen pounds to the acre, and may be rolled in, a process which, if performed by a hand roller, will rather serve than injure the flax.

If the seed is sown in March, the flax will blossom from the latter end of June to the middle of July, and, if intended for thread only, it may be then pulled; great care being taken how the work is performed, which is by catching the flax with the right hand about eight inches from the top, doubling what is over the hand by compressing the left hand upon it, and then with a gentle and sudden, but not violent, jerk, drawing it from the ground. The flax should be then tied up in small sheaves and taken to a pond of clear water, where it should be deposited and allowed to remain for at least six days, after which it should be examined each day, by drawing a few stalks from one of the sheaves, and trying whether or no it has been sufficiently steeped to admit of the thread being drawn out of the outside lining, just as you would try whether or no the season would admit of oak trees being barked, by ascertaining if the strip runs freely; which will generally be the case when the wind is in the south or the west. When the thread can be easily separated from the outside covering, then the sheaves may be taken from the pond and spread thinly over a grass field or clean stubble, where it should be allowed to remain until it is perfectly dry, and until it has acquired a yellowish colour. It may be then tied up in small bundles as thick as a man's leg, and stacked like corn for a day or two if the weather is fine, after which it should be stored away in a dry place, with a hurdle under it, five or six feet from the ground, and with a good current of air.

As soon as the long nights drop in, the family may begin to manufacture the flax, the several processes of which are performed as follows: – It is first pounded, which may be performed either with mallets, a round polished stone, or by a flax pounder, which last instrument I recommend, and merely mention the two former as substitutes which are frequently used; however, as I before stated, each district will be very likely to have a sufficiency of machinery for the more easy performance of all such jobs, and therefore I shall calculate upon the flax being pounded by a pounding machine. This process softens the bark, and the flax is then ready for scutching, which is performed either by holding a lock of the flax twisted round the left hand, and hanging over a board about three feet high, along the side of which it is slashed, with a scutching handle which resembles a cleaver, being, however, much longer, and about five inches wide, and sharpish at the edge.

There is another instrument used for scutching flax which may be described as follows; it is about eighteen inches long, six inches wide, and hollowed out like the handle of a knife; a wooden blade about five inches wide and of equal length with the handle is fastened at the end with a wooden rivet and made to open and shut freely. This is placed upon the ground, and the woman holding the blade about the centre in the right-hand, puts the flax under the blade and continues to ripple it through this machine until it becomes so fine that it will run freely, although compressed nearly to the bottom of the handle; that is, at first the flax is merely drawn through as the blade and handle meet, and by degrees, as the process goes on, the blade is closed more and more after every five or six ripplings, until at length it runs freely, although the edge of the blade should nearly touch the bottom of the groove, and after which the flax is held in the left hand and slashed over with the right, until all the loose fibres of tow are removed from it.

This process takes the coarse tow off the flax, and prepares it for 'heckling,' a process which is performed by rippling the flax through the teeth of the heckle, of which there are various descriptions used, according to the fineness which it is intended to make the linen. As soon as this process has been performed, the flax is then twisted into hanks, after which it is spun into thread, and subsequently wove into linen, while the coarse and fine tow mixed together make good sacks or winnowing sheets.

As I mean in my rules for the Management of Small Farms, to assign a portion of each for the growth of flax, I have thought it necessary to give instructions for its cultivation in this preliminary number. No house-keeper should be without a plot of flax, and it is no excuse to say, either that he can have it dressed cheaper at the mill, or that he can buy linen cheaper than he can manufacture it, for experience will teach him that in both calculations he is mistaken, if he sends it to the mill, his family will be idle just at the time when they might be agreeably and profitably employed, and if he purchases his linen he will soon find out the difference between his own and that of his neighbour who has manufactured it for himself.

A great prejudice has been most ridiculously created against the growth of flax, from a belief that it impoverishes the ground, whereas there never was a greater error, as I have seen excellent crops produced after flax when the seed has not been allowed to ripen, and in which the whole damage to the land from a crop of flax consists. There is no better plan for growing clover than that which I have described, it admits of the seed being sown in the very best season, while the act of pulling the flax loosens the ground, and is of great advantage to the young shoots which have not, up to that period, deprived the flax of any of the required sustenance.

CLOVER.

Clover may be classed amongst the great variety of other artificial grasses; however, as it is my desire to steer clear of all complexity, I shall merely treat of that description which should constitute the small farmer's crop. I am, then, decidedly in favour of the broad leaved 'red clover.' I have before described how it should be sown with flax; however, as it may suit some to sow it alone, I shall give instructions for that purpose. Though clover requires but little covering, it will come to the greatest perfection in deep rich soils; however, land of a very moderate quality, if properly treated, will yield an abundant crop.

The best time for sowing is early in March, when the ground should be made perfectly fine, and well rolled in order to procure an even surface. The seed may be then sown and covered slightly by raking the ground well with a close-toothed rake. If care is taken in selecting fresh seed the crop seldom fails, and, as it quickly covers the ground, it stands in no danger of being choked with weeds. When the first crop is fit for cutting, the small farmer, when going to perform that operation, should take with him a wheelbarrow-full of the finest compost, and as soon as he has cut as much as he requires for the day, he should give the stubble a good sprinkling of the compost.

By this means he will ensure three or even four cuttings in the season of the very best description of food for cattle, growing pigs and sheep, the only caution necessary, being, care to bring cows to their full feed by degrees and never allowing them to drink water for some time after feeding; clover should be given scantily at first, and by degrees cattle may be brought to a full feed of it, but, if given too profusely in the outset, cows are very apt to burst. If it can be avoided clover should not be mown for cows in wet weather, or with a dew upon it, until they shall have been used to it for some time. There is no food upon which cows will give richer or more milk, or upon which growing pigs will thrive better. The difference in the appearance of a cow fed upon clover and upon vetches is very apparent – those fed upon clover will have plumper quarters and tighter carcase, while those fed upon vetches will have lank quarters and loose dropping bellies.

Clover will fat a cow, vetches never will, however, they are fine wholesome food and very efficient in bringing a new calved cow to a full flow of milk. If clover is sown without any other crop, about four pounds more seed may be used than if sown with flax or wheat; indeed, I am not very favourable to the practice of sowing clover with wheat for this reason, if it is sown too early it becomes so high at harvest time that the wheat must either be cut very high or a large quantity of the clover must be reaped with it, thereby losing the best of the straw in the first case, or rendering it necessary to delay saving the wheat until the clover is perfectly saved to prevent heating in the stack in the second case.

REMARKS.

My objection to keeping land in pasture has been already stated, and in order to support that objection, I have devoted the previous chapters of this work to the consideration of the means by which the use of grass may be rendered wholly unnecessary; indeed, when a writer undertakes to expose any system which to him appears erroneous, it becomes his duty, if he has any other to propose as a substitute, to develope it in all its features and details so fully that, as a whole, it may be considered complete. I have thought well upon, and have had much practical experience in, farming, before I ventured upon so bold a step as that of a complete change of system; however, the more I think, the more I hear, and the more I read upon the subject, the more firmly am I convinced that the government of England will be compelled in less than one year from this date, to make the question of home colonization the principal feature of legislation. The erroneous system of agriculture which has been hitherto practised in this country, has, very fortunately, been a kind of savings bank, of husbanding much richness in the land, which may at any time be abundantly yielded to a proper description of labour. In many previous chapters I have touched upon the rapid improvements to which the increased propagation of the turnip crop have led, while hitherto I have abstained from mentioning the greatest advantage which the higher classes of society have derived from the introduction of that root, as well as others, as winter food.

Before the English farmer had been instructed in the art of stall feeding cattle, it was customary to slaughter the required number of oxen for winter provision at that season of the year when grass feeding had lost its virtue, and when cattle were likely to fall off. This practice imposed the necessity of eating salt meat during the winter and spring months, whereas the present system of winter feeding with roots enables the farmer to bring his stock to market every day in the year, the supply being in some degree regulated by the demand. This alteration has led to the greatest improvements in the breed of cattle, by crossing the blood, until the best and most profitable description had been procured; while I would venture to assert that a natural consequence of a change from salted provisions to fresh food has been found most beneficial to the human race. If then, the change from salt to fresh meat has been beneficial to man, I think we may come to the same conclusion that fresh fodder for cattle during the winter months, would be an excellent substitute for dried up hay.

I may be told that hay is indispensable for some purposes. I deny it, or that it is at all necessary that one cock of hay should be grown throughout the empire. As it is my intention to conclude the second number of this work in the present chapter, it may not be amiss to devote a portion of it to facts which I have witnessed myself.

Some years ago a relation of mine purchased a two-year old filly, the produce of a pony mare by a stolen leap, the breed of which had been in my family for a great number of years. The name of the gentleman was the Rev. John Henry Madras and the history of the filly was this: she was fed upon boiled potatoes and nothing else, and his son hunted her from three years old to six, astonishing the field with her performance, and she was always fresher at the end of the day than any other horse. I resolved upon having the mare at any price when she was six years old, and I tempted the owner with a large price and bought her. I was sceptical upon the point of potatoes constituting her only food, and I tried her with the best hay and oats, both of which she refused; I then treated her to her old dish, and for two years that she was in my possession she seldom or ever tasted any other food than boiled potatoes. She was not even a large pony, and I have seen her hunted with the fastest fox hounds, which I was obliged to part with because they were so fast that the gentlemen in the neighbourhood could not ride with them, and I have seen that pony carry the huntsman up to their tails three days in the week, and never tire. Again, after riding her back during the whole week of the Clonakilty races, and having ridden her on Saturday from one o'clock till five, at that hour I put her into a handicap with five other horses, some of them thoroughbred, with more weight upon her than any of the rest, for two mile heats; she lost the first heat from being over weighted, when I changed the jockey, putting up a lighter boy without a saddle, she won the second heat; and distanced the field the third heat, and carried me afterwards a distance of some miles, prancing the whole way, and supped comfortably off a bucket of boiled potatoes. Now who will say that boiled potatoes are bad for the wind, or that hay is indispensable to the keep of horses?

Having now treated of the different crops which should constitute the produce of a four acre farm, I shall proceed in the next number to a developement of the means whereby the working classes of this country may become possessed, and at once, of a sufficient quantity of land to carry my plan into very extensive practice. I shall then proceed with minute and detailed directions for the proper management of small farms, with unabated confidence of success provided those most interested in the undertaking shall cheerfully co-operate with me in its accomplishment. Though but a short time has elapsed since I commenced this work, every day teaches me that stern necessity is bending the mind of the supporters of the old system to the expediency of change, while I am buoyed up with strong hope from the deep interest that the working classes are beginning to feel in the subject.

HOW THE PROJECTED PLAN IS TO BE EFFECTED.

In the two previous numbers I have given directions for the cultivation of the several crops that I consider most necessary for the small farmer, while I have abstained from clogging the work with any notice of matters not necessary for him to know anything about in the outset: and the next duty that I am called upon to perform, is that of instructing the working classes as to the means by which land may be acquired for carrying out the plan. The morbid and insensate submission of the working classes of this country to the rule, dominion, and controul, not of the laws, but of the slave-owners, would have discouraged me from my present undertaking, had I not witnessed a desire upon the part of the people themselves to discover some practical means whereby they may rid themselves of the galling yoke of capital, more, far more, oppressive than the utmost tyranny of the law. Bloody as the English laws formerly were, they were mild in their bloodiest form, tame in their most savage aspect, moderate in their utmost vengeance, and preserving in the midst of the most reckless destruction, when compared with the havoc, the desolation, the persecution, and wholesale murders committed by the capitalists of England.

If you hear of a political prisoner being badly treated in prison; if you hear of a fellow-creature who has died in a poor-house; if you witness the execution of a murderer, whose guilt may either be doubtful, or mitigated in heinousness by some extenuating circumstances; you damn the law, denounce the institutions, and revile the government; while you tamely witness the victims of the capitalist, to whom death in any shape would be a relief. You see men of thirty years of age withered and prematurely decayed, reduced to the dire necessity of sweeping the streets for their taskmasters, although their virtuous parents had given large premiums for their instruction in some trade, protection for which, they vainly hoped, was guaranteed by the laws of England. You see these men, and wandering paupers still more destitute, and the only feeling that their condition arouses is, that of comparative satisfaction, that, *as yet*, your lot is preferable to theirs. The laws have not injured those men in any respect: on the contrary, there are laws upon the statute-book unrepealed, which, if administered, would protect them; and which are not administered because money has become more powerful than law, and money, not justice, is consequently the fountain of English law. This is a great and crying grievance, arising out of a great national debt, the payment of the interest of which absorbs all other considerations, and turns our houses of representation into banking concerns and offices for the transaction of money matters, rather than legislative assemblies for the good government of the people.

Every country has a peculiar interest upon which its institutions are based, and all laws are made with reference to the main or leading interest; and eight hundred millions, with a cavalcade of hirelings and mercenaries, parsons and paid sycophants, being the pivot upon which our laws must turn, all are made, directly or indirectly, with the view of upholding this principal interest. Formerly, agriculture was the primary interest of this country, and hence laws were formerly made with reference to agriculture. Manufactures then sprung up, and laws for their government were grafted upon our agricultural stock. The great ambition to ensure ascendancy for the latter, embroiled us in expensive wars with the world, and the debt, the fruit of those wars, has exhausted both stock and graft, and our government is consequently compelled to sink all consideration of agriculture and manufactures, further than they may be made subservient to our monetary system. Hence, then, we arrive at the conclusion, either that the debt must be wiped off or compounded for, or that some expedient shall be devised, which will have the effect of relieving the non-debtor from its pernicious effects, and of saddling it upon the real debtor, who will very speedily find a remedy for an abuse which only affects himself, while he will be slow in looking for it as long as other shoulders bear its weight.

In my several communications to the working classes upon the land question, I have endeavoured so to familiarize their minds with the subject, as to prepare them for the adoption of the small farm plan upon such a system as would be most likely to lead to a successful result. One thing is quite clear, and all I believe have now seen it, it is this – that the government is not inclined to make any organic change in the constitution, while, without such change, it is not able to suggest any plan for the correction of those social evils which afflict society, without incurring the disapprobation and opposition of the several classes who have lived, thriven, and prospered upon things as they are. Having, therefore, arrived at the conclusion that the people have nothing to expect in the way of change from the government, it becomes the paramount duty of their friends to point out how the required change in their condition can be effected without force or fraud. And although it is quite clear that such change would be unpalatable to the revellers in abuse, if produced by an angel from heaven and in strict accordance with the Almighty's will and in conformity with the terms of his imperishable laws, yet have I ventured to brave all opposition for the general good. Not only have I been opposed by a portion of the press; but, still worse, I have met with the ignorant snarl of some working men, or rather men who profess to work for working men, and whose opposition is based upon personal vanity, disappointed ambition, hostility to myself, and a jealousy founded upon their own ignorance of the subject.

It is a very lamentable fact, that, in the midst of general distress, the people's professing friends invariably meet propositions, which do not originate with themselves, with a cold-blooded and vindictive opposition. Some foolish egotists have gone so far as to draw conclusions from the present state of Ireland, where they assert that the small farm system has produced slavery, dependency, and misery, for the purpose of discouraging the English working classes from an agricultural life. Such writers are mere wordy copyists, puffing theorists, ignorant dogmatists, self-sufficient coxcombs, who know no more of Ireland than they know of Japan, and who are as hopelessly ignorant of the capabilities of the land, as the ox that treads, or the bird that flies over it. The curse of Ireland has been, not the small farm, but the large farm system, while the requirement for a provision for the poor has arisen out of the abrogation of small allotments. I never approved of the political use made of Irish forty shilling freeholders; while the disfranchisement,[1] and consequent ouster, of that numerous body has led to the present state of pauperism by which Ireland is cursed, and has given rise to a bad system of poor-laws as a substitute.

Those who are ignorant upon the question of Irish agriculture, and who desire instruction upon the subject, will do well to read the work of that excellent gentleman, Mr Blacker, upon Small Farms;[2] always receiving it with great caution, for the following reasons: – firstly, it is written by the land-steward of a nobleman, who would not find it his interest to go into a searching enquiry of the title, the powers, and the uses made of those powers by the landlord-class. Secondly, it merely developes the result of some very trifling experiments made with success, without reference to any general principle. Thirdly, he speaks more with reference to the improvement of the land than with reference to the improvement of the tenants' condition; the one being permanent, and conferring a permanent benefit, through increased rent, upon the landlord, while the other is merely temporary, and is too often the cause of ouster, as a means of acquiring increased rent, while it entails an additional rent upon the improving tenant on the expiration of his lease. But, above all, the objection that I have to showing any conclusions from Mr Blacker's book beyond the irrefutable proof of the capabilities of the soil which it affords, is, that in almost every one of his reported cases we find improvement tested by the addition of a horse to the small farmer's stock; although his holding may not consist of more than seven or eight acres. Moreover, the average size of farms treated of in Mr Blacker's book usually consist of from four to five times as much land as one man can profitably manage.

As it is necessary that I should answer the sophistries of those ignorant parties who would urge the state of Ireland in opposition to the small farm plan, I may here remind them that every advance in the large farm system has led to

---

1 When the county franchise was raised to £10 in 1829, in part exchange for Catholic Emancipation.

2 William Blacker, *The Improvement to be Made in the Cultivation of Small Farms* (Dublin, 1834).

increased pauperism in Ireland, while it has contributed to an increased glut of Irish labourers in the English market. The first proof that I adduce in support of this assertion is, that the ousting of the forty shilling freeholders led to great distress. The second proof that I adduce is, that the ousting of Catholic tenants from small holdings, upon which the Reform Bill conferred the franchise, has considerably augmented that distress. The third proof that I adduce is, that the rage for introducing Scotch farmers, to carry out the system of feeding upon turnips, has induced many landlords to oust small tenants, with a view of possessing themselves of the farms, in the hope of redeeming their shattered fortunes by an improved system of agriculture; while, under a general summary, it should be understood that my system of small farms would be incomplete unless based upon the principle of a real 'fixity of tenure;' the want of which in Ireland operates more injuriously against the small farmer than it does against the large farmer. Thus, the large farmer, with a lease, or accepted proposal on blank paper, which, when stamped at any time the tenant pleases, may be converted into an equitable title, may contend against the legal persecution of his landlord; while neither lease nor accepted proposal are any protection whatever to the tenant who only occupies fifteen or twenty acres of ground, and who is unable to resist the demand of the landlord for its surrender, whenever he may think proper to require it. Hence the ability of the landlord to repossess himself of a small farm discourages the tenant from increasing its value even by industry, as the improvement is sure to lead either to additional rent or a turnout. This very system of bidding over the heads of small farmers with leases, who have improved their little holdings, has led to more murders than any other circumstance – to more murders, nay, to every murder that has been committed in Ireland for the last forty-three years, and each and every one of which are chargeable upon the tyrant landlords, land-sharks, land-agents, and middlemen, and not upon the maddened, plundered, infuriated peasant, who, in the wildness of despair, takes that vengeance in lieu of the satisfaction which the law denies him.

From these facts, then, the English reader will learn that Irish pauperism, Irish crime, Irish slavery, and Irish murders, are consequences of oppression and misrule, and that the want of the small farm system, and not its existence, is the immediate cause of Irish distress. I defy any man living to point out any single act of treachery committed by an Irish peasant arising out of any dispute in the adjustment of which he had received anything approaching to justice. The fact is, that foreign invaders have possessed themselves of the country, and would stigmatize the natives as barbarians for their virtuous resistance to the most cold-blooded tyranny, committed under the plea of loyalty, necessity, and devotion to English connection. Here, though out of place, I may be permitted to say, that the English people never have been the oppressors of Ireland, while the Irish-English have been the ruin of both countries, invariably constituting the English minister's strength for the maintenance of Church ascendancy and suppression of popular rights. To correct the several evils of which all now complain, to reconcile the people of both countries in a bond of union and brotherhood, to destroy the social inequality so destructive of peace, prosperity and harmony, I see no remedy

but an abandonment of our present artificial position, and a nearer approximation to the laws of nature. With these views, then, I proceed to develope the
means by which society may acquire a footing so firm, that its peace shall not be
in danger from the madness of despair, from agricultural restrictions, commercial
speculations, or ministerial change.

Since I first broached my plan for acquiring a sufficiency of land wherewith to
carry the small farm system into extensive practice, I have made it a portion of
my daily business to enquire into the probability of being able to accomplish the
object without the intervention of parliament; and in my research I have discovered that so great is the pressure of the times, which means the pressure of
gambling-debts, mortgagees, and creditors, that land may be purchased in the
wholesale market with as much facility as cotton, woollen, or earthenwares. I
have arrived, then, at the conclusion that the land may be had, and our next consideration is naturally directed to those means by which it may be acquired. In
this latter consideration, however, a collateral question very naturally arises; it is
this: – As the clubbing of the pence of the poor people is the only means whereby
the system can be carried out, we must investigate the several causes that operate
against it. Firstly, then, the people have discovered that even the wealthy, the
favoured, and the law-protected, have not been able to guard themselves against
the machinations of bubble companies, banking companies, improvement societies, mining societies, colonization societies, emigration societies and the
thousand and one other traps that are enticingly baited with fascinating prospectuses, wherein even the possibility of failure is the one only thing never
mentioned, while the certainty of success is confidently insured.

Want of confidence, then, is one very natural cause that will operate against
the success of the plan. Another great difficulty which presents itself arises from
the fact that a much greater number must become contributors to the fund than
could derive immediate benefit from it; for instance, suppose one million persons
to subscribe sixpence a-week each, it would amount in one year to £1,300,000,
which sum, if laid out in land worth a pound an acre, would purchase 65,000
acres at the usual rate of twenty years' purchase. As it is my desire to make every
thing so plain that every man who reads it will be able to understand the meaning without applying for assistance. I must tell you how land is bought. Suppose
an acre of land lets for a pound a-year, the way to estimate its value, if bought
out and out, is by multiplying the amount of yearly rent by the number of years'
purchase at which it can be bought, and that is the price given for the land for
ever; for instance, an acre of land let at a pound a-year can be bought for ever for
£20, or twenty years' rent being paid down for it. The sixty-five thousand acres
which may be purchased with the produce of the funds subscribed by a million
contributors, if subdivided into farms of four acres each, would only yield 16,250
allotments, thereby only admitting of 16,250 of the one million subscribers
being gainers by the project.

As, however, it would be extremely unjust that there should be so many
blanks to so few prizes, that is, sixty blanks to every prize, I would propose the
following remedy, which I think would give general satisfaction, and, in order to

explain it in the most simple way, I will make my calculations upon one allotment of four acres, and which would require the contributions say of sixty to purchase it. If, then, sixty men subscribe eighty pounds in one year, and if that eighty pounds will only purchase four acres, only one man can derive benefit from the scheme. When the land is purchased however out of the general fund, if A gets the four acres by lottery, he returns a rent of four pounds a-year, or a pound an acre for it, thereby leaving to the fifty-nine less fortunate speculators the whole amount that they had subscribed, as well as his own subscription, to be divided amongst them, that is, he has four acres of land for four pounds a-year as his share, and they have the four pounds a-year for ever for their share; thus, while one of the sixty is more fortunate than the others, none of them are great losers.

However, in all cases where a very extensive project is to be carried out, there must be some amount of risk, and it is my object to reduce that loss to the lowest possible amount, and at the same time to preserve the subscribers from risk as far as possible. In order then to break down the great inequality between the one who draws the prize, and the fifty-nine who draw the blanks; while I am unable to hold out the prospect of a prize to each I would submit the following as my plan for reducing the chances of loss. Now, let me be distinctly understood, and if the reader shall pass over all other chapters without much thought, I beg, I implore, nay, I pray of him, to bestow his very best attention upon the plan which I propose for his redemption.

PLAN OF DISTRIBUTION.

Sixty persons subscribe eighty pounds in one year, which eighty pounds is to be laid out in the purchase of four acres of ground, worth four pounds a-year for ever – only one person can become possessed of the land. Supposing the land to have been purchased by an individual, or a society, for the benefit of the sixty subscribers, those sixty subscribers go into a lottery, wherein there are fifty-nine blanks and one prize. A gets the prize, and with it a lease for ever of four acres of ground, at four pounds a-year, executed by the individual or the society in trust for the following eight persons: – after the fifty-nine blanks have been drawn, the fifty-nine persons drawing them go into another lottery, wherein there are eight prizes of ten shillings a-year for ever each, that is, the four pounds rent conditioned to be paid by him who draws the land, is divided into eight shares of ten shillings each; the parties who draw those eight prizes will have thus received ten shillings a year for ever for twenty-six shillings subscribed, and which at five per cent. would sell for ten pounds. Thus, out of the sixty, one would have received four acres of land at four pounds a-year as his share, and eight others would have received ten pounds for twenty-six shillings paid, making somewhat more than one good prize in every seven ticket-holders; while, if the speculators were anxious to reduce the chances of risk still lower, they may divide the four pounds a-year into sixteen prizes of five shillings each, and worth five pounds each, and thus there would be seventeen prizes in every sixty, or in the proportion of two prizes to seven blanks, thus reducing the chances of either extraordinary gain upon the one hand or injurious loss upon the other.

The scale which I have laid down for the disposal of four acres would equally apply to four million acres, or any quantity of land. I will suppose, for instance, a district of one thousand acres, distributed by lottery amongst two hundred and fifty holders, paying four pounds each, or a thousand a-year; and suppose that to have been purchased with funds raised as I have described, we are then to con-sider the means whereby those who are entitled to the ten shillings a-year each, or five shillings a-year each, are to be paid. The land, subdivided as I have described, would be worth five years' more purchase, in consequence of the increased security that the additional labour would confer upon it. However, I leave that out of the question, or for after consideration. If it was worth five years' more purchase, each farm of four acres would produce a capital of twenty pounds more than was originally given for it, that is, in the wholesale market, at a pound an acre, it was worth twenty years' purchase, or eighty pounds; whereas, in the retail market, it would be worth twenty-five years' purchase, or one hundred pounds.

However, the thousand acres, subdivided into two hundred and fifty farms, would not want a purchaser of the rent of a thousand a-year, paid by the several holders, for twenty-four hours. It would constitute better stock than any for which the government are security; while, with the lease for ever, the tenant would be made wholly and entirely independent of the purchaser. The purchase-money would pay the sums to which the several parties who drew money-prizes were entitled, and thus, in less than one week in each year, the whole business may be transacted.

It may be asked, how a hand-loom weaver who may become possessed of four acres of land is to commence operations? and, in order to provide for such a happy necessity, I will lay down another plan. Suppose a thousand acres of land to be in the market, worth a thousand a-year, or twenty thousand pounds to buy it out and out; a very usual practice in such cases is, to pay ten thousand pounds – one half the purchase-money – allowing the other ten thousand pounds to remain as a mortgage upon the estate. In such case, if twenty thousand pounds had been subscribed to purchase the thousand acres, ten thousand of that sum would be applied as purchase-money, and the other ten thousand may be divided into shares of forty pounds each, which would leave that amount for every one of the two hundred and fifty occupiers between whom it was divided to commence business upon; and admitting that such subdivision increased the value of the land by five years' purchase, or by the amount of twenty pounds in every four acres, that sum, added to the forty, would leave a capital of sixty pounds to com-mence business with.

I have now developed my scheme in its most simple, most harmless, and most democratic form; yet, I doubt that I have developed it in the most fascinating shape, inasmuch as the people themselves, the very working classes, are more captivated by fascinating prospects than perhaps any other portion of the com-munity; and I do not blame them; it is natural; and I can well understand sixty working men who have subscribed eighty pounds for any particular object, unanimously preferring a chance to the whole, with the risk of losing their subscription, to the chance of being moderately compensated for the loss of the great prize. In such case, then, it would be quite competent for the subscribers to agree amongst themselves upon all questions of risk, increasing the comfort of the most successful by diminishing the chances of those more moderately so.

Another plan by which my scheme could be carried out immediately is, by the appropriation of funds at the disposal of the several trades, benefit, and other societies; and as the parties in such case may be brought into immediate contact, without the interference of a third party, I should be glad to find the several trades accomplishing the double good, of securing good interest for their own funds while they may be the means of conferring happiness upon their poorer neighbours. In fact there is no class of society in England which has so great an interest in the cultivation of our domestic resources as the several trades. Carpenters, builders, tilers, stonemasons, slaters, nailors, painters, plumbers, glaziers, blacksmiths, ironmongers, miners, colliers, bricklayers, block-printers, hatters, stationers, bookbinders, silversmiths, goldbeaters, tailors, shoemakers, butchers, bakers, sawyers, and toymakers, and all persons who are engaged in building, repairing, furnishing or supplying houses, are beginning to discover that every cottage abandoned for the cellar is a competitor against those who build, and the loss of a customer to those who supply. And whilst speaking of the trades, I must say of them to my sorrow, that, with the exception of a very few, and, generally speaking, with the exception of those of Manchester, Aberdeen, and a few other towns, they are the most prejudiced, the most haughty, the most imperious and time-serving class in the community. The good sense, however, of those who have reasoned upon their position, is now forcing the hitherto apathetic of that body into thought and action, and to that improved state I look for the assistance of the trades in carrying out my project. In truth, I would prefer the experiment being made by them, inasmuch as it would divest the scheme of all liabilities to jobbing and speculation, because their officers are for the most part men of business, men of character, and men of talent.

I shall then proceed to lay down a scale whereby the plan may be carried out by a trade society. I will suppose twenty thousand pounds to be at their disposal, and inasmuch as the great object to be achieved by political economy is to set the producing powers as actively and profitably to work as possible, and as capital, when judiciously applied, may be considered an essential for carrying out the project, I shall here say a word as to the relative value of ready money, when profitably and unprofitably applied. At present money is dear at two per cent., because there is more in the market than is required for the working of the system; whereas, if the retail labour market was opened, I unhesitatingly declare that the required amount of money to give an impetus to the required amount of labour, would increase its value from two per cent., at which it is now dear, to twenty per cent., at which it would be then cheap. Not that I would anticipate such a rise; not that such a rise would or could take place, because free labour would speedily create capital for itself; but I mention it preparatory to entering upon a consideration of the propriety of trades' societies vesting their money in the purchase and improvement of land.

Suppose, then, that a society having twenty thousand pounds at its disposal purchases a thousand acres of land, by paying ten thousand pounds down and five hundred a year, or five per cent., upon the remaining ten thousand pounds as rent; and supposing seventy pounds is required for building a suitable house upon every four acres: as the thousand acres would be subdivided into two hundred and fifty farms, it would require seventeen thousand five hundred pounds to erect the necessary buildings; obliging them to raise seven thousand five hundred pounds to add to the ten thousand pounds remaining after the purchase-money. If we add to this ten pounds capital for each to begin with, we would require two thousand five hundred pounds more, making altogether a capital of thirty thousand pounds expended, and five hundred a-year, equal to ten thousand pounds more, payable in rent – in all forty thousand pounds. For such a house and four acres of ground they would receive fifteen pounds a-year, and it would be a very moderate rent. For this they would have expended forty thousand pounds, and would receive annually three thousand seven hundred and fifty pounds, or fifteen pounds a-year for each farm of the two hundred and fifty; so that it would leave them over nine per cent. interest for the capital expended; while each small farmer would have a good house with the requisite quantity of out-offices, four acres of ground, and ten pounds in hand, for fifteen pounds a-year, a rent which the milk of one cow would more than pay.

The farmer, guaranteed in such a holding for ever, would have no difficulty in raising the required amount for furnishing his house, and supplying himself with the necessary stock. If a division of labour is considered good, a division of capital must be also good; and in order to relieve this plan from all ambiguity or difficulty, the act of purchasing may be confined to the trades' society, while possession, with a lease, would insure competition amongst capitalists in the erection of the necessary buildings, and for which the land and labour would always constitute more than an ample security. However, in the performance of any great undertaking it will be necessary that suitable machinery should be put in motion, and if I shall have been in any way instrumental in leading to the invention of new machinery, or the improvement of the old, for working out so desirable an object, I shall have fully discharged my portion of the duty, and all that I have to desire is, that those who are sceptical or obstinate will well weigh the proposed system as a whole, rather than at once damn it from their ignorance of any part of it, or their personal dislike of the author.

The public mind is now strongly leaning on the hope of change of some sort or other, while two plans only are proposed by the leaders of public opinion. The one is, to insure high wages, cheap bread, and plenty to do, by what is called such an extension of trade as would render the employment of all our surplus population profitable to the master manufacturers as producers, and also to the Exchequer as consumers. The other is, a scheme of colonization, or of locating the population made surplus by machinery upon the lands of foreign countries, in the hope that their colonial dependency upon England will make them profitable consumers of the produce of their brother slaves. Now, these are the two plans; the one free trade, contended for by the manufacturer: the other emigration, supported by the landlords. We have had so much discussion upon the question of free trade already, that I shall abstain from further remark upon that subject, and shall say merely a word upon the subject of emigration, and the purposes which it is intended to serve. I have been obliged, and most reluctantly so, to mix up a little of politics in this work, and I am again compelled to do so, in order to reconcile the anomaly of agricultural labour being patronized by English landlords when applied to the improvement of the land in British colonies; while they use all and every means, in conjunction with the master manufacturers, for substituting artificial for manual labour at home.

The strong hope with which landlords and manufacturers rely upon commerce with our colonial dependencies, arising altogether out of the improved state of agriculture in these colonies, must at once convince every man of the value of an improved state of agriculture; while the same circumstance must lead all men to enquire wherefore it is that agriculture, to which so much importance is attached, firstly, as a means of employing our surplus hands; and, secondly, as a means of creating a market for our artificial produce, should be so much neglected at home. Would not the rational man suppose, that if the labour of an Englishman, expended in Australia, the Canadas, or New Brunswick, would be beneficial to England, the labour of the same man, if expended in an English county, would be still more beneficial? And if he arrives, as I have done, to the conclusion that it would be so, he will then naturally ask why it is not encouraged? and this is the question which I shall answer. It is not encouraged, because our strong government at home can hold our weak colonists in subjection; whereas, if the land was opened as a free-labour market at home, the English labourer would very speedily discover his own value, and once having arrived at a knowledge of that fact, he would demand such protection for it, as would ensure him in the possession, not of such portion as may be spared to him after the wants of an idle aristocracy are supplied, but in the full enjoyment of the whole, after his just contribution towards the maintenance of such institutions as were necessary for the protection of his rights and privileges.

The aristocracy of this country, that is the owners of land and the owners of money, will try every shift and device before they will allow Englishmen the means of judging of the real value of their labour; and the land being the only market in which the standard can be established, from that they will exclude them until tempted or bullied; and, as I prefer temptation to intimidation, I have suggested the plan by which the former may by carried into effect. One thing must be always borne in mind; it is, that although the prejudices of a class may be clubbed and united against the people, nevertheless their power, if clubbed and united, may be made the means of destroying and breaking down the strongest union of their opponents. For instance, the landlord who has an estate to sell, will not allow his prejudice to operate against his interest, and he ceases to be a member of the landed union the moment that he is tempted by a union of the popular funds to estrange his property. Thus I have shown, firstly, that the landlords are opposed to the subdividing system, because the possession of social comfort leads to a demand for political power; and, secondly, I have shown how the union of the working classes, if complete, would break down the prejudices and the strongest union of the landlord class.

It is very probable that my readers may consist, for the most part, of the working classes, many of whom will bear in mind the fact, that now for more than nine years I have endeavoured to instil into their minds the great power they possess. I have shown them upon more than one occasion the position that they might very easily acquire, by husbanding a certain amount of their wages annually. I have explained how the labourers, in a few years, may become possessed of the whole Church property of the country, or of any other description of property, in the purchase of which they chose to invest their funds. The mere gratification of a whim is one thing, and their capability is another thing; – the last I shall treat of.

Suppose, then, that five millions of the industrious classes of this country, and under which head I class small shopkeepers and tradesmen, were to save the sum of two shillings per week, it would amount to more than twenty-five millions per annum and would purchase one million two hundred and fifty thousand acres of land of more than an average quality, and which, if subdivided into farms of four acres each, would make three hundred and twelve thousand five hundred allotments, and, allowing five to a family, would support in affluence one million five hundred and sixty-two thousand five hundred persons upon the land, while it would create a population of professional men, shopkeepers and trades, of at least one-fifth of that amount, or three hundred and twelve thousand five hundred, making in the whole a happy community of nearly two millions; returning an interest of nine per cent. for the capital expended, and creating surplus produce over consumption, or, in other words, leaving for expenditure in the artificial market the sum of THIRTY-ONE MILLIONS TWO HUNDRED AND FIFTY THOUSAND POUNDS ANNUALLY; made up of one hundred pounds worth produced annually by each farmer. I am not so extravagantly enthusiastic as to look for anything like such a fulfilment of my plan, and I merely state the fact for the purpose of showing that the amount of money paid for the support of a state church, a standing army, and useless navy, in one year, would purchase land enough for ever to make one-seventh of the population happy for ever, to leave nine per cent. interest for the capital expended, and over thirty-one millions annually for expenditure in the artificial market. If we had expended what was unjustly paid to the West India planters for the manumission of their slaves in locating our own slaves upon our own land, England would by this time have been the happiest, richest, and greatest nation upon the face of the earth.

Before I propose the machinery for carrying out my scheme, I beg leave to submit the following simple facts, authenticated by ample authority, and the reader having full power to satisfy himself by an application to the parties referred to. In the *Labourer's Friend Magazine*, I find the following account, which I submit to the reader whole and entire.

CHEAP FOOD AND GOOD WAGES.

The following extraordinary instance of what may be accomplished by spade husbandry has been furnished by a correspondent who took the particulars himself from Samuel Bridge, in the presence of another gentleman, steward to a nobleman, and we have his authority for saying he will be happy to answer any enquiries our friends may wish to make on the statement he has given.

Samuel Bridge, of Stock Green, near Feckenham, in the county of Worcester, has occupied four acres of very inferior stiff clay land, on the blue lias, for twenty-seven years. He grows two acres of wheat and two acres of potatoes every year, and sells all his produce, even his wheat straw. The stubble from the wheat, and the tops from the potatoes, serve to bed down his pigs, and the manure from this source, and from his privy, is all that he gets for the use of his farm.

The crops obtained are not at all extraordinary for the result of spade husbandry; but it is very extraordinary that such crops, with so little manure, and from bad land, could have been obtained for a quarter of a century together; and, coupling the duration of the operation with the quality of the land, it must be admitted that nothing more is needed to prove the superiority of the spade system over the plough system; for although the same crops are obtained by the plough on good land, it is quite certain that the plough would fail to compete with the spade on equal qualities of soil.

The produce obtained on the average of a quarter of a century, by this exemplary man, is twelve tons of potatoes per acre, and forty bushels of wheat per acre, and the following account may be taken as a close approximation to the truth:

Sold annually –

		£	s	d
24 tons of potatoes, at 2l. 10s. per ton		£60	0	0
80 bushels of wheat, at 7s.		28	0	0
4 tons of wheat straw, at 50s.		10	0	0
		£98	0	0

Deduct as under –

	£	s	d			
Manual wages, 4l. 6s. 4d. per acre per annum.	£17	5	4			
Seed potatoes for two acres	5	0	0			
4 bushels of seed wheat (being dibbled) at 7s. 6d.	1	10	0			
				23	15	4
Subject to rent and parochial payments				£74	4	8

It may be safely stated that the average of all the land in England, under cultivation, does not yield 5l. per acre gross produce, and also that 20s. per acre per annum is more than is paid in manual wages; whereas, in this case, of very inferior land, above 28l. per acre gross produce is obtained, and 4l. 6s. 4d. per acre per annum paid in manual wages; or, in other words, you get by the spade, on small allotments, near six times as much produce, and employ four times as many people, as by the plough.

It is only necessary to add, that this useful member of society has bought his four acres of land many years since, and paid for it out of his savings. He has also built himself a comfortable cottage and out-buildings thereon, and is the owner of considerable property besides.

It should be mentioned also, that, during two years of the period of twenty-seven years, Samuel Bridge got his land ploughed gratis by his neighbours, but found the injury so great by the treading of the horses, that he reverted to the spade, and says it answers his purpose better to pay for digging than to have it ploughed gratis.

If that extract, authenticate as we must suppose it to be, and bearing the very strongest marks of truth, while it is rated much under what might be produced from it by a complete system, does not open the reader's eyes, I cannot hope to make much impression by mere assertion borne out by practice. It will be seen that the gross amount set down is 98*l*., while the potatoe crop is estimated at an immoderately low rate. That, further, from 98*l*. is deducted the price of labour which Bridge appears to hire, having by his industry acquired an honourable title to that ease which he has honourably purchased. It will be seen that the labour expended upon those four acres is only estimated at 4*l*. 6*s*. 4*d*. per acre, or 17*l*. 5*s*. 4*d*. upon the whole four acres; and the consequence is a restriction to two crops, the one wheat, being not of one-third part the value of several others which may be produced, while I allow the expenditure of an able-bodied labourer's work every day in the year upon the four acres, and also make allowance for the assistance of his wife and children in such labour as they should be engaged in; so that if we take the calculation of Bridge thus, we find that the profit upon 17*l*. 5*s*. 4*d*. worth of labour amounts to about 70*l*., leaving 4*l*. 4*s*. 8*d*. for rent, which is more than, from the description of his land, we are warranted in setting it down at. Bridge, it will be found, sells all his straw and relies upon labour as a substitute. He sells his potatoes instead of consuming them and returning the manure to the ground, and yet, allowing his labour to be worth three shillings a day, or say a pound a week for seventeen weeks' labour in the year, he receives 90*l*. over and above rent, rates, taxes, and seed, or nearly one pound a day for every day's labour expended.

In holding up Bridge's industry and success I must be careful, however, in cautioning the reader to receive the account as a mere comparison between the best large farm system and the worst small farm system. The best large farmer in England, say cultivating a thousand acres, could not make a profit of 22*l*. 10*s*. an acre, or 22,500*l*. a year of the thousand acres, while it would be impossible to practice a more injurious system than that followed by Bridge, and by which it appears he has nearly a hundred a year for about a hundred and twelve days labour. The facts narrated, however, fully bear me out in two important assertions – the first is, that upon each farm there may be produced more than a sufficiency of manure for its most perfect cultivation by the application of labour, and, secondly, that, by a very few years' industry, the working farmer has it in his power to purchase any quantity of land that he is able to cultivate to advantage by his own labour. It appears that Bridge has refused to allow his land to be ploughed for nothing, and that when ploughed the crops fell off; and it also appears that, by his own industry, he has become possessed of considerable property, whereas, had he confined himself to the growth of only one acre of wheat, one acre of potatoes, and the remainder to the production of green crops, and had he not sold his produce raw, he might by this time, that is, at the end of twenty-seven years, if he is a single man, have purchased two hundred and fifty acres of land and more, worth one pound an acre for ever.

I shall now proceed to put the reader in possession of the machinery by which I hope to see my plan carried into full effect, and my object shall be to divest it of all those drawbacks which I have mentioned in the beginning of this chapter, as being calculated to dishearten working men from entering into any specula-tion. If, however, I can inspire them with a belief in my plan, and confidence in the machinery for carrying it into effect, I have the most thorough conviction that in one year from the date of its commencement, such a universal feeling of surprize, delight, and satisfaction would be the result, as was never felt by the working classes of this or any other country.

MACHINERY FOR WORKING THE SMALL FARM PLAN.

All those who have been in favour of the allotment-system, and those who have recommended attention to the land, in a sweeping or particular manner, as well as those who have experienced disappointment from the bad working of any partial system that has been tried, and that has failed, will exclaim, Oh! we have seen all this before, and it has failed. However, I must observe in the outset that a principle must be tried before it is condemned, and in order to its fair trial, it is indispensable that it should be worked with its own, and not with machinery conveniently borrowed from another principle. Now, such is the complaint that I have to make, such are the reasons for my asserting that the plan has never yet been even tried. It has been so mixed up with prejudices, follies, and absurdities, of one sort or another, that everything like fair trial has been prevented. I will state some of the causes that have hitherto operated against the success of all those experiments that have been made, and, as a sweeping illustration, I may direct attention to the great dissatisfaction caused by the failure of the co-opera-tive store system.[1]

That system was an approximation to the community-of-labour principle; and from the fact of its investing one man or a committee of men, with power over the property of other men, it failed to possess that invigorating spirit of self-inter-est so essential to the success of any undertaking. The fellow-feeling, or *esprit de corps*, considered so necessary for holding individuals together in one common cause, actuated by one common feeling, and leading to one common object, is an essential to the well-being of that community, consisting of individuals having one common interest. If, however, a disparity exists between individuals, that want of fellowship fails of giving to the body that individuality of feeling so nec-essary to its existence.

---

1 Referring in particular to the labour exchange movement of 1832–3.

I have framed my plan, then, after long and mature deliberation, with a view to the removal of those several difficulties which have hitherto stood in the way of fair trial. I cannot, for the life of me, be brought to believe that a hundred men clubbing their labour will feel as strong an interest in the general undertaking as they would individually feel if each man relied upon his own resources, and enjoyed the undivided fruits of his own labour. For instance, I feel convinced that a community consisting of one hundred men, occupying four acres each, would be a more contented body, a more industrious body, and a more united body, than a hundred individuals located upon the same four hundred acres, managed by the master minds of the whole body; while the community of self-acting individuals would have the advantage of the superior knowledge and skill of the master minds of their body. I believe that in what is called the community-principle, improvement is likely to stop or flag at that point at which moderate comfort is insured; whereas it goes on to the extreme limit to which it can be pushed, if impelled by individual emulation.

I am quite prepared to justify and to recommend the co-operative system of labour with individual responsibility and possession – thus suppose twenty occupiers of four acres each to constitute a section of a district community, and suppose the season for performing any particular work should last for twenty days, and that the performance of that work would take the labour of one individual for twenty days, or the labour of twenty individuals for one day: again, suppose of the twenty individuals the harvest of some is ready while that of others is unripe, in such case those whose harvest is likely to be late will give their labour to those whose harvest is ready, thereby enhancing the value of their own labour, not immediately required, to that amount which it would be worth at the highest price, having insured, by the exchange, the labour of their neighbour at the moment when his assistance will be of the greatest value. This makes his labour, not particularly valuable to himself, of its full value when required by the man whose harvest is ripe, and makes the return equally valuable when his own is ready for the sickle.

In the case of the twenty men clubbing their labour to take advantage of the season – suppose in planting potatoes – there, each farmer has his whole work done in one day, instead of being twenty days at it, while it is all done within the prescribed season. It may be said, yes, but one poor fellow has to wait till the last; well, suppose he has, it would be so in community; for allowing that the same number in community had the same number of acres under potatoes, the last acre that was planted would represent that of the man whose last acre was planted under the co-operative system. Again, if the clubbing of twenty would be too precarious, ten may limit the work to two days, and thus vary the system, and as I have no doubt that the necessity for such a co-operation would very speedily manifest itself, the arrangement for carrying it into perfect practice would be made by those parties to whom it would be an advantage.

I attach something of a more limited definition to the term 'home,' than the mere politician, and would rather prefer that limitation which the poet assigns to it. I do not think that 'country' designates a man's home. I do not think that a compulsory residence in any part of that country constitutes what the poet calls 'home, sweet home.'[1] I think home means a residence in the selection of which man has something like a choice, and for that reason I have always objected to the necessity under which the community-system compels strangers to migrate from different parts of the country to one common habitation.

As I never speak at an abuse, having, I trust, the manliness to attack it openly if it requires exposure, and as my remarks under this head may be supposed to be directed against the plan put into practice by Mr Owen,[2] I beg leave in the outset to state, without giving any opinion of the social principle, that I look upon the experiments made by Mr Owen for the improvement of the physical condition of all classes of society, but more especially the working classes, as having far exceeded in utility those of any other individual who has ever lived before him. It is all very fair for those who differ from Mr Owen upon questions of religion, to hold up his peculiar notions upon that subject to such contempt as can be enlisted against them; while it would be sycophancy of the vilest order to reject his plans for social improvement, because his religious opinions do not square with the notions of other men. I very much prefer the community-principle as practised by Mr Owen, to the present system; while I very much prefer the co-operative system, with individual responsibility and possession to the community principle.

A healthy state of body is indispensable to a healthy state of mind. A diseased body will lead to a disordered mind. A healthy body will lead to a vigorous mind, and as I believe religion, pure religion, can stand investigation, give me the man who will best prepare the human mind for that state wherein it will be best able to judge for itself. One object, then, that I have in view is, to give to every member of society some choice in the selection of his home; and for that purpose I propose a general plan for the management of the general principle, while I would so arrange its details that a Yorkshireman should not, in compliance with the principle, be dragged to Cornwall, or the Cornishman to Cumberland, or *vice versa*.

For this purpose I shall first develope the general machinery, by which I propose to put the whole plan in motion, and I shall then explain by what means the benefits may be most pleasingly and advantageously administered to the subscribers. I have already explained the mode of administering the funds; I shall now enter upon a consideration of that subject which is of even more importance. If any one circumstance more than another has tended to the uncontrolled power of the few, it has been owing to the total want of confidence upon the part of the working classes for the proper direction of their strength, and the proper, just and honest administration of their funds.

If all those political leaders who were with the people in 1839 had remained true to their own pledges, the working classes would have achieved their rights

---

1 From the opera, *Clari*, by John Howard Payne.

2 Robert Owen (1771–1858), socialist philanthropist and factory reformer, who aimed to creative 'home colonies' of co-operative industry and agriculture with property owned in common.

before this time. If the several managers of the people's funds had at all times given a satisfactory account of their appropriation, the people would have *purchased* their liberty long since; and even yet it is not too late, nor can I blame the oft-burned sufferers for that caution, which, as politicians and contributors to funds, they have recently manifested. In the hope, however, to inspire them with confidence, and to attach responsibility where character is the security, I propose the following as the plan for insuring the safe custody and proper appropriation of the poor people's pence. I propose,

That Thomas Duncombe,[1] Esq., Sharman Crawford,[2] Esq., and John Fielden,[3] Esq. shall constitute a Finance Committee.

That a Treasurer shall be appointed, with an allowance of £2 per week to pay a Secretary, whose whole time shall be devoted to the furtherance of the plan, and to pay postage.

That each town where there are subscribers shall have a committee of three, whose duty it shall be to receive the weekly subscriptions on Saturday and having received them, they shall, by that night's post, transmit them to the general treasurer in London; and, upon failure of so doing, that the Treasurer report such failure to some person who shall be appointed by the body of subscribers for that purpose.

That the general treasurer, in acknowledging the receipt of the week's subscription, shall transmit a notice, from one of the finance committee, to the committee residing in the town from whence the subscriptions came, to the effect that their monies, together with all others, have been deposited in the Bank of England, to the joint credit of the Trustees and Treasurer, and whose signatures will be required for drawing out the funds.

That the whole amount received on Monday in each week shall be published, and stated to be lodged, as per receipt, in some daily paper, published on Tuesday, setting forth the gross amount received from each town, and thereby enabling the subscribers throughout the country to have the earliest information as to the receipt and disposal of their funds.

That the whole list of subscriptions be also published weekly in the *Northern Star* – that is the amount sent from each town; thereby affording the several subscribers a double opportunity of comparing the acknowledgment of the general treasurer with the account of the local committee.

I propose that no officer, with the exception of the Secretary, shall receive any salary, with the exception of the Solicitor, who shall be paid his taxed bill of costs for any legal services which may be required, such as investigating title of land about to be purchased and such like.

As the duties of the local committee will be very trifling, they should not receive any salary; and good men will be always found ready to discharge the

---

1 Thomas Slingsby Duncombe (1796–1861), radical MP for Hertford 1826, 1830, 1831, and Finsbury 1834, who presented the Chartist Petition in 1842.

2 William Sharman Crawford (1781–1861), MP for Rochdale 1841–52.

3 John Fielden (1784–1849), MP for Oldham 1833, 1835, 1837, 1841, and factory reformer.

duties, care being taken that they should be chosen from amongst the largest subscribers, and that a guarantee be given conjointly by the whole three that any defalcation in their weekly account shall be made up out of the monies that they themselves have subscribed as individuals.

The accounts to be published under a general head and a district head – a county constituting a district – and all the funds subscribed within that district to be appropriated to the purchase of land within that county, and to be distributed, as I have already described, to subscribers to that particular fund. For instance, to avoid the inconvenience or disinclination that a Cornishman may be placed under if compelled to go to land purchased in Cumberland, and with a view of locating as many as possible in their own counties; all the monies subscribed to the Lancashire fund would be appropriated to the purchase of land in that county, and would be distributed amongst the subscribers.

However, as our manufacturing system has led to the wanderings of those of one county to another county, and many if not all, of whom would wish to go home, suppose a Dorsetshire man, working at Manchester, he may subscribe at Manchester to the Dorsetshire or any other fund, and thus have all the advantages that he would derive from having subscribed in his own locality.

I would further propose that two or more counties may have the privilege of borrowing from each other; for instance, suppose Lancashire, Cheshire, Nottinghamshire, and Derbyshire, were not any of them in condition to purchase an estate offered for sale in one of those counties – in such case I would suggest that the Finance Committee, the Treasurer, and one member from each of the local Committees of counties so situated, should constitute a body in such emergency for the purpose of making the most of circumstances, by aiding a purchase in one county by a loan from other counties, giving such security for the reimbursement as shall not only be satisfactory, but conveniently available to those subscribers who have lent it.

Now, I will explain what I mean; suppose Lancashire to have a fund of £20,000; Cheshire of £3,000; Nottingham of £7,000; Derbyshire of £5,000; and Cumberland of £5,000; making in all £40,000; and suppose an estate in Lancashire was worth forty thousand pounds, in such case loans may be made from those other counties for the purchase of the Lancashire estate, and, possession being the great thing, no distribution should take place of the Lancashire estate until Lancashire had repaid the amount borrowed, which would be done out of the growing funds. Upon the other hand, suppose Cheshire subscribers, with their £3,000, could purchase an estate for £10,000, funds may be advanced by other counties, holding the Cheshire estate in trust and undistributed, until the debt was discharged.

This precaution of not distributing the estate would be necessary as a means of guarding against any fraud; for instance, if Lancashire got an advance of £20,000, and immediately proceeded to the distribution of the property, the subscriptions would cease; the most fortunate would be in possession of the land, and the lenders would never get back their money; and, further, holding the estate in trust until the whole purchase money was paid would be necessary for the protection of those parties who may draw money-prizes in the lottery.

I shall now explain the great service that such a system would render to the general purpose. I presume, and indeed I feel convinced, that every district would be able to purchase a large amount of land every year; while, by this plan, Manchester, or any other county, may purchase a large estate at the end of three months; all liabilities upon which would be discharged by subscriptions for the remaining nine months at the end of the year; and I presume that no trustees can have better security for the repayment of monies, than the certainty of subscribers continuing to pay up their subscriptions for an estate which had been purchased, and to all benefit of which they would forfeit all claim, in the event of failing to pay up their subscriptions.

The reader will see that my whole plan is arranged with the view of preventing fraud, or of leading to such an immediate discovery of it as would render it as harmless as possible; to an economical mode of managing the affairs of the society, and to a saving of one shilling of incidental expences.

As a matter of course, the most perfect, and legal, and satisfactory arrangements would be made to prevent anything like a failure of the plan, and to insure the speediest results from its operation. Under the controul that I have mentioned, I shall most cheerfully act the part of Receiver of Weekly Subscriptions, and shall deposit them as soon as received, publishing the amount, as I have already proposed, while I shall see to the complete performance of all the required duties by a Secretary, who will be responsible to me, and whose time will be at my disposal. In the event of my being absent from London it will be necessary to appoint a Sub-Treasurer, who would supply my place while absent, and the person most fit should be decided upon by the Committee of Finance.

The plan is now before the people, and the material questions for their consideration are, Firstly, do they believe in its practicability? Secondly, if practicable and carried out, do they believe in its efficiency as a means of redressing the present national complaint, and of preventing its reappearance? Thirdly, have they confidence in the persons whom I have named as trustees of their funds? And, Fourthly, would they consider the risk of the loss of twenty-six shillings sufficiently compensated for; firstly, by the chances of remuneration presented; and, secondly, by the removal of a portion of the surplus-made population of idlers? I shall say just a word under each of those heads.

Firstly: do they believe in its practicability? Perhaps the wholly uninstructed will delay answering this question, until I shall have located a peasant upon four acres of ground, and shall have laid down easy rules for its management, explained its capabilities, and have shown the returns, after the expenditure of one man's labour; while, for the present, I may direct the attention of such persons to the account of Samuel Bridge, which I believe to be well authenticated; and further add from myself, not only that I believe, but that I have not a shadow of doubt, that any moderately industrious labouring man will be able to purchase for ever that amount of land which he can cultivate well by his own labour in less than three years, and without abridging a single one of his comforts for that time.

Further, I am confident that an industrious man, by three hundred days' moderate labour in each year, with a lease for ever, can feed himself, and lay up, after good living, good clothing, and payment of rent, rates, taxes, and casualties, more than one hundred and fifty pounds. In fact, I am ready to hazard the fate of my plan upon the success of the experiment; and, with the view of testing it, it is my intention to locate a good, honest, industrious labouring man upon four acres of ground, which for three years I will give him rent free, and supply him with the required capital, and if that man is not worth four hundred and fifty pounds, over and above all charges and liabilities, at the end of three years, I will allow that I am a fool, and turn corn-law repealer.

Secondly: if practicable and carried out, do they believe in its efficiency as a means of redressing the present national complaint, and of preventing its reappearance. While my observations under the first head are also strictly applicable under this head, I may further add, that surely, even admitting many disadvantages, it furnishes many fascinations to all those who are now idle, or only partially employed. Firstly, the chance of being provided for; or, if not successful in that respect, of supplying the place of those who have been.

Thirdly: have they confidence in the persons I have named as Trustees of their funds? Under this head I have only to observe, that in Mr Duncombe, Mr Crawford, and Mr Fielden, I have the most unlimited confidence; and, I believe, the working classes have the same confidence in me. However, observing that rule of law, which presumes the necessity of treating every man as if he was a rogue, I have limited the power of the officers to commit fraud, if inclined, to that point which would render the fund comparatively trifling, and lead to its immediate detection. But I can go further, and render the Treasurer a responsible officer, without leaving it in his power to commit one single act of peculation. Thus, the Trustees may open an account with the Bank, and the monies may be sent from the several districts direct to the banker, to the credit of the Trustees; while the Treasurer would be able to publish the balance sheet each week from the banker's accounts, just the same as if he had deposited the monies himself; and, in truth, this latter plan I very much prefer, as it will relieve me at once from the necessity of dabbling in any way with public funds; while it will also do away with the necessity or reposing confidence in a sub-treasurer during my absence from London.

Moreover, I should think the time of a Secretary would be sufficiently occupied in corresponding with the several district committees, while our lodgements would be large enough to make it worth the while of a banker to keep a clerk, if necessary, whose sole business it would be to attend to the affairs of the society, while he would have no power of touching the cash. But of all things we must take care and make the Bank of England our bank of deposit, for I can well imagine the temptation that it would be to an honest *firm* to fail, with a million of the people's money, just as their trustees were about to vest it in the purchase of estates; and I can easily suppose the feeling of indignation which would naturally exist in the minds of those who were ruined or disappointed by my indiscretion.

Further, the security required from the district Treasurers would make it not worth their while to commit fraud; while the publication of the weekly receipts would put it out of their power to repeat it, as it would be discovered upon the first attempt, and within the first week.

Fourthly. Would they consider the risk of the loss of twenty-six shillings sufficiently compensated for; – firstly, by the chances of remuneration presented; and, secondly, by the removal of a portion of the surplus-made population of idlers? As the observations under this head are most applicable to the poorest class of subscribers, to whom twenty-six shillings would be of great importance; arising, firstly, from the want of employment; secondly, from the probability of being unable to continue their subscriptions, and thereby forfeit what had been paid; I shall make a comment or two, with particular reference to such members, both as to the importance of the amount, and the possibility of loss, from inability to keep up the subscription.

I believe, then, that the very poorest working man spends much more than twenty-six shillings a year, or sixpence a week, and many, more than five times that amount, in tobacco or drink of one kind or other, and if he prefers the enjoyment of those luxuries, as he may term them, to the prospect of being moderately able to enjoy them in after life by one year's abstinence, I should say that he well merited that calamity which, knowingly, stupidly, viciously, and sinfully he had brought upon himself and his innocent family. But as it is a maxim of even our bloody laws, that it is better that ninety-and-nine criminals should escape punishment than that one innocent person should unjustly suffer, so in our regard for the interest of the virtuous who may be rendered poor from circumstances over which they had no control, we are compelled, in justice towards them, to enact a general law which would equally save the vicious from loss, arising out of their own wickedness.

This healing law may be established as follows: – All shareholders should be entitled to transfer their shares to a purchaser for the exact amount paid up, and no more, to prevent gambling upon the eve of the annual distribution of prizes, whereby an act framed for the special protection of the weak may be turned to the advantage of the wily and strong. A clause should be inserted, giving the trustees the first option of purchasing up the shares, in order that it may be used for the protection of the society, if it should ever happen that a few middle class men should attempt to consolidate the national fund, by purchasing up a number of shares; which, however, I would further provide against, by not allowing any man to have more than one share, be it large or be it small, be it sixpence a week or a pound a week, allowing each at the same time a chance for every share paid up, according to the general standard; that is, if there were a million subscribers, and if the general standard of subscription was sixpence a week, the man who paid sixpence would, at the end of the year, have one chance; the man who paid a shilling would have two chances; and the man who paid a pound would have forty chances; and quite right they should; while, if there was so large a number of subscribers of different classes, it might be a question whether or not a classification of subscribers would not be prudent, that is, that all from five shillings and upwards should be thrown into one class, and from sixpence to five shillings into another class, preserving the graduated scale of distribution according to the amounts subscribed, as I have before explained. Or it may happen that a more extensive classification may be deemed prudent; however, that would be all matter for after consideration, in the arrangement of which the people themselves would have most interest, and all the power. Further, I would suggest the propriety of a clause compelling the Trustees to return subscriptions, at any time that they may be demanded, to those who are too poor to continue them; and, for this reason, it is but a simple act of justice to the unwilling defaulter, while it commits no injustice against any member of the society.

Now, I have been particular, most particular, in anticipating every objection that malice or ingenuity may bring against my plan. I have, and I rejoice at it, hit upon an expedient whereby I can discharge the most onerous duty without other responsibility than that which, I trust, will ever attach to any service of mine in the people's cause; while I have relieved myself from any dabbling with the people's money; and while I further have it in my power to render those services gratuitously, thereby leaving the undiminished treasure of the poor to be administered free from peculation for their own sole use, behoof, and benefit.

I have now entered into a general consideration of those means by which I hope and trust to render myself an extensive benefactor to the human race. If I am allowed to proceed, I shall take care so to fence the interest of my clients by all that legal protection so necessary for their preservation; while, in the watching over their interests, in the administration of their resources, and in the direction of their capabilities, I shall exert my every faculty to make the plan as available as human ingenuity, energy, perseverance, attention, and honesty will admit of. My plan differs from all others in the one great essential, namely, the funds cannot be dissipated by officers, committees, directors, managers, and lawyers; it must be applied whole and entire to those purposes for which it is subscribed.

If, then, the people themselves have confidence in those whom I have selected as their trustees; if they believe in the capabilities of the land, and in the value of their own labour when unrestrictedly applied for their own benefit; if they believe in the necessity of some plan for meeting and arresting the increasing influence of capitalists in the artificial market; if they have a desire to have a fair day's wage for a fair day's work; to live independently upon their own resources; to be free, without that freedom trenching upon the rights of others, while it will limit and ultimately destroy the peculation and injustice of their oppressors; if they can abstain from pernicious luxuries, that they may be enabled to purchase virtuous enjoyment; if they see, as I see, the means of egress from the land of bondage; I would implore them to follow me, and I will lead them from their present sinking and degraded state by purchasing their freedom, or I will originate such an opposition and aversion in the minds of their oppressors as will place them in a situation to achieve that deliverance by force which was refused to justice, and for which they were willing to pay.

Let those, then, who are tired of slavery raise the standard of freedom in their several localities; let the necessary arrangements be made forthwith; let subscriptions commence; and let the motto be, – 'Englishmen so loved peace, and abhorred bloodshed, that they have resolved upon buying their liberties, and woe be unto those who refuse the just price of their redemption.'

POPULATION – ITS APPLICATION.

Although the working classes, for whose benefit I write, have come to the conclusion that what is called the surplus-population of this country does not consist of a surplus beyond what the country, if properly governed, would support; yet it will be necessary for them to be armed at all points against the sophistries of free-traders, by which they may be led to a belief that a repeal of the Corn-laws would do for them as much and more than I propose; while such change could be acquired by a simultaneous demand, in which the only labour imposed upon the working classes would be, to shout, to cheer, to defy, and, if necessary, to threaten revolution.

Now, changes achieved by those easy means always present fascinations in proportion to the labour required for their accomplishment, and in a vicious state of society, with an uninformed people to contend against, I should have but slight hope in the success of a plan which proposes some delay accompanied with purchase money, when compared with the more fascinating mode that I have stated above. However, as I have an enlightened public mind to deal with, and as that mind has discovered that changes brought about upon a sudden, and by violence, are seldom productive of lasting benefit, and never to that extent vouched for by the leaders of excitement, I have a confidence in the steady exertions of the whole people in behalf of their own order. When we consider the vast resources of this country, and think of a large portion of the working classes being in a state of absolute beggary, while the cultivation of those resources would confer happiness upon all, I feel myself justified in digressing now and then from the practice of agriculture to a consideration of those means by which alone society can be restored to its proper position.

The great difference that exists between the leaders of the three political parties who now contend for power is this: the Whigs and the Tories differ but little in their political notions, indeed no further than in the belief each have in their own power of making ends meet. Neither has got any defined or distinct plan to propose as a permanent remedy for those grievances the existence of which is admitted by all. In their own councils there is division, hesitation, and disunion; while in the Chartist body there is now a perfect union of political sentiment, and a thorough belief in the one remedy for all their grievances. That remedy, however, being one which presents so great a change, all classes with anything to protect oppose its progress, not from any doubt that can be justly entertained towards it as a means of benefitting the working classes, but from a foolish apprehension that such change would lead to the confiscation of that property amassed under the old system. These prejudices naturally lead me into a discussion upon the merits of my plan, and, after fair and full investigation, I think it will be found that all the people contend for is the means of so increasing the productions of this country, as by increased produce, and an equitable distribution of it, to place themselves in a most independent position; while that independence could not possibly require the sacrifice of any other class.

Every man who casts his eye around and sees the uncultivated state of the land in every county in England, and who calculates the difference between its present state and that to which it might be brought, must at once confess that to such improvement we must ultimately look for escape. Those who have witnessed the pernicious system by which our mines, minerals, and fisheries, a large portion of our domestic resources, have been mismanaged, will at one see in a better system a means of providing for a large portion of our unemployed, system-made, surplus population. And here I must enter rather minutely into the indirect injury caused by machinery to those to whose trade it has not as yet been applied, and even to those for whose work it cannot be substituted. I shall consider it more with reference to the consumption of those articles which exclusively come under the head of home manufacture, and for the home market; and the supply of which is made for the most part by persons working upon their own account, constituting a valuable class of society, and whose poverty as a class is a great national calamity, and a much greater national evil, than the failure of a large capitalist, who, in whose own person, represents a body over which he has exclusive controul.

That there should be some rule by which the supply may be apportioned to the demand, is a fact which I presume even free-traders will admit. I shall now proceed to explain how machinery operates against those several trades, the work of which is not performed by machinery. No machinery has been applied to making shoes, and yet we find the shoemakers much distressed, if not more so than the manufacturing operatives, and why? because the operatives cannot afford to buy shoes, in consequence of the reduced state of their wages, caused by machinery; and, therefore, being no demand, there is no supply. The very same argument holds good in the case of tailors, for whose work no machinery has been invented. The same with regard to hats; and, indeed, if diminished wages leads to diminished consumption, it will be found that this malady not only affects those trades and classes who are nearest to the condition of the working people; but that it pervades all classes of society, even to the very payment of rents, and more especially the payment of ground rents for cottages left desolate by the removal of the operative to an underground cellar; a change brought about exclusively by the operation of machinery.

I think we may go even farther than merely arguing the relative effect that machinery has upon society at large, and trace it a little beyond those limits by which society is bounded. We then find that the malady enters into the Exchequer, and that the throne itself is not free from its infection, its symptoms being manifested in the obligation imposed upon the monarch for submitting to the payment of the Income Tax. Now, machinery, and machinery alone, has been the cause of this Queen-taxing necessity. Again, a man with a family and out of employment becomes a dangerous competitor in a market to which his labour has not been before brought. For instance, an able bodied operative, ousted by machinery, will look abroad for some other market for his labour; if he has never cleaned a horse, he may learn to clean a horse, and the owner of the horse will tolerate his incapacity in the beginning, if induced by a lower rate of wages; thus, if A is a horse-keeper, getting sixteen shillings a-week, and if B, an operative out of work, offers to do it for ten shillings a-week, the master will make allowances for the difference of skill, B will get the place, and will soon be as handy at his work as A, while the master will save six shillings a week by the change. So with light porters; so with colliers; so with ship carpenters, whose work is now for the most part done by apprentices, who receive little or no wages, and who can be very speedily instructed in much of the trade, and who, by the judicious mixing of a journeyman with three or four apprentices, become in a very short time not only competitors with, but monopolists of, the whole trade, while the masters make all the profit; a circumstance which, in my opinion, has led to the loss of very many vessels, and especially those built in Greenock, where the system of employing Highland trampers and Irish emigrants has been extensively practised. In short, literature, the arts, the sciences, trade, commerce, manufactures, agriculture, polite society, and the stability of government, all, one and all, depend upon the condition of the working classes, and their condition depends upon the profitable application of their own labour for their own benefit; the proceeds from that labour being the source from whence every other class must draw their means of support. Upon the other hand, the more extensive the inventions and improvements in machinery, under the small farm system, the greater would be the benefit to all classes in society, while against none could it be a competitor. The great aim and object therefore should be to apply labour to those purposes which will, firstly, make the labourer independent, and, secondly, to insure from his independence all those advantages which society is sure to derive from his improved condition. Let us hear no more then of foreign corn as the breakfast, dinner, and supper of the English slave; let every man who chooses to work have the power to place his own meal upon his own table from his own field, produced by his own labour. This will be a change in which all would have a benefit; while all others are but patchings, botchings, and mendings in the hope of 'MAKING THE THING LAST OUR TIME.'

Such, then, are the outlines of that plan by which I hope to do for the working classes what their rulers are not inclined to do; and, if inclined, what they could not accomplish. All the machinery by which any scheme calculated to improve the condition of the working classes must be arranged by themselves, and for their own sole benefit; while I am unfashionable enough to believe that the advantages derived by all other classes from their improvement, would increase in the same ratio, caused thereby in the condition of the working classes themselves.

In discussing questions of political economy, I can afford to admit the truth of several principles contended for by the disciples of Malthus;[1] so on questions of

---

1 T. R. Malthus (1766–1834), population theorist.

agriculture I can afford to admit the truth of the reasoning of many of my opponents; but those principles and truths so much depend upon system, that their supporters are only able to present them as a choice of evils, holding up opposing doctrines as dogmas, untried experiments, and dangerous innovations. This is not wonderful; because we find that any innovation upon ancient theory or long practice, is met in the cradle by the opposition of the striding giant 'custom,' until by perseverance the new light extinguishes the flame of prejudice; and then, wonder is expressed that we could have lived so long and so contentedly under the old system. My object, then, is to direct the public mind to the improvement of the most valuable of all our domestic resources, and to promote a love for the science of agriculture, through cultivation of which, as I have before observed, the greatness of England would be found to consist in an aggregate of happy individuals.

The comparative insignificance of the yearly value of the land, as compared with the value of that labour which would be required for its highest cultivation, at once establishes the great value of the land as a raw material; while the value of labour will be discovered in the surplus over rent which one man can produce from the cultivation of the exact amount that he is able to manage. Upon the other hand, land not being a raw material that can be brought into the artificial market for improvement, capital is not so likely to be invested in its manufacture as it is in the manufacture of other articles upon which extensive speculations are entered into. This is a reason why the capital of the country has been abstracted, during times of a pressing demand, from the cultivation of our own domestic resources. I rejoice, however, to find that the tariff of Sir Robert Peel, the wisest, the most statesman-like, the most comprehensive and patriotic measure ever proposed by a British minister, has had the effect of turning the eye of the landed proprietors to a consideration of the value of their own land, as compared with the land of other countries, and that it is leading them to the conviction that they have been too long dabbling in the wholesale market, and must, sooner or later, bring their wares into the retail market, and which can only be done, profitably, by presenting advantages to those who have a sufficient amount of capital, by which I mean labour, to insure a profitable return for such holdings as may conveniently come within their capability.

Nothing has gone further to open the eyes of the working classes to the value of English land than the great importance attached to the produce of the land of other countries. The most ignorant working man sees that he is able to accomplish for himself that which the free-traders propose to do for him by law. He knows that the cry is for wheat; that land, with the required expenditure of labour, produces wheat, and that there is under his nose, whichever way he turns, a sufficient quantity of land, if labour was applied to it, to make him independent of all foreigners. Hence, his thirst for wheat created by the League, has been changed into a thirst for land, from which wheat is produced. He has learned, also, that the great value attached to home-production is, that it opens a market for domestic industry, while it increases the demand for artificial productions.

As I have answered a question which sceptics may put to me, as to 'why political landlords do not bring their land into the retail market, and thereby considerably enhance its value?' I shall also anticipate a question which a freetrader may possibly ask, it is this: while I assert that the application of much labour to the cultivation of the land would considerably increase our home trade in artificial goods, the free-trader, or the half instructed, or wholly ignorant, may ask me, 'why, then, if such was likely to be the result, should manufacturers withhold their assistance from any plan calculated to increase their trade?' The answer, however, is easy and may be given thus. Although the domestic demand for manufactured goods may be five times as great as it is at present, yet the price of labour in the artificial market being regulated by its value in the natural market, would leave a less profit upon the increased demand than they have now, holding exclusive dominion over the slave-market, upon the lesser amount.

Having now developed the whole plan, and having commented upon it under several heads, and having assigned what, to me, appear good and sufficient reasons for the proposed change, I shall now proceed to the spirit of my work by showing man what he ought to be, and how he can be made so.

SMALL ALLOTMENTS.

As the practice of taking land and subdividing it into garden allotments is now being extensively acted upon in many parts of the country, and lest my system should be tested by the result, I desire to say a word or two by way of comment upon the difference between the two plans. I believe that there is no way in which the labourer will receive so much wages as from the application of his labour to the soil. Throughout all my writings upon the subject of labour and capital, it will be discernible that my sole object in giving up society, ease, comfort, and every enjoyment that a gentleman could desire, has been with a view to enable the workman to discover his real value in society, and that object can be only achieved by making him wholly independent, by placing him in such a situation as will invite him to industry. I fear, then, that the purchase of land by communities, with a view of expending hired labour upon it, would retard improvement, while it would fail of presenting an inducement for the expenditure of man's industry. In fact, after the fascinations of novelty had passed over, the community of original experimentalists would merge into a corporation of landlords.

I write against circumstances, and not against men; and I feel convinced that man can place no reliance whatever upon his fellow-man, or a community of men, when circumstances operate upon his or their minds, the influence and effect of which would be stronger than any abstract notions of justice. For instance, if a community of labouring men purchase a quantity of land, and hire labour for its cultivation, however just their intentions and pure their motives, they will nevertheless feel themselves justified in raising the price of the land, according to the improved value conferred upon it by the labour of the hired workman. This power of stealthily trenching upon the rights of others is one of the greatest disadvantages against which the labourer has to contend; and those hired by a community, at the end of twenty years would be in no better condition than they were at starting; while the community of proprietors would have increased the value of their property twenty fold; that is, they would have robbed those labourers, by whose industry the value was increased, of nineteen shillings in the pound.

In a previous chapter I have stated, that, in my opinion, a labourer can purchase for ever, any amount of land that he can cultivate to advantage in three years; but a labourer working for a community would not be able to purchase it at the end of twenty years; and it is, therefore, that I have thought it right to caution people against drafting any unfavourable conclusions upon the landed question from the community system, unless, indeed, those communities will grant leases for ever of such allotments as shall come within the scope of one man's capability, instead of hiring labour to give an improved value to their own land.

As I feel the necessity of inspiring the working classes with a thorough knowledge of their own power; and as I feel no apprehension of danger from the possession of all their rights, I shall devote a chapter to the consideration of their value, as compared with the value of all other classes of society.

VALUE OF LABOUR.

Of such great importance was the labourer in olden times, before his rights were trenched upon, and his place supplied by artificial power, that we find the statutes of old teeming with enactments for his protection. So minutely interwoven was the interest of the landlord and the workman, the master and the hand-loom weaver, the employer and employee of every description, that the complaint of the employed was sure to arrest the attention of the employer, and to receive that correction which their mutual interest demanded. In those days there was no poor laws, but as art became substituted for nature, that is, when Henry the Eighth deprived man of his natural title to the soil, man lost his position in society, his interest was separated from that of the capitalist, and the consequence was the introduction of a state provision, as a substitute for that which, if justice was done to him, the labourer would have insured for himself.

As this artificial system increased, feuds, jealousies, and dissensions also increased; until at length we find the whole of society cut up and subdivided into sectional interests, warring against each other, with completely separate interests, and foolishly relying upon an amalgamation of all, as a means of representation, and as the source of justice to all. The great disparity that this ascendancy of art has created between the several classes is now the cause of that increasing demand for popular representation. It has been truly said by one of the ablest writers, that in politics are included morality, religion, and instruction; how then is it possible to write a work, the object of which is to make the people moral, religious, and educated, without treating of politics.

However sorry I may be, then, or however I may regret that necessity which compels me to introduce politics into this little work, nevertheless I feel it indispensable to do so, as politics are the cause of all our present dissensions and disagreements, and as the severance of the interest of master and man has led to this angry political feeling; the whole contest now is for political power; while, formerly, the practical liberty enjoyed by the labourer, either with held all consideration of politics, or satisfied him with the amount of power which he possessed, arising chiefly out of the identity of interest which then existed between master and man. In those days, when there was no such thing as pauperism, there was no necessity that the right of appeal, in the shape of a petition, should be vested in those who had no votes; any injustice done to them was very speedily felt by their masters who had votes, and immediate correction followed the appearance of abuse.

When the right of petitioning was conceded, it was an implied admission that new differences were likely to spring up between electors and non-electors, and in the exact proportion in which we find the social interests of master and man separated, in the exact same ratio do we find the petitions of the non-electors against the acts proposed to be done by the representatives of the masters, neglected and despised; until at length so widely separated have those interests become by the improvement in artificial power, that the petitions of the people are now laughed at with the most contemptuous scorn. And however theorists, metaphysicians, historians, and speculating logicians may attempt to eulogise the beauties and perfections of the British Constitution, I defy them to disprove, however fine drawn their theories upon British liberty, yet has the English labourer lost every vestige of that practical freedom which he enjoyed under the implied contract that he had a right to live; that he was the first claimant upon the land; and that however his right was changed from actual possession to trusteeship; from trusteeship to parish relief; and from parish relief to commissioners' caprice; that nevertheless that original right was vested in him, and its reassumption in its original form is what he now contends for.

The character in which the capitalist delights to represent a working man is that of a producer; while his non-consumption, or meagre consumption, of late years, has convinced both the capitalist and the landowner that he is still more valuable as a consumer. They have also learned that machinery, which has become a substitute for his labour, fails in that essential point, it is not a consumer; and hence destructive as a producer, so long as it commands the labour-market, and can be only made a medium of general improvement and advantage when brought in aid of, instead of into competition with, manual labour. I shall now test the value of free-labour in a general sense with the value of hired labour; commencing with its application to land.

We seldom find a farmer retiring from his occupation, because it furnishes him with amusement and gratification, while it insures him enough to eat, good health, and wherewithal to make himself comfortable in life. I shall suppose the farmer to hold a hundred acres of land, and I think I may assert that in ten years time he will not have saved sufficient amount of money whereon to retire in idleness, or wherewith to purchase one quarter of the hundred acres. This inability proceeds from the fact, either that his capital is insufficient for the employment of that amount of labour required to bring it to perfection, or from his ignorance of its capability; both obstructions militating against the general interests of society. Upon the other hand, I shall suppose the hundred acres to be subdivided into farms of four acres each, or twenty-five farms, and will allow that each labourer, after consumption, realises and puts up no more than fifty pounds a-year; that is, the twenty-five labourers, after having comfortably maintained and educated their families, will save £1,250 annually. They would save £100 a man and more; but I am now writing for the sceptic, and prefer placing myself out of his reach.

In ten years, then, the twenty-five labourers would have saved twelve thousand five hundred pounds, which would purchase six hundred and twenty-five acres of land, worth a pound an acre at twenty years' purchase; that is, while the one man, cultivating the same hundred acres with hard labour, could not, after ten years, purchase twenty acres of it, twenty-five men after living upon it and supporting their families out of it, would have saved enough, I contend for it, to purchase one thousand two hundred and fifty acres of the same description of land, while, for argument sake, I only allow them to be able to purchase six hundred and twenty-five acres at the end of that time. Again, during the ten years the one occupant will have employed say four labourers, whose families, at seven to a family, would amount in the aggregate to twenty-eight half-fed, half-naked, wholly uneducated slaves; while within the same period the same one hundred acres would have supported and educated twenty-five families, making in the aggregate one hundred and seventy-five; and, beyond that, while the four slave families, and the single occupant, would have conferred little or no benefit upon society, the twenty-five free labourers and their families would have contributed very largely towards the support of tradesmen of every description.

Hence, I show the manner in which a bad system of cultivation limits production, stagnates trade, and pauperizes those engaged in the unproductive pursuit; while, upon the other hand, I show how a proper system would increase production, encourage trade, and furnish that sweetest of all sauces to labour, the prospect of amassing in manhood a sufficient amount for old age to retire upon in idleness, independent of parish relief, and not subjected to the tender mercies of a cruel overseer, or to those galling reflections which must haunt him through life, that the day would assuredly come when he would be torn from his aged partner, from his own children, from friends, from society in the world, and consigned as lumber to linger out the winter of life, an object of jealousy to those who had fattened upon his young blood, and to whom he had become a loathsome burthen.

I now turn to a consideration of the act of employment of capital in the artificial market, and I shall take the very lowest estimate of the capabilities which the present system affords capitalists for amassing fortunes by artificial power. I suppose a manufacturer to commence business with ten thousand pounds, over and above his original capital. I may be told that it is not usual for a manufacturer commencing business with ten thousand pounds to retire in ten years with a hundred and ten thousand pounds, I admit it; but it does not arise from his inability to do so, but is in consequence of the great fascinations which success presents; and which become an inducement to extend his trade; however, the fact is undeniable that the smaller returns from such business are the exceptions, and that the larger profits are the rule; and I must not be answered by losses sustained in bad times, when failures have been brought about by injurious speculations and over-production, all militating against the labour class, and none furnishing any fair set-off against the injustice done to the labourer, while the lost fortunes were being accumulated.

There is a very fanciful notion abroad that you have no right to interfere with speculations, or to interpose any obstacles in the way of industry. This may be all very true, if the system which presents those opportunities was equally protective of the rights of all; but it becomes an injustice when it subjects the fortunes of the many to the caprice of one. Feeling myself justified, then, in setting down the profits from the employment of a hundred men's labour at a hundred thousand pounds in ten years, we will see how a more equable distribution might be made of the accumulated sum: if the master retired with his ten thousand pounds original capital, and if to that was added twenty thousand pounds of the accumulated profits, he would be well paid by receiving two thousand a year for his overseership for ten years, while the remaining eighty thousand pounds, if divided amongst the hundred hands, would leave the sum of eight hundred pounds as the retiring salary of each individual.

Suppose, for argument sake, that the man only added forty thousand pounds in ten years to his original capital, thereby having accumulated fifty thousand pounds within ten years, and the superintendance of the work being equally onerous; suppose he draws one half of the whole accumulated profit as his share, it would still leave twenty thousand pounds to be divided amongst the one hundred hands, or would leave a retiring salary of two hundred pounds for each labouring man; an amount which would purchase him four acres of good ground for ever, and leave him a capital of one hundred and twenty pounds, to build a house and supply himself with the necessary stock. If then a lad begins to work at the age of sixteen, after he shall have received a proper education, he will have earned wherewithal to support himself during life when he attains his twenty-sixth year; thereby relieving the country from the expence of a standing army to suppress his treasonable designs against the system which consigns him to beggary and starvation; and releasing society, who has derived the benefit from his labour, from the necessity of supporting him in premature old age, after the capitalist shall have used him up.

I have now shewn the effect of withholding a sufficiency of labour in the natural market, and also the effect of the application of capital to the employment of labour in the artificial market; and I shall now treat of it under a more general head; its effect upon the shop-keeping class. It will at once be seen that my object is to shew the disadvantages which the present system impose upon the great majority of society, and the consequent injuries inflicted upon the great majority of all classes. Suppose a shopkeeper then, a grocer, or tobacconist, or corn-chandler, or any description of shopkeeper you please. He stands in the position of an active agent between the product and the consumer; he makes no profit whatever of the producer, but, on the contrary, the producer through him, as an agent, makes a profit upon each consumer. Suppose this man to start in business with one thousand pounds, a very fair capital, and more than in the general run of business is invested by those who deal in consumable, and for the most part perishable articles. That thousand pounds at five per cent. would produce him no more than fifty pounds a year, a sum less than many mechanics can earn; but so great is his confidence in the ability of labour to support him, that he enters into an engagement to pay the whole interest of his money and more in rent and taxes, thereby at once embarking his all in speculation upon consumption.

Now, a man having vested a thousand pounds in shop-keeping, will live and support his family very much better than if he had invested his money, received fifty pounds a year for it, paid ten pounds rent and taxes, and lived upon the remaining forty pounds, while, with fair business, at the end of twenty years he would consider himself unfortunate, if, after living well, and having educated his family well, he was not able to retire with ten thousand pounds, his business being worth a thousand pounds, or the original sum invested when he embarked in it. This is perhaps the most honourable description of accumulation, and let us see the position in which it places the speculator. The ten thousand pounds saved by his agency would purchase five hundred acres of land of good quality for ever, and those five hundred acres, subdivided into one hundred and twenty-five farms of four acres each, would support eight hundred and seventy-five individuals, besides the demand for increased trade occasioned by their independence; and would further produce an annual capital from their savings of twelve thousand five hundred a year.

I have thought it essential to enter minutely into this part of my subject, because it comprehends what I consider to be the most important branch of political economy, namely, the means whereby the labour of the country may be so applied as to relieve the country from all those impositions which its misappli-cation imposes; and at the same time sweetening labour, nay slavery itself, with the fond thought that the harder the task, the nearer is the hour of retirement. I believe that every professional man, every commercial man, every manufacturer, every trader, and every shopkeeper, receives a spur to his industry from the hopes of his being one day able to retire from the bustle of life to that retreat where he may enjoy that ease which he has honourably purchased, and where he may spend the winter of life without the toil of business, and relieved from the anguish occasioned by dependency.

If, then, this hope gives a spur to what may be called sedentary life, why, I would ask, should not the toil of him who has contributed towards the ease of others be sweetened by the same anticipations? Why should not the labouring man, by whose industry all thrive, be allowed to thrive himself? Why, when he sees those retiring from amongst him who have grown rich upon his toil, should he be subjected to the galling necessity of slaving on till a new batch has fastened upon his resources, looking not to an honourable retirement, but to a cold Bastile as his last retreat, and to death as his last resource? Can he love your system? Can he honour and obey the king, and all that are placed in authority under him? Can he submit himself lowly and reverently to his spiritual teachers, pastors, and masters, who speak to him of the blessings of eternity, while they consign him to beggary, starvation and want here below? Do you want him to be loyal? Can you expect that he will be religious? Can you hope that he will be moral? It is because it is contrary to nature that he should be so, that I seek to place him in that position wherein he is sure to be so.

AMERICA.

The present number being intended as a preface to the practical mode of managing four acres of ground by the labour of one man, and agriculture being a science of which the English working classes are, shame to their rulers, wholly ignorant, I have thought it right to place the capabilities of the land, and the value of their own labour when applied to its cultivation, in such light as, without a practical knowledge of agriculture, may induce them to reflect upon the subject. Again and again I must state as a reason for diving into the question in all its bearings, that no work has ever yet been written upon the same plan, and had I at once jumped to a consideration of how four acres of land were to be managed, without developing the means by which it was to be acquired, or without giving the reader a taste for the science, I should have been justly chargeable with extreme folly.

The reader will see that I have been compelled to refute a great many free trade arguments that have appeared in newspapers, and that I have also felt the necessity of contrasting the value of labour in the natural labour market, and the artificial labour market. And as some of our writers upon political economy have attempted to contrast the condition of the American operative with that of the English operative, supposing that the same prospects were open to both, I shall just make a comment upon the subject.

The free-traders have so jumbled and conglomerated what they call principles of political economy, that I scarcely know how to saddle each inventor with his own folly; and shall therefore treat this part of the question as a piece of absurdity that seems to meet with the acquiescence of the old school. It is this: in their endeavour to prove the great value of an increased trade, and the advantages that it confers upon the operatives, they say, look to America! and there we find that, although there is an abundant demand for agricultural labour, yet do the working classes prefer working in the factory to working in the field; now, can any thing be more absurd, more ignorant, more ungenerous, or more ridiculous? Do not these writers upon political economy know full well, that, if they had argued the question out fairly, they must have come to the very same conclusion that I have in a previous part of this work.

It is quite true that an American operative will prefer factory to field labour, and what does it prove? Why, precisely what I have asserted; that the preference for the artificial labour is based upon the higher rate of wages with which the manufacturer is compelled to tempt the operative to leave the natural market. This is just the case. There is an abundant demand for agricultural labour in America, and yet, where the opportunity presents itself, the American labourer prefers working in the factory to working in the field, but why? Firstly, because he is tempted by an offer of higher wages in the artificial market than that which has been established in the natural market; and secondly, that he may, by the higher rate of wages, be able to purchase a plot of ground for himself and thus provide a free market for his own labour; thus clearly showing his ultimate object to be the cultivation of the soil. So it was precisely in this country, the agricultural labourers were seduced from their natural labour by the tempting prices offered in the artificial market, and many could in those days have laid up wherewithal to insure a happy retreat, had the same opportunities been presented to them that are presented to the American; but as they are not, the attempted contrast is incomplete.

The political economists have failed to tell the people that the law of primogeniture, which precludes the possibility of the Englishman purchasing a small plot of ground, does not exist in America, and that the consequence of its existence in England is now daily seen in the overstock of professions, trades, and dealers of every description. The speculations to which the most fortunate adventurers in the artificial market betook themselves, rested upon a belief that the prosperity was to increase and every branch of business was to be extended to suit the advance in wages of the working classes; and now, the poverty of those several speculators is not a consequence of the diminished rate of wages, occasioned by improvements in machinery. Our shop-keeping market, our trade market, our commercial market, were all extended to meet the improved condition of the people, and their total failure is a consequence of the poverty of the people, while, in the midst of that poverty, the subtle owners of that artificial power have got hold of all the money that ought to belong to those speculators, the shop-keepers, and to the people.

The grievance is not poverty arising out of a want of money there being more money, and more money's worth, in the country than ever there was before; the grievance is, that machinery came upon us with a hop, step, and jump; that, in its infancy, it presented such fascinations to the Chancellor of the Exchequer, that it allowed to remain uncontrolled, until at length its owners got so far a-head, and became so wealthy, that they are now able to dictate terms to a government, whose existence depends upon the confidence of the capitalist.

If, upon the other hand, one-tenth part of the money that was expended in speculations to meet the improved condition of the working classes, had been expended for the improvement of agriculture, no artificial circumstances whatever could have checked the growing prosperity, and had the retail land market been open for the operative, as it is in America, thousands upon thousands would have purchased in it to the full amount of their earnings; but, horrible to say, to write, or to think of, the necessity of upholding a corrupt system, renders dissipation and immorality necessary, and I unhesitatingly assert, that, if I had proposed my present plan at the time when the working men were prosperous, and had I succeeded in converting a portion of their wages into a Savings Bank, and thereby abstracted a portion from gin duty, tobacco duty, malt duty, hop duty, and all the other accursed duties, the Chancellor of the Exchequer, under the advice of the Attorney-General, would have charged me with the crime of endeavouring to make her Majesty alter her measures, by depriving her of those means by which she is compelled to uphold them; and I have as little doubt that some honest judge and middle class jury, would have seen danger to their order, in the improved condition or the working classes, and would have found me guilty of that offence.

If I am right in my conclusions, then, it is manifest that the law of primogeniture, which does not exist in America, presents an insurmountable barrier in the way of the English operative, and leads us once more into the field of politics; and also to a consideration of that power apart from government control, which is vested in the people themselves, and which no government can destroy. It is a truism, that a combination of the political mind directed to any common object, must establish itself as the foundation of the government of the country. It is folly, childish and absurd, to talk of the difficulty of such concentration if the majority are oppressed, and if their union will relieve them from oppression, and if they will not unite, then are they willing slaves, and the government of the union of the weaker party is justified in looking upon the people as satisfied with their measures.

This rule especially holds good, when the service required from the people as a test of union is not dangerous, while, upon the other hand, if there is danger in the mode by which the union of the people is to be exhibited, there is danger in proposing it, and its failure is followed by increased weakness; for instance, a month's cessation from labour is a plan that a majority of the people would have gladly adopted as a means of evincing their union, while their incapacity to carry it out but shewed their weakness. In the plan which I propose there is no danger, because there can be no failure; while its adoption would break down the law of primogeniture altogether, because, although it precludes the possibility of selling estates in patches, yet it does not prevent the trustees of the place from purchasing estates and subdividing them into the very smallest allotments.

Thus, then, I show the means whereby that strong bulwark of the English aristocracy can be knocked down by a union of the people. Again, the national debt is a great burden, and a great stumbling block in the way of all improvements, yet, if the people were to conspire not to drink any intoxicating drinks for one year, the government would be compelled either to abandon the national debt, or to throw the whole burthen of it upon the owners of property, and thus the law makers being made the tax payers, they would speedily rid themselves of a grievance of which they never felt the weight when they saddled it on the backs of the working classes.

Again, the church is a great grievance; and yet if all the industrious classes of society came to a resolution not to enter any place of worship where a tithe minister preached, and if they united into one large dissent congregation, taking up their stand in view of the church, preaching there, and exhibiting their numbers to those who had attended the tithe church, offering no offence, behaving decorously, and thus giving a practical illustration of the injustice of making the many without pay for the few within, this union of dissent would very speedily overcome the injustice of a state church.

Union, in fact, has never failed of accomplishing its end, if legitimately used, and it is because I feel perfectly convinced that a union established for the purpose of locating the people upon the land cannot be obstructed by any factious means, and because it cannot be weakened by adventitious circumstances, that I hail it with great joy and pleasure as one that must go on and prosper. I believe that its very establishment, and the purposes for which it will be formed, will lead to an improvement in the morals and the character of the people, from the very inducement that it holds out of a better remuneration than a head-ache, and vomit, incapacity, and loss of character from their little savings; in fact, I think that the working-man who can scrape sixpence or a shilling together on a Saturday night and who prefers spending it in drunkenness to vesting it in the land fund, deserves all the misery that his own recklessness can entail upon him, and I, for one, shall never pity the forlorn condition of such a suffering slave.

I think I may triumphantly refer to those letters which I addressed to the Irish landlords from York Castle, in 1841,[1] wherein I predicted their present condition, and wherein I foretold the outbreak of August, 1842, the means by which it would be brought about, the parties who would bring it about and those who would suffer for resisting the attempt. Those letters have been widely circulated, and have aroused the working classes to thought. Emboldened then by the fulfilment of my prophecies of 1841, I shall now venture upon a prediction in 1843.

I prophecy, then, that before this day twelve months the question of national faith will be passionately discussed in the House of Commons; that the tariff landlords, and the free-traders, having lost the confidence of the people, and being more powerful than the owners of funded property and the church party, will put their heads together to devise measures whereby they may rid themselves of both incumbrances and divide the spoil between them; that the minister will be compelled to abandon all artificial speculations, and to turn his attention to our natural resources; that many of our colonies will be given up; that a state provision, payable out of the consolidated fund, will be applied by a graduated scale to the support of all ministers of all denominations; that bishops will be thought a nuisance; that Scotland will demand the expenditure of her own revenues in Scotland, or a repeal of the union if such proposition is resisted; that the surplus money, now valueless in the market, will be applied to agricultural purposes; that the great 'WEN' will be reduced; that many of those stately mansions by which London is surrounded will be uninhabited, and that the present occupants of loathsome cellars will be removed to the country air; that agriculture will be an honourable science; that a minister of agriculture will be added to the cabinet, and, to prevent revolution, the aristocracy, thus clipped of the means of

---

1 See *The Remedy for National Poverty* (1841), vol. 2 of this edition, pp. 333–57.

keeping up corruption, will begin to enquire how the franchise may be safely extended to those whose altered position gives them an interest in security of life, liberty, and property, and in the preservation of peace.

Always bearing in mind that war is to trade what the hot-bed is to the plant, which forces it but strengthens it not in its growth; while peace is as the pure air from heaven, which forces it not but strengthens it in its growth until it arrives at a wholesome maturity. It is quite true, that much of the above prophecy will depend for fulfilment upon the conduct of the people themselves. However, I have made it, and time alone will prove whether I am right or wrong. All classes of society are panting for change, and the question is what that change shall be. Nearly thirty years of European peace has turned the public mind to a consideration as to how its blessings may be preserved, and they will find no means so effectual as those which will give the working classes an interest in the preservation of those institutions under which they live.

TO THE PEOPLE.

In order that I may be perfectly understood, and in order that the working classes may be prepared to answer all the objections started by the wily against my plan, I have to beg it as a compliment at their hands that they will, in their several localities, appoint good readers to read this number, if they pass over all others. Let them appoint political evenings in each weak for reading and discussing it chapter by chapter, and if there is any emendation which they can point out calculated to make the plan more perfect, all such proposed alterations may be submitted with great advantage to the governing body. There are many circumstances connected with the life of a working man of which I may be ignorant, and a knowledge of which is indispensable for the completion of the machinery.

So anxious am I that this subject should be extensively discussed, that I would much rather that one number only was taken and read to ten thousand persons until they thoroughly understood it, than that five thousand of those ten thousand bought a number each, while the remaining five thousand remained in perfect ignorance of the subject. My particular objects cannot be too often repeated. Firstly, I hope to establish the real value of labour in the natural labour-market, below which the labourer will not work in the artificial market. Secondly, I wish to impress upon the minds of all, the double good that the carrying out of the plan would effect; that of not only conferring upon a large number the means of living happy during the whole of life, but of also removing them as competitors from the artificial labour market. For instance,

Suppose ten thousand persons were the exact number required to perform all the work in a certain district, and that their wages were regulated by that steady demand for their labour; and suppose that an additional two thousand came into that market to compete with them, it would be much more to the advantage of the ten thousand to club their entire wages, and to divide it in equal portions amongst all, including the two thousand idlers, than to admit them as competitors in the labour-market, as they would very speedily find that the surplus of labour would lead to such a reduction of wages, as would compel the twelve thousand to work for a less amount than the ten thousand, which constituted the proper supply for the demand, were in the habit of receiving.

I would beg of all money-clubs, and all societies having monies at their disposal, to consider my plan dispassionately, and of all things to bear well in mind the fact that they are not called upon to abandon the control of their funds to the management of others; while I would impress upon the working classes the absolute necessity of appointing the ablest of their body as lecturers, not to live upon the excitement that the subject may cause, but who will be able, without speechifying, to explain a homely plan in homely language, so that all may understand it. From a proper observance of such advice I anticipate much good, because the subject being a novel one, and, in my mind, a captivating one, will gain daily strength from discussion.

Many persons have already expressed their determination to take shares, in the hope of forwarding the interests of the working classes, while that excellent gentleman, Mr David Weatherhead, of Keighley, has embarked several hundred pounds in the speculation, and our friend Mr Linton, of Selby, and others anxious to furnish practical illustrations of the system, have successfully engaged in the cultivation of small allotments. I have started at four acres, because I believe that to be about the amount which one man can cultivate to advantage. However, circumstances would materially guide us as to amount; while I would be most cheerfully governed by the opinion of those upon whom those peculiar circumstances operate.

And, now, in conclusion, as I have stated that the main interest in a country will always be the mainspring of legislation, I hope, ere long, to see our laws based upon common sense instead of upon fiction, and that those laws will be framed by all for the benefit of all. While in an undertaking like the present, although I may take credit for the performance of one man's work, yet I cannot withhold that praise which is due to the great architect, without whose projection all my labour would be lost. My superstructure is to be built upon common sense, and the adored Father Mathew[1] is the architect who has marked out the site, and furnished me with a sound foundation. If the plan should succeed, of which I have no doubt, I shall claim the credit due to a good workman; while to that greatest benefactor that the world ever produced shall be accorded the merit of having manufactured the tools with which the work is to be done, and my only hope is that his gigantic exertions may be crowned with success here below, and rewarded with eternal glory in the world to come; and to which, in my opinion, he is endeavouring to establish a title. GOD BLESS HIM.

---

1 Father Theobald Mathew (1790–1856), Irish temperance advocate.

INTRODUCTION TO THE PRACTICAL MANAGEMENT OF SMALL FARMS.

The great success with which my endeavour to familiarise the mind of the working classes with the landed question has been crowned, (one publisher alone having sold over 3,000 numbers of this work) leads me to a very sanguine hope as to the result, and to a belief that ere long the subject will be considered of importance far outstripping all others. It was no easy task to have digested anything like a poor man's plan out of the rude and complicated absurdities, technicalities, and legal restrictions with which, through all time, landed proprietors, law makers, political economists, and interested writers, had entangled the question. Indeed, it would appear as if some magic spell hung over the land of these countries, whereby it was made barren and sterile, whereas the incapacity lay not in the land but in the system under which it has hitherto been managed. Before I proceed to the simple work of laying out that quantity of land; which, according to the present population of the country, I deem the requisite amount to allot to each individual, I shall state the leading inducement which should operate upon the minds of all, and which should ensure the co-operation of all, in furtherance of the object.

Under our present artificial system, the one great evil of which even the most fortunate complain, is uncertainty. Risk is a term very generally used by manufacturers, merchants, and traders. Risk means uncertainty, and that uncertainty is occasioned wholly and exclusively by the uncertainty that prevails in the labour market. Whatever a working man's condition in society may be, and however satisfied he may appear with his condition, the uncertainty of even a bad lot, is a cause of fretfulness, anxiety, and unsettledness, to which no legislature can reconcile him, from which no philosopher can relieve him. It is right that the reader should understand precisely what I mean by uncertainty. By uncertainty in trade, I mean the probability of speculations being entered upon, attended with great risk, in consequence of the uncertainty that prevails in the labour-market, and by which market all speculations must be regulated. Uncertainty in the labour market, more than even the ruinous reductions in wages, occasioned by the unrestricted use of machinery, is the greatest evil of which the working classes complain, while, under the present system, it is wholly out of the power of any government to legislate between artificial power and manual labour, while the existence of an uncontrolled, *non-consuming*, producing power is incompatible with certainty in the labour market.

The channels through which governments and commissioners profess to arrive at the state of the labouring market, are erroneous and deceptive. The Commissioners, in making their reports, set down not only the highest amount of wages returned by the masters as paid to their hands, but they further neglect to state the number of days in any given period in which the men are compelled to remain idle. Thus, there is very little sympathy for spinners, miners, power loom weavers, mechanics, block printers, engravers, and others of the labouring classes, who, by returns, appear to have received from thirty to fifty shillings a week, whereas it not unfrequently happens, that parties employed in those several works may have been one-half their time idle, either owing to bad trade, which means over production, or to a strike against a reduction of wages, or to some other cause. Over those casualties the working men have no controul whatever, they are always on the defensive, and their object always is to arrive at something like certainty of employment. There is very little doubt that a working man would much prefer the certainty of a salary of £40 a year to the chance of receiving £60, and, therefore, certainty of employment is the great object that I have in view.

The owners of that surplus capital now lying idle, complain of the very limited sphere allotted for its circulation, as well as of the uncertainty and risk consequent upon its investment. To the land alone, then, and to the land at home too, and to that only, can capitalists look as a certain field for the investment of their monies, while, to the same source, and to it only, can the labouring classes look for certainty of employment. The man who occupies four acres of ground, and who would otherwise be a pauper living upon the industry of others, would have a certain market wherein to expend his labour, and wherefrom to draw with certainty the proceeds of his labour, and thus would the country be at once relieved of the whole system of poor laws, so galling, so grinding, so revolting and expensive. A class of farm labourers whose profits were thus reduced to something like certainty, would create a certain market for all classes of traders, whereas I much doubt that they would require any of those expensive establishments now considered necessary for reconciling the pauper to his lot; while the proceeds of industry thus equitably circulated and distributed, would constitute an abundant resource, from which a minister may draw the necessary taxes requisite for maintaining a just system of cheap government; a system made cheap by the substitution of certainty for uncertainty.

Some portions of the press have taken exceptions to my work because I have found it necessary here and there to introduce political subjects, but I would ask how it is possible to write upon a system wholly of a political nature without adverting to politics? Is not the question of a repeal of the Corn Laws made one of great political prominency, and is not the question of home production inseparable from that of foreign importation? Is not the means of acquiring a sufficiency of wheat, the one question of all absorbing political importance? Is it not from the land that wheat is produced? And how then is it possible to separate the question of a repeal of the Corn Laws from that of the home production of wheat? However, I have only touched upon politics, where, to have avoided them, would have rendered illustration incomplete, and, if fault can be charged, it must be upon those who have so cunningly mixed up political with social questions.

No plan can be made perfect in the outset, and further consideration has led me to the suggestion of a great improvement upon a portion of my plan as laid down in Number 3. In Number 3 I have described a plan, by which risk to the several shareholders may be limited as far as possible, while I found it impossible to devise a scheme altogether free from risk. The plan which I suggested in

Number 3, for the distribution of land and the subsequent appropriation of the purchase money amongst a portion of the shareholders, is attended with considerable speculation; and the following I think will be considered as a great improvement upon that portion of my plan. Possession of the land is the one great object that the people have in view, and how to make that possession as extensive as possible should be the great object of the society. The improvement, then, that I propose is as follows: – Suppose the society were possessed of one hundred thousand pounds to lay out in the purchase of land, instead of selling it after it had been allotted for ever to the various holders, and of distributing the purchase money amongst a portion of the shareholders, I would recommend the sale of the land after allotment in the same manner as proposed in Number 3, while, instead of appropriating the funds to repay any portion of the shareholders, I would recommend that the purchase money be applied to the purchase of more land, upon which other shareholders may be located, and thus, with any given sum, say one hundred thousand pounds, the society may become possessed of every estate offered for sale in the market.

Possession is the one thing needed, and one thousand acres of land, subdivided amongst two hundred and fifty able-bodied men, would be far better security to any purchaser than the same one thousand acres would be in the possession of the most improving individual. Suppose an estate worth a hundred thousand pounds to be in the market, and purchased by the society; as soon as it is purchased it should be allotted, in farms of four acres each, to those subscribers selected by ballot from the general body; each holder should then receive a lease for ever of his land, at a rent regulated by the price at which it was purchased. This gives him possession for ever, independent of any purchaser who may become the landlord. The estate is then sold with the additional security that increased labour would give to it, and the purchase money is at once laid out in the purchase of more land, to which another batch of shareholders are also appointed by ballot, and so on.

Now, I am aware that your first-principle men will deal with this subject as an unjustifiable interference with national property, and the only answer that I can give unto the ninety and one hundredth generation men yet to come, is, that when my plan presses hardly upon generations yet unborn, let those generations in their day do as we hope to do in our day, leave the world better than we found it. For the next three hundred years and more the population of Britain without being thinned by plague, pestilence, war, or famine, could live under the provisions of my plan, while each succeeding year would ensure for it improved machinery, through increasing population to make it perfect and still more perfect, while it is the only means by which the blighting influence of the law of primogeniture, reliance upon foreign states, and dependence upon the artificial labour market, can be successfully combated.

The most dogged and stupid must admit that something must be done. All must see that England has become too small for the speculations of the owners of a non-consuming producing power; that they have swallowed up a large portion of the land of England by converting artificial labour into purchase money of real property, that that land, however valuable, is of minor consideration when compared with the rapidity with which fortunes may be accumulated with ficti-tious money and a non-consuming producing power, and that having thus possessed themselves of a large portion of the lands of Britain, they will hence-forth play for those of Poland, of Prussia, and the continent of America, if not stopped by doing beneficially at home, that which they purpose to do for their own advantage abroad. Once more then repeating the principal objects that I have in view, I shall proceed to the practical management of a four acre farm. The objects that I have in view then, are as follows. –

Firstly. To create certainty in the labour market.

Secondly. To establish an unerring standard of the value of labour in the free labour market, whereby its value in the artificial market may be ascertained.

Thirdly. That the capitalists who make fortunes by other men's labour shall henceforth hire that labour in the free labour market, wherein every man will have arrived at a knowledge of its full value, instead of, as at present, hiring that labour from the reserve of a system-made surplus population, and which is reg-ulated wholly and entirely by the amount of system-made paupers in the market.

Fourthly. To insure some wholesome regulation as to demand and supply, whereby the capitalists will be prevented from drugging the markets of the world with the produce of cheap labour.

Fifthly. To enable the legislature to make laws for the promotion of morality instead of living upon depravity.

Sixthly. To enable us to dispense with that heavy load of taxation now said to be requisite for keeping the dissatisfied in subjection.

Seventhly. To create a feeling of self-respect in the minds of the working classes, by making each component part of the human family, and thereby attaching all to those institutions which render them protection in return for their support of them. And

Eighthly. To destroy my own and all other demagogues' trade, by enabling the people to do for themselves that which they now rely upon political traffickers to do for them.

RULES FOR THE PRACTICAL MANAGEMENT
OF A FOUR ACRE FARM.

In the previous numbers I have entered upon general topics connected with the management of land, and in the consideration of which I have stated the result of several experiments made by myself and others. As a matter of course the result of those experiments also led me into the field of assertion, but by no means to an extravagant amount. In those rules however which I shall lay down for the management of Small Farms the reader will expect certain data to be taken as the foundation upon which the system shall be built; as the object is the one nearest of all others to my heart, I shall so confine myself within the limits of moderation as to defy refutation. It is not my intention to state extravagantly what the land may be made to produce, it is merely my desire to state that every man may make it yield. I do not take the highly cultivated market gardens by which I am surrounded as specimens of the state of perfection to which the land may be brought, although I would be justified in shewing that every article produced in those gardens are raw materials, produced by labour, from which bread, butter, beef, mutton, bacon, pork, lamb, milk, cheese, honey, poultry, eggs, wool, leather, and fur are one and all manufactured. We have not population for such a system of refined cultivation, and therefore I shall confine myself to the most profitable application of the producing power to the productive means of the country.

In order to accomplish my purpose with satisfaction to the public and to myself I must base my reasoning upon some general and indisputable data. I must shew what four acres are capable of producing by the labour of one man, I must shew the most profitable application of the produce, while I shall be required to state the residue after consumption of the labourer, his wife and family. The first point then upon which all are agreed, and which Mr Cobbett[1] has placed beyond doubt, is the fact, that a quarter of an acre of ground of moderate quality is capable of supporting a cow throughout the year. The second point relied upon by all is, that one cow will make a sufficiency of manure within the year for an acre of land, and the third and most important admission is, that one man by sixteen days' labour will be able to support a cow from the produce of a quarter of an acre. – If then we can rely upon those calculations, I would be justified in coming to the following wholesale conclusion as to the value of one man's labour applied to the cultivation of four acres of ground: – if a quarter of an acre supports a cow with sixteen days' labour, four acres will of course support sixteen cows with two hundred and fifty-six days' labour; and supposing a cow for eight months in the year to give twelve quarts of milk a day at three half-pence a quart, the milk of the sixteen cows will amount to over £285, and, if one cow makes enough of manure for one acre, sixteen cows will make enough for sixteen acres, leaving a sufficiency for twelve acres more than the farmer requires; and which, valued at five pounds an acre, would be worth sixty pounds, which, added to the price of milk £285, would make £345.

Now it may be argued that the amount of labour for attending so large a stock could not be bestowed by a single individual. I admit it; while I feel myself justified in adopting so much of the plan as would relieve it from a charge of impossibility, while I shall state minutely the probable produce of every perch of ground; the seasons at which the several crops should be sown or planted; the times at which they would be fit for use; the length of time they would last; the amount of labour expended in their cultivation; the purposes to which they should be applied, and the profit after the support of the family that they would leave.

1 William Cobbett (1762–1835), radical reformer.

THE SEVERAL CROPS, TO THE PRODUCTION OF WHICH FOUR ACRES OF LAND, WITH THE LABOUR OF ONE MAN, MAY BE MOST BENEFICIALLY APPLIED.

1 Acre of Potatoes.

1 Acre of Wheat.

1¾ Acres to be appropriated as hereinafter described – and ¼ of an acre for kitchen garden.

The stock to be fed upon the produce of the land so cultivated to consist of –

4 Cows.

6 Pigs.

6 Sheep.

Poultry.

As I propose the acre of potatoes to constitute a large portion of the food for feeding the cows and sheep, as well as the sole food, with milk, of the pigs – and as the wheaten straw will also constitute a large portion of food for the cows, it will be seen that, independently of such food, I assign two acres of ground, or nearly so, to the support of the four cows, thus so far differing from Mr Cobbett and others inasmuch that I allow nearly three quarters of an acre to the support for each cow instead of a quarter of an acre, while I have the assistance of six pigs, six sheep and a quantity of poultry to aid four cows in making a sufficiency of manure for four acres, while I further discharge the labourer of many days' work by holding more than half the land in wheat, potatoes, and grass, which would not require that amount of labour that would be necessary for a succession of crops, while I further allow him the assistance of his wife and family in performing a large portion of the required service.

This arrangement is meant to apply to the system when it should be got into good working order; not presuming that any man will at once be able to step into four acres of ground with the required stock. However, apart from the confidence which possession would inspire in capitalists around him and from whom in many instances the needful may be procured, yet from a different management for the two first years he would live better than the best mechanic now lives, while at the end of that time he would be in a situation to purchase more stock than he would require. For instance, in the first year of his tenancy he may purchase four yearling heifers for three pounds each that would calve at the commencement of the third year. In the outset pigs of lower value may be purchased, and, until his stock came round to complete the plan, he may produce other crops which, though not equally remunerating, would nevertheless pay him well for his labour. When it is borne in mind that £12 will buy four yearling heifers, and that at the end of two years they will constitute the principal stock of the small farmer, the want of capital cannot in any way operate as a barrier against his success.

Indeed, it is absolutely necessary that all the operations should be progressive, and two years is as short a period as could be assigned for bringing the whole into good working order. I shall, therefore, start from that point when the farmer would be in possession of four milch cows, six pigs, and six sheep. Supposing him to be in possession in May, 1844, his arrangements would be completed in November, 1845. I state November as the period, because under any circumstances his cows, which would have calved before, would be dry or nearly so at that time. Thus, after eighteen months from the time of entering upon possession he would find his arrangements for future operations perfect.

It now becomes my duty to point out the manner in which the land is to be subsequently applied. In November, 1845, he will have stock, four in calf heifers to calve in May, six pigs, and six sheep; and his food for their support till the middle of April, will consist of an acre of potatoes, less the family's consumption, eight hundred sheaves of wheaten straw, the produce of his acre of wheat, a quarter of an acre of rape, and a quarter of an acre of winter cabbages, to be applied as follows: – of course varying the food, taking care to give more straw with rape and cabbages than with potatoes. As much as thirty-five tons of potatoes have been produced off one acre, while twenty tons is by no means an extravagant though a large crop. I average the produce, however, at sixteen tons, and dispose of it thus: –

	Tons
Firstly, consumption of family from 1st of November to the 1st of June, thirty weeks, at 16lbs. a-day, or 112lbs. per week, making	1½
Six full sized pigs, a stone and a half each per day from the 1st of November to the 1st of March, when five should be sold and the best killed for family use, about	6½

Of course the pig intended for family use would for the last three weeks be fed upon oats, peas, or barley, in a raw state, and the saving of potatoes would much more than pay for the oats, peas, or barley, while the pigs, being fat all through the summer, I have allowed much more than a sufficiency of food for the last sixteen weeks, and, as the dry feeding of pigs upon peas, oats, or barley, for a month or three weeks before killing, is indispensable for insuring good bacon, we may set it down that the six tons and a half of potatoes would much more than feed them in the best style, and, indeed, as will be learned from all my calculations, the potatoes, if sold, would bring more money than the profit on the six pigs from November to March. A ton of potatoes at fourpence per stone would be £2 13s. 4d., or for the six tons and a half £17 6s. 8d. I prefer, however, consuming everything on the farm, so that the labour may be sold in the highest state of manufacture; and in order that as much manure as possible may be made. There then remain eight tons of potatoes to constitute a portion of the winter food of four cows and six sheep.

Those eight tons, together with the wheaten straw, a quarter of an acre of rape, and a quarter of an acre of winter cabbages, is to constitute the whole provender, from the 1st of November to the 20th of April, when the winter tares, as hereafter described, will be ready for use. I beg it to be observed, that the calculations in which I am now engaged are but preliminary to a perfect table which I shall submit in a subsequent chapter; wherein I shall set forth the mode of cropping, the crops to be used, the time of sowing, planting, harvesting, and using;

appropriating every inch of the ground to those purposes to which it should be applied with a succession of crops.

We will estimate the time from the 1st of November to the 20th of April at six months, and apply the quantity of food that I have allotted for that time, regardless of the particular seasons at which each crop shall be respectively given, a matter in which the farmer himself will be regulated by the state and condition of his cows, the forwardness of his rape, and the appearance of his cabbages. For instance, if the cows are still giving a good flow of milk in November, he must not use straw, which has a tendency to dry them up, but he should rather hold it over to that period when they ought to be dried. Under those circumstances, then, I shall shew how long each crop would feed the stock, leaving it to the farmer to judge of the proper time for applying it. I allow three stone of steamed potatoes a-day for each cow, or a hundred weight and a half for the four. That may be set down as a ton a fortnight as I have allowed overmuch for their keep – six tons for three months. Eight hundred sheaves of straw would weigh two ton and a half, and at two stone a-day for each cow would be a hundred a-day, and would last the four cows fifty days. We have, then, after consuming the potatoes and straw, to provide for less than six weeks, and for which the farmer has got a quarter of an acre of rape, and a quarter of an acre of winter cabbages, with two tons of potatoes; quite sufficient to feed four cows for four months, the residue furnishing more than ample for the six sheep for six months. The sheep may be fed upon raw potatoes, rape, and cabbages.

Here again, when I come to calculate the value of gross produce, it will be found, that I apply nearly twenty pounds' worth of potatoes, two tons and a half of straw, a quarter of an acre of rape, and a quarter of an acre of winter cabbages, to the support of the stock, at a time when the cows are rendering comparatively little profit. We have now to provide for the stock from the 1st of May to the 1st of November, and to do that we have an acre and three quarters of ground, the remaining portion being under wheat, potatoes, and kitchen garden.

A half acre of winter vetches sown in September comes into use first, and will be ready by the 1st of May; and at the rate of nearly three perches a-day, there being eighty perches in a half acre, will be ample for six lambs, the state at which I shall recommend the sheep to be laid in, six pigs of six months old, and four cows, for the month of May, when half an acre of soiling grass will be fit for use, and which will be ample for the stock for the month of June.

In July, a quarter of an acre of spring vetches sown after the winter crop had been cut, together with a quarter of an acre of early cabbages planted in the remaining quarter of an acre of winter vetch ground will be ready, and will feed the stock till the tenth of August, when the grass cut in June will be ready for the second crop, which will last the stock till the middle of September, when a quarter of an acre of clover sown with flax will be ready for use and will last the stock to the end of September, when a quarter of an acre of early turnips, and a quarter of an acre of cabbages, will be ready for use and constitute the food of the stock, pigs excepted, during the month of October.

I have not here taken into calculation the picking to be had off the half acre of grass in October, the period at which it should be well manured, and before which it may be eaten bare by the sheep and cows being turned upon it. Nor have I mentioned the bran which will be taken from sixty stone of ground wheat, and which constitutes excellent food for cows, pigs, and poultry.

This whole process would not take two hundred and twenty days of a moderate workman's labour, while with the assistance of his wife and family, who would milk the cows, weed, do some little in the kitchen garden, feed the poultry and stock, it would not take more than one hundred and eighty days' labour or one half the year; nor indeed ought it, for when we deduct fifty-two Sundays we leave a hundred and thirty three days for wet weather, when work may be injurious not only to the man, but to his land, and for holidays, and instruction. And now let us see what that man (made a rebel from unwilling idleness, and disinherited from society by machinery, now a beggar at the door of the capitalist for license to linger or to live upon the slavery of his wife and little children) could earn after supporting himself and his family by those hundred and eighty days labour.

I shall place him in the very worst condition, by making him sell the entire produce in the wholesale market, whereas a large portion of it may be more profitably disposed of in the retail market. Not again to travel over the old ground, and to avoid complication, I shall estimate the produce of the cows, although to be sold in the wholesale market, by putting a very low value upon the milk, and the following is the amount of provision which I deduct in the first instance from the gross amount of produce: –

One bacon pig	20 stone.
Flour	1 stone per week.
Potatoes, 16lbs. a-day	8 stone per week.
Milk, or butter made from the milk	3 quarts per day.
Eggs, poultry, vegetables and honey, as much as they can consume.	
For clothing, 30lbs. of wool, the produce of six sheep at five lbs. a fleece, and the produce of a quarter of an acre of flax.	

Such, I think, would be amble provision for the family, while all would be wholesome, fresh, and nutritious, instead of being purchased at twice the value in a truck shop, or bought rotten in the market at a late hour on Saturday night, when the respectables had stripped the stall of the best and left the pawed refuse for the hard-working man. The produce, after consumption, I set down as follows: –

	£.	s.	d.
Produce of four good cows from the 1st of May, the time at which they should calve, to the 1st of November, average sixteen quarts a-day each, or sixty-four quarts at 1½d. per quart	73	12	0
Profit upon five bacon pigs for the year	25	0	0
Profit upon six sheep	6	0	0

	£.	s.	d.
Produce of an acre of wheat, (160 stone, less by sixty stone consumed by the family), 100 stone at 1s. 6d. per stone	7	10	0
Value of four calves at 10s. each	2	0	0
Eggs, poultry, honey and vegetables over what would be required for consumption	10	0	0
Value of produce after consumption	124	2	0
From which deduct for rent, tithe, and taxes	24	2	0
and we find that it leaves the sum of	£100	0	0

over and above all charges, demands, and liabilities, for the labour of one hundred and eighty days, besides the best of good living, and the means of laying up more woollen and linen fabric than would be required for three families. Indeed, we may safely calculate that the surplus of woollen and linen fabric, after supplying the family with an abundance of both, would furnish them with coals, candles, shoes, and hats.

Perhaps I may be asked why I estimate the profits upon the cows according to the amount they are supposed to yield? whereas I have appropriated three quarts a-day to the use of the family. I have done so. But it is to be understood, that from the end of October to the end of January the cows will give more than three quarts a-day each, and that I have only assigned the quantity for the use of the family during those three months, and which I have not brought into account in the gross produce. Twelve quarts a-day for three months in the year, is equal to three quarts a-day for twelve months in the year. Nor, in my calculation, do I intend to say, that a cow will give the same quantity of milk in September that she has given in May, or the same quantity in October that she has given in June, but she will average that quantity; giving the largest quantity for the four months after she has calved, and falling off from the latter end of August after she has been served, and allowing her to remain completely dry for three months before she calves.

In the above calculation, I can scarcely be said to have taken the quarter of an acre for kitchen garden into account, while I have allowed the land to be cultivated in rather a rude state, whereas, had I drawn my conclusions from the unrefuted assertions of others, I might have set down the value of produce after consumption at three hundred pounds, allowing forty-five pounds for the maintenance of the family for a year. Suppose, for instance, that I go upon the data of others, and make my calculations upon the application of one man's labour to two acres of land, allowing that a quarter of an acre will support a cow, upon even twenty days' work, and that a cow will make enough of manure for an acre of ground. If we estimate the value of a cow's milk for the whole year at £15, eight cows, supported upon two acres with one hundred and sixty days' labour, will produce

	£.	s.	d.
Milk	120	0	0
Eight calves at 10s. each	4	0	0

and leaving all the manure of the eight cows for the two acres, we find that the man, upon a hundred and sixty days' work applied to two acres of ground, can earn £124. Or, if we choose to reduce it to the occupation of one acre, which would only take eighty days' labour, we find that a man's labour for those eighty days is worth £62.

It is folly to talk to me of the necessity of a good dwelling, and the required amount of stock in the first instance, as there are other means beside, those afforded by feeding stock for making profit of land. Let those who are now disinherited get possession of the land, and within four or five miles of it they will find a better, a more healthy, and more cheerful residence than in the cold damp cellars of Leeds or Manchester, and until there is a sufficient return from their labour to enable them to build suitable residences, and to supply themselves with the required stock, let them walk four or five miles to their work and four or five miles from their work, and they will walk the distance with light heart and step, knowing that it is labour bestowed for themselves. And until they can procure stock let them grow potatoes, wheat, and vegetables; let them feed some pigs, and, like Samuel Bridge, in a very short time they will find themselves in a condition not only to build a house and offices and to procure the required stock, but to purchase the fee simple of their farm. The one thing that they must bear in mind is this: – that their labour is the only capital that can be applied to the land, and that labour when profitably applied is the best description of manure; and instead of at once looking for a well built and well finished cottage with suitable offices and the required stock, that if they only get hold of the land, those are advantages which will assuredly follow in quick succession if they are but moderately industrious and moderately prudent.

However, I would implore those who are now destitute in consequence of the impossibility to procure work in an overstocked labour market, to consider well what their condition must be if not altered by their own determination, while I would emphatically impress upon the minds of those who are as yet more fortunate than their disinherited brethren, the fact, that their day also will assuredly come; for the same process which has caused the distress of others is day after day adding to the general calamity, and that they will not be spared. It is because I see the possibility of converting that which is now man's curse into man's blessing that I seek shelter for those upon whom the curse has fallen.

SUBDIVISION OF FOUR ACRES OF LAND INTO THE REQUIRED ALLOTMENTS, FOR CARRYING OUT THE SMALL FARM SYSTEM.

Of all things I wish to guard myself against the idea that I expect anything like a complete observance of my plan. On the contrary, I do not suppose that every small farmer will have four cows, six pigs, or six sheep; some may have more cows, some may have only one cow and more pigs; others may have more sheep, others may have no sheep; some may sell their potatoes in the market, and keep stock of my description or another fed upon green food to assist in making manure; some may have more wheat, some may have none; some may keep breeding pigs, and indeed may very profitably apply the whole farm to rearing them to that state when their neighbours would require them. Some may rear young stock to renew that of their neighbours: others may breed lambs; others may have more flax, and dress and sell it; others may keep a sufficient number of horses to put out manure, to draw produce to market, and so-forth; but what I do contend for is, that no man who works a hundred and eighty days, and who is moderately assisted by his family, can fail of insuring the living that I have set down, and the profit that I have calculated upon. In fact there is no reason why any other man should not make as much profit of four acres of land as I could make, and I undertake to test the success, by making two hundred pounds clear profit of four acres of middling ground, over and above what shall be consumed by an able-bodied man, his wife and family, besides housing them well, and clothing them well, and not allowing them to want a single comfort that a working man is entitled to, and ought to enjoy. With those preliminary observations I shall now proceed to subdivide four acres into those allotments necessary for carrying out the plan before mentioned, leaving to all the power of making such alterations as circumstances and their own will may point out.

ALLOTMENT.

As we must start from some point, I shall begin with the first of May, when the following will be the disposition of that portion of the land assigned to what may be called annual crops, or that may be kept in constant use as kitchen garden.

		A.	R.	P.
Annual crops,	Wheat	1	0	0
	Potatoes	1	0	0
	Soiling Grass	0	2	0
	Kitchen Garden	0	1	0
		2	3	0

Such we shall suppose to be the disposition of the farm in May, 1844, showing two acres and three roods in crop, and an acre and a rood to be disposed of.

	A.	R.	P.
Winter Vetch to be cut in May	0	2	0
Flax and Clover	0	1	0
Cabbages for Autumn	0	1	0
Turnips for ditto	0	1	0
	1	1	0

SUCCESSION OF CROPS.

		A.	R.	P.
1845. Wheat after potatoes	[1]	1	0	0
Winter Tares, after wheat	[2]	0	2	0
Rape, after ditto	[3]	0	1	0
Winter Cabbages, after ditto	[4]	0	1	0
Flax after No. 3,	[5]	0	1	0
Spring Vetches after No. 4,	[6]	0	1	0
Ditto after No.2,	[7]	0	1	0
Cabbages after No. 2,	[8]	0	1	0

Nos. 5, 6, 7, 8, are successions after 1, 2, 3 and 4, leaving the farm
thus. In the autumn of 1845 –

	A.	R.	P.
Wheat	1	0	0
Potatoes	1	0	0
Nos. 5, 6, 7, 8, stripped	1	0	0
Soiling Grass	0	2	0
Kitchen Garden	0	1	0
To which may be added for early Turnips	0	1	0
Making	4	0	0

1845. Nos. 1, 2, 3, 4, succeeded by 5, 6, 7, and 8, as last year, after
wheat.

	A.	R.	P.
1846. Potatoes, after 5, 6, 7, and 8,	1	0	0
Wheat, growing after potatoes of 1845,	1	0	0
Wheaten Stubble, as disposed of in Nos. 1, 2, 3, and 4, succeeded by 5, 6, 7, and 8,	1	0	0
Soiling Grass	0	2	0
Kitchen Garden	0	1	0
Turnips	0	1	0

So the succession goes on, year after year, always taking care that the ground where flax is sown shall be changed, so as not to produce two crops in less than five years off the same ground. By this process the land will become richer and richer every year; while the improvement in the crops will astonish even the labourer himself. And now I shall point out the time of sowing each crop, and the probable period at which the several crops will be fit for use.

After the wheat is reaped, which will be about the tenth of August, a quarter of an acre of winter cabbages should be taken from the seedling bed in the garden, and transplanted with a sufficiency of manure. A quarter of an acre of rape should be the next crop sown in the wheaten stubble, and, after those crops, a half acre of winter tares, with a sprinkling of rye-grass or oats, for standards, should be sown in the other half acre, from the middle till the 20th of September. I have given directions in Number 2 for cultivating those crops. The rape will be fit for use any time after Christmas, and should be cleared off by the first of March, to make way for flax, which should follow it. The cabbages will be fit for use shortly after the rape, and should be cleared off about the same time, to make way for the first sowing of spring tares. A quarter of an acre of early cabbages should be planted in No. 2, after the winter tares; and spring tares should be sown in the remaining half.

The clover should be sown with the flax, and the crops which succeed those that were sown after the wheat crop being all off before autumn, that portion of the ground, amounting to one acre, should be trenched up for potatoes for the following spring; so that we'll say in July of each year the disposition of the farm will stand as follows: –

	A.	R.	P.
Wheat	1	0	0
Potatoes	1	0	0
Soiling Grass	0	2	0
Kitchen Garden	0	1	0
Early Turnips	0	1	0
Early Cabbages	0	1	0
Spring Tares	0	2	0
Flax and Clover	0	1	0

By this table it will be seen that the ground from which the crop of spring tares had been cut would come into earlier use for winter cabbages and rape than the wheaten stubble would, nearly by a month, and that the farmer might commence planting winter cabbages or rape in the ground that had been cleared of spring tares each day, for the use of the cattle. This and many other improvements his own observations would very speedily suggest.

There are many other things that must be left wholly to the discretion of the farmer. For instance, many may prefer mangel wurtzel to turnips, as I do; others may prefer more ground under cabbages and less under tares, as I certainly should; but my object has been to deal rather with a rude than refined system; well knowing that the science would be yearly improved by that class of men whose industry, while employed, made England the envy and admiration of surrounding nations, and whose poverty has reduced the country to the degrading position of a sea-bound dungeon.

With respect to a close following of the plan as laid down above, a word or two of advice may not be unnecessary. In a former number, under the head 'Wheat,' I gave my reasons for not assigning that wonderful importance which most writers do to the wheat crop. And although I have assigned a whole acre, or one-fourth of the holding, for producing wheat annually, yet, by comparison with any other crop, it will be found of less value, and, simply, because less labour is required for its cultivation. A good acre of potatoes will be richly worth £40 and more, while I only estimate the value of a crop of wheat at £12; this is, one hundred and sixty stone, at 1s. 6d. a stone. A good acre of cabbages would be worth £30 for feeding cattle; and in the neighbourhood of a town, if in good season, may produce £70, leaving a quantity of outside leaves for feeding stock. An acre of rape, if allowed to run to seed, would be worth £20; while the stalk, if burned, would make a valuable manure. A good acre of clover will feed four cows for four months in the year; and, averaging their milk even at one shilling and sixpence a-day each, or six shillings for the four, will produce £36 worth of milk, besides a quantity of manure.

Even an acre of the best weed, as I call grass, will produce in hay, besides after-grass, nearly as much as an acre of wheat, and, therefore, I am not to be understood as advocating the system of taking a wheat crop every fourth year, or, in other words, of having one-fourth of the land constantly under wheat. A half acre of wheat upon four acres would but call upon the land for a wheat crop every eighth year; while, if attention was paid, only one crop of flax would be taken off in sixteen years, that is, one-sixteenth of the four acres only would be under flax in each year. Now, of all things it is essential that the farmer should have the whole question before him, and not merely draw his conclusions from four acres of this kind or that kind or the other kind of land – the man with heavy stiff clay-land arguing the expence of spade husbandry, and the unfitness of the soil for tur-nips, potatoes, and most green crops – the reader must take at least one thousand acres, or what may be called a small farm district, into his calculation; and he must also look upon that quantity as yielding, though not exactly the produce that I have laid down, yet the same amount in return for the labour expended. For instance, one man may devote the whole of his farm to the support of horses for working a threshing-machine, a draining-plough, or heavy roller, or breaking stiff soil with the plough, or putting out manure, and for Sunday or holiday excursions, or drawing produce to market. Another man may devote the entire of his farm to the keep of stallions, bulls, boars, and rams, for the use of the dis-trict. Others may keep a portion in hay, which would be always in demand at retail price; a little here and a little there for a sick cow, and so-forth. Others may grow nothing but potatoes and wheat. Others may grow oats; others may grow flax. Others, building upon the partial neglect of some, may grow all kinds of seed required for the use of the district. Others may very profitably rear lambs of a good breed, or heifers, to renew the stock of those who keep milch cows; while others may keep all pigs, either for breed or fatting. But upon the whole I mean to assert, that the two hundred and fifty farmers, occupying the one thousand acres, and cultivating it as they may, would feed their families as I have described, and have each one hundred pounds and more at the end of the year.

Some rules must be invariably observed, and their observance would be criti-cally enforced even upon the most dull and inattentive by those advantages which the careful would derive from an observance of them; for instance, no man should keep a bad cow for a second week, nor should he boggle at any price for a good one. Every day that he keeps a bad one is increasing his loss, and the sooner he replaces her with a good one the sooner he will repair his loss. I have estimated the average milk of a cow at sixteen quarts a-day for six months in the year, and only three quarts a-day for the remaining three months in the year out of the nine that she should give milk; but if the cows are good, and properly attended, and milked three times a-day, as I have recommended, I am very much below the average.

In the second volume of the Library of Useful Knowledge, entitled 'British Husbandry,' I find the following statement, and, as I have before observed, this, of all others, is the most valuable work, at all events in my opinion, that has been published upon practical farming. The following is the extract: – 'Regarding *quantity and quality of milk*, there are few persons who have not heard of Mr Cramp's cow, which during four years – from 1805 to the end of 1808 – yielded the extraordinary amount of 23,559 quarts of milk, producing 2,132lbs. of butter, and various instances of nearly equal productiveness have been cited in many publications. The largest average product which has been stated by any writer in whose practical experience confidence can be placed, is, however, that of Mr Aiton,[1] who rates the yearly average return of the best kyloes at 4,000 quarts within three hundred days, or until they run dry; thus –

				QUARTS.
First	fifty days,	24	quarts per day	1,200
Second	"	20	"	1,000
Third	"	14	"	700
Fourth	"	8	"	400
Fifth	"	8	"	400
Sixth	"	6	"	300

And he cites an extensive Ayrshire dairyman, as saying – 'That he would not keep a cow on his farm that did not yield her own value, or her weight in sweet-milk cheese, every year.' He, however, admits – 'That many cows will not yield more than half that quantity; and that, probably, six hundred gallons in the course of the year may be about a fair average of the Ayrshire stock: if equalled, we believe it will not be found exceeded by any other breed in the kingdom.'

Now, from the above calculation of the produce of Mr Cramp's cow, as well as many other instances which the writer says has been cited of nearly equal produce, we find, if we estimate the value of the butter at a shilling a pound, the whole made in the four years amounted to £106 12s.; while, by the usual mode of estimating the milk at one-half the value of the butter, which would be £53 6s., we find that Mr Cramp's cow, and several others, have yielded £159 18s. worth in four years, or within sixpence of £40 a-year; while I only allow £18 8s., or less than one half, for the produce of a good cow for a year; while I see no earthly reason to prevent any small farmer having just as good stock as those referred to in the above extract. And, then, if it is admitted that a quarter of an acre of ground will support a cow for the year, four acres would support a sixteen cows for that time; and if each cow was as good as Mr Cramp's, or the several others referred to in the extract, the produce of the four acres would amount to six hundred and forty pounds a year: while I am satisfied with less than a fifth. If we estimate the amount of milk given by Mr Cramp's cow at three halfpence a quart, we find that it leaves for the four years £147 19s. 10½d., or for each year, £36 19s. 11½d.

There always appears to be some insurmountable difficulty in the way of performing very easy work, and I cannot for the life of me see why equal

---

1 William Aiton (1760–1848), Lanarkshire agricultural writer.

improvements in agriculture to those made in machinery may not leave the experiments of Mr Cramp and others as far behind as the power-loom has left the hand-loom. My own impression is, that at the present moment the science of agriculture is in the cradle. I cannot give a better illustration of the value of labour than the following anecdote will furnish. My father had a tenant whose name was Phelim Conolly, who was a remarkably large man, and still more remarkable for the immense size of his head and hand. It was the practice for the wife or one of the children to carry the man's dinner to the field during harvest, or when time is precious. Conolly's wife took his dinner to him when he was occupied in reaping a field of wheat; while he was eating she was binding, and when she came to the 'head-land,' that is the part upon which the horses turn while ploughing the field, and which is consequently the best worked, she found the sheaves twice as thick upon the 'head-land,' and the wheat much better than upon any other part of the field; 'Wisha, Phelim,' says she, 'how is it that this strip along here is so much before the rest of the field?' 'Ogh!' replied Phelim, 'my jewel, it's the head-land.' 'Wisha, then,' rejoined Mrs Conolly, 'bad luck to your chuckle head and platther fist, why the devil didn't you make head-lands of all the field.' Now, rude as this dialogue may appear, yet it furnishes a very happy illustration of what may be done with the land, while, had Phelim's head-land been as well cultivated as it might be, it would have yielded more than double, than even that which excited the admiration of Mrs Conolly.

So far I have described what a cow may be made to produce, and I have illustrated the effect produced upon the wheat crop by additional labour; and now I shall cite a very high authority in support of my general view of the capability of the land when applied to other purposes than those of producing wheat, milk, or butter. I find the following vouched for by the Editor of the *Leeds Mercury* newspaper, and as that journal is, out of all comparison, the ablest and most consistent organ of free-trade, as well as the highest authority upon all commercial questions, I presume that the facts vouched for upon the faith of the individual by whom they have been furnished, will not for a moment be doubted. The following is the extract as it appeared in the columns of that journal: –

'GROWTH OF POTATOES. – A correspondent who takes a good deal of interest in the production of potatoes, and who on a former occasion furnished us with a communication on this subject, sends us the following as the result of his labours. The experiments may be found very useful to those parties who are just now engaged in cultivating small plots of ground. The plan has been pursued for two years; the month of March in both years being selected for planting. In order to show which plan is the most productive, every row of potatoes is reckoned ten yards long, and the first row to produce forty pounds: –

	lbs.
1st. – Ashtop Potatoes, size of a hen egg, cut in two, but planted before they begin to sprout; many small ones when ripe	40
2nd. – Ashtop Potatoes, cut in two, but sprouted one inch before they were planted; the tops were shorter, and the potatoes ready for use fourteen days sooner; when ripe, few small	30

                                                                            lbs.

3rd. – Ashtop Potatoes, the size of a goose egg, planted whole, and sprouted
   one inch; when full grown very bushy, and few small   40
4th. – Ashtop Potatoes, cut in two, and sprouted one inch; they were ready
   for use fourteen days sooner than the above   45
5th. – Ashtop Potatoes, cut in two, and planted before they began to sprout;
   when ripe, part small   40

It appears in this statement that one Ashtop potatoe, the size of a hen egg, cut
in two, produced the same weight as the size of a goose egg set whole: the only difference is, that there were less small in the latter; and it will be found that a potatoe
cut in two, will, after having made its appearance above ground, in the course of
ten or fourteen days, appear more promising than a whole potatoe; in about a fortnight afterwards, however, the whole one will take the lead, but the cut potatoes
will be ready for use first.

6th. – Prince Regent Potatoes, the size of a wall-nut, planted whole, before
   they began to sprout   80
7th. – Prince Regent Potatoes, cut in pieces, so as to leave only one eye for
   a plant; very weak   30
8th. – Prince Regent Potatoes, the size of a cricket-ball, cut in two, but
   sprouted one inch   160
9th. – Prince Regent Potatoes, sprouted one inch, and planted whole   120
10th. – Prince Regent Potatoes, cut in pieces, so as to leave only one eye for
   a plant; strong tops   60
11th. – Whole Prince Regents, the size of a child's ball, planted with long
   stable litter   22

All the potatoes (excepting No. 11) were planted with manure, composed of
ashes, road-scrapings, lime, soot, night soil, &c., well mixed together.

The land is rich black soil, clay, sand, and red earth, and in order to insure a fair
trial, six rows of each sort of potatoes were planted in different parts of the field;
and potatoes have been grown on the same land for four years, and the last crop
has been the best.

Our correspondent formerly sent an account of ten yards ten inches producing
10 stones 5 pounds, the tops weighing 7 stones 3 pounds; out of twelve rows, meas-
uring ten yards each, he obtained 70 stones 5 pounds; or, out of one hundred and
twenty yards, 985 pounds of potatoes: twenty-four of these potatoes weighed 28
pounds.

Ashtop Potatoes. – The ridges were twenty inches asunder.

Prince Regents. – The ridges were thirty inches asunder.'

Now, as there are 4,480 square yards in an acre, it follows that if 100 square
yards produce, as the *Mercury* asserts, and as I sincerely believe, 1,920 lbs., an
acre, cultivated in the same way, will produce 92,928 lbs., and four acres will produce 371,712 lbs.; and estimating a bushel of potatoes, weighing 72lbs. at one
shilling and sixpence, or something about three pence halfpenny a stone, we find
that the *Mercury* estimates the value of the produce of four acres at something
more than £487. Now, suppose that we deduct so large a sum as £87 for manure,
seed, and rent, we find that one man, by cultivating four acres in the year, can
earn four hundred pounds, or more than a pound a day, wet days, Sundays, and
holidays included.

Now, suppose we adopt the scale by which we have reduced Mr Cramp's profit, and apply it to the above calculations, that is, if we halve the amount, we find that a man will have two hundred pounds for the labour of a year, being yet considerably more than I have allowed; while it will be borne in mind, that in addition to the testimony of Samuel Bridge, who has produced alternate crops of potatoes and wheat for twenty-seven years, we have the authority of the correspondent of the *Mercury* bearing testimony to the fact, that the process, so far from exhausting, enriches the soil. He says, 'the land is rich black soil, clay, sand, and red earth, and in order to ensure a fair trial, six rows of each sort of potatoes were planted in different parts of the field; and potatoes have been grown on the same land for four years, and the last crop has been the best.'

Having so far explained the means by which a labouring man may support his family, and save one hundred a year to be expended in the commercial market, I may now ask those who so loudly call for an extension of trade, what the commerce of the world would be, compared to such a home-market as one million heads of families located upon four million acres of land would furnish, leaving a hundred millions a year of good and substantial produce, such as bacon, mutton, milk, butter, poultry, woollen and linen fabric, to be exchanged for the produce of machinery, regulated in its price by the ability of the consumers to purchase it.

Without going deeply into the science of political economy, the two contending parties will find it difficult to reconcile the working people to that system which starves them in the midst of a superabundance produced by their own hands. Surely the promised benefits from free-trade should be regulated by some graduated scale; and if the tariff has gone to the extent of reducing prices, those who cultivate the soil should find a better remuneration from the change than that miserable and squalid condition which the advocates of free-trade describe them as being in. Upon the other hand, if the promised benefit was to confer all the anticipated blessings, each extension should be followed by an increase in the comforts of those who are engaged in the trade. But while the agriculturist is consigned to starvation in the midst of abundance of his own creation, and while the operative is in nakedness while surrounded with a superabundance of that, in the production of which he is engaged, what language, what art, what logic, what eloquence can inspire him with confidence in a system, under which he grows daily worse and worse.

BUILDINGS.

In my frequent experiments I have always found that the great advantage I had over my neighbours was derived from my capacious out-offices, having very nearly ten thousand square feet for farming purposes, and built of the very best materials; and, therefore, I attach great importance to a sufficiency of farming offices.* There is no person who has not in the winter time frequently observed a

* I have had under roof, and lock and key, at the same time, a sufficiency of turf for twelve months, fifty tons of hay, twelve thousand sheaves of corn, with houses to receive the straw when

poor horse or cow shivering under a hedge, and especially in Ireland, where the very largest farmers' stock are allowed to remain in what is called the night-park during the whole of winter. Not only does this practice lead to the great detriment of the stock, but it also leads to the sacrifice of a large quantity of manure. If any person should be at all sceptical as to the effect produced upon cattle that are allowed to remain unhoused during the winter, they need but take the trouble of comparing their appearance with those that have had shelter from the weather.

My own opinion is, that an in-calf heifer, which, if housed during the winter, would fetch ten pounds when about to calve, that the same heifer, unhoused during the winter, would not fetch eight pounds. And, as regards sheep, I have constantly housed from a hundred to a hundred and fifty every night in the year, and, by proper attention to the sheep-house, I have found that my flock has always escaped those diseases occasioned by continuous wet, while their wool has always been better than my neighbours. I do not remember having lost a sheep from any disease, and I believe that most diseases are occasioned by a heavy fleece of wool being constantly wet. One great object therefore, and, indeed, the very next in importance to the house for the family, is that of houses for the stock. I know full well that a man possessed of four acres of ground, and who had to walk some distance to his farm, would be very apt to throw up some kind of a hovel wherein to thrust himself as speedily as possible. His first care, therefore, should be to secure the means of building himself a suitable dwelling, and as that purpose could only be effected by profit made of his stock, I would recommend him to commence with his out-offices, and which should consist of the following buildings: –

A COW-HOUSE. – If for four cows, twenty-four feet long and ten feet wide, divided into four stalls, each partition being four feet high; thus allowing the cow to have perfect freedom to lie down and get up with perfect ease, not being tied, or in any way confined. The expence of this building, if economically set about, would be very trifling, for this reason, because in my plan of a farm-cottage I propose that the back wall should be shedded down to constitute the required offices. The back wall of the house would consequently constitute the main wall of the cow-house, and the only other building that would be required to complete it would be two end walls six feet high.

SHEEP-HOUSE. – A sheep-house of five feet wide and ten feet long, that is, the width of the cow-house constituting the length of the sheep-house, would be more than ample for six sheep; and which, with the end walls of the cow-house, and the twenty-four feet allowed for that building, would occupy thirty feet six inches; the six inches being the outside wall of the sheep-house.

---

thrashed, one hundred and fifty sheep housed, thirty-five head of cattle, each having a separate house, twelve horses, each having a stable to himself; a large quantity of manure under sheds; the produce of several acres of potatoes housed, and sixteen men threshing, with calf-houses, fowl-houses, dairy, and over forty pigs, with a considerable quantity of room to spare besides having all the farming implements under cover.

PIG-STYE. – As I propose allowing forty feet in the clear for the family dwelling, we have left nine feet of the back wall against which the pig-stye should be erected; thus, having all the offices, with the exception of fowl-house, dairy, and privy, we may say under the same roof; and requiring no additional brick or stone work beyond the mere erection of the partitions. The pig-stye would admit of sufficient room for sleeping, and a yard for feeding.

DAIRY. – The dairy should be shedded down at one gable end of the house, and its dimensions should be twelve feet by ten feet, and, as the width of the house in the clear would be eighteen feet, the remaining part of the end wall would leave eight feet by twelve for potatoes and fuel. At the other gable should stand

THE FOWL-HOUSE, AND A SHED FOR FARMING IMPLEMENTS, with a sufficiency taken off for a commodious privy.

All except the dairy should front to the yard, and the dairy, for the advantage of light as well as appearance, should be entered from the front. So far I think I have very minutely explained what my intentions are with respect to the necessary out-offices, and now for

THE DWELLING HOUSE.

I do not seek to restrict any man's fancy to that description of house which takes my own, and which is as follows: – I propose the plan, of which the woodcuts in the two following pages give an outline, as well for the dwelling-house as the out-offices, and, by reference to that, the whole may be comprehended in a single glance. The dwelling-house is forty feet long in the clear, and nineteen feet wide, consisting of five rooms, and no stairs or back door which is always a nuisance.

No. 1. – Porch; six feet square, with benches for wash-tubs and sink.
" 2. – Kitchen; sixteen by eighteen feet.
" 3. – Parlour; ten feet by twelve.
" 4. – Front Sleeping-Room; ten feet by twelve.
" 5. – Sleeping-Room; twelve feet by eight.
" 6. – Sleeping-Room; twelve feet by eight.
" 7. – Dairy; twelve feet by ten.
" 8. – Potatoe and Fuel-house.
" 9. – Pig-stye.
" 10. – Sheep house.
" 11, 12, 13, 14. – Cow-houses.
" 15. – Privy.
" 16. – Fowl-house, and Shed for Farming Implements.

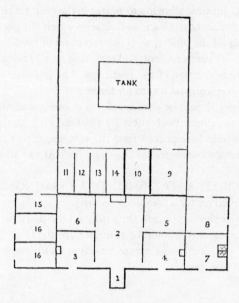

GROUND PLAN OF DWELLING HOUSE, OFFICES, AND FARM YARD.

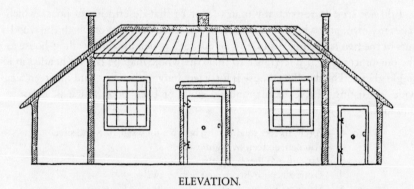

ELEVATION.

Now such would constitute the whole amount of buildings required by a four-acre farmer, as I take it for granted that every man who had corn would take advantage of the threshing machine.

FARMYARD.

The farm yard should consist of the width of the house, forty feet in the clear, and should extend about forty feet; that is, may be forty feet square, and need not be enclosed, nor do I think that a single lock or key would be required for the whole district. However, as tank water and manure would be the two only things in the yard, they would require no protection. In the centre of the yard a tank, twelve feet square and five feet deep, should be made and flagged at the bottom, and bricked up at the sides. There should be a fall from all the houses into the tank; that is, to the rear of the cow-houses, sheep-house, and pig-stye there should be an over-ground channel, inclining from each end to the centre of the cow-house, where a grate should be fixed, and thence communicating by a covered sewer with the tank; the remainder of the yard would be appropriated to heaps of manure. This would be kept inexpensive, and would be more than fourfold paid for in the first year by the tank water. There is nothing more sinfully neglected than the preservation and application of this admirable manure. I will be bound to prove that four cows, six pigs, and six sheep will furnish, within the year, a sufficient amount of tank water to manure four acres of ground. Indeed, I have calculated that, allowing somewhere about seventeen thousand cabbage plants to an acre, one cow will furnish enough to admit of a pint to each plant, and which, if applied shortly after being transplanted by a watering pot without the rose would soon show its value. For carrots, for potatoes, especially early ones, in the dry season, for cabbages, or mangel wurtzel, to all of which it can be so immediately applied there is no better manure; while it surpasses all others in producing a heavy crop of grass. In fact, a good tank is indispensable; it is always come-at-able, and may be applied at seasons when other manures cannot.

MODE OF ERECTING BUILDINGS.

We have heard so much of mud-cabins, and the horrible destitution suffered in them by the Irish people, that, were it not for the good sense of those for whom I write, I should be afraid to mention the subject. However, my object is to prove the great advantages that nature presents if we would only take advantage of them. I trust I am above those vulgar prejudices that have been so artfully fostered by those who have brought the people to their present artificial state. Before I give my own opinion as to the durableness, the cheapness, and sufficiency of clay as a material for building both dwelling-house and out-offices, I beg leave to submit the following extract, taken from a very able work, published within the present year, entitled, 'The Improvements in Agriculture and the Arts of the United States, as set forth luminously and at length in a Report to the Congress of the United States.'

MODE OF CONSTRUCTING HOUSES.

Another improvement relating to a cheap mode of constructing houses where timber is scarce, which shall be at once durable and comfortable, as it has a most important bearing on the vast unoccupied lands of the several States and the nation, may not be inappropriately mentioned. Its full advantages may be appreciated by an examination of the plan, which will be found in a detailed statement, for which see 'Document' No. 15. Many who have been made acquainted with this method have deemed it most desirable to have it published for the benefit of the country at large.

PLAN OF CHEAP COTTAGES.

After selecting a suitable spot of ground, as near the place of building as practicable, let a circle of ten feet or more be described. Let the loam be removed, and the clay dug up one foot thick, or, if clay is not found on the spot, let it be carted in to that depth. Any ordinary clay will answer. Tread this clay over with cattle, and add some straw cut six or eight inches long. After the clay is well tempered with working it with the cattle, the material is duly prepared for the making of brick. A mould is then formed of plank, of the size of the brick desired. In England they are usually made eighteen inches long, one foot wide, and nine inches thick. I have found the most convenient size to be one foot long, seven inches wide, and five inches thick. The mould should have a bottom. The clay is then placed in the moulds in the same manner that brick moulds are ordinarily filled. A wire or piece of iron hoop will answer very well for striking off the top. – One man will mould about as fast as another can carry away, two moulds being used by him. – The bricks are placed upon the level ground, where they are suffered to dry two days, turning them up edgewise the second day, and then packed in a pile, protected from the rain, and left to dry ten or twelve days, during which time the foundation of the building can be prepared. If a cellar is desired, this must be formed of stone or brick, one foot above the surface of the ground. For cheap buildings on the prairie, wood sills, twelve or fourteen inches wide, may be laid on piles or stones. This will form a good superstructure. Where lime and small stones abound, grout made of those materials (lime and stones) will answer very well.

In all cases, however, before commencing the walls for the first story, it is very desirable, as well in this case as in walls of brick, *to lay a single course of slate*; this will intercept the dampness so often rising in the walls of brick houses. The wall is laid by placing the brick lengthwise, thus making the wall one foot thick. Ordinary clay, such as is used for clay mortar, will suffice, though a weak mortar of sand and lime, when these articles are cheap, is recommended as affording a more adhesive material for the plaster. The wall may safely be carried up one story, or two or three stories, the division walls may be seven inches, just the width of the brick. The door and window frames being inserted as the wall proceeds, the building is soon raised. The roof may be shingles or thatch. In either case, *it should project over the sides of the house, and also over the ends, at least two feet, to guard the wall from vertical rains*. The exterior wall is plastered with good lime mortar, and then with a second coat pebble-dashed. The inside is plastered without dashing. The floor may be laid with oak boards, slit, five or six inches wide, and laid down without jointing or planing, if they are rubbed over with a rough stone after the rooms are finished. Doors of a cheap and neat appearance may be made by taking two single boards of the length or width of the doors; placing these vertically, they will fill the space. Put a wide batten on the bottom and a narrow one on the top, with strips on the side, and a strip in the middle. This door will be a batten door, but presenting two long panels on one side and a smooth surface on the other. If a porch or a verandah is wanted, it may be roofed with boards laid with light joints and covered with a thick paper dipped in tar, and then adding a good coat, after sprinkling it with sand from a sand-box or other dish with small holes.

Houses built in this way are dry, warm in winter, and cool in summer, and furnish no retreat for vermin. Such houses can be made by common labourers, if a little carpenter's work is excepted, in a very short time, with a small outlay for materials, exclusive of floors, windows, doors and roof.

The question will naturally arise, will the wall stand against the rain and frost? I answer, they have stood well in Europe, and the Hon. Mr Poinsett[1] remarked to me that he had seen them in South America, after having been erected 300 years. Whoever has noticed the rapid absorption of water by a brick that has been burned, will not wonder why brick walls are damp. The burning makes the brick porous, while the unburnt brick is less absorbent; but it is not proposed to present the unburnt brick to the weather. Whoever has erected a building with merchantable brick will at once perceive the large number of soft and yellow bricks, partially burned, that it contains – brick that would soon yield to the mouldering influence of frost and storms. Such brick are, however, placed within, beyond the reach of rain, and always kept dry. A good cabin is made by a single room twenty feet square. A better one is eighteen feet wide and twenty-four feet long, cutting off eight feet on one end for two small rooms, 9 by 8 each.

How easy could a settler erect such a cabin on the Western prairie, where clay is usually found about fifteen inches below the surface, and where stone and lime are often both very cheap. The article of brick for chimneys is found to be quite an item of expense in wood houses. In these mud houses no brick are needed, except for the top of the chimneys, the oven, and casing of the fire-place – though this last might be well dispensed with. A cement, to put round the chimneys, or to fill any other crack, is easily made by a mixture of one part of sand, two of ashes, and three of clay. This soon hardens and will resist the weather. A little lard or oil may be added, to make the composition still harder.

Such a cottage will be as cheap as a log cabin, less expensive than pine buildings, and durable for centuries. I have tried the experiment in this city, by erecting a building 18 by 54 feet, two stories high, adopting the different suggestions now made. Although many doubted the success of the undertaking, all now admit it has been very successful, and presents a convenient and comfortable building, that appears well to public view, and offers a residence combining as many advantages as a stone, brick, or wood house presents. I will add what Loudon says in his most excellent work, the Encyclopaedia of Agriculture,[2] pp. 74 and 75:

'The great art in building an economical cottage is to employ the kind of materials and labour which are cheapest in the given locality. In almost every part of the world the cheapest article of which the walls can be made will be found to be the earth on which the cottage stands, and to make good walls from the earth is the principal part of the rustic or primitive builder. Soils, with reference to building, may be divided into two classes: clays, loams, and all such soils as can neither be called gravels nor sands, and sands and gravels. The former, whether they are stiff or free, rich or poor, mixed with stones, or free from stones, may be formed into walls in one of these modes, viz: in the pise manner, by lumps moulded in boxes, and by compressed blocks. Sandy and gravelly soils may always be made into excellent walls, by forming a frame of boards, leaving a space between the boards of the intended thickness of the wall, and filling this with gravel mixed with lime mortar, or, if this cannot be got, with mortal made of clay and straw.

'In all cases, when walls, either of this class or the former, are built, the foundations should be of stone or brick, and they should be carried up at least a foot above the upper surface of the platform.'

---

1 Joel Roberts Poinsett (1779–1851), US ambassador to Britain 1825–30.
2 John Loudon, *An Encyclopaedia of Agriculture* (1830).

We shall here commence by giving one of the simplest modes of construction, from a work of a very excellent and highly estimable individual, Mr Denson, of Waterbeach, Cambridgeshire, the author of the Peasant's Voice, who built his own cottage in the manner described below:

'*Mode of building the mud walls of cottages in Cambridgeshire.* After a labourer has dug a sufficient quantity of clay for his purpose, he works it up with straw; he is then provided with a frame eighteen inches in length, six deep, and from nine to twelve inches in diameter. In this frame he forms his lumps, in the same manner that a brickmaker forms his bricks; they are then packied up to dry in the weather; that done, they are fit for the use as a substitute for bricks. On laying the foundation of a cottage, a few layers of bricks are necessary, to prevent the lumps from contracting a damp from the earth. The fireplace is lined and the oven is built with bricks. I have known cottagers, where they could get the grant of a piece of ground to build on for themselves, erect a cottage of this description at a cost of from £15 to £30. I examined one that was nearly completed, of a superior order: it contained two good lower rooms and a chamber, and was neatly thatched with straw. It is a warm, firm, and comfortable building, far superior to the one I live in; and my opinion is, that it will last for centuries. The lumps are laid with mortar, they are then plastered, and on the outside once rough-cast, which is done by throwing a mixture of water, lime, and small stones, against the walls, before the plaster is dry, which gives them a very handsome appearance. The cottage I examined, cost £33, and took nearly one thousand lumps to complete it. A labourer will make that number in two days. The roofs of cottages of this description are precisely the same as when built with bricks or with a wooden frame. Cow-house, sheds, garden walls, and partition fence, are formed with the same materials; but in all cases the tops are covered with straw, which the thatchers perform in a very neat manner. – DENSON'S *Peasant Voice*, p. 31.[1]

Above, then, the reader has the testimony of persons who have not only seen, but who actually live in clay houses. Mr Cobbett objected to potatoes in consequence of their easy production making the Irish people an easy prey to the oppressor, and not because he would have limited the use of the potatoe when applied to its proper purposes, so perhaps the growler may object to a clay house, because the Irish are known to suffer great destitution in such buildings; however, I will add my testimony to that already given, and will further suggest some improvements upon the plan. A great objection to clay houses is, that they are in general infested with vermin, whereas that proceeds from the mode of roofing and that alone; clay houses being usually thatched with straw, whereas they may be slated or tiled just as brick or stone houses, and would be then much freer from vermin than either of the latter.

I have seen in Ireland clay houses in perfect repair that have been inhabited for more than two hundred years, and many of them two stories high, free from damp, warm and comfortable. I have also seen walls inclosing large parks and wholly exposed to the weather that have stood for centuries and are now sound and solid. Indeed, we need not go to Ireland for proof of this assertion, as the traveller may see many of a similar description still standing between Loughbor-

---

1   John Denson, *A Peasant's Voice to Landowners* (1830).

ough and Leicester. I do not however agree entirely with the plan laid down in the above extract, because I am of opinion that the whole house may consist of one brick, thereby saving the expence of moulding and of mortar.

The plan universally adopted in Ireland is as follows: – the site of the house is first laid out, and from the space intended to constitute the interior, and that which is intended for the 'bann' or yard, the earth is dug, the stones are picked out, it is then wetted and well trampled, after which chopped straw is mixed with it, when it is tempered to the consistency of mortar fit for use, and, when in that state, the walls of the house are erected as if by magic. The plan however which I recommend as an improvement upon the foregoing is the following.

MODE OF ERECTING A CLAY HOUSE.

The place intended for the tank should be excavated, and to it should be added a spit from the space intended for the house, and as much more as would be required should be taken from the farm yard. As soon as there is a sufficiency of earth it should be screened as gravel is screened, in order to rid it of the stones. It should be then brought together in the most convenient place for use, wetted, and trampled with cattle; after which chopped straw, as directed in the extract, should be mixed through it, and then, without a stone or brick foundation, it will constitute as good materials as either brick or stone for making a house of any dimensions of two stories high. The walls may be a foot and a half thick, and may be made with the greatest accuracy by applying a frame of the same dimensions, say ten or twelve feet long, three feet high, and a foot and a half wide, merely consisting of two planks, ten or twelve feet long and three feet wide as a gage.

When the wall is perfectly dry it will be ready for the roof, which should be slate or tiles. The outside should be pebble-dashed after it has got a coat of lime mortar, and the inside may be plastered and made ready for either paint or paper, and when perfected I would rather live in it than in either a stone or a brick house. It will last for centuries. It will be free from damp, it will be warm, free from vermin and never require any repairs.

The Dairy, the Fowl house, and the Potatoe house may be all built of the same materials, so that nature has placed the means of building a habitation within the reach of every man. It must be distinctly understood, however, that, in districts where brick or stone are plenty and prejudices strong, every man would be at perfect liberty to follow his own taste, while my object is to get over the eternal obstacles that casuists, political economists, and free traders ever interposed between the working man and comfort, always leading him to a belief that without the intervention of capital he should starve.

I have now concluded my work so far as relates to the practical management of Small Farms. Had the condition of those for whom I write justified me in writing a larger, and consequently a more expensive volume, I might perhaps have entered more into detail; however, after a very close examination, I cannot discover that I have omitted any thing necessary for a Small Farmer to know.

In a previous number I have directed the attention to the great advantage that might be derived from sowing a small portion of each allotment with French furze, a food to which cows and horses are very partial; but, as I did not consider it a question legitimately connected with agriculture, I abstained from giving it a place under any general head, while I esteem the practice of so much value as to recommend its adoption, and the more especially because the preparation for the crop would in the outset furnish the small farmer with a large quantity of the very best manure wherewith to commence operations. Suppose, for instance, that he should decide upon having a quarter of an acre of ground under furze, he may take two or three feet of the surface for manure, and the substratum will produce a better crop than the richest surface would have produced, while the rich mould taken from the surface, if made into a heap and frequently turned when the farmer has nothing else to do, will furnish an abundance of the very best description of manure, and, if mixed with lime, so much the better. Throughout the winter the furze of the year's growth will supply his cattle with excellent food, and which they very much prefer to the best hay. The mode of using it is as follows: the year's growth should be mowed down with a strong scythe, as required for use, the furze should be then bruised in a machine or pounded in a stone trough with a heavy mallet, and may be given to cattle until they begin to blossom, after that they engender worms and should be discontinued. As I before stated, I have followed the practice myself for many years and have discovered its advantages, and would strongly recommend its adoption by all farmers. The mode of renewing the crop is very simple and inexpensive, and is performed as follows: when the stick or stump becomes coarse, and when the plant presents an unhealthy appearance, the whole should be burnt down during the first fine weather in Spring, after which the young sprouts will shoot through the ashes from the level of the surface and will be fit for use in the same season. This operation will not require to be performed oftener than perhaps once in ten years, and it is a crop which never fails, and which no weather affects, and therefore a safe and inexpensive one.

Since I commenced my work upon the Practical Management of Small Farms, many persons having spare capital have commenced experiments upon the land, and from all from whom I have heard upon the subject, I learnt that my calculations, as to profits, are likely to be more than realized. Upon the other hand, I receive numerous letters from persons who are anxious to commence operations, but who are also desirous to receive answers from me on several points upon which they are ignorant: had those parties waited for the completion of my work, they would have found the required information, while they must admit, that it would have been impossible for me to enter into correspondence with each individual who may desire special answers to their communications. From the progress that the landed question is making, not only among the working classes who have been heretofore wholly ignorant upon the subject, but from the degree of attention which it must receive from capitalists and the government, as the only means of righting the country, I may, ere long, feel myself called upon to publish a more elaborate work upon agriculture. The commission now prosecuting its labours in Ireland upon the question of landlord and tenant, and also the increasing importation of foreign stock, will lead the public mind to consider the landed question with more attention than it has hitherto bestowed upon it.

For my part, I feel convinced that there now remains no method whereby the higher and middle classes can be relieved from the threatening distress, other than an improved system of agriculture, and whereby all our non-consuming system-made surplus population might be profitably employed. If I could bring myself for a moment to believe in the anticipated benefits from what is called Free Trade, I should still more urgently press the necessity of the small farm plan, not more from my conviction of the ruinous disappointment which would otherwise inevitably follow the establishment of the free trade principle, than from a desire so to regulate the labour market, that demand and supply may be governed by wholesome regulations. I stated in the outset that the greatness of a country must consist in the aggregate of happy individuals, and not in the concentrated wealth of speculating bodies. England is now strong in the latter, but weak in the former ingredient. I have set plainly before the reader the immense advantages which a natural state of existence presents over that artificial and dependent state to which the present system has brought them; I have laboured hard and incessantly for many years to inspire the industrious of all classes with self-respect, and a knowledge of their own value to society. Neither have I laboured in vain, as we find than the question of the land in one shape or the other is made the foundation of all grievances and complaints, while the necessity of dealing with it in one shape or the other has at length forced itself upon the consideration of the cabinet, and as population increases the necessity for the adjustment of the question will necessarily increase with it. All the dicussions in the House of Commons and out of the House of Commons upon the question of free trade, and any law that may be made upon the subject, will all end in talk and disappointment, as the accomplishment of the full desires of the free trade party must inevitably, and after a very short trial, lead even to their own dissatisfaction. Foreign countries will not allow the English parliament to give and take as it pleases.

Free trade is a game at which two can play, and those who have the controul over the raw material, and who also constitute our best customers for the manufactured article, have at least two to one in their favour. Upon the other hand, is it not monstrous that while other nations are directing their every attention towards making themselves independent of England, that a class of Englishmen should the while be engaged in an endeavour to make Englishmen still more dependent upon foreign states. If it is wise in the foreigner, and the wisdom is admitted, to do for himself that which England has been in the habit of doing for him, surely it would be equally wise of the Englishman to do for himself that which will make him independent of the foreigner! Over all English produce, save the produce of the land, foreign states have controul, and their legislation thwarts and destroys our best intentions. If we seek to depreciate their produce by the production of cheap labour, their people, with more controul over their government than our people, demand and receive protection, and, therefore, the question of free trade is not an English but a universal question, one in which all nations will have their fair share, while no other government in the world can interfere with any legislation affecting English agriculture.

I entertain but very little doubt that the next session of parliament will be almost exclusively devoted to the landed question in one shape or other. In fact, in my letters written to the Irish landlords from York Castle, in 1841, I predicted the very state of things which is now fast coming about; and I now assure the landlords of both countries that the question is whether they or others shall do what the present condition of society demands. It is wholly impossible that the present system of keeping land in the wholesale market for the purpose of monopolizing legislation can co-exist with a rapidly increasing population. The system of stopping holes, of patching up, and of mending, has gone too far; society must be based upon a new and stable foundation, that foundation is the land. Our artificial system has centralized wealth and poverty; the wealth confined to a very few, and poverty raging amongst the many. It has also centralized opinion, an opinion by which the system must be tried, indeed it has been tried and condemned, and lives at the present moment, now upon ephemeral prosperity, and again upon the law's rigour; temporary quiescence existing, while order are being hastily executed, and dissatisfaction suppressed by brute force upon the return of idleness. It is against this system of uncertainty that I the more particularly write. The working classes will not much longer tolerate it, while the declining tradesman will find that upon him at last devolves a great portion of the evil, inasmuch as he is compelled to maintain the hands of the speculators during the season of idleness, while he receives no share of those profits which the masters have wrung out of them, during the season of toil. It is this inequality that leads to dissatisfaction; it is this injustice that requires correction; it is to this adjustment that government must direct its attention. The old system of allowing class to feed upon class cannot be carried on much longer, and for this very simple reason, because one very small class has, through the instrumentality of a non-consuming producing power, contrived to appropriate to themselves all the monies that should belong to all, and no law can be framed to get at an equitable distribution of the national wealth so usurped. They would be compelled to vest their surplus capital in the landed market if that market was once opened, while the equalization of wages would establish a more equitable standard of competition in the manufacturing market, and place all, as heretofore, upon something like an equality.

All must now be awake to the awful inroads made upon the social comforts of the working classes. Perhaps the best picture that can be drawn of the present gamblers in human labour is to represent them in their former character, and in their present position. In the olden times, when a good understanding existed between the master, and some twenty or thirty manual labourers, they played for pence and the game was fair. If the profits of the masters were comparatively small, it was because an equitable distribution was made of the profits to all: and society was seldom disturbed by any misunderstanding, which the good sense of the interested parties did not very speedily reconcile, without the interference of the law, the military, the special constables, or the police. At that time, the small masters were not invested with the double character of employers and justices!

When machinery was introduced, and as it progressed, they began to gamble for shillings in the first instance, and the pennies were put out of play. As new inventions or improvements went on, they began to gamble for pounds, and the shillings were also put out of play. As soon as the accumulated property was able to contend for representation with the landed interest, the gamblers in pounds were able to achieve an amount of representation, which compelled their government to appoint them to the magistracy of the country; and thus, armed with the two edged sword, the power of capital to reduce wages, and the power of the magistrate to coerce into an acquiescence, they began to gamble for hundreds, and put the pounds out of play; until at length they have not only rendered all the real money in the world incapable of representing their stakes, but have gone to the extent of gambling for the produce of foreign states; Great Britain and Ireland being too narrow a field for gambling speculations.

We believe it was during the vice-regency of lord Townshend,[1] in Ireland, that the demands for patronage by the Hutchinsons[2] and Beresfords[3] became so extravagant that the viceroy, upon one occasion, observed – 'I do believe that if the Hutchinsons and Beresfords got a gift of England and Ireland, they would want the Isle of Man for a potatoe garden.' So it is precisely with our manufacturers. They have gambled for all at home. They have cheated until they have won all. They have placed it out of play by a non-consuming producing power; and now they ask for some higher stakes to represent their power of cheap production.

It may not be unimportant to shew the immediate effect that this progressive spirit of gambling is likely to have upon the parties engaged. Let us group them, and mark their progress. Suppose that a number of persons sit down at a gambling-table, to play for penny stakes. As long as the play is confined to those stakes, the penny will represent something, and have its value in the market. If the play is changed to shilling stakes, the pennies are put out of play, and out of the market; and he will be considered impertinent who offers to pay a shilling in pennies. The shilling then becomes valuable as it represents the stake played for. If, however, the gambling increases to pound stakes, the shillings are put out of play, and out of the market; and the man who attempts to stake twenty shillings would be laughed at. As the blood warms and the desire to speculate increases, the stakes increase with it, until at length they arrive at hundred pound stakes, when pounds are put out of play: and it not unfrequently occurs that the hundreds are put out of play by bonds, bills, I.O.U.'s, post obits, and mortgages, rendering what may be considered real money but an inadequate representation of the gambling speculation. Observe then, the effect which those altered stakes will produce, as if by magic. As long as a penny represents a stake, it was of

---

1 George Townshend (1724–1807), fourth Viscount, Lord Lieutenant of Ireland 1767–72.
2 E.g. John Hely-Hutchinson (1757–1832), Baron Hutchinson.
3 E.g. John Beresford (1738–1805), MP for Waterford 1760–1805.

certain value; and four or five pennies would be looked at twice before they would be given, say to a messenger who bought a note. When the stakes increased to a shilling, however, the pennies would be freely given in handsful, as they represented nothing, while passing importance would be attached to the shilling. And this, again, when put out of play, would be as freely given as the pennies were; and so on: each increase of the stakes rendering comparatively valueless those smaller amounts which were previously played for.

Now such precisely is the position of our present speculators in human labour. They have got more artificial power than would supply the world with produce; and, in the wildness of speculation, they have lost all thought of the land at home, so inadequate to represent the stakes they play for. If the system be not checked, no power on earth can much longer suppress that popular fury which, though long pent up, will in its rage destroy the whole system, leaving no trace of what is called England's greatness. Machinery has put manual labour out of play and rendered it comparatively valueless in the gambling market.

However, the book, the first practical book upon the subject, is now before the working classes: it has been written for the purpose of instructing them, and of producing a change which must be beneficial to all. In perusing it, they will take it as a whole, they will either reject or require satisfactory explanation upon points which they cannot understand, while I rest satisfied in the belief that even my errors, should they be ever so numerous, will lead to a further illustration of the subject. I shall perseveringly prosecute my labours until I am convinced of my ignorance or until I convince others of their ignorance. When I undertake a project, however great it may be, or however long the period it may require to be brought to maturity, I am not to be diverted from it; and as the convenient subdivision of the land for the support of all who wish to cultivate it has occupied more of my attention than any other subject, I shall continue to press it in one shape or other upon the consideration of all, until I, or those who may come after me, shall see my justification in the happy results which its completion is sure to produce.

ENROLMENT OF THE MILITIA
FOR IMMEDIATE SERVICE!!¹

[1846]

This measure is actually contemplated. The circumstances are such as demand the attention of all classes of the community. Every man will be liable to be drawn for the service who is between the ages of 21 and 45. The enrolment is proposed to take place by ballot; and the service to continue for three years, and then to be repeated for three years more after the expiration of six years, unless the Militia troops can be induced to become regular soldiers by volunteering into the lines.

Read the following extract from the TIMES and MORNING CHRONICLE, of December 27th, 1845, in both which papers it substantially appeared.

'The letters which we lately published of the Secretary of State for the Home Department, and of the Secretary of War, leave no doubt of the intentions of the government as to the enrolment of the Militia for immediate service.' 'Our readers must not treat the matter with any degree of levity, as it relates in a great measure to every person in the kingdom, without any distinction whatever.' 'It must be understood that the Militia will not on this occasion be raised, as incorrectly reported a short time since, by beat of drum, but according to the old system of ballot or process, which no one above the age of 21 need flatter himself that he can avoid. It appears that of the number at first enrolled in a single district – say Sussex – one-third will be called on for duty for three years, when they will be discharged (each man having the option of volunteering into the line), and will not again be required for at least six years. It is understood by those connected with the Militia, that government have not determined upon enrolling that body through any fear of War, but with a view of affording the Canadas, New Zealand, and other portions of the colonies, additional military force.' 'The attendance of those enrolled will consequently be continually required at the barracks for the above-mentioned period. The barracks, of course, in which the army on home-service are now stationed, will be occupied by the Militia troops.' 'The vacant adjutancies alluded to in the letter of Sir James Graham, will be principally filled up by half-pay officers. There are altogether, including those of England, Wales, Scotland, and Ireland, 129 regiments, exclusive of private bodies.'

---

1 One edn, 1846, 2 pp. By William Lovett (1800–77), Chartist and Owenite.

FELLOW-COUNTRYMEN, look at this proposal. There is not a moment to be lost. Parliament will meet in two or three weeks, and you should be all ready with petitions against it. It will add 42,000 soldiers to the army at once. It will do this by ballot, from which no man within the prescribed ages can escape. It will separate those who serve from their wives and children, and shut them up in barracks for three years, subject to all the rigours of military training and discipline. It will forcibly withdraw them from their own useful occupations, to make them soldiers. It will deprive them of their liberty to act as they please, and rob the community of all their valuable services. It will press most heavily upon the labouring classes. Other classes may be burdened to pay the money, but the labouring classes will supply the men. And all this at a time of general peace. Is it right?

We ask you seriously to consider whether the system and practice of War be not altogether opposed to the character and precepts of our holy religion; whether it be not fraught with innumerable mischiefs in every form which it assumes; and whether this particular form of it be not especially objectionable? Will it not go far towards making us a nation of fighting men? Will it not inflict serious injury upon the moral and religious habits of the people? Will it not hinder the onward progress of our commercial prosperity? Will it not greatly interrupt the laudable efforts of the middle and lower classes to improve their leisure hours by mutual instruction in general science and literature? Will it not tend to endanger our personal liberties and our social peace? Must it not awaken the jealousy of other nations, and induce them to do likewise? Is this the way to shew that we love our neighbours as we love ourselves?

You cannot approve of this measure. We ask you to oppose it, by all peaceful and legal means. Meet at once and PETITION against it. Tell the legislature that you have most decided and religious objections to the War-system altogether, and to this Militia-system in particular. Let the voice of the British people be heard on this question. Public opinion respectfully, firmly, unitedly uttered, cannot be uttered in vain. Every subject of these realms, of adult age, has a right to express his and her opinion, by signing a Petition. Again we remind you that prompt action is indispensable.

MEET AT ONCE, AND PETITION.

PROPOSAL
FOR FORMING A PEOPLE'S LEAGUE,

ADDRESSED TO THE RADICAL REFORMERS OF THE UNITED KINGDOM.[1]

[1846]

FELLOW COUNTRYMEN,

Desiring the *peace*, *prosperity*, and happiness of our country we deem it our duty to address you at this eventful period; believing that correct views, just feelings, and *a cordial union among all classes of reformers* would be the most effective means of peacefully removing all unjust obstructions to our national prosperity, and would form the best security for the advancement of our people.

But in inviting your aid for the formation of such a union, we deem it necessary to declare that we are opposed to every description of outrage or violence, and that we have no intention of interfering with the present constitution of the realm. We only wish the Common's House to be a true representation of the industry, intellect, and good feeling *of the whole population* that our reforms should be peacefully and justly effected – that the security of person and property should be maintained – that our trade, commerce, and enterprise should be justly extended – our brethren improved and educated – and that our country should progress *politically* and *socially* the first among the nations of the world.

We have faith also to believe that all this can be effected *by peaceful and moral effort*; as our combined industrial energies, our united capital, *our moral courage*, our *intelligence* and *will* alone, give strength to our state, and constitute the only power of our rulers.

But, fellow-countrymen, judging from the legislative effects and burthens of the last few years, we have just cause for apprehending that the longer reform is delayed in every department of the state the more difficult will it be to effect it – the more destructive will be its results to the middle and working-classes – and the greater will become the danger lest an impoverished and oppressed people overturn, in their frenzy, the accumulated wealth, power, and improvement of ages.

---

1   One edn, 1846, broadsheet. By William Lovett. Lovett, in *The Life and Struggles of William Lovett* (1876), p. 335, gives the founding of the People's League as soon after the French Revolution of 1848.

For should our present system of privilege and corruption be prolonged, we may confidently predict that our *Manufacturers* and *Traders*, overburthened by taxation, cramped by monopolies, and fettered by exclusive laws, will year after year find it the more difficult to compete with less burthened countries; and that their markets being thus restricted will afford less profits on labour and capital, and will cause less employment for our continually increasing population.

Our ingenious *Artizans* and industrious *Mechanics*, and *Labourers* compelled to strive with each other for such limited employment, would inevitably bring down their present inadequate wages to the subsistence point; and with that would speedily come the fast deterioration, the pauperising and destruction of our country's hope and pride, her intelligent and industrious people.

Our *Shopkeeping* and *Middle-classes*, chiefly dependant on the consumption of the industrious millions, would most assuredly sink with them, as, in addition to their loss of business and profits, they would have to sustain the burthen of that pauperism and misery such a state of things would engender.

With an unemployed and impoverished people would come turbulence and disorder, for a people steeped in misery will not always listen to the dictates of prudence, and, to escape such a state of commotion, the *capital*, the enterprise, and the intellectual stamina of our country would wing their way to other lands, as we have seen in the case of unhappy Ireland.

But, fellow-countrymen, with all our apprehension of the future, we need not to point beyond present evils to afford abundant cause for awakening your sympathies, and stimulating your benevolent resolves.

Misery, starving wretchedness, and ill-requited toil, have been proclaimed by our rulers to be the daily lot of millions of our working-class brethren. Over-burthening taxation, restricted trade, debts, bankruptcy and insolvency, are making rapid inroads on the industrial energies and previous accumulations of our middle and upper classes; and yet, amid all this social deterioration our rulers are adding burthen to burthens, and seem resolved to perpetuate them.

The Commons House, which ought to be a true representation of the wants and wishes of the whole people, and composed of men whose aim and object it should be to reduce and keep down our present extravagant expenditure, and to determine how the mental, moral, and industrial energies of our people should be developed and extended, so as to add to the prosperity and happiness of all, seems but a mere instrument in the hands of our privileged orders for maintaining their monopolies, perpetuating their unjust powers, and taxing our population.

For the present franchise being so limited and unequally distributed, and the means of bribery and corruption so extensive, the legislative efforts of the few representatives of the people in that house are generally neutralised, or rendered hopeless, by the overwhelming power of aristocratic nominees, army, navy, or mere privileged representatives.

Fellow-countrymen, the intellectual and moral energies of reformers have for years been contending against this power of corruption. Thousands of lives have been sacrificed, and millions of money have been spent in striving to make the

House of Commons an instrument of progress, an organ for effecting the welfare of our country. To move every reluctant step, it has been compelled to take, a social tornado has been required, and that subsiding, it has again sought to retrace its progress, and to build up and strengthen its oppressive powers.

Believing, therefore, that the House of Commons must truly and justly represent *the whole people* before it can become effective for lessening our burthens, removing restrictions and monopolies, or for helping onward the intellectual, moral, and truly religious progress of our people; we invite the good and true among all classes to unite with us for the forming of a PEOPLE'S LEAGUE, the chief object of which shall be to obtain the equal and just representation *of the whole people* as set forth in the *People's Charter*, with such alterations and amendments in its details as may appear necessary.

But in adopting the principles of this document we deem it necessary to state that we adopt it in the spirit of those with whom it originated; whose object it was to create and extend an enlightened public opinion in its favour, and to endeavour to unite all good men for peacefully obtaining its legislative enactment.

At the same time we repudiate, with all earnestness and sincerity, the violent language and mischievous conduct which selfish and unprincipled individuals have associated with that measure of political justice – persons who have sought to maintain their notoriety and to acquire an ascendancy over the multitude by lauding their vices and administering to an intolerant and persecuting spirit. By which malevolent conduct they have fostered and perpetuated divisions between the different classes of society, given support to oppression, delayed the cause of reform, and consequently prolonged the poverty and misery of the millions.

Hopeful however that the time is now arrived for a union of all true reformers, and having full faith that there is sufficient intelligence, moral energy, and religious feeling among our countrymen for restraining all acts of violence and folly – and for peacefully effecting all those reforms necessary for the prosperity of our country, and the elevation and happiness of our people, we resolve to attempt the formation of such a union, and invoke the blessing of Heaven for our success.

We remain your sincere fellow-countrymen,

ADDRESS OF THE COUNCIL
OF THE PEOPLE'S INTERNATIONAL
LEAGUE.[1]

LONDON:
PRINTED BY PALMER AND CLAYTON,
CRANE-COURT, FLEET-STREET.
1847.

---

1 One edn, 1847, 16 pp.

At a public meeting, held on Wednesday, April 28, at the Crown and Anchor, Strand,

Dr BOWRING, MP,[1] in the Chair,

Resolved, –

That an Association be now formed, to be called the 'Peoples' International League,' the Objects of which shall be as follows: –

To enlighten the British Public as to the Political Condition and Relations of Foreign Countries;

To disseminate the Principles of National Freedom and Progress;

To embody and manifest an efficient Public Opinion in favor of the right of every People to Self-government and the maintenance of their own Nationality;

To promote a good understanding between the Peoples of all Countries.

That the following gentlemen shall be the Officers of the League for the ensuing year: –

TRUSTEES.

MR W. H. ASHURST,[2]   MR P. A. TAYLOR,[3]
MR JOS. TOYNBEE.[4]

COUNCIL.

MR W. B. ADAMS,[5]	MR DOUGLAS JERROLD,[6]
— W. H. ASHURST,	—W. J. LINTON,[7]
— GOODWYN BARMBY,[8]	— R. MOORE,[9]
DR BOWRING, MP,	— J. H. PARRY,[10]
MR WM. CARPENTER,[11]	— W. SHAEN,[12]
— THOMAS COOPER,[13]	— J. STANSFELD,
— WM. CUMMING,	— P. A. TAYLOR,
— T. S. DUNCOMBE, MP,[14]	— P. A. TAYLOR, JUN.,

---

1 Dr John Bowring (1792–1872), linguist and diplomat, MP for Clyde Burghs 1835–7 and Bolton 1841.

2 William Henry Ashurst (1792–1855), radical solicitor.

3 Peter Alfred Taylor (1819–91), later MP for Leicester.

4 Joseph Toynbee (1815–66), surgeon.

5 William Brides Adams (1797–1872), civil engineer.

6 Douglas William Jerrold (1803–57), dramatist and man of letters.

7 William James Linton (1812–98), engraver, poet and journalist.

8 John Goodwyn Barmby (1820–81), Christian socialist.

9 Richard Moore (1810–78), originally a wood-carver.

10 John Humffreys Parry (1816–80), barrister.

11 William Carpenter (1797–1874), radical journalist.

12 W. Shaen (1821–87), solicitor.

13 Thomas Cooper (1759–1839), shoemaker, teacher, journalist and poet.

14 Thomas Slingsby Duncombe (1796-1861), radical MP for Hertford 1826, 1830, 1831, and Finsbury 1834, who presented the Chartist Petition in 1842.

DR EPPS,[1]   — R. TAYLOR,
MR W. J. FOX,[2]   — J. TOYNBEE,
— S. M. HAWKES,   — H. VINCENT,[3]
— THORNTON HUNT,[4]   — J. WATSON.[5]

AUDITORS.

MR AUSTIN,   MR H. MITCHELL,
MR SOLLY.[6]

SECRETARY.

MR W. J. LINTON.

---

1 John Epps (1805–69), homeopathic surgeon.
2 William Johnson Fox (1786–1864), Unitarian minister.
3 Henry Vincent (1813–78), radical journalist and lecturer.
4 Thornton Hunt (1810–73), radical journalist.
5 James Watson (1799–1874), radical publisher.
6 Henry Solly (1813–1903), Christian reformer.

ADDRESS, &c.

The insularity of England among the family of European nations is more than that of mere geographical position. Self-contained and self-contented, her people, as a people, seldom extend an enlightened regard or a warm sympathy beyond the narrow sphere of cares and interests involved in the progressive development of the internal powers and resources of their own country. That high, earnest, and ever-watchful Public Opinion, the Palladium of the rights and immunities of Englishmen, is concentrated on the affairs of their own island-home; *foreign* relations – as the mutual affinities and interdependencies of communities are styled – being regarded as the exclusive and peculiar province of statesmen and diplomatists. In this field the wholesome jealousy of power, characteristic of the English mind, either works not at all, or works in ignorance of the true bearings and tendencies of the transactions which it seeks to control. That 'proud indolence,' in regard to 'foreign affairs,' with which the statesmen of a neighbouring country charge us, or the 'apathy' of which many of our own political writers have loudly complained, is at once selfish, impolitic, and unjust. The Unity of Humanity, which expresses the law of individual intercourse, also includes the law of the inter-communication of nations. The sentiment, enthusiastically responded to by the human instincts of a Roman audience, even in Rome's most corrupt days, Christian England has yet to extend and apply to international interests. WE ARE A NATION, AND NOTHING THAT CONCERNS OTHER NATIONS DO WE DEEM FOREIGN TO US. Through good and evil report, to this principle we must firmly adhere, if we would have our claim of 'teaching the nations how to live' held for more than an idle boast. It is not enough that we have established, and are resolute to further and maintain, our own freedom and nationality. Our wishes and endeavours must tend to secure the same blessings for other countries. As no man will reach heaven who seeks to reach it alone, so no nation will ever develop the highest and most enduring forms of national life, while it is contented to remain the passive and uninterested spectator of the onward and upward struggles of kindred peoples. A recluse tribe is as anomalous as a single anchorite. Seclusion is an indulgence that can, in neither case, be gratified except at the sacrifice of duty, and duty is never sacrificed except at the cost of interest. For self alone, no man, no people lives. Multiplicity in Unity is the law and type of National Progression. The varied forms of opinion, character, and institution, by which the nations of Europe are respectively distinguished, are all aggregate elements in the great unit of European civilisation; and the nation which in selfish solitariness resists the interchange of these God-ordained influences, sins against that law of moral gravitation which knits communities in the same self-asserting bonds of relationship by which classes and individuals are held together. Though many, the nations of Europe are one, and all members one of another. In the well-being of each all are interested, for all share, consciously or unconsciously, in the mixed good and evil which affects each.

An isolative national policy, which we have seen to be morally wrong, we might naturally, nay, must necessarily presume to be politically imprudent. It encourages Absolutism to interfere with national rights in a way that Absolutism would not dare to attempt if nations were fully alive to the importance of the common interest which unites them. The popular indifference in England to the course of continental policy invites despotic aggression abroad. It does more. It paralyses the power of any honest Government at home to adopt the measures of beneficent intervention necessary to repress meditated outrage, or to redress committed wrong; while it offers impunity to a false and fatal compliance with the views of despots, on the part of rulers who may be adverse to the principles of pacific social progress. How small the amount of enlightened public opinion that can, in the present eventful crisis of our country's external relations, be brought to bear upon British Statesmanship! How few Englishmen but are either uninformed or misinformed in regard to the character, connexion and consequences of the recent circumstances under which the policy of the Peace of 1815, from time to time undermined, has finally been demolished by the hands which reared it. In the ranks of the great industrial classes of this country, the substantial depositary of political power, beyond the ill-considered cry of 'Peace, peace,' when there is no peace, absolutely *no symptom of public opinion* exists on the subject; and the settlement of a grave question, involving interests of primary importance to England and to Europe, is left to the discretion or caprice of a Government, under conditions that curb and cripple a good Minister, and leave a bad Minister free to run his unchecked course. These things ought not to be. Englishmen should be cognisant of the processes through which the progressive destinies of Europe are being worked out, so that whenever European affairs may call for interference, they may be in no doubt as to the course to be pursued. Our people must learn to bring to the consideration of foreign questions the same vigilance, prudence and sagacity which they bestow on home questions. They must not indolently abdicate their right to adjudicate on such matters, in favour of uncontrolled and irresponsible diplomacy, but be themselves able and ready to pronounce judgment in a tone and spirit worthy of freemen, conscious of their position and duty, with the calmness of collected thought, and the firmness and power which only knowledge can impart. For the progress we have already made in our internal policy, for the removal of restrictions, religious, political, social and economic, for the views and hopes of a higher liberty, which still open to us in distinct though distant vista, we are indebted wholly and solely to the influence of enlightened public opinion upon the action of Government and legislation. Should not this consideration inspire the endeavor, in regard also to our foreign policy and relations, to create a public opinion, which, trusting to our past history and our national character, may ultimately do that for the cause of European progress, which a like agency has done for the liberties of our own country?

To place England in this position of knowledge and matured opinion is the aim of the proposed Peoples' International League. Of all practicable means within the compass of English laws and English sympathies it will avail itself, for the purpose of working out its ends. The result, with the help of God and of all earnest men, will be to infuse new strength, morality and prosperity into England's social life, by harmonising under one high principle of Justice, Truth and Duty, her political and economic energy, her national and international influence and agency.

The present position of general European politics, independently of the considerations above submitted, justifies – were justification needed – the formation of our League. The virtual abrogation of the Treaty of Vienna, by the recent suppression of Cracow, seems to open a new era to Europe. The political system established and guaranteed by that treaty had already undergone repeated change and modifications. It needed only this public disclaimer of its obligations, to destroy any opinion that might remain as to the influence it yet exercised upon the destinies of Europe. France had long since thrown out the elder branch of the Bourbons, for whom especially the Congress of 1815 seemed to have provided. Portugal had changed her dynasty. Belgium had severed herself from Holland. The new kingdom of Greece had sprung up. And now the three great Powers of Eastern Europe have proclaimed their absolute independence of its provisions. To what further aggressions this may be the prelude, it is impossible to foretell: enough that these Powers have shown that their usurpations are not restrained by treaties, however solemnly contracted. And while the absolute Powers are thus intent upon their own aggrandisement, the oppressed people of Europe are equally determined to assert, and sooner or later will achieve, their rights of Nationality and Self-government.

In the division of Europe among the several Powers, at the Congress of Vienna, an immense error, not to say a great iniquity, was committed. The natural peculiarities of character – the indications of different destinies, the diverse natural tendencies of various peoples – deducible from their languages, creeds, habits, historical traditions, and geographical position, were altogether overlooked or disregarded. Questions of the balance of power, of imaginary equalities, calculated by ciphers, representing square miles or millions of men – not human ideas, human wants, human tendencies, – were the considerations that decided the partition of Europe. It was a hurried, an ill-advised, and improvident work, concocted, on the one hand, by Powers that had nothing in view but their own despotic interests and aggrandisement; on the other, by politicians looking no further than their own time, seeking only for present peace, frightened at, and weary of, the convulsions through which Europe had just passed, and without faith in the future; men anxious merely to reconstitute the old system which Napoleon had broken down, and who had given neither time nor sympathy to the study of those vital elements out of which a new system might be constructed, and upon which alone permanent peace and progression can be established.

And what has been the result? First a hidden, then an open, struggle against the established order of things. The spirit which God has breathed into the Peoples, in furtherance of his providential plan – the Spirit of Progress – is more powerful than any diplomatic arrangements, and will not be long dammed up, nor diverted from its natural courses. Since 1815, at sundry times and in diverse manners, that Spirit, which speaks in deeds, has uttered its protest: successfully, in Greece, in France, and in Belgium; unsuccessfully, hitherto, in other places, but unceasingly, with ever-growing power, and with sure promise of ultimate success.

The question now at issue throughout Europe, at the bottom of all European movements, is the question of Nationality – of national rights and duties.

We have but to cast our eyes over the map of Europe, to see that it is so. We have but to watch, during the short space of a month, the symptoms now manifesting themselves in almost every part of Europe: signs of old things verging to decay, of new ones rising in their stead, prophetic sounds of no uncertain meaning, voices from the deep, telling us with unmistakable plainness of the spirit working underneath.

Poland. – See how her often-baffled but never-conquered determination to recover her right of Nationality, of distinctive life, has continually disturbed the peace of Europe since the first days of her spoliation; how impossible it is to tread out that determination, to eradicate the hate with which she regards her oppressors, to destroy the will which eventually must conquer.

Italy. – Mark how clearly the character of the agitation there is manifested; how visibly it has descended from the few to the masses; how it has compelled concessions, reforms, and promises from the Italian Governments; and how neither local remedies nor partial improvements stay its progress. It is no material interest that may be appeased by fiscal arrangements. There is an Idea here at work, – the idea of Unity – of Nationality. The land of Dante,[1] Petrarch,[2] and Machiavelli,[3] yearns to fulfil their prophecy. It wants to be One. It is not an internal question about forms of government: it is a national question. Twenty-four millions of men, tried and disciplined by three hundred years of common bondage and martyrdom, want to unite in one compact body, to have some weight in the scale of nations, some recognition of their part and mission in the life and destinies of Europe.

Greece. – Called to a second life after a death of ages, can we think that the arbitrary barriers of diplomacy will be strong enough to repress her growing aspiration to re-unite in one common nationality all the Greek populations now in the hands of Turkey; to rally round her, her children of Thessaly, of Macedonia, of Candia; and to build up a living Greece which ancestral memories may visit without breathing a reproach?

---

1 Dante Alighieri (1265–1321), Italian poet.
2 Francesco Petrarca (1304–74), Italian poet.
3 Niccolò Machiavelli (1469–1527), Italian politician and writer.

Switzerland. – Discontented with the constitution imposed upon her by the Allied Powers, in 1815, which has been a source of perpetual strife and weakness, she, too, desires change – to make herself a Nation, united in one Federal Bond, under which, while the local Cantonal Sovereignties will still continue to exist for Cantonal government, the general Swiss interests shall be represented by some central power not at present existing: the Diet being now composed of representatives of the Cantons, not of the Nation; representatives of local and partial interests, intrusted with imperative mandates from each Canton, not with the mission of representing all that constitutes Swiss life, Swiss independence, Swiss progression.

SLAVONIANS. – A race of eighty millions (including the Poles and Russians), spreading from the Elbe to Kamshatka, from the Frozen Sea to Ragusi on the shores of the Adriatic: five millions of Tcheks, in Bohemia; two millions of Moravians, scattered through Silesia, Hungary, &c.; two millions of Slovaks, in Hungary; two millions of Croatians and Slovents, in Styria and Carinthia; the Serbes, Bulgars, and Bosniaks, in Turkey; the Dalmatians, Illirians, and Slavons, in Austria: they, too, are looking to a new era in Europe; they, too, having risen from a literary movement entirely unknown in England, to a political one equally unknown, are demanding the common life and unity of Nationality; they, too, are prepared to start into being, at the first energetic and prolonged appeal of Poland, to form four nations (if we reckon Poles and Russians) bound in one great Federal Bond.

And, behind them, perhaps, as regards ripeness, yet still firmly bent toward the same point of National Unity, comes Germany. Her tendencies were clear enough in 1813 and 1815, when the popular spirit was aroused against Napoleon; and, though betrayed by her Governments, the same spirit lives and works toward the one end.

From all this, the position of Europe, the volcano on which it sleeps, may be learned.

But must the explosion come? Is it not possible, by a wise foresight, to avoid the danger? May not a calm and peaceful evolution avert the threatened strife? Why cannot these Nationalities be recognised – as each proves the justice of its claim, be set free to develop each its own peculiar growth, to fulfil each its own special mission, so to work out God's providential plan? for, if this is not God's plan, languages, tendencies, traditions, geographical characteristics, have no meaning. When a People is struggling to embody its inner life in new forms of outward institution, why not hail the event, and assist, instead of hindering, its ascent to the dignity and capacity of a Nation? Is not the will of the People the will of God? Is not England, for one, ready to welcome any new power, any new element of activity and civilisation?

There are, in Europe, three Powers representing Absolutism: the principle that denies man's right to self-government, self-development, and, consequently, progress towards the Right and Good, – that denies the right of national and individual freedom, – that virtually denies even the providence of God, by asserting that his gift of national character, of peculiar genius, is so aimless and accidental that it may be thwarted or controlled by any arbitrary convention of despots. These three Powers are leagued together for any foul deed that may subserve their designs; and none are leagued against them.

There is in Europe, at the present time, no representative of the Good Principle: there are three of the Evil One.

And thus the question is left to force, – force between the oppressors and the oppressed; and by the assumption, 'for peace' sake,' of an utter indifference, by refusing to throw into the balance of European destinies the weight of a peaceful, but firm and generous assertion of the principles of Eternal Truth and Justice, by the denial of even passive sympathies with the oppressed and their aspirations, the nations of Western Europe compel those who are struggling for freedom to look to insurrection as their only hope. The consequences of this ignoble and fatal indifference are manifest enough. Cracow is swallowed up when Russia chooses; Poland is not even a name; Switzerland and Italy are threatened with intervention; treaties are set at nought, and protests mocked at. In the same speech in which the King of the French congratulates his subjects on the completion of a commercial treaty with Russia, he is forced to contradict that gratulation by the acknowledgment that Russia is no respecter of treaties. International faith is gone. There is security neither against political aggression nor for commercial enterprise. Having on our side abdicated that course of public duty which faith in God and Humanity points out, and which would have insured us the respect of Europe, we have now no hold upon these Powers, except through their interests, which may or may not be the same as ours. They have neither respect nor fear for us. They do not hesitate to hurl their defiance at us: – 'We shall rule, for we have the daring of Evil; we act: you have not the courage to stand up for Good.'

Such a state of things cannot last: it is atheistic.

Are we not all of us, by God's will, one single family, endowed with the same rights, bound by the same duties, invested with the same mission of development and progress? Is it enough that we egotistically vindicate our own rights, if Eternal Right is every hour violated at our doors? Is it enough that we proclaim in ourselves the law of God (a law of duty and responsibility – and, therefore, necessarily of liberty), if we neglect to recognise this law for others? Is it enough that we call ourselves Christians, if we desert our brothers at their utmost need, struggling in a holy cause at fearful odds? Is it enough to care for national honor when some fancied slight affects the private interests of diplomacy, and to refuse all interference when the most solemn treaties are violated in our despite, when the honor of humanity is concerned? Is it enough to proclaim philanthropy and liberate the Blacks, when our fellow Whites are groaning around us? Is it enough to preach peace and non-intervention, and leave Force, unchallenged ruler over three-fourths of Europe, to intervene, for its own unhallowed ends, when, where, and how, it thinks fit? Is it enough, in short, to call ourselves God's servants, while we leave Evil uninterfered with, and refuse to intervene between Right and Wrong?

Let all Englishmen who believe in one God, in one Duty, in one common brotherhood of mankind, think of this earnestly and deeply! Let them examine what, in this matter, is right and what wrong, and then decide. But, having once decided – whether with us or against us – let them speak and act in accordance with their decision. If nations are indeed to settle their own Governments – if, in international questions, non-intervention is to be the rule of their conduct, let it at least be fairly and logically carried out. Let it be indeed non-intervention to which they pledge themselves – a consistent policy, which, though it will leave the destinies of a God-ordained nation to struggle upward alone and unaided against the tyranny of Force, will at least require from others an observance of the rule to which it binds itself; not the policy which has hitherto obtained – non-intervention, on our own part, in the struggle with which we cannot but sympathise, and, at the same time, an allowance of any intervention on the part of those who are openly leagued together to act against the cause of Truth, Right, and Justice. This is not so much non-intervention as indifference. Through our indifference we abdicate our claims to Christianity – to Humanity. Can it be that, after eighteen centuries of Christianity, we reach no higher faith than the ignoble 'Every one for himself'? Can it be that, regardless of that Divine law which, requiring the best devotion of each for the best development of all, binds together all members of the human family, England – the England of the Reformation, the England of Elizabeth[1] and of Cromwell,[2] self-centred in immoral indifference, gives up Europe to the dictatorship of Force; to the blind rule of the Powers representing that principle which, by her institutions, by her belief, she declares to be the Evil One? And was it but to yield submissively to *such* a dictatorship, that England for so many years poured out her treasures, and the best blood of her sons, in the contest against Napoleon?

And let Englishmen seriously meditate on the consequences which such an indifference must produce on even the future influence and the material prosperity of England! Suppose England persists in her carelessness and apathy, suppose she quietly looks on, without uttering a single word of sympathy for the struggling Peoples of Europe. The explosion comes. The Austrian empire vanishes from the map, under the combined influence of its Slavonian and Italian subjects. Two Slavonian nations, and one Italian, arise out of its ruins. The Mediterranean and the Danube are in the hands of new powers. Greece lifts up her voice on eastern questions. Europe is altogether remodelled. What will England do? Will not her old alliances be shaken? Will the new nations readily take for their ally, for their partner in commercial activity, for their fellow-worker in the new channels opened to industrial energy, the Power which, while they were suffering and struggling, turned contemptuously away, and said, 'I know you not'? Has English statesmanship no concern for the future?

There is no thought in this of any armed intervention in the affairs of Europe, no thought of England embroiling herself. Let her only speak out firmly and

---

1 Elizabeth I (1533–1603), Queen of England and Ireland 1558–1603.
2 Oliver Cromwell (1599–1658), Lord Protector of England during the Interregnum.

decidedly: her voice will be listened to, if it is felt that she is in earnest, – that the voice of her statesmen expresses the feeling of her people, – that her aspirations, as a nation, are ever for the Right. Her present apathy encourages aggression, and so does more than aught else to make the sword the sole arbiter of right. It is emphatically for Peace that the League is founded. Not the pretence of peace now existing, not the peace of Galicia; but peace founded upon right, and insured by justice. Peace for the progress of humanity, for true civilisation; – for the free growth of national peculiarities of character; for the unlimited development of the boundless resources of varied clime and country; – for facilities of transit from place to place, from country to country, that the world's goods may readily be exchanged, that every man may have the opportunity of placing himself in that sphere in which his energies may be turned to the best account for the public service; and, that each country may thus be the gainer, not only by the immigration of useful members from other countries, but, also, by the emigration of such of her own members as cannot find at home a profitable investment of their faculties; – for a constant inter-communication of ideas and information, for the benefit of all countries; – and for that free trade, that unrestrained interchange of natural products and manufactures, by which alone the material wants of nations can be supplied, states become not only prosperous but the assurers of each other's prosperity, and a sufficient scope be given to that boundless activity of man, which, if not allowed to fructify for the general good, continually expends and wastes itself in worthless schemes, in narrow, unassisted, and abortive efforts, in costly and disastrous wars, or in barren measures of precaution, of protection and prohibition, only necessary while nations are not in co-operation for the common weal.

We have now, as far as could be done in a first address, indicated the motives of our course, the object we have in view; and, by that excluded from our sphere of action, all we did not include. With political questions, except this question of Nationality, we, as a League, have nothing to do. With forms of Government, with contests between Democracy and Privilege, we, as a League, cannot interfere. Ours (we repeat it) is an International League, – a League proposing to aid the People of this country in forming a correct judgment of the national questions now agitating Europe; proposing to preach the Right of Nationality, and to promote a cordial understanding between the Peoples of all countries. The business of the League is solely with international questions. Our League seeks liberty for God's life to manifest itself everywhere; and let the form under which it will manifest itself be decided altogether by the natural tendencies, the state of education and enlightenment of each and every People! To interfere, to control that life, or to dictate its method, would be, in fact, a contradiction of our own principles. We claim for every People the right to choose their own institutions, to determine their own way of life. What we now ask, through this our League, is free room for growth. Let the growth be as God wills!

Our means, as already indicated, will be such as, within the bounds of English law and sympathy, time and circumstance may suggest. Through the medium of the Press, the Platform, and the Lecture-room, our endeavor will be to enlighten the public, to give information on all that can help Englishmen to form a sound opinion upon European questions. We shall supply the elements of judgment, and trust the consequences to English sense. By the diffusion of information obtained from unimpeachable sources in every foreign country, we hope to be able to correct errors, to destroy prejudices, to give a true version of all that passes in Europe, of all important events that would interest Englishmen, careful either for the honor or for the prosperity of their country.

And thus we shall lay a sure foundation for that real Holy Alliance of Peoples which God has ordained, and for which, through all struggles and strivings, his Spirit has been unceasingly preparing mankind.

CONDITIONS OF MEMBERSHIP.

All persons agreeing with the objects of the League may become members on enrolling their names, and paying an annual subscription of *one shilling or upwards*.

Offices of the League: 85, Hatton-garden.

AN ADDRESS TO THE CHARTISTS OF THE UNITED KINGDOM,

ON THE ATTAINMENT OF THE CHARTER BY MEANS OF BUILDING SOCIETIES,[1]
BY
ALASTOR.

LONDON:
PRINTED FOR GRATUITOUS CIRCULATION.
1847.

---

1 One edn, 1847, 8 pp.

ADDRESS TO CHARTISTS, &c.

> 'Rise like lions after slumber,
> In unvanquishable number!
> Shake your chains to earth, like dew,
> Which in sleep had fallen on you:
> Ye are many – they are few!'
>
> Shelly.[1]

FELLOW CHARTISTS,

Again we are arrived at one of those times of political struggle, when the two great conflicting factions, who, careless of the true happiness of the people, contend for place and power; while we, the unenfranchised millions inactively stand by without the power to snatch from tyrannous grasp those inestimable rights for which every honest heart has long and hitherto vainly beaten.

Again the few enfranchised Chartists are doomed to put forth ineffectually, though determinedly, their little strength, which will again rekindle whiggish hate and tory scorn; again we must submit to be ignominiously and contemptuously trampled down, or at best to be but the balance weight upon faction's see-saw.

The time is not yet arrived when our bigoted, tyrannical task-masters will honestly open their eyes to, and acknowledge that great undying truth that, 'of one blood God made all nations of men.'[2] Having set before them no better object than self-aggrandisement; no higher ambition than from an easy throne planted upon a nation's liberties, to sway the sceptre of misrule; it is impossible that, from their hands can come the establishment of those much cherished and long demanded rights, which inalienably belong to humanity, and ought to form a part and parcel of our very existence.

A melancholy truth it is, that we have yet to toil and struggle on in that well worn, slave trodden path which has been cut out for us by the unceasing efforts of good and brave spirits in all ages, who, loving the whole human race as themselves, despite the efforts of malicious intolerance and freedom-hating bigotry, have still applied their untiring energies to the onward march of truth, to the universal progress of mankind; their prophetic souls pushing forward into the depths of futurity, to that glorious time of man's independance when it shall no more be said

---

1 Percy Bysshe Shelley, *The Masque of Anarchy*, stanza xxxviii.
2 Acts 17: 26.

'Man's inhumanity to man
Makes countless thousands mourn.'[1]

And now fellow-chartists let us not slacken in our exertions, let not a link in the great toil chain be severed, but let us rather apply ourselves still more ardently to this well-doing, and thereby earn for ourselves a well-deserved companionship, with our brave fathers who have done so much for those who were to come after them; never relinquish the struggle until we have fully, fairly and freely established our rights upon the rock of truth, where they shall live and flourish despite the clamouring storms of moloch and of mammon, and the blasting breath of prejudice and bigotry.

Now friends, at last oft-baffled hope dawns in reality on our work. The charter is at length within our reach. The long-looked-for haven, where our toils shall cease, is now attainable, aye, and will be easily attained. 'Union is strength,' and union amongst Chartists of the united kingdom, will now, by one grand and determined effort, convert that very money power, which has hitherto been the strong-hold of our enemies alone, and by means of which our liberties have been held captive, into a bulwark of defence, whence shall be begotten and disseminated a power, that shall lay bare and prostrate the knavery and malevolence of mitred mountebanks and sceptered simpletons, and all their attendant crew of servile parasites before the high altar of universal love, well founded peace and eternal truth.

Thanks to the first projector of Building Societies, though it is scarcely possible that he could forsee the mighty results consequent upon his enterprise. By these societies it will be evident to all who will demonstrate the truth for themselves, that the number of parliamentary votes may be increased to an extent that at first sight appears almost incredible. If the Chartists of the united kingdom will now exert themselves as energetically as the good cause demands, and as from past observation of their zeal and devotedness it is believed they will; there can no longer be a doubt of the success that must inevitably result from their efforts. But let me advise every man, and especially every poor man, who joins a Building Society for the purpose of procuring a house, and by virtue of that house a vote, to look well at the frame work of the society, that is to say, let him ascertain that its principles are good and just towards all, that it does not, as some societies do, enrich one member at the expence of another, in which case it is invariably the poorest member who pays dearest for his whistle. I have given great attention to the rules and prospectuses of many societies, and have carefully watched their working; and after strict examination of the thousand and one plans before the public, many of which I believe to be good and sound – I have arrived at the unbiased conclusion, that those societies founded upon the principles laid down by Dr Bowkett,[2] are decidedly best and safest for a working man to invest his hard earned savings in. My reasons for this unqualified preference

---

1 Robert Burns, *Man Was Made to Mourn*, ll. 55–6.
2 Probably Thomas Edward Bowkett.

are these. These societies are without exception the most economical. They are conducted by men, who, having at heart only the good of their fellow-men, do not require to be extravagantly paid for their time and trouble. The monthly or weekly subscriptions are low, and within the reach of every prudent, industrious man. They are strictly democratical, inasmuch as no one member can take undue precedence of another; each and every member stands upon the same footing with his neighbour; all share alike; no one suffers for anothers benefit. These then are the societies for Chartists, who, generally speaking have to earn their daily bread by daily toil, and glad am I to see there are already many societies in London alone founded upon these principles, one of these I may especially mention, 'The Finsbury Economic,' which although only nine months old, has already done much good, and is monthly increasing its power to do good.

Seeing that by a union of small weekly savings so much good may be achieved, where I ask is there a Chartist in the land who will not put his shoulder to the wheel, and while actually creating for himself a pecuniary benefit, a house and home – assist in urging forward that glorious reform which shall prove a benefit to the whole human race. And let there be no time lost, the sooner we set about the work the sooner will it be accomplished. It will be well if the reader can pay up back subscriptions to join some already established society; if he be located in a small town where no society at present exists, let him use his influence to establish one, remembering that societies formed upon the principles before alluded to do not require a vast number of members to work it out effectually. The plan is equally available to a society of one hundred, or even of fifty members, as to one of a thousand. The amount of monthly subscriptions may be fixed according to the ability of the members, but of course the higher the amount of subscription, and the greater the number of members, the more rapidly would the society be able to make appropriations and purchase houses, and thereby accumulate elective power. I will be bold to say that if the whole body of Chartists would spontaneously set forward at once, in this easy path, the Charter, in fighting for which so many years of ceaseless toil have been expended, and for which so many martyrs have sacrificed their liberty, aye, and shortened their lives, would become law in less than seven years. In two years the present insignificant number of voters would be doubled, and in three years at least a million of names might be added to the list; we should go on every year proportionately increasing, until at length, the factions in power who now laugh at our insignificance would tremble before our irresistible numbers.

The iron heel of toryism, which for ages has been almost immoveably fixed upon our liberties, finality-mongering whiggism, which insolently says to the immutable law of progress 'thus far shalt thou come, and no farther;' an intolerant, ignorant, and blood-stained church, with its hypocritical, pharisaical, perjured priesthood, which have ever been a stumbling-block in the way of reason and of truth, will with all their arrogance, buffoonery and folly, be driven before the accumulating and irresistible strength of numbers; and no longer prove a barrier to the march of intellect, and natural progress of humanity.

And, Chartists, all this may be done by peaceful means; means legalized by act of parliament; moral force alone is sufficient for all our wants; we need no more dungeoned martyrs to pine away their lives for conscience sake, we have not now to risk our lives in the battle field, as our fathers did, when, in the seventeenth century they bearded an insolent king, who spurned and trampled on their rights, and taught him, and taught the world that no pampered puppet, clothed in 'purple and fine linen' should with impunity enslave a people upon whose bounty he depended, and from whose industry were wrung the means of maintaining the contemptible pomp and merry-andrewism[1] of a court.

Long have we been taunted with our non-qualification, we have had thrown in our teeth the standard cant of the day, 'O it is not right to enfranchise a parcel of lawless fellows who have no stake in the country.' Ay, Chartists, remember this, those praters of liberty and lovers of tyranny, the whigs, tell you you have 'no stake in the country.' They grant you the privilege of toiling almost incessantly, and paying taxes. You may prove that you have mental capacity; you may prove undeniably that from your ranks have sprung nine-tenths of the really great and useful men that ever adorned and enlightened the world; you may prove indisputably that it is impossible to find among the unenfranchised, men less capable of rightly exercising the suffrage than thousands of the present electors. All this is admitted. Yes, Chartists, you have intelligence, you have *brains*, but you have '*no stake* in the country.' That is to say, you have no house, shed, hovel or mud hut worth forty shillings a-year; you have not the brick and mortar, or mud and straw '*stake* in the country.' And now, shall we not teach these half whig, half tory mongrels an unmistakeable lesson? Shall we not prove to them, that being conscious of our right and of our might, we are determined to exert our might for the acquirement of our right? Shall we not lay hold of the opportunity now afforded to relieve ourselves from the thraldom of factions – to erect our rights and liberties into a law, to shake the chains of slavery from our mental limbs – the badge of serfdom from our nation. Aye, friends, now is the time to prove ourselves true-born Chartists. Deeds not words must be our motto. While others talk we must *do*. Let every Chartist, who means what he says, show himself in his true colours. Act decisively and at once; and we will soon carry out triumphantly, and by peaceful means, that good work so long since begun in hardship and suffering, when rampant kingcraft and priestcraft were in the zenith of their glory, and consequently the laborious millions sunk deepest in the slough of oppression. Let every man prove himself a man, let him look in future to the welfare of himself and fellow-men, let him learn, and know and teach the grand truth, that 'the few were made for the many, not the many for the few.' Let him acquire and disseminate knowledge to the full extent of his ability; 'knowledge is power.' Yes it is that power, which, together with its twin sisters, wisdom and justice, shall eventually controul the world, when ridiculous titles or nicknames shall be known no more, when the lordling worm of to-day shall stand upon a level with his poorest fellow worm, when contemptible conventionalism, and degrading bigotry, and

---

1 After a humorous physician of the time of Henry VIII.

mind-enslaving dogma shall fade away before the ever-growing light of reason; when a new order of things shall be established on just and honest principles, rendering to every man his due, and to no man more than his due; giving to every man an unfettered right of thought and speech; making no one man's will a nation's law; doing away for ever with that most monstrous of all monstrous impositions a state church. A church which preaches 'thou shalt not steal' and at the same time with bare-faced impudence robs its dissenting neighbour of his goods and chattles. A church which boasts of its prescriptive right, and was concocted and established by a gluttinous, wife-killing king, and a batch of heretic burning bishops. A church ever prating of 'good will and peace among men,' and yet is ever ready to open the dungeon's doors to those who deny its authority, or as Rathcormac's annals inform us, to shoot the widow's sons dead at her feet, when they, directed by filial duty, implanted in their minds by no other hand than God's, came to defend their widowed mother and her home against a reverend robber. A church with its meek and lowly, fox-hunting, drunken priesthood, who while professing to be called by the Holy Ghost to the cure of souls, daily exhibit a miserable lack of everything approaching to religion or morality, themselves being the worst patterns that could be set before the eyes of their deluded dupes; and many of whose names, never known for their good works have become familiar to the public by frequent and dishonorable mention in police sheets and the Newgate calendar.

O men of England. Chartists of England, think upon these things, forget them not; know that for you was reserved the glorious task of demolishing the evil. Will you do it, or will you not? Remember what I have said about the suffrage, and the means of procuring it. You can obtain it, and you must. Leave not your duty undone, it is a duty you owe not merely to yourselves, but to futurity also, and you must perform it; let there be no flinching, no hesitating, no thought of failure, a thorough true-born Chartist dreams not of failure. The charter we must have, the means of obtaining it are in your power, votes may be multiplied under existing laws; we may obtain our rights without seeking it as a boon from whig or tory government. This rapid accumulation of power is no delusion, no utopia, every county may soon be in the hands of the Chartists; it is a fact easily demonstrated, and which every good and honest man, desiring the welfare of humanity and downfall of faction, the increase and spread of knowledge, and annihilation of dogmatical ignorance, will do well to act upon. But let us be speedy in our movements, for I would not answer for the continuance of the present law of building societies; in truth I believe it will be altered, seeing that by it faction is jeopardized, faction will doubtless attempt to smother it; quick then to work, and hasten the good time when every man shall possess a vote and a house of his own; when every man shall be able steadfastly to look his fellow in the face; when none shall be able to chain down another's thoughts, but when all shall be free to follow the dictates of their own consciences; when God shall be worshipped instead of mammon, and men shall be politically and theologically free, and each and all shall have and enjoy a 'stake in the country,' and

> 'Man to man, the world o'er
> Shall brothers be for a' that.'[1]

> I remain, Fellow Chartists,
> Your humble adviser,
> ALASTOR.

London, July, 1847.

Note. – ALASTOR will feel obliged, if when the reader has done with this pamphlet, he will give it to some working man.

---

1   Robert Burns, 'Is There for Honest Poverty', ll. 39–40.

REPORT OF A PUBLIC MEETING,

HELD AT THE CROWN AND ANCHOR TAVERN, STRAND, ON MONDAY, NOVEMBER 15, 1847, 'TO EXPLAIN THE PRINCIPLES AND OBJECTS OF THE PEOPLE'S INTERNATIONAL LEAGUE.'[1]

The first public meeting of the Peoples' International League was held at one o'clock on Monday, November 15, at the Crown and Anchor Tavern, Strand. The small room was entirely filled at the hour of meeting, and an adjournment to the large room became necessary before the commencement of the proceedings. Nearly 1,500 persons were assembled.

Dr BOWRING,[2] MP for Bolton, having been called to the chair, addressed the meeting as follows: – The object of this meeting is to give greater publicity to the views and intentions of the Peoples' International League. It is the belief of the Council that, when those views and intentions are known, they will excite great sympathy, interest, and co-operation on the part of the British public; because we are acting under the conviction that nations can be no more isolated and separated from each other than individuals; that they are dependent one upon another; that the interests of each are common to all; and that we are bound to aid one another, as far as we are able, to put down anarchy and despotism, and to assist the cause of civilization, emancipation, and universal liberty. Happily, the voice of England, when England speaks, finds an echo through the wide and universal world. Indeed it is to be regretted that the voice of England has not spoken as loudly and as often as it ought during the great controversy that is every where being carried on between the oppressor and the oppressed. Now, the opinion of England must be in favour of those who are struggling for the rights which we, to some extent, have happily attained. Look where we will, there is much to interest us; and I venture to say, that every word of encouragement that is uttered from this land causes thousands of bosoms elsewhere to throb with anxieties and hopes, and encourages men in multitudes to persevere in that honourable course in which they are engaged. Let us look where we will, interesting objects are presented to us. Travel we to the far East? Let us look upon that Greece where Plato[3] spoke and Homer[4] sung; –

---

1 One edn, 1847, 16 pp.

2 Dr John Bowring (1792–1872), linguist and diplomat; MP for Clyde Burghs 1835–7 and Bolton 1841.

3 Plato (*c.* 428–348 BC), Athenian philosopher.

4 Homer (*fl.* 1000 BC), Greek epic poet.

> 'Where grew the arts of war and peace,
> Where Delos rose and Phoebus sprung;
> Eternal summer gilds her yet.'[1]

And shall that beautiful land be without England's sympathy? Shall it be given over to Bavarian dulness and Bavarian despotism? Look again to Portugal, where a struggle is going on in that little land which discovered and founded empires, – the land of the Albuquerque,[2] of Vasco di Gama[3] and Camoens.[4] Are not we interested in the redemption and salvation of Portugal? I believe there is not one among you that does not desire that Portugal shall be happy and free. Look again at Spain, that renowned, that romantic land, which has so often and so nobly repelled the invader; that land in whose history there are so many bright and brilliant pages; that land whose people once – the people of Arragon, before they conferred sovereignty on their monarch – held this magnificent language – 'We, who are as worthy as you, make you our king and lord, on the condition that you preserve to us our rights and liberties; and, if not, "No."' I hope the same conditions will be exacted hereafter in Madrid, which, of old, were exacted within the walls of Saragossa. Look, again, at France. Why, can any one believe that, after the great and magnificent outbreak of 1789, and after the three glorious days of July, in 1830, that matters are to end with that noble country being delivered over to the corruption, pollution, and dishonour which are now found in its Government? Again, look at Italy; that country of which one of its poets pathetically said, that she was doomed,

> 'Conquering or conquer'd, still to vassalage.'

And another poet, fully estimating the character of the national mind, how truthfully has said, –

> 'True, we are slaves; but yet indignant slaves.'

And the indignation of Italy has broken out, and she is marching – led by that illustrious man who occupies the Papal chair – from darkness into light and liberty. The blessing of God and the blessing of freeborn Englishmen, whether Catholic or Protestant, be upon her; and we cannot doubt that that bright and lovely land will be distinguished for her free institutions hereafter, as she has been always distinguished for the intellectual superiority of her sons. And can we forget Poland? – Poland, whose mind's existence despotism has sought to trample under foot! No doubt we have prayed, and we have protested, and we have never recognised that foul and impious deed which said – 'Poland shall exist no longer.' But let every Pole – be his wanderings where they may, or his mournings where he will; let him know that there are millions of Englishmen who are waiting for the day of salvation for his country; and that it does not depend on despots

---

1 George Gordon, Lord Byron, *Don Juan*, III. 691–3.
2 Alfonso de Albuquerque (1453–1515), founder of the Portuguese East Indies.
3 Vasco de Gama (1460–1524), Portuguese navigator.
4 Luis Vaz de Camoes (1524–80), Portuguese poet and soldier.

whether Poland shall or shall not be free. I now call upon the Secretary to read our first Report.

The following Report was then read by the Secretary (Mr W. J. Linton):

REPORT.

When, last year, in defiance not only of justice, but of their own Treaties, the three Absolute Powers of Europe violated the neutrality and destroyed the independence of the Republic of Cracow; when the rest of Europe, beholding that wrong, did nothing to redress it; and the British People, whatever their indignation, scarcely so much as echoed the protest of their Government; then, observing that general abdication of national duty, that carelessness of national honour, and the want of anything like intelligence upon what are called foreign questions, it was felt by some few men that the time was come for an organisation, whose aim should be to rouse the public mind to a recognition of the rights and duties of Nations, and to furnish, from trustworthy sources, the necessary information through which a healthy public opinion might be formed upon all international questions.

In pursuance of this idea, a public meeting was held on Wednesday, the 28th of April last, at the Crown and Anchor Tavern, Strand (Dr Bowring, MP, being in the chair), at which meeting the following resolutions were passed: –

That an Association be now formed, to be called the 'Peoples' International League,' the objects of which shall be as follows: –

To enlighten the British Public as to the Political Condition and Relations of Foreign Countries.

To disseminate the Principles of National Freedom and Progress.

To embody and manifest an efficient Public Opinion in favour of the right of every People to Self-government and the maintenance of their own Nationality.

To promote a good understanding between the Peoples of all Countries.

That the following gentlemen shall be the officers of the League *for* the ensuing year: –

TRUSTEES.

MR W. H. ASHURST.   MR P. A. TAYLOR.
MR JOS. TOYNBEE.

COUNCIL.

MR W. B. ADAMS.	MR DOUGLAS JERROLD.
— W. H. ASHURST.	— W. J. LINTON.
— GOODWYN BARMBY.	— R. MOORE.
DR BOWRING, MP.	— J.H. PARRY.
MR WM. CARPENTER.	— W. SHAEN.
— THOMAS COOPER.	— J. STANSFELD.
— WM. CUMMING.	— P. A. TAYLOR.
— T. S. DUNCOMBE, MP.	— P. A. TAYLOR, JUN.
DR EPPS.	— R. TAYLOR.
MR W. J. FOX.	— J. TOYNBEE.
— S. M. HAWKES.	— H. VINCENT.
— THORNTON HUNT.	— J. WATSON.

AUDITORS.

MR AUSTIN.   MR H. MITCHELL.
MR SOLLY.

SECRETARY.
MR W. J. LINTON.

That all persons agreeing with the object of the League may become members on enrolling their names, and paying an annual subscription *of one shilling or upwards*.

The following have been the proceedings of the League since its formation: –

In the first place the Council issued an Address explanatory of the principles of the League, its objects, and the course to be pursued. The Address referred to the changes which had taken place in Europe since the Treaty of 1815; to the open breach of that Treaty by the Absolute Powers; to the question of Nationality manifestly lying at the bottom of all European movements; and to the apparent imminence of a fearful struggle. It endeavoured to show that such struggle might be avoided if there were in Europe any strong League of public opinion for Good to counteract the alliance of the Despotic Powers for Evil. It declared the course of action to which the League would be confined – that its business would be solely with international questions, claiming liberty for God's life to manifest itself everywhere, leaving the form in which that life should be manifested to be decided altogether by the natural tendencies and state of enlightenment of each individual People; and it explained the means to be used – to give, through the medium of the Press, the Platform, and the Lecture-room, such information, from unimpeachable sources, as should enable the public to form a sound opinion upon all important European questions, supplying them with elements of judgment, and trusting the consequences to the good sense of the People.

This Address (accompanied by a circular requesting co-operation) was forwarded to the Members of both Houses of Parliament; to the entire Press of Great Britain and Ireland; to a large number of public institutions – literary and political; and to several thousand individuals, including as many as possible of foreigners resident in this country. It was favourably noticed, and occasionally reprinted, by a number of the British and of the Continental Press. Among the latter may be mentioned: in France 'The National,' 'The Réforme,' and 'The Démocratie Pacifique,' besides provincial journals; in Belgium 'The Brussels German Gazette;' in Germany, 'The Bremer Gazette,' 'The Frankfort Journal,' 'The Berlin Gazette,' 'The Upper Rhenish Gazette;' in Italy, 'The Alba' of Florence; and in Switzerland 'The Helvetic' of Berne, 'The Swiss National Gazette' of Basle, 'The Nouvelliste Vaudois,' 'The Narrator' of St Gall, 'The Review' of Geneva, &c., &c.

Many of these journals have given repeated notices. The Address has been translated into French, Spanish, German, Italian, and Polish. Other manifestations of strong sympathy from almost all parts of the Continent have also reached the League; and in Switzerland its formation has been celebrated by public demonstrations in Berne, Lausanne, Basle, and Geneva; and responded to by resolutions of several Swiss associations to support and join the Peoples' International League.

The Council of the League have also published a pamphlet on the important question at present agitating Switzerland. This has been distributed among the Members of the League, – to the Press (by whom it has been extensively used), – to the Members of the House of Commons, – and to a number of literary and other institutions. It has been translated into French and German; and its statements approved by most of the Swiss journals.

Beyond this, the Council of the League have been actively employed in establishing communications with the principal cities of the Continent, for the purpose of obtaining correct and ready information on all important questions.

During the past seven weeks seventeen lectures have been delivered in different parts of London, upon the present political condition of Italy and Switzerland, by Mr R. H. Horne, Mr Thomas Cooper, and Mr W. J. Linton. To most of these lectures the public have been admitted without charge.

A statement of the Italian Question is now in the press; and it is purposed to publish similar pamphlets as occasions offer.

The publications, lectures, and other expenses of the League have been met by the funds already subscribed. The number of members enrolled amounts to nearly four hundred. The names of Colonel Thompson, MP,[1] Mr George Thompson,[2] MP, Mr Hamer Stansfeld,[3] of Leeds, and Mr Joseph Biggs, of Leicester, besides those of several foreign gentlemen of eminence resident in London, have been added to the Council; and it is now confidently hoped that the Peoples' International League may be considered established; and that it may claim, in virtue of its principles, and of the earnest of well-doing it has already given, the extended sympathy and support of all those who consider it a part of their public duty or of their private interest, to care for the protection of national rights, for the performance of national duties, or for the preservation of national honour.'

The FIRST RESOLUTION was moved by Colonel THOMPSON, MP for Bradford, in the following speech: – Let me begin with congratulating the meeting and its movers upon the agreeable disappointment we have met with in the outset, in having our feet set in a large room. We began, like modest men, with taking a small one. I had heard it intimated that we were busybodies, whom nobody would attend to hear. See the nobodies that have been brought together! If I have any skill in physiognomy, I see before me earnest, intelligent citizens, able to comprehend their own interests, and to carry them into execution by all those means which are happily within reach of the citizens of a free country. It may be that public concerns, as connected with foreign relations, have for many years too little attracted the attention of the community. One thing, which I know full well, they have done, – they have paid for them; and if they are prudent men, they will not think a few minutes in any day, or in every day, thrown away in endeavouring to create and accumulate that public opinion which shall operate to cause their government to walk in the way in which it should walk, and let alone the paths which it ought not to follow. The resolution I have to submit to you is this: –

'That it is our duty as a (free) nation to inform ourselves fully upon all matters bearing on the conduct and policy of our Government, whether at home or abroad; and that our relations with foreign nations, and their social and political manifestations and progress, demand at the present time an especial and increased share of our interest and consideration.'

Now, what is there in that which any man can find fault with? Are we a free nation, or are we not? (Cries of 'No.') Perhaps not so free as we *hope* to be. I might

1 Thomas Perronet Thompson (1783–1869), general, MP for Hull 1835–7, Bradford 1847–52, 1857–9.

2 George Thompson (1804–78), MP for Tower Hamlets.

3 Hamer Stansfeld of Leeds (1797–1865).

add a bolder word, and say, as we *mean* to be; but we are freer than many of our neighbours, and thereby a duty is laid upon us to consult for the interest of those whose condition is less fortunate than our own; and if we have been in some sense the firstborn of liberty in Europe, though there be specks on our 'scutcheon, let us improve the powers we have, and endeavour to secure to ourselves and others the advantages we have not. What would be the use of freedom, if we might not employ it thus? Let nobody tell me that our Chairman, for instance, wants to be Secretary for Foreign Affairs, or that we who stand here mean to put the office into commission, and be the commissioners ourselves. Not one bit of it! We want you, as men regretting there is not more knowledge in the country on the subject of our relations with foreign countries, to form a society to direct the attention of your countrymen to those objects. And you will do your part by joining us, – by assisting us in the promulgation of all that goes to the creation of information and interest; and so I trust we shall not die without leaving some good behind us from this very meeting that is held here to-day. It is a stirring time. There is much good and much evil to be done at this very moment. There has been a great deal of evil done before, and a great deal of good omitted to be done; but, inasmuch as we cannot go back and undo, there is nothing left but to try to improve what is to come. Now look abroad on the continent of Europe: do you not see one large portion of that continent – the Italian States – moving together under the direction of a potentate who has done more towards destroying religious feuds than any man, perhaps, who has appeared since the days of the Apostles. Is there a man here who will throw in any controversial questions to diminish the delight with which we see the Pope – for, though not born under the Papacy, we cannot be blind to his good deeds – moving forward to increase the liberties of his country, and making to himself, I hope, a name which shall last for ever? Is this a time for us to be dumb? Is it your interest, either at home or abroad, that such an effort should not be assisted? There is the question of Switzerland next. You know, I doubt not, how Switzerland has been for centuries one of the bulwarks of public liberty in Europe. You know that when your forefathers of the civil wars – the founders of English liberty – were driven into exile, the honest Swiss offered them homes at the peril of the wrath of all the powers in Europe; and you may see now the monuments of those men in the church at Vevay, if you wish to have ocular testimony of the fact. These are all reasons why you should feel an interest in their concerns. Let us hope the end will be some peaceful arrangement, and that they will refrain from shedding blood, and that we shall see that men in a free country can settle their disputes without having recourse to bayonets and cannon. In France you know full well that the spirit of freedom is struggling, and wants nothing so much as encouragement from this country. Was it anything but the encouragement given by the British community, that caused the Revolution of 1830 to pass over in comparative peace, and prevented the invasion of France by foreign powers to put it down? In Spain, things look as if they grew worse and worse; but you know, by experience, that this is often a proof that they are going to grow better by-and-by. Let us hope this will be the case in Portugal too. I wish we could shut our eyes to all that has been done there. If we wanted evidence of the importance of our knowing something about our own affairs in the matter of foreign relations, we might point to what has been done in that unfortunate country. So much for Europe. But there are other quarters of the globe besides. I look abroad and I see a country which calls itself a republic, – a country in which we once had hope and confidence, and men in this kingdom were proud to bear the name of republican, though to their peril and damage. I see that country going forth to invade its unoffending neighbour, and giving such evidences of a reprobate and cruel spirit as can hardly be paralleled in the worst of the bad annals of our own or any other monarchical country. But the principle we must here be ready to protest against is, that two blacks make a white. We know that our governments have committed enormities unspeakable; but that is no reason why we honest men, who have struggled against such acts of our government, and have still to struggle against their repetition, should be put down by the allegation that our government has done as badly in its time. Now, see what these republicans have done. The American troops were ordered to pass a boundary, where they knew they must be fired on, and then they said, 'American blood has been shed, and we must "annex."' Never was there a ruder exhibition of the principle of brute violence. And see how the war has been conducted. Are there any Irishmen here? (Cries of 'Yes.') Well, then, to you I speak. Fifty Irishmen were found to have deserted, no uncommon thing in any army; but these men had not deserted for drink, – nor for women, – nor for good quarters, – nor for a dislike to fight, nor any of those motives which ordinarily cause soldiers to desert. They had deserted because they were being led against the religion of their fathers, and the interests of their own country. These poor men, whose bodies now swing in the desert, had a sharper eye to these things, I suspect, than some of our Ministers of State. But you will hear it said, 'When a soldier deserts he must be put to death.' Not always; and not always by fifties. (Hear.) Those of you who have read the histories of ancient wars in Europe, may have been puzzled with the mention of 'six covered carriages' stipulated for when a town surrendered. What were these 'six covered carriages' to do? I will tell you what it was. European humanity knew that there were in the town men who, from one cause or other, had gone over from the one side to the other; and into these carriages European humanity stowed away these unfortunates, that their blood might be on the heads of nobody. See what a horrible contrast. I used to be proud of calling myself a republican under compact; and now the utmost I can say is, let there be fair play for republicanism, but not one bit beyond. The prestige is gone for ever which led men to believe that republicanism is a security for good conduct or political honesty. The truth is, that honest republicans will make an honest republic; and the contrary. And what was this Mexican republic which is now to be destroyed? Was it not the firstborn of English liberalism, the earliest evidence of our Government's abandoning the Alliance miscalled Holy, and telling mankind it meant to stand up for justice and human rights? What, then, have their successors been doing while all this has been going on? It is now nine years since I heard in the

House of Commons an honest Tory, Mr Barlow Hoy,[1] make a motion on the subject of Texas, at which time it wanted nothing but to direct a sloop of war to ask what flag the invaders of Texas came under, and it would have prevented the occupation of that country, and all the mischief that has followed. But nobody would stir. The Secretary of State said nobody could suppose the Americans would be so naughty as to seize on Texas. And so, unless you rouse them, will the case be now. The despotic powers of Europe are looking on with interest and hope; for they trust to see a monarchical government re-established on the ruins of an honest republic. Surely we all might agitate a little here. We might, at all events, express our thoughts. Would there, for instance, be any great danger in calling 'Stop thief!' Every honest man makes opposition of some kind when extreme occasions arise. We have friends who conceive it to be their duty to make a protest against all war; but even they do not object to call 'Stop thief!' And in extreme cases I strongly suspect they would go further. I need not impress on you how great a glory it was for England to have taken the lead in the abolition of slavery and the slave trade. Political slavery is a grievous evil, but personal slavery is political slavery ten times over. Depend upon it, if any man has ever tried it, he will tell you this is true. I firmly believe there has been no such horror in human history, as this scheme of the Americans for planting the banner of slavery through the American continent, and through the world; for that is what it comes to. The Romans conquered, but they conquered to civilize, and not to enslave; and we stand here instances ourselves of the fact. Had the Roman theory of conquest been like the American, we should all have been hewers of wood or drawers of water at this moment, unless our ancestors had been worn away in mines, or otherwise made away with, as is to be the fate of those unfortunate races on the continent of America. Have I then shown you anything, worthy citizens, intelligent citizens, which may properly occupy a leisure hour, and induce you to spend a short time now and then in attending to the subjects for which you are now assembled, and strengthening our hands in the good cause, which, if it be young and feeble now, will, I trust, before many years have passed, be strong and victorious in the hands of our posterity?

The Secretary having read a letter from Mr Douglas Jerrold (who was to have seconded the resolution) expressing the warmest sympathy with the purpose of the meeting, and apologising for his compelled absence,

Mr P. A. TAYLOR, Jun., in seconding the resolution, said: – In attempting to give vitality to the principles of the Peoples' International League, so far from apprehending that we are going out of our way, and meddling with affairs that do not actually concern us, we hold that we are merely fulfilling a simple duty, and acting upon an eternal principle of right, as well as carrying out the traditions of our country. Our great patriot-poet, John Milton,[2] said, that it was 'England's prerogative to teach the nations how to live.' It is not very easy to perceive how we can exercise this prerogative, if we feel not even sufficient interest

---

1 James Barlow Hoy, who retired as MP for Southampton in 1837.
2 John Milton (1608–75), republican poet.

in what concerns our brethren of Europe, to acquire any knowledge whatever of their position, prospects, history, and hopes. As well might a man be said to be fulfilling the duty of guardian to a person of whose character and tendencies, of whose very name, and whereabouts, he was nearly ignorant. And, indeed, it appears to me that this reasoning from a nation to an individual, from a unit in society to a unit among nations, offers more points of analogy than at first sight one might have been led to expect. In either case, the individual has his *double* life to fulfil – his external, as well as his internal life to live: and, while the latter concerns only all that works round the pivot of his own individualism, the other and larger embraces everything within its influence – everything which the mind can reach, or the sympathies can act upon. To omit this larger sphere of action, even though in such isolation the individual may become wise and the nation free, is a selfish and immoral course; and, so far from tending towards the better fulfilment of other and nearer duties, as we are sometimes told it does, it is simply a repudiation of our noblest duty – a negation of our highest mission – in truth, an actual abrogation of vitality. As no good man, when he hears outside his house the screams of suffering, or the raging of fire, locks his door, closes his shutters, and satisfies himself with saying, 'I have enough to do with my own affairs; I have my family to provide for, and I cannot afford to run the risk of burning my fingers in assisting to aid the miserable'; so no great nation can worthily or safely say, 'We interfere not in the concerns or doings of other peoples; we have enough to do with our own.' *Philanthropy should begin at home.* True – we say so too; *but should it end there?* Our question is, Who are they who best fulfil their home and lesser duties? Those whose interests are the narrowest, and who are constantly fearing lest they should be dragged beyond their individual sphere, or those whose sympathies are world-wide – whose interests are bounded only by the boundaries of humanity? Moreover, our national pride need not shrink from the avowal that we require the assistance, co-operation, and sympathy of other peoples, as they do ours; and that not more in relation to the supply of our physical and material wants, than of our intellectual and spiritual requirements. The Anti-Corn-Law League, by its success, has established the principle that it is good for the labour of this country to be free to purchase the corn of America, the wine of Spain, and the silks of France: be it the higher object of our League to establish, by its triumph, that it is good to have free-trade in the productions of the head, in the aspirations of the heart; and, surely, a nation that has sought its highest art in Italy, its noblest philosophy in Greece, and its purest religion in Palestine, need feel no shame in acknowledging, much as it may prize the tendencies and characteristics of the Anglo-Saxon race, that these may be improved, elevated, purified, by a combination with them of the many noble tendencies and characteristics of the peoples of other lands. Moreover, I for one feel that England owes a deep debt to the liberties of Europe. Without entering here into the history of the past, it is sufficient to allude to the now seldom disputed fact, that within the last fifty years we have impoverished ourselves and our descendants, and, worse still, wasted our moral strength and influence for good, by waging unjust wars; undertaken, not to obtain peace, or maintain justice, but to secure the throne of France for an unworthy and infatuated family. In addition to these considerations, it must not be forgotten that the question is not whether England shall or shall not exercise her judgment and influence upon foreign affairs; her position and power render it impossible that she should be a cipher. The question is, How shall this judgment be formed – this influence exercised? Shall her foreign policy depend upon the caprice of a too irresponsible department of the Ministry for the time being, or shall it derive additional strength and influence from being recognised as the result of a matured, deliberate, intelligent public opinion? Shall we say to the various peoples of Europe, 'Friends, we feel the deepest sympathy for your sufferings; the most earnest desire for your emancipation and progress. We know the voice of England is powerful to assist you, if it be raised. We have an office somewhere in Downing-street; go and ask our representative what he will do for you; we hope he'll do what he can for you.' Shall we – the people of England – say this? – we, who are so jealous of authority, that an irresponsible beadle would be unbearable to us here at home? Or, shall we not rather say, 'Brothers, march forward on your road to freedom and to justice; we know the rights you seek, for we have won them; we know the battles you must fight, for we have fought them. Onward, then! we have heads to think with you, hearts to suffer with you; and a country whose history and traditions necessarily place its influence on your side.' On all these grounds we hold it our inalienable duty to obtain and circulate information on all that relates to the position and prospects of the Peoples of Europe; and, if a duty at all times, how peculiarly so now! Surely never has there been a time when the illustration of our principles was more imperatively called for than at this moment! Never a time when change, revolution, and a struggle for progress have been more visibly marked on the face of Europe. Almost every kingdom seems to be a centre and nucleus for the operation of forces which cannot much longer be controlled. Besides that unceasing element of struggle existing in all States – of the old against the new – the onward against the retrograde – the love of change against the fear of innovation – the privileges of the few against the rights of the many – the spirit of aristocracy against that of democracy; besides this world-wide element of struggle, there is now the coarse and selfish one of family and dynastic interest to add its fearful quota to the dangers to progress, civilization, and freedom, which now threaten Europe. Be it ours, if possible, to secure a peaceful solution to these grave problems by obtaining for the right that strongest, justest weapon – the deliberate judgment, the powerful moral influence, exercised through the public opinion of an intelligent and free people. Not now the time to lecture upon the condition of the various nations of Europe! The very recital of many of their names is sufficient to suggest the fact which I wish to enforce, namely, that if ever our efforts were a duty, they are *now* pre-eminently so. France, Spain, Portugal, Austria, Italy, Switzerland, Prussia, Russia, Greece! Is there one here who does not feel this list is incomplete? Is there one here who does not miss a name which, although it may not be found in the last map of Europe; though no longer hinted at in protocols, or mentioned in treaties; though no longer even considered as a 'geographical term' by kings and statesmen: yet, while there are twenty millions of human beings speaking a common language; clinging to a common nationality; kneeling before the altars of a common faith; looking backward to the glorious associations of their country's past; and, better still, looking onwards in confident anticipations of glories yet to come; while there are twenty millions of human beings whose hearts beat quicker, whose eyes flash fire, whose hands grasp at an unseen weapon when the name of their country is heard; while there are twenty millions of human beings to whom – while kings and statesmen trample them in the dust – priests whisper that they were framed in the image of their God; oh! whilst there is power in truth, and truth in God, never be omitted that name by Englishmen met to talk over the nations that shall be; never, oh never, be omitted the name of Poland the heroic! It may be – it has been objected to us – that we propose to carry out no object not undertaken by the Press. 'If,' it is said to us, 'your object be simply to obtain and circulate information, to acquire and distribute facts, why not leave this to the Newspaper Press, whose very business this is; whose vast establishments are formed, and whose interests are best served by this procuring and circulating the earliest intelligence – foreign and domestic? Are you not wasting your energies in doing that which the Press is able to do more effectually?' To this we answer, that we have no Press in this country so to look to – so to trust. We have a Press to act upon, and to carry forward a public opinion when formed – *none* to originate it – and none, or few, so free from the influence of dishonest aims, or public ignorance, as to be depended upon for giving truth for truth's own sake, without reference either to Ministerial cajolery or popular clamour. Do we not find it so in our struggles at home? When does the Press create a great public movement? It is but the reflex of the prejudices and opinions of the class it represents. The League had to be 'a great fact' before 'The Times' ceased to deride its acts and its promoters, and so must we before we shall derive much assistance from the Press; and we may be more sure of faithful, impartial, and ungarbled reports from abroad, when our League is in action to correct the error and to brand the falsehood. I say this in no spirit of general reprobation of the Press; we owe it much, and, upon the foreign questions now so interesting to us, I may mention two journals which have been distinguished for their fairness and impartiality – I allude to 'The Morning Chronicle' and to 'The Daily News.' We have no quarrel with the Press generally; in what I have said, it may be I have only traced a necessary and inevitable tendency, namely, that writers who please to live must write to please: my business has been to defend our action, not to attack theirs. I must now, in justice to ourselves, and to our cause, leave this language of general argument and criticism in relation to the Press, and advert to errors and misstatements which are not to be classed with those of necessity or ignorance, but which have evinced an attempt on the part of a leading member of the London Press to deceive and mislead the public upon the Italian and Swiss questions; an attempt, systematically made, and followed up day by day, and week by week, for some time past. (Cries of 'The Times.') Yes, I allude to 'The Times' newspaper; and I here charge that journal with wilfully, systematically, and deliberately endeavouring to mislead its readers upon the subject of the Italian and Swiss movements. Be it borne in mind, I have nothing here to do with opinions that might be honestly held, although not ours – with statements which might be believed, although we knew their fallacy; but, I repeat it, I allude to the systematic and wilful attempt which 'The Times' has made to mislead the British public by false statements and sophistical arguments; and that this attempt has been made, I am sure I shall find no difficulty in proving to the satisfaction of every impartial mind. It is not to convince those who are here that I speak of the dishonest partisanship of 'The Times'; I take their presence to be an evidence of their interest in these questions, and that interest a sufficient guarantee that they have detected its misdoings; but I speak that the public at home and abroad may have such opportunity as I can give them of estimating the credit to be given to – the confidence to be bestowed upon – 'The Times' newspaper. I will not dwell upon those small arts by which a journal is able to insinuate error without directly compromising its honesty – such as the insertion of reports partly true, as though they were the whole truth; the insertion of all that tells in favour of the one party, with an entire omission of all that contradicts or throws doubt upon such statements from the other. I will not arraign 'The Times' where it has outstepped the modesty of probability, but only where it has outrun the possibility of honesty. One such case, however, a rather flagrant one, I must give in illustration of the kind of self-evident trickery to which I allude. On the 23rd of October 'The Times,' in its leading article, gave, for the purposes of its argument against the Swiss Diet, an account of the circumstances attending the seizure, by the Vaudois, in the Canton of Neufchatel, of some arms which were *en route* to the Sonderbund cantons; not merely utterly untrue in itself, but even in contradiction to the account of its own correspondent, dated from Berne, and published in its own columns some few days previously! I will allude now to 'The Times' article upon our League, which appeared on its establishment some few months back, and I do so, not because the opinion of 'The Times' concerning the usefulness or desirability of the League is in itself of any interest or importance, but because in the spirit of the article may, I take it, be found a key to the policy which 'The Times' has adopted on the questions now agitating Italy and Switzerland. What was our avowed object in the formation of a League? – to obtain and circulate sound information from trustworthy sources: not the propagation of particular opinions; not the upholding of particular parties; not the attempting to lead our countrymen to any particular conclusions; but, in the words of our address, 'to supply the elements of judgment, and trust the consequences to English sense.' Now, it would have been perfectly legitimate for 'The Times' to have said, 'We doubt, gentlemen, whether you can do this; we doubt whether you can obtain this information; or, if you do, whether you can effectually communicate it. In either particular we think that by supporting the Press, whose proper avocation it is, you would be rendering more service to the cause of truth; so far, therefore, from supporting your League, we advise none to join you.' All this would have been fair enough, and quite within the bounds of legitimate criticism; but when we find 'The Times,' instead of adopting any such tone, sending forth one of those blatant, bullying, truculent articles, known so well to all the readers of that paper, as the weapons by which it attempts to 'write down' any subject or person; one of those coarse and violent effusions which are only protected from general contempt by the conventional license allowed to the oracular and editorial 'We'; when, I say, we see such an article levelled at an association with such objects, we are driven to the conclusion that it is not our failure that is feared, but our success; that, in fact, 'The Times' and 'The Times'' masters, whoever for the nonce those masters may be, have a purpose and a cause to serve, which loves the darkness rather than the light. Again, on the question of the Italian movement, I quarrel with no opinions or anticipations, however much they may differ from ours; but I do quarrel with the paper which, relying upon English apathy and English ignorance, deliberately set itself to the task of misleading its countrymen by means of false assertions, dishonest omissions, and untenable deductions. Had 'The Times' said, 'The Italian movement will not, cannot, ought not to succeed; the Italians are neither powerful to obtain nor worthy to enjoy the freedom they demand'; this would have been, at least, a tangible and comprehensible line of argument; but when 'The Times' could see nothing in the struggle but a noble effort of the Pope and other Italian princes to lead on their subjects to some degree of independence and freedom, why, then, I think, 'The Times' trusted too much to the faith or to the ignorance of its readers. Englishmen can scarcely so completely have forgotten the condition of Italy for year after year; the alternation, nay, almost the continuity of outbreaks, persecution, and wholesale legal butchery; they will scarcely have forgotten that the throne of Pius IX[1] seemed no bed of roses on his accession; they will scarcely be driven to any other conclusion than that Italy is now in hopes to gather the fruit which has ripened on the tree of suffering. All honour to Pius IX; it is enough that he has shown himself worthy of his time. Were not his people ready for him, his deeds would prove him a Quixote, not a patriot; – he is that he is, because not in vain has the exile toiled and languished on a foreign shore; because not in vain has the prison echoed with patriot groans; the scaffold reeked with patriot blood; because the blood of martyrs is the seed of liberty, and because that tree of Italian liberty is firmly rooted in its classic soil, and the shadow of its branches already extends from Sicily to the Alps. What worse than mockery in 'The Times' to denounce as ungrateful and blood-thirsty the people of those states, where the sword has been made the arbiter between their rulers and themselves; whilst it praises the moderation and virtue of those whose struggle has been unstained with blood; knowing, as it must full well, that not in the demands or temper of the People has this difference arisen, but in the real or presumed power of their rulers to arrest their onward course. Again, on the Swiss question: who, to read the constantly reiterated denunciations of 'The Times' against the tyranny of the Diet; against the overbearing attempts to crush the liberties of the smaller Cantons by the larger: who, I say, would have supposed it possible that the political portion of the question simply resolved itself into the desire of a large majority of the Swiss People (a majority, it is said, of four-fifths) that their views and opinions should find a fitting illustration in a National Assembly of their country? How

1 Giovanni Maria Mastai-Ferretti (1792–1878), Pope Pius IX 1846–78.

can we as Englishmen, whose boasted constitution and liberties are founded upon the principle of representation, and government by a majority, reconcile the fulminations of 'The Times' against a People who seek to give expression to the will of such a majority, with the commonest principles of consistency and honesty? And, if it be answered that tyranny may be exercised upon a minority as well as upon a majority; and that, if the different Cantons differ in opinion, there should be a partition of Swiss Nationality; then, I say, such reasoners are bound, not merely to join in the cry for Irish Repeal, but even if the little Isle of Wight should demand a separate legislature and different rule, then they should denounce as tyranny the power which denied such wish, and as a wicked coercion the exertions of the six London policemen who might be requisite to quell the movement! Again, with respect to the exclusion of the Jesuits from Switzerland, 'The Times' would make its readers believe that it is simply a question between Catholics and Protestants, of religious bigotry and priestly persecution: the fact being (as 'The Times' cannot but know), that there is no such line of demarcation between Catholic and Protestant in the religious part of the question. All the Catholic Cantons do not belong to the Sonderbund; still less do all the Catholics of Switzerland, – nay, it is said, that even of the Catholics throughout Switzerland, there is a majority in favour of the Diet. It is a contest, and not the first, between Jesuitism and freedom. It is not for their religious opinions that the Jesuits have long been feared, but that they make their religion the leverage for political action; and that that action is ever on the side of political tyranny and of subserviency to despotism. Why, there is scarcely a country in Europe from which at one time or another this sect of Religio-Political schemers has not been driven; and, from the massacre of St Bartholomew[1] to the massacres of Gallicia, how many crimes have received their sanction and support! I must here once more reiterate that I have nothing here to do with the policy or justice of the expulsion of the Jesuits from Switzerland. I have only to show that 'The Times'' version of the dispute, as a religious one between Catholic and Protestant, is not merely not the true one, but is one not reconcileable with honesty of intention. Shame! oh, shame upon the paper which can so prostitute its high mission – its immense influence for good – by so pitiful a paltering with common honesty! But shame! tenfold shame – when, from misrepresentations of principles and facts, too much sanctioned by custom, I must confess, as only *politically* wrong, it adds thereto personal and individual calumny, and, with a stroke of the pen, attempts to crush an individual whose fall it thinks will weaken the principle to which he is devoted. Such an attempt has lately been made, and I deem it but justice to that individual, as well as to my case against this paper, to take notice of it here, as at the time I did, through the columns of an honester member of the Press. There is a man in this country – a man known to many of those present personally – to all by reputation, and not more widely known than esteemed – respected – loved; a man who has borne evidence to the earnestness of his opinions by a long martyrdom of

---

1 The Massacre of St Bartholomew (24 August 1572), which began the killing of some 50,000 French Protestants.

exile; for all the prime of a yet middle life he has lived an outcast from his country, – a stranger to the ties of kindred and of family; yet in all these weary years he has never, I may, perhaps, say, for an instant, despaired of the ultimate triumph of the principles for which he suffered, of the ultimate regeneration of his own loved land; nay, not content with living for that end only, glorious though it be, he has thrown himself into the literature and moral atmosphere of our England; and here, also, he has been a light to guide our steps, – a voice still stimulating us to fresh exertions and increased devotion: a man who, though every political scheme that had ever passed through his brain should moulder and die, would still, by his very life, have done more for humanity than falls to the lot of most men, by his high example of devotedness and elevation. And this – this is the man who has been singled out to be denounced by one of the basest terms that can be applied to man, one that describes at once an utter selfism of object with a brutal blood-thirstiness of means; by a term applied only to the most reckless of demagogues – the worst of tyrants; this man has been denounced as 'SAN-GUINARY,' – this man *'sanguinary'* who, while he has done so much to advance his country's liberties, has striven no less to stop useless bloodshed and to put down Carbonarism in Italy! *This man is Joseph Mazzini,*[1] *and this slanderer is still 'The Times.'* (Cheers.) It only remains for me to thank you for the attention with which you have heard me, and to reiterate that – holding it the bounden and eternal duty of all, without distinction of colour, class, or country, to unite their powers for their mutual advancement – that, inasmuch as there are peculiar cir-cumstances at present rendering this duty more than usually imperative; and that – as I have shown – the Press partly *cannot* do our work, and, in one impor-tant instance, *cannot* be trusted to do it: so I conclude with calling upon you to support this resolution, and to strengthen our hands in the performance of the task we have undertaken.

Mr WILSON rose to move an amendment to the first part of the resolution. He said, – The objection I have to the wording of the resolution is, that, while we in this country are struggling for freedom, to state that we are free, does not appear to me consistent with the condition of the great body of the working classes. How can a man be behind freedom more than he is in England when he is disfranchised? We say, if a man is disfranchised, he is a slave to all intents and purposes. But while we, the unenfranchised portion of the industrious classes of England, do sympathise, in the strongest possible manner, with the struggles of other countries, with their march for freedom; yet most certainly I cannot submit to see a resolution passed which conveys the idea that the people of this country are as free as they wish and ought to be. (Hear.) I say that this resolution does appear to me to signify that this country is in such a condition. I shall be glad to see the people unite against the aristocracy everywhere; because the aristocracy of all countries are leagued together for the purpose of keeping the working classes in all lands in their present position. It is because I feel strongly that the aristocracy of every country do so, that I am inclined to take the position that the

---

1 Giuseppe Mazzini (1805–72), Italian revolutionary.

working classes, even though in this country disfranchised, should sympathise with those of other countries who are now struggling for freedom. Now, look at the present troubled state of England and Ireland; and for a meeting of this description not taking into account the things that appear of the highest degree necessary, but taking into account matters abroad when we find hundreds and thousands of our fellow-countrymen starving, – when we find that the present state of things can hardly be pictured in any country of the world, – when we see all these things, and when I say all these things are the consequence of the disfranchisement of the great bulk of the working classes of this country and of Ireland, – when we know this, I should not be satisfied to allow the first part of that resolution to pass without raising my voice against it, and against the word 'free,' while we in this country are struggling for freedom. I say that will appear to be a manifest untruth with reference to the present position of the people of England. A suggestion has been made to strike out the word 'free.' If that be done, I am quite willing to submit. I am perfectly satisfied; and should feel that I have done my duty.

Colonel THOMPSON supported the amendment.

The CHAIRMAN then put the resolution in the amended form, striking out the word 'free' before the word 'nation.' The resolution was then carried unanimously.

Mr GEORGE THOMPSON, MP for the Tower Hamlets, moved the SECOND RESOLUTION: –

'That, in order to bring to bear upon the foreign policy of this country the beneficial influence of public opinion, it is of the greatest importance to obtain and circulate accurate and systematic information concerning the political condition and relations of foreign countries, to disseminate the principles of national independence and progress, and to promote a good understanding between the people of this and all other countries; and that these being the objects of the Peoples' International League, that Association is entitled to our warmest approval and support.'

Anything in the shape of an attempt to prove that the interests of nations are identical would, I think, on this occasion be idle. We are so intimately bound up, commercially and otherwise, with the nations of the world at large, that nothing interesting to them is foreign from our own pursuits, and our own individual interests. But we have a duty to discharge beyond this. It is our duty to sympathise with all in every country who are struggling to obtain the liberty – partial though it may be – that we ourselves possess, and to do for them that which existing compacts and treaties between the heads of governments often prevent those heads from doing. A minister in this country may sympathise with a movement abroad personally and privately, but he may be so shackled by the treaties, compacts, and negotiations which have previously existed and gone on between one government and another, as to render it utterly impossible for him officially or otherwise to testify that he does sympathise with the people of another country whom he considers in the right. Now we can aid an honest minister, and we can rebuke a dishonest one; we can often accomplish by small measures a positive good, and we are certain that all such associations as these, if they do nothing else, have a tendency to prevent evils. But, if we could not even promise ourselves so much usefulness as this we know from personal experience that in affliction, difficulty, and danger, even where the evils that menace are not removed by the friendly sympathy of another person, our ability to bear the burthen and to face the evil is greatly augmented by an honest and fraternal assurance of personal sympathy and of a disposition to aid. Now, I would not have the cry of distress uttered without an echo being sent from this country; we should then become one throughout the world in the general struggle for the amelioration of the governments under which the millions of the earth live. I look with hope to this society because, from all I have seen of it in its official documents, it is a society to promote peace; to bring about a friendly understanding; to encourage those who, like many in this hall to-day, are aiming virtuously and intelligently to arrive at a higher position as members of the body politic than that which they now fill. We ought to wish them God speed. I was extremely glad that our friend's only objection to the resolution was, that it seemed to assert for the people of this country the enjoyment of an amount of freedom, politically, which they really do not possess. I am glad he did not show any sympathy with those who think that an attention, temporarily and occasionally, to one good cause ever hurts the progress of another. It does not; it helps it. It multiplies the number of those who sympathise with it; it ennobles our own nature; it expands our sympathies and enlarges our views by an identity of feeling and of objects with men in every other part of the world. We are strengthened in the race we are running ourselves, placing before us a nobler and loftier good than the attainment of mere local and personal advantages – the great object being the advancement of humanity itself. I hope as an association our movement will be distinguished by wisdom and prudence, that it will be a self-improvement association; not as though we had already attained to a perfect and profound knowledge of foreign policy, still less to the ability to sway it by our own counsels or views to the ends at which it should arrive; but as a society seeking constantly for information, trying it by every test that can prove its accuracy, and then disseminating in a popular form information touching the condition of foreign countries universally. It is my earnest desire that this League may have its ramifications throughout the entire country, and its corresponding friends throughout the globe at large, until at last we shall be able to say with the American poet –

> 'There is a voice on every wave,
> A sound on every sea,
> The watchword of the brave,
> The anthem of the free.
> From steep to steep it rings
> Through Europe's many climes,
> The knell of despot kings,
> The sentence on their crimes.
> Where'er a wind is rushing,
> Where'er a stream is gushing,

> The swelling sound is heard;
> And man to freeman calling,
> And broken fetters falling;
> And, like the carol of a cageless bird,
> The bursting shouts of Freedom's rallying word.'

Mr J. Williams, MP for Macclesfield, having to leave the meeting,

Mr LINTON seconded the resolution: – Of the principles upon which our movement is based – what I may call our Confession of Faith, I would say some few words before I ask you, by carrying this resolution, to pledge yourselves to support the League. We believe that there is something like order and harmony and intended progress in this world of ours; that the affairs of this world, the course and destinies of nations, are not the mere consequences of chance combinations, but the result of natural laws. We recognise growth, not accident, as the world's law; order, not anarchy. We believe that nations are but parts of one great whole – the world; that they bear the same relation to that whole which individuals bear to a family; that, while each nation should be free, as an individual, to develope in its own way its own peculiar character and resources, all should act harmoniously together for the common weal. And we are convinced that no such combination or co-operation of nations can ever obtain, while the national genius of a people is subjected, as in Italy and Poland, to the domination of another people, careless of its wants, its wishes, and its tendencies. We believe that it is of the highest importance for the world's peaceful growth, that, wherever a people contains within it the germ or capability of becoming a nation, no foreign interference should hinder its progress. We consider the characteristics which indicate a nation, or what should be a nation, are not to be found merely in difference of language or geographical position, but in the continuous desire of the majority of a people, arising from peculiarity of character and from the consciousness of having some special mission and business in the world. We believe, also, that nations, like individuals, do not live for themselves alone; that as an individual has not only a duty towards himself, but also a duty towards his neighbours, so nations have their duties towards other nations; that the foreign policy of nations should correspond with their domestic policy; their conduct abroad with their institutions at home; that the same principles should regulate both. We see this consistency in absolute Governments, such as Russia and Austria, which, ever despotic at home, always uphold despotism abroad; and we cannot but think that this country should not be less consistent: that we, who are ever striving for free, and yet freer institutions at home, should be ever ready to give our voice, our hearty aid, if need be, to the advance of freedom abroad. We think, also, that such consistent conduct is, if possible, even more necessary now, when there exists throughout Europe a close alliance of the Powers that represent the old order of things – the maintainers of things as they are against that power of growth and continual improvement which is God's spirit and law in the world, while there is no combination or common purpose of the more liberal States; now, when, in default of any international law universally recognised as the basis of public right, in default of any international law save that of treaties, compromises between governments acting against, rather than for, the people they pretend to represent, the mere chance of Brute Force is enthroned in the place of Justice as sole arbiter of the destinies of nations: – Brute Force that dismembered Poland; that yet tramples upon northern Italy; that has so lately destroyed the independence of Cracow; that at the present moment insolently menaces Switzerland, and the States of the Pope. We believe that it is neither right nor useful that such a state of things should last: not right, because that which is immoral in individuals only becomes more monstrously immoral in nations; not useful, because it occasions and prolongs a state of struggle and confusion, a state of oppression and necessary revolt and war, during which there is no security either for political relations or commercial intercourse between country and country. We believe, further, that the only remedy for this state of things is in the wide spread of information, which shall enable nations to form correct views of each other's wants and wishes, in order that public opinion may influence governments, either to support them in a just course of policy, or to stay their arms when upraised for evil. We have no thought of interfering in the internal affairs of other nations: from that we debar ourselves by our very principle – that every people has a right to self-government and the maintenance of its own nationality. Neither do we presume to instruct other nations; all we would do is to set an example, to obtain information for our own guidance, to care for our own duties; and so, we trust, to take the first step towards a good understanding with our neighbours; to form the first link of a real Holy Alliance, not of kings and cabinets, but of free and enlightened nations. Towards such a holy and peaceful result we believe that the world is destined, and progresses. This is the faith of the Peoples' International League, this its guiding principle, this the end at which we aim. If you consider that end desirable; if you deem our principles sound; if, from the report of what we have already done, and what you have heard of our intentions, you are induced to believe in our earnestness, to look upon us as men really working, through reasonable and well-considered means, towards the accomplishment of a great purpose – then, and not else, hold up your hands for the resolution I am seconding, and pledge yourselves to stand by us, and carry on the work we have begun.

The resolution was carried unanimously.

The thanks of the meeting having been given to the Chairman,

Dr BOWRING returned his acknowledgments, and added: – This meeting is a memorable one; for the enthusiasm and, I may say, unanimity which have been exhibited here will, I have no doubt, give to the meeting the most important results. But do not believe that in coming here you have done all the work that is to be done. This is a subject which, now having launched, we confide to your care. You must talk about it at home; you must interest your friends and families in it; you must induce people to give us the means of circulating information upon it, and that information, I venture to promise you, shall be valuable. We are seeking truth because we know that truth is the ally of virtue and freedom. What we want to do is to exhibit to this great country the position of other lands. As I said before, be assured that the expression of your sympathy, and the knowledge of the fact, that you, the people of England, are really interested in what is passing in the wide world – the knowledge of that fact will encourage the champions of freedom in their earnest and most perilous struggle with their oppressors, and the words which have been spoken this day will forward the cause of truth and liberty throughout the universal world. (Loud cheers.)

The meeting then separated.

THE FRATERNAL DEMOCRATS.

ADDRESS OF
THE FRATERNAL DEMOCRATS
ASSEMBLING IN LONDON,
TO THE MEMBERS OF THE NATIONAL
DIET OF SWITZERLAND. [1]

[1847]

HONOURABLE GENTLEMEN,

This Association, composed of men of different nations, desires to congratulate you, the representatives of the noble Swiss people, on the glorious and happy termination of the troubles which recently distracted the Helvetic confederation.

Although from the commencement of the division which for a brief period divided Switzerland into two hostile camps, we deplored the infatuation which induced a misled minority to arm against their countrymen, still we regarded that unhappy division as a question essentially Swiss, with which other nations had no concern. It was evident that right and reason, as well as the force of numbers, were on the side of the Diet, and thus armed the triumph of the majority was from the first certain.

Now that the contest is at end, it may be permitted to the friends of democratic liberty, wherever residing, to express their admiration of the course pursued by your honourable body, and of the heroism of the Federal troops, combined with that humanity and generosity to the vanquished which should ever characterise the soldiers of liberty. All hail! to the brave defenders of Swiss sovereignty, who have shown themselves at once competent to conquer faction, and worthy of the victory which has rewarded their bravery.

Far be it from us to cast any reflection upon the courage of the misled sons of Switzerland who, lured from the path of duty, by the falsehoods and calumnies of a 'rebel faction,' dimmed the bright page of their history by taking up arms against the majority of their fellow-countrymen. The children of William Tell, and his compatriots, are dear to the friends of liberty throughout the world; dear for the services which their great forefathers rendered to the general cause of human liberty, and we would utter no word which should imply doubt of their

---

1 One edn, 1847, broadsheet.

bravery, or their public and private virtues. Vanquished in the late contest, they were so because they had placed themselves in a false position, and arrayed themselves against the immense majority of their fellow-citizens, the interests of their country, and the very recollection of their forefathers' patriotic deeds. What wonder that with so bad a cause they were speedily compelled to succumb? But, we repeat, the citizens of the seven cantons were partly misled, and partly coerced into acts of hostility against the public weal; but now that their deceivers and oppressors have been driven from the soil of Switzerland, we are persuaded that those citizens will at once re-unite with their Helvetic brethren, and in the event of their services being required to defend their country from the attacks of jealous tyrants, they will be found amongst the foremost and the bravest of Switzerland's defenders.

Besides offering our congratulations to your honourable body, we have another reason for sending this address. We have witnessed with less of alarm than of disgust and indignation, the conduct of certain governments who have insolently presumed to offer what they have called 'mediation,' between the legitimate Government of Switzerland and the 'rebel faction,' which, for a moment, impiously raised the standard of unjustifiable insurrection. The offer of such 'mediation' (under any circumstances uncalled for), is at once insulting and ludicrous when offered after the treasonable faction has ceased to exist, when, in fact, there is not the shadow of a party opposed to the Diet, and consequently, no parties between whom to 'mediate.' We cannot sufficiently express our admiration of the unanswerable reply of your honourable body to the offered 'mediation' of the French Government. That reply – a model for statesmen of all countries menaced by intermeddling powers – must command the enthusiastic approbation of all nations.

But, what is the meaning of those gatherings of troops on the French and Austrian frontiers of Switzerland? Are they intended to intimidate your honourable body into negotiating a compromise with the beaten, dissolved, and dispersed faction? Or, are those forces collected with the vain view of Polandising Switzerland? The evil intentions of the Governments which assisted the Sonderbund with arms and money cannot be doubted; we think, however, that even those Governments will pause before committing themselves to a contest, the issue of which may be more fatal to them than to Switzerland.

Governments, which are the incarnations of corruption or assassination, and, therefore, hated by the nations they govern, would act very unwisely for themselves by provoking a 'war of principles.' The perfidy, violence, and political pollution from which the people of France have suffered during the past seventeen years, are not the best guarantees against social convulsion, and such convulsion is more than probable in the event of an European war. Besides, the people of France are too democratic to quietly acquiesce in the desecration of the tri-coloured flag, and will never submit to see that flag joined with the colours of despotism against the Republican banner of Switzerland. The confiscation of Cracow is not yet forgotten or forgiven, and the blood of the victims of the massacres of Gallicia yet cries to Heaven for retribution. There are more nations than one who pray for the hour when they may burst the fetters imposed upon them by the hereditary enemy of Helvetia. The ring of the first Austrian shot fired against Switzerland, would reverberate through Germany, Poland, Bohemia, Hungary, and Italy, and not Swiss rifles alone would answer the vollies of the armed slaves of a detested despotism.

The other 'powers' may assure themselves that the nations over which they rule, will neglect no opportunity of achieving their emancipation; and such an opportunity would be afforded by a crusade of kings against the liberties of Switzerland.

To you, legislators of a free and glorious people, is entrusted the safeguard not only of your country's liberties, but also of the hopes of the down-trodden nations who yet bow beneath the tyranny of irresponsible rulers. Europe, weary of the misery of slavery, finds hope and consolation in witnessing the devolopement of Swiss institutions, anticipating the time when those institutions, established in every nation, shall secure to its people the blessings enjoyed by Switzerland. Patriotism and philanthropy – duty to your fatherland, and duty to your fellow-men of every nation, alike enjoin you to defend the sacred interests committed to your charge. Faithful to your trust, you would, if the need existed, find a nation of warriors on your own soil, quite capable of successfully defying all the armies of all the enemies of Switzerland. But your warriors would not be left alone to fight the battles of freedom against tyranny. The sympathy and the support of every people in Europe would be arrayed on the side of the Helvetic Confederation.

Legislators of Switzerland, stand fast by your country's liberties, undismayed by the roaring of the blatant beasts of despotism, or the howlings of their jackals. While respecting the rights of others, you will be prepared to defend your own. While sacredly guarding the rights of each individual citizen and the liberties of each canton, you will nevertheless perfect the unity of the Confederation so as to concentrate the national will and the national power for national purposes. While protecting the rights of conscience, and the freedom of religious worship, you will best provide for the general good by curbing fanaticism, and crushing, with a heavy hand, every attempt to subject the people to the yoke of a tyrannical Theo-cracy. While rendering your political institutions models of democratic perfection, you will ensure the Equality, Liberty, and Fraternity they are intended to guard, by promoting that wise organisation of industry which will prevent pauperism, and save the Swiss labourer from the misery which is the condition of millions of the children of labour in other countries. Thus acting, you will earn the gratitude of your own fellow-citizens, and the admiration of the world.

Very respectfully we tender to you this expression of our profound esteem, and our earnest wishes for the prosperity of Switzerland, and the happiness of all her children.

Signed by the secretaries and members of the committee, in behalf of, and in the name of, the Association,

G. JULIAN HARNEY,
ERNEST JONES,   } Great Britain
CHARLES KEEN,
THOMAS CLARK,

J.A. MICHELOT,
H. BERNARD,   } France

CARL SCHAPPER,
JOSEPH MOLL,   } Germany

J. SCHABELITZ (of Basle)
H. KRELL, (of Lucerne) } Switzerland

PETER HOLM,
— LUNTBERG,   } Scandinavia

LOUIS OBORSKI, Poland

CARL POHSE,
P. BLUHM.   } Russia
London, Dec. 13th, 1847.

PRINCIPLES AND RULES OF THE SOCIETY OF
FRATERNAL DEMOCRATS.

This society, composed of natives of Great Britain, France, Germany, Scandinavia, Poland, Italy, Switzerland, Hungary and other countries, has for its

OBJECT

the mutual enlightenment of its members; and the propapaganda of the great principle embodied in the society's motto: —

'All men are brethren.'

The members of this society agree to adopt the following

DECLARATION OF PRINCIPLES.

In accordance with the above declaration of the brotherhood of the human race, we renounce, repudiate, and condemn all political hereditary inequalities and distinctions of 'caste;' consequently, we regard kings, aristocracies, and classes monopolising political privileges in virtue of their possession of property, as usurpers and violators of the principle of human brotherhood. Governments elected by, and responsible to, the entire people, is our political creed.

We declare that the earth with all its natural productions is the common property of all; we therefore denounce all infractions of this evidently just and natural law, as robbery and usurpation. We declare that the present state of society, which permits idlers and schemers to monopolise the fruits of the earth and the productions of industry, and compels the working classes to labour for inadequate rewards, and even condemns them to social slavery, destitution and degradation, is essentially unjust. That labour and rewards should be equal is our social creed.

We condemn the 'national' hatreds which have hitherto divided mankind, as both foolish and wicked; foolish, because no one can decide for himself the country he will be born in; and wicked, as proved by the feuds and bloody wars which have desolated the earth, in consequence of these national vanities. Convinced, too, that national prejudices have been, in all ages, taken advantage of by the people's oppressors, to set them tearing the throats of each other, when they should have been working together for their common good, this society repudiates the term 'Foreigner,' no matter by, or to whom applied. Our moral creed is to receive our fellow men, without regard to 'country,' as members of one family, the human race; and citizens of one commonwealth – the world. Finally, we recognise that great moral law, 'Do unto thy brother, as thou wouldest thy brother should do onto thee,' as the great safeguard of public and private happiness.

RULES.

I. – Democrats of all nations, wherever residing, may become members of this society.

II. – Candidates for membership must be proposed by two members at any one of the regular meetings, the proposers being held responsible for the democratic principles and moral character of the person they nominate. The person nominated to be elected or rejected by a majority of votes of the members present.

III. – That to provide for the cost of postage, printing, and other necessary expenses, each member shall contribute a sum of not less than one shilling annually. The shilling to be paid (or otherwise held as due from each member from) the 22nd of September in each year. The contribution may be paid by instalments.

IV. – That a general secretary be selected from each country represented in this society; the whole of their names to be affixed to the members' cards, and to all public documents issued by the society. The general secretaries to choose from among themselves one or more corresponding secretaries.

V. – That a committee, consisting of the general secretaries, and one additional member selected from each country represented in this society, shall be appointed to prepare and manage the general and financial business of the society.

VI. – That a treasurer and financial secretary be appointed.

VII. – That the regular meetings of the society shall be holden on the first Monday in every month, at which besides the members one or more 'friends' may be introduced by a member, (the names of the 'friends' to be made known to the chairman of the evening), persons unknown to members present, may also be admitted on satisfying the doorkeepers that they belong to the National Charter Association, or the French, German, Polish, or other Democratic Societies.

VIII. – Special meetings may be called whenever the committee shall consider such meetings necessary,.

IX. – That the order of business at the monthly meetings shall be as follows:-

Chair to be taken at eight o'clock.

Minutes of the previous meeting to be submitted for confirmation.

Correspondence to be read.

The general secretaries to report when necessary on any event, either favourable or hostile to democratic progress.

Discussion upon any question introduced by the committee shall then take place; any question introduced at a previous meeting and not disposed of at that meeting, shall have precedence, unless a majority of the members present shall determine otherwise.

A chairman and two doorkeepers to be appointed for the next meeting.

The chairman to vacate the chair at ten o'clock.

X. – A quarterly financial statement shall be laid before the members at their meetings in the months of March, June, and December. An annual balance sheet shall be submitted to the members at the meeting on the first Monday in September.

XI. – The officers of the society shall be elected annually, at the meeting on the first Monday in the month of September.

A PROPOSAL FOR THE CONSIDERATION OF THE FRIENDS OF PROGRESS.[1]

BY WM. LOVETT.[2]

LONDON:
PUBLISHED BY JOHN CLEAVE, 1, SHOE LANE,
AND SOLD BY ALL BOOKSELLERS.
Price One Penny.

---

1 One edn, 1847, 8 pp.
2 William Lovett (1800–77), Owenite and moral force Chartist.

A PROPOSAL, &c.

FELLOW-COUNTRYMEN,

Millions of our brethren, from their ardent desire to promote such changes, social, political, moral and religious, as they conscientiously believe will remove, or greatly abridge, the present lamentable amount of poverty, misery, vice and crime, may justly be considered *friends of progress*.

Knowing that vast numbers of those friends are actively engaged in their respective societies, as well as individually, in forwarding each their peculiar views, too often midst difficulties and discouragements ending in disappointment destructive of future efforts, I have long been desirous of seeing some combined effort made by which, as I conceive, all the various objects of reform they are separately in pursuit of may sooner be realised than can possibly be effected by individual or isolated effort; while at the same time they are cultivating principles of peace, union and brotherhood, which doubtlessly form the best foundation for social happiness and national advancement.

To effect any great improvement in this country, politically or socially, we have learnt from experience the great effort that is needed, as well as the amount of money that must be spent before public opinion can be formed and concentrated so as to influence our legislature in favour of even *one* measure of reform, and yet very *many* are needed to effect our social and political salvation.

Owing to this slow and tardy process of reform, misery, vice and crime are perpetuated; thousands are born and die in ignorance and vice; and thousands too often lose health and hope in the continuous and protracted struggle to make men wiser, better and happier than they found them.

This slow progress for good is evidently to be attributed to the great variety of measures advocated by different bodies of reformers; to the contentious feelings too often engendered in their onward progress, and the consequent difficulty of uniting our brethren in favour of any *one* object; and, above all, in the great difficulty of *abrogating old laws, or instituting new ones* necessary to effect or facilitate the reform desired, by any particular body of reformers, or portion of the people.

But as all those various classes of reformers are *equally the friends of progress*, all zealous and desirous of benefiting their fellow-men, and, it may be, all equally active in promoting the especial object they have espoused, it will be useless to call upon any of them to give up their particular object in favour of any *one* measure that may by some persons be considered more practical and important than another; for such appeals have frequently been made, and as often disregarded.

As measures of progress they are *all* doubtlessly important, if not equally so, and as they are all equally desirous to check evil and promote good, and, it is presumed, *anxious to live to see the realization of some of the objects they are contending for*, the question arises, whether, upon the Good Samaritan principle, of each helping his fellow man, they can be brought to unite the sooner to realize *the objects they are severally in pursuit of*, and thus to carry forward simultaneously all those measures necessary for accomplishing the greatest good in the shortest possible period.

In reflecting on the difficulties in the way of progress it has struck me that something might be done to facilitate such a desired object, in the formation of a GENERAL ASSOCIATION OF PROGRESS, in which might be combined *all those measures of social and political reformation for which societies are established, or mankind individually are now in pursuit of*, as well, indeed, as any other measure calculated to aid the great cause of mental, moral, and political progression.

Anxious that something should be done in favour of some combined effort for the progress of humanity, I have presumed to address you, as well as to direct your attention to the following proposal, as an outline explanatory of my views on the subject, which may be improved or altered by any persons disposed to promote or aid such an undertaking.

PROPOSAL FOR FORMING
A GENERAL ASSOCIATION OF PROGRESS.

Its first object being to unite in one general union of progress all those who are now separately, or in small bodies, seeking the attainment of the following *political* and *social* objects. Secondly, to devise some *practical measures* for unitedly promoting and realizing such objects in a shorter time than can possibly be done under present arrangements, and this without interfering any way with the internal regulation of any present association.

Political Objects of Progress.

1st. The EQUAL and JUST REPRESENTATION of the whole people.

2nd. The abolition of all STATE RELIGION; and the right of conscience and opinion secured.

3rd. The ABSOLUTE FREEDOM OF TRADE, and the abrogation of all custom and excise laws.

4th. The ABOLITION OF ALL TAXES UPON KNOWLEDGE, such as the tax and securities on newspapers, stamps, and advertising duties, taxes on paper, books, pamphlets, &c.

5th. The GENERAL REDUCTION OF TAXATION, and a more rigid economy of its expenditure.

6th. DIRECT TAXATION on PROPERTY, and the abolition of all *indirect* means of raising a revenue.

7th. The Abolition of all POLITICAL MONOPOLIES and UNJUST PRIVILEGES.

8. The Legislative improvement, impartial execution, and cheapening of LAW and JUSTICE for the whole people.

Social Objects of Progress.

9th. GENERAL EDUCATION for the whole population, provided *by all*, and carried out and enforced *by all*, with the least possible government interference.

10th. The promotion of SCIENTIFIC INSTITUTIONS, SCHOOLS for ADULT INSTRUCTION, and LIBRARIES for general circulation among the whole population.

11th. The Promotion of TEMPERANCE, SOBRIETY, CLEANLINESS, and HEALTH, amongst all classes; and the securing of places of rational recreation for the people, *apart from intoxicating drinks*.

12th. The devising means by which the working and middle classes may have COMFORTABLE HOMES, and be gradually enabled to become MANUFAC-TURERS, TRADERS, or FARMERS, on their own capital.

13th. To labour for the general abolition of WAR, SLAVERY, and OPPRES-SION, and the promotion of GENERAL CIVILIZATION and CHRISTIAN BROTHERHOOD throughout the whole world.

SKETCH OF THE GENERAL ORGANIZATION.

That any number of individuals uniting, or already united, to promote any of the above objects may become members of the association of progress, by complying with the following conditions:

1. That they be united for one or more of the objects specified, and be classi-fied, for purposes herafter mentioned, one hundred persons in each class.

2. That they individually subscribe 2*d.* each towards a general fund weekly, the same to be collected by one of their own body, and paid into the District Bank of the Association.

3. That they signify by resolution that any sum their class may secure by lot (or otherwise) shall not be divided or applied otherwise than for their declared object.

4. That they appoint one of their members to form a *Committee for the District*; such Committee to see that the sums collected by the Classes within the district are paid into the Bank, as well as for promoting the objects of the Association within their respective districts.

General Committee.

That each District Committee appoint two members annually to form the *General Committee for the Association*, such Committee to meet in London (or other large town alternately) for the division and application of the money thus raised, according to the rules agreed to; as well as for the promotion of the general objects of the Association, by all just and peaceful means.

Application of the General Fund.

That the fund so raised be annually divided by the Committee, into portions of £2,000; such portions to be appropriated by lot (or any other approved means) among the different classes of the Association, and immediately handed over to those who may be so successful; the same to be applied by them in promoting their declared objects, without any further intervention.

Such is a mere outline of the plan proposed. It will be seen that I have sought to include under the heads of *political* and *social* reform all those measures which are now advocated and contended for by different bodies, as well as others which I deem desirable and necessary, before right, knowledge and happiness can be effected for our fellow-men.

I have not thought it necessary to enter into the details of Rules and Regulations, as those can be best matured by such persons as may be disposed to form such an association.

As however a mere outline of the plan is set forth, it may be necessary to explain, that the chief object of the classification *into hundreds* is for the appropriation of the fund raised, as well as to afford facilities for persons not included in any existing Association to form a part of the Association of Progress. As, for instance, 100 men, known to each other, may unite for the purpose of building themselves comfortable habitations, for raising means to take a farm, to commence manufacturing, or trading, or for any social or political object embraced by the Association, and in this manner may obtain £2,000 capital to commence or forward their undertaking; or if not successful directly in a pecuniary sense, they will, by their union, be indirectly benefited by the reforms they would unitedly be able to effect.

If in this manner the friends of progress were only combined to the extent of *one million*, that number, paying *2d. each* per week, would raise money enough to give £2,000 *capital to 216 different classes every year*.

The mere pecuniary advantages however would be trifling, compared with the great and paramount object, A UNION OF ALL FRIENDS OF PROGRESS, all aiding each other, in the spirit of Christian Brotherhood, the better to accomplish the reforms they are anxious to effect; acting in concert for the promulgation of their respective views and objects; seeking to smooth down those contracted, prejudiced and contentious feelings which now so much impede the progress of reform; and uniting hearts and minds to remove the poverty, misery and oppression of their land, and to extend the blessings of peace, prosperity, knowledge and happiness among all the nations of the earth.

That the friends of progress may speedily perceive the necessity for some such plan of union, is the sincere wish of

WM. LOVETT,
16, South Row, New Road.

Dec. 31st, 1847.

No. 1.
TRACTS FOR FUSTIAN JACKETS AND SMOCK FROCKS.

STATE OF THE POLL,
MASTERS AND MEN AT ELECTIONS.[1]
BY THE REV. B. PARSONS,[2]
OF EBLEY, STROUD.

[1847–9]

> 'I was a father to the poor,
> The cause of which I knew not
> I searched out.' – JOB.[3]

FELLOW-WORKMEN,

You will allow me to address you as companions in labour. Society is a complex thing and very full of wants. To supply its necessities an almost incalculable amount of toil is requisite. 'Arts, trades, and mysteries,' must be learnt and practised; some must work with their heads and some with their hands; and moralists, philosophers, and operatives, are all essential to perfect society and to render mankind happy. A great deal has been said about the *respectability* of trades and professions, and one occupation is often extolled as more dignified than another, when the real fact is that all honest employments, whether of the body or mind, are essentially *honourable*. The scavenger who sweeps on streets and keeps our drains clear, does more for public health than the most skilful physician in the land. The former *keeps away* disease, the latter only *cures* it, allows that '*prevention is better than cure.*' 'Tis true the doctor may be the more polite and learned man of the two, but then that is not the fault of the scavenger. If the clergy and gentry, &c., had done their duty, the man who sweeps our streets would have been, in his manners and morals, as perfect a gentleman as any other person in the land. The clergyman who delivers the sermon, and the clown who reduces it to practice, are *equally honourable*, except in those cases in which the preacher neglects the rules he prescribes to others, for in every such instance the peasant

---

1 Nos 1–18, 1847–9.

2 Benjamin Parsons (1797–1855), originally a tailor's apprentice, Congregational minister at Ebley, Stroud, 1826–55; active in local education and temperance movements.

3 Job 29: 16.

is by far the better and *more respectable* man. The day labourer may be rude, and the priest polite, but then as the rudeness of the former is to a great extent the *crime* of the latter, no one ought to be taunted with a fault to which he has been doomed by the negligence and injustice of those who had his manners and destiny in their hands, and were actually *paid* to perfect his education.

I must then maintain that all useful labour is essentially *respectable*, and indeed was so esteemed by our wise and unsophisticated ancestors: hence palaces and mansions were the manufactories of antiquity, and the principal *mill girls* were *queens* and *princesses*: and these not only wove the cloth but took it to market, or made it up into garments for both sexes, and not unfrequently kept open a shop for ready-made clothes. I make these remarks, because many of you have occasionally been scowled upon and called mean, vulgar, and low, and I fear that some have begun to imagine that this contempt is your due, and that both yourselves and your various employments are really dishonourable. Now you will never rise in society until you *raise yourselves*, and you will never raise yourselves until you duly estimate the essential dignity of your nature and of your occupations. The fact is, you make, or help to make, all the respectability of the land. I am sure you will not abuse these remarks by not rendering 'honour to whom honour is due;' and should any of the wealthy treat you with insolence or rudeness, you know that your highest revenge will be to show them that you have *better manners*, and that you have learnt from the Bible to '*honour all men*,' whether rich or poor. Every human being is a *child of God*, and our Heavenly Father feels himself dishonoured when any member of his great family, whether prince or peasant, is treated with injustice or contempt. Hence he who calls his 'brother a fool is in danger' of everlasting perdition. But we hope to bring out these facts more fully on some future occasions.

I address you as the Fustian Jackets and Smock Frocks of the neighbourhood, not only to compliment you on your useful and respectable garb, but, because from some observation on society, I have learnt that you have among you the largest amount of plain common sense. This valuable article is sometimes a rare qualification among those who are conventionally called 'the higher ranks;' indeed, common sense is not mentioned as a school accomplishment, and for want of it, 'the March of Intellect' in certain quarters means that Intellect has marched away. A waggish professor gave the following as a reason why our Universities are the seats of learning. He said, 'that every person came out more foolish than he entered, and therefore must have left a portion of his wisdom behind him to enrich the schools.' I have known some hundreds of people spoiled by schools and colleges, and it really is one of the blessings of your existence that you have escaped the calamity of a University education; and on that account I address you in these tracts. To talk about '*Human rights*,' '*Liberty for all*,' '*Justice to all*,' and such like matters, in our great National schools, or to dedicate tracts on these subjects to Doctors in Divinity, &c. &c., would in many cases be just as effectual as to reason with a hop-pole. It is a humbling fact that the noble, the learned, and the wealthy, have generally been the last to receive the truth. 'Not many wise men after the flesh, not many mighty, not many noble are called.' Till the Fustian Jackets and Smock Frocks had made the Anti-Slavery question *respectable*, princes, peers, bishops, and members of parliament could not see the *injustice* of *selling*, *branding*, and *cart whipping men* and *women* like cattle: and had not you rallied round Cobden[1] and Bright,[2] the cruelty of taxing the poor man's loaf to increase the overgrown wealth of the rich, would to this day have been deemed the quintessence of equity.

You should consider that every measure for the welfare of the nation has generally to be enacted and passed by the voice of the people out of the Senate, before it obtains the sanction of Parliament or the Royal signature. And this is as it ought to be. The *People* of England form the *Third Estate* in the Constitution. Our Government is 'a *three-fold cord*,' and, when all the strands are good, 'not easily broken.' It consists of Monarch, Lords, and Commons: and hence the 'Sovereign people,' or 'the Majesty of the people,' are phrases quite as correct as the Majesty of the Monarch. The Commons are intended to represent the whole people, but how can they do this unless you hold public meetings and use other legitimate means to make them acquainted with your grievances and wishes. '*The right of Petition*' has this object especially in view.

Now you must have observed that for a very considerable time there has been a tendency in what used to be called the '*People's House*,' to set your reasonable and equitable requests at defiance. Your petitions have been treated as waste paper. And the parties most guilty in this affair have been the *Whigs*, who used to be deemed the bulwarks of 'Civil and Religious Liberty.' When you asked to eat *untaxed bread*, the Whigs proposed to make a bad matter worse, by enriching the revenue at your expence with an Eight Shilling duty; and thus, if they could have had their way, they would have burdened the already over-burdened masses with a new impost. The *Dissenter's Bill*, which was intended to give a legal right to property which had been obtained by unjust means, was carried in the face of public opinion, and was a more wanton insult to the Church of England than to Dissenters. The Maynooth Grant[3] was not asked for. Many even of the Catholics saw its insidious tendency, and united with Churchmen and Dissenters in protesting against it: and, indeed, so strong was the opposition, that had not the *Whigs* – these very popular Whigs! – voted in greater numbers than the Tories, the measure would have been lost. The people were reviled for expressing an opinion on the subject. Macaulay,[4] whom the Electors of Edinburgh have sent about his business, and by this one act have immortalised themselves, poured forth the most vulgar abuse on one of the most enlightened meetings that was ever held in Exeter Hall, because delegates had assembled from all parts of the realm to express the nation's wish; and seeing Exeter Hall was denounced in St Stephens, we had this insolence reiterated elsewhere.

---

1 Richard Cobden (1804–65), anti-Corn Law leader.
2 John Bright (1811–89), liberal politician.
3 Sir Robert Peel's 1845 increase in the annual funding for the Catholic College at Maynooth.
4 Thomas Babbington Macaulay (1800–59), historian, MP for Edinburgh 1839–47, 1852–6.

The new Measure of Education has not a single good trait to recommend it, and yet this is another of the exploits of the *Whigs*. How it disgraces the Church, and especially the *wealthy* and the *Evangelicals*; how it degrades the Government; how it *taxes* the people, and must in the end enslave them, I have exhibited in another tract, No. 4. I merely refer to the subject here to show you that these *Whigs are no more to be trusted. To multiply Commissioners, places, offices, and pensions*, has been their study for some time past, and if you allow them to go on, the glory of our country will set for ever. On the Continent, the almost endless creation of Government Offices, &c., was intended to render the great mass of the people dependent upon the State for daily bread, and destroy every vestige of liberty. Could the plan only be brought to bear upon England, tyranny, far worse than that of the dark ages, would a second time scourge the nation.

My object in writing these tracts is to sound the alarm and call upon you to prevent this dire calamity. In looking at the country just now, I find that you are the chief persons to whom I can turn. Noble families in all ages have been the first to sell their liberties. Tacitus,[1] one of the most philosophical of historians, tells us that Rome was thus betrayed. I could adduce plenty of proofs of a similar character respecting the downfall of other nations and empires: and the same tragedy will soon be played in England unless you come to the rescue of your country. See how anxious the wealthy classes are to transfer as much power as possible from the people to the Crown, and thus to violate one of the most glorious principles of the Constitution. What a rush there is among the *respectable!* and the rich for Government Offices. Many retire from honest trade that they may deal in corruption: and others, who have not as yet stained their hands, have long since polluted their souls by acquiescing in this iniquity and denouncing all who attempt to stop its progress.

The state of the Poll at the late Election is one of the most ominous events that has occurred for many years. Dr Arnold has justly observed that England owes an immense debt to its *Political Parties*. The opposition of Whig and Tory has given to England its most invaluable blessings. Each of these ambitious sects has alternately courted the people, and promised you something for your patronage: and the violent sectarianism of the senate has been in no small degree the salvation of the country. But for the opposition benches the nation had long since been enslaved, and thus the evil has been far over-balanced by the good. But a new era has dawned, and Whigs, Tories, and Radicals are becoming one, and in the rage for *centralization*, and the *offices*, *powers*, *salaries*, and *pensions*, which this system involves, the real interests of the people have been forgotten. Factions may be bad, but *coalitions* are ten thousand times worse. Unless you arouse yourselves, John Bull will very soon be in the condition of the flat between two sharps. To prove what I have been saying, only look at the doings of the late Parliament or the votes of the present Election. The *Whigs out of office* always profess to be your friends, but *in office* they give you a graceful bow and turn to the Tories. When not in power, the know that if they propose a good measure you will support

---

1 Cornelius Tacitus (*c*. AD 55–120), Roman historian.

them, and forsooth they are the friends of the people; but let them gain office, and the tables are turned. They then feel assured that to keep their places they must court the abettors of arbitrary power, and that if their measures are only bad enough, they shall have very cordial support from your opponents. Ever since the passing of the Reform Bill the Whigs have been thus temporising and going down. If they wanted any unconstitutional work done they knew where to look for assistance, and their gratitude has been almost boundless in the payments they have made to their new friends. Look at the 'Maynooth Grant,' the 'Dissenter's Bill,' the 'New Poor Law,' and the 'Education Plan,' for proofs of these facts.

The last Election tells a most instructive tale. In Leeds, the *Whig* – aye, the *liberal Whig!* mind ye – had *five hundred* Liberal votes, and upwards of *fifteen hundred* Tory supporters! while Joseph Sturge,[1] the *real friend of the people*, had upwards of *nineteen hundred* Liberals. At Halifax, one Whig gave place to a Tory, and the other Whig was brought in by Tory votes. In London, the election of Lord John Russell[2] was secured by the Tories. But for them his Lordship would have been out. A letter in the *Morning Herald* says, that unheard-of bribery was also resorted to. You know how the Tories voted at Stroud, and how proud the Whigs were to boast of this occurrence. Now the Tories have always been very attentive to their own party, and not one of these votes would have been given had they not felt assured, that their own interest would be best served by returning these very liberal Whigs.

From these truths you ought to learn the great lesson, that you cannot look to the present Parliament for friends. You must now resolve to befriend yourselves, and if you thus determine, these passing events will produce the happiest results for the country. Too long have you asked – what will the Parliament do? and have been most grievously disappointed. The good that Parliament men will do, will be just as much as you influence them to effect. 'Put not your trust in princes,' is a command sent us from heaven. 'Cursed is the man that trusteth in man,' is also a declaration of one of the inspired prophets. You should then attend to your own affairs. Every man, woman, and child should become a politician. This is one of your most solemn *christian duties*. You must read on these topics; you must discuss them in your houses and work-shops, and have public meetings and lectures to elucidate and enforce them. To be ignorant of the constitution of your country and the doings of Parliament should be condemned as a sin, second only to ignorance of the bible. The Almighty never intended that any one man, or any body of men, should be trusted with irresponsible power; and our late senators have given us ample proofs of their unworthiness of such confidence. Many of them have exhibited the grossest ignorance of political economy, and their speeches and actions have been in favor of arbitrary power. The Franchise, not only in several of the Counties, but in the Boroughs, has been trampled in the dust; and the Elections have been in numerous instances a most perfect farce, and this treason

---

1 Joseph Sturge (1793–1859), anti-slavery and anti-Corn Law League reformer.
2 Lord John Russell (1792–1878), Home Secretary under Melbourne.

against the constitution of the country and the people, is allowed to pass without a word. You must – you Fustian Jackets and Smock Frocks – you who enrich the country with your labour and give wealth and comfort to all – you must make yourselves acquainted with these facts, and lift your voice against them.

There never was a time when you had such opportunities as now to redress your grievances and to check the power of those who disregard your rights. You have books in abundance, the press is free, and you may meet for public discussion. Many of the middle classes are on your side, and the dissenters, with few exceptions, will soon join your ranks. The Conservatives also are making their court to you, Bishops and Curates profess to take a deep interest in your rights, and therefore all you have to do is to test their sincerity by enlisting their aid to effect your political emancipation. You will, if they are sincere, have the clergy demanding for you the suffrage and the ballot. The man who would give you wash-houses and baths, or supply you with soup, coals, and blankets, but deny you your political emancipation, is your enemy; even his proffered charity is the grossest uncharitableness. Obtain your constitutional rights, and you can honourably help yourselves.

You may gather much hope from the scene that took place on the Hustings and in the Victoria Rooms at Stroud, and elsewhere, at the conclusion of the last election. After the Returning Officer had declared the poll, I analysed Mr Stanton's[1] votes, and stated that a labouring man had informed me that he 'had been called into the counting-house before his master and Messrs Scrope[2] and Stanton, and asked whom he intended to vote for.' The man had no idea that I should repeat it again, nor indeed did he mention the circumstance with any degree of ill-feeling. It was quite *usual*. I am happy to say he had courage to speak for himself and vote as his judgment directed him. We shall never forget the consternation that the reference to this circumstance produced. A volley of voices called out, 'Name him,' 'Name him.' I did not name the man because I feared I might injure him, but I promised the gentlemen that if they would form themselves into a committee, we would investigate the matter. I have not heard that the committee has been formed, or that Messrs Scrope and Stanton have come forward to declare that in no instance were any of the operative Electors brought into the counting-house, or that they themselves accompanied the masters into the shops or dwellings of the workmen. This avowal would at once settle the question. Since the election I have been told by gentlemen of great respectability of at least five cases besides the one I referred to on Friday evening; but as the matter is probably to drop, I do not here introduce the subject so much for the purpose of detailing these reports, as for the sake of letting you know how anxious many of your employers are that you should enjoy perfect political freedom.

The scene on the hustings was really distressing. Some cried one thing and some another. One shouted, 'Name him, Name him.' Another seemed almost furious. Some had all their good manners paralysed, and uttered words which I dare not print. A young clothier, belonging, I believe, to a firm in the neighbourhood,

---

1 William Henry Stanton (1790–1870), MP for Stroud 1841–52.

2 George Julius Poulett Scrope (1797–1876), geologist and political economist.

went almost so far as to forget that he was a gentleman; and I think it was a companion of his who was so smitten that he nearly lost the gift of speech, and actually kept on repeating the same word over and over again, as if all the other words of his mother tongue had completely deserted him. *No one can be offended with what I am here narrating without acknowledging himself guilty, or that he is the patron of those that are.* Besides, I want you to take these demonstrations of indignation as tokens of the great change *in your favour*, that has come over the hearts and consciences of certain gentlemen who were once supposed to be far from favourable to your voting as you pleased. I have long known masters who would not canvass their workmen, because they would not in the least degree influence them. If they did canvass at all they went into another district where their presence could not be construed into an intimidation. I have heard a large manufacturer declare that he would not ask for a single vote among his workpeople, because he wished them to vote as freely as himself. This was not only honourable, but *right honourable*, and the master who sets such an example is more worthy of a monument than Wellington.[1] Still there have been strange tales of a contrary character, and some poor fellows are said to have had no alternative but starvation or political annihilation.

Things however now wear a different aspect, for if the bare mention of one poor man being called into a counting-house made so many gentlemen almost faint, you must perceive that such conduct is now esteemed the most execrable abomination. For to suppose that any individual who had been guilty of such a dirty trick, could foam and rage, profess the most unmanagable indignation, and keep on shouting, '*Name him! Name him!*' when he knew that if the truth came out his own name would be mentioned, is such a piece of audaciousness and hypocrisy that is rarely heard of, except among the most abandoned culprits. It reminds one of the accomplished plunderer who had just robbed a shop, and then, to prevent detection, ran through the street crying, '*Stop, thief! Stop thief!*' You must therefore take the scene on the Hustings and in the Victoria Rooms as a pledge that there will be no more *counting-house* work, no more bribery or intimidation, and that hereafter you may all be freemen in the best sense of the word. For should any Election tricks be resorted to hereafter, I think it would not be unseasonable to remind the guilty parties of the Victoria Rooms, on Friday evening, July 30, 1847. Of all *miscreants*, he who traffics in votes, whether by bribe or intimidation, is the *vilest* and *lowest*. You cannot imagine an occupation more *mean, disreputable,* or *treasonable*. But though noblemen may thus degrade themselves, or masters in other districts may thus far sacrifice their reputation, we of course shall never again hear of such an occurrence in the immaculate Borough of Stroud.

One fact I had need explain for the satisfaction of my readers. I am told that at one of the Polling Booths several men voted contrary to their own inclinations, so that they remind us of the brute beasts mentioned in the book of Samuel, which, in opposition to all the instincts of nature, left their calves behind and

---

1 Arthur Wellesley (1769–1852), first Duke of Wellington, soldier and Tory Prime Minister 1828–30, Foreign Secretary 1834–5.

drew the Ark home to the Israelites;[1] their *'lowing'* for their offspring showed that their conduct was involuntary. So the complaints of many a poor operative showed that he was not his own master. Still, as the scene on the hustings must be taken as a demonstration that the masters could have had no hand in this unnatural proceeding: – and as *politics* are too *abominable* for any *good christian* to touch them, and therefore, of course, too iniquitous for the interference of Providence: – and further, as we do not believe in magic, or that masters resort to legerdemain, political, or otherwise; – the only alternative left, is to conclude that these poor men were influenced by evil spirits, and in their conduct illustrated the old adage, *'that needs must when Satan drives.'* I have some hope, however, that the occurrence will not take place again, or if we should be threatened with it, that the Clergy will make matters straight. A very wealthy Lord of a Manor, a hoary-headed old gentleman, once told me, that 'the grand proof of the vast superiority of the Clergy over dissenting ministers consisted in the fact that *the former could lay evil spirits whenever they liked.'* If this opinion be correct, I trust the Clergymen will see to it that none of the demons of bribery or intimidation may make their appearance in any future Elections. I do firmly believe that if they only do their duty, we may yet see the poor elector enjoying his constitutional freedom, and quite delivered from all adverse, human, or satanic influence.

In conclusion, I again say, that you must work out your own political salvation, and that you must do it by *moral* means alone. Not a pike, a blunderbuss, a brick-bat, or a match must be found in your hands. In *physical force* your opponents are mightier than you, but in *moral force* you are ten thousand times stronger than they. The best way to prove that you deserve your rights, is to show that you respect the rights of others, and that you will not redress even a wrong by revenge, but by reason and justice alone. Your manners ought to demonstrate that *Fustian Jackets* and *Smock Frocks* have no necessary connection with rudeness or vulgarity. You can now rescue yourselves and your country from that corruption and slavery with which it is threatened, and we trust you will read, think, and act worthy of yourselves, remembering that not merely 'England,' but that *Christianity,* 'expects every man to do his duty.'[2]

Since this Tract was written, Parliament has met, and our most painful forebodings have been realized. We have a coalition of all the worst elements of Whigs and Tories. What it would have been but for the downfall of Louis Philippe[3] and the revolutions in Europe, we cannot tell. The sudden overthrow of the French Monarch seemed for a moment to alarm it, but it has nearly recovered its disposition to set the people at defiance. Certain it is, that our representative system is the greatest piece of deception that ever duped the world. It is now seen that the persons who set at nought the laws and the constitution, are not the *Fustian Jackets* and *Smock Frocks*. The most orderly part of the nation is to be found among the *working classes*. The men who ask for justice and constitutional government, are the *operatives* and *peasants*. While nobles, bishops, squires,

---

1 Samuel 6: 11.
2 The phrase associated with Horatio Nelson (1758–1805), admiral.
3 Louis-Philippe (1773–1850), duc d'Orléans, King of France 1830–48.

clergymen, and not a few dissenters, are the persons who actively commit, or tacitly allow, the grossest outrages upon equity and common sense. The prerogatives of the crown and the rights of the people are monopolised by the aristocracy, so that the Queen is made a mere cipher and the masses political non-entities. The present parliament, strong in its majorities, laughs at the wishes of the nation. Indeed, *'laughing and cock-crowing,'* if we believe the newspapers, are some of its most prominent qualities. It is now admitted on all hands that the most disorderly assembly in the country is too often to be found in St Stephens. Fustian Jackets and Smock Frocks would behave ten thousand times better. We want a few working-men elected to sit among these gentlemen, and teach them, not only justice, but good manners. It is a remarkable fact in the town of Stroud, that disturbances at elections and public meetings generally originate with those who claim to be esteemed the *respectables*! The working classes set an example to those who call themselves their betters, and if report be true, the senate of the land not unfrequently has exhibited behaviour which would never be tolerated in the meetings of the peasantry. Only think of a *laughing* and *cock-crowing* legislator!! Have not the *property qualification*, the £40 *freehold*, the £10 *franchise*, *open voting*, and *septennial parliaments*, worked well and wrought wonders in sending men to the House who never open their mouths but to hiss like a serpent, to laugh like a hyæna, or crow like a cock? And what is worse than all, these *gentlemen – property qualification* men – never exert their talents so energetically as when it is proposed to correct some glaring abuse, or to agitate some great question of justice or humanity. Well, it is said that all things in the universe have their use, and therefore our laughing and cock-crowing representatives must not be despised. Arguments in favour of an enlarged franchise, vote by ballot, &c. &c., seem to have been lost upon the middle classes. They boasted that THEY – that THEY ALONE – were fit to choose the senators of the empire, and have set the masses at nought, as being formed in a baser mould and made of more ignoble stuff; and the result is a *'laughing, cock-crowing'* House, under whose extravagance these very middle classes are to be ground by taxation into that very pauperism which they have so frequently treated with contempt! The fact is now written as with a sunbeam on the mind of every patriot, that a worse House of Commons than the present could not have been chosen by the most ignorant of the peasantry; nay, that a wiser and better assembly of senators might have been selected, almost at random, from 'the hewers of wood and drawers of water.'[1] The present parliament will teach the middle classes that to avoid ruin they must fraternise with their unenfranchised brethren; and thus laughing and cock-crowing at law, liberty, and justice, will eventually minister, like Louis Philippe and Guizot,[2] to the downfall of iniquity, the elevation of the masses, the prosperity, and the salvation of the nation.

---

1 Joshua 9: 21.
2 François Guizot (1787–1874), French historian.

Nos. 2 & 3.

TRACTS FOR FUSTIAN JACKETS AND SMOCK FROCKS.

THE BIBLE
AND THE SIX POINTS OF THE CHARTER:
UNIVERSAL SUFFRAGE, THE BALLOT, NO PROPERTY
QUALIFICATION, PAYMENT OF MEMBERS OF PARLIAMENT,
ELECTORAL DISTRICTS, ANNUAL PARLIAMENTS.
BY REV. B. PARSONS,
OF EBLEY, STROUD.

'He hath put down tyrants from their thrones
And exalted them of low degree.' – MARY'S SONG.[1]

Who has heard of Chartism or the People's Charter without feeling queer? Pikes, blunderbusses, brick-bats, and lucifer matches almost instantly seem to bristle and flash through the country, and all the horrors of the Revolution of 1790 are enacted again. 'Only grant the six points of the Charter,' say they, 'and neither life nor property will be any longer secure.' Such doubtless not long since were the direful forebodings of an excellent and amiable minister when he gave utterance on a platform to the following exclamation: *'Atheism, Chartism, and every other ism that comes from the bottomless pit.'* No man has deeper at heart the welfare of the working classes than the very kind-hearted individual who uttered these words, and therefore I have long felt it to be a christian duty that some one should endeavour to disabuse him and the public of that misapprehension respecting the Charter which dictated this sweeping condemnation: for I am persuaded that the patriotism and philanthropy of our friend are such that if he saw that this same Chartism would work well for the country, and especially for the operatives, he would be the first to advocate its adoption.

There is a general misunderstanding respecting the Charter. Many imagine that it originated lately with a few extravagant radicals. But this is a mistake. Some time before the present century, Fox[2] and a number of *noblemen* and gentlemen are said to have turned their attention to the subject of Parliamentary Reform by means of the true representation of the people, and to have adopted

---

1 Luke 1: 52.
2 Charles James Fox (1749–1806), radical Whig leader.

as the basis of their movement the following principles. 1. – Universal Suffrage. 2. – Vote by Ballot. 3. – No Property Qualification. 4. – The Payment of Members of Parliament. 5. – Annual Elections. 6. – The Division of the Country into Electoral Districts. Now these six points are the whole of the Charter, and therefore whatever there is of radicalism, or treason, or disorder in these points, must be referred, not to the Chartists of these times, but to the renowned Fox and the lords and gentlemen that agreed with him. We have reason to believe that Charles James Fox was a more complete *Chartist* than any of the present day. In 1798, at a numerous meeting of the Whig Club, he proposed as a toast, '*the Sovereignty of the people.*' Now Fox was not a disloyal man, but he clearly perceived that the only way to secure the throne, was for the people to assume their full constitutional power as one of the integral parts of the government. He was for the elevation of the country. He saw that *representation* was become a *farce*, and therefore laboured to arouse the people. '*To talk any longer about Parliament,*' said he, '*is idle, the nation must exert itself, or prepare to suffer the consequences of its opprobrious tameness.*'[1] A cheap tract containing the substance of Fox's liberal principles would be a powerful means of quickening the dormant patriotism of the present day, and would tend especially to awaken the middle and working classes to agitate for the full possession of their rights.

Another mistake respecting the Charter is very general. As soon as you mention the word '*Chartist,*' or '*Chartism,*' there are not a few who immediately turn to the Newport riots,[2] and imagine that every advocate of the *six points* is favourable to physical force, violence, and anarchy. But they should reflect that the *Charter* is *one thing*, and the *mode* of obtaining it another. There are now several ways of going to the great metropolis, but no one in his senses would affirm that *London*, and the *roads* to London, are words of the same meaning. Surely in this enlightened age, men, and especially gentlemen and christians, ought not to confound the *means* with the *end*. There are two modes of endeavouring to obtain the Charter, the *one* by *physical*, the *other* by *moral force*. Now as all the people have been educated in *physical force principles*, and as *physical* rather than *moral means* have for centuries been resorted to by masters, educators, clergymen, warriors, and monarchs, it really is not surprising if the masses have been led astray by the pernicious examples of those whom they are taught to revere. Indeed, with these facts before them, it is a great wonder that the operatives have confidence in anything else but violence for the attainment of their rights. However, we are proud to say that the most enlightened views respecting the impotence of *physical force*, and the *omnipotence* of *moral force*, are to be found among the masses. It is a fact – a glorious fact – that in this particular the people are wiser than their teachers or their rulers. Very few, if any, of the operatives have now one particle of faith in violence or intimidation of any kind. Give to justice a *tongue*, and it asks for no other arms: indeed all other weapons would be worse than weakness and sure to

---

1 For which he was ejected from the Privy Council. See Earl Russell, *The Life and Times of Charles James Fox*, 3 vols (1866), vol. 3, p. 168.

2 The 1839 uprising led by John Frost.

fail. 'He that killeth by the sword will be killed by the sword.'[1] Still, it is clear as a sunbeam, that if every Chartist in the country were as firm a believer in *physical force* as the Duke of Wellington, this could make no difference to the *Charter*. What we have to do is to look at the *six points,* and not at *this* or *that mode* of making them the law of the land. Thousands have thought that Christianity ought to be propagated, like Mahomedanism, at the point of the bayonet; indeed, I saw it printed on good authority, not long since, that a protestant minister in Ireland went about his duties armed with a pistol, and thus was ready to give his fellow creatures bullets or the gospel, and conduct them to heaven or blow them to the other place, according to circumstances. But this folly does not in the least degree alter the claims of the religion of the bible. We are commanded to '*Scrutinize the Scriptures,* instead of gathering bugbears from the folly, madness, or inconsistencies of worthless believers.' So we say, 'scrutinize the *six points* of the Charter, and not waste time about the imperfection of *any,* or *all,* of the Chartists.' Newport riots have just as much to do with the Charter as the *fires* of Smithfield with the *benevolence* of the gospel. Bonner[2] and physical force Chartists belong to the same category. There is no more Chartism in violence than there is of the bible in the burning of Hooper[3] and Latimer.[4]

Look the six points fairly in the face, and it will be seen that instead of being classed with the wickedness 'that cometh from *beneath,*' they belong to the 'wisdom that cometh from above.'[5] Let us examine them for a moment.

I. – The Charter asks for *Universal Suffrage,* or that every male person of *twenty-one years of age,* who is not insane or condemned as a criminal, shall be deemed qualified to vote for a member of Parliament. This may be called *radicalism* – so it is, for it would *eradicate,* or pull up by the *roots,* an immense amount of injustice and corruption – but then it is none the worse for that; indeed this is one of its high commendations and shows how thoroughly it accords with the gospel, for Christianity is the most *radical religion* in the world. But without basing an argument, which we could, on this fact, let us turn to the first chapter of the Acts of the Apostles, and we there find that the first public transaction of the Church after the Saviour went to heaven, was to choose an apostle to fill the place of Judas, and that in doing this they proceeded in accordance with this doctrine of the Charter, for they adopted *Universal Suffrage.* The assembly consisted of one hundred and twenty names, or persons, Acts i. 15, and they were all addressed and all voted. In this case there were *women* present, and *they* had the same liberty to vote as the men. The gospel knows nothing of the '*mental and moral*' inferiority of sex, for 'in Christ Jesus there is neither male nor female:' so that here you have suffrage on a larger scale than the Chartists propose. There is also nothing said about *age.* We have reason to believe that in the first Christian churches there

---

1 Revelations 13: 10.
2 Edmund Bonner (*c.* 1500–1569), Bishop of London.
3 John Hooper (d. 1555), Bishop of Gloucester and Worcester.
4 Hugh Latimer (1490–1555), church reformer.
5 See John 3: 31.

were many members under twenty-one, and yet they voted in the election of all the officers of the church, and here we find all the members present were called upon to give their suffrages in the choice of an *apostle*. This practice of *universal suffrage* was common in all the apostolic churches, nor was it abrogated until the grossest corruption prevailed.

It will be objected that all these had a moral qualification. But there is no force in this remark, because we demand a moral qualification now. All who are not convicted of a crime, are, in the sight of the law and the constitution, considered *good* citizens. Should any opponent further demur, we may ask, if the £10 or 40s. franchise has any respect whatever to *moral* qualifications, or affords the least security respecting the piety of the voter? The morality required under the present system is the morality of *Bricks and Mortar*, or of *Pounds, Shillings, and Pence*!! The greatest miscreant in the country, provided he sins so craftily as to keep out of jail, and has the property qualification, is permitted to vote. His ignorance and wickedness may be notorious, but if his rent is £10 a year, or his freehold worth 40s. per annum, his franchise is as good as the most profound philosopher or enlightened Christian. It is therefore the very climax of inconsistency for those who advocate the continuance of the present system to demand moral qualifications for the further extension of the suffrage. Besides, we are continually told that we must not mix *religion* and *politics*. It is almost a crime for a good Christian to give a vote. His piety rises in value a thousand per cent. in the estimation of some pious people, should he refuse to go to the poll!! Politics are especially to be turned over to satan and his angels, plainly intimating that civil affairs are become so infamously bad that no one can touch them without endangering his piety. According to this popular doctrine, only wicked men are fit to be Members of Parliament, or Electors to choose them. *Immorality* is therefore the great *desideratum* for Representatives and Voters!! And yet these selfsame transcendental pietists ask for a *moral* qualification if you enlarge the suffrage. This is to blow hot and blow cold with the same breath, and completely to overturn their own theory; for as there can be no morality without religion, and as religion and religious people must not mix nor meddle with politics, then the moment you make a man a Christian, his *moral* qualifications unfit him to be an Elector or a Senator!!

But if this doctrine, which is held by many of the educated and spiritual classes, should appear as absurd as it really is, and if they still insist upon a *moral* qualification, then we must demand of them in the name of common sense and consistency, to unite to abolish the present *brick and mortar* qualification. The £10 and 40s. franchise exclude a large portion of the intelligence and morality of the country. There are thousands of persons among us of the highest mental and moral character, who because they have not a paltry freehold of forty shillings a year, are deemed political nonentities, and treated as untutored and demoralized paupers. – Yea, paupers are ranked above them. For I have seen the wretched being whose miserable hovel was crumbling to dust, or was mortgaged far beyond its value, and who was himself not worth one sixpence, but actually living upon charity, and his mental powers so shrivelled by ignorance that he knew no more of the duties of a Senator than a broomstick – I say, I have seen this prodigy of poverty, ignorance, and irreligion, conveyed in a carriage and pair to the poll booth to vote for a Knight of the Shire; while the wealthy, intelligent, and pious citizen, because he did not own a forty shilling *nothing*, was deemed destitute of any qualification for so high an honour! Why the present system does not even do what it pretends to do. It does not represent the real property of the country; and therefore is indefensible on the very ground on which it is said to be based.

We have also among us what may truly be called, *the real 'Young England'* of our day. We have hosts of Sabbath School Teachers and others who are men of sound knowledge, of distinguished piety and morality, and yet deprived of the right of voting. These are already the most active and efficient agents in the intellectual and moral renovation of the country; and were they only endowed with the franchise, they would soon regenerate the representative system and the Senate. To talk of moral qualifications for voters, when we are excluding the largest and best part of the morality of the country from the poll booth, is the extreme of folly.

I might further ask, is there a dissenting minister in the country who will confess that he has any man in his congregation beyond the age of *twenty-one* who is unfit to vote for a Member of Parliament? To be the professed enlightener of a congregation, and to have so far neglected his duty as to have men under his charge who are too ignorant or wicked to be trusted with the franchise, is a reproach which few men will be ready to avow. My own congregation is not less than a thousand, and they are, I am proud to say, mostly operatives; but I should be sorry to think that there is a single person above the age of twenty-one unfit to receive and use his political rights. There is no danger of granting this constitutional privilege to the dissenters of the country; and as to the Church of England, if we believe the Bishops and Clergy, matters are ten thousand times better there; for all persons baptized by these successors of the Apostles, are, the catechism asserts, 'made members of Christ, children of God, and inheritors of the kingdom of heaven.' Episcopalians measure the number of square feet in the Chapels of dissenters, or count the heads that enter the door of the conventicle, and then claim all others as their own. All the rest are, forsooth, regenerated, and therefore cannot but be fit to vote for Members of Parliament. To say that '*a member of Christ, a child of God, and an inheritor of the kingdom of heaven,*' is too ignorant or too wicked to be entrusted with the franchise, is a libel on the Clergy, on the Church, and on Christianity. Every Clergyman to be consistent must be an advocate for the extension of the suffrage. To deny its constitutional character would prove him ignorant of the political rights of man: to deny its equity would convict him of being unacquainted with the first principles of christian rectitude: and to affirm the unfitness of any of his flock to exercise this power, would demonstrate his own unfitness for the sacred office, his guilty inattention to his flock, and at the same time impeach the boasted efficacy of sacramental grace. To oppose universal suffrage on the ground of the mental or moral imperfections of the people would not only be grossly inconsistent with the present principles of representation, but a bitter reproach on the Churchmen and dissenters of our day.

If the masses are not fit for the suffrage, then in the name of justice what have the over-paid clergy been doing with their time and learning?

But marvellous to say, these working people, who must not be trusted with their own rights, have at the same time the whole country committed to their hands. Theirs is nine-tenths of all the practical skill of the empire; they produce the chief of its wealth; they watch over our property; they fight all our battles; and yet they are such a base ignorant rabble that they could not be trusted to choose that modern Solon,[1] a member of Parliament! Surely, before we utter against them so sweeping a condemnation, we ought to be able to show our own extraordinary wisdom in this respect. And in so doing, to what parliament shall we turn? I wish the Privy Council would issue a commission to inquire into the state of education among Parliament men, and would have them examined in *history, political economy, morals,* and *religion,* and then print their answers. After this exposure, we should never hear another word about the gross ignorance of miners and factory boys. We should even have the education scheme given up, unless Mr Kay Shuttleworth[2] introduced a '*New Minute,*' to include the lords and commons. Let any one read the history of the last House of Commons, and then let him say whether taken as a whole, the unfranchised operatives could have chosen a worse? whether we look at the present voters or the men they send to St Stephens, every thinking man and woman must perceive that an enlargement of the franchise, instead of an injury, would be of immense advantage to the nation and the world. We should have *better electors, better legislators, better laws,* and consequently an immense increase to the morality, prosperity, and happiness of the empire. What a perfect political hoax, to trust our persons and property in the hands of the working classes, and then profess to tremble to give them the franchise. It is not the *evil* but the *good* of such a step that many persons dread. Political and Ecclesiastical corruption would be abolished, Taxation would be equalized, Commissions and Sinecures for placemen and the poor nobility would be swept away, and industry, honesty, intelligence, and morality would be the only avenues open to honour and affluence. When left to themselves to choose stewards for their clubs, &c., the masses always show ten thousand times more judgment than the Electors of England have ever yet exhibited in the selection of members of Parliament; and when they obtain the suffrage, the same prudence and common sense will guide them in using their votes. We have *despised* them, *overworked* them, *overtaxed* them, and in many instances *underpaid* them, and yet we have not feared to trust the country in their power; for we have chosen our *servants, watchmen, policemen,* and *soldiers* from their ranks, and they have nobly honoured our confidence; and if under insolence and injustice their conduct has been beyond all praise, surely we need not fear the consequences of giving them their rights and using them well.

I trust them I have met every argument that might be advanced against the intellectual and moral qualifications of the masses for the exercise of the

---

1 Solon (*c.* 638–558 BC), Athenian lawgiver.

2 James Phillips Kay Shuttleworth (1804–77), first Baronet, educational reformer.

franchise. If there are some errors among them, a few Lectures from such patriots as *George Thompson*, who is now, to the honour of the Electors, returned for the Tower Hamlets – or *Henry Vincent*, that most eloquent advocate of the people's rights, and of everything that can advance the real interests and glory of the country and the world – would soon set everything straight. Cobden and Bright found among the masses a faithful response to every word of truth and equity that fell from their lips. The chief opposition they had to encounter proceeded from the upper classes. From the days of the Saviour until now it may be said of all reformers, that *'the common people have heard them gladly,'* and such will be the case until corruption and oppression shall come to an end. This was known by our Lord and his apostles, who always appealed to the *common sense* and *common justice* of the *common people*: and hence the doctrine of universal suffrage was not only taught but practised by the apostles in the very first Ecclesiastical transaction of the church. The chapter in which this fact is recorded tells us that the Redeemer, during the forty days that elapsed before his ascension, spoke to his disciples *'of the things pertaining to the kingdom of God,'* and as the apostles did nothing authoritatively in the church without his word or the inspiration of the Holy Spirit, we may rest assured that the *universal suffrage* which they adopted was from *Heaven*; and if in the important matter of selecting an apostle this principle was practised, we have a divine example which we may justly follow in the election of members of Parliament. Our countrymen over twenty-one are just as qualified to select senators as these 120 primitive converts were to give their votes for an apostle. According to the Church of England we are all christians if we have been rightly baptized, and therefore must be qualified to choose the *ministers of religion*, and consequently pre-eminently fit to elect our secular representatives.

Instead, then, of this equitable doctrine of the right of all to be represented and to choose their representatives, being an emanation of the prince of darkness, we believe that there is nothing which he more dreads. Give the people of this country the enjoyment of their full political rights, and the empire of Satan would totter throughout the earth. The God of this world is pre-eminently the *God of Tyrants and Slaveholders*. His kingdom is based upon *corporal, mental, civil, political, and ecclesiastical slavery*. Let mankind have perfect emancipation, and the empire of the 'old serpent' is at an end, and hence the divine John in the apocalyptic vision as soon as he saw the downfall of all political and ecclesiastical tyranny, immediately introduces the 'binding of Satan for a thousand years,' and at the same time, shows us the emancipation of mind, truth, liberty, and religion under the type of the *'First Resurrection.'* The first step towards the exaltation of Britain was the enfranchisement of the middle classes; and the last step to perfect our liberties is the enfranchisement and consequent elevation of the masses. Let this be consummated, and reformers may then hail the commencement of that millennium for which so many have panted, laboured, and shed their blood.

II. *'Vote by Ballot.'* Universal Suffrage without the Ballot would inflict a great injury on multitudes of our countrymen. For though increasing the number of Electors must render bribery a very expensive business, and from this circumstance would lessen it, yet many a poor voter would be sacrificed to strike terror into the rest. There are in this country those who have so little English blood in their veins, that they would ruin the tenant or the labourer who should dare to use his vote in a *constitutional* manner. These persecutors, be it remembered, are to be found among the educated, the wealthy, and *noble* of the land! They boast of being the guardians of the laws, and of good order, and yet they trample the Constitution of the country under their feet. They inherit the spirit of Nero[1] and Bonner, for, although they may not rekindle the martyr's fire, yet, by dismissing men from their farms and their labour, they propose to *starve* them to death. Language cannot furnish epithets sufficiently strong to brand the meanness, the tyranny, or the treason, of these despots. If transportation were proper under any circumstances, these are the people that ought to be banished from civilized society. How any christian man can behold such cruelty and be silent, is a problem not easily solved. My countrymen – especially you, who wear fustian jackets and smock frocks – must demand – peacefully, rationally, and firmly demand – *the Ballot*. They say that secret voting would be '*un-English*,' and yet these very men practise it in their clubs, to shield themselves from the unpleasantness of being called to account for their votes; but they refuse you this protection. What folly to talk of equal rights, when they thus institute one law for the rich and another for the poor. '*Un-English*' to vote by Ballot: – then it is *un-English* to carry a shield or erect castles and bulwarks, or defend the oppressed from the cruelty of the tyrant. The rich man and the lord have now the power of robbing their tenants and dependants of their constitutional rights or of their daily bread; and in many instances use it with all the despotism of a Turk; and then charge you with cowardice if you propose to protect yourselves or your fellow citizens from their despotism.

Some of our Solons tell us that to introduce the ballot would be '*an organic change*.' The remark hardly merits a reply. If we saw a number of intelligent citizens with a ring through their nostrils, chained to a goose, and doomed to be led by the nose through rivers, ponds, and quagmires, what could we think of the sagacity or even humanity of the being who should object, that to loose these citizens from being the slaves of these geese would be an organic change which would endanger the constitution! And yet until we have the ballot, we shall have freemen of the highest intelligence doomed to loss and starvation, unless they submit to be led by human bipeds of a far lower order than those who traverse the ponds in the farmers' yards.

But the *Bible* sanctions the Ballot. I have shown, from the Acts of the Apostles, that Universal Suffrage was the doctrine of primitive Christianity, and the very same chapter tells us, that in choosing a minister to fill the place of Judas, the church adopted the *Ballot*. Every scholar knows that Acts ii. 26, might be translated, 'And they gave their *Ballots*, and the *Ballot* fell upon Matthias, and by means of the *Ballot* he was numbered with the eleven Apostles.' Now there never was a body more free from party spirit or less in danger of being influenced by

---

1 Nero (AD 37–68), Roman Emperor 54–68.

any after feeling of envy or jealousy than this primitive congregation, and yet they adopted the ballot, and did so under divine direction. In this instance we may safely say that God himself was the author of the Ballot, and therefore that Vote by Ballot comes from heaven. Joseph, the rejected candidate, could not tell who they were that voted against him, and Matthias knew not those who preferred him or opposed his election, and thus the possibility of any anger or bitterness was entirely prevented. And if in so holy and benevolent an assembly as this, our adorable Redeemer saw that vote by ballot was necessary, then how much more essential is it in those elections where it is expected that the electors and the elected will be destitute of every particle of christianity. It is a fashionable doctrine now that 'Christian men should have nothing to do with politics!' and therefore, confessedly, all who use the franchise and all who are chosen by it, must be bad men, and if bad men they must have bad passions, and consequently the contention may resemble a bull fight or a bear garden. Indeed we have had plenty of instances of this. Nobles and gentlemen, notwithstanding the vaunted gentleness! of their education and manners, often become brutish during a contested election, and resolve, not indeed, thanks to the law, to tear their opponents to atoms, but what is far more cruel, to rob them of their trade – to deprive them of daily bread – to turn them out of house and home – and if possible starve them to death. – Well saith the scripture, 'the tender mercies of the wicked are cruel,' and how strikingly this test is illustrated at every election. Talk of the violence of the masses, why these are gentle as lambs until the gentle-men have inflamed them by falsehood, or bribery, or drink. But if you want the counterpart of a menagerie let loose, you must turn to the coronetted, knighted, educated, and, not unfrequently, clerical, apostolical, monsters, who haunt the streets or crouch in their dens, to ruin any dependent elector who dares to use the right which the British Constitution has put into his hands. Let us either shield men with the Ballot, or cease to curse them with the franchise, or to mock liberty and equity with the present farce of representation. The divine Author of Christianity who made all men of 'one blood,' and fashioned their 'hearts alike,' and who demands equal rights for all, and therefore ordained Universal Suffrage in his church as an example for all other elections, foresaw that open voting might engender strife and empower political and ecclesiastical tyrants to crush the poor, and therefore he instituted 'Vote by Ballot,' as the only security of the oppressed against the violence of the oppressor, and as the best guarantee for peace and concord among mankind. 'Vote by Ballot,' then, as well as 'Universal Suffrage,' is an Apostolic Institution, and therefore an Orthodox doctrine of the sacred volume.

III. – No Property Qualification. Moral excellence is the only qualification recognised by the Bible and the God of the Bible, and as money is no guarantee for the wisdom or piety of its possessor, the mere accidental attribute of wealth can be no commendation to the King of kings. He is the universal Father, His tender mercies are over all his creatures, and therefore his poor children are especially dear to him. Their wants and necessities, and the ignorance to which they have been doomed by their wealthier brothers and sisters, are matters of deep interest

to him, and will undergo a very searching scrutiny at the great day. On that
solemn period, how many a lord and squire will wish that they had been born
hedgers and ditchers. Their rank and wealth, and their consequent responsibility
if not properly used, will be the mill-stones that will sink them below the lowest
in perdition. 'How hardly shall they that have riches enter into the kingdom of
God.'[1] 'It is easier for a camel to go through the eye of a needle, than for a rich
man to enter into the kingdom of heaven.'[2] 'The love of money,' says the apostle,
'is the root of all evil, which while some have coveted after, they have erred from
the faith and pierced themselves through with many sorrows.'[3] From Genesis to
Revelations we have denunciations against the ungodliness of the rich, and at the
same time the most tender sympathy towards the poor. Ministers of religion tell
us that the Bible is the standard of truth and morals, and the Statute Book by
which every human being is to be judged. But where, we may ask, in any of the
pages of the Old or New Testament, do we read one word about property conferring an intellectual or moral qualification upon its possessor? We may find rich
men, in the scriptures, filling high offices in the state and the church, but never
is it once hinted that they were raised to those stations because of their *wealth*.
Many of them were elevated from, what some would term, the very dregs of society; their only commendation, rank, and nobility, was their piety. The Redeemer
was so poor that he had not where to lay his head. The Apostles were entirely
dependent upon their labour or the benevolence of their friends. The first christian church knew nothing of a property qualification. All were on an equality.
Universal Suffrage was practised, and the vote of one member was just as good as
that of another. Now we call ourselves a christian people, and are either what we
profess to be, or a nation of hypocrites. But to be christians we must be ruled by
the laws of Christ, and if we are guided by his laws we must at once abolish the
Property Qualification.

What can be more irrational than to suppose that mere rank or wealth can
confer mental or moral excellencies? Not a few of the sons of noble families and
of the heirs to immense possessions have been idiots. Some of the wealthiest of
men have been the basest and the most foolish. Multitudes have become rich by
the practice of every species of iniquity; the steps by which they conducted themselves to glory and affluence were those of murder, oppression, plunder, or the
meanest sycophancy. They swam to their honours through a sea of blood. Thousands, because they were rich, have neglected the cultivation of their minds, and
have despised the claims of morality and religion. They have been surrounded
with minions and flatterers who have praised their folly, pampered their vices,
and even extolled their crimes. The history of the baneful influence of titles and
wealth is one of the blackest pages in the records of human depravity. Milton[4]
tells us that Mammon was

---

1 Mark 10: 23.
2 Mark 10: 25.
3 1 Timothy 6: 10.
4 John Milton (1608–75), republican poet.

'The least erected spirit that fell from heaven;'[1]

and if we may judge of the god from the conduct of his votaries, the poet is not far from the truth. Such a perfect root of *all* evil has the love of riches been, that you can hardly mention a crime which has not been perpetrated either in obtaining or spending them. To choose men to office because they have the *Property Qualification*, is to prove that we are the worshippers of mammon and guided by that root of all evil, the love of money, and are opposing ourselves not only to the word of God, but to the plainest dictates of common sense.

It is said that the possession of property is a pledge of the wisdom and respectability of its owner: but this assertion is contradicted by fact. The follies and ignorance of many rich and noble personages are proverbial, and their licentiousness, injustice, and irreligion, exhibited to the world without shame, and therefore the dimensions of a man's purse or estate can never afford any evidence respecting his knowledge, his talent, or integrity. A *Tinker's Qualifications* would be a far more rational requirement for a member of Parliament, because a certain amount of intelligence is necessary before any man can mend or make pots and kettles; but a gentleman may possess £300 or £500 a year, and thus, according to our present law, be fit for a Senator, and yet, so destitute of any natural ability, as to have been incapable of learning the least mechanical of all trades. Need I ask my readers to examine the history of British Senators for the confirmation of this statement. Could we not have chosen labourers and operatives from the fields and factories at random, who would have legislated far more in accordance with truth, justice, and humanity? Are there none in the present House of Commons whose only qualification is their purse? Take away their wealth, and would any one dream of making them senators?

The *Property Qualification* has been and is still the bane of our country. Hundreds of upright and intelligent men are excluded from exercising the franchise, because they do not rent a house of £10 a year, or own a 40s. freehold. Here the property qualification robs the citizen of his constitutional right of representation: and the requirement of a certain income per annum before any one can be a member of Parliament, deprives the nation of the services of some of the most judicious and disinterested patriots. You have *good* men excluded from the poll and the senate because they are not possessed of a certain amount of riches, and you have irreligious and foolish men exalted to the dignity of Legislators, whose only qualification is their worldly rank or property. Is it any wonder that Slavery – that outrage on humanity – was advocated: that the Corn-Laws should have cursed the country for four hundred years, by starving the poor and paralysing trade: – that we are overwhelmed with a national debt, rendered more than doubly burdensome to the poor by a most iniquitous system of *indirect taxation*: – that we have a corrupt establishment, and an enormous army and navy, supported for the sake of keeping down liberty, and providing pensions and places for the penniless sons of pauperised prodigals and gamesters? If we had

---

1   John Milton, *Paradise Lost*, I. 679.

demanded a weaver's qualification for the senatorial honour, is it not probable that we should have had more than enough of legislation in favour of weavers? Or if, in our wisdom, we had decreed that every member of Parliament should be a *bona fide* periwig maker, then is it not almost certain that we should have had hosts of laws in favour of wigs and wig manufacturers? and therefore it is not strange, that having fixed upon the worst of all qualifications, we find these Property Qualification senators, almost perpetually labouring how they may increase their own wealth, and burden the poor and needy with the most unequal and unjust load of taxation.

We are told that property must be protected. We reply that property has always the honourable means, independent of partial and dishonourable laws, of protecting itself: and therefore the great object of legislation should be to afford a shield to all, but especially to the *poor* and the *defenceless*. How often the word of God calls upon Governors '*to judge*' or '*do justice* to the needy and the oppressed,' 'the fatherless and the widow.' Doubtless the Property Qualification is as old as Sodom, or Egypt, or Nineveh, or Babylon, or Rome; but still we know that the privilege it conferred of crushing the weak, brought all these nations under the curse of heaven, and ended in their ruin. To make men voters or legislators because they possess wealth, is a practice at utter variance with the rights of man and the doctrines of the Bible. Christianity, our country, and the world, demand wise, intelligent, just, philanthropic, and disinterested legislators: let us have these, whether chosen from the rich or the poor; and universal peace, prosperity, and happiness, will go far towards giving the property qualification to every human being.

IV. – The Charter demands that '*every Member of Parliament should be paid.*' It is a doctrine of the word of God, that 'the labourer is worthy of his hire.'[1] The Senator is a working man, or at least ought to be so; and as such, should be paid for his toil. It may be said that these gentlemen are too proud to receive wages; but then it is a notorious fact, that crowds haste to Parliament for the sake of the immense *direct* or *indirect* gains thus placed within their reach. If we do not pay them, most of them take good care to pay themselves. If they are too proud to receive money in the form of hire, they are not too high-minded to take it out of our pockets, by means of monopolies, patronage, pensions, sinecures, and exemptions from taxation. To give six hundred Members of Parliament £500 each would cost about £300,000 annually, while our Corn-laws alone, not unfrequently, robbed the people of *thirty* times that amount in the course of a single year. Talk of £300,000 per annum, to be divided among a certain number of Senators: who would think that any Right Honourable Gentlemen would receive such a paltry sum, when at present they can divide millions among themselves and their relatives? and what is more, can legislate so nicely as to transfer no small portion of the burden of taxation from themselves to the shoulders of the *fustian jackets and smock frocks*. Not honourable indeed to receive pay for being a

---

1 1 Timothy 5: 18.

Senator! Why Sir Robert Peel[1] told us that he would not give his recipe for our state diseases until he had his *Fee*, and who will deny the disinterested patriotism of Sir Robert Peel? Let the profit of the Peel Family from state revenues be calculated, and it will be seen that cotton spinning was not resigned for nothing. Lord John Russell and his ancestors have not carried on the business of Senators for *nought*. How often you find men giving up trade, as they call it, and immediately trafficking in Church or State, Army or Navy, corruption. Depend upon it John Bull pays dearly enough for being waited upon by servants, who instead of having a fixed salary, undertake to remunerate themselves. For every shilling he saves, the poor fellow has to pay many a pound.

Then this so-called '*non-payment of members*' keeps a number of really honest men out of Parliament. There are among us individuals of first-rate talent and character for legislators, who cannot afford to leave their present occupations and bear the expense of a seat in the House: and further, these are persons whose integrity excludes the possibility of their being Whig or Tory minions or sycophants, and therefore no crumbs will ever be thrown to them from the ministerial table, and if they were, these patriots would never stoop to gather them up. The rage of late years has been to increase State offices, and hold out pensions to needy adventurers, and thus to centralize power in the government, and prostrate the spirit of liberty and patriotism in the people. The trick has succeeded wonderfully on the continent. Many of the wealthy in our own country are hurrying to sell themselves and posterity for these wages of unrighteousness, and unless the middle classes and operatives bestir themselves, all the blessings which our fathers bought so dearly, and bequeathed to us so faithfully, will be lost for ever. We must have wise, honest, and disinterested senators, but to obtain these we must pay them for their services, and thus place them above want, and render them independent of the smile or frown of ministerial patronage. Besides, what can be more unjust than to desire our fellow citizens to represent us in Parliament, and yet for us to refuse to bear their expenses? We cannot all go to St Stephen's, and if we could what a loss of time and money there would be; and therefore the individual who takes our place and faithfully discharges our work, should be viewed as a public benefactor, and ought not to be called upon to spend one single sixpence from his own purse. To demand the labour of a ploughman or weaver for nothing, and pick his pocket into the bargain, would be the same kind of justice, as to ask a fellow citizen to take our place in the House of Commons for six months together – to sit up until all hours in the morning – to bear his own expenses, and spend several hundreds on treating, bribery, and other abominations! Instead of looking upon the patriotic candidate as conferring a benefit upon us, there are electors who imagine that they make him their debtor by giving him their votes, and demand to be carried to the poll and back in a carriage, and treated with a dinner and punch to boot. If this is not enough to make legislators selfish and dishonest, then we may ask what is? The best recipe

---

1 Sir Robert Peel (1788–1850), second Baronet; MP for Tamworth from 1833, Conservative Prime Minister 1834, 1841–6.

for making servants thieves is to pay them badly, or not at all. To put a member of parliament to £500, to a £1000, or £10,000 expense to procure his seat, and then expect him to use no means to refund himself, is as silly as it is unjust. We have already paid a heavy price for this folly, and now, if nothing else can do it, our dearly bought wisdom should render us sufficiently honest to send members to Parliament without costing them a single penny, and also to award them a sufficient salary for their services.

V. – To divide the country into *'Electoral Districts'* is another equitable and rational provision of the People's Charter. Nothing could be more absurd than the present partition of Counties and Boroughs. Granted that the Chartists are hairbrained men, but then what shall we say of the sagacity of those legislators who invented electoral towns and shires? Men who live in glass houses should not throw stones. Let any one look at a map, or calculate the population and at the same time let him compare the present system with this proposition of the Charter, and we are not afraid of his imputing madness to the advocates of Chartism. Here is a man dwelling on one side of a stream, or a hedge, or an old wall, and on account of this mere accident, if his rent is £10 a year, he has a vote, and is deemed a meet and proper person to choose a Member of Parliament. He may not be able to read or write, his character may be execrable, and his mind hardly one remove from idiocy, still he pays £10 a year rent, and therefore is taken to the poll booth in a carriage, amidst music and hurras! On the other side of the same brook, hedge, or wall, as the case may be, there dwells an individual whose character is the boast of the neighbourhood, whose wisdom and intelligence are of the highest order, and further, he rents a house worth £40 a year, but alas! it is on the wrong side of the hedge or the stream, and therefore he is a political nonentity, and altogether unfit to be trusted with the franchise. Who could tell whether the throne or the very sky might not fall, if a man on that unlucky side of the wall should be rendered eligible to vote for a British Senator? The same unfortunate gentleman also may have an income of £500 a year, but still as he has no 40s. freehold, he is rejected from the poll book as unfit to enjoy one of the most constitutional rights of a free citizen! And this is not all. That poor half-witted neighbour on the other side of the hedge has a 40s. cottage, mortgaged far beyond its value, and therefore he has a vote for the county as well as for the borough. Perhaps he may also have in other divisions several 40s. mortgaged nothings, and as a consequence he can assist in making ten or twenty senators, while his intelligent, upright, and wealthy brother citizen, has no more political power than the rooks or jackdaws. Surely there is no one after looking this matter fairly in the face, who will assert that a system so unequal, ridiculous, and absurd, ought to be tolerated, or to insult the common sense of the nation for another year. Let every man above *one and twenty* have his vote, let there be *one vote*, and *one vote* only to *one man*, and let the whole country be divided into convenient Electoral Districts, and into as many of these as shall be deemed equitable to all, and best adapted to answer the purposes of a just representative system, and then the great end of the British Constitution will be realized.

No man ought to have *two* votes, or if this boon is conferred on any one, it ought to be given to the poor. Property can protect itself, but the working classes, the *fustian jackets and smock frocks*, have in all ages and countries been oppressed; and therefore every law of God and man demands that these, if there must be any partiality, should be especially protected. We know there have been and still are wealthy patriots, and of course we intend no censure on these. Indeed we condemn none but the *guilty*, and hence none but the *guilty* can be offended. Tell us not that the people are unfit to exercise their constitutional rights. If they are not, then shame on the ministers of religion, who in neglecting to prepare them for their political duties, have omitted one of the most important obligations of the christian teacher. We may be told that the bible says nothing about Electoral Districts – granted; nor does it say anything, in so many words, about a House of Commons – but then it does what is better, it demands equal rights for all, and especially requires that there should be no injustice to the poor or the operative. In the primitive times the christian population consisted of distinct divisions, or *independent Churches*, and thus exactly corresponded with the '*Electoral Divisions*,' proposed by the Charter. No Christian had any right to interfere, except by persuasion or remonstrance, with other churches; and thus again we see that Christianity and Chartism are not in any respect opposed to each other.

VI. – *Annual Parliaments* are asked for by the advocates of the Charter. Surely there can be nothing unjust or unscriptural in this demand. Members of Parliament are the servants of the country, and to settle with them once a year cannot be too frequent. The responsibility of a representative is so great, and so much depends upon the discharge of his office, that every caution should be used to prevent any error in judgment or abuse of power. And further, the man who is unwilling to submit his conduct to the scrutiny of his employers, must be either weak or wicked. He feels conscious of having neglected his duty or done what will not bear investigation, and therefore shuns the light. There is a tacit confession of folly and guilt in the demand of *seven years*, or even *three years*' immunity from the review of his deeds. A wise, judicious, and *right honourable representative* would hail the opportunity of annually meeting his constituents. Here again the bible is on our side: – in its beautiful language we are told that 'He who doeth truth cometh to the light, that his deeds may be made manifest.'[1] But it also declares concerning the wicked, that 'Every one who doeth evil hateth the light, neither cometh to the light, lest his deeds should be reproved.'[2] What a misnomer to call a Member of Parliament a '*Right Honourable Gentleman*,' and yet at the same time, for this very *Right* Honourable Gentleman to assert that he cannot look his employers in the face more frequently than once in seven years! There must be something radically bad about the man who thus dreads to have his political conduct examined.

Besides, *seven years* of irresponsible power is too long for any mere man to be trusted with, especially in these days when despotism is doing everything to

---

1 John 3: 21.
2 John 3: 20.

regain its sceptre. My Lord John Russell read the electors a long lecture on daring to influence their representatives on the Education Scheme, thus shewing that he wishes Members of Parliament to be as irresponsible and despotic as the Emperor of the Turks. These sentiments from the mouth of a *Russell* speak volumes, and should have been met with a remonstrance from the whole country. His resignation as the prime Minister of a free people ought to have been demanded. No wonder that members, who could hear in silence this unconstitutional language, should dread to face their constituents except at very long intervals. Only think of the mischief that may be done in *seven years*, or even in *three*, and then judge whether Annual Parliaments would be too frequent? Tell us not of the confusion that would be occasioned. There is nothing more healthy to the nation, or more invigorating to the body politic, than a public election when properly conducted. Every general election places the country a step in advance of what it was before. It is national education on a large scale, and always leaves the country wiser than it was previously. Stagnant ponds grow putrid, and where there is nothing to stir the popular mind the political waters become corrupt and pestiferous. Britain owes its present measure of social health and vigour, in no small degree, to the excitements of its popular elections. Only give us Annual Parliaments, and it shall speedily become the giant that Milton and other patriots have foretold. As for the confusion, the good effected will be an ample compensation for that; besides, when we have *Universal Suffrage*, *Vote by Ballot*, and *Annual Parliaments*, Bribery will be abandoned, Canvassing will most probably be given up; Workmen will no more be *closeted* in counting houses, nor Tenants threatened with ejection from their farms, and men who are too foolish or too wicked to admit of the yearly examination of their parliamentary conduct will keep away from the hustings. We shall then have independent and judicious voters, and *Right Honourable Senators*, who will recognise the scriptural doctrine of man's social responsibility to his fellow man, and especially the obligations which representatives owe to those who placed them in office.

I trust the facts thus briefly stated, and the arguments advanced, are sufficient to show that there is nothing unreasonable or unconstitutional in *the People's Charter*! but that its demands are founded in justice, involved in the British Constitution, and sanctioned by the word of God; and therefore, men, women, and children, it is a sacred duty that you owe to yourselves, to posterity, to your country, to the world, and to pure religion, to become politicians, and agitate until this great principle of truth and equity shall become the law of the land. But in demanding your rights, it is of the utmost importance that no breach of the peace should in any respect be committed. Nothing would so much delight those who oppose your liberties as your resorting to violence. The grossest slanders are uttered against you. There are those who would gladly bribe the police to provoke you to violate the laws. The gold of the men who live by corruption would be liberally bestowed on any miscreants who, by breaking lamps and windows, and other depredations, may bring the Chartists into disrepute. You must prove by your peaceable conduct that you are worthy of the rights you ask. Show that you are *intelligent, industrious, equitable, and moral* citizens, and no one will dare refuse your constitutional demands.

The French Revolution has burst like a volcano on Europe and the world. A monument ought to be erected to Louis Philippe for what he has done. By carrying despotism to the utmost limit of craft, perfidy, and corruption, he has magnanimously hurled himself from his throne; and as a royal wreck, he speaks more emphatically to his brother oppressors, than has been done for many an age. Such a sermon they have rarely heard. It has already been published in all the languages of the continent, and read in all courts. Philosophy, history, humanity, morality, religion, the rights of man, and the laws of heaven, spoke to them in vain. Led on by Louis Philippe, a golden age of despotism occupied their visions by day, and their dreams by night. A new era was promised them, when the press would be enslaved, public meetings prohibited, freedom of speech punished, liberty overthrown, and the world reduced to civil, political, commercial, military, mental, ecclesiastical, and royal vassalage. Pensions and places were to be multiplied without end, until such a thing as an independent human being was not to be found on the face of the earth. Centralization was to transfer all power from the people to the aristocracy, or the crown; and the human family were to become a mere mass of puppets in perfect subservience to the will of imperial, aristocratical, or military showmen. Their souls were to be stereotyped by state schoolmasters and Educational *minutes* of Privy Councils. Every action to be superintended by state functionaries; all were to be made military slaves to rivet each other's fetters, to be corrupted by salaries and pensions, or impoverished by taxation. O what a glorious man was Louis Philippe! All the courts of Europe blessed him; all the aristocrats adored him; all the priests of Antichrist gave him their benediction. Encouraged by his seeming success, our own government had grown arrogant. What a host of places and pensions have been created of late. Corruption promised a golden harvest to adventurers and the penniless sprigs of nobility. The income tax was to do wonders; it was to increase in per centage until it had made paupers of the middle classes, mendicants of the operatives, wealthy hirelings of sycophant commissioners, inspectors, and placemen, and the whole nation was to be drilled into subjection by government pedagogues, or awed into submission by military minions. The petitions of the people were treated as waste paper, and with a Louis Philippe at his elbow, a prime minister could lecture the electors of the country on their audacity in asking their *representatives* to *represent* the constituencies they *had vowed to represent!* All things were fast going to ruin. The glorious constitution which your fathers reared at such labour and sacrifice was about to be destroyed, and not a few of the middle classes, among those who boasted that they were the *more respectable* and *religious*, were looking on with indifference or lending a hand to precipitate their country's fall – when lo! to the amazement of every one, in one short week, Louis Philippe is an exile, his throne burnt, and France a republic!! The dial of liberty, which was moving backward at such a terrific rate, by this event has been put forward a century, and the world is a hundred years nearer the millennium than it was on the 20th of last February. Despotism, then at a premium, is now at a discount, and our own income tax, out of pure sympathy, has fallen *two per cent*. It is said that the nerves of certain statesmen have been so shaken that they have sought the sea breezes to recruit their health. What, in former years, took centuries to accomplish, France has done in a few days, and the great *Bible doctrines* of *Liberty, Equality, Fraternity,* which the believing nations of Christendom had branded with infamy, are now proclaimed by a people long since reproached for their *unbelief.*

Doubtless every effort will be made to render this grand movement abortive. There may be traitors in France who will endeavour to move the emancipated masses to licentiousness, and perhaps English gold may not be wanting to aid in so base a work. But the people of this country must be faithful to the truth, must proclaim their sympathy and brotherhood with the French patriots, and, at the same time, resolve that our own national abuses shall be redressed, the constitution preserved, and the British sceptre rendered 'a sceptre of righteousness.' To accomplish this work, we have the shield of our laws. We may meet, we may publish our grievances, appeal to the great principles of justice and liberty, and by constitutional means legally annihilate every unrighteous statute, and enact whatever may conduce to the prosperity and happiness of the country. Violence in this work would be the superfluity of madness. To have recourse to such folly, would show that the masses are as ignorant, cruel, and unjust, as many of those who seek to oppress them. Truth and equity are eternal and omnipotent; give to these a tongue, and the redemption of our country and the world will not long be delayed.

The TIMES says, '*While all our neighbours are having their revolutions, we must have a revolution of our own – one of the quiet and constitutional sort. All Europe is making a start. Every country is contributing something to the movement. France expects to get something by her change. The British people will be ashamed to be beaten in this respect.*' These words, remember, are from the leading journal of Europe. The *Herald* and *Morning Post* are speaking out in reference to the neglect of the people's rights, showing that a response to the calm, peaceable, and just demands of the masses may be anticipated from quarters where it was least expected.

TRACTS FOR THE FUSTIAN JACKETS AND SMOCK FROCKS.

No. 4.

'GOODY GOODY!'

OR STATE EDUCATION A NATIONAL INSULT.

BY THE REV. B. PARSONS, OF EBLEY.

'No one can be offended with what I say, without owning himself guilty, or that he is the patron of those who are.'

STROUD: R. BUCKNALL,

Sold also by F. W. HARMER, and W. A. BAYLIS, MATTHEWS BROTHERS, Bristol. J. SNOW, London.

1847.

There are some people who say, *yes*, to everything you utter. Tell them the sun runs round the world and they respond with their '*yes*,' or reverse the matter, and affirm that the earth revolves round the sun, and still you are saluted with their omnipresent '*yes*.' I once knew an individual who resolved to try the extent of the credulity of one of these happy assenting and consenting gentlemen. He told him that 'dipping in the river Severn' was an effectual cure for the bite of a mad dog, that a 'swarm of bees had lately been so unfortunate as to be bitten, and that the owner had taken the whole hive to the Severn and one single immersion had cured every bee!' The credulous listener immediately answered '*yes!*' On another occasion he was informed that the mail coach on the King's highway from London was robbed by a French privateer in the English Channel, and our friend, with equal simplicity responded, '*yes!*' You may tell me the fellow was a simpleton, but alas, we have many among us, both learned and illiterate, who say '*yes*,' to everything. With these people whatever *is*, and whatever *is not*, is right, for their faith is as perfectly satisfied with a fiction as with fact. And this reminds me of a tale which I once heard of a doctor of large practice. Proving the power of the mind over the body, he never croaked nor attempted to bring back the age of miracles by assuring the patient that the diseases which he *hoped* to cure were perfectly *hopeless*. Nothing of the kind. In his nomenclature, every thing was '*Perfectly Right*,' and he had used this said phrase, '*Perfectly Right*,' with such constancy, that on all occasions it spontaneously dropped from his lips. The most opposite treatment of the same disease, or the most contradictory symptoms were '*Perfectly Right*.' A peasant's wife, whose poverty rendered crotchets hopeless, and therefore was lucklessly doomed to use that rare article, called *common sense*, was not a little provoked at the perpetual reiteration of this '*Perfectly Right,*' and one day thought she would try the *Reductio ad Absurdum*, to see to what extent the complacency of the doctor would go. The medical gentleman made some searching inquiries concerning her husband's appetite, and the good woman told him that the patient was very capricious about his food, but that lately he felt a very great longing for *eggs*, '*Perfectly Right! Perfectly Right!*' exclaimed the doctor. A few days after when this skilful son of Esculapius called, he very anxiously inquired respecting the eggs, 'O,' said the wife, 'he liked them so well that he actually swallowed them *shells* and all,' '*Perfectly Right, Perfectly Right,*' was the immediate response.

My worthy patron, the Rev. Rowland Hill, to whom I am deeply indebted, was, as every one knows, very fond of remarkable stories, and never experienced any squeamishness about introducing them into the pulpit. He had no idea that Christianity was intended to give long faces or disfigured gloomy countenances to its votaries. That people should sigh all the way to heaven as if they would not go there if they could help it, was to him as absurd in itself as it was contradictory to the genius of the Gospel, and therefore he felt no fear that provoking a smile would corrupt his audience. One day he was employing his exquisite and withering sarcasm against those very liberal and good natured souls, who, like our present advocates of State Education, pronounce all Religions equally good. These people say, '*Yes,*' and '*Perfectly Right,*' to every thing, however contradictory, provided it bears the name of Religion. He stated that some hearers received whatever came from the pulpit, whether good or bad, orthodox or heretical. 'Call it a sermon,' said he, 'and whatever its qualities, these *toad eaters* will be sure to exclaim '*Goody Goody! Goody Goody!*' They reminded him, he continued, of a certain old lady in her dotage, who was very fond of syllabub, and invariably on tasting it, exclaimed, '*Goody Goody! Goody Goody!*' To the very great vexation of her servants she often called for it at the most unseasonable hours. One day as the maids were busy at the washing tub and anxious to finish their work, the old gentlewomen sent and demanded her favorite beverage. Nothing is generally more irritating than a bucking, and therefore a hinderance at such a time is doubly provoking, and these girls would most assuredly have lost their temper, had not the dexterity of one of them interposed. Every one knows that syllabub, which is a composition of white wine, sugar, nutmeg and new milk, has in appearance very near resemblance to *soap suds*, and it was immediately suggested that a tumbler should be filled with the latter material. This was directly done, and the delicious draught was taken to the lady, who on tasting this mixture of soap, water, and filth, exclaimed '*Goody Goody! Goody Goody!*'

It may perhaps be as well not to be too merry at the old lady's expence, lest in so doing we should condemn ourselves. What crowds among us say, 'Goody Goody! Goody Goody!' to everything. Give them the veritable syllabub, and it is 'Goody Goody! Goody Goody!' or fill their glass with soap suds, and they no sooner taste it than you hear the very same exclamation. All sorts of sermons, all sorts of books, all sorts of speeches, all sorts of religions, though the most absurd and contradictory, are 'Goody Goody! Goody Goody!' What is most remarkable and most humbling to the pride of rank is, that this 'Goody Goody' spirit is especially prevalent among the higher castes in our country. – The rich and the educated are often far worse than the operatives. Make a man a bishop because of his love to the gospel and desire to preach it, and it is of course *'Goody Goody,'* or choose him because of his skill in playing at cards, and still, though he may be as unregenerate as a wild bushman, yet Puseyites[1] and Evangelicals alike bow down and exclaim 'Goody Goody, Goody Goody!' aye, and what is worse than all, the Deans and Chapters assure us that the Holy Spirit has actually chosen him to his office!! We defy any Infidel to invent blasphemy of a deeper character than is thus uttered and practised; and yet, thousands of your bettermost people, as they call themselves, acquiesce, say *'yes,'* pronounce it *'Perfectly Right, Perfectly Right!'* and exclaim *'Goody Goody! Goody Goody!'* And woe to the poor wight who dissents from this ignorance and folly or exposes its absurdity. I once heard of a book whose title was, *'The World without souls';* – if the wag that wrote it was alive now he would have ample materials for composing many a volume on this point, for the men and women who are ever uttering their 'goody goody' and 'perfectly right,' are either soulless, or what is worse unworthy of a soul – aye and will remain so until the Fustian Jackets and Smock Frocks shall arouse them to think.

The concoctors of national education belong to these goody goody people. With them all contradictory religions are *'perfectly right.'* They want all creeds to be taught, all to be endowed from the public purse; and thus wish to make the whole nation accomplices in their folly and irreligion. Tell them Trinitarianism is right, and like the man and the bees they say *'yes.'* Assure them that Unitarianism is the only orthodoxy in the world, and still they say *'yes.'* Teach high churchism or low churchism; teach Puseyism or Evangelicalism; teach Popery or Protestantism; teach Socialism or Paganism! and they exclaim 'Goody Goody! Goody Goody!' That crafty man who has enslaved France;[2] that heavenly minded evangelical who rejoices in the Prussian throne,[3] and whose piety exults in an empire of sabres; that Austrian despot[4] who kisses his subjects one moment and dooms them to worse than the scaffold the next; that blessed pattern of humanity who rules Russia with a sceptre of iron;[5] and that beautiful Macaulay,[6] whose pious pen alike extols Jesuits or the Clapham sect, – most perfectly sympathise with each other, and in paying for the teaching of all contradictions, patronize and labour to perpetuate all contradictions, and thus pronounce them all 'perfectly right,' and wish the people, whose hard earnings they tax, to follow their example. If you instruct the young in the everlasting obligations of the law of God, it is *'perfectly right!'* or tell them that the law is abrogated, that Jesus Christ died to

---

1 Followers of Edward Pusey (1800–82), Regius Professor of Hebrew at Oxford and supporter of Anglican revival.
2 Louis Napoleon Bonaparte (1808–73), President of France 1848–52.
3 Frederick William IV (1795–1861), King of Prussia 1840–61.
4 Franz Joseph (1830–1916), Emperor of Austro-Hungary 1848–1916.
5 Nicholas I (1796–1855), Tsar of Russia 1825–55.
6 Thomas Babington Macaulay (1800–59), historian.

purchase us a licence to be wicked, and it is still *'perfectly right!'* Tell the children that to worship the Virgin Mary is the road to heaven, or that the adoration of this same lady is the surest and shortest way to perdition; tell them that fidelity and universal love are graces indispensable to every christian, or assure them that every real believer is under no obligation whatever to keep faith with heretics, and that it is his duty to torture them and burn them the first opportunity; – and these State Educationists exclaim respecting all these creeds and contradictions, all this morality and immorality, 'Goody Goody! Goody Goody!' Here, too, you have Herod[1] and Pontius Pilate[2] become friends. Dr Bunting[3] and Wesleyans; the Rev. Hugh M'Neil[4] and the Evangelicals of the Church of England; Roman Catholic Bishops and their Clergy; Unitarians and their leaders; wealthy orthodox dissenters, with Doctors of Divinity at their head; – all met together, all telling Government that their religion is exhausted; and in spite of their antipathy to politics, begging the political power to pick their pockets to teach true religion, false religion, or no religion, and as they rob each other and carry away the cash, exclaiming with the old lady and the soap suds, 'Goody Goody! Goody Goody!'

In this race of absurdity what a host of competitors! The Government of late years has been playing the old Absalom farce. It takes every man by the beard and kisses him and pronounces his affairs good, whether they are good or not, and wishes for nothing so devoutly as to be made the head of all things, Civil and Ecclesiastical. The state craft of the son of David is so instructive and so applicable to the present age that I shall be excused for giving the brief narrative recorded in 2 Sam. xv. 1–6. 'And it came to pass after this that Absalom prepared chariots and horses and fifty men to run before him. And Absalom rose up early and stood beside the way of the gate, (the Parliament House or Guildhall,) and it was so that when any man that had a controversy came to the king for judgment, then Absalom called unto him, and said "of what city art thou?" and he said "thy servant is of one of the tribes of Israel." And Absalom said unto him "see, thy matters are good, but there is no man deputed of the king to hear thee." Absalom said moreover, "Oh! that I were made judge in the land, that every man which hath any suit or cause might come unto me, and I would do him justice!" And it was so that when any man came nigh to do him obeisance, he put forth his hand and took him and kissed him. And in this manner did Absalom to all Israel that came to the king for jugdment. So Absalom stole the hearts of the men of Israel.' I hope the women of Israel would have had more sense than to be thus duped and plundered – but be that as it may, we have here a beautiful specimen of the state craft of our own day. Every government has its runners. The great object of centralization is to provide plenty of places and pensions, and placemen to run after them. Louis Philippe, the king of Prussia, the emperor of Austria, my

1 Herod the Great (*c.* 73–4 BC), Roman ruler in Palestine.
2 Pontius Pilate, Roman governor of Judaea AD 26–36.
3 Jabez Bunting (1779–1858), Methodist minister.
4 Hugh McNeile (1795–1879), Dean of Ripon.

Lord John Russell, and the Whigs have all laboured hard to obtain these 'chariots and horses and fifty men to run before them.' The pious ejaculation of every one of them is 'Oh that I were made judge in the land!' Only let any one do obeisance to them, and they instantly put forth their hand and embrace him and cover him with kisses. By these infamous means the heart of the nation has been stolen; national sycophancy has superseded patriotism, and instead of the noble manly heart of our forefathers, we have a race of flatterers who sigh for government offices and pensions, and cry 'Goody Goody!' to every thing, however absurd or tyrannical, that these Absaloms may broach. What a host of men government patronage has raised up to shout, *'Perfectly Right, Perfectly Right!'* The army and navy consist of necessity of human machines so drilled as to say *'Yes,'* to all sorts of orders. The Church obtains nine millions a year, and shows its pious gratitude by exclaiming *'Goody Goody'* to all state creeds and state prayers. One of the great objects of Oxford and Cambridge is to unman the men they teach, and change them from thinking beings into machines who will repeat their obsequious *'Yes'* to all that the state may enjoin on the abject Hierarchy. To be ready to adopt every sort of religion projected by the state as the perfection of modern churchism, and therefore that much ridiculed vicar of Bray,[1] was after all one of the best models of our vaunted successors of the Apostles.

But this Absalomism works wonders also among your members of parliament. We have men who having made their fortunes by trade, become tired of business and ashamed of the occupation to which they owe their wealth. Their olfactory nerves can no longer bear the smell of such vulgar things as oil and manufactories; they must have something more ambrosial, and therefore turn to the putrescence of the battle-field and that sink of simony – the church. To these humane birds of prey the smell of carnage is the purest anodyne, and the spiritual charnel-house, in which souls are bought for gain and buried in perdition, sends forth an odour far more delicious than the incense that arises from Araby the blest. But then promotions in the army, the church and the navy, depend more upon patronage than upon talent, virtue or religion, and as centralization has placed hosts of good things in the hands of the government, men who deal in corruption crowd to enter parliament that by doing obeisance to Absalom they may get the state kiss and something more. What numbers appear on the hustings and unblushingly declare that their claim on your suffrage rests on the stupendous qualification that they are going to St Stephen's to say *'yes,' 'perfectly right,'* and cry *'goody goody'* to all that my Lord John Russell or Sir Robert Peel shall propound. And what is worse, you have not merely selfish, uneducated squires and lords adopting this pious, patriotic course, but you have learned barristers running before Absalom, and shouting 'goody goody' more loudly than any one else. Some of these men were actually radicals, at least in profession, so long as the whigs were worth anything, but have proved renegade to the people and worshippers of the whigs just in proportion as the latter have practically denied all their former professions. What a charm there must be in places and pensions

---

1 Vicar of Bray: equivocator, or fickle person.

when a promising learned man will even sell his soul to a political apostate and therefore to a worse than Satan, and do so for the sake of office and a retiring salary! Oh! what a blessed thing is state education! Only give us this boon and we shall have pensions for bribes; schoolmasters converted into state puppets; and the people a race of machines who will be as pleased with soap suds as syllabub, and be as ready to smack their lips and exclaim 'goody goody' to the one as the other. In my work, *'Education the Birthright of every Human Being,'*[1] I have shewn that the effect of government education in France, Prussia, Switzerland, &c., &c. has been to demoralize and enslave the people and strengthen the hands of despotism. Formerly the soldier, the sword and the dungeon were the chief instruments of tyranny, but modern ingenuity has discovered that the state schoolmaster is a far more efficient agent. His is the magic power of paralysing mind and educating a race of slaves who will fawn on tyrants, and not only kiss their fetters, but actually manufacture them and fight for the honour of wearing them and riveting them on their sons and daughters. All the despots of the continent know full well that England is the battle-field of truth, liberty and religion, and that her operatives – her *'Fustian Jackets and Smock Frocks,'* – are the noble spirits by whose energy she has achieved her greatness, and that until these are vanquished, tyranny must tremble throughout the world. To corrupt the noble and wealthy has long been an easy task. Foreign tyrants read our newspapers, and perceive that a patriotic speech, except from the mouth of an operative, is a modern prodigy, and that for a wealthy man to be a christian patriot, is to lose caste among his compeers. How many Hampdens[2] or Sydneys[3] could the last parliament boast? Who so much hooted by their own caste as Cobden or Bright, until the millions made them respectable? Here then is the rub. This many headed monster – *the people,* – must be subdued before despotism can enter on its millennium. But how can this be effected? Swords and artillery would be tried in vain, and therefore something else must be resorted to, and what so effectual as state education? Every where this has succeeded. Look at the Continent. Aye, look at home. Have not Oxford and Cambridge done well? The moral history of these schools cannot be written, it would pollute a pandemonium; and what enthusiast would dream, though he dreamt till the day of doom, of a patriot being formed in either of those universities? Men who say *'yes'* and *'perfectly right'* to all kinds of injustice and absurdity are the usual offspring of these celebrated seats of learning. Here we have thousands of minds annually unmanned by state education. Enlarge this governmental power and let it provide schools for the masses, and England's 'bold peasantry' will become like her bold and patriotic barons, – a thing of yesterday; and in their stead a people such as the Prussians or our Oxford scholars, who will utter their *'goody goody'* respecting all absurdities and contradictions, will be the result.

---

1 Benjamin Parsons, *Education the Birthright of Every Human Being, and the Only Scriptural Preparation for the Millennium* (1845).

2 John Hampden (*c.* 1595–1643), leader of the opposition to Charles I's demand for ship-money.

3 Algernon Sidney (1622–83), republican politician.

But Government Education is not merely adapted to raise a nation of mental and moral slaves, but the very proposal itself is a national insult. It supposes,

I. – That the people are unwilling to educate themselves. This is a libel on all classes but especially on the operatives and peasantry. Past experience must not be pleaded. Lords, Squires, Clergymen and others have for years been protesting against the education of the people. They have declared that if our operatives were instructed they would not work, and that neither Church nor Throne would be any longer secure. The bliss of ignorance has been sung from land's end to land's end, and even the pulpit has dwelt on its praises. We need not go back ten years for the verification of these statements. Why there are thousands now in this country who dread the progress of knowledge, and the only thing that reconciles them to it is the thought that the Church and State by taking it in hand, will render it as efficient in the production of patriotic christians as the tuition of Oxford or Cambridge. The people have been literally dinned with the sentiment that knowledge would make them unhappy and that even 'a little learning is a dangerous thing.'[1] Poor souls! many have believed these false prophets and on the authority of the learned gentry and clergy have neglected the education of their offspring. But further, they have been oppressed in their wages and thus in many instances have been deprived of the means of education. Men who were gaining princely incomes from their trade or estates, have ground the faces of the labourers to whom they owe their wealth, and cursed themselves with the guilt of extortion, and their dependants with the scourge of poverty and ignorance. But if instead of this misrepresentation and injustice, the masses were shown the importance and duty of educating their children and were furnished, as they ought to be, with the power of accomplishing it, there is not a person among them but would gladly perform this most pleasing task. I have never yet found a peasant or operative but mourned the hard lot which doomed his family to ignorance. The Fustian Jackets and Smock Frocks of this country do not want to live on alms. They neither desire charity bread, charity clothing, nor charity education. Their language is 'Give us a fair day's wages for a fair day's work and we will feed, clothe, and instruct our children ourselves.' The system of state education is only another trick to keep down the people. The question of wages and direct taxation is to be burked, the poor are to be crushed, and, to prevent their complaining, their minds are to be drilled into obsequiousness or bribed into sycophancy by state pensioners, and the very funds by which they are to be enslaved are to be taken, in the most extravagant manner, from their own pockets. Government Education will cost the people four times as much as they would have to pay if they taught themselves. And as the masses, by our present foolish and unjust system of taxation are doomed to pay *nine tenths of all the taxes*, and in some instances more than an hundredfold beyond their due proportion, the burden must fall most heavily on themselves. If the concocters of National Education were sincere, they would bring forward a plan of direct taxation, – they would remove every restriction on trade, – they would repeal all taxes on knowledge, –

---

1 Alexander Pope, *An Essay on Criticism* (1711).

they would abolish all sinecures, – they would lessen the national expenditure, – they would study the principles of peace and do away with that disgrace to Christianity and humanity, a standing army – They would use for the good of the nation the overgrown wealth of the Church, and thus to the utmost of their power lessen the burdens of the country, and consequently give the people the means of educating themselves. Till they do this, all their zeal about National Education will be open to the charge of an attempt to enslave and oppress those whom they profess to benefit. It is a gross libel on the poor to say that they are unwilling to pay for the instruction of their families. In no grade of society is there such pure and fervent natural affection as among the working classes; and one of the foulest blots on our age is the injustice which so systematically prevents them from gratifying the spontaneous, the heaven-inspired dictates of parental love. Go ye libellers, ye despisers and oppressors of the men and women who produce your wealth, and like guardian and ministering angels, protect your property and create the comfort of your dwellings; – go and learn from the Bible 'to do justly, to love mercy, and walk humbly with God, and instantly a self educated people shall demonstrate that the poor have a greater love for knowledge, truth, and religion than the clergy or nobility.

II. – Government Education is an insult to the wealthier classes. It intimates that they refuse to pay wages sufficient to support their workpeople, or to give for the articles they purchase a price which will remunerate the labourer and the operative. The condemnation is deeper than this, for the necessity of Government interference intimates that these gentlemen, though rolling in wealth, yet, if not compelled, would leave the poor around them to perish in ignorance and depravity. These are the Cains of our day, who destroy their own species and then exclaim 'am I my brother's keeper?' The Greek term used in the new Testament for an *extortioner* is of the same origin as the word '*harpy*,' whoever, therefore extorts unrenumerated labour and oppresses the hireling in his wages or the tradesmen in is lawful profits is a '*harpy*,' and by the word of God excluded from the pale of Christianity. With this fact before us let us only look at the spectacle of a Lord or a Squire receiving his £50,000 or £100,000 a year – every penny obtained through the hard toil of the labourer; – only think of these gentlemen going to Parliament and unblushingly declaring that their servants are so ground down by poverty that unless the starving paupers are burdened with a heavier tax they will very soon become a race of '*untutored savages*!' Can the whole history of depravity exhibit any form of shameless iniquity equal to this? But let us glance a little further. These very advocates of compulsory taxation for education are many of them so wealthy that they actually fool away their money to get rid of it. What a scene will be presented at the last day when the great judge of all shall reckon with these men and women for the sums which they wasted on the very '*pomps and vanities of this world and all the sinful lusts of the flesh*' which they had solemnly vowed before God, angels, and men to renounce! and yet these self same persons stand up in the senate house, and before the nation, attest that unless compelled by the strong arm of the law – unless the money be extorted from them by a tax-gatherer – they will allow their own brethren and sisters 'to

perish for lack of knowledge.' Listen to that hue and cry over yonder hill and dale.
– What a magnificent sight; there you have an innocent stag or fox, pursued by
a crowd of cowardly dogs, followed by a host of senseless horses, spurred to their
utmost speed by a set of nondescripts in human forms, who are willing to risk
body and soul for the pleasure of seeing a helpless animal torn limb from limb by
a multitude of bloodthirsty hounds!! The folly we pass over – but tell me the cost.
To keep up those savage sports treasure is wasted to an extent amply sufficient to
give physical comfort, intellectual culture, pure morality, and celestial hope to
the whole needy population of the land; and yet the men who thus voluntarily
waste the resources of the country on game, dogs, and horses, are the very persons who tell the world that the poor around them would die of famine and perish
in crime unless compulsory taxation provided them with food and education. The
wealthy men who thus demand government aid and state tuition proclaim their
own infamy in terms that language cannot exaggerate.

III. – Government Education is an insult to the Clergy and the Church. Man
was made to be religious, but without liberty there can be no religion or morality;
and therefore the only spiritual influence that one man can exercise over another
is persuasion. The human soul is especially a believing thing, so much so, that a
rational scepticism was intended to be its shield against credulity. Persuasion or
faith move the will and lead to voluntary or moral action, and one of the chief
offices of a clergyman or minister of religion is to '*persuade men;*' – if he does not
accomplish this he is unfit for the duties he has undertaken. Men can be persuaded christianity is the most credible religion upon the face of the earth. Its
chief argument and evidence is its doctrine of universal love. If Clergymen who
are employed to persuade, and paid *nine millions* a year to teach the people to
exercise charity – cannot or will not persuade, then they are unfit for their offices.
You might as well have ploughmen who cannot plough, or spinners who cannot
spin, or cooks who cannot cook, as clergymen or dissenting ministers who cannot
persuade. The swaggering weaver, who does not weave, but demands wages for
work which he will not do, is not a greater swindler than the vaunted successor
of the Apostles who receives pay to persuade people to be liberal and yet never
uses the means in his power to accomplish this object. The clergy are appointed
to raise up a religious people, a nation of voluntaries – for *involuntary* religion is
nonsense; – and these men loudly demand their pay, but at the same time are
unblushingly telling parliament and the world that they have not done their
work. Their failure is entirely their own fault. They have in the Scripture the most
beautiful and sublime, yet simple and heart touching religion that divine love
could reveal; they have hearers capable of being attracted and moved; they have
the promise of Omnipotent grace to make their ministry effectual, and yet from
sheer idleness they leave the people to perish and then pray the Parliament to
interfere and exact by compulsion what these priests will not effect by persuasion.
They sound a trumpet before them to proclaim that they have made their hearers, all of them to a man, '*members of Christ, children of God, and inheritors of the
kingdom,*' and yet they tell the government, that *these same* '*members of Christ, children of God* and *inheritors of the kingdom,*' though many of them are rolling in

wealth, are so fond of drinking, racing, hunting, gambling, and every species of dissipation, folly and vanity, that unless compelled by the strong hand of the law, they will allow old England to go back to barbarism! Many of the Evangelicals, and some of the dissenters are also as loud as any one in thus making Christianity the scoff of pagans and infidels. Tell us no more of an insulted church, or dishonoured priesthood, we defy any demon whatever the depth of his malignity to invent a reproach equal to that with which the church and its ministers cover themselves, when Bishops, clergy, and lay members declare that they will not do their duty and therefore invoke the aid of what they do often brand as a '*Godless Parliament*,' to exert its unholy influence to compel, bribe and corrupt men to become religious.

But some of these gentlemen attempt to reason and assert that, 'the Government has no right to punish crime which is the result of ignorance, without first affording the means of knowledge.' We are not afraid that the Fustian Jackets and Smock Frocks will be led astray by this fallacy. If secular knowledge could prevent crime, why did Thurtell,[1] Fauntleroy[2] and others come to the scaffold? Morality is the only thing that can produce virtuous citizens, and every school boy knows that there can be no morality apart from religion. Religion is a *bond*, *an obligation*, and what is morality but fulfilling our *obligations* to God and man? If therefore the government must afford the means of preventing crime, it must provide moral teaching, and consequently become a religious teacher. But then what religion must it teach? To teach only *one* religion and compel all sects to pay for it would be injustice and persecution: – to teach *all* religions would be nonsense, because it must then teach all sorts of contradictions: – to teach *no* religion would be to teach *no* morality, and could not prevent crime; and therefore its only legitimate course is to let all religious teaching alone. The fact is, governments were never instituted to be religious teachers, nor 'to manage, control, or pay' for national education. The civil government is only a legislative and executive body, and in its executive capacity it is nothing more than a magistracy and a police to take up and punish offenders. In the Jewish nation, which was a Theocracy, the magistrate had nothing to do but to settle civil and criminal disputes according to the law, to punish the guilty and defend the innocent. To '*bear the sword*' is the office assigned to the civil ruler in the new testament. Among the Jews the judge might sometimes be a prophet and a priest, but these offices were perfectly distinct, and neither Samuel nor any other person had a right to teach or institute religious teaching or pay for religious instruction *because* he was a *magistrate*. It would be just as correct to say that no justice of the peace has a right to condemn crime, that no judge on the bench has a right to pass sentence on murder, unless he has first tried by religious teaching to prevent it, as to affirm that government has no right to exercise its civil functions in punishing offenders unless it should first assume the office of religious instructor. Religious teaching is the duty of every one, and ought not, and cannot be, undertaken by the state. The

1 John Thurtell (1794–1824), son of the mayor of Norwich, murderer through gambling.
2 Henry Fauntleroy (1785–1824), banker, executed for forgery.

government might as well attempt to be religious for the people, or to make the nation religious by state compulsion as to interfere with the duties of parents in educating their children. There can be no true morality without faith and repentance; there can be no true faith and repentance without the regeneration of the Holy Spirit, and if the right of the magistrate depends on his making the people religious and moral, then his right must depend upon his doing what he cannot do, and on this principle the State never can have any right to punish crime. State-Church regeneration leaves the people 'untutored savages,' and their educated betters a race of vandals who would rather waste their money on dogs and dissipation than attend to the dictates of justice or mercy respecting their poor brethren. State Education is one of the worst of all monopolies, for it robs the people of their money, their liberty, and the privilege of attending to one of their most delightful religious duties. The Jewish magistrate was a mere policeman, judge, and executioner. – The law of God gave him no authority to exact taxes for the support of the State for tithes for the Church. He might receive them but he had no right to seize them if the people were unwilling to give them. Our Lord paid tribute not because there was any law to compel him or that he was in danger of being summoned before a magistrate and fined, but to prevent himself and Peter from being blamed. In fact, compulsory taxation of any kind is not a law of the Scriptures. Where there is *patriotism*, there is no need of compulsory revenues for the national expenditure: where there is *humanity*, there is no necessity for poor rates: – and where there is *real christianity*, tythes, church-rates, and educational taxes would be deemed a libel not only on religion but on human nature. Compulsory taxation for civil, parochial, or religious purposes, has a tendency to paralyse patriotism, christian charity, and religious benevolence – it spares the rich and crushes the poor – it produces sinecures, pensions, and placemen – it makes patronage and sycophancy rather than talent and virtue, the stepping stone to office, and raises up crowds of 'goody goody' flatterers who are willing to do any thing, or be any thing, or say any thing, provided the Church or the State will repay their adoration of mammon. The tendency of the age is to add to this Augean abomination, and State Education is only another effort to increase the burdens of the people and the patronage of the government. Already it has polluted the pulpit and the press, and the people have few patrons left, and therefore must become their own liberators. Our only hope is in the Fustian Jackets and Smock Frocks. You must demand that the government shall not interfere with your rights – you must teach the senate that its duties are merely legislative and magisterial – that it may punish vice but that it has no right nor power to produce virtue – you must resolve to send your children to no school supported by State taxes, nor to attend any place of worship sustained by compulsory revenues – you must leave government churches and government schools empty, and thus demonstrate that you are not a race of slaves who will exclaim 'yes,' 'Perfectly Right!' and 'Goody Goody!' to every thing that may be propounded by men who for the sake of power, place, and pensions are willing to sacrifice the rights and liberties of the noblest people upon the face of the earth. Educate yourselves, educate your children yourselves, repudiate every idea of physical violence, be men, 'quit you like men,' by clothing yourselves in all the dignity and omnipotence of moral force, and you shall become your own benefactors, the renovators of your country, and the emancipators of the world. Christian patriotism driven from the church and the senate, seeks her last asylum among you – become her protectors and heralds, and a thousand generations shall call you blessed; but reject her appeals to your patronage, and ages of tyranny may be the result. Liberty and despotism are now almost equally poised and it rests with the Fustian Jackets and Smock Frocks to turn the scale in favour of all that is dear to humanity and for the glory of God.

In this tract I have not responded as I had intended to Mr Symons' letter to the people of Stroud.[1] On reading it a second time I found little but what I had fully answered. – Besides the book has not sold well and a gratuitous circulation was therefore deemed prudent. Little mental effort would be necessary to expose its sophistry, but why slay the slain? To recall it from oblivion would do him more harm than I have any wish to inflict. To all whig worshippers, placemen, and pension hunters, we cordially wish a better occupation.

---

1 Jelger Cookson Symons (1809–60), miscellaneous writer.

No. 5.

TRACTS FOR THE FUSTIAN JACKETS AND SMOCK FROCKS;

RADICALISM
AN ESSENTIAL DOCTRINE OF CHRISTIANITY.
BY THE
REV. B. PARSONS,
OF EBLEY.

'I have this day set thee over nations and over the kingdoms,
To ROOT OUT and to pull down, and to destroy and to throw down,
To build and to plant.' JEREMIAH.[1]

STROUD: B. BUCKNALL,
Sold also by F. W. HARMER, and W. A. BAYLIS. PARTRIDGE, Nailsworth:
HARPER, Cheltenham: J. SNOW, London.
1847.

A few years ago the term '*Radical*' was as terrific as the name '*Chartist*' is now. What a tremendous being was a *Radical*. The monster was a kind of political and religious bugbear conjured up on all occasions to frighten the great boys and girls who have long been out of their teens and all the old ladies of the masculine gender. Mention a radical to some of these spoilt children whose education had been so shamefully neglected, and they almost wanted a smelling bottle. By the bye, the history of terrific names would be rather an amusing tale. 'Give a dog a bad name and hang him,' is a very old adage, or rather we might say, a very old trick, and has worked so well that it has been almost universally adopted. There has been nothing good in this world, but Satan or his angels have given it some dreadful name. Our Lord was called a Nazarene, a demoniac, a destroyer of the temple, and an enemy to Caesar. And how admirably the thing answered. All the rich and the learned, the doctors of divinity and the priests were frightened out of their wits at the mention of his name. Who would sit at the feet of a Carpenter from Nazareth, or listen to the preaching of one who was inspired by Beelzebub? Only think of being led by a madman who was going to destroy the temple and build it in three days, or overturn the throne of the pious and heavenly minded Tiberias Cæsar! Well might they ask, 'Have any of the rulers believed on him?'

---

1 Jeremiah 1: 10.

Of course, only the rabble, 'the people who knew not the law and were cursed,' were wild enough to give him a hearing. Why even his followers were probably for a while deterred from assuming his name. All the more prudent believers, whether Jews or Gentiles, were alarmed at the idea of being called '*Christians.*' Was there ever a name covered with so much odium and infamy? What a common carpenter, a lunatic, who, on the authority of the university men of his day, had 'a devil and was mad,' an agitator who stirred up the people throughout all Jewry, and who at last was executed as a criminal and died the ignominious death of a slave on the cross; – who in the world that had the least respect for himself or religion would for one moment endure the thought of being called by his name? What a calamity when some of the enemies of truth at Antioch fastened on the disciples, the despised cognomen of *Christians*! Talk of the infamy of the terms *Methodist*, *Dissenter*, *Radical*, or *Chartist*, why there never was a name so covered with odium, so loaded with curses as the name of the Son of God. The Saviour foretold his disciples that their '*name* was to be cast out as evil,' and that they were to be called worse than Beelzebub. There was no small amount of courage needed in the men, who could glory in wearing such a name, and rejoice in suffering the consequences. But the trick answered admirably. Doubtless thousands admitted that Christianity was not a bad thing after all, if it were not for the *name*. Alas the rose would have smelled sweet but for the *name!* It was the name, not the thing to be sure, only the name, that was so horrible! Nicodemus[1] was frightened at it, and went to consult the Saviour by night, and even that sensible and honourable barrister, Joseph of Arimathea,[2] was afraid to own him while he was alive. The history of the treatment of the name of Jesus, is one of the most humbling records of the folly of respectable people (?) and university men, that was ever read. No satire could be so cutting, no sarcasm so severe, and yet the learned and the wealthy portions of society are as proud of being duped to day as they were in the days of Herod and Pontius Pilate. The Fustian Jackets and Smock Frocks, are now as distinguished for the use of *common* sense as were the '*common people*' who heard the Saviour gladly, while many of the modern successors of the Apostles and their votaries glory in nothing so much as their having inherited the prejudices of the Scribes and Pharisees. '*Temperance*,' said a great dandy six feet high, the other day, – 'Temperance is very good, and the fact is, I would become a Total Abstainer, but there is that abominable name *Teetotaler*, why I would not join your ranks on any account so long as you retain it.' And so the poor fellow kept on drinking poisons and actually poisoning himself, rather than bear one of the most innocent and harmless names that ever was invented. *Chartist* again. Who would be called a *Chartist*? Every person who reflects or has studied the British Constitution, or political economy, knows, that the six points of the Charter, contain in them the germ of social, political and even religious reform, but then who can bear that insufferable name *Chartist*? Only think of a Doctor in Divinity or a Squire being called a Chartist! And yet a better name as

1 John 3: 2.
2 John 19: 38.

expressive of a constitutional principle was never invented. You may say that it was once good, but that it has been disgraced by the extravagance of some of its adherents. Well and what of that? Has not Christianity been disgraced by its professors? Go almost into any parish in the country, and hear the old men describe the clergymen of the olden time, and the narrative is too polluting to be written. Look at the lives of the Christians that Voltaire,[1] Gibbon,[2] Byron[3] and Shelley[4] conversed with, and can any one wonder at their infidelity? Nothing, nothing, has ever been so thoroughly, so constantly disgraced as Christianity. The pagan lives of some of its vaunted, first water votaries, must make demons blush, and yet there are people who notwithstanding all, glory in the name. Surely then we ought not in these days to allow ourselves to be frightened at a word, because some who have used it, have disgraced their principles.

What has been said above may be applied to the term *Radical*. Whig, *radical*, dissenter, papist, unitarian, and infidel, have formed a string of sounds, which has helped many an uneducated gentleman to an enunciation, when the lack of wit and wisdom caused his tongue to cleave to the roof of his mouth. But the whigs have out-toried the tories, and are now become very nice men; Mother Church by the aid of her Tractarian sons is going so fast to Rome that Popery is one of the most honoured religions in the country: – The state has lately so fondly embraced the Unitarians and the political dissenters who ask the Government to take the money out of their pockets to pay for their schools, that heresy and dissent are no longer a reproach, – and finally, the radicals have laboured to plant so many more evils than they have plucked up, that even this much abused epithet may be borne without any fear of being stoned or anathematized. No one therefore will be alarmed at our saying that '*Radicalism is an essential doctrine of Christianity.*' Some years ago the thing would have been frightful, but now even Louis Phillippe and the Emperor of Russia can sleep without dreaming of the radicals. Most of these gentlemen both in Parliament and out, are so anxious to do every thing by legislation, to advance centralization, and thus, by vesting vast powers in the state, are sapping every principle of individual and constitutional liberty, that a modern radical is quite a pet with the upholders of arbitrary power. I make these remarks because in this tract I am going to use the word, *Radical*, not in its present diluted, but in its *original* and *natural signification*.

Radical comes from the Latin, '*Radix, a root,*' and therefore, '*Radicalism*' was intended to signify that system of reform which goes to the '*Root*' of every evil, and *eradicates it*, or *roots it out*. Now this kind of Radicalism is the dictate of virtue, of equity, of benevolence, of pure religion, in fact, the religion which spares any evil, any injustice, or unkindness, is unworthy of our notice and ought to be exposed, condemned and banished from the earth. Not that we would use physi-

---

1 François-Marie Arouet de Voltaire (1694–1778), leading philosopher of the French Enlightenment.
2 Edward Gibbon (1737–94), historian and religious sceptic.
3 George Gordon (1788–1824), Lord Byron, romantic poet.
4 Percy Bysshe Shelley (1792–1822), romantic poet.

cal force to accomplish such an object. Unholy means must not be employed to bring about holy results. The end can never sanctify the means. We have seen enough of 'doing evil that good may come.' The logic of the sword, the bayonet, the cannon, the jail, or the gibbet is as absurd as it is cruel. Persuasion is omnipotent for all the purposes of truth and rectitude. Every child knows that the only religion which deserves the name, is the one which instructs us *to avoid everything that is wrong, and constrains us to do everything that is right*. Such a religion needs not the evidence of miracles or prophecy to prove its heavenly origin. These gifts in an ignorant or vicious age might have been of immense advantage as seals to the truth, but in a rational and enlightened generation, such interpositions of the Creator are unnecessary. Every one must see that '*to avoid everything that is wrong, and to do everything that is right,*' is the highest species of Godliness that man can conceive or the Deity reveal. Such a religion has the stamp of heaven upon it. Heathen fabulists tell us that their Gods found a difficulty in concealing their divinity when they conversed with men. If they became visible, their features and especially the eye told their Olympian birth, if they spoke, the voice sounded more than human – if they walked, the step was divine, and spontaneous flowers sprang up to mark the path which had been trodden by their feet. Probably these imaginations originated in the deep rooted conviction that the heavens are more pure and sublime than the earth, and that God is greater than man, and therefore that whatever comes from above must be pre-eminently good. He who is not infinitely good cannot be God, and a being who is perfectly just, wise and benevolent, should he give a religion to his creatures, must leave on his laws the impress of his own perfections, and hence it is not difficult to prove which system of morals is from heaven. Here, the wayfaring man, though a reputed fool, cannot err. There is none good but one and that is God. In the Deity we have unmixed good, in demons we have unmixed evil, in man we have good and evil blended together; and hence, a religion from beneath would be undiluted iniquity; a religion invented by man would be partly right and partly wrong; but a religion from the Creator must be altogether 'holy, just, and good.' No one will deny these propositions. Could we announce them to an assembled world all would consent to their truth. But this assent shows that the religion of heaven must be the irreconcilable antagonist of every thing wrong, unjust, or unkind. It will propose to *root* up every moral evil upon earth, in a word, it must be a *radical religion*, for if it is not, it is not divine. To suppose that it can wink at sin, or sanction viciousness in the rich or the poor, in the church or the state, in the monarch or the slave, in the priest, the merchant, or mechanic, would be at once to sacrifice its claims to a celestial origin: and consequently the title of my tract is proved, for if the religion of the bible is from God, then *radicalism* must be one of its essential doctrines. The transcendental spiritualism of some may have been shocked at the assumption of this title, but should they deny its propriety, they must at the same time give up the divine authority of their religion. To tell me that a good man sanctions injustice, is to utter against him the greatest libel, or to impeach his piety. To aver that any man can be a christian who does not wish and labour for the entire *eradication*, or *rooting* up of every evil, is to blaspheme christianity; and therefore to teach or insinuate that the God of heaven approves of any crime is to dishonor him to the last degree. He who does not hate vice cannot be God, but if he hates it he must naturally seek its destruction, and the religion or gospel which he reveals to man must be a *radical* gospel. In fact a gospel which is not *radical* is no gospel. Gospel is *good news*, but good news to man must include his emancipation from evil, and therefore the gospel is radicalism, and *real* radicalism is the gospel. And hence if christianity is from God every real christian must be a thorough radical. To object to the truth of these remarks is to abjure the divine origin of the scriptures, 'to deny the faith, and be worse than an infidel.'

But I am writing to those who wear *Fustian Jackets and Smock Frocks*, and need not be tedious. Your plain common sense intuitively tells you that what I am saying is correct. And further, you have a vested interest in the great truths of Radicalism. You have for years groaned under the iron sceptre of injustice. Long ago you ought to have been well employed, well paid, well fed, well clothed, well lodged, and well educated. Christianity and the God that made you demand all these blessings for the industrious labourer and mechanic. – Aye, and enjoins that you should have all these without charity. The means of procuring them by honest and honorable industry ought to have been placed in your hands. Your Creator has made the most ample provision for your sustenance and comfort. Your great destroyer has been your fellow man. He has scowled upon you as his inferiors. He has taxed your means to gratify his barbarian lust of war, and has poured out your blood as a libation to this ambition. Missionaries make you horror sick as they tell of the human sacrifices of paganism, but every field of battle consists of hecatombs of immortal beings voluntarily offered by professing Christians at the shrine of the heathen Mars. And when the peace comes, you have been too often deprived of its blessings. Those who have returned from the battle field and its means of plunder, have not unfrequently entered the senate to wage war with your industry and with the prosperity of other nations. Talk of peace, we have never yet been at peace with the world. When we retire from Blenheim or Waterloo, we go to the Parliament to carry on a destructive battle with the trade and commerce of the whole world. When we cannot summon them to stand before our bayonets or cannon, we tax their industry and use tariffs instead of steel or gunpowder. And this constant warfare with foreigners is a perpetual scourge to ourselves. It is cutting off our own nose to spite our own face. Whatever injures the trade of other countries injures our own, and then, as a consequence you are the chief sufferers. Our corn laws and restrictions on trade have cost us and the world more treasure and blood than the last ruinous war. Thousands have been pauperised and died of want and starvation: and yet, which is more horrible still, you have had priests who endeavoured to persuade you that the King of kings approves of all this injustice, and that you ought to be passive and not utter a complaint. We do not wonder if some of you have become sceptics. Your infidelity was more acceptable to heaven than the faith of these false prophets. They caricatured the gospel, and blasphemed the God of love by making him the accomplice of tyrants, and it was your duty to disbelieve their misrepresentations. They call you an infidel rabble, we deny the charge. You are not 'faithless but believing,' only you demand that the religion which claims your assent should be impartial, should be just and pure and benevolent. You have not been sophisticated by the schools and therefore are not sufficiently blind to call it justice to *tax* the *poor* to *enrich* the *rich*, – to hang the murderer of *one* man and to reward and applaud the destroyer of *thousands*; – nor are you profane enough to throw the shield of religion over these abominations. He is the infidel who makes the gospel the pander of ambition, the sycophant of the rich, and the patron of tyranny, injustice and hypocrisy.

You are too wise to attempt to redress any of these evils by violence. To employ physical force would only make a bad matter ten thousand times worse, and would show that you are as corrupt as those who have crushed you by injustice or misled you by false statements respecting religion. No one was ever reformed by being shot or burnt. Besides every man is our brother and we are bound to do him 'good and not evil all the days of our life.' Persuasion is the only legitimate agent for the regeneration of society. Truth is an omnipotent weapon. The bayonet can only pierce the body, but the words of equity can penetrate the inmost soul and slay the tyrant without killing the man. The noblest slaughter of our foes would be to convert them into friends. You must meet often, and show to the world your rights and your wrongs. The genius of reformation commits her mantle to you. The barons of Runnymede have long been buried and have scarcely a successor; patriotism has for many a day been exiled from the mansions of the wealthy; a reformer in the church is more detested than Lucifer; many of the rich dissenters are slumbering or reviling those who will not drink their opiates; the parliament for years past have practically told you that he is 'cursed who trusts in man;' and therefore you must look to yourselves. England expects every man to do his duty, not by slaughtering his foes, but by firmly demanding that the British sceptre shall be the sceptre of righteousness, that the rights of the poor shall be regarded and that all iniquity shall be rooted up. Trust in God and yourselves, but rely not on others to perform the duties which Heaven has delegated to you. Remember that the Gospel is a radical religion and therefore divine, and that as such it arms you with omnipotent authority to labour rationally and constantly to eradicate all injustice and regenerate society.

It is of everlasting importance that you should look at Christianity, as it is revealed in the scripture and not as it is debased by many of its priests, or degraded by the lives of thousands of its professors. To say a ready made prayer, and read or hear a ready made sermon, to pass through all the genuflexions, sittings, standings, bowings, courtseyings, and turnings to the east, *à la mode ecclesiastique*, is the very climax of the christianity of millions in our day. But then this *puppetism* is not the gospel. Mind, I do not call it *puppyism*, because a puppy has a *will* of his own and is a *voluntary* agent, but the very mention of the *voluntary principle* or of *voluntaryism* in religion makes not a few of our modern successors of the apostles almost faint. Only think of any person praying, or giving, or going to heaven as a *voluntary*! Who but a madman would dare utter such heresy? Now *compulsoryism* is *puppetism*, but *puppetism* is not radicalism and therefore is not christianity. There is as much religion in a steam engine as in the man who is pious from compulsion. These *involuntaries*, you may be sure, will do no more than they are compelled, and will rather encourage than root up the injustices of the day. In fact many of them have a great relish for political and ecclesiastical corruption. It is said to be an orthodox proof of a gentlemanly palate to prefer game the nearer it approaches putrescence; and I need not say how perfectly the sensual and the moral taste of many of these highly educated individuals agree. But then their christianity is not the christianity of the scriptures, and you might as well judge of the talents of Raphael[1] by the fox and geese on a boy's slate, as to decide respecting the gospel from the conduct of these evangelical patrons of injustice and formality.

No, if you would know what the gospel is, you must look at it in the Scriptures. There you find a religion which commands us to exert ourselves to root up every vice from among mankind. The gospel is so perfectly *radical* that it spares nothing that is unjust or wrong. As a dispensation of mercy, it of course proposes to pardon the guilty, but then one of its immutable and inflexible conditions is, that the sinner shall repent and undergo a thorough *radical* reform of heart and life. Should he retain the love of but *one* sin, however small, mercy holds out to him no hope. This requisition may be strict, but it is the strictness of righteousness; and further, to enable us to comply with it, God gives his Holy Spirit to all who ask him, and he who is born of God must hate all iniquity. To talk of a 'child of God' sanctioning injustice or winking at vice is an absurdity. Such a one abhors his own imperfections. He labours to *eradicate* his own sins. *Radicalism* enters into all his tears, all his prayers, all his efforts. This is the beauty of the gospel, it proposes to make every individual a personal reformer, and constrains him to go first to the root of the evil in himself. His zeal and his charity begin at home, but they do not end there. Sin is that abominable thing which his soul hates, he loathes it in himself first and most, and he detests it everywhere, and hence becomes a *Radical Reformer*. The wickedness and injustice of individuals, and the iniquities of public bodies, whether civil, political, or ecclesiastical, are alike condemned in the scriptures. The vices of none are to be spared. The master who robs a servant or the servant who defrauds a master are both called upon to repent and reform by the gospel. Here you have no respect for persons, poverty is not an excuse, and riches are not a shield. 'Know ye not that the *unrighteous* shall not inherit the kingdom of God?' 1 Cor., vi. 9. The apostle says 'know ye not?' intimating that everybody ought to *know* so plain a truth, that heaven bars its gates against the '*unrighteous*,' and therefore the church on earth which recognises such moral monsters as her members, cannot be a church of God. The fiat of the last judgement concludes, 'He that is *unjust*, let him be *unjust still*,' and we defy the gloomiest imagination to depict a deeper hell than that of a being banished from God and doomed to the unmitigated remorse of conscious *injustice*.

But the apostle continues, 'Be not deceived, neither fornicators, nor idolators, nor adulterers, nor effeminate, nor the abusers of themselves with mankind, nor

---

1 Raffaelo Sanzio (1483–1520), Italian painter.

thieves, nor covetous, nor drunkards, nor revilers, nor extortioners, shall inherit the kingdom of God.' Here you have *radicalism* or perdition. You must labour to *root* up all these evils or be excluded from the true church in this world and the next. Only think of the extent of that reformation which calls upon all mankind to forsake these vices. Give us the practical radicalism of the gospel and you have no longer a single unchaste, obscene, debauched or dissipated person on the earth. Insobriety would be unknown and slander would be heard of no more. Every man would be really and truly manly, for effeminacy is abhorrent to the genius of Christianity. Thieves, misers and extortioners would cease from the world. And there would not be merely the absence of these vices, but every human being would be clothed with all the graces of the spirit. People would not only be *negatively* good by the abandonment of vice, but *positively* good by the practice of every virtue. They would *first*, 'deny themselves all ungodliness and worldly lusts,' and then, *secondly*, 'they would live soberly, righteously and godly in this present evil world.' And the gospel, be it remembered, never spares the ungodliness of the wealthy or of public bodies. Rich men among us are often fawned upon and flattered, though stained with crimes which would have ren- dered a poor man an object of execration. Rank or money can now cover a multitude of sins. Had Charles II[1] or George IV[2] been operatives, they would have been shunned as monsters in iniquity, but they were kings, and the clergy insulted heaven and earth by pronouncing them the '*most religious*' persons in the world. Here you had 'the wicked justified for a reward,'[3] for when it came to this that the *living* must be lost, or the mendacious prayer repeated, the falsehood was preferred, and 'men's persons were held in admiration because of advantage.'[4] And sadder still, the evangelicals said this. These men knew better and yet were bold enough to tell their Creator that these royal profligates were superlatively religious. Evangelical religion has too often been so exclusively preached as to encourage vice. Indeed it has of late become so fashionable that most of the scrib- blers who write manuscript sermons for the clergy have orders to make them evangelical. What a blessed gospel that is which never disturbs the conscience of the selfish, the bigot, the niggard, or the extortioner! Yonder squire would give up his pew if the stern morality of the bible were brought home to his soul. That curate will never have a living if he boldly proclaim the whole counsel of God, – Mitres rarely have been made to fit the heads of those vulgar men who have so 'reasoned of righteousness, temperance, and judgment to come' as to make Felix tremble.

'Thou shalt not follow a multitude to do evil,' was an ancient prohibition, but modern conventionalism allows you to be ungodly in a company or a public body. Parliament may commit what sins it likes without any fear of reproof from the chaplain or the bishops. The men who says least about religion in the senate are

---

1 Charles II (1630–85), King of England, Scotland and Ireland 1660–85.
2 George IV (1762–1830), King of Great Britain and Ireland, 1820–30.
3 Isaiah 5: 23.
4 Judges 1: 16.

the lords spiritual. Some have thought they act thus because they fear to cast their pearls before swine. But surely they ought not to forget that all the temporal lords have been made by baptism 'members of Christ, children of God, and inheritors of the kingdom of heaven,' and therefore ought to be willing to suffer the word of reproof or exhortation: and, besides to deem these 'children of God' swine, is not very complimentary either to the men themselves or the church that regenerated them. But be that as it may, the morality of the gospel is rarely brought to bear upon companies or legislative assemblies. 'To frame iniquity by law,' is one of the commonest acts of senatorial justice. And then all these things must be passed by without notice or reproof. The ministers of religion must be dumb, the professors of christianity must not open their mouths because that would interfere with the sacred duties of the priesthood, and thus vice in our day can live unscathed. Formalism can atone for it, or the righteousness of the Saviour may cloak it, or rank and wealth render it respectable, or public bodies and senatorial authority can change it into a virtue. What would be gross injustice in a clown or a single individual, becomes reputable in a squire, and the climax of rectitude in a body of legislators.

People profess to wonder how it is that the world is so wicked, if christianity is so good; but there is no mystery in the affair. What, if nothing was done to root up the noisome weeds on an estate, would any one be surprised to find 'thistles growing instead of wheat and cockle instead of barley?' The gospel is a *radical religion*, it condemns iniquity every where, in every one, and every thing; but then this *radicalism* is not practised and in thousands of places of worship is never preached, and as a consequence 'iniquity abounds and the love of many waxes cold.' Bring the gospel to bear upon the church and the state, upon individual and senatorial ungodliness, and you would immediately have the millennium. All the ancient patriarchs, prophets, apostles, and martyrs were perfect radicals. These men spared nothing that was unjust or unholy. Noah, though he stood alone, was a radical before the flood; and his radicalism saved him, and, had the world listened to him, the deluge would have been spared. The radical preaching of Lot, if attended to, would have saved Sodom and Gommorah. Job was 'perfect and upright, he feared God and *eschewed* evil;'[1] and his defence to his friends, in which he fully avows his principles, shows that he was a consummate radical. He was especially the advocate of popular rights and justice to the poor. – See Job xxix, xxx, xxxi. What could be more radical than the laws of Moses? Not a single act of iniquity or injustice but was condemned in the most severe terms. It was announced to the Jews again and again, that their neglect of the poor would be their ruin; and these threatenings were afterwards fulfilled to the very letter. Samuel was a perfect radical: and the Psalms of David show that the royal son of Jesse was deeply imbued with this selfsame spirit. His prayer for Solomon, in the 72nd Psalm, is the finest specimen of radicalism that has ever been uttered. What shall we say of Elijah, Elisha, and Micaiah? If these men had been obeyed, every evil which oppressed the people would have been eradicated: so fully did they

---

1 Job 1: 1.

blend religion and politics. We have reason to believe that these old fashioned seers thought that one great object of religion was to purify politics and render them equitable and beneficent. The prophesy of Isaiah is full of all sorts of social, ecclesiastical, and spiritual radicalism. Jeremiah was divinely educated from a boy to be a radical. The commission which he received from heaven reads thus – 'And Jehovah said unto me, behold I have put my words in thy mouth, see, I have this day set thee over the nations and over the kingdoms, to *root out* and to *pull down*, and to *destroy* and to *throw down*, to *build* and to *plant*.' Here was a mere child trained in politics from his cradle, baptized by the spirit of God to be a radical reformer, and appointed by the King of kings to take society to pieces, to eradicate its vices and construct it afresh: and what may seem more marvellous still, we do not find that his politics at all injured his spirituality. Ezekiel and Daniel are so full of politics and radical reform that many preachers take the liberty of reproving them by misinterpreting and spiritualizing them. The glorious truth that real evangelicalism is perfect radicalism, is not as yet, very extensively understood. The books of the twelve minor prophets might be printed alone and would form a body of the most complete radical tracts that ever issued from the press. I need not add that the grand object of the birth, life, miracles, preaching, death, resurrection, ascension, and intercession of the Son of God, was the perfect radical renovation, reformation, and consequent salvation of the whole world. He is so bold a reformer and his language concerning tyrants, oppressors, and ecclesiastical formalists and hypocrites, is so awful, that many of his modern professed followers cannot agree with him. Their hyper-spirituality prevents them from interpretating or quoting his words. The last sermon I preached before I went to college was from the text 'ye serpents, ye generation of vipers how can ye escape the damnation of hell,' but you may be sure that I was sorely rebuked for taking so uncomfortable a text. Read the Acts of the Apostles, the Epistles and Revelations, and what have we but personal, social, political, ecclesiastical, and spiritual radicalism from beginning to end? The Apostles threatened to turn the world upside down. Their radical doctrines spread consternation among priests, philosophers, kings, captains, and in fact among every body and every thing. These men let nothing that was wrong, or unjust, or unkind, or unholy alone: Poor Demetrius was not the only *craftsman* whose *craft* was endangered; priest craft, king craft, and every other ungodly craft trembled before them.

Such is the brief sketch of the radicalism of the bible. It condemns every thing that is injurious to the temporal and spiritual welfare of mankind, and commands us on the authority of the God of heaven to seek its complete and entire eradication; and should we disobey, our salvation is periled. Heaven never unbars its gates to any monarch, bishop, priest, presbyter, dissenter or private christian who is not a radical reformer. Radicalism, then, is an essential doctrine of the gospel, and he who is ignorant of this fact has 'need to be taught which be the first principles of the oracles of God.' I have not time in this tract to say more, but were space allowed, I would show that there is not an evil in our social or ecclesiastical condition which the scriptures do not condemn and exhort us to eradicate or root out. The millennium is to be the effect of radicalism, and will not come until a perfect radical reformation shall have been achieved by the rational and moral means enjoined and furnished by the Son of God. Remember, that in every great change for the benefit of the world, the people have been the first to receive the truth. The Saviour himself was an operative; the Apostle Paul in these days would have worn a *'fustian jacket,'* several of the prophets were *'smock frocks,'* and those desperate radicals, James, Peter, and John, were Gallilean fishermen. Appeals to the rich respecting radical reform are generally vain. 'Not many wise men, not many mighty, not many noble, are called.' 'How hardly shall a rich man enter into the kingdom of God.' 'God hath chosen the foolish things of the world to confound the wise, and God hath chosen the weak things of the world to confound the mighty, and base things of the world, and things which are despised, hath God chosen; yea, and things which are not, to bring to naught things which are, that no flesh should glory in his presence.'[1] In all ages the Fustian Jackets and Smock Frocks have been the most efficient radical reformers, and therefore the most enlightened and practical gospellers; and our own day tells us that we must look to the working men and working women for the emancipation and salvation of the world.

---

1 1 Corinthians 1: 29.

TRACTS FOR THE FUSTIAN JACKETS AND SMOCK FROCKS.

'THE CHIEF OF THE SLAUGHTER-MEN'
AND
OUR NATIONAL DEFENCES.
BY THE
REV. B. PARSONS,
OF EBLEY.

> 'Put again thy knife into its place,
> For all that use the knife
> Shall perish with the knife.' MATT. xxvi. 52.

Going through the book of Daniel a little time ago, with my bible class, I was struck with the plain and expressive terms used in the fourteenth verse of the second chapter, to designate a military officer. A person is there introduced whom our translators have called 'the *captain of the king's guard.*' In the margin they tell us that he was '*the chief of the slaughter-men.*' Now this latter rendering is a literal version of the original Chaldee. It is worthy of observation that the very phraseology of the court of Nebuchadnezzar,[1] was employed by the Egyptians as early as the days of Pharaoh; for Potiphar, to whom Joseph was sold, is also termed 'the captain of the guard,' or according to the Hebrew, '*the chief of the slaughter-men,*' see Gen. xxxvii. 36; and xxxix. 1. There is great simplicity and expressiveness in these terms. Soldiers, in the olden time, were deemed '*slaughter-men,*' and consequently those who presided over them were '*chiefs*' of these *slaughter-men.*' We have now a great many grandiloquent names given to the officers of the army and navy, and in such words as majors, colonels, captains, generals, admirals, commanders in chief, &c., &c., men seem to forget that the profession of arms is the profession of blood, and ought always to be so designated. We pay men large salaries, we dress them up like mountebanks or harlequins, we give them fine names, and then imagine there is something really respectable in their occupation, when instead of this, to use the language of one of the heroes of the late Indian war, '*the profession of arms is one of the most damnable occupations under heaven.*' These words the newspapers tell us were used by that gentleman in a speech at

---

1 Nebuchadnezzar (b. 530 BC), King of Babylon.

a dinner given to celebrate his victories. We are glad to find a soldier thus speaking out and only regret that any individual who calls himself a christian should continue to follow a trade which is not only worthy of execration in this world, but will most assuredly be visited with tremendous condemnation in the world to come. What person who has the least regard for his eternal interest would be an Alexander,[1] a Cæsar,[2] a Napoleon,[3] or a Nelson[4] at the day of judgment? That excellent man, Bishop Porteus,[5] in his poem on 'Death,' has justly observed, 'One murder makes a villain, Millions, a hero!' His lines on this subject are so just, and withal so unusual as coming from a bishop, that I will give them in full. Speaking of the death of Abel, he says: –

> 'First envy, eldest born of hell, embrued
> Her hands in blood, and taught the sons of men
> To make a death which nature never made,
> And God abborred; with violence rude to break
> The thread of life, ere half its length was run,
> And rob a wretched brother of his being.
> With joy ambition saw and soon improved
> *The execrable deed.* 'Twas not enough
> By subtle fraud to snatch a *single* life!
> Puny impiety! *Whole kingdoms* fell
> To sate the lusts of power: more horrid still
> The foulest stain and scandal of our nature
> *Became its boost! One* murder made a *villain;*
> *Millions, a hero!* Princes were privileged to kill
> And *numbers* sanctified the crime!
> Ah! Why will *kings* forget that they are *men,*
> And *men* that they are *brethren?* Why *delight*
> In *human sacrifice?* Why burst the ties
> Of nature that should knit their souls together
> In one soft bond of amity and love?
> Yet still they *breathe destruction*, still go on
> *Inhumanly ingenuous* to find out
> New pains for life, new terrors for the grave,
> *Artificers of Death!* Still monarchs dream
> Of universal empire growing up
> From universal ruin. *Blast the design*
> *Great God of Hosts*, nor let thy creatures fall
> *Unpitied victims at ambition's shrine!'*

This bishop we are told was one of the most amiable of men, but here his love to his species suggested the strongest terms of condemnation as the mildest words which his benevolence could use to brand the deeds of the warrior. The murder of Abel was an *'execrable deed,'* but he tells us that *'ambition saw it with joy,*

---

1 Alexander the Great (356–323 BC), King of Macedon.
2 Gaius Julius Caesar (100–44 BC), Roman general and dictator.
3 Napoleon Bonaparte (1769–1821), Emperor of France 1804–14, 1814–15.
4 Horatio Nelson (1758–1805), admiral.
5 Beilby Porteus (1731–1808), Bishop of London from 1788.

and improved' upon it. To the hero *one* single death is *'puny impiety,' 'whole kingdoms'* must fall to sate his lust of power. Conquest by means of blood, he asserts to be the *'foulest stain and scandal of our nature.'* He implies that if *'one murder makes a villain'* then he who is the author of a million must be a million times more vile. War he justly designates *'murder,'* and *'princes'* who engage in war are consequently murderers. He intimates that *'kings'* who countenance it, 'forget that they are *men,'* and that all who assist in these *'human sacrifices'* are *'inhumanly ingenious,'* and the *'artificers of death,'* and he solemnly invokes the *'God of Hosts'* to *'blast the designs'* of these desolators of mankind.

Alas! how few ministers of religion have sympathized with this prelate in these just, humane and scriptural feelings. The churches of Christendom have still a great relish for slaughter. Read the following extract from the speech of the bishop of Winchester on consecrating colours which were presented to the 49th regiment in 1844. This prelate, it should be remarked, is said to be highly *evangelical*, and to have supplicated the privilege of making the following observations, after praying for God's blessing on the *colours* which were then given to these *slaughter-men!!! 'I must bid you,'* said he, *'look back to the recollection of those days when you won glory in Holland, Copenhagen, and Quebec, and since in Affghanistan and China. I remember well the stirring phrases used by the great captain of the age, the duke of Wellington,*[1] *when he asked for the thanks of parliament to the army in India. Those were stirring phrases indeed – they were well worth living to hear,* AND WELL WORTH DYING TO DESERVE'!!!

Only think of a minister of peace, who is paid thousands a year to teach men *'to love their enemies,'* uttering this language of blood, extolling the glory of the Copenhagen massacre,[2] and the other sanguinary deeds which sent myriads of souls unprepared into the presence of their Judge! The newspaper, whence we have quoted, tells us that a portion of the glorious deeds at Quebec consisted of a *'Sergeant Frazer stabbing seven Americans to the heart!!!'* Winchester, it would seem, is particularly famed for warlike bishops. Some years ago one of these meek successors of the Apostles actually exhorted all the clergy of his diocese to take up arms. Talk of physical force chartists, why here you have *physical force bishops*; and we may add that these Winchester dignitaries do not stand alone, for when of late, in the House of Lords, have we heard these supposed favorites of the *Prince of peace*, utter one word in deprecation of war? Here you have a body of *'slaughter-men'* told that to have the praises of *'the chief of the slaughter-men'* 'was worth living to hear and worth dying to deserve!!!' Language more befitting the lips of a Vandal was never uttered. According to the creed of this bishop, the Idolaters of India are unfit for the kingdom of heaven, and at death are shut up in endless woe. From that misery his Lordship believes there is no redemption. – 'The worm never dies, the fire is never quenched.' In the late Indian war FIFTY THOUSAND, at least, of these unhappy pagans had their bodies mangled in the battle

1 Arthur Wellesley (1769–1852), first Duke of Wellington, soldier and Tory Prime Minister 1828–30, Foreign Secretary 1834–5.
2 Presumably in reference to Nelson's actions at the battle of Copenhagen, 2 April 1801.

field, and amidst the roar of cannon and the groans of death, their souls were launched into everlasting misery; and a bishop tells the soldiers who took part in this *double* massacre – this slaughter of body and devastation of soul – that to be praised for such a sanguinary act 'was worth living to hear and worth dying to deserve!!!' Hear this ye heavens, ye celestial hierarchies – hear this, ye philanthropists, and ye savages; – hear it ye demons, and learn, to the confusion of all justice, mercy, and humanity, and to the everlasting honour of barbarians and fiends – that the thing worth living for, worth dying for – is to be praised for having unnecessarily and prematurely hurried thousands of immortal souls into the bottomless pit! Tell us not that they were barbarians and our enemies! If bishops and clergymen and British christians had done their duty to these children of the East, every soul of them would have imbibed the pacific principles of the gospel, and instead of warring with us, would have embraced us as their brethren. Not a lance or a cannon ought ever to have been exported from this country to India. One missionary, with the arts of civilization and the gospel of peace would have done more for the salvation of our eastern empire and the wealth and glory of our souls, than an army of forty thousand soldiers or *slaughter-men*; and at the same time have saved millions of treasure and rivers of blood.

Now we want you Fustian Jackets and Smock Frocks to look at things in their own light and call them by their proper names. A soldier is a *slaughter-man* or a butcher, and a commander in chief is the *'head of these slaughter-men.'* The bible says so, and bishops and clergy tell you that what the scriptures assert is true. I have just shown that when humanity and religion are allowed to speak, even a bishop can call war, *'murder;'* soldiers, *'artificers of death;'* and invoke the 'God of Hosts to blast their designs.' Still stronger language was used by bishop Warburton[1] – *'I look'* said he, *'upon war as the blackest mischief ever breathed from hell upon the fair face of creation.'*[2] The learned and eloquent Dr Jortin[3] tells us that war is *'no better than robbery and murder.'*[4] Our illustrious reformer, Wickliffe,[5] exclaims, *'Lord, what honour to a knight that he kills many men? The hangman killeth many more and with a better title. Better were it for men to be butchers of beasts than butchers of their brethren.'*[6] Here you have soldiers called *'butchers,'* not of beasts, but of their own *'brethren,'* and their occupation said to be far more dishonourable than that of the common hangman. In some eastern nations, and especially in China, the military man is actually looked upon as a kind of *'Jack Ketch.'*[7] Lord Brougham,[8] in a speech at Liverpool, branded *'war'* as *'the greatest curse of the human race and the*

---

1 William Warburton (1698–1779), Bishop of Gloucester.

2 See William Warburton, 'The Alliance between Church and State', *Works*, 11 vols (1788), vol. 4, p. 40.

3 John Jortin (1698–1770), ecclesiastical historian.

4 See John Jortin, *Sermons on Different Subjects*, third edition (1787), vol. 7, p. 131.

5 John Wycliffe (*c.* 1320–84), religious reformer.

6 See *Select English Works of John Wyclif*, 3 vols (1869), vol. 3, p. 137.

7 John Ketch (d. 1686), famous executioner.

8 Henry Peter Brougham (1778–1868), first Baron Brougham and Vaux, Lord Chancellor 1830–4.

greatest crime, because it involves every other crime within its execrable name.[1] I need not introduce these authorities to prove to your plain common sense that war is *butchery* – is *slaughter* – is *murder*, on a large and extensive scale; but I have given them to show that though in these degenerate days evangelical ministers can eulogise bloodshed, and it is deemed heresy to advocate the cause of mercy and humanity; yet there have been men who were distinguished for rank and learning, who dared to call the battle field by its appropriate name – aye, and were extolled for doing so. When lord Brougham uttered the passage quoted above, the whole company rose and greeted him with deafening applause. We have the highest authority on earth and in heaven on our side when we designate the soldier as a trained destroyer of his species, and all the leaders of armies nothing more than the chiefs of these human slaughter-men. A common slaughter house is ten thousand thousand times more glorious than the field of battle: in the one, you have *animals* slain to feed mankind, but in the other, you have the *blood of your own brethren* poured out like water; you have this done, not speedily and at once, but under every species of cruelty that even demons could wish; and not merely bodies cut, blown, and trampled to pieces, but you have souls, if the bible is believed, sent unprepared to their eternal home. Language cannot depict, cannot express, the horrors, the cruelties, the eternal consequences of war; and therefore to call soldiers '*butchers*,' and their leaders the '*chiefs of these slaughter-men*,' is to use terms of the softest and mildest import compared with what the magnitude of this execrable vice deserves. We write that you may take up the subject and resolve no more to be the dupes of those who call themselves your superiors, and who ought to set you an example of justice and humanity. They are generally too cautious to expose themselves. The hands that are to perpetrate all this wickedness are drawn from your ranks. The money that is wasted on these chiefs of *slaughter* is taken in a very large proportion from your pockets; and therefore you must arouse yourselves and put a stop to this waste, carnage, and death.

I need not tell you that unless you bestir yourselves no effort will be wanted to perpetuate this inhumanity. You cannot look to the lords to interpose and stay the shedding of blood. Alas! many of them have no small portion of their relatives maintained by this accursed trade in human gore. You cannot look to the ministers of the church to denounce this barbarity. These men are ready to insult heaven and earth by praying that the Father of mercies will miraculously interfere to give courage and cruelty to one body of men to send thousands of his children to the bottomless pit! The church and the army and navy have too long been refuges for destitute paupers who are too proud and too idle to earn their bread in an honourable and humane occupation. You cannot look to squires or members of parliament generally to take up the cause of peace and mercy. Many of these have a vested interest in slaughter, and not a few, when by profitable trade they have risen to affluence, are ashamed of the occupation to which they owe their wealth, and become dealers in commissions, traffickers in carnage, and the sycophants of the prime minister of the day, that their sons may be promoted

---

1 *The Speeches of Henry Lord Brougham*, 4 vols (1838), vol. 3, p. 586.

and roll in luxury purchased by taxes wrung from the hard earnings of peasants and operatives. Aye, and after exacting the last penny from your pockets, have the insolence to look down upon you as a mean and vulgar race. You must then be up and doing and peacefully but firmly oppose these abominations. You must execrate war and denounce its abettors. You yourselves must resolve not to engage in such a vile occupation. You must assemble and protest and petition against being burdened with taxes to support a system of wholesale murder. You have humanity and truth and justice and mercy, and above all the God of mercy, on your side, and therefore if you exert yourselves you must prevail.

You have lately heard of the trick to alarm the country about the supposed insecurity of our national defences, and a hireling press has done its utmost to produce a general panic. An old man, who is near his dotage, if not actually there, and who will soon have to face the spirits of those armies which he assisted in sending unprepared into another world, has attempted as a last effort to awaken the demon of slaughter, and place in hostile array nations which were made to live in love and amity. Wellington and Napoleon will have to meet their troops again and to reckon before an impartial tribunal for the carnage of Waterloo. The French do not want to slaughter us, and there is not one of you that wishes to massacre the French. You cannot find the blood thirsty men among the Fustian Jackets and Smock Frocks of France or England. In the time of Napoleon when such a demand was made on the youths of France to repair the armies of that tyrant, many disabled themselves rather than become the murderers of their species. And those who obeyed the conscription often shed tears of blood at the thought of being thus led forth like beasts to the field of slaughter. Think too of the appliances of false hopes, false glory, maddening liquor, and cruel discipline, that have been resorted to before you could have a race of English peasants and operatives so unmanned and unmanly as to sell themselves for thirteen pence a day to shoot others or be shot. The people, the common people, of all humane countries, deprecate war. In christian nations it requires the sophistry of the schools, the steeled hearts of iron dukes, the craving avarice of a needy aristocracy, the heartless sycophancy of a degenerate gentry, who are aping the vices of reckless ambition, and the hardening influence of an ungodly priesthood, to render men so base as to engage in the destruction of their fellows. The masses are not so deaf to the voice of humanity – and hence in the last war, Dibdin[1] received a large salary from the state to write military songs to inspire the people with false notions and make them thirst for the blood of the French. The drum, the fife, the floating banner, the beer barrel, the press gang, the militia draft, and even the pulpit and an interested body of priests, had to be employed to deceive or paralyse the natural aversion to blood, before the unsophisticated labouring classes of the country could be reconciled to war. The language of Thomas Carlyle,[2] in his 'Sartor Resartus,' is exactly to the point: –

---

1 Thomas John Dibdin (1771–1841), actor and dramatist, whose *The Mouth of the Nile* (1798) honoured Nelson's victory.

2 Thomas Carlyle (1795–1881), Scottish historian and critic.

'What,' says he, 'speaking in unofficial language, is the net import of war? To my knowledge, for example, there dwell and toil in the British village of Dumdrudge some five thousand souls. From these by certain *"natural enemies"* of the French, there are successively selected during the French war, some thirty ablebodied men; Dumdrudge, at her own expence, has suckled and nursed them; she has not without sorrow, fed them up to manhood, and even trained them to crafts, so that one can weave, another build, another hammer, and the weakest can stand under thirty stone avoirdupois. Nevertheless, amidst much weeping and swearing they are selected; dressed in red and shipped away at the public charge, some two thousand miles, or say only to the south of Spain; and fed there until wanted. And now to that same spot in the south of Spain, are thirty similar French artisans from a French Dumdrudge in like manner wending; till at length after infinite effort, the parties come into juxtaposition, and thirty stand fronting thirty, each with a gun in his hand. Straightway the word, *"Fire,"* is given, and they blow the souls out of one another; and instead of sixty brisk, useful craftsmen, the world has sixty dead carcases, which it must bury and anon shed tears for. Had these men any quarrel? Busy as Satan is, *not the smallest*. They lived far enough apart, were the entirest strangers, nay, in so wide a universe, there was even, unconsciously, by commerce, some helpfulness between them. How then? Simpleton, their governors had fallen out; and instead of shooting one another, had the cunning to make the poor blockheads shoot.'[1]

This 'cunning' of designing rulers has been at the bottom of most of the wars that have desolated the earth. The masses have not quarrelled with the masses of other countries, the Fustian Jackets have not thirsted for the blood of their fellows. Vulgar as the Smock Frocks have been, they have not been sunk so far below tigers and wolves as to long for the murder of their species. No, this spirit of carnage has been the genius of courts, the foster child of the schools, and the pulpit lauded angel of the clergy. You had to unmake mankind by ambition, avarice, false education and false religion, before you could bring them delight in pouring out the precious blood of their brethren. An analysis has been made out of 280 principal wars waged, since the days of Constantine, by nations calling themselves christians, and the following is the result: '44 wars of ambition to obtain extent of territory; 32 wars to plunder; 24 wars of retaliation and revenge; 8 wars to question some question of honour or prerogative; 6 wars arising from disputed claims to some territory; 41 wars arising from disputed titles to crowns; 30 wars commenced under the pretext of helping an ally; 23 wars originating in jealousy of rival greatness; 5 wars which have grown out of commerce; 55 civil wars; 28 wars on account of religion.' In these encounters, the principal agents and abettors have been princes and educated aristocrats or gentlemen. The people never fly to arms unless goaded by injustice, and even then would have settled the matter amicably, if their superiors had not laboured so hard to imbue them with a recklessness of life.

---

1 Thomas Carlyle, *Sartor Resartus* (1901), p. 140.

Thousands of millions of the human family have been slain in war, and yet the masses have had no interest in these contests; their chief part has been to furnish the treasure and the blood, hence the poet has justly said,

'War is a game which, were their subjects wise,
Kings would not play at.'[1]

The world is waiting for the *fiat* of the Fustian Jackets and Smock Frocks to put an end to these desolations. And of all beings on earth you are the most interested in peace. A French writer has calculated that during the last four thousand years *'Six thousand, eight hundred and sixty millions'* of the human family have been slaughtered and destroyed by war. His calculation runs thus,

	Millions.
Killed in battle	980
Severely wounded	2,940
Famine and suffering	2,940
	6,860 Millions

This would give an average of above one million and a half annually sent prematurely and unprepared to their final account. Every soul that falls fighting goes to the presence of its Judge stained with blood, and therefore hardly fit for an empire of purity and love. The majority of these, be it remembered have been the working classes, and this tremendous sacrifice of body and spirit is one of the boons which the people owe to an ambitious and heartless aristocracy. Dr Dick[2] tells us that the persons slain in war, would be sufficient, if they held hand by hand at arms length, to encircle the globe upwards of *six hundred times*.[3] It has been said that the wealth wasted in wars, would purchase every foot of land upon the globe, would clothe every man, woman and child in an attire that kings and queens might be proud of, would build schools, academies, colleges, and temples for the whole world and supply them all with well paid teachers, professors, and ministers of religion. In a word, would drive poverty, wretchedness, ignorance, vice, and irreligion from the earth and after giving mankind the millennium, would have millions upon millions of treasure in hand.

But I must not conclude this tract without one word about our National Defences, you are told: −

I. − That our country is insecure. But if so, what becomes of the enormous sums we spend from year to year? We are taxed for war to the amount of nearly *twenty millions of pounds* annually, and yet we are said to be the most defenceless people upon the face of the earth!! If so, then there must be a deal of bad management. We are spending more in war than any other people on the globe. Look at the four great powers of Europe. The annual military expenditure of Austria is not *seven millions*, of Prussia not *four millions*, of France about *thirteen millions*, while the whole revenue of Russia does not yield enough to pay our war expences. We

---

1 William Cowper, *The Task*, v. 187.
2 Thomas Dick (1774–1857), scientific writer.
3 See Thomas Dick, *The Christian Philosopher*, eighth edition (1842).

have also been increasing our hostile apparatus for years at a most extravagant rate. The cost of army, navy and ordnance in 1792, was *four millions*, in 1836, *twelve millions*, in 1846, upwards of *sixteen millions*! In 13 years we have spent upwards of ONE HUNDRED AND NINETY FIVE MILLIONS OF POUNDS on warriors and the apparatus of war, and now are told that we are perfectly defenceless!! Where is the money gone? But a precious little of it comes into the hands of the common soldiers. These poor fellows have sold body, soul, liberty, and all that is dear to humanity for a most pitiable price. So small indeed, that the farmer or manufacturer who demanded such sacrifices for such wages would be called after through the street. Surely we ought to enquire who pockets the money? Nearly twenty millions annually spent and the country defenceless shows that there is extravagance, waste, or plunder going on somewhere. Why if we believe the duke's letter, we are not so safe as we were when we had no stand-ing army, so that all our money is worse than thrown away. What a proof that there are other leeches, beside the horse-leech that continually cry 'Give, Give.' In thirteen years, taken at random from the last twenty, the civil government has cost us TWENTY MILLIONS; the justice department FIFTEEN MILLIONS, during the same period, the presidents of our war establishment have spent nearly TWO HUNDRED MILLIONS of our money and yet we are now per-fectly defenceless. We defy avarice or impudence to find a parallel to this barefaced extravagance, insolence, and audacity.

II. – You are told that the French are likely to invade us. This is an insult and a libel on France and Frenchmen. It is calling them a nation of unprincipled, bloodthirsty villains. If I tell my neighbour next door, that I believe him to be a thief and a murderer, and therefore begin to build fortifications round my house, to plant cannon and police, to line my doors and shutters with iron, to double my locks and bars and bolts, and when I go out arm myself with a sword and a pistol, what do I do by all this but insult him to the utmost and proclaim to the world that he is one of the most execrable monsters in a human form? Would any one wonder if one day I was shot for my impudence and folly? Now what is this duke's letter but the most aggravating piece of hostility that ever was offered to the people of any nation? Hundreds of wars have been waged for trivial provoca-tions compared with this most unprovoked insult. The French people do not want to plunder or slay us. They would rather meet us in the market than in another Waterloo. None but coffin makers, undertakers, sextons, and resurrec-tion men, prefer dead customers. I was once at a funeral, and when the undertaker entered, a gentleman who sat next me said, that fellow is one of the most marvellous beings in the world, for the other day he came to me and bow-ing very low, said, 'Sir, I had the pleasure of burying your grandfather, and I had the pleasure of burying your father, and I hope I shall have the pleasure of bury-ing you!' Now this simpleton was too much of a simon to perceive that in burying this gentleman he would commit to the grave one of his best customers. The French, however, are not so moon stricken, they are neither sextons, poor curates, parish clerks, coffin makers, undertakers nor resurrection men, and would far rather deal with us alive than dead.

III. – Supposing we are defenceless, what dreaming old woman in pantaloons would run about and tell every one of it? If I tell my neighbour he is a great thief and a foul bloodthirsty miscreant, and then at the same time inform him that all my friends and property are without the least protection, what would any one say, but that first I insulted him and then invited him to come and murder my children and plunder my house? This is just what we are at present doing to the French. We tell them that they have neither honour, honesty, nor humanity, and then we assure them that our whole country is at their mercy. We believe that if any commander in chief, in any age, except in this degenerate one, had thus exposed our own nation and insulted another, that his name would not have remained twenty four hours among the servants of the crown.

It may be asked, how is it that this insolence and folly is allowed to pass with so little reprobation? The answer is not difficult. *The Naval and Military Gazette has let the cat out of the bag.* This *Mark Lane Express* of the military traders tells us, *'that increasing the regular army as well as establishing an army of reserve, will no doubt give a certain amount of promotion and employment to many who now are nearly without hope or languishing on half pay.'* In connection with this you must remember that we have *'one hundred and forty'* members in the House of Commons who are directly interested in war, and perhaps twice as many more who, though not military officers themselves, have relatives who are. And then in the house of Lords you have *one hundred and eighteen* naval and military men, and hardly a nobleman in the country who has not some of his kindred receiving pay for his profession as a *slaughter-man*. In France matters are no better, there you have hosts of the upper classes, as they call themselves, living on the taxes raised for war. For a while then the insult will be pocketed, but by and bye, there will be a Dumdrudge diversion, and to make a show that these increased preparations were necessary, a war will be hatched, ten thousand of the best blood of England will be called out to shoot and mangle ten thousand of the best blood of France, and when enough have been launched into eternity to satisfy the lookers on; the men who expect promotions, enlarged pay and pensions, will mutually march up to their knees in gore, and shake hands, the clergy will sing 'Te Deums' over this murderous scene, and the countries on both sides will have the blessing of peace, of an increased standing army and heavier taxation! The men languishing without hope, the pauper gentry and nobility will thus be provided for and the people again ground to the dust. The present panic is very opportune, seeing the corn laws are abolished, and the privilege of taxing your bread is gone. To make up for this loss a desperate effort is made to regain the whole in the form of military pay and pensions. Every thing is now done to increase government offices, commissioners and hangers on. The State Education scheme has this at heart. The reports of the commissioners, especially in Wales, are the most shameless one sided pieces of misrepresentation that perhaps ever saw the light, all having one object in view, the increase of government influence, the support of placemen, and the degradation of the masses. Wellington has received upwards of *two millions and a half of our money* for his services! Other men, his compeers in the trade of slaughter have not been left penniless, and, in taking such large sums have impeached their patriotism and morality. Indeed it could easily be shown that the war spirit and true patriotism are utterly incompatible. He who delights in bloodshed cannot be a patriot. Nations have never gained any thing by war. All said to be effected, might have been obtained far easier without shedding one drop of blood. *Seventeen and sixpence* out of every *pound* we pay in taxes is levied for our past or present military and naval expenditure. View it however you will, war is a loss. It is hateful to God, and the direst curse of man, and must be abolished. Again we say, that to accomplish this glorious object, our chief hope is in the Fustian Jackets and Smock Frocks. You must meet and protest against this crafty stratagem to induce you and the French to tax yourselves and shed each others blood. Let your brethren in France know that you possess a christian spirit, and have no sympathy with the slaughter-men of another order. Train your sons and daughters to abominate war, and if the clergy will not do their duty then become preachers yourselves, and show the gentry and nobility that, of all occupations, bloodshed is the lowest, the most unmanly, dishonourable, and accursed. If they have pauper sons, let them spin, weave, and dig, collect old bottles or old rags, become porters or scavengers, but never sink so low as to be slaughter-men or subsist on taxes wrung from the hard earnings of peasants and operatives. – Or if they *will* fight, then let them be manly enough to shoot one another, but not be so base as to sacrifice useful artisans, to glut their vengeance, feed their avarice, or gratify the most execrable ambition.

Let me entreat the Fustian Jackets and Smock Frocks, as the strength, the glory, and wealth of the country – as the chief tax-payers – as the men whose blood is soon to be called for – as the women who are to be made childless, brotherless, and widows – to lift your voices against these abominations. Ambition, like a vampire, has for ages been fattening itself on your blood. It is now more thirsty than ever, and unless you arise, will bring your country to utter ruin. Make yourselves acquainted with these facts; call public meetings; expose the injustice, the cruelty, and the avarice, of war, and let the government and the world know that you are the SONS AND DAUGHTERS OF PEACE; and that if the French or Dutch are to be shot, the work of plunder and blood shall be executed and paid for by the gentry and aristocracy. As the slaughter field is so glorious, then let the squires, the clergy, and the nobility enjoy the whole of its glory. If you make a proper use of this crafty alarm you can give the war spirit of the country and the world a deeper wound than it ever yet received. Remember, *Cobden* and *Bright* and *George Thompson*[1] are again in the field waiting once more to lead you on to a certain and bloodless victory.

---

1 George Thompson (1804–78), anti-slavery advocate.

No. 7.

TRACTS FOR THE FUSTIAN JACKETS AND SMOCK FROCKS.

THE KNIFE AND NOT THE SWORD, OR CIVILIZATION VERSUS WAR & DESOLATION, A FEW WORDS ON OUR LORD'S COMMAND 'TO BUY A SWORD.' LUKE xxii. 35. BY THE REV. B. PARSONS, OF EBLEY.

'And he said unto them, "When I sent you forth without purse, or scrip or shoes, lacked ye anything?" And they said, "Nothing." Then said he unto them, "But now he that hath a purse, let him take it, and likewise the scrip, and he that hath no sword, let him sell his garment and buy one; for I say unto you that this that is written must yet be accomplished in me; and he was reckoned among the transgressors, for the things concerning me have an end." And they said, "Lord, behold here are two swords," and he said unto them, "It is enough."'

Among thousands of errors that might be mentioned, none has been more prevalent than the belief that christians have divine authority for engaging in war. Because there are instances mentioned in the bible in which God commanded his enemies to be destroyed by the sword, many have supposed that *without any command or authority from the Most High*, war might be waged and countries desolated. In the former example we have *divine justice* directing the execution of criminals, in the later we have *human revenge*, in spite of God's command to forgive and bless our enemies, sheathing its sword in the heart of a brother. God has said 'vengeance is mine,' intimating that it is his prerogative and that no one except himself shall exercise this awful attribute with impunity, and yet impious men, often on the most trivial occasions, arrogate to themselves the right of most unmercifully and barbarously destroying their fellow immortals. How slow have professing christians been to imitate the mercy and benevolence of the Creator, and yet how anxious many have been to wield the weapons of his wrath!

The text at the head of these remarks is frequently quoted by those who delight in war as a proof that the Saviour approved of the use of warlike weapons. The following observations are intended to show that the Son of God had no reference whatever to offensive or defensive arms, and that he merely commanded his disciples to furnish themselves with the common necessaries of life.

I. – The Greek word '*machaira*,' rendered '*sword*,' means an iron or metal implement with an edge. In Hebrew, '*kara* or *chara*,' signifies '*to cut*,' and as the Jews were accustomed to prefix an *m* to some of their roots to form them into nouns, the term '*machaira*,' comes very naturally from '*ma-chara*,' a *cutting instrument* or *edge tool*. Now history allows us to say that when cutting instruments were first invented the same edge tool was used for cutting food, for cutting and carving wood, &c., for sacrificing, and for wounding or slaying enemies. The distinction between knife and sword therefore did not at first exist. When art was sufficiently advanced to make every description of cutting implement, so that there might be an edge-tool for every particular use, then a variety of names would of course be adopted, but until this was the case, the name '*machaira*,' edge-tool or cutting instrument, would be deemed sufficiently definite as the appellation of a knife or sword. In our day the term sword has in most cases a definite signification: but the Greek word '*machaira*,' which our Lord used, and which our translators have rendered '*sword*,' was not thus limited. If we examine the lexicons we shall find '*machaira*' interpreted by the terms '*an instrument to fight with*,' '*a sword*,' 'a cleaver, chopper, or carving knife,' 'a sabre,' 'a scymitar,' '*a knife*,' *a razor*,' 'a sword of justice.' That '*machaira*' sometimes signifies a knife, will be evident from the following quotations taken from Herodotus[1] and Homer.[2] Speaking of the superstitious regard which the Egyptians paid to animals, the former says that they would not use a Grecian knife, &c., because the Grecians were considered unclean, especially so, as they paid so little deference to the beasts which the Egyptians had deified.' His words, book ii. chap. 41, are, 'Therefore no Egyptian, neither man nor woman, use the *knife*, spit, or caldron of a Grecian, nor taste even consecrated flesh if it has been cut with a Grecian *knife*.' Here we have the term '*machaira*' used twice, and in each place it refers to a *knife* rather than to a sword. Homer shows that at an early period the '*machaira* or *knife*' was distinguished from the sword. In the 270th line of the third book of the Iliad, he says, 'Then Atreides with his hands drew his *knife*, (machaira) which always hung near the large sheath of his sword, and cut the hairs from the heads of the lambs.' This quotation intimates that the knife was carried in a sheath as well as the sword, and that both were suspended from the belt of Agamemnon.[3]

In the book of Genesis, chap. xxii. 6 and 10, Abraham is said to have taken a knife. The Hebrew word which the sacred historian employs is '*makeleth*,' it is derived from the root '*akal*,' food, and means a provision or sacrificing knife. Now it should be observed that in each of these verses the Greek translators of the Bible have used the same word, '*machaira*,' which was employed by our Lord in the text we are examining.

---

1 Herodotous (*c.* 484–424 BC), Greek historian.
2 Homer (*fl. c.* 1000 BC), Greek epic poet.
3 Agamemnon, King of Mycenae and Argos during the Trojan Wars.

In the days of our Lord, knives and forks were not at all common; indeed forks are supposed to be of very recent origin, and there is reason to believe that at that period clasp knives were little known, and therefore not only the sword but the knife was carried in a *sheath*. Hence Agamemnon drew his knife from its sheath, and Peter also drew his knife and cut off the ear of the servant of the high priest. Cutlers in those days were comparatively few, and cutlery was by no means common, nor was it customary to have pockets in the loose garments of those countries, the knife therefore was carried in a sheath and suspended from the girdle. It was then usual for the head of the family to carve with the knife which he carried at his side. In many cases he was the only one at the table that had a knife, the rest of the company were entirely dependant upon their fingers and their teeth. This state of things made it expedient that the washing of the hands before meat should be attended to not merely as a religious ceremony but also as a matter of cleanliness. Modern travellers inform us that in different eastern countries at the present time, the carver is the only person at the table who uses a knife, and that the guests for the most part use their fingers. The term '*machaira*' is not the only name of a cutting instrument which has a generic signification. The Latin word 'culter' stands not only for the coulter of a plough, but also for a knife and a razor. Our Saxon term knife was formerly a generic rather than a specific appellation and very frequently was used for a sword. Chaucer[1] says,

> 'Myne handes been not shapen for a KNIFE
> As for reven no man of his life.'

Spenser,[2] Shakspere,[3] Fletcher,[4] Dryden,[5] and other of our poets often employ the word knife to express a sword, or dagger, or some other instrument of destruction. Indeed it is far from unusual for barbarous or half civilized nations to have their knives so constructed that they may use them either at their meals or to deprive their enemies of life.

II. – Having thus shown that the word, '*machaira*,' was the name of a '*knife*' as well as of a '*sword*,' we must now turn to the verses in question and endeavour to learn from the scope of our Lord's directions which of these instruments he desired his disciples to procure. Nearly all words taken separately were ambiguous, and therefore the context, not the lexicon or dictionary, must settle the meaning. An extensive knowledge of authors and of lexicons would show us the various significations which the same word may bear in different writers, hence if we would settle the exact sense in which any term is to be understood we must carefully examine the sentence in which it is used, the other sentences with which it is connected, and the intention of the writer or speaker in employing it. Let us apply these rules to the word in question and most persons will perceive that our Lord did not command his disciples to buy swords.

---

1 Geoffrey Chaucer (*c.* 1340–1400), poet.
2 Edmund Spenser (*c.* 1552–99), poet.
3 William Shakespeare (1564–1616), dramatist and poet.
4 John Fletcher (1579–1625), dramatist.
5 John Dryden (1631–1700), poet.

I. – The number of the disciples and the number of '*cutting instruments*' which the Saviour said was '*enough*,' prove most satisfactorily that he did not refer to offensive or defensive arms. As soon as he had given his directions respecting purse, scrip, and knife one of the disciples said, '*Lord, behold here are two knives,*' and he said unto them, 'It is enough.' Now it should be remembered that they were twelve men, and if he had intended to make warriors of them, instead of saying, 'two swords are enough,' he would rather have exclaimed, 'two swords are surely not enough for twelve soldiers, by all means sell your coats and buy ten more.' *Twelve* men with only *two* weapons would be but poorly equipped for the battle-field, for at best they could only fight two at a time! On the face of the text therefore we see that the Saviour did not refer to implements of destruction. But supposing that the Lord Jesus wished the apostles to furnish themselves with the necessaries of civilized life, then as long as the disciples remained together, two knives would be sufficient, and when they might be scattered from each other, common foresight and common decency would suggest that each one should supply himself with so valuable an instrument. It is evident that the disciples understood the words in this sense. For instead of saying, 'master, we have but two swords for twelve of us!' their language intimates that they thought themselves well supplied in that they had *two knives*, seeing for so small a family as they were one knife would have been quite enough. At the passover for which they were preparing, only *one* knife would be requisite to kill and to carve the paschal lamb, so that in their two knives, they had one more than would be necessary at the feast.

II. – Our Lord is here contrasting the hospitality with which they were received in their last mission, with the unkindness which they would have to encounter in their future labours in spreading the gospel. 'When,' said he, 'I sent you forth without purse, or scrip, or shoes, lacked ye anything?' and they said 'nothing.' In a former mission when he sent them forth, he commanded them to take neither 'purse nor scrip, nor two coats, nor shoes, nor staves.' They attended to his injunction and found all their wants amply supplied without any foresight or providence of their own, but then their ministry had been confined to their own countrymen, for they were prohibited from going into the way of the gentiles, and from entering any city of the Samaritans; – they were to seek 'the lost sheep of the house of Israel.' Now hospitality to a stranger and especially to a prophet or religious teacher, was a well known characteristic of the Jews. It would therefore have been a reflection on their countrymen for these early preachers to have cumbered themselves with a purse, a knapsack, or any provision for their journey. They went forth without any of these things, and when they returned, they could say, we have lacked 'nothing.' But there was a fear that the faith which this successful mission had inspired might produce presumption and lead to indolence and improvidence, and as they had little knowledge of the world, and of the manners and customs of other nations or the hostility that the gospel would provoke, they were in danger of concluding that all other lands were like their own and that economy and providence would always be unnecessary to a disciple of Christ; most effectually therefore to remove such an impression from their minds, he here contrasts their former reception with what they had to expect in future. 'When I sent you forth,' said he, 'without purse or scrip or shoes, lacked ye anything?' And they said, 'nothing.' Then said he unto them, but now he that hath a purse let him take it, and likewise his scrip, and he that hath no knife, let him sell his garment and buy one.' Every one must perceive that these instructions are placed in exact contrast with those of their previous commission. In their former journey they were exhorted to make no provision, but now they were to supply themselves with every necessary. They were to take 'a purse,' or money bag. Pockets were then, for the most part, unknown, and the purse was generally fastened to the girdle. Judas carried the bag or purse for our Lord and the Apostles. The '*scrip*' was a provision bag, a kind of wallet or knapsack, in which the traveller deposited his food, clothes &c. The knife also was a useful article, and far more valuable than a sword. It is one of the most important badges of civilization. To refine the iron from the ore and then form it into a cutting utensil, places the civilized man at an immense distance above the savage. Hence all rude nations set a high value upon an iron instrument with an edge. The barbarian must use a flint, or a piece of hard wood, or else his fingers and his teeth, but the man who comes from a civilized country has his knife. Without iron, without edge-tools made of iron, the world could not be reclaimed from barbarism. Hence without an age of *iron*, there could be no *golden* age, a knife therefore might be adopted as the appropriate emblem of arts and refinement.

III. – Our Lord was about to send his disciples to all nations, but he did not wish them to go forth as paupers and mendicants, and therefore he commands them, to take both a money bag and knapsack. He did not wish that they should tear their food to pieces like tigers or savages, with their fingers and their teeth, and consequently he tells them by all means to furnish themselves with a knife. He lays great stress upon this injunction, 'He that hath not a knife let him sell his garment and buy one.' He here uses a common phrase employed then as well as now, when importance is attached to the possession of any article. We say, a man ought to sell his coat or his shirt rather than be without such and such books or utensils. Maimonides,[1] a Jewish Rabbi, has a similar expression. If we consider that knives at that time were scarce and very dear we shall probably see that between the price of a good knife in a sheath and that of a garment there was not so great a difference as at the present day. Iron has two uses. In the form of a useful instrument with an edge, it can do much towards advancing the savage to the highest degree of civilization: in the form of a sword, it can reduce civilized man to a savage. The knife is an emblem of refinement, the sword is the ensign of desolation and death. Now we ask any considerate person to reflect on the character of our Lord and his gospel, and then to decide whether the Prince of Peace commanded his disciples to furnish themselves with the weapons of death, or, with the useful implements of domestic comfort and the arts? We are persuaded that there can be but one conclusion, namely, that Jesus Christ wished the apostles to be honest, provident, respectable men, and in that character to appear among all

---

1 Moses Ben Maimon (1135–1204), Jewish philosopher.

nations and publish his gospel. But this they could not be unless they made proper provision for their missionary enterprise, and the purse, the knapsack, and the knife, were the most appropriate emblems of this preparation that could have been selected.

IV. – His instructions at other times show he did not command his disciples to furnish themselves with warlike weapons. When 'Peter drew his knife and cut off the ear of the servant of the high priest,' the Saviour rebuked him, and said, 'put up again thy knife into its place, for all who take the knife shall perish with the knife.' The context here sufficiently proves that the Lord Jesus refers to taking the knife as an offensive or defensive weapon. Knives were often used by the ancients in this manner, and when we consider that the same term in Greek stands both for a knife and a sword, there was a play upon the word '*Machaira*,' (cutting instrument) which at first sight is not apparent to an English reader. To show most emphatically that he did not intend that real swords should be drawn in his defence, the Saviour, in rebuking Peter, adds 'thinkest thou that I cannot now pray to my Father, and he shall instantly give me more than twelve legions of angels.' Instead of encouraging his disciples to arm themselves or use any weapons of defence, he commanded them to offer no resistance to their enemies. They were never to avenge themselves. They were 'to bless them that cursed them, and pray for those who despitefully used them and persecuted them.'[1] 'If smitten on the one cheek they were to turn the other also.'[2] They were 'to agree with their adversaries speedily.'[3] They were not to offer a gift or prayer without first forgiving their foes. After this manner they were to pray, 'forgive us our trespasses as we also forgive them that trespass against us,'[4] thus making their own exercise of mercy a pattern for the God of mercy to follow. Generally we are called upon to imitate God, but in praying for forgiveness we are to call upon Jehovah to imitate us. Christ forbade his apostles to avenge themselves. He told them to 'love their enemies' and thus prove that they were 'the children of the Highest who maketh his sun to rise on the evil and the good, and sendeth rain on the just, and the unjust.' In being *merciful* as their Father in heaven was *merciful*, they were to prove that they were '*perfect* even as their Father in heaven was *perfect*,' plainly teaching us that mercy to enemies is the greatest proof of moral perfection that any rational being can give.

In accordance with these sentiments, the scriptures, both in the old and new testament, give the command, 'if thine enemy hunger, feed him, and if he thirst, give him drink.'[5] We are also told that unless we feel and practice that love which beareth all things, we are nothing. But how any human being can show that he loves God, and loves his neighbour as himself, at the same time that he carries a sword for the purpose of destroying his enemies, is a problem too absurd to be

1 Luke 6: 28.
2 Luke 6: 29.
3 Matthew 5: 25.
4 See, e.g., Mark 11: 25–6.
5 Romans 12: 20.

mentioned. How strange then it would have been, if the religion of Jesus had in one breath commanded us to exercise universal love and in the next, exhorted us to sell our garments that we may buy swords and destroy our enemies! How inconsistent to arm us with the weapons of vengeance and yet tell us, on pain of everlasting misery, that we must forgive our enemies and never in any wise avenge ourselves. The word of God cannot be charged with such contradictions, nor, in the text under consideration, is it probable that the Saviour had the least reference to a sword. He merely directed his disciples to be provident and prepare themselves with every thing necessary for the missionary enterprize in which they were about to engage.

V. – That the apostles did not think our Lord referred to a sword is further evident from the fact that we never read that they armed themselves with warlike weapons. Peter it is true 'drew his knife and cut off the ear of Malchus,'[1] but we have no reason to believe that what our translators have called a *sword* was anything more than a common *knife*, which fishermen and others were in the habit of carrying in a sheath suspended from their girdles. The apostle Paul says that 'a bishop should be no striker,' and we never read that either himself or any of his brother apostles showed any disposition to violate that heavenly injunction. But if Christ really did mean that the disciples should carry swords, why then their not doing so was a gross violation of the command of their master. 'Let him sell his garment and buy a knife,' is a precept uttered by the same authority that gave the ten commandments, and if the apostles paid no attention to it, they were rebels against God, and consequently not the disciples of Christ after all. If the Saviour intended that his followers should carry arms, and his words were understood in this sense, it is rather strange that we do not read more about these carnal weapons in the Acts of the Apostles, and the Epistles. The primitive church ought to have been a large repository of swords and spears. Every convert to christianity ought to have been furnished with an implement of destruction, and large revenues should have been exacted from believers to supply the whole body of the faithful with these deadly weapons. But instead of this, Paul tells us that, 'the weapons of their warfare were not *carnal*.' He commanded the Romans 'to overcome evil with good,' and the context proves that he did not mean a good broad sword, but forgiveness and kindness. Christ's words were 'I say unto you that ye resist not evil, and when they persecute you in one city flee unto another.'[2] Wars were fast bringing the world back again to barbarism. There was no need of a teacher from heaven to encourage mankind to buy swords. They were already quite pugnacious enough, and no religion which encouraged the shedding of blood could have deserved the name of '*gospel*,' or 'glad tidings.' No nation or people have ever as yet been heard to exclaim 'how beautiful upon the mountains' are the feet of warriors threatening desolation and death to their foes: but 'peace on earth and good will toward men' have always been grateful. 'How beautiful upon the mountains are the feet of him that bringeth good tidings, that

---

1 John 18: 10.
2 Matthew 10: 23.

publisheth peace,[1] is a sentence that finds a response in every human heart. Now the apostles were charged with this message, and never dreamt that they were to impeach their pacific embassy by carrying swords or staves. They never resisted their persecutors. They neither wounded nor slew their foes. We never read of any man, whether robber, assassin, or persecutor, being slain by the apostles. Like their divine master they came 'to save men's lives and not to destroy them.'[2] Hence, if persecuted in one city they fled to another. They had courage to run away, and were willing to bear the obloquy of so doing. If they had drawn swords against every adversary their mission of mercy had been a mission of blood, and soon would have terminated, for 'he that killeth with the sword must be killed by the sword.'[3] 'Here was the patience and faith of the saints;'[4] – they used nothing but moral force. They warred with error and wickedness, and the only suitable weapon was persuasion. They delivered their message of peace and then hasted to another city, that they might proclaim it there also. Had they stopped to fight with swords they would soon have been killed and their embassy had been ended, and their consistency been a laughing stock. It may suit modern folly to offer men *bayonets* or civilization – *bullets* or the gospel, but both sacred and profane history alike testify that the early christians were never guilty of such madness, and in the first centuries not a christian could be found to engage in war! We may therefore justly conclude that the disciples did not understand the commands in question as an injunction to supply themselves with swords.

VI. – The reference which our Lord made to his death and the predictions which concerned himself and his kingdom are a still further confirmation of the correctness of the interpretation adopted above. He reminds them that he was to be 'reckoned among the transgressors,'[5] and that 'the things which concerned him were to have an end.'[6] These expressions intimate –

I. – That Divine justice was about to treat him as a transgressor. He was to be our sin or sin-offering, that is, he was to be treated as our sin deserved to be treated. God might have made an example of us and have punished us, but he is merciful as well as just; and therefore he laid on Christ the iniquities of us all. 'He was wounded for our transgressions,'[7] and thus in his death we have the brightest display of divine justice and divine mercy. But the atonement of Christ concerned every human being. – 'It was a ransom for all to be testified in due time.'[8] Now if it is to be testified, proper witnesses must be raised up and sent to all nations, and here we find the Saviour giving the most appropriate directions for the universal diffusion of the gospel. His words contain the platform for a missionary society for the whole world, and render it imperative that his disciples should

1 Isaiah 52: 7.
2 Luke 9: 56.
3 Revelations 13: 10.
4 Revelations 13: 10.
5 Luke 22: 37.
6 See Romans 10: 4.
7 Isaiah 53: 5.
8 1 Timothy 2: 6.

furnish from among themselves both means and men, that the whole human family may hear the 'faithful saying that Jesus Christ came into the world to save sinners.' In this great work carnal weapons were never to be employed. Nothing could be either more unseemly or useless to the preachers of the gospel than military weapons.

II. – These words suggest that not only Christ himself was 'to be reckoned among the transgressors,' or among the *lawless*, but that the odium attached to himself would for a very long period follow his religion and all who possessed it. Like himself, his followers would be reckoned among the '*lawless*,' and instead of the hospitality that marked their first mission, they would now 'be hated of all men for his name's sake.'[1] Unless therefore they made provision for their work, instead of '*lacking nothing*,' they would lack every thing. Still, in this state of exigency, swords could afford them no relief. The purse, the knapsack, and the knife, would make them independent of their foes, and as far as temporal provision went fully equip them for their embassy.

III. – 'All things concerning Christ are to have an *end*,' or as the words mean, *to be fulfilled*. All the predictions concerning the efficacy of his death, the general promulgation of his gospel, the means by which it was to be diffused, the opposition it was to encounter, the success with which it would eventually be crowned, and the universal peace and happiness which it was to establish, were all to have an end, or be gloriously accomplished. – And to be accomplished through the medium of human instrumentality. But not with swords or weapons of war. Only the sword of the spirit is to be drawn – nothing but moral suasion is to be tried – the world is to be saved by being taught. Those who have employed carnal weapons have ever been the greatest obstacles to the spread of the gospel. The Redeemer knew this, and therefore we may rest assured did not command the apostles to arm themselves with weapons of destruction.

These observations show, that the text we have examined holds out no encouragement whatever to offensive or defensive war; and thus exonerate the meek and lowly Saviour from the charge of having sanctioned, in any of his commands, the shedding of blood.

The following tables will afford much instruction to the Fustian Jackets and Smock Frocks and will show them that other motives besides patriotism may induce men to plunge the country into a war. How many useful artisans have bled and whitened the soil with their bones! – How many thousands have died of want and starvation to procure the Iron Duke the extravagant revenue contained in this catalogue of the profits of military glory. What shall we say of the patriotism of any man who would accept such sums from a country ground down by taxation and in which thousands annually perish for want of bread? Millions of facts show that there is no patriotism in war. The subjoined bill of the wages of slaughter has appeared in many newspapers, but is here quoted from the *Patriot*, Dec. 30, 1847.

---

1 Luke 21: 17.

THE WELLINGTON PENSIONS.

'I consider no pension I ever made worth one year's interest of the money it cost.'
FREDERICK THE GREAT.

AN ACCOUNT OF PAY, PENSION, AND VOTES OF MONEY, LEVIED ON THE PUBLIC, FOR THE SUPPORT OF THE DUKE OF WELLINGTON AND HIS HEIRS TO 1847. INCLUSIVE!

	£	£
Money received as pay since he entered the army up to 1818		
		30,000
Ditto as Commander-in-Chief in Europe		
Ditto as his share of prize money in Spain, said to be upon £800,000		
Ditto ditto prize money in France, said to be upon £1,000,000		
Ditto as Salary whilst Ambassador to France and Vienna		50,000
1811. – Pension of £4,000 per annum – this has been paid 37 years		148,000
1812. – Grant per 53rd of Geo. III	100,000	
36 years' interest thereon	180,000	
		280,000
1812. – Grant per 53rd and 54th Geo. III	400,000	
1813. – 35 years interest thereon	700,000	
		1,100,000
1814. – Grant per 55th Geo. III	200,000	
34 years' interest thereon	340,000	
		540,000

(The 2nd of Victoria recites the several grants – together £700,000.)

1815. – Vote per parliament after the battle of Waterloo	60,000	
33 years' interest thereon	99,000	
		159,000

Interest is charged as above, as the public have to pay the interest on the war debt.

Pay as Field Marshall, 1818 to 1847, 30 years, at £2000 per ann.	60,000
The Duke has since obtained, in addition, the following lucrative appointments; –	
1820. – Appointed Colonel of Rifle Brigade, pay £285 15 per ann. 28 years	6,872
1826. – Ditto Constable of the Tower £947 22 years	31,262
1826. – Ditto Warden of the Cinque Ports £474 22 years	10,428
1827. – Ditto Colonel of 1st Regt. of Guards £1,200 21 years	25,200
1827 to 1830. – Ditto Commander-in-Chief, £3,458 4 years	13,832
1842. – Re-appointed ditto £3,458 6 years	20,748
	£2,464,914

The emoluments of the Duke's sons, brothers, nephews, and other relations are also very great in the army, navy, and church.

364 CHARTIST MOVEMENT IN BRITAIN: VOLUME 4

The parliamentary vote for the office of Commander-in-Chief is upwards of £16,000 per ann.

Frederick's fightings and the Wellington fights were no doubt equally worthless, yet under these two warriors, tens of thousands of poor men were led out, – and perished.

I here add three tables, accompanied with remarks by Dr Campbell,[1] from the British Banner of January 26th, 1848. –

'The following table presents a selection of THIRTEEN out of twenty years, ranging from 1827 to 1847, – a period during which we have expended on powder, brass, and steel – the pomp and circumstance of war, the sum of nearly TWO HUNDRED MILLIONS sterling! The items of the account comprise the army, navy, ordnance, and some miscellaneous matters chargeable upon the annual grants: –

	£					£		
1827	15,970,327	0	6		1840	13,984,076	0	0
1828	15,642,054	15	10		1841	14,119,418	0	0
1829	14,376,881	4	3		1844	14,513,917	0	0
1830	14,716,694	0	9		1845	13,961,245	0	0
1835	14,430,402	3	10		1846	15,664,169	0	0
1836	14,058,076	11	1		1847	20,296,325	15	1
1839	12,720,750	0	0					
					£195,454,336	1	4	

Let our readers ponder these columns. Let them moreover, well weigh the fact, that the increase in this department has become FOURFOLD since the year 1792, as will appear from the following: –

EXPENDITURE ON THE ARMY, NAVY, AND ORDNANCE IN 1792 AND 1846.

	Army. £	Navy. £	Ordnance. £	Total. £
In 1792	1,814,800	1,943,892	463,601	4,222,283
In 1846	6,699,699	7,803,464	2,361,534	16,864,697

But the most alarming part of the case still remains. The expenditure for 1847 is actually near FIVE MILLIONS more than in 1836, that is to say, it is £4,751,729, or 39 per cent INCREASE. And now it is gravely proposed it shall be increased further still! One should think, that if we are not sufficiently defended, we are at least paying enough for soldiers and sailors, and that if the supply of protection be incomplete, it is time to reduce the cost of it. But as things of this sort are best understood by contrast, we shall subjoin the entire cost of our Civil Government for the same period. The matter stands thus: –

Civil Government, under the heads, Civil List, Privy Purse, Salaries of the Household and Tradesmen's Bills, the allowances to the several branches of the Royal Family, the Lord Lieutenant of Ireland's Establishment, the salaries and

---

1 John McLeod Campbell (1800–72), theologian.

expenses of the Houses of Parliament (including printing), Civil departments, (including superannuation allowances,) and Annuities, Pensions, Civil List, &c.

	£					£		
1827	1,621,239	4	8		1840	1,634,683	0	0
1828	1,598,028	6	9		1841	1,721,577	0	0
1829	1,596,899	17	4		1844	1,626,219	0	0
1830	1,578,969	19	0		1845	1,618,265	0	0
1835	1,700,090	4	4		1846	1,562,887	0	0
1836	1,207,032	15	10		1847	1,689,146	7	2
1839	1,672,000	0	0					
						£20,827,035	15	1

Thus it appears that the defence of one year costs the country as much as the government of thirteen years! But it may be worth while again to compare the expense of our War-defence with that of JUSTICE during the same period of thirteen years. The matter stands thus: –

Justice, under the heads Courts of Justice at home and abroad, Police and Criminal Prosecutions, Correction, &c.

	£					£		
1827	1,023,950	5	0		1840	1,438,976	0	0
1828	1,000,592	18	6		1841	1,397,603	0	0
1829	1,004,598	18	4		1844	1,782,469	0	0
1830	993,678	2	2		1845	1,857,205	0	0
1835	857,203	6	10		1846	1,557,756	0	0
1836	430,652	17	11		1847	847,753	17	10
1839	1,532,338	0	0					
						£15,819,777	6	7

Here, again, the expense of thirteen years' justice has been only THREE-FOURTHS of that of our army and navy for the one year just expired!

These, then, are facts for the consideration of the Electors. Within the short space of some fifty years, besides the debt of 800,000,000, we have seen the annual expenses of this department increasing fourfold! And all this for the defence of the nation! If things go on in this ratio another fifty years, even without the recurrence of war, the expense of the army and navy will exceed the sum of EIGHTY MILLIONS per annum! Is it not, then, time for the electors, and the people at large to deal with this question! We pay the electors, – for the bulk of the members, and the class to which they belong, of the house of commons, find their account in the augmentation, and hence the quiet indifference with which these expenses have been allowed, year by year, to increase. It is a fact, which the people should know, that frequently when these millions are being voted, there are barely so many members present as to make a house! So sure as effect follows cause, a continuance of these things, and other things with these connected, will lead to troublous times.'

From what has been said in these pages it will be seen that war has no sanction from the discourses and example of our Lord or his apostles; and from the tables appended we have shown that it is a most expensive pursuit, destructive to the prosperity of nations and the patriotism of citizens. What millions of treasure and rivers of blood have been shed, and all to no purpose. Some of the greatest and most energetic minds have been degraded by it to a level with savages and barbarians. At the great day of retribution, Alexander, Cæsar, Napoleon, Nelson, and all their abettors, must take their stand with the murderers and plunderers of mankind. Alas, that the plain dictates of humanity and the bible are so little understood! Not a few of those who lay claim to the highest order of sanctity and benevolence are the advocates of blood, and proclaim in the face of high heaven that it is lawful to send men amidst the greatest torture, cruelty, revenge, and blasphemy, to the bottomless pit. *The Fustian Jackets and Smock Frocks* must teach these desolators of the world that there is no gospel in war, but that the occupation is one at which demons would blush. As the present electors of the country pretend that they are the *only* persons fit to exercise the franchise, let them show the working classes that they are the foes of tyranny, slaughter, and extravagance, and give us a parliament of wise, humane, equitable, and patriotic legislators. Until they do this they demonstrate that they have no qualities for voting beyond those of the unrepresented and oppressed operatives.

No. 8.

TRACTS FOR FUSTIAN JACKETS AND SMOCK FROCKS.

THE RADICALISM OF MOSES.
BY THE
REV. B. PARSONS, OF EBLEY, STROUD.

Thou shalt love thy neighbour as thyself. LEV. xix. 18.

I have been told that it is profane to talk of the *Radicalism of Christianity*. The objection shows how very imperfectly the scriptures are understood. Perhaps there is no volume so little studied as the bible. I refer not to unbelievers, but to those who profess to be governed by holy writ. There are thousands who believe in the divine origin of the old and new testaments who have never read them through, and thousands more who read without rationally studying or understanding their contents. Is it any wonder that these people feel shocked at hearing of the *radicalism of the gospel*. Many of them do not know the true meaning of *radicalism*, and as they have not attentively examined the word of God, they cannot tell whether *radicalism* is there or not. Had they attended to our Lord's command, *'search the scriptures,'*[1] they would have found radicalism expressed or implied in almost every page of revelation. Let the essential attributes of the Deity – the eternal principles of equity – the relations of man to man, and of man to God – the heinous character of sin and iniquity – be understood, and instead of its being accounted profane to call christianity a *radical religion*, it will be seen that *radicalism* must be a necessary element of any divine scheme of salvation for a guilty world. Take away this sacred characteristic, and the seal of its divinity is gone. Hence those are the *profane* and the *blasphemers* who deny that the gospel is intended to eradicate all error and vice.

I have said in Tract, No. 5, that *radicalism*, in its true and appropriate sense, means the *uprooting* of everything that is unjust, unholy, or unkind; and hence *true radicalism* is *true conservatism*. Suppose I am a medical man and a patient is brought to me who is afflicted with the leprosy. – If I entirely eradicate from his frame the malady under which he labours, I preserve or conserve the man, and thus my *radicalism* is complete *conservatism* to him. The same remark applies to all kinds of moral diseases, whether personal, political, or ecclesiastical. Hence the

---

1 John 5: 39.

wisest of monarchs has said 'Take away the wicked from the presence of the king and his throne shall be established in righteousness.'[1] In the moral world nothing is stable but what is right. *Wickedness* is *weakness*, the lowest, meanest, basest description of imbecility. The religion, the church, the throne, or the government based upon it, or polluted with it, is built upon the sand, and is sure to fall. If christianity is not a *radical* religion then it is a *wicked* and consequently a *weak* religion, and its doom may be foretold with the most unerring certainty. *Radicalism* would have saved Egypt and Babylon, and Greece and Rome, and all the kingdoms and empires that have crumbled to nothing. *Radicalism* would have saved Louis Philippe and can save England, but banish the *eradicating* principles of true equity from the country, and our ruin is not very distant.

We propose in this tract to exhibit a little of the *radicalism* of Moses. We say a *little*, because to bring forward *all* would require many volumes. You perceive it in almost every sentence of his five books. Genesis, Exodus, Leviticus, Numbers and Deuteronomy are thoroughly impregnated with it.

One of the most glorious doctrines of radicalism is the *natural equality and fraternity* of mankind, and in no writings upon the face of the earth do we find the *universal brotherhood* of the human family so distinctly stated, or based on so firm a foundation as in the writings of the Jewish lawgiver. There we are told that the body of man is from the dust and his spirit from heaven. His material frame is a divine formation. The stamp of divinity is upon his bones, his blood, his digestive, breathing, and circulating organs. His muscles, nerves, brain and senses proclaim the Godhead of his creator. What finite skill could form such a wonderful machine? His body demonstrates that God is his father. And then if we look at the powers of his mind, we have in them a reflection of the Deity. We wonder not that an apostle tells us, that *'we are the offspring of God.'*[2] Man is a noble, a divine, creature. And this natural dignity belongs to every human being upon the face of the earth. It is as much the prerogative of the savage as of the philosopher – of woman, as of the other sex. Moses tells us that God made a *helpmeet* for *man*, or as the Hebrew may read, *'a help corresponding to his dignity,'* and this equality was at once recognized by our discerning forefather. As soon as he saw Eve, he exclaimed, 'This now is bone of my bone, and flesh of my flesh, she shall be called *woman*,'[3] or as the original means, 'she shall be called a *female man*.' All the animals had a female associate, but when they came to Adam to be named, there was among them no helpmeet for him, no sympathizer, no companion, no one of whom he could say, 'This now is bone of my bone, and flesh of my flesh.' There were *female* lions and tigers, and serpents, and doves, but until woman appeared there was no *'female man.'* From this happy pair, – these children of the Most High God, – these perfect creatures – whom he formed in his own image and likeness – the whole human family have sprung, and hence all are brothers and sisters. Yonder barbarian and savage is my brother, and so is yonder monarch. Some of

---

1 Proverbs 25: 5.
2 See Revelations 22: 16.
3 Genesis 2: 23.

our relatives are black, some are red, some are copper colour, and some are pale, but these variations can be accounted for on physiological principles, and do not in the least degree afflict our brotherhood. Queens and princesses are as much our sisters as washerwomen or kitchen girls; and the poorest and lowest are as closely related to us, as those who wear crowns or glitter in diamonds. God has 'made of *one blood* all nations of men for to dwell on the face of all the earth,'[1] so that if there is *royal blood anywhere* there is *royal blood everywhere*. The minister of religion who denies this truth is an *infidel*, because he disbelieves the scriptures, and if he is afraid to publish it, then he is unfaithful to the plainest dictates of nature and revelation. Let the chemist examine the blood of the negro, the savage, the serf, the mill girl, the princess, and the monarch, and there is no difference, except that perhaps the blood of the poor is less polluted with luxury. Let the metaphysician scrutinize their minds and you have the same essential attributes and powers. Accidental circumstances may have elevated some and depressed others, so that various developments of mental vigour or weakness appear, but still all souls are alike. Nor will it do to taunt the negro or the peasant with the want of intellectual energy, so long as we have in history and in the living world such hosts of imbecile and corrupt princes, nobles, squires and ecclesiastics. No one can be offended with what I say without owning himself guilty. That titles, pensions, and corrupt universities are as degenerating to moral vigour as the prairie or the desert, is now generally admitted. You have more cruelty and plunder in the wars and injustice of civilized Europe than in the wilds of Africa. The refinement of theft and bloodshed among the moderns, instead of diminishing, enhances their turpitude. Pope in his Dunciad, has ably exposed the degenerating influence of the peerage, and the Quarterly Review, that favoured organ of the tories and the church, has just quoted his words with much zest; –

> 'How quick ambition hastes to ridicule
> The father made a peer, the son a fool.'[2]

intimating that you have as many little souls among civilized lords as in barbarian clans. We hardly find a person and scarcely a family that have intellectual and moral stamina sufficient to bear up against the debasing and paralizing influence of aristocratical rank. Still, we must remember, that the blast which has withered the powers of the nobleman or the savage, of the prince or the pauper, is a calamity which does not in the least invalidate the native dignity or brotherhood of man. All are originally great, and by a due cultivation of their powers might have been the glory of earth and the boast of heaven.

Now this original greatness – this divinity of the human family – this close affinity of body soul and spirit, which unites all mankind together – is one of the most important radical doctrines of the books of Moses. Because if all men are thus equal – are the real children of God – and are brothers and sisters to each other – then there ought to be no injustice, or oppression, or cruelty, or

---

1 Acts 17: 26.
2 Alexander Pope, *The Dunciad* (1728), ll. 547–8.

bloodshed, in the world. If kings and queens felt this truth they would no longer oppress, and instead of impoverishing their brethren by taxation, would deny themselves for the good of those they undertake to govern. 'I was a king, and *therefore* I was a tyrant, a sensualist, a spendthrift, and a scourge to my species,' will form no excuse at the great tribunal of heaven. If legislators, if merchants, if tradesmen, if masters, if servants, if neighbours, if nations recognized this brotherhood and acted according to its dictates and duties, all injustice, cruelty, selfishness, dishonesty, malignity, and uncharitableness, would cease. Warriors would give up their traffic in human blood, no man would murder or hang his brother, no one would oppress, or rob, or slander. There would be a holy emulation as to which should do most to elevate and bless his brethren and sisters. Every one would look on himself or herself as a missionary sent from heaven to communicate blessings to all around. Without state education all would be educated. – In fact, government education would be viewed as the greatest libel upon the human race. There would be no need of poor-laws, union houses, or jails. There would be labour for all, ample wages or all domestic comfort and intellectual and moral pleasures for all. The practical recognition of the great truth taught by Moses, that we are all brethren and that God is our common father, would soon eradicate injustice, tyranny, and ignorance and render mankind a happy family. To injure any human being is to injure a child of God and an heir of glory. Our father will not hold us guiltless if we rob, neglect, despise, insult, tyrannise over, or in any way harm any of his children. We are to love them as we love ourselves; and our love of God is to be tested by our obedience to his command to 'love our brother also.' It has been fashionable to set Moses and Christ at variance, and represent the law as the antagonist of the gospel, and in too many cases evangelical doctrine has been hailed as affording not only an indemnity for past iniquity but an indulgence for future transgressions, and hence we see every where faith and works separated from each other. Some ministers wonder that there are not more conversions, seemingly forgetting that it is necessary to make men the disciples of Moses before they can be the disciples of Christ, and that faith to be worth any thing must work by love, and in the exercise of that love practically recognize God as our father and all mankind as our brethren. The christianity of many in our age is a sickly, selfish, imbecile, proud, arrogant, aristocratical thing. Unbelievers cannot see it. It is like the talent very 'carefully wrapt up in a napkin,' or the light kept 'under a bushel.' Sceptics wonder at our audacity in asking them to embrace so barren a faith – a creed which has done us so little good. We must convert the church to Moses before we shall convert the world to Christ. We must destroy the *practical* infidelity of professing christians before we can hope that infidels will join our ranks. As long as any Gibbon, or Voltaire, or Tom Paine[1] has any reason to ask 'what do ye more than others,' scepticism will abound and immorality will flourish. If we are to believe the statements of some of those who are so pious that they say to others 'stand by thyself and come not near us, for we are holier than thou,' we should conclude

---

1 Thomas Paine (1737–1809), republican political theorist.

that real christianity is one of the most puerile religions that has ever been taught. According to these professors, the really spiritual christian cannot do his duties as a citizen without endangering his piety! He cannot bring his principles to bear upon the correction of civil, political, and ecclesiastical corruption without great injury to his spirituality! To make a public effort to terminate intemperance, to stay the demon of war, to curb the tyranny of despots, to lessen the power of a domineering aristocracy, to lighten the burdens of a people groaning under a crushing load of taxation, to unfetter trade, to unmanacle liberty, to unsecularise the church and drive 'a den of thieves' from the temple of God – alas! alas! to do such wicked deeds as these would pollute the sacred garments of your modern pietist and unfit him for public and private prayer. Were he really and *practically* to recognize the brotherhood and consequent equal rights of mankind, he would be unable to look with a devout spirit and say 'Our father who art in heaven!' His ability to acknowledge, with a pious spirit, Jehovah as our *universal parent*, must depend upon his neglecting his duties to his *brother* man! Is is any wonder we have empty churches and chapels when such a religion as this is palmed upon the world as the christianity of the gospel. Especially, seeing many of these eminently spiritual people are not always so over squeamish in all their deeds and transactions. They do not undeviatingly 'renounce the devil and all his works, the pomps and vanities of this wicked world and all the sinful lusts of the flesh.' The love of money is not entirely abandoned, nor do they always prove that avarice is incompatible with their supposed hyper-spiritual mindedness. They can follow every fashion, and almost adore wealth and rank though associated with ignorance, vice, and manifest hypocrisy. The outrage on common decency, and the falsehood, farce and impiety exhibited in the choice of bishops and archbishops, they are too holy to attempt to abolish. Large livings for drones and starvation for real labourers, they approve by their silence. They can neglect the education and elevation of the masses without any compunction and then brand these their poor brothers and sisters as low and vulgar. – In a word, the vaunted christianity of the age is not the christianity of common sense or of the bible, and therefore has justly exposed itself to the censure of the sceptic and the scoff of the profane. The world wants a manly religion, a religion of justice to all, a religion of brotherhood and love; and until professing christians will demonstrate by their deeds that they possess this religion they must be content to mourn the paucity of conversions and the spread of scepticism.

Now it is only for any one to study the books of Moses to perceive that his precepts are all based on justice. The sum and substance of the ten commandments is universal love. Love to God and love to man is all they enjoin. Sin is the transgression of the law of love, and the whole ceremonial law was intended to teach us that man must be cleansed from iniquity or for ever forfeit the favour of heaven. All the judgments inflicted, and all the wars waged under the sanction of heaven, were to punish crime. The old world was deluged because the earth was corrupt and filled with violence. Sodom and Gomorrah were destroyed for their vices. In those cities the crimes were the usual transgressions of a proud, idle, heartless, aristocracy, for Ezekiel tells us, chap. xvi, ver. 49, that the iniquity of Sodom consisted of '*pride, fulness of bread, and abundance of idleness, neither did she strengthen the hand of the poor and needy.*' One might almost think that the prophet had lived in these times, and that instead of describing Sodom and Gomorrah, he is depicting the idle nobility, the luxurious landowners and capitalists, the lordly bishops and endowed clergy of modern days. We have plenty of pride and fulness of bread – we have abundance of idleness, and a great outcry against any one who would give the people their rights, or practically recognize the brotherhood of man, and thus really and permanently strengthen the hand of the poor and needy. Were special judgments now to burst forth in volcanos, or descend in storms of fire and brimstone, we have reason to fear that a very large portion of the British empire would be doomed to destruction. The inhabitants of Canaan also were sunk in vice, and therefore Eternal Justice, after giving them three hundred years to repent, employed Joshua to cut them off. All the plagues of Moses and the final overthrow in the Red Sea, were brought upon the monarch and aristocracy of Egypt for their despotism, injustice, and cruelty – 'the children of Israel sighed by reason of their bondage; and they cried out and their cry came up to God by reason of their bondage; and God heard their groaning, and God remembered his covenant with Abraham, Isaac, and Jacob, and God looked upon the Children of Israel, and God had respect unto them.' Exod. ii. 23–25. Our religious people will do well to recollect that the crying thus spoken of was a *political cry*, and further, the *political cry* of a very *ignorant, debased, irreligious people*, for we can hardly imagine a more degraded and ungodly race than the Israelites in Egypt. And yet the God of heaven heard the *political cry* of these irreligious victims of tyranny; showing us that a *political cry* against *political oppressors*, though uttered by ungodly persons and unheeded by man, 'enters into the ears of the Lord God of Sabaoth.' It is of no use to refer to the covenant with Abraham as the sole reason why this political cry was heard, because the promise to the patriarch was that all the families of the earth should eventually be blessed, or made happy through him, and therefore the Abrahamic covenant embraced all mankind, and consequently all races of men, and at the same time included *political* as well as *spiritual* redemption. The Almighty may not always, in this world, punish tyrants so signally as he did Pharaoh, for he is long-suffering to monarchs as well as to other persons, still he is the same determined foe to injustice now that he was then, and the *political cries* of those who groan under French, or British, or Austrian, or Prussian, or Italian, or Russian, or Chinese despotism, reach the ears and touch the heart of our Heavenly Father now as truly as they did in the days of Moses. And Jehovah intended that the judgments upon Pharaoh should be a warning to the kings and rulers of all ages and nations and that his attention to the *political cries* of the Israelites should encourage the oppressed of every time and country to seek the redress of their wrongs, and in doing so to remember that they have the sympathies of the God of heaven. He himself raised up Moses and Aaron as *political agitators* to demand *civil and religious* liberty for their brethren, and commanded them to indoctrinate the elders and tribes of Jacob with their own political sentiments. History hardly affords an example of such perfect *out and out radicals* as Moses and Aaron, or of such *complete radicalism* as that which emancipated the sons of Abraham from Egypt. Here you have heaven and earth conspiring to accomplish the glorious event.

It is a great mistake to suppose that the King of kings only listens to prayers for spiritual redemption, or, that the covenant with Abraham refers merely to the salvation of the soul. The Almighty looks with pity and compassion upon all his erring children. He knows that their ignorance, crimes, and even the vulgarity with which the poor are taunted, are in too many cases, the result of oppression and injustice on the part of their superiors, and of neglect on the part of the religious people and the priesthood; and he is too holy to despise these sons of need because their brethren have made them wretched, or to reject their cries because they are poor and despised or even wicked. It is a glorious truth that the supplication for mercy enters within the veil, but it is also a most consolatory fact that those who groan under civil, political, and ecclesiastical tyranny, have, in the governor of the universe, a friend who hears their 'sighs,' and will eventually send them deliverance. The seed of Abraham, the Messiah, the annointed Saviour of the world, is a *political* as well as a spiritual Redeemer. The *political* and *spiritual* salvation of the world are more intimately connected than legislators or divines have hitherto imagined. In my tract on the radicalism of king David, I shall show, that his prayer, Psalm 72, for his son Solomon, was, to a great extent, a *political* prayer, a *radical* prayer, and that he especially supplicated that his son might be a *radical monarch*, who would 'administer justice to the poor of the people, and save the children of the needy, and break in pieces the oppressor;' and as it is allowed by all interpreters that this psalm has reference to David's greater son, the brother and saviour of the human race, it is very evident that he expected that the Lord Jesus Christ would be the *political* emancipator of all the sons of need and oppression. Past records of the overturning of empires have demonstrated, that God's providence as well as his word, has waged an incessant warfare against tyrants, and passing events show that the iniquity of despots is nearly full. The cup, to use the expressive language of that *radical* prophet Jeremiah, is passing round to them all, and their only security is in becoming *radical reformers*. They must submit to Christ, acknowledge themselves to be men, embrace all mankind as their brethren, and grant equal rights to all, or – their sceptres will be broken. The best advice to them all is the royal exhortation of the son of Jesse in the second psalm. – 'Be wise now therefore, O ye kings; be instructed, ye judges of the earth; kiss the son, lest he be angry and we perish from the way, when his wrath is kindled but a little.' What a sermon the overthrow of Louis Philippe preaches from those inspired words of our Lord's mother –

> 'He hath put down dynasties from their thrones,
> And exalted them of low degree.'[1]

I have said enough to show that Moses was a *political agitator* and a *radical reformer* and that he received his commission to be such from the King of kings and Lord of lords. A crafty aristocracy and a hireling priesthood, have wished to

---

1 Luke 1: 52.

impress on the public mind that Moses and the prophets were only *spiritual* instructors, and thus have laboured to frighten religious men from engaging in the political renovation of the world. They very well knew, that persons of sound religion and morality are the only agents qualified to eradicate corruption from the country, and therefore, if men of principle could be duped to resign politics to Satan and his angels, the reign of civil and ecclesiastical extravagance and despotism might hope for a long impunity of licentious misrule. Alas! they have been but too successful, and an age of imbecile spiritualism is the result; and as a consequence christianity is a byeword, the bible is dishonoured, and the sanctuary neglected. The church is a pensioner and sycophant of the state, and totters at every political breeze. Her very sons that eat her bread, declare – most unblushingly declare before God and man – that they would not support education or christianity unless *compelled* to do so by an ungodly race of senators. No drunkard, scoffer, or infidel laughs so loudly at VOLUNTARY RELIGION as bishops, clergymen and other pious evangelical episcopalians. Is it any wonder, seeing the glory is departed from the temple and Ichabod written upon her walls, that irreligion prevails. If christianity is formalism, or mere symbolism, if the really pious man is so debased by his sanctity that he cannot perform his duties as a citizen, or seek the political regeneration of the world, without endangering his heavenly mindedness and the salvation of his soul, then we ought to be infidels. What, to be so morbidly pious as to be unable to attend to the sacred obligations of banishing iniquity from the state and the church, and purify the political Augean stable of its corruption!! Such a religion is neither acceptable to God, nor worthy of anything but reprobation from man, and such a vile caricature of the christianity of heaven, deserves all the ridicule and unbelief with which it has been assailed.

The religion of Moses, which is nothing more than the gospel in an antique form, is of a more manly and equitable character, and in an especial manner, the shield of the poor. To prevent overgrown wealth on the one hand, and hopeless pauperism on the other, the Jewish lawgiver instituted a redivision of the land every fifty years, and thus, at every jubilee the children received again the fields which their fathers by misfortune or extravagance had lost. That none might forget their mean origin and their common brotherhood, each person, when the nation at the great festival presented the first fruits as an offering of gratitude to their divine benefactor, was commanded to make an annual confession, '*A Syrian ready to perish was my father.*'[1] Kings, as well as paupers, had to use these words, and to acknowledge that the blood in their veins was common blood derived from a *starving foreigner*. To the *poor*, the *labourer*, the *stranger*, the *fatherless*, and the *widow*, the laws of Moses paid a special regard. If money was lent to the *poor*, no interest was to be required. If his garment was taken for pledge, it was to be restored before the sun went down, or else, says the King of heaven, 'When he crieth, I will hear, for I am gracious.'[2] Every seventh year the land was to rest and

---

1 Deuteronomy 26: 5.
2 Exodus 22: 27.

lie still, that the *poor* might eat. The corners of the field were not to be reaped but were to be left for the *poor* and the *stranger*. It was a divine command 'Thou shalt open thy hand *wide* unto *thy brother, thy poor*, and *thy needy in the land.*' They were not to harden their hearts nor shut their hands against a *poor brother*. The *hired servant*, whether an Israelite, or a *foreigner*, was not to be oppressed, but his hire was to be paid before the sun went down, lest he should have occasion to cry out unto God against his employer and the Almighty should take up the cause. The *judgment of the poor* was not to be wrested, nor was the *stranger* to be oppressed. Now these laws show that the religion of Moses was a religion which paid particular attention to the wants of the poor and indeed was their shield. Here you have no aristocracy paid to do nothing, nor any laws made to secure their rank, after they were bankrupts in property, intelligence, and morality. Kings were not instituted by Moses. He rather told all the people, mechanics, and labourers, – the fustian jackets and smock frocks of those days – that they were to be 'a kingdom of priests or princes,' which expressions Peter and John have interpreted in the new testament by the words, 'a royal priesthood,'[1] – 'kings and priests unto God.' In the scriptures, royalty and nobility consist, not in *blood*, but in *intelligence and morality*, and thus the *operative* may be as *princely* as the monarch or the peer. In ancient days, kings were labourers, mechanics, shepherds or tradesmen, and queens worked at the loom, in the field or the bakehouse. Their state revenues were the *voluntary* offerings of the people. In the records of Moses, a prince was merely a magistrate or the leader of his tribe or family. He was no aristocrat, his blood was common blood, his rank was official, and he was expected to bless rather than fleece his brethren. Till the nation became corrupt, their leaders were *too patriotic* to accept of pay for serving their country. The priesthood were the public instructors of the people, and they taught *politics* as well as religion. In the laws of Moses, these two are so blended that you cannot separate them without doing violence to the scriptures. The modern mode of taking texts, rather than expounding the whole bible, is very convenient, because it enables the preacher to pick and choose and reject those portions of revelation which do not suit his creed, his system, or his audience. But Moses was not afraid of politics. His spirituality was of too manly and divine a character to be hurt by them. The God of Israel did not deem it meet to exclude politics from his word. Politics are a most important branch of the morals of nations, and to prevent religion from sanctifying them, is one of the greatest civil and moral curses that can visit the earth. The exclusion of pure rectitude from governments has been the downfall of every monarch and empire that have been overthrown. The King of kings foresaw this, and he made his priests *political* teachers, and had the sons of Levi done their duty, and the nation hearkened to their voice, the Jews would never have lost the promised land. In the pentateuch, politics and religion are not so much *united as one*, and it was the separation of the former from the latter that brought the nation under the wrath of heaven and made the Jew a wanderer upon the face of the earth. The priests of Israel were national schoolmasters without government

---

1 1 Peter 2: 9.

pay. The tithes to remunerate them were to be *given* on the *voluntary* principle. There was no law empowering the magistrate to demand them by force, to seize them by violence, or to fine the defaulters for non-payment. The punishment of the offender was left to the Almighty. And as the salary of the teacher depended upon the *voluntary* gifts of the people, you may be sure there was no lord bishop corrupted by his £10,000 per annum, nor any poor starving curate,

'Passing rich on forty pounds a year.'[1]

Nor were the priests to be a proud, haughty, aristocratical sort of men, but brethren to the poor and needy, men who 'could have compassion on the ignorant and them that were out of the way.' What politicians, what radicals, aye and what patriots and christians we should all be, if we only believed and obeyed the divine religion of Moses.

Here then we have perfect radicalism sanctioned by the God of heaven – the divine legislator and judge, – at whose tribunal we must all stand. The histories and laws of Moses form a magnificent base to the other part of revelation, and explained by the new testament, exhibit a perfect system of political and religious economy. His characters are either splendid examples of virtue, or disgusting specimens of vice. His wars and executions were undertaken by divine command, and therefore, until we have the same authority from heaven, we have no right to imitate the one or the other, still they were all *radical* in their tendency. Pharaoh, and Sihon king of the Amorites, and Og, king of Bashan, and all the kings of Canaan were consummate tyrants – the scourges of the earth. And God took them away as a warning to future ages and that he might show his sympathies with the poor and oppressed, and hence *king* David tells that he did so *'because his mercy endureth for ever.'* He who rules the universe cannot err, and if he punishes his enemies by famine, by the volcano, the deluge, or the sword of a Moses or Joshua, no one has a right to say unto him 'what doest thou?' But then vengeance is his prerogative, and therefore we have no more right to assume his executive than his legislative authority; and until we have a direct command from him have no licence to take away life. Besides, christianity commands us to love and forgive our enemies, and consequently prohibits us frown slaying them. Political injustice cannot be corrected by the sword; bayonets and cannon are poor radical reformers. Tyranny that has been overturned by slaughter has generally been replaced by a worse kind of despotism. The demon has too often returned with seven other spirits more wicked than himself, and the last state been worse than the first. All we want now to obtain the rights of the people, is reason, religion, argument, firmness, agitation, a free press, free discussion, union, and concentration of purpose. These abolished slavery and the corn laws, and are still omnipotent for every good purpose. I have said enough to show that Moses was a perfect *radical*, that his books are *radical* books, and that the God of Abraham approves of political agitation, and sympathizes with all who firmly but peaceably labour for the downfall of political and ecclesiastical corruption and the social

1 George Crabbe, *The Village* (1783), I. 303.

regeneration of the world; and therefore we earnestly exhort the operatives, the Fustian Jackets and Smock Frocks, to take courage at the thought that Jehovah is on their side; remembering, that in seeking justice for all they are doing the will of God, are coming to the help of the Lord against the mighty, and, in this holy warfare are fighting under the banner of the King of kings and shall, without doubt, be more than conquerors. Despotism and injustice arrayed against equity are mere butterflies threatening to overturn omnipotence. 'He that sitteth in the heavens shall laugh; Jehovah shall have them in derision and dash them in pieces like a potter's vessel.'

No. 9

THE FUSTIAN JACKETS
AND SMOCK FROCKS.

THE SHAKING OF THE NATIONS
AND DOWNFALL OF TYRANNY.
BY THE REV. B. PARSONS,
OF EBLEY, STROUD.

'For thus saith the Lord of hosts: –
Yet once, within a little while,
And I will shake the heavens and the earth,
And the sea and the dry land;
Yea, I will shake all nations:
And the desire of all nations shall come.'
HAGGAI ii. 6 & 7.

It is unnecessary to say that the word '*shake*,' in the text which I have quoted above, signifies to '*agitate*.' The Almighty intends that all his *real* disciples should be *political* as well as *religious agitators*. He generally works by *instruments*, and while he makes use of the elements, and even of the wicked, to accomplish his purposes, yet, there are no agents that he approves of so thoroughly as the devoted followers of Jesus Christ. These, in the truest and noblest sense of the word, ought to be moral reformers, and consequently *agitators*, bent on the entire overthrow of all that is unjust, oppressive, or ungodly. That the world is to be revolutionized is one of the plainest doctrines of the scripture. The Jews expressed a great and glorious truth when they exclaimed, 'the men that have turned the world upside down are come hither also.' The great design of the Saviour's mission, teaching, miracles, and death; – the grand object which patriarchs, prophets, apostles, and martyrs have kept in view; – has been the intellectual and moral revolution of the whole world. But then the moral includes the domestic, the civil, and political overturning of everything that wages war with the liberty, the rights, and the happiness of man. One design of this tract is to awaken the *fustian jackets and smock frocks* to become *revolutionary agitators*, by using all *rational*, *constitutional*, and *moral* means to uproot whatever is contrary to equity, wholesome law, and good government. There was a time when anarchy and treason were supposed to be confined to the masses; when property, rank, and titles were deemed guarantees of respectability and obedience to the laws of rectitude. But the tables are turned. The masses are becoming the well ordered citizens, while some of the worst swearers, sabbath breakers, and sensualists are to be found in the higher ranks of society. If you would see awful specimens of the want of human sympathy, or the most unblushing avarice, and disregard of the laws of the land; you must turn to the aristocracy; – you must read the history of our game laws, our corn laws, our slavery laws, our taxation, our sinecures, pensions, election bribery, our ecclesiastical, military, and naval corruption. And one of the worst signs of the times is the fact, that you have ministers of religion boasting that they are the successors of the apostles, and yet actually participating in all this iniquity and flattering those who are its most guilty agents and abettors. The wisdom of these men is from beneath and is 'earthly, sensual, and devilish.' They seem especially inspired and ordained by the prince of darkness to bring christianity and the gospel into contempt, and are the chief occasion of the infidelity of the land. Who, in these days, expects to see a clergyman a reformer? Who, but would be surprised to hear that the universities had produced a patriot? When men become worth £1000 a year, they too often eschew such vulgar things as national justice, bible christianity, and rational liberty. Well is it said, 'how hardly shall a rich man enter into the kingdom of heaven!' The poor fellow who a few days ago was not worth sixpence and talked loudly and largely about the rights of man and universal brotherhood, since he has made his fortune has greatly changed his views. – He now wishes the mob, from which he sprung but yesterday, to be put down. The corruption of the church must not be touched, because, forsooth, wealth renders it respectable; political oppression and injustice he is too nervous or too pious to oppose; and thus property and rank not unfrequently render their possessors the most worthless or baneful beings that crawl the earth.

Interpreters of the sacred volume are generally agreed that the words 'heaven,' 'earth,' 'sea,' and 'dry land,' are figurative expressions, and that 'the heavens' represent the political and ecclesiastical powers; and 'the earth,' the people who are governed by them. 'The sea,' some have thought is employed to represent the masses; and 'dry land,' the supposed fixed and established institutions of society. Let us look at them separately; –

I – 'The heavens.' The influence of the heavens over the earth is a great physiological fact. The atmosphere, the clouds, the winds, the lightning, the thunder, the sun, the moon, and the stars, greatly affect this lower world, and may be said to preside over our destiny. Without the air and the rain and the sun we should all die, and for ages the moon and the stars were the guides of the husbandman, the sailor, and the traveller; – hence the doctrines of the astrologer and the worship of the heavenly bodies. We therefore cease to wonder that men should have seen in these celestial signs the emblems of political and moral government, or that kings and priests should have been called suns or stars. Political and ecclesiastical tyrannies, then, are the heavens which the prophet tells us that God will shake or agitate. Governments shed a benign or deadly influence over the earth. When wise and equitable they resemble a genial sun and make our earth a paradise; but when they are corrupt and despotical they blast every thing within their sphere, and are ten thousand times more destructive to mankind than the scorching heat, the bolt of the thunder, the shaft of the lightning, or the overwhelming flood. This beautiful earth of ours has been for ages cursed with bad government and rendered a desolation. Where the tyrant reigns, rich soils, genial skies, luxuriant vegetation, the most seraphic mental powers, are all withered. The bottomless pit cannot send forth upon this lower world a heavier plague or a deeper curse than a bad government. – We beg pardon, there is one other pest still more baneful, and that is an ignorant, arrogant, ungodly, and dominant priesthood. Here you have a race of incarnate fiends to whom Beelzebub especially delegates his sceptre. These possess the baneful art of unmanning the soul, of withering its divine powers, and cursing it for ever. They indeed carry the keys not only of heaven but of the lower abyss. They may well boast of anathemas and excommunication, especially seeing there are none whom they anathematise so completely as those whom they mislead and pretend to bless. The only persons safe from their curse are those who reject an ungodly hierarchy and a domineering priesthood. The union of church and state is nothing less than a confederacy of two of the most malignant pests that have ever visited the world. Here you have political and ecclesiastical corruption amalgamated. The state endows and throws its shield over every ecclesiastical abomination; and the church in return becomes a sycophant, flattering and even using God's name to bless all the iniquity of the state. As we have said before, a clerical reformer is so unusual that he is esteemed an eighth wonder in the world. Even the evangelicals pronounce their benediction, or throw the shield of their charity over government injustice. Were it not too profane, they might sing –

'O no, we never mention her!' –

Now it is these political and ecclesiastical 'heavens,' these 'nests' of corruption, 'built,' as they boast, 'among the stars,' that the God of mercy intends to shake or agitate. 'Yet a little while,' saith the Lord of Hosts, and 'I will shake the heavens.' The agents that will be employed to accomplish this work we will mention hereafter.

II. – '*The earth.*' If the '*heavens*' represent the ruling powers, then it naturally follows that '*the earth*' must stand for the people who are under their government; and the prediction foretells that these are to be shaken or agitated. Nothing is more fatal to truth, justice, and liberty than an inert mass of citizens, ready to be any thing, or do any thing that a foolish or tyrannical government may command. Nations, like stagnant waters, unless agitated, become putrid. This fact is well known to despots; and therefore to impoverish and render the people spiritless by taxation; to intimidate them by policemen and standing armies; to enslave them by bad laws; to corrupt them by places, pensions, and sinecures; to paralyse their mental powers by state schoolmasters, state creeds, state prayers, and a state priesthood; and to rob them of all power by centralization; have been the various stratagems of despotic rulers, to render their subjects a body of mere puppets to move or stand still as their governors may command. But vain are the hopes of ungodly princes. The King of kings hath said 'I will shake the heavens and the *earth*.'[1]

---

1 Joel 3: 16.

III. – '*The sea and the dry land*,' are supposed to be only a continuation of the same thought; to show that this 'shaking' shall embrace every thing and every one, and that nothing shall escape. Instead of using such words as *universe* or *universal*, the Jews often employed an enumeration of the objects included, and therefore by such expressions as 'the *heavens*, the *earth*, the *sea*, and the *dry land*,' embraced the whole creation. According to this interpretation the prediction refers to the rulers and the ruled, and to every thing influenced by their tyranny or obsequiousness. But there are those who imagine that other explanations may be given to the words. In the language of the bible, the term '*sea*' often stands for the west, and '*dry land*' for the continent, which of course was to the *east* of the great sea. According to this exposition Jehovah foretells that the west and the east are to be shaken, or that all the then known world was to be agitated. And as the sea or the west stands first, it has been thought that the western nations or islands were to take the lead in this agitation. History shows us that this has been the case, for the Gothic nations, and our own little island in particular, have had no small share in shaking the despotism of the world, and liberty, born and cherished in our country, has erected an empire in the western continent of America, which has done more to agitate tyrants, and develope the powers and capabilities of man for self government, than any other fact that has ever occurred.

But another meaning has been attached to the words. In the sacred volume, the terms, '*waters*,' and '*sea*,' are often used to represent the people or the moving masses. It is said that the Hebrew word for '*sea*,' signifies *tumult* or *agitation*; and therefore very properly expresses what we generally understand by our opprobrious epithet '*mob*.' Indeed our idea of a '*mob*' is that of a moving tumultuous crowd, and hence we have borrowed this expression from the Latin '*movere*,' to move. The ancients used to call the people the '*incertum vulgus*,' or *uncertain, unsteady, multitude*. These expressions are not inapplicable; for so long as you have unjust rulers and oppressed ignorant subjects, you will have a mass of heaving soul, which like the agitated ocean, will not unfrequently sweep away every barrier and spread desolation around. The only safe way to prevent such a catastrophe is that peaceful and moral agitation for the right of man which the gospel prescribes, and which shall eventually destroy the power of tyrannical priests and princes, and make 'wisdom and knowledge the stability of the times.'[1] But if the '*sea*' is supposed to prefigure the moving masses, the '*dry land*' may signify the establishments and seemingly *fixed institutions* of the world. The great object of tyrants has been to establish and concentrate injustice. – Hence you have military and naval establishments, and educational and ecclesiastical establishments. By means of the former, princes have agents prepared to slay the bodies of mankind, and by the latter, they have already destroyed millions of souls. The bottomless pit is chiefly peopled with victims who have been slain by the sword or poisoned by ungodly priests. And yet most of them can boast of state support and governmental establishment. But the '*shaking*' has begun. State hierarchies are

---

1 Isaiah 33: 6.

perpetually crying out *'church in danger!'* It is marvellous, but *'established'* *churches* are the only sects that utter this doleful cry. None of the other denominations need be alarmed. However, it is a comfort that the agitation has commenced in the right place. All establishments founded on injustice, whether civil, military, or ecclesiastical, are doomed of heaven and even now are tottering. The fact is, the masses are opening their eyes – are becoming acquainted with the greatness of their strength and where it lies; and as they shake their locks and feel for the pillars of the temple of iniquity, a mighty shaking is felt. When the fustian jackets and smock frocks, the Sampsons of our age, shall arise in the majesty of moral power, Dagon must fall.

IV. – The prophet himself furnishes an explanation of the metaphors he has used. 'I will shake *all nations*,' is nothing more than a commentary upon the words, 'the heavens, the earth, the sea, and the dry land,' and teach us that this agitation is to affect all mankind. Not a people under the sky shall be free from this shaking. Monarchs, priests, middle class men, and the masses must be universally shaken before the desire of all nations shall come. Not a corner of the earth shall escape the convulsion. 'All nations,' the barbarians and the civilized; the rude and the learned; the pagan, mahometan and the christian, shall be agitated with the condemnation of injustice and the demand for liberty and equity. Wickedness is weakness; tyranny and oppression are preeminently wicked, and therefore essentially weak, and hence they naturally tremble. Almost every zephyr that breathes shakes them to their centre, but nothing so thoroughly alarms them as the *radicalism* of the word of God. The Bible is especially *'The People's Charter,'* drawn up by the King of kings, and sealed with the blood of his only Son. This fact has been kept back by the priesthood, and the consequence has been the infidelity of millions. The unbelief of the world is chargeable upon the church. The truth has not been fully taught, or those who have professed to teach it have denied it by their lives. But the Eternal has decreed that his gospel shall be propagated throughout the whole world, and that its great doctrines of *universal* brotherhood, universal liberty and universal justice, shall agitate all the nations of the earth.

It may here be asked, who shall be the agitators? We reply that they are many and various.

I. – Monarchs take a prominent part in this agitation. Not that they wish to be co-workers in this glorious enterprise, but they cannot help themselves, for so long as their sceptre is cruel and their laws unjust, their measures must produce dissatisfaction, and consequently render their subjects disaffected. There is an old proverb,

> 'Tread on a worm
> And it will turn,'

as if even that reptile had implanted in its nature a keen sense of injustice. But whatever may be said of worms, man, every man and woman is 'the offspring of God,' was created in the divine image, and ordained to feel and protest against wrong and oppression. Hence tyrants are hated, and the first opportunity that presents itself, their subjects overturn their power. Fortunately, an injured people have a natural and a vested interest in the destruction of tyranny. This fact is well known to despotic rulers, and therefore every stratagem is employed to keep down the masses, and every precaution adopted to barricade themselves against the indignation of their outraged subjects. Conscious guilt makes the hair of the tyrant stand erect and horrifies his thoughts by day and his dreams by night. The loaded pistol is under his pillow; the glittering sword is suspended from his tester; an armed force watch his bedchamber; royal guards surround his chariot; his food must be tasted, for fear of poison; and he makes all his servants swear, in the name of the Eternal, that they will not take away his life!! What a timid, a horrified, an expensive thing is injustice! To protect it from the effects of its own violence you must gag the press, suppress freedom, and surround it with bristling bayonets and standing armies. On the other hand, justice is the cheapest thing in the world; it is its own shield and defence. Hence in the expressive phraseology of scripture, '*righteousness* and *peace* kiss each other.' 'The work of righteousness is *peace*, and the effect of righteousness *quietness* and *assurance* for ever.' But 'the wicked flee when no man pursueth them; they are like the troubled sea, which cannot rest:'[1] and it is after all scarcely a problem which is the most miserable, the wretch who groans under injustice, or, the monster who inflicts it. Louis Philippe did not sleep on a bed of down while he wore the crown of the French. He had all the misgivings and mistrust of tyrants. He was his own agitator – his own evil genius and fiend. But he was more, he was the O'Connell[2] of France, the great agitator that stirred the souls of the most patient people on earth to rebel. No man in the world could have done the work so well. He seemed to say to other agitators, 'give place to me.' The press was silenced; the ministers of religion were bribed by state pay; his political advisers were rendered obsequious; reformers were easily disposed of; and the monarch had the stage to himself; and there, by his tyranny, he galled and goaded his subjects to arise against his iniquity and hurl him from his throne. Henceforth let him be called the royal agitator, – the shaker of the nations; for he not only convulsed France to its centre, but aroused other nations and summoned them to mutiny against oppression. Louis Philippe stands not alone in this work. Every age can boast of his royal compeers in agitation. It is fashionable to charge national convulsions upon the mob. Poor souls! they have been the essence of obsequiousness. There has rarely been a throne overturned by the people until injustice had compelled them to rise and burst their fetters. The greatest instigation to violence on the part of the masses is the previous violence of princes. The world asks for nothing but righteousness. Give to the masses freedom and equitable government and the sceptre of the world might be swayed by an infant. 'A little child shall lead them,' is the language of the prophet respecting that age when oppression shall cease, when 'the lion shall dwell with the lamb,'[3] and men shall no longer 'hurt nor destroy.'

---

1 Isaiah 57: 20.
2 Daniel O'Connell (1775–1847), Irish politician.
3 See Jeremiah 65: 25.

You, to whom I address these tracts, – you, the *fustian jackets and smock frocks*, are ready by millions to attest the truth of what I write. You ask for nothing but justice, and you never assemble to the dismay of tyrants until you have been summoned to do so by the invasion of some of your most sacred rights. Let history be searched and it will be seen that the most active agitators of nations and desolators of thrones have been the tyrants that sat upon them. The eternal God has decreed that injustice and oppression shall seal their own doom, and if moral principle be too weak to call for reform, then the aggression of ungodly rulers shall awaken the spirit of the oppressed and shake the nations.

II. – Men in authority not unfrequently become the coadjutors of princes in this work of agitation. What wonders have been done by a Guizot[1] in France, a Metternich[2] in Austria, and not unfrequently by a prime minister and an iniquitous parliament in England, Hampden and Cromwell were created by tyrants. Despotism called them forth and gave them immortality. How often has this nation been convulsed by premiers, royal favourites, and privy counsellors. Who so adapted as the flatterers of Charles[3] to bring his head to the block, or as Judge Jefferies[4] to banish his master from the throne? My Lord John Russell and his laughing, cockcrowing parliament, will do more to 'shake the nation' than all the chartists in the world. John Bull does not like to be laughed at, especially by those who have brought him into trouble. *Minutes of education, more Bishops, no retrenchment of expenditure, no decrease of army and navy, new placemen*, and a *permanent income tax*, will do wonders in awaking that sluggish animal, the British lion. The coalition of the whigs and tories, by destroying the hopes of *all parties*, are a windfall to radicals and reformers. It was a saying of antiquity, that, 'the gods inflicted madness on the men whom they wished to scourge, and then they brought destruction on themselves.' History in every age has attested the truth of the sentiment, tyranny naturally becomes licentious and besotted, and by its folly overthrows itself. England is to have another shaking. We have laws and taxes and extravagance that paralyse the energies of the middle classes especially, and to appeal to parliament is to be laughed to scorn. The consequence will be a firm, peaceable, equitable, constitutional, agitation, which will sweep oppression from the land. Soon the middle classes will discover that to depend upon the aristocracy is to lean not merely on a reed, but a spear; that to fraternize with the wealthy is to seek sympathy where there is none, to attempt a union of materials as heterogeneous as the iron and the clay in the feet of the monster which Daniel saw.[5] All power is vested by the God of heaven in the people. Monarchs, governments, and parliaments are the creation of their subjects. They produce the wealth of the nation, they supply our armies, navies, and policemen; they create and pay the taxes; physical power is theirs, and moral power is theirs. It is true

---

1 François Guizot (1787–1874), French historian.
2 Klemens Wenzel (1773–1859), Prince von Metternich, Austrian foreign minister 1809–48.
3 Charles I (1600–49), King of England, Scotland and Ireland 1625–49.
4 George Jefferies (1648–89), judge.
5 Daniel 2: 33.

that the state Delilahs have shorn them of their strength and sent them to the mill to grind, or called them forth on special occasions to make sport for the laughing Philistines and cockcrowing legislators, but their locks are growing and their enemies shall soon feel their power. A real union, a perfect fraternization of the working and middle classes is about to be formed which shall spare nothing that is unjust or oppressive, but shall call for perfect radical reform in everything, and thus shall render the British sceptre 'the sceptre of righteousness.'

III. – The bishops and a corrupt priesthood are a glorious race of agitators. The tyranny, the ungodliness and madness of the church called forth Luther,[1] Zuingle[2] and others. The iniquity of the spiritual Canaanites was full. Never had we heard of Wickliff and Huss,[3] but for the depravity of the hierarchy. The reformers were the creatures of circumstances; the hypocrisy, impiety, sensuality, and avarice of men in holy orders called them into being. We know that God inspired them, but then had there been no ecclesiastical hydras to be slain, no Augean stables to be cleansed, their divine prowess had never distinguished them, or raised them to an eminence above their brethren of more peaceable times. And thanks to the priesthood of England, the nation shall have a shaking yet. Your Harrys of Exeter,[4] your Samuels of Oxford,[5] your Dean Mereweathers,[6] and your Hampden controversies, will work gloriously. Acts of uniformity in former years called forth the puritans. State creeds are blessed things for dissenters. The church catechism has yet a vast work to do in shaking the church, and increasing nonconformity. Church rates are a great boon to agitators. To take by violence men's tables, bibles, to carry away gunpowder from shops, tea pots, silver spoons and even favourite dogs from private dwellings, – to demand three or four times as much as the rate prescribes – and to do all this to purchase wine and bread for the sacrament of the squire, and to pay for the washing of the sacred vestments of the parson, who though he has an income of £300 or £500 a year, would wear a dirty surplice, if the poor dissenters were not mulcted of their property to find soap and a washerwoman – these abominations in the name of religion, will yet arouse even those dissenters who are asleep and make thousands of churchmen blush for a hierarchy and a priesthood who can descend to such meanness, because forsooth it is the law of the land, and being founded in *injustice* is a favourite statute with our modern successors of the apostles! The imprisonment of Toogood,[7] Simmonds, and others will tell on the nation with powerful effect in favour of the anti-state-church movement. Horse racing, card playing, hunting, shooting, drinking, debauched clergymen will do more than all the O'Connells

---

1 Martin Luther (1483–1546), religious reformer.

2 Ulrich Zwingli (1484–1531), Swiss Protestant reformer.

3 John Huss (*c.* 1373–1415), Bohemian church reformer.

4 Henry Phillpotts (1778–1869), Bishop of Exeter.

5 Samuel Wilberforce (1805–73), Bishop of Oxford.

6 John Merewether (1797–1850), Dean of Hereford, opposed the election of Hampden to the see of Hereford in 1847.

7 Presumably John Thorogood, a Chelmsford dissenter imprisoned for failing to pay church rates.

in the world to agitate the 'heavens.' Ignorant, bigotted, and puseyite priests, – men who have slept so soundly at Oxford that they have forgotten the time, and are still dreaming the age is nine and not nineteen centuries old; these are our ecclesiastical agitators that will shake the very foundation of their church. God has ordained that iniquity in any shape, but especially in a sacred garb, shall produce dissatisfaction and disgust, and impel its victims to rebel.

IV. – The agitators I have just mentioned are *indirect*. They never intended to produce such an effect; but there are others whose *immediate* object is the shaking and overthrow of tyranny and oppression. Here we may mention THE PUBLIC PRESS. DESPOTS should never allow their subjects to read, nor leave books or newspapers without a censor. France, Austria, Prussia, Italy, and Russia, feared the power of the press. Tracts, pamphlets, periodicals, and newspapers have shaken church and state a thousand times. Providence has made large use of this mighty engine. Almost every operative now reads the news of the day, and especially the empty speeches, the foolish proceedings, and disorderly conduct of infatuated senators. Editors freely expatiate on these doings and thus open the eyes of the masses to see right and wrong and seek the entire overthrow of injustice. *Public* meetings also are terrific objects to the patrons of church and state corruption. In these assemblies every abuse is exposed and the soul of the nation stirred to demand its rights and liberties. But these conventions to be effective must be peaceable. If oppressive rulers were to speak out they would bestow their highest honours on the madmen who persuade the oppressed to resort to violence. In former years men were actually employed by the government to provoke the people to rebel against order and the laws, that an argument might thence be derived in favor of absolute power. We do not charge the present ministry with having employed and paid the speakers who lately talked so loudly in favour of physical violence; but this we know, that nothing could have been more favourable to aristocratical injustice or more detrimental to popular freedom. It gave the abettors of war a pretext in favour of standing armies and the continuance of our present extravagant expenditure. Lord John ought to give pensions to the principal actors, seeing they did more to aid his falling power than any thing that has occurred for many a day. Again we repeat, that public meetings to be effectual must be rational and peaceable. Nothing but mischief can arise from the spread of alarm. To put life and property in danger is to produce the greatest prejudice against the masses. To match violence with violence, or injustice with injustice is as little conducive to rational liberty as the fighting of two bull dogs, or the baiting of a bull, a bear, or a badger. *Justice* is the only true and triumphant antagonist of wrong: and it is when the people can meet as they did in the antislavery and anti-corn law agitation, and peacefully demand the repeal of oppressive laws, that the government trembles and is compelled to give way. Truth and equity come from God and are omnipotent for all the purposes of reform. Ten thousand thousand thousand bayonets arrayed against the voice of reason and rectitude are as impotent as so many blades of grass. Hence real reformers never carry swords; their tongue touched with a live coal from the celestial altar is their only weapon, and with it they become more than conquerors.

Intellectual and moral agitators are the agents which the Lord of hosts more directly employs. With these he intends 'to shake the heavens and the earth, the sea and the dry land.' All nations are destined to feel their power, and hence every true christian is anointed of God to be a *radical* and an *agitator*. He who is not one and yet bears the name of the Redeemer, is a 'wolf in sheep's clothing.' Moral reformers are the only men fit to overthrow tyranny and renovate the world. Here we have an energy which costs nothing; an invincible power which every *fustian jacket and smock frock* may use, and with it shake the throne of despotism until its empire falls. The fishermen of Gallilee were the poorest of all men; they carried neither 'purse, nor scrip, nor club,' and yet they convulsed the world. Millions of tyrants have fallen before them, and still 'the heavens and earth' vibrate from the impulse of their stroke. Nor shall these agitators cease until truth has triumphed – until 'the oppressor is broken to pieces,' the world is emancipated, and mankind are universally free and universally blest.

TRACTS FOR THE FUSTIAN JACKETS
AND SMOCK FROCKS.

THE WORKING CLASSES
THE BEST REFORMERS.
A FEW WORDS FOR THE CHARTISTS.
BY THE REV. B. PARSONS,
OF EBLEY, STROUD, GLOUCESTERSHIRE.

'Can there any good thing come out of Nazareth?'
'Come and see.'
                    THE GOSPEL OF JOHN.

A few words for the Chartists! A minister of religion too, undertaking to say
a few words for the Chartists! And above all to do so after the never to be forgotten 10th of April 1848!! To speak not a *few* but *many* words *against* them, that
would be tolerated as highly christian, spiritual and evangelical, but to speak a
word *for* them! – Alas! alas! what times we live in! Surely these are the last days!
Tis true that every miscreant if he can find a *fee*, can obtain an educated man in
wig, gown and bands, who will plead his cause. The criminal is a thief or a murderer, and this is pretty well known to the advocate, and yet you can procure
men, who, to use the words of *Young*,

'Earn dirty bread, by washing Ethiops white,'[1]

and do so without hardly any one's doubting that they are scholars, gentlemen
and apostolical christians who have been regenerated by the church, and by their
own modest avowal, are the only *really*, *truly* and *perfectly sanctified* persons on the
face of the earth. Now if money can thus cover a multitude of sins; if even the
vilest monster can be defended for money; if to keep their places, *alias*, their *fees*
or salaries, ten thousand men, some of them evangelicals, were willing to insult
heaven and earth, by calling Charles and George IV 'THE MOST RELIGIOUS'
beings upon earth – if this could be responded to by all the people of rank and
education in the land – and if it was deemed important to repeat this great
untruth many times a week in the temple of the living God, lest christianity and
the constitution should be annihilated, then surely it may be forgiven, though a
few words should be said for the Chartists. It is well known that men who have
no merit but have *money* can be defended and applauded, and therefore it ought

---

1 Edward Young, *Night Thoughts* (1742–5), l. 353.

not to be an unpardonable sin, if a word or two should be uttered on behalf of citizens who however destitute of money, are not, as I will show, entirely free from merit. By the bye, this reference to money suggests the great fact, that one of the blackest things in the circumstances of the chartists, is their supposed poverty. That some of them have used violent language would be pardoned if they had more wealth, because lords, dukes, squires, and clergymen often have been guilty of this offence, which was rendered quite venial by the imagined *property* qualification of the sinners. That some of the masses have been foolish enough to talk of physical force is a pity, but then they have been taught this by their vaunted betters. Louis Philippe was a physical force monarch, and yet we have had his downfall bewailed, and men in holy orders have tried to whitewash him and to show him up as the prop, not of the wiliest despotism, but, of the wisest policy.

Perhaps before we proceed any further we may as well define what we mean by a chartist. The six points of the charter are, '*Universal Suffrage, Vote by Ballot, No Property Qualification, Payment of Members of Parliament, Electoral Districts and Annual Parliaments.*' These I have shown in '*Tracts*' 2 & 3 to be in accordance with the word of God. They are also included in the British constitution and indeed are essential to the full development of its character, and the proper and equitable working of its principles. Until these are granted there will be no security for the people against oligarchical despotism. Now *a chartist is one who advocates these six points of the charter.* Hence the *Newport riots, physical force, national conventions, monster meetings, or metropolitan processions*, have no more to do with the six points of the charter than the fires of Smithfield and the burning of heretics with christianity. If bad advocacy, foolish or violent advocacy, is sufficient to prove that the thing advocated is bad, then we must all become infidels; for nothing could have more outraged humanity and common sense than the means which thousands have adopted to propagate the gospel. But then, persons of thought and reflection always separate the cruelties of Harry VIII,[1] Mary,[2] Elizabeth,[3] Charles II, and their obsequious flatterers and minions from the religion of the new testament. And yet it would be as fair to charge the bible with the crimes of any of the popes or of Louis XIV[4] as to taunt the chartists as a body with the indiscretion of those who have thought, that a just cause might be carried by unjust means. Surely we ought not for the nine hundredth and ninety ninth time to have to say, that the *six points of the charter* are one thing, and the mode of advocating them another. In speaking a few words for the chartists, I am not about to defend the creed, the morals, or the language of every chartist. All mankind, even the holiest believers, are imperfect. Who would say that Abraham, or Moses, or the apostle Paul was perfect. Absolute perfection is the property of no one except the Deity, 'there is none good,' – none perfectly and entirely good – 'but one, that is God.' Compared with him, every creature is imperfect, and therefore 'the heavens are not clean in *his* sight,' and 'the angels *he* chargeth with folly.' If we were

---

1 Henry VIII (1491–1547), King of England 1509–47.
2 Mary I (1516–58), Queen of England and Ireland 1553–8.
3 Elizabeth I (1533–1603), Queen of England and Ireland 1558–1603.
4 Louis XIV (1638–1715), King of France 1643–1715.

to give up every good principle that is either *imperfectly* advocated, or advocated by *imperfect* men, then we must abandon truth and righteousness and benevolence altogether. My readers then need not be alarmed lest I should try to make it appear that the chartists are without fault. I could not undertake this for the nobility, or bishops, or clergy, or dissenting ministers, or even for the chief of saints. Nor is it necessary. The church of England, in the estimation of its *modest* members is the *very best* form of christianity in the whole world! aye better than the christianity of the new testament, from which it so thoroughly dissents, and yet the holy church of England has been advocated by the most brainless, furious, blaspheming, sabbath breaking, debauched beings that have ever walked the earth. These advocates too have had the blessing of the bishops and clergy, without any of them insinuating that the *thing* was bad which had such miserable and ungodly defenders. I have known one of the most inveterate sceptics come forward and plead for the church; I once heard a gentleman, to defend the church, keep on shouting 'Tipperary!!' 'Tipperary!!'[1] – now there was no piety in the one, or common sense in the other, and yet the kindness of the defenders was gratefully accepted. The matter put into a syllogism, stood thus –

If a gentleman, a noted sceptic, defended the church by talking nonsense that would have disgraced a national schoolboy, then the church of England is an apostolical church! A gentleman, a well known sceptic, did defend the church by talking such nonsense! *therefore* the church of England is an apostolical church!! Or take the other case,

If an educated gentleman can cry 'Tipperary!' then the church of England is a godly church! An educated gentleman did shout 'Tipperary' *therefore* the church of England is a godly church!!!

Every clergyman and school boy knows that I could fill volumes with the wickedness and foolishness of those who have undertaken to protect the *established* church when *tottering*, and yet no one of the clergy will admit that episcopalianism is bad because many of its defenders have been as destitute of rhyme, or reason, as they were of religion. Now I ask just as much, and no more, for the '*people's charter*,' and the chartists, than is thus daily conceded to the hierarchy of our land. The charter, like mother church, may have been defended by men to whom it might be said,

> 'Ye brainless wits! ye baptized infidels;
> Ye worse for mending! washed, to fouler stains!'[2]

But this does not alter the question a whit, for the church and the charter may be good for all that. Truth and righteousness, like the Deity, are absolutely perfect, are so positively good, as to admit of no comparative or superlative degree – are eternal, immutable, and incorruptible, and hence cannot be altered by the folly or wickedness of men. If the charter is based on truth and right, receive it, if not, confute it and reject it, but in the name of common sense and consistency,

---

1 Presumably symbolising Catholicism in general.
2 Edward Young, *Night Thoughts* (1742–5), ll. 233–4.

do not mix up with the six points of the charter, the imperfections of any of its defenders, or if you persist in doing this, then by all means be consistent, and at once abandon not only the church, but truth and christianity.

But a few words for the chartists, or those who believe that the six points of the charter are founded in justice, are perfectly accordant with christianity, the constitution, and the rights of man, and therefore ought to become the law of the land. I know that many, that perhaps the majority, are to be found among *the fustian jackets and the smock frocks*. Ye men and women of hard hands and hard fortune, and hard fare, your chief fault in the eye of thousands, is not your chartism but your poverty. Could you boast of rank purchased by the plunder, the infamy, or sycophancy of your ancestors; could you recount wealth obtained by slaughter, by injustice, or pensions for doing nothing; were the diplomas of literary blockheads, the coronets won by Norman Vandals, or the 'barbarian pomp' of senseless vanity, yours, then your chartism would be extolled by all the bishops, clergy, aristocratical dissenters, and the haughty *gentle*-folks of the land, but alas! alas! you honestly earn your daily bread – you produce the wealth of the land – you make many rich, and therefore of course your charter is a bad thing. You often hear the old exclamation, 'Can any good thing come out of Nazareth?'

It would not after all be amiss, if those who possess leisure and opportunity would reflect, that the masses in all great questions have been oftener right than the wealthy and the aristocracy. This was preeminently the case respecting the slave trade, slavery and the corn laws. Were history investigated the same fact might be shown from the records of all ages and nations. And even when violence has been resorted to, that very cruelty has been taught by the example, and elicited by the tyranny of the great and the noble. The masses have not rebelled until patience and forbearance have been outraged in the most shameless manner. It is an incontrovertable fact that virtue moves upwards but wickedness downwards. The people wear the vices of the aristocracy as they do their livery or their old clothes, and even the vulgarest form of modern depravity can be traced back to the halls of the barons of another age. Luxurious ease and aristocratic privileges have been a political and moral pest-house, from which the greater part of the ills that have scourged this world have emanated, these more than anything else, have emasculated and corrupted humanity. It is fashionable to throw all the blame of popular ignorance and crime upon Adam, upon Lucifer, upon predestination, or even, – we shudder at the blasphemy! – on the Almighty himself! and thus to screen the guilty agents from deserved condemnation; but let the matter be investigated, and the natural history of all wickedness is as easily traced as the source of the Nile or the Thames. But if vice works downwards, virtue moves upwards. 'You see your calling brethren, that not many wise men after the flesh, not many mighty, not many noble are called. But God hath chosen the foolish things of the world to confound the wise, and God hath chosen the weak things of the world to confound the things which are mighty, and base things of the world and things which are despised hath God chosen, yea and things which are not to bring to nought things which are, that no flesh should glory in his presence.' It is worthy of remark that the apostle here is speaking of the masses, the common people, and he calls them not *persons*, but *'things;'* because in the language of proud Greece and Rome they were mere goods and chattels, *'things'* without a gender, sex, individuality or personality. Our brethren in Jamaica and elsewhere, were *'things'* only a few years ago, and could the aristocracy and clergy have had their desire, they would have been *'things'* to this very day. America makes liberty a mockery by holding such a multitude of her subjects in bondage, and though black slavery does not exist among us, yet thousands of our poor brethren, – the wealth producers of our age, are treated more like *'things,'* than persons of equal birth with the monarch, and the very offspring of God. From such *'things'* as these, God in all ages has chosen the reformers of the world. 'The sons of God are born, not of *blood* nor of the will of the flesh, nor of the will of man, but of God.' In the whole field of missions in modern times, you have neither nobles nor squires. These you may find in shoals among the 'slaughter men' and desolators of the earth. What dangers have they not braved to massacre mankind, but what have they done to save their brethren? At home they unblushingly tell us that they would not support religion nor educate the masses unless the state took the monies out of their pocket by force! There is but one Howard[1] in St Pauls, the majority of the other statues are erected to men who 'fell *gloriously*!!' in the very act of killing their fellow immortals and launching them amidst oaths, revenge and blood, into the presence of their judge; and worse than all, the slaughtermen themselves presumptuously rushed before the Almighty covered with their own gore and that of their brethren, expecting that their inhumanity and malignity would be rewarded with a crown!! I here enumerate these facts to show, that wisdom, philosophy and philanthropy, have had comparatively few votaries among the wealthy. The reformers have generally been called from the poor or needy, and the history of the charter and chartism, will add another laurel to the people's crown. The carrying of the charter would be one of the most glorious political reforms, and yet this grand movement has hitherto been conducted by men, who like the fishermen of Gallilee, are deemed unlearned and illiterate, and indeed the very 'offscouring' of all things. To us this is one of the charms of the movement. The nobility and gentry have generally some vested interest in corruption, and therefore are sure to mar, if possible, any reform which they can touch, but the people have a vested interest in justice to all, and hence they become perfect *radicals*. They, unless state priests or state school masters have unmanned them, have no sympathies for despotism, and if they had power would apply the besom of destruction pretty freely to all civil, political, and ecclesiastical injustice. Your bit and a bit reformers, your half and a half philanthropists, your men that heal the hurts of the nation slightly, your state quacks who cover the wound and leave the poison at the core, are always to be found among your respectables, your educated, your wealthy inhabitants, but your real out and out regenerators, who would provide none of the pestiferous carrion of political or hierarchial corruption for the black coated ravens, or the more *noble* birds of prey, must be chiefly sought among *the fustian jackets* and the

---

1 John Howard (1726–90), prison reformer.

smock frocks. Let not then the poverty to which aristocratic ingenuity has doomed the masses, be brought as an argument against the chartist movement. In all ages the people have been the best reformers, and but for them the world had long since been reduced to barbarism. For though the philanthropist who may have originated some glorious agitation, has been a person of rank and influence, he has been indebted for sympathy, power and success to the common people who have heard him gladly.

But a great objection is urged against the chartists because they are politicians. It is said that *fustian jackets and smock frocks* have nothing to do with politics. This observation would hold good if politics had nothing to do with the masses, but seeing there is not a man, woman, nor child in the country, but is affected by politics, and to a great extent injured or benefitted by the political laws of the land, then is it the duty of every one, but especially of the operatives, to bestir themselves in this very important branch of human affairs. It is rather amusing to hear people talk on this subject. We are told that good men ought to have nothing to do with politics, because politics would injure their piety! and, on the other hand, that bad men are not fit to manage them. Christians must not touch them because they are *good men*, and chartists must not touch them because they are *bad men*! At this rate we shall soon send the civil government to limbo, or the 'fool's paradise.' The legislature must consist of neither religious nor irreligious persons, but of a race of nondescripts who neither understand nor practice either right or wrong. What a blessed thing to have governors and politicians who are destitute of souls and consciences! Some people are so foolish as to think that we have had enough of this. But if heartless men make the best politicians, what nonsense for the clergy to pray that '*the lords of the council and all the nobility*' may be endowed '*with grace, wisdom and understanding*,' because as soon as they have 'grace, wisdom and understanding,' they will be good people and consequently unfit to be politicians. However a change is coming over the public mind, especially the more pious part of the community, for we have lately had the church in raptures at the thought that a popular preacher of the gospel had become the editor of a newspaper.[1] We do not say one word against this only we must entreat the christian men and women who have extolled this proceeding, to be consistent with themselves and allow other persons besides tory clergymen and doctors in divinity to use their own discretion in this matter. And surely the plebeian chartist who is crushed to poverty, deprived of his political rights, and taxed beyond his last penny, ought not to be branded as a traitor or a Vandal, because he asks for simple justice, and asks it too of a superlatively sanctimonious christian legislature. For I speak a well known truth, when I assert that my lord John Russell and the other episcopalian lords and commons are in their own modest estimation the most sanctified believers upon the face of the earth. Their piety is such that they tax every body else to pay for the support of their religion, and actually take by violence dogs! gunpowder! bibles! cigars! and silver spoons! from their

---

1 Possibly in reference to Edward Miall (1809–81), Independent minister and editor of the *Nonconformist*.

neighbours to pay for their sacramental bread! I must confess that nothing has pleased me more in this movement of the chartists than its *political* character. Until the working men plead their own cause, show their wrongs and demand their rights, they must groan under oppression. It is said that they should leave their cause with their betters. Poor souls! they have done this long enough, and the consequence has been the bitterest injustice and neglect. Why the man who, either in the House or out of the House, pleads for the rights of the working classes is sure to be slandered or persecuted, and by none so much as by those wealthy persons who profess to be endowed with a more than common share of christian piety. (No one can be offended with what I say without owning himself or herself guilty.) Look at the laughing cockcrowing parliaments, that the middle classes have chosen from the nobility and gentry, and then see if it is safe for the masses to commit their cause to the hands of their superiors. The chief good that the whigs are doing by keeping in office, is, that they are showing their own worthlessness, and perfectly disgusting the nation. What will the present session effect for England, Ireland, or the world? What mischief was it not ready, by extravagance and increased taxation, to do, if the British Lion had not shaken his mane and shown his ire? The *fustian jackets and smock frocks* must become politicians and demand good government, and render the British sceptre a sceptre of righteousness, before the nation can have peace and prosperity. For years the wealth of the world has been within our reach, but aristocratic folly and class legislation have chained our hands and paralysed our energies, and therefore the chartists in arousing the masses to awake and think and ask for justice have done a noble work for which posterity will embalm their names and very cordially forgive the errors with which some may have been chargeable.

But it is objected that they are bad politicians. This charge comes with a poor grace from those who make it, seeing not a few of these accusers of the chartists are among the very worst political economists. And besides, men are allowed to be *bad* politicians, provided they have property or learning, or their fathers were lords! Is there any one in the country so infatuated as to expect a good legislator or elector from either Oxford or Cambridge? Are not the sympathies of the clergy proverbially on the side of despotism and corruption? Is not the exception a rare occurrence? To hear a lord or a man of wealth talk good politics is almost a prodigy, and sure to make him lose caste among no small portion of his equals. Indeed many of the gentry have been so badly educated that they cannot rise to speak without claiming the indulgence of the operatives on whose patience and good sense they so unsparingly trespass. How often they cough, and how loudly you must clap to help them along. The mountains are evidently in labour to bring forth a mouse. It is actually not expected in these enlightened days that a gentleman should be a good speaker or a good politician. If any of them, to whom these remarks apply, should read my words and resolve, by reading and thinking to render themselves intelligent and intelligible I shall thank providence that I have not written in vain. If you want the most humbling specimens of bad politics badly delivered, you must go to the parliament house or read the daily press. And not a few of our newspaper editors are so fascinated with bad politics when falling from the lips of a lord or squire that they do their utmost to diffuse the oracular nonsense. Now it is an old saying that 'there ought to be the same sauce for the goose as the gander.' If a lord, or a duke, or a clergyman may be not only forgiven, but actually extolled for talking bad political economy, then surely some pardon should, in common justice, be accorded to the poor illiterate chartist; especially, when it is remembered that oppression has doomed him to poverty, and this very poverty has limited his education. Besides, any educated or thinking man who ventures to associate with the chartists, to lend them his advice, is condemned as an outlaw and a monster. That distinguished philanthropist and christian, Mr Samuel Bowly,[1] whose character stands so deservedly high throughout the city and county of Gloucester, was lately called upon to defend himself for having attended a meeting of the operatives that he might give them the aid of his counsel. − The religious people were almost in hysterics on the subject; some seemed ready to faint. Had he gone to the hall and clapped his hands while a sprig of the aristocracy, hardly out of his teens, had insulted the county by a mock election and vowed to pursue a course of politics which, if persevered in, would inevitably endanger the throne and bring the country to beggary, then the good people would have eaten their suppers and said their prayers without first charging their pistols, lest a member of the Peace Society at the head of the chartists should break into their houses. There was some time ago a law passed in America that no slave should be emancipated unless he could read; and then another was immediately enacted that any person who taught a slave to read should be transported! Now the same thing is conventionally decreed in our country by the respectable and pious people of the present time. − First, every chartist shall be a bad man, and especially a bad politician. Secondly, no good or intelligent man shall go among the chartists to correct any thing that may appear to be wrong. And thus the christian prudery of the age dooms a large portion of its most intelligent citizens to neglect, and then, if they happen to make a blunder, holds them up to universal contempt. I charge to the clergy, the gentry, and the religious people, all the ignorance imputed to the chartists. I do not lay the sins of this ignorance to the account of the government. − Government has nothing whatever to do with the education of the people; but the ministers of religion, the wealthy classes, and the electors ought long ago to have redressed the wrongs of the masses, and thus have put them in a position to educate themselves; and where necessary, the rich should have furnished from their own voluntary offerings every thing requisite to further this work. I am no advocate of popular ignorance, no apologist for unsound political economy. Every one who reads what I have written, or examines what I have done, knows that I need make no defence on this point. Still I must demand justice for the chartists, and that those who extol injustice when uttered by a lord or squire will exercise a little candour towards their poor brethren, if, when struggling for their rights, a sentence which will not bear to be grammatically or politically parsed should escape from their lips. The charter shows that they are the soundest, the wisest, and most equitable

---

1 Samuel Bowly (1802–84), Quaker, Gloucester cheese factor.

politicians of the day, and if some sentiments on other subjects, broached by a few of their number, have not displayed the discernment of Solon, then let the middle classes associate with them and correct their errors. The mistakes of individual men have nothing to do with the principles embraced in the six points. The chartists are also willing to learn. Their conduct since the 10th of April has shown that as a body they have no wish to disturb the country. Had they been as bad as they are said to be they might have agitated the nation to a fearful extent. If their power is contemptible, why were £200,000, or more, spent to protect the city of London; or ammunition prepared, enough, as a gentleman told me, to blow the masses to atoms for fifteen days? Was not alarm convenient to a government waning in popularity? A threat of civil war was a windfall to men wishing to have an excuse for a standing army, a pensioned aristocracy, and increased taxation. The chartist who talked about physical force was no small favourite with the friends of despotism. But again we repeat that these things have nothing to do with the charter. We would earnestly recommend to our timid friends an article on the chartist movement in the May number of the 'Evangelical Magazine.' Give the people their rights, and 'a little child may lead them;' and never call them bad politicians while they advocate by peaceable means that full share of liberty which is their due; – for which the fathers and founders of the British nation contended and bled; and which is all that is demanded in the people's charter. We are glad to see so many of the *public journals* doing homage to the wisdom of the chartists. Some are willing to have *three* of the points, some *four*, some *five*, and one leading journal has said that there is nothing so very objectionable in the *six*. One editor, who has taken the *five* points only, omits '*the payment of members of parliament*.' But this proposition is actually one of the best. If you do not pay your members they will pay themselves. Many of them now get double or treble. Besides, for want of remunerating our representatives hundreds of *good men* are excluded from the legislature. And above all, *justice* demands, that if we use the services of our fellow citizens they ought to be paid. We are always safe if we take our stand by the side of justice. Wherever members are paid it has answered well. – Look at Norway for example. '*Be just and fear not*,' must be our motto. This is what is asked for by those bad politicians, the chartists.

But we are told again that the chartists are in favour of *physical* force. This is not true of the body. Some who have been duped by spies who wish to drive the working classes to extremes that their cause may be ruined, and the men may be shot, may have talked about pikes and firelocks, but all enlightened chartists, and they are the majority, know that an appeal to brute force would be the most insane thing upon earth. The chartists ask for justice, for constitutional liberty, for *practical* christianity, but in demanding these boons, they will not hurt the hair of any man's head. They know that murder is not reformation. He who stabs a tyrant is himself a bloodthirsty man and as little to be trusted with power, as the victim he slew. The *only real conqueror* is he, who by solid argument, by kindness and perseverance, convinces his opponent and converts him into a friend. But it would not be a wonder if some of the operatives should have been led astray by the example of the respectables. Thousands of these are *physical force* men and women, and of course ought to be avoided. My Lord John Russell is a *physical force* man and therefore is unfit to be a premier. The house of lords and the bishops perhaps to a man are physical force gentlemen, and consequently unfit for their high stations. The house of commons can hardly name a member who belongs to the Peace Society. The idea of such a thing would make that merry cockcrowing house laugh for the next month. The clergy and a great portion of the dissenting ministers have faith in *physical force*. 'To beat swords into ploughshares,' is ridiculed. What a pity it is recommended in the Bible. Is not the book damaged by such outlandish advice? Now with all this array of *physical force* wisdom and respectability, with standing armies and navies, with cannons, firelocks and bayonets, saluting him everywhere, with flags of war in churches, sermons in favor of war in chapels, statues of men *'who fell gloriously'!!* while murdering their innocent fellows, is it any wonder if a few poor chartists have been led astray by their superiors, and supposed that arms might be taken in defence of RIGHT? Taking these matters into consideration, the wonder is that so many of *the fustian jackets and smock frocks* have risen so far above their learned and wealthy and noble and consecrated neighbours, as to protest against the use of any thing but *moral force* to obtain their rights. Here again we have 'the foolish confounding the wise,' and these bad politicians actually a century ahead of the schools, the university and the church. *Physical force* is the *impotence* of hell, *moral force* is the *omnipotence* of heaven.

Finally, the chartists are irreligious and especially sabbath breakers. What will be said next to condemn the poor chartists? Until now it has been proclaimed from the pulpit that religious men should have nothing to do with politics, but lo! these objectors blow hot and blow cold with the same breath, for the chartist must not be a politician because he is not religious! were he religious, then they would tell him he must not ask for justice because he *is* religious!! and now they say he must not seek his rights because he is *not* religious!! so the poor fellows are to be done either way. With a notoriously irreligious race of senators, we are told that the chartists must be religious before they ask for constitutional freedom and equity! Well but they meet on Sundays and break the sabbath. I am sorry that they should violate the day of rest. My views of the sacredness of the sabbath would be laughed at by those spiritual people who cry out against the chartists. I knew the wealthy deacon of a church, who kept his servant girls at home cooking and his man at home cleaning knives and shoes, while he very piously went to the sanctuary, to pray for the salvation of the world. The fact is we have a sabbath breaking nobility, gentry, and clergy. The working classes are not only taught by the example of the wealthy to set at nought the sabbath, but are doomed, on pain of starvation to trample the fourth commandment under foot; and is it any wonder, if poor creatures who have rarely had a day of rest, who have been robbed of God's day from their childhood, is it any wonder if these children of neglect and oppression have no higher ideas of the sacredness of the sabbath than lords, bishops, railway companies, doctors in divinity, and deacons of churches? Here we ask justice for all. Ye who condemn the irreligion of the chartists, lift your voice against the sabbath breaking of monarchs, of lords, of bishops, of ministers, and professors of religion. 'Physician heal thyself.' To the chartists I would say never hold another meeting on a Sunday! If not for religion, for policy sake, take that handle from the mouths of your adversaries. To the religious people and ministers of the sanctuary, I would add, make the house of God attractive by showing to the operative that the gospel is the true charter of man for both worlds, and demonstrate by your deeds the sincerity of your words, and you shall not have to complain of empty temples, or sabbath breaking chartists.

But, 'Mr O'Connor,' say they, 'is a bad man.' I never spoke to Mr O'Connor, but I have heard that he is a zealous member of the church of England and therefore of course no infidel but a regenerated man. 'But his land scheme is horrible.' Have a little patience, if good, it will work well, if not, the thing will show itself. He and his plans are before the country and the whole nation is the jury, and facts will decide their judgement. You who do nothing for the people and croak at philanthropy of every sort, should be silent or else set a good example. But Mr O'Connor is not the charter, the land scheme has nothing to do with the six points. Were Mr O'Connor an angel or a demon, were 'Snig's End'[1] a paradise or a purgatory, the charter would not be affected by one or the other. What then is the guilt of the chartists? they ask '*Universal Suffrage*,' the very thing taught in the word of God, this is *crime* ONE; they ask for '*Vote by Ballot*,' that the poor may be defended from the rich, this is *crime* TWO; they ask for a *rational* division of the country into '*Electoral Districts*,' this is *crime* THREE; they ask that '*Annual Parliaments*,' should render representatives responsible to electors, this is *crime* FOUR; they ask for the abolition of that absurdity, '*the Property Qualification*,' this, though practised in Scotland, &c., is *crime* FIVE; they ask that '*Members should be paid*,' this demand of justice is *crime* SIX. These, these, are their crimes, therefore let no one speak on their behalf. Send missionaries to India or Africa, let your sympathies embrace outcasts at the antipodes, but let no pious man, no Samuel Bowly, attempt, on pain of being deemed a christian outlaw, to guide with his discretion the counsels or movements of the chartists! Is it thus decreed that these sons of toil, poverty and oppression shall be abandoned and abandoned because they ask for JUSTICE? Then we need not wonder if our philanthropy should be questioned, and our zeal for religion be deemed problematical.

---

1 A Chartist Land Company settlement.

TRACTS FOR THE FUSTIAN JACKETS AND SMOCK FROCKS.

THE 'POWERS THAT BE' AND THE 'POWERS THAT BE' OF GOD.
BY THE REV. B. PARSONS,
OF EBLY, STROUD, GLOUCESTERSHIRE.

'Let every soul be subject to supreme authority,
For there is no authority but from God.' Rom. xiii. 1.

'The powers that be!' What a boon this text has been to tyrants! And what a stumbling block to sceptics and rational divines! If every soul is obligated by the command of heaven to be subject to *'the powers that be,'* then if they order us to steal, we must steal; or to kill, we must kill; or to swear, we must swear; or to play the hypocrite, we must do as they bid. What a blessed scene of royal confusion the world would present if this injunction were literally obeyed! But, gentle reader, you need not be alarmed. The text is badly rendered, or rather, I ought to say, *politically* translated to suit the tastes of despots and the friends of arbitrary government. James I[1] was a tyrant of the first water, though he was said by the bishops to be especially inspired from above and the very Solomon of his age. I should be sorry to disfigure this tract with the disgusting portrait of this monarch which the historians of his day have handed down to us. It seemed quite in character that so perfect a ruler should emphatically insist on the doctrine of *'the divine right of kings.'* Plenty of minions and flatterers surrounded him and laboured to gratify his vanity and ambition, and none more so than the priesthood. Even the scriptures were translated to disturb as little as possible the fears of the prince. We have shown in tracts 5 and 8 that the bible is the most *radical* book in the world. Like its divine author it is no respecter of persons, and therefore spares the wickedness of none. Royal culprits are not excused because they wear crowns, and more vulgar iniquity is not passed over in silence because the transgressors were clothed in rags. We need hardly say that a plain version of such a book would be no favourite with worldly minded bishops, a corrupt aristocracy, or oppressive monarchs. As a proof of the correctness of these remarks take the following examples. The Greek word *'episcopos,'* is generally rendered *'bishop,'* but

---

1 James I (1566–1625), King of England 1603–25.

in Acts xx. 28, the term *'overseers'* is adopted, because, had *'bishops'* been used, all the poorer people would have seen that the apostolic *episcopacy* of the primitive church was a very different thing from the episcopacy of the English hierarchy; for instead of having *one lord bishop* over many churches, you have *many bishops* over one church, and you have no *lord* bishop at all; for the context shows that they were labourers or mechanics, and instead of wearing mitres and lawn sleves were clothed in fustian jackets and smock frocks, or what, in those early times, were used by the operatives as a substitute for those honourable garments. Human beings, and especially professing christians, were not then sunk so low as to need gowns and bands or £10,000 a year to render them respectable. Alas! alas! what havoc would be made of priestcraft and despotism if the clergy would but give unto the masses a literal translation of God's own word. We are not without hope that our working people will, before many years, determine to study Greek and Hebrew, and thus prevent themselves from being led astray by a *political* church. But let us look at another specimen. In Revelation xvi, 10, the fifth angel is said to pour out his vial on the *'seat of the beast.'* The Greek word is *'thronos,' 'a throne;'* but to suppose that an angel would pour out a vial on *'a throne'* though the *throne of a beast* would have sorely disturbed the monarch, and the softer word *'seat,'* was adopted. Mary, the mother of our Lord, was a perfect *radical*, – for radicalism in those days was an important part of piety and patriotism, and *women* were as radical and piously patriotic as the other sex; – aye, and shall be so again before many years. Well, Mary was a radical, and embodied no small part of her radicalism in her song of praise. She was so wicked as to mix religion and politics together. In the *'magnificat'* so regularly read in our churches, after commencing her thanksgiving with –

'My soul doth magnify the Lord,
And my spirit hath rejoiced in God my Saviour,'

she adds –

'He hath put down POTENTATES from their THRONES,
And exalted them of low degree.'

Was it not very profane thus to introduce politics into religion? What must our pious people think of the blessed Mary? And then not for a man, but for a *woman*! – 'Tell it not in Gath!' for a woman to be thus political! Is not the church of England, which forsooth so thoroughly nauseates politics, polluted by using Mary's Song within her consecrated walls? Why do not the bishops ask permission of parliament, to dispense with its use. Stop, courteous reader, mother church is wise in her generation, and therefore has spiritualized the verse, for in the prayer book she has given another turn to the passage. We there read –

'He hath put down the mighty from their seats,
And exalted the HUMBLE AND MEEK.'

Very prudently, and in consistency with her character as the *'poor man's* church,' she omits the reference to the *fustian jackets and smock frocks* which Mary made, (for her husband was a carpenter,) and substitutes a moral qualification. Had this poor woman only alluded to the *property* instead of the *poverty* qualification, no liberty would have been taken with her inspired words. However, the matter answered marvellously, and James could read the *'magnificat'* without alarm; when, had it been literally translated, the idea that 'the God of heaven putteth down *potentates from their thrones'* would have disturbed his dreams for many a night. But the 'throne is established by righteousness.' Princes and governments that act justly have nothing to fear from their subjects, and therefore have no need to falsify the scriptures. The best way to silence the radicals is for monarchs and rulers to become *radicals* themselves, and *eradicate* all civil and political injustice and corruption, and then tumult and anarchy will cease. The greatest anarchists and revolutionists are iniquitous legislators and tyrannical princes.

I might adduce other proofs to show that a great effort was made in translating the bible to render it an aristocratical book, but the text which has furnished a title to this tract is sufficient evidence of this. The verses should be read –

'Let every soul be subject to supreme authorities, for there is no authority except from God; those which are authorities have been ordained by God. So that he who setteth himself against this authority resisteth the institution of God, and those who resist shall receive in themselves condemnation. For these rulers are not the terror of good works but of evil. Dost thou wish not to be terrified by this authority, practice goodness, and thou shalt have praise of the same. For God's servant is thine for good. But if thou doest evil, fear, for he beareth not the sword in vain. For God's servant is righteous in his wrath towards him that doeth evil. Wherefore it is necessary to be subject not merely on account of wrath but also for the sake of conscience. For this cause also pay ye tribute, for the servants of God pay especial attention to this very thing. Render therefore to all persons the things which are due; tribute to whom tribute is due, custom to whom custom is due, fear to whom fear is due, honour to whom honour is due. Be in debt to no one, except to love one another; for he that loveth another hath fulfilled the law.'

All the clergy know that I have given a faithful translation of this inspired text, and I will now offer a few words of explanation.

I. – It is a question whether the text has any particular reference to civil or political governments, but if it has, they are here called not *'powers,'* but *'authorities,'* for the Greek word *'exousia'* has this signification. The distinction is a very important one, because *power* and *authority* are very different ideas. A man may have *power* to crush, oppress, or murder his neighbour, but he has no authority from God to be thus cruel. Cain had *'power'* to slay Abel, and Nero to behead the apostle Paul, but neither of them had any *authority* from heaven to commit these crimes. *Authority* then is *delegated power*. It is permission to exercise power, and in the text, it means *permission from God*. Our judges have *authority* to pass the sentence of the law upon certain offences. Like the centurion in the scripture, they are *'under authority,'* and if the laws that sanction their proceedings accord with the word of God, they have authority from heaven, but if not, they are notoriously wicked for taking a salary to administer unjust or cruel laws. The hangman has the authority of the judge to murder his fellows with the rope, but neither he nor the man in ermine has any right according to the laws of christianity, to take away human life for any offence whatever.

II. – The paragraph before us sufficiently defines *what authority* it means, for the text tells us that there is '*no authority but from God,*' and, that those '*who are authorities have been ordained by God,*' and thus we have explained what is signified by '*supreme authority.*' '*Supreme authority*' means the *highest authority,* but the only '*supreme or highest authority*' is the authority of the 'King of kings and Lord of lords.' No authority therefore can be supreme unless it be that of the Creator or so exactly accordant with his word as to be identical with his will. It need not here be asked, how can we know whether an authority is agreeable to his mind, because the bible fully reveals to us the statutes of Jehovah. Here the word of God is our supreme arbiter. 'To the law and to the testimony, if they speak not according to this law they have no *truth* in them,' and we may add, that if they act not according to this law they have no true authority. When the text says that 'those who are authorities are ordained of God,' it asserts that their *authority is* '*set in order, defined, determined, or prescribed,*' by the universal lawgiver. Such is the signification of the Greek. The Apostle also uses the perfect tense of the passive voice, and the rendering may be, '*those which are authorities have been determined of God.*' The thing is not *to* be done, it has been effected already by the wisest and best of beings in the universe; and if it be asked 'where?' we reply, '*in the scriptures.*' God is our supreme lawgiver, the supreme lawgiver of kings and rulers, and consequently the King of kings and Lord of lords. Hence the monarch of England is called the '*servant*' *of God.* The clergy for years used the words, '*thy servant Charles, George, William,*' &c., as the case might be. A servant is one who obeys his master or lord, and if the English monarchs are the *servants* of Jehovah then of course they observe the laws of heaven, otherwise it is a mockery to call them God's servants. Now the laws of Jehovah are in the scriptures. There he has already '*set in order, defined, determined, or prescribed,*' every thing that kings, rulers, legislators, or their subjects ought to do; and we are not at liberty to add a single letter to his law, nor to alter or take away one jot or tittle; if we do we are threatened to have our names taken away from the book of life and to have every plague denounced against such rebels and blasphemers poured out upon us. It is at our peril, it is at the eternal peril of any prince, emperor, or senator, to legislate contrary to the laws of Jesus Christ. The person who does so is guilty of high treason against him who is the blessed and only potentate, the King of kings and Lord of lords. Wherever we have God's law to direct us in what we do we have God's *authority,* and consequently '*supreme* authority.' How definitely the verse before us explains itself. – First, we have '*supreme authorities*' mentioned: then, we are told that there is '*no authority but from God:*' and thirdly, that '*those which are authorities are defined of God.*' They are therefore '*supreme,*' because they are '*from God,*' and are, '*defined*' in his word. Here then, you have a sure test by which you can decide whether governors have any real authority or not. If they legislate and judge according to the laws of the King of kings their authority is from above and we are bound to obey them; but if they enact what is contrary to the word of revelation they are guilty of rebellion against the universal sovereign, and we are under no obligation to submit to them. 'We must *obey God rather than man*.' This is the doctrine taught by the precept and the examples of the Apostles. They never hesitated one moment when the commands of rulers clashed with the revealed will of their divine master, but preferred the scourge, imprisonment, and death to the guilt of yielding obedience to a law which was opposed to the will of their maker. Civil rulers, then, as now, had *power* to punish disobedience, just as Cain had physical *power* to murder Abel; but then they had '*no authority from God*' to take away the liberty or lives of any of his subjects because these virtuous persons preferred allegiance to their rightful and divine sovereign. The emperor Nicholas has a greater right to slay an Englishman for obeying the laws of queen Victoria and rejecting the statutes of Russia than any earthly prince has to perse- cute or prosecute a human being for preferring the laws of God to the laws of tyrants and despots. What a pity that rulers and princes will not learn that the best way to render their '*authority supreme*' is to study the scriptures and take heed that all the statutes of their realm shall exactly accord with the bible. If they did this every person that rebelled against their authority would be guilty of treason against the Lord of Hosts. Monarchs might then talk of the '*divine right*' of their laws, and the throne would be established by righteousness. The Jewish judges and princes when they ruled according to the bible had the sanction and blessing of Jehovah, but when they legislated contrary to his word they became feeble, and all the good people, the real patriotic citizens, felt themselves bound by their duty to the Most High to disobey such usurpers. The greatest enemies to rulers are those who persuade them or aid them to make unchristian laws; and the peo- ple who obey such statutes are also guilty of treason, not only against heaven but against the very sovereign whom they thus encourage to trample upon human rights and the authority of God. The moral, as well as the physical world, is made to be governed by the laws of the Creator, and every statute that opposes this grand design is an act of treason against the Lord of Hosts. The Lord Jesus must reign until all enemies are under his feet; his is the only '*supreme power*' in the uni- verse, and human '*authorities*,' to prove themselves '*supreme*,' must demonstrate that their laws are in exact accordance with the perfect law of love taught by the Redeemer. We shall then have supreme authority in the world, every legislative enactment will be an embodiment of divine benevolence, every human being will have his rights, the world will be happy, and revolutions heard of no more. The rich will not oppress or despise the poor, nor will the poor be guilty of any injus- tice towards their wealthy brethren. It is said of the Lord Jesus, 'with righteousness shall he judge the poor, and argue with equity for the oppressed of the earth; and he shall smite the earth with the sceptre of his mouth, and with the breath of his lips shall he slay the wicked. And righteousness shall be the gir- dle of his loins and faithfulness the girdle of his reins. The wolf also shall dwell with the lamb and the leopard shall lie down with the kid, and the calf and the young lion and the fatling together, and a little child shall lead them.' Govern the people with the laws of the Saviour, which is only another word for saying, govern mankind with the law of love, and then, the sceptre of the whole world might be swayed by a 'little child.' We should no longer have any of those governments whose empires are called by that radical prophet, *Daniel*, the empires of *'beasts.'* We should have no royal lions, no aristocratical bears or tigers, and no priestly wolves or serpents. The kids, the calves, the oxen, and the lambs – the useful and peaceful and laborious portions of the world – the *fustian jackets and smock frocks of society* – would then be no more despised or oppressed, but the rich and poor would form one brotherhood of love, would all enjoy equal rights, and dwell together in harmony. Such will be the results of adopting the scriptures as the text book of legislation, and rendering human laws and human authority *'supreme'* by conforming them in every respect to the will of the God of heaven.

III. – The word *'authorities'* in the text under review is in the *plural* number, consequently there is no *one* particular authority referred to. A bishop has lately attempted to make this text support his ideas of a monarchy; but every one must see that there is not the least allusion to monarchs, oligarchs, emperors, popes, or republicans. The text teaches neither aristocracy, episcopacy, or democracy. It leaves all these things to be settled between the people and their rulers: it merely takes up the question of *'authority'* and tells us who has and who has not authority. All that act or rule according to the definite laws of christianity have the *authority* of heaven for their conduct, and all who violate God's universal law of love, are rebels against Jehovah and destitute of any divine authority whatever. The Almighty leaves it to the nations to choose that mode which may be best adapted to secure to all the people their rights. Peter tells us that kings are a *'human creation.'* His words are 'submit yourselves to *every human creation* for the Lord's sake, whether to the king as supreme,' &c., I Peter, ii, 13. In this text the king is called a *'human creation.'* It is true our translators have used the word *'ordinance'* instead of *'creation,'* but the latter rendering is the true sense of the Greek. King James and the bishops would have been frightened out of their wits if the country and the masses had been informed that kings were a *'human creation'* especially after they had been trying to make every one believe that they were of *divine origin.* The apostle not only says that kings are a *'human creation,'* but he also limits our obedience by the phrase, *'for the Lord's sake;'* intimating that we are to be in subjection only so far as we can do it in accordance with our duty to the Lord Jesus. *'For the Lord's sake'* does not mean that we are to submit to worship idols, to break the Sabbath, to destroy life, and trample upon the rights of our fellow creatures if any of these *'human creations'* command us to act thus, but that we are to yield obedience as far as we can do so without transgressing God's law of universal love. To suppose that we are exhorted by the Lord to disobey the Lord that we may please tyrants, or that we are to transgress the will of the Lord *'for the Lord's sake!!'* is an absurdity, because this is to teach that our Redeemer, who came into this world for the purpose of making us *religious,* has also commanded us to be *irreligious* if human governors should require it!! There is no common degree of blasphemy in this sentiment! Sceptics are not the only or the worst contemners and scoffers of God's word. Were we delivered from the infidelity, the presumption, and the blasphemy of the priesthood and the church, we should have nothing to fear from the opposition of unbelievers. To persuade men that *human creations* are *divine creations*, and that such monsters as Nero, Constantine,[1] Julian,[2] Harry VIII are to be obeyed rather than a God of love, is infidelity of a worse kind than any that has ever yet been exhibited by your Voltaires, or Tom Paines. The fact is, the bible does not dictate to us what forms of government we are to set up, but it commands what is far better, it tells us *how* we are to regulate our *civil*, *political*, and *ecclesiastical* affairs, and that we are to take care that all our laws shall exactly accord with its spirit because there is '*no authority but from God.*' The people have power to create kings, emperors, presidents, protectors, or republics, but no power on earth has any right to delegate or exercise an *authority* whose equity does not accord with the christianity of the new testament. There may be many kinds or forms of governments, and yet after all, there is but one '*supreme authority,*' and that is the eternal law of rectitude – '*thou shalt love thy neighbour as thyself.*' Now we want the people, especially the *fustian jackets and smock frocks*, to consider this great and glorious truth, that the scriptures give no shadow of authority to princes, priests, or rulers to be unjust, oppressive, or tyrannical. They command that all human statutes shall accord with that great principle of jurisprudence – '*whatsoever ye would that men should do unto you do ye also unto them, for this is the law and the prophets.*' Were governments to observe this golden rule they would have divine authority for their proceedings, and there would be no such thing at a tyrant, a slave, a soldier, or a rebel, on the face of the earth.

IV. – Verse the second, in this paragraph, tells us that '*he who sets himself up against this authority, resisteth the ordination, or arrangement of God, and they that resist shall receive in themselves condemnation.*' The '*authority*' here is '*the authority of God*' spoken of in the former verse, and therefore the words bear more hardly upon rulers than subjects, because they are the chief culprits, if they set up or assume an authority which is contrary to the bible. By so doing they oppose or resist God's revealed '*arrangement*' that his creatures shall be governed by his laws. The greatest rebels that have ever lived are those who have governed contrary to the scriptures. These attempt to dethrone the Eternal, and demand that his creatures should obey men rather than God! These are the kings, spoken of in the second psalm, 'who set themselves, and the rulers who take counsel together against the Lord and against his annointed, saying, let us break their bonds assunder and take away their cords from us.' These are the men at whom 'he who sitteth in the heavens shall laugh, the Lord shall have them in derision.' These are they who 'wage war with the Lamb.' A Nero, a Constantine, a Henry VIII, a Nicholas, or a Louis Philippe or an American president or congress setting themselves up against the plain dictates of humanity, equity, and benevolence are nothing less than rulers resisting the *ordination*, the *arrangement*, and the *authority of God*. How wickedly this text has been interpreted to serve the tyranny of despots and crush the people! The only persons, forsooth who can resist authority are the poor fustian jackets and smock frocks! Rulers to be sure are never thus guilty. Charles II,

---

1 Constantine the Great (*c.* 288–337), Roman Emperor 306–37.
2 Julian the Apostate (*c.* 331–63), Roman Emperor 360–63.

that mass of corruption, was called his *'sacred majesty,'* and *'a most religious king,'* and what is worse, the clergy were guilty of this abomination. The Puritans who obeyed the laws of heaven and acknowledged God's authority were condemned as bad men, and the rulers who trampled *divine authority* in the dust and set up *human authority* in its place, were of course good men. The bible has been thus perverted by its professed followers. Scarcely any text has been so grossly abused as the one before us. It has been applied exclusively to subjects when its chief reference is to princes and legislators. For though it condemns every one, whether monarch or slave who opposes the scriptures, it especially pronounces condemnation on those governors who set up their own power in opposition to the laws of God's anointed.

V. – This text tells us that, *'these rulers are not the terror to good works but of evil.'* *'These rulers'* are the *'authorities'* mentioned in the first verse, who legislate according to the scriptures. There is a peculiarity in the Greek which shows that 'these rulers and authorities are identical. And the apostle keeps up this idea by adding that, *'these rulers'* are 'not a terror to good works.' Show me a government that refuses liberty of conscience, or imposes fines, or any sort of punishment on 'good works,' and you at once point me to 'powers which are not of God.' The American president and congress are, or wish to be, a terror to those good men and women who are opposed to slavery and war, and therefore 'are not of God.' In Russia, Austria, Spain, &c., &c., the rulers have generally been a *terror* to *good* works, and not to evil. To be the favourites of these governments, you must be so wicked as to be the enemies of God and man; and yet these are *'the powers that be,'* which, according to the false interpretation of these words, ought to be implicitly obeyed! In reference to the rulers in the text, the Holy Spirit says, 'Dost thou wish not to be terrified at this authority? Do that which is good and thou shalt have praise of the same.' But to have praise of those governors who set the bible at defiance, you must do what is *evil,* or else, instead of having praise, you will be blamed. The English government, though greatly reformed by the people, yet still continues to be a terror to a variety of good works and a praise to wickedness. How it smiles upon the sycophant bishop, the ignorant and ungodly clergyman; and how it frowns upon the dissenter, however pious or learned he may be. How long it caressed the dealers in human flesh and blood; and the aristocrats who taxed the poor man's bread. How it praises the priests and officials who seize the goods of poor nonconformists to pay for the bread and wine which the squire consumes at the sacrament. How it lauds and pensions your slaughtermen who sell their liberty that they may slay their brethren. Even the hangman has its benediction. Were the society of friends and other dissenters to write a *'Book of Martyrs,'* the cruel days of queen Mary would be thrown into the shade. Considering the limits of its sway, the church of England is more deeply stained with blood than the church of Rome, and these cruelties were sanctioned by the ruling powers. Hence the authority spoken of in this passage of scripture is not the authority of England, France, or America. Those who have God's authority are not a terror to good works but to evil, and never legalize iniquity, or any thing that is contrary to the liberties and rights of the whole population.

VI. – This authorized ruler is called, in verse fourth, 'God's servant;' and is said to be ours 'for good:' in the latter clause it is added 'that he is righteous in his wrath towards him that doeth evil.' Him we ought to 'fear and reverence,' for 'he beareth not the sword in vain.' This text beautifully explains itself. First, it tells us that the ruler which it commends is '*a servant of God.*' Now 'a servant of God' is one who obeys the laws of God. Those senators or princes who make or administer laws contrary to the scriptures are not the servants of God. You might as well call Balaam, or Pharaoh, or Nero, the servants of God. Secondly, it is here added, '*God's servant is thine for good;*' but wicked rulers are not ours for good, but for mischief. Thirdly, we are exhorted to fear or reverence these servants of the Most High; but rulers who make statutes contrary to the Saviour's law of universal brothethood and love are not the servants of Christ but the ministers of Satan and therefore are not to be feared. Fourthly, '*the servant of God:*' the ruler who legislates according to the scriptures has authority, and 'bears not the sword in vain.' By the sword here we are only to understand the emblem of authority and the power to punish those who transgress such laws as are sanctioned by God's word. The expression is a metaphorical one, like the word '*ax*' or '*fasces*' among the Romans, but it by no means countenances the taking away of human life. Thieves and murderers, &c., may be punished by the magistrate, but we have no divine authority for hanging them. Fifthly, 'The servant of God is righteous in wrath towards transgressors.' Our translators have improperly used the word '*avenger*' in their version; '*righteous*' is the proper term. Now we have seen hosts of rulers who have been *unrighteous* in their wrath. They have first made ungodly laws and then have executed them in a most ungodly manner. These were not God's authorities, God's rulers, or God's ministers, for they trampled the laws of the bible in the dust and were nothing better than traitors and rebels against the laws of nature, of nations, and of heaven.

VII. – We are here commanded to obey, 'not for fear of wrath or punishment but for conscience sake.' The rulers whom we are to venerate are those whose laws have God's authority as set forth in the scripture. Conscience here means a good conscience or a proper sense of *right and wrong*. But no conscience can be good unless it is guided and enlightened by the scripture. God himself, in his word, is the only arbiter of conscience, and consequently a good conscience can never direct us to obey a wicked law. To obey for conscience sake is to yield obedience because the civil or political statute is in exact accordance with the letter and spirit of christianity.

VII. – On this ground the apostle directs us 'to pay all their dues, tribute to whom tribute is due, &c.' Wicked rulers demand that we should pay tithes, taxes, and rates, which are NOT DUE; and that we should exercise '*fear*,' and bestow '*honour*,' when NOT DUE; but the bible only demands what is DUE to every one: and it is added in the text that the servants of God pay particular attention to this very thing. This does not mean that rulers are to be such a mercenary race as to pay particular attention to taxation, &c. but that those subjects, who are the servants of God are especially concerned to give to every human being his DUE. In fact, this divine sentence advocates *voluntary taxation*. In ancient days men had hearts and every thing was done on the *voluntary principle*. – The church, the state, and the poor, were all supported by the *voluntary* offerings of the people. But we are fallen on an age of men and women without souls. Their loyalty is such that they would not support the throne or the civil government if they were not *compelled* to do so. Their religion is so base that they would not sustain the church unless forced to do so by the strong arm of the law; and their humanity is so thoroughly paralysed that they would leave the poor to starve and famish unless the money was taken out of their pockets by a collector of *rates*. Such at least is their own tacit confession. Christianity teaches rulers to 'be just, and to rule in the fear of the Lord,' and then it demands *voluntary* obedience and tribute. – In a word, it enjoins voluntary loyalty to a good government, voluntary religion, and voluntary provision for the poor. But alas, many of our modern interpreters of God's word seem to have no idea of any spontaneous loyalty, patriotism, religion, or charity. To such a degraded state are we sunk by our *national church* and *national christianity*, that bishops, clergy, and senators, laugh aloud and treat with the utmost contempt any one who is so mad in these enlightened days as to imagine that man can be any thing more than a puppet or machine. Morality and compulsion are at the antipodes to each other, and therefore where there is no *voluntary* religion, loyalty, or charity, there is no *morality*; and consequently those who teach that there is no *voluntaryism* in the country teach that there is no christianity. Thus, after all the regenerations, prayers, and sermons of the clergy, we have so far retrograded as to have lost the power of true religion. Is not such a result an ample compensation for the *ten millions* a year paid to the hierarchy?

IX. – In the conclusion of this paragraph we are exhorted to 'owe no man anything,' except 'LOVE.' Here is a debt which we shall never discharge even through eternal ages. To enforce this obligation the apostle lays it down in verse 10, as a divine axiom in morals, that '*love is the fulfilment, the fulness,* and *completion of law,*' and for this very solid reason that 'love worketh no ill to his neighbour;' and consequently, 'he who loveth another hath fulfilled the law.' For this, thou shalt not commit adultery, thou shalt not kill, thou shalt not steal, thou shalt not bear false witness, thou shalt not covet, and if there is any other commandment, it is briefly comprehended in this one saying, namely, '*thou shalt love thy neighbour as thyself.*' Here then we have the fulness of all law, – a grand principle of jurisprudence for all senators to follow, and which if they obeyed, all their statutes would be stamped with universal benevolence, and their 'authority would be from God,' would be 'supreme,' and accord with divine ordination. We should then have no princes or legislators incurring 'damnation,' by 'setting themselves against the authority' of 'the Lord and his anointed;' but rulers would be 'God's servants,' and ours for 'good,' their wrath would be 'righteous,' their power would be 'feared,' for they would be a terror, not to good works, but to evil, a good 'conscience,' would lead their subjects to obey them, and voluntarily render all 'due fear, honour, tribute, and custom.'

I have thus shown that there is a great difference between '*the powers that be*' and '*the powers and authorities that are of God*;' and from the preceeding remarks, which I am prepared on critical grounds to defend, it must have been seen that this text has been most grossly perverted for the purpose of upholding despotic power and oppressing the masses. It does not say a single word about *kingly, priestly, republican,* or *democratical* power as such; it speaks solely of the authority of God as revealed in the scriptures, and affirms that all human legislation to be supreme must conform itself to the great maxim *'thou shalt love thy neighbour as thyself.'* Every statute enacted according to this sacred standard is stamped with *divine* and consequently *supreme* authority; but all others have no sanction from above and those who frame them are guilty of high treason against the King of kings, and, unless they repent 'shall receive to themselves damnation.' I am deeply anxious that *the fustian jackets and smock frocks* should duly weigh these remarks. The principles of arbitrary government and despotism which the clergy have attempted to father upon christianity, have laid the foundation of the most fearful scepticism. My firm belief is that the church of England is the bulwark of *tyranny, infidelity, and irreligion,* and in the language of Mr Binney,[1] *'that it destroys more souls than it saves.'* I am grieved that any good man or woman should yoke themselves to this last and most complete form of antichrist, and I most earnestly intreat the masses to withdraw themselves from a system which does all it can to rob them of their rights in this world, and, by its heresies and blind guides, threatens them with perdition in the world to come. In some future tract I shall show that I have good reason for concluding that it is respecting the protestant state antichrist that the voice from heaven cries *'come out of her my people, that ye partake not her sins, and that ye receive not of her plagues.'*

---

1 Thomas Binney (1798–1874), Nonconformist divine whose *Sermons* were published in 1875.

No. 12.

TRACTS FOR THE FUSTIAN JACKETS AND SMOCK FROCKS.

WHO ARE THE LEWD FELLOWS OF THE BASER SORT?
BY THE
REV. B. PARSONS,
OF EBLEY, STROUD, GLOUCESTERSHIRE.

With the bible as my guide I will condemn what is vicious in the rich or poor, and no one can be offended with what I say without acknowledging himself guilty or that he is the patron of those who are.

> 'Howe'er it be, it seems to me
> Tis only NOBLE to be GOOD;
> True hearts are more than coronets,
> And simple faith than Norman blood.'
> ALFRED TENNYSON.

'Lewd fellows of the baser sort' are generally supposed to belong to what are called the lower orders of society. To imagine that a squire, a lord, a priest, a bishop, or a monarch, may be as lewd and base as any of the masses would almost make some of our modern sentimentalists faint. In our day, money and rank are every thing. – If you have these, you may drink, swear, break the sabbath, be a blasphemer, a gourmand, a sensualist, an obscene debauchee, and an oppressive despot, and yet thousands both of the godly and ungodly will bow down to your pecuniary or aristocratical virtue. Were the chartists one hundredth part as ignorant, foolish, and irreligious, as some of the gentry and nobility, we should have a large demand for special constables. I must here remind my readers that I am stating plain facts, well known to all who study ancient or modern history, nor can any one be offended with what I say without proving that *he is either guilty himself* or *the patron and advocate of those who are*. What can be more preposterous than that the vices of the rich and noble should be passed over in silence or dealt with more leniently than those of the working man. Common sense and common justice would dictate that if an extenuation of ignorance and irreligion can, under any circumstances, be admissible, it can only be conceded to those who have been by oppression and poverty deprived of the means of a christian education. For kings, nobles, and squires, no excuse can be pleaded. I was amused the other day, when on board the Chinese Junk, to observe how perfectly and unblushingly the spirit of aristocracy had entered into the religion of that people. On the upper deck there is an oratory for the common sailors, the god is only a few inches long, with only two hands and two feet; the shrine also is a very small affair, and every thing bespeaks the plebeian character of the worship; but when you descend to the cabin, you have a large god, finely decorated, and furnished with *eighteen* or *twenty* hands! So partial even in China are the gods to the rich and the aristocracy! We perhaps very piously thank God that we are not as these poor Chinese, and yet a little examination would prove that we are worse. For we know better, because we have an impartial, and therefore a better religion. Shame on us, shame on our ministry that it should be loud in condemnation of the sins of the people, and so silent respecting the crimes of the wealthy! Perhaps there is not one person in a thousand who has ever dreamt that *'lewd fellows of the baser sort'* have been found in mansions, cathedrals, and palaces; and these not the menials or the livery servants, but the *bona fide* heirs to crowns and coronets. We feel persuaded that until the nation shall abandon its idolatry of wealth and rank, and acknowledge no aristocracy but that of intelligence and virtue, not only will the God of heaven frown upon us, but vice and vicious government will scourge the empire.

It may perhaps be proper to define in the first place what we mean by *'lewd fellows of the baser sort.'* We find this sentence in Acts xvii. 5. and it will greatly aid us in understanding its true import if we refer to the original text. The Greek term rendered *'lewd fellows,'* is *'andras ponerous,'* literally, *'wicked men.'* Now *'ponerous'* has many significations. It means, *'bad, unsound, diseased, calamitous, malignant, wicked, impious, slothful, envious, covetous,'* and sometimes, 'the *evil one,'* or *satan.* It is therefore applied to physical and moral evil. In the latter sense it includes all kinds of lewdness or depravity. We are told that our saxon word, *'lewd,'* signifies *'to crave,* or *lust after,'* and consequently is a proper epithet to designate persons who are *wicked, profligate,* and *licentious,* and in gratifying their own desires pay little regard to the rights of others. In lewd persons you generally have the two vices of avarice and profligacy united. Extravagance reduces them to want, want makes them crave what they do not possess, and as soon as they obtain the means they become licentious; a lewd fellow therefore is a compound made out of the worst moral materials. The term translated *'baser sort,'* is *'agoraion,'* and is derived from *'agora,* a *market,* a *forum,* or *place of public concourse.'* An *'agoraios'* was 'a *base, mercenary, lounger,'* ready to be hired out to do any dirty work provided he could be well paid. We have reason to believe that it was in those days applied not only to the idlers in the market, but to those gentlemen who hung about the forum waiting for a brief, and were ready to make white, black, or black, white, if they could secure a fee. We have thus arrived at a tolerable view of the characters of these *'lewd fellows of the baser sort;'* they were *avaricious, profligate, idle,* and *mercenary,* ready for all sorts of mischief if they were well paid. It is difficult to imagine a viler moral mixture than entered into the composition of these gentlemen of the 'baser sort.' I have called them gentlemen, because my readers will remember, that the *operatives,* the *fustian jackets and smock frocks* of those days were for the most part slaves, and their owners took care that they should have something else to do beside lounging in the markets or the forum. The freemen, the citizens, the gentlemen of that age, were the *agoraioi*, – the persons too noble to work, but not too proud to receive pensions for doing nothing, or wages for doing mischief. Hence the terms are descriptive not of rank but of character, and may be just as applicable to the *rich* as the *poor*, to the *noble* as the *plebeian*. Yea, a monarch who is avaricious, licentious, profligate and mercenary, is far more deserving of the title of a 'lewd fellow of the baser sort,' than the peasant or mechanic that earns his bread by the sweat of his brow and thus obtains an honest living.

Some may tell us that in using this language we are 'speaking evil of dignities,' but we deny the charge. Every school boy and school girl knows that there is no '*dignity*,' or *worthiness* about avarice, licentiousness, idleness, profligacy, and venality. It is not in the power of wealth, noble or royal blood, hereditary estates, titles, coronets or crowns, to impart dignity to a wicked man. Indeed the higher the worldly rank, the greater the possessions, and consequently the means of learning and morality, the more vile and base must the individual be who though surrounded with all these advantages, yet wallows in iniquity and curses the world with his tyranny and viciousness. Such characters are not '*dignities*' but *indignities*. If you record or rebuke the deeds of these men, you must pollute your pages with what is loathsome. Truth here is disgusting, and yet in many of these cases what is disagreeable must be told; 'them that sin rebuke before all, that others also may fear.'[1] The apostle Jude, in complaining of those who speak '*evil of dignities*,' or as the Greek reads, '*blaspheme worthy and glorious stations or persons*,'[2] does not prohibit us from condemning wickedness; for he himself was doing this very thing, and exposing the crimes of many notable and distinguished personages. Nor is the language which our translators have put into his mouth the most respectful, for he is said to call some of them, '*filthy dreamers*.' The fact is, wickedness must be exposed and condemned, nor is it either '*blasphemy*' or railing to do so. Nothing has tended so much to corrupt and ruin monarchs, nobles, and squires, and overturn thrones, as the leniency with which the vices of the great have been treated or the silence with which they have been winked at and passed over. The sacred penman felt none of this squeamishness. They were not the obsequious flatterers and sycophants of noble or royal profligates and despots. They always spoke out and took the consequences, and hence have left us a book distinguished for the perfect impartiality with which it condemns the offences of princes or slaves, of saints or sinners, of churches or states. Had the writers of scripture been partial their inspiration might have been questioned, for the God of the universe must be 'holy, just and good,' and therefore as he bears an equal affection to all his children would not, could not, commission prophets and apostles to denounce the faults of his poor sons and daughters, but at the same time caution them to be very mild and gentle to the vices of nobles and kings. If there might be any leaning towards either party, that privilege, if privilege it be, should

---

1 1 Timothy 5: 20.
2 2 Peter 2: 10.

be shared by those who have been condemned to ignorance by the oppression of their rulers. But for kings and nobles no excuse can be pleaded, and the bible shows no gentleness to their sins. Despotic rulers are called 'BEASTS,' to intimate to us that they were undeserving of the names of men, and the royal David has told us, that God *'will cut off the spirit of princes; he is terrible to the kings of the earth.'* The kingdom of Jesus Christ is to break in pieces all ungodly kingdoms upon the face of the earth, and 'the dominion under the whole heaven is to be given to his saints.' His people are 'to bind kings in chains and nobles in fetters of iron. Such honour belongs to all the saints.' Now as he prohibits all physical force and violence, and as the followers of the Lord Jesus cannot be warriors or appeal to arms, these splendid predictions teach us that, 'the saints,' – or as the hebrew word imports, holy, just, benevolent and merciful persons, – are to publish their principles, and in the name of God to condemn the crimes and oppression of all, but especially princes and statesmen, and to demand that the affairs of this world shall be conducted according to the equitable and beneficent dictates of the gospel. These *'saints,'* or really *good men and women*, are to throw the restraints and obligations of religion around kings and nobles, and thus bind them with fetters more durable and effective than iron or adamant. *'This honour,' this greatest of all honours, 'belongs to all the saints,'* and he who does not use it neglects one of the most glorious privileges and powers that God can bestow on a creature, and impeaches his own claim to the rank of a follower of the Lamb. In the following pages then if we should show that *'lewd fellows of the baser sort,'* may be found among the wealthy and the noble, we shall not in any respect violate the injunction which prohibits us from 'speaking evil of dignities,' or rather, *'from blaspheming and calumniating honourable persons.'* To narrate and rebuke vice is neither blasphemy nor slander, if it were, the bible would be the most scandalous book, and the prophets the greatest calumniators in the world. We suppose that there is not a person to be found who has so little regard to virtue as to assert that a lewd person can be a *'dignity,'* or that in publishing the sentiments of scripture respecting injustice and ungodliness, we are *'speaking evil of dignities.'* The man who can utter such an absurdity, must first confound religion and irreligion, dignity and indignity together.

History tells us that many who have sat on thrones have but too literally proved that their characters belonged to the *'baser'* portion of mankind. We presume, though Louis Philippe may have his admirers, yet there are few who would speak a word for Pharaoh, Nebuchadnezzer, Belshazzar,[1] Tiberius,[2] Nero, or Caligula.[3] The doings and courts of kings have been the staple of history; and though in many instances the writers have been the flatterers of thrones, yet the details are very far from being creditable to our species. Indeed, had any of the common people been half as guilty as not a few of these monarchs were, they would have been executed, though possessed of a thousand lives. Can we read the

---

1 Belshazzar (*fl.* sixth century BC), Babylonian general.
2 Tiberius (42 BC–AD 37), Roman Emperor AD 14–37.
3 Caligula (AD 12–41), Roman Emperor AD 37–41.

royal history of France, Spain, Germany, Russia, &c., without blushing that we are men? The avarice, the profligacy, the sensuality, cruelty, and irreligion which characterized many of these monarchs very far surpassed any thing recorded in the Newgate Calendar. And we fear if we make the bible our standard of virtue that the annals of England will be far from flattering. We presume there is not an Englishman who can say one word for the piety and moral character of William the conqueror. His birth conferred on him no honour, his life no real dignity. Avarice and ambition brought him to our shores. His march was tracked with devastation, plunder, and blood. He murdered the Saxons, burnt their houses, and took possession of their lands. His valour was mere brute force and his sceptre a rod of iron. There perhaps was hardly a human being that regretted his death; even his sons exhibited few marks of natural affection. Much as the country may then have been beset with banditti yet there was not a culprit executed who was a thousandth part so criminal as the chief magistrate. Who would be William the conqueror at the bar of God, or in the day of judgment? Could we bring back his sons to the world is there one of them that would congratulate himself on the fortunes of his father? How Cardiff castle, during upwards of twenty years, must have resounded with the wailings of poor Robert of Normandy! There was not a pauper in the land which he did not envy. Twenty-eight years in a dungeon for the sole crime of having a title to the crown was a dear price to pay for his father's conquests. And then the thought that all this suffering was inflicted by a heartless brother, who had usurped his throne and plundered him of every thing, must have filled his cup with every bitter ingredient. William II fell, perhaps we might say was executed, by the just indignation of heaven, in the forest which his father had stolen; and Henry[1] – the unnatural implacable Henry – found probably to his everlasting cost, that the crown which he had obtained by robbery and cruelty was from first to last lined with thorns. Can we more appropriately designate the morals of these men than by saying that they were 'lewd fellows of the baser sort?'

If we proceed further down the stream of history the same dark scenes present themselves, with but little variation. – What shall we say of Stephen,[2] of Richard *coeur de lion*,[3] of John,[4] of Henry IV,[5] Richard III,[6] Henry the VII[7] and VIII? The characters of Mary, James I, Charles II, and James II[8] have long been an execration, and there are others whom we could name whose lives have left a foul blot on humanity. The following words of an historian who lived in the age of Henry II will give us some idea of the morals of that prince and his attendants. – Peter of Blois,[9] who was a friend of the king, says, that 'his train consisted of knights,

---

1 Henry I (1069–1135), King of England 1100–35.
2 Stephen (*c.* 1097–1154), King of England 1135–54.
3 Richard I (1157–99), King of England 1189–99.
4 John (1167–1216), King of England 1199–1216.
5 Henry IV (1367–1413), King of England 1399–1413.
6 Richard III (1452–85), King of England 1483–5.
7 Henry VII (1457–1509), King of England 1485–1509.
8 James II (1633–1701), King of England 1685–8.
9 Peter de Blois (*fl.* 1160–1204).

nobles, throngs of cavalry and foot soldiers, baggage waggons, tents and pack horses; players, prostitutes, and marshals of prostitutes; gamesters, cooks, confectioners, mimics, dancers, barbers, pimps, and parasites; and at the setting forth of the day's march there was such jostling, overturning, shouting, brawling, that you might have imagined that hell had let loose its inhabitants.' Here you have crowds of 'lewd beings of the baser sort,' including persons of all ranks; but none so guilty as the monarch and his courtiers who encouraged, and indeed required, these degraded and abominable satelites to minister to their pleasures. When this assembly of incarnate fiends, which to an intimate friend of the monarch seemed to issue from the bottomless pit, had to appear face to face before the bar of God, none stood so deeply implicated as the prince and his nobles. We cannot, and if we had space we dare not, pollute our pages with the doings of other monarchs and courts. Can savage life present a viler monster than Henry the VIII, who notwithstanding, was constituted the *head* of the church and 'the defender of the faith?' If we are to believe history, James the I was one of the most despicable of men; and the writer who should dare to give a full, true, and particular account of the courts of Charles the II would publish a book that might make demons blush. Who can help shuddering as he reads of the blood that has been shed by the revenge and ambition of princes? What a black catalogue of slaughter the wars of the roses present. 'In the field or on the block, there fell, the *duke* of York,[1] his son Rutland,[2] three successive *dukes* of Somerset,[3] the likes of Exeter and Buckingham,[4] three *earls* of Northumberland,[5] the *earls* of Salisbury, Devon, Wiltshire, Shrewsbury, Pembroke, Rivers, Warwick, Montacute, Worcester, Leeds, Audley, Beaumont, Egremont, Bonville, De Roos, Hungerford, Cromwell, Saye, Wenlock; *Sirs* Kyriel, Erey, Woodville, Lisle, Audley, Rose, Clifton, Gainsby, Carey, Tresham, Owen Tudor;[6] who are particularly named, besides a whole host of others. In the battle of Northampton alone, 300 knights and gentlemen fell; and six barons were beheaded with the earl of Northumberland after the battle of Towton. And it is calculated that not less than 100,000 of the *people* were sacrificed.' Who does not sicken as he looks at the almost incessant executions of Henry the VIII, and his worthy daughters, Mary and Elizabeth? or those of Charles the II, and of Jefferies, sanctioned by James the II? We owe it to a miracle of grace that the people of these realms are not the most bloodthirsty on the face of the earth. The example set them by kings and nobles

1 Richard (d. 1460), Duke of York.
2 Rutland (son of above).
3 Edmund Beaufort (d. 1455), second Duke; Henry Beaufort (1436–64), third Duke; and Edmund Beaufort (*c.* 1438–71), fourth Duke.
4 Humphrey Stafford (1402–60), first Duke of Buckingham.
5 Henry Percy (1394–1455), second Earl; Henry Percy (1421–61), third Earl; and Henry Percy (1446–89), fourth Earl.
6 Richard Neville (1400–60), first Earl of Salisbury; James Butler (1420–61), Earl of Wiltshire; John Talbot (*c.* 1413–60), second Earl of Shrewsbury; William Herbert (d. 1469), Earl of Pembroke; Richard Woodville (d. 1469), first Earl Rivers; Richard Neville (1428–71), Earl of Warwick; John Tiptoft (*c.* 1427–70), Earl of Worcester; Robert Hungerford (1431–64), third Baron; Anthony Woodville (*c.* 1442–83); Thomas Tresham (d. 1471); Owen Tudor (d. 1461).

was enough to corrupt a nation far more humane than the English have ever been. Our annals are baptized with blood, often shed in the most treacherous, cruel, and wanton manner. The aged Countess of Salisbury[1] was confined for two years in the reign of Henry VIII,[2] and then brought out for execution. She was then seventy years of age, but refused to lay her head on the block, saying, that 'her head had never committed treason, and if they would have it they must take it.' The executioner tried to seize her, but she moved swiftly round the scaffold tossing her head from side to side. At last, when her grey hairs were covered with blood – for they struck her with their weapons – she was held forcibly down and the axe severed her neck. But if women were not exempt from such cruelty we also find that they not unfrequently were the instigators, and quite willing to yoke themselves to those very monsters who had sacrificed their nearest relatives. Sometimes the most deadly purpose was concealed under the most fulsome professions of affectionate regard. James I was noted for hugging and kissing his favourites. 'The king,' so Rushworth[3] tells us, 'had a loathesome way of lolling his arms about his favourites, and the messenger whom he had commissioned to arrest the earl of Somerset, found him thus embracing his victim and exclaiming, as the officer bore him away, "when shall I see thee again? when shall I see thee again?" and as soon as Somerset was gone, he added, "now the devil go with thee, for I will never see thy face more!"'[4] An eye witness has described the last sabbath evening that Charles the II spent in this world. – 'I shall never forget,' he says, 'the inexpressible luxury and profaneness, gaming, and all dissoluteness, and as it were, total forgetfulness of God, – it being Sunday evening, – which this day se-night I was witness of; the king sitting and toying with his concubines, Portsmouth,[5] Cleveland,[6] Mazarin, &c.; a French boy singing love songs in that glorious gallery; whilst about twenty of the great courtiers and other dissolute persons were at basset round a large table, a bank of at least £2,000 in gold lay before them, upon which two gentlemen who were with me made reflections. *Six days after all was in the dust!*' Will any one believe a thousand years hence that there were ever found in any part of God's universe, men in holy orders so sunk in depravity as to call these infamous rebels against God and man '*most religious and gracious kings,*' and bury them 'in sure and certain hope of a resurrection to everlasting life?' The avarice and profligacy of the latter monarch induced him to do his utmost to sell his country to France, and for this villany was to receive from Louis the XIV[7] a pension of £200,000 a year; and while he was actually in the pay of that monarch received £400,000 to go to war with France, and as he took the money was laughing with the French ambassador at the 'credulity of his good English subjects.' If, according to Cowper[8] –

---

1 Margaret Pole (1473–1541), Countess of Salisbury.
2 Henry VIII (1491–1547), King of England 1509–47.
3 John Rushworth (c. 1612–90), historian.
4 See John Rushworth, *Historical Collections* (1659), p. 157.
5 Louise de Kéroualle (1649–1734), Duchess of Portsmouth.
6 Barbara Villiers (1641–1709), Duchess of Cleveland.
7 Louis XIV (1638–1715), King of France 1643–1715.
8 William Cowper (1731–1800), poet.

> 'Kings, then, at last have but the lot of all;
> By their own conduct they must stand or fall,'[1]

and if we are to judge their deeds by the scriptures of truth, we have no alternative but to conclude that a very large number of those who have wielded sceptres, have belonged to men whom the bible designates as 'lewd fellows of the baser sort.' Avarice, profligacy, indolence, cruelty, and venality were the most prominent attributes of their characters.

Whatever virtue there may be in noble or Norman *blood*, we are sorry to say, that mental and moral greatness has been an exception to the general rule in the history of aristocracies. What crowds among these have belonged to the basest and most lewd of mankind. They are sometimes said to be the bulwarks of law, loyalty and order, but if we are to draw our conclusions from the numbers of their august rank, who have been executed for *treason*, we fear that their loyalty and patriotism will bear but a poor comparison with that of the common people. In modern times it is generally thought that the throne has nothing to fear except from a few physical force chartists, but there was a period when the nobility were the ringleaders in almost every effort at anarchy and insurrection. The history of English rebellions would exhibit but a very poor display of the loyalty of our aristocracy. It may be said that of late years they have greatly improved, but this has evidently arisen from the greater amount of influence which they now exercise over the crown and the people, and the vast revenues which their cupidity has extorted or wheedled from the wealth of the nation. If *'lewd'* signifies *lusting* or *craving*, and if the Greek word rendered *'baser sort'* means *mercenary*, then *'craving fellows of a mercenary character,'* is one of the most appropriate phrases, to describe the lives and conduct of the generality of aristocracies. We reproach no man with his origin. The son of a chimney sweeper, as far as birth is concerned, is just as honourable as the son of a duke. Lord Thurlow[2] used to boast that he thought his grandfather was a *carter*. The same nobleman when reminded in the House of Lords, of the meanness of his ancestry, very justly retorted that a lord who is a lord because his father was a lord, is *'the accident of an accident'*! An hereditary peer has no more natural honour than an hereditary pauper, and it is rather remarkable that among the nobility, the sublime and the ridiculous not unfrequently meet, for the peerage has generated the most consummate race of unblushing paupers. When common sense shall prevail, it will be deemed the greatest indignity that can befall a human being to owe his respectability to his fathers. As Young says –

> 'Each man makes his own statue, builds himself –
> Pigmies are pigmies still, though perched on Alps;
> And pyramids are pyramids in vales.'[3]

---

1 William Cowper, *Table Talk* (1782), ll. 107–8.
2 Probably Edward Thurlow (1731–1806), Solicitor General.
3 Edward Young, *Night Thoughts* (1742–5), ll. 309–12.

Who cares anything about the parentage of Milton, Howard, Newton,[1] Whit-field[2] or the apostle Paul? The noblest ancestry would have added nothing to their real dignity; nor would their fame have been injured a jot, though their parents had been paupers, slaves, or criminals. We then cannot disgrace or degrade the aristocracy by referring to their fathers. Norman means Northman, and our Norman countrymen were starving Northmen, who became murderers and plunderers for a living. They extorted Normandy from the French, and then by mere brute force took possession of England, and in the most heartless manner slaughtered the Saxons and appropriated their lands. No nobleman therefore who has any respect for his progenitors will refer to the Norman founders of his line. Not a few of our other nobility owe their present rank to the immorality of their mothers. They are dukes or lords because their progenitors were destitute of virtue. Others again had ancestors who rose to power because their forefathers were sycophants, or the unprincipled minions of the court. It is true that this is no disgrace to their children, nor should we allude to it were it not that we are continually dinned with such canting phrases as *'noble ancestry,' 'noble blood,'* &c. Goodness is the only true greatness, and when this is the offspring of an enlarged and liberal mind, we have the highest dignity that any human being can obtain. Every fustian jacket and smock frock in the country has the patent for this divine peerage within his reach. But if we judge of aristocracies generally by this rational standard, we fear that a very large number must be struck out of the list. The Saxon chronicler has left us a graphic description of the character and conduct of the nobles of his day. 'All this king's time, all was dissension and evil and rapine. The great men soon rose against him. They had sworn oaths but maintained no truth. They had built castles which they held out against him. They cruelly oppressed the wretched people of the land with this castle work. They filled their castles with devils and evil men. They seized those whom they supposed to have any goods and threw them into prison for their gold and silver, inflicted on them unutterable tortures. Some they hanged up with the feet and smoked with foul smoke; some by the thumbs or the beard, and hung heavy coats of mail on their feet. They threw them into dungeons with adders and snakes and toads. They made many thousands perish with hunger. They laid tribute after tribute upon towns and cities, and this in their language, they called *tenserie,* (chastisement.) When the towns had nothing more to give, they set fire to all the towns. Thou mightest go a whole day's journey and not find a man sitting in a town nor an acre of land tilled. The poor died of hunger and those who had been well to do begged their bread. Never was more mischief done by heathen invaders. To till the ground was to plough the sands of the sea. This lasted the nineteen years that Stephen was king, and it grew continually worse and worse.' We leave the reader to judge whether or not these nobles were 'lewd fellows of the baser sort.' The following *nine* particulars include some of the more glaring vices of aristocracy

1 Isaac Newton (1642–1727), natural philosopher.
2 George Whitfield (1714–70), leader of the Calvinistical Methodists.

and prove to us, if proof be wanting, that there is no real nobility in birth, blood, or political rank.

I. – *Treason*. Our history gives us a tremendous list of dukes, lords, and their offspring who, from time to time have been fined, imprisoned or executed. I was once cutting off the heads of some poplars, and a person who was passing by asked me if I was about '*to make lords of them?*' I did not at first understand the question, but she replied that 'noblemen had so often been guilty of treason and beheaded for their crimes that it was usual among the common people in that locality to say when a tree was lopped that it was made a lord of.' We cannot read history attentively without coming to the conclusion, either that our kings have been notoriously cruel, or that our peers are preeminently rebellious. At any rate the nobility of these realms can hardly be so indiscreet as to charge the masses with having sprung from an ancestry addicted to sedition. Compared with the aristocracy *the fustian jackets and smock frocks* have been paragons of loyalty and order. It may be said that of late years things have been better, but we fear that anything rather than a regard to the rights of man and the dictates of equity has produced this seeming change. They have enslaved both the crown and the people, monopolized a large portion of the wealth of the nation, and have legislated for their own cupidity, and now forsooth are obedient to their own unjust legislative enactments.

II. – *Disregard of the constitution of the country and its best laws*. The various ways in which the peers transgress the statutes of the realm would be a long tale, we shall therefore only glance at our public elections. Is it not notorious that in the face of the constitution – the penalties against bribery – and the right of the British people to be represented in parliament, – the most complete and refined tyranny is exercised over the greater part of the counties and many of the boroughs? Bribery of the most unblushing character is employed and yet the poor bribed tradesmen and farmers are expected to be ready to swear before God and man that they are free from this crime! Of all miscreants upon earth, the lewd fellow who sells his vote is one of the vilest, the only monster that excels him in viciousness, is the *ig*-noble traitor who buys it. Now the tradesman who votes to save his business, or the farmer who polls to please his landlord and save his farm, is as much a bribed elector as the more open villain who receives his £5 or £10 or £20 for his vote. And, why, we may ask, do the aristocracy who are too high-spirited to carry on any honourable trade, thus *deal* in corruption? The reply is obvious. They want to put their hands into the public purse and keep all the abominations of a standing army, of an ungodly hierarchy, of sinecures, pensions and places, and to do this they must have a corrupt parliament, and, to have a corrupt House of Commons, they must have a corrupt constituency, and thus they poison the nation at the fountain head. For if the senators are immoral and avaricious, the patrons of bribery and the violaters of law, order and the constitution, what are we to expect from the laws they frame, or the people they oppress and contaminate? It is no wonder that these men dread the virtue that would arise from *universal suffrage and the ballot*. In this one act of despotism exercised by the aristocracy over the liberties of the electors and employed for the sole

purpose of obtaining as large a portion as possible of the nation's wealth, you
have a most striking proof that *'craving fellows of the mercenary sort,'* are by no
means confined to the uneducated portion of the people: especially when you
consider that the men who countenance this corruption, and trample the constitution in the dust, almost annually exhibit the farce of making laws to prevent
the wickedness of which they themselves are the sole authors and perpetuators!

III. – *Unwillingness to pay taxes.* If you look at our system of taxation you will
find that every thing has been done to save the aristocracy from bearing their just
proportion of taxation. Poor souls! some of them have only the paltry sum of
£100,000 a year, some alas! not more than £1,000 a week to live upon, and of
course they can hardly make two ends meet and therefore the depth of their poverty has prompted them very generously to *relieve themselves* from the trying task
of contributing their share to the public revenue! They delight to *take* from the
national purse by the million; but the chief task of supplying the treasury they
throw upon the hardworking masses, and hence in numerous instances the *eight
shillings* a week of the labourer is taxed more than fifty per cent beyond the
£1,000 per week of the lord or baronet! These poor people have by the sweat of
their brow not only to produce the wealth of the nobleman, but to starve themselves that they may, from their paltry pittance of an income, screen the pockets
of the rich from equitable taxation. Only mark how things are done. By all manner of tricks, the aristocracy laboured first to obtain possession of the land of the
country. By various impeachments, confiscations, &c. they have gained possession of thousands of acres which were the rightful property of better men than
themselves; and by being the sycophants and tools of Henry VIII they grasped
immense possessions from the church; and now, the next thing was to save this
property from equitable taxation. Hence being legislators, they passed a law that
the tax on land should be a mere fraction. In 1842, the land tax of France was
£23,200,000, whilst that of England was only £1,214,430. The land in France
pays *half* the national revenue, while the land in Britain does not supply *one
twenty-fifth part* of our taxes. The poor widow who has a legacy of £100 must pay
£10, or more than two years' interest to the government, while the nobleman
who inherits an estate worth £50,000 a year is not taxed one farthing! When the
house tax was in existence, the mansions of the great were in many instances not
taxed to half the amount of those of our tradesmen. Common sugar for the common people must be taxed 96 per cent., while double refined for lords and squires
pays only 34 per cent. duty! The same may be said of tea and a variety of other
articles. The fact is the aristocracy, if we may judge of them by their unwillingness to pay taxes, have neither loyalty nor patriotism. They regard neither the
crown nor the masses, and if ever the throne in this country is overturned, it will
be by the cupidity and lawlessness of the nobility. In many instances, nearly *one-
half* of the income of the labourer goes in taxes, while the lord pays scarcely a fraction of a fraction of his immense revenue. Rent is only wages for houses or land,
and our corn laws arose from a periodical strike of the lords for higher wages for
doing nothing, and the bread of the poor labourer, who had only 8s. a-week was
often taxed 2d. a quartern to eke out the income of the poor landowner who

could not maintain his family out of £100 a day. And this very year, 1848, we have men in the House of Commons to tell us that unless we go back again to *protection* and tax the poor man's loaf, the aristocracy will not be able to live! We are threatened with another strike for protection, *alias* rent, *alias* wages, on behalf of the pauper nobility, who in some instances have only £1,000 a week to live upon! I leave my readers to judge whether or not these are examples of lewdness of the most iniquitous character. Let the matter be enquired into and the plain facts of history brought forth, and we believe that the more respectable of the aristocracy will come forward and either reform their house or lay aside their titles. That *the fustian jackets and smock frocks* should exhibit a higher order of honour, patriotism, and virtue than the nobility, must be a very humbling truth to every respectable nobleman.

Our space is exhausted, and we shall therefore continue this subject in our next tract. We shall then dwell a little on *pensions, sinecures, gambling, sensuality, the law of primogeniture, and freedom from arrest*. We intend also to show that 'lewd fellows of the baser sort' may be found among the clergy, squires, merchants, masters, servants &c., &c. In the mean time we congratulate the operatives on the glorious truth that nobility does not consist in riches, birth, or blood, and earnestly intreat them to acquire that real dignity which consists in intelligence and goodness, and which is within the reach of all, and without which, coronets, or even crowns, can impart no real honour.

No. 13.

TRACTS FOR THE FUSTIAN JACKETS
AND SMOCK FROCKS.

WHO ARE THE LEWD FELLOWS OF THE BASER SORT?
BY THE REV. B. PARSONS,
OF EBLEY, STROUD, GLOUCESTERSHIRE.

With the bible as my guide, I will condemn what is vicious in the rich or poor, and no one can be offended with what I say without acknowledging himself guilty or that he is the patron of those who are.

> 'Howe'er it be, it seems to me
> Tis only NOBLE to be GOOD;
> True hearts are more than coronets,
> And simple faith than Norman blood.'   ALFRED TENNYSON.[1]

In my last tract I showed the meaning of the words, '*lewd fellows of the baser sort,*' and produced examples to prove that it is an egregious mistake to suppose that such characters are found *exclusively* among the working classes. History informs us that not a few of the most infamous of our race have belonged to the gentry and nobility. In these pages I condemn no good man or woman, no really noble person of any age or country. We believe that there have been truly digni-fied individuals who have worn crowns or coronets, but then we as firmly maintain, that it was their *goodness* and not their *civil or political rank* that consti-tuted their honour. Indeed rank, without intelligence, justice, and philanthropy, is the foulest degradation. It is worse than placing a pigmy on a pyramid. All countries have been bitterly scourged with the adulation and adoration of wealth and titles. Nothing has tended so much to emasculate nations, as the heresy that men can be *great* without being GOOD; and one object in writing these tracts has been to aim a blow at this basest species of idolatry, and to show the working classes, that they are born with as much nobility in their blood, and divinity in their souls, as any peer of the realm. True nobleness or meanness are moral and not civil distinctions, and therefore must be our own work. No monarch can issue a patent to make any person really great. If we are mean it is our own doing, and if we would be noble we must achieve it ourselves, and as I have hinted before,

---

1 Alfred, Lord Tennyson, 'Lady Clara Vere de Vere'.

there is no dignity worth having which is not within the reach of *the fustian jackets and smock frocks*.

In my last tract, I proposed to notice *nine* of the more glaring vices of the aristocracy. Space allowed me only to mention '*treason*,' '*disregard of the laws and constitution*,' and '*unwillingness to pay taxes*,' we shall now offer a few remarks on the other six.

IV. – *Pensions*. We believe that the custom of giving pensions is one of the great sources of national corruption, and especially pauperising to the circumstances and minds of the recipients. Every human being ought to be economical and provident, 'Go to the ant, thou sluggard, consider her ways and be wise,' is a divine command. All the servants of the state should have sufficient remuneration to enable them to make provision for sickness and old age; but no reason in the world can be shown why a lord chancellor, or commander in chief should be pensioned from the public revenue, rather than a common hedger and ditcher or a chimney sweeper. The lord chancellor, including his salary as speaker of the house of lords, has only about £14,000 a year coming in, and of course ample means of providing for a rainy day. My lord Brougham, it is said, has a retiring pension of about £5,000 a year to give a few comforts to his old age. Where are all his revenues from his former profession and offices? Were they insufficient to provide for his retirement, and as a consequence must he become a state pauper? If so we may exclaim, 'How art thou fallen O Lucifer, son of the morning!' and fallen by being exalted to the peerage! The man who went from Jerusalem to Jericho and fell among thieves who stripped him and wounded him and left him half dead, was not in a worse plight than this *quondam* advocate of the rights of the people. In the good time coming, no patriotic man or woman will accept of a pension. They would rather gather bones or rags. But if *pensions* were proper under some circumstances, who can say a word for those which have been granted to lords and ladies for doing nothing? And yet we have numbers of these. Indeed many of our nobility are continually craving for a share of the taxes which the masses earn by the sweat of their brow. Yonder poor peasant with his *six shillings a week* has not only to provide for his own wife and half a dozen small children, but also to aid in maintaining in indolence the families of not a few of our renowned nobility. We could fill this tract with the names of lords and ladies who receive pensions to which they have not one hundredth of the equitable claim that the pauper in the union has. Some high minded dames do not scruple to take from the public revenues so small a sum as £97 per annum: there are other persons who are more fortunate and get their £1,000 a year. It is said that we have still to pay for the sensuality of Charles II and that one family which owes the peerage to illegitimacy, has, in about 170 years, received from our taxes upwards of TWO MILLIONS of the people's money, and at the present day a scion from this very stock obtains more than £10,000 per annum. Now no individual, except the basest and the lowest, will accept of pay for doing nothing. Our nation groans under the load of its taxation. Thousands among us have to deny themselves the common necessaries of life, because they are so heavily taxed. Their children have to go without bread because their parents' wages are charged with a high per centage to find pensioned lords and ladies in luxuries. A generation of real nobles would be ashamed of this, and therefore as soon as the clergy shall do their duty and instruct the aristocracy in the commonest laws of christian morality, we shall have a voluntary abandonment of every pension.

V. – *Sinecures*. The word *sinecure*, is from '*sine curâ*,' and means '*without care*,' or '*payment without labour*.' What should we think of the tradesman who brought in a bill for goods that he never had, and never intended to deliver? or of the labourer who demanded weekly pay for work that he never did, and determined never to do? We should deem each of these persons dishonest, 'lewd fellows of the baser sort,' and especially if the man they wished to defraud was in straitened circumstances. Now John Bull is very poor, and has not a penny but he works for. His indigent children have 'to rise up early, and late take rest, and eat the bread of carefulness.' These sons and daughters of toil make the wealth of the country. They are, taken as a whole, the most *peaceable, industrious, reasonable, honest, and honourable* beings upon the face of the earth. 'They are poor and yet make many rich.' Is it not then a burning shame that these hardworking people should be doomed to pay a large portion of their earnings to support a number of idle pensioners and sinecurists? Is not the God of heaven insulted by this cruelty to his poor children? Are not humanity and religion, especially christianity and the *bible*, outraged by this injustice and meanness? To rob the rich is bad enough, but what language can sufficiently execrate the conduct of him who plunders the poor? Common sense and common justice assure us, that every sinecurist must be the meanest of the mean, and therefore preeminently and essentially '*a lewd fellow of the baser sort*.' About such a being there can be nothing great, noble, humane or christian. I would as soon believe in the christianity of Satan as of such an idle, dishonest mass of impiety. The fustian jackets and smock frocks only ask a fair day's wages for a fair day's work, and are nobles and princes compared with these treasury paupers. And yet not a few of those who thus receive wages from the people for doing nothing, actually scowl upon the masses, and call them mean and vulgar, or load them with all kinds of opprobrious names if they ask for that simple justice which the constitution and statutes of the realm as well as the laws of christianity demand for all men.

VI. – *Gambling*. This is one of those vices against which our legislators have from time to time enacted very severe penalties. But what is the use of laws when the senators themselves are the chief transgressors? Here again we have another instance, that many of our educated gentry and nobility are the most notorious violators of the statutes of the country, and consequently the patrons of disorder. Were the masses half so guilty, the '*Habeas Corpus Act*' would be suspended to morrow, and my Lord Ashley[1] would complain of our '*untutored savages*.' Alas! his lordship is too partial to perceive the tutored ungodliness which fosters more than half of the un-educated impiety of the land. Need we say that a gambler is a '*lewd fellow of the baser sort?*' The places in which these depraved beings meet are very characteristically called 'HELLS.' And it is not necessary to add, that the

---

1 Anthony Ashley Cooper (1801–85), seventh Earl of Shaftesbury, Tory politician.

fiends who frequent these pandemonia are not *the fustian jackets and smock frocks*. I knew a bishop who was raised to the episcopal chair because of his skill at cards. He had ruined himself by gambling and was placed on the bench to assist him in paying his debts, yet he protested, '*Noli episcopari*' that he was '*unwilling to be a bishop*,' although he longed for it as much as the Dean of Hereford. Whist qualified him for the sacred office, and the dean and chapter declared that the Holy Spirit had chosen him to preside over the church! I knew a clergyman who had £2,000 a year from his living, but through gambling became a bankrupt. His debts were about £25,000. I have heard of a duke who would stake £1,000 on the sublime result of one snail beating another in crawling over a given space. Another nobleman has bet largely respecting the number of pieces into which he could dash a glass bottle. Some of these bright spirits, though heirs to immense revenues, are the most abject paupers, and all in consequence of gambling. They are obliged to pension their families from the taxes paid by the working classes. But for the law against arrest, they would have been sold up again and again, and must have gone to work or the union. Before Epsom and other races, the sabbath is especially devoted to betting. We heard sometime ago of the brother of a *quondam* premier who had pocketed £14,000 from gambling. But volumes might be written on this vice as practised by many of the gentry and nobility of our day? And this vice is not alone, it is connected with a host of others. Who could write or read the abomination of a race course or a London hell? Yet the patrons of these haunts of crime, and generally, the chief agents in them, are termed the *higher* classes. But for these, the gambling houses would be closed and the race course deserted. Strange to say, but the clergy inform us that these culprits against whom so many stringent laws have been enacted, are pillars of the church, have been regenerated by baptism, and are 'members of Christ, children of God and inheritors of the kingdom of heaven!' Blasphemy equal to this was never uttered by any Voltaire or Tom Paine. No one I am sure will dispute with me respecting the propriety of designating *gamblers*, as 'lewd fellows of the baser kind.'

VII. – *Sensuality*. On the crimes involved in this word, I have facts for volumes, although I confine myself to the aristocracy alone. But the narrative would be too obscene to be perused. Ancient history is polluted with it in almost every page. And be it remembered, that the annals of former times take but little notice of the masses, so that these stereotyped crimes were the vices of the great and noble. We are thankful that things are not so bad now, but still when an effort was lately made to pass a law to prevent females from being kidnapped and sold to minister to the appetites of our gentry and nobility, the House had to deliberate with *closed doors*. The newspapers would have been polluted and the whole country contaminated if the facts had been told publicly. When we are informed, that agents are sent through the country, – that registrar offices for servants, and railway stations are beset – and that not unfrequently £100 are paid for new victims, we need not say that the miscreants who employ this worse than infernal agency are not the fustian jackets and smock frocks. The cruelty of the system beggars description. Beelzebub must feel himself a prodigy of morality when he compares himself with these wretches and their aristocratical employers. If there are any persons

whom more than others the common damned will shun, they will be these titled
and wealthy seducers. They inveigle and destroy, often with the most horrid
oaths and protestations, the fairest portion of God's creation. And then when
they have worse than slain their victim, for a woman without a character is more
than 'twice dead,' they turn her upon society to be a moral pest and at last to
perish in neglect, vice and want. The average life of these poor creatures, while
on the town, is FIVE YEARS. Why did not the seducers employ their pistols or
prussic acid to end the scene. Barbarous as this would be, yet it would be the
essence of humanity compared with the course they pursue. One of the monsters
who conducted a house of ill fame for the *gentry, nobility and clergy*, began business
for the 'villains' without a penny, but although she rented a house worth £450 a
year and lost £500 a year in bad debts, she gave her daughter, who is still living,
£3,000 on her wedding day and left her £20,000 more at her death. When she
retired from her infamous trade in blood, she treated her visitors with a ball;
twelve noblemen, she tells us attended, and a duke high in royal favour, and a great
pillar of the church, presided on the occasion. We must not describe the rest.
Again we say, that these worse than beasts in a human form are not the low and
vulgar masses, although the latter, poor fellows! have to work hard to assist in
paying for this sensuality, brutality and death. We might dwell on the luxury,
gluttony, excessive drinking, and every species of waste and extravagance as practised by the aristocracy of all countries; but the facts are before the public in the
pages of the past and of almost every modern newspaper. The avarice, lewdness,
and mercenary deeds of men of wealth and title are no small portion of the staple
of history.

VIII. – *The Law of Primogeniture*. Were this outrage on humanity and violation
of the ties of blood, a crime of the working classes, the pulpit would ring with the
abomination, and my Lord Ashley would shed torrents of tears. Some of the facts
already advanced have manifested that there are those among the aristocracy
who have few of the common feelings of humanity; but this infamous law – this
blot of the age and the statute book – shows that they are cruel towards their
own flesh and blood. What should we think if the eldest son of a spinner or
labourer took possession of the small substance which his father left, and by so
doing reduced all his brothers and sisters to beggary? Such an act of voluntary
plunder would stamp the perpetrator with the foulest infamy. Now there is no
difference between such inhumanity and the law of primogeniture. By this unjust
statute the eldest son takes all, and very often reduces his brothers and sisters to
pauperism, so that they must be supported by pensions or sinecures drawn from
the earnings of the vulgar operatives. In many instances the poor sisters of the
nobleman are literally sold to wealthy husbands for the sake of obtaining a living.
We may be told that it is the law of the land. – But what a subterfuge! Who
made the law, and who sustains it? The lords themselves enacted this injustice,
and, if they wished, could abolish it to-morrow. They might bring in a bill, and
read it *first*, *second*, and *third* time the same day: aye, and would do so if they
allowed the plainest dictates of natural affection to guide their proceedings.

What a brother, to rob his brothers and sisters by an act of parliament, which his unnatural progenitors passed in a barbarous age, and which he, in the most unfeeling manner, advocates in this year of our redemption, 1848! The artist has never been born capable of constructing a coronet that could give dignity to a brow thus dishonoured by injustice. But the evil not only scourges every aristo-cratical family, alas! the whole nation has to suffer from it. – Look at the army, the navy, the church, and the pension list. The estimate of our war department for the current year is about £20,000,000. Only think, £20,000,000 to be spent in fostering the trade in blood. This in a christian age too, and in a christian coun-try!! Our governors also want to increase the sum, and why? Not that there is the least necessity for such extravagance, but to find places, wages, and pensions for the younger sons of the nobility, who are in a starving condition because the eldest brother has taken possession of all the estates of the family. The church too, is made a refuge for the destitute, and *useless Commissions* are instituted that these scions of the nobility may be fed, clothed, and supplied with pocket money for gambling, sensuality, and luxury, at the public expense, that thousands have been pauperised, enslaved, and ruined for both worlds, by this worse than Vandal law of primogeniture. Can we have a better personification of 'lewdness of the baser kind' than is thus exhibited in the perpetuation of such cruelty and injustice?

IX. – *Freedom from Arrest.* The design of this law is to give to lords and mem-bers of parliament the liberty of running in debt without their creditors having the power to obtain their due. Some of these honourables have £20,000, some £50,000 some £100,000, and some still larger incomes *per annum*, but the poor creatures cannot pay their way, and therefore they have very considerately and mercifully enacted laws to keep their creditors at bay. What should we think of the grocer or draper who required an act of parliament to save himself from arrest? And yet the commonwealth would be a far greater loser by the imprison-ment of useful tradesmen than from the incarceration of a few tens of the aristocracy. They can vote by proxy, forsooth, wherever their bodies and minds may be; and if not, the state would lose little by being deprived of their obstruc-tive talents and influence. And surely gamblers and debauchees can be of no very great use or credit to any country, especially as legislators. Here again we shall be told that it is the law of the land; and in reply we must again ask who made this insulting law, and who are they who keep it on the statute book? There are among the aristocracy and members of parliament some men of noble principles – who owe their dignity neither to parentage or wealth, but to themselves. The Byron, the Ducie, and other distinguished families have not been amateurs for places or pensions. In the commons there are burgesses who pay their way and never dread a sheriff's officer; and we trust that a time will speedily come when these noble and right honourable men will protest against having their names and characters defamed by an infamous law that none but swindlers or such like lewd fellows of the baser sort could desire or tolerate. Surely our queen, when she takes the matter into consideration, will refuse to have her levees and ball rooms dishonoured by persons who must be shielded from arrest by an act of parliament, lest the sheriff's officer should take them from the palace to durance vile,[1] or put in a writ to sell their goods and chattels to pay their creditors.

Every nation must and will have its aristocracy, but then it ought to be an aristocracy of intelligence and virtue. Every other description of rank is a bane both to the titled pigmies themselves and to the country which such an order of imbeciles invariably scourge. In these pages we have said, and shall say, nothing that can offend any honest or honourable individual. We have exposed and condemned nothing but vice, cruelty, and injustice. The principles of true greatness which we advocate would raise the nobility above any dependence upon pensions, titles, diplomas, or coronets. Children of a larger growth may prize these toys and gewgaws, and, if they can be of the least use to any one, by all means let them be continued. But still we must protest against the idea of any man's imagining that the greatness of his father, the patent of the sovereign, the robe of a lord, or the mitre of a bishop, can confer the least honour. We feel more respect for the *jim crow*[2] or the labourer than we do for all the mitres or coronets in the world. We 'honour all men,' as men, because they are the offspring of God. The scavenger is in our estimation as honourable as a baron. We especially revere the *truly good*, seeing they belong to the peerage of heaven. Their patent came from the King of kings. But men guilty of treason against God and man – who trample the equitable laws of the country in the dust – who are unwilling to pay either to Caesar or Caesar's Lord, his due – who covet pensions and sinecures – who are gamblers and sensualists – and who require especial laws to enable them to beggar their own kindred or rob their creditors – for such ignoble beings we have no respect, nor do we apply to them any unjust epithet when we say that they belong to the '*lewd fellows of the baser sort*.'

We are afraid, if we turn to the church, we shall find too many who belong to the baser characters that have infested society. The scriptures tell us that Jeroboam 'made priests of the lowest of the people.' This does not mean '*the lowest*' in rank, but the most degraded in principle. Here you have a blessed example of the union of church and state. The priests were made by the king. They were not God-made ministers. The *conge d'elire* came from the monarch. Intelligence and piety were by no means requisite. Indeed the lower they were in virtue the more suited were they to be the minions of the state. The church of Jeroboam was a political institution in a religious garb. It was the tool of the government to enslave the people. No man of principle would or could enter it. Pious men in the sacred office would have been as distasteful to the prince as evangelical ministers were to Mr Pitt[3] and my lord Eldon[4] of blessed memory. And in every country where you have a state hierarchy with vast revenues, and where the patent for the priesthood is in the civil power you may expect plenty of priests of the *lowest*

---

1 Imprisonment.

2 Slang for black American slaves.

3 William Pitt (1759–1806), Chancellor of the Exchequer and Prime Minister 1783–1801, 1804–6.

4 Sir John Scott (1751–1838), first Baron Eldon, MP, Attorney-General 1793–9.

description. 'Lewd fellows of the baser sort' are sure to crouch to the state for the sacred office. Men unfit for any useful occupation will aspire to the desk and pulpit – many of them so destitute of intellect and piety that you must have a spiritual warehouse to supply them with ready made prayers and sermons. Even the sacramental bread and wine they participate, and the washing of their canonicals, must be paid for out of the pence and farthings of the operative and pauper. I knew a case in which the pious churchwarden swore lustily at a poor fellow who had spent his last *penny* on a cake for his dinner because he had not saved *three farthings* out of it to pay for the sacrament of the squire and the washing of the surplice of the indigent priest, who could not, out of his £600 a year, afford pence to remunerate the washerwoman, and therefore was in danger of performing duty in a filthy garment. If *'lewdness'* means *'craving,'* if *'baser sort'* signifies *'mercenary,'* here you have a rich supply of both, invested with the outward sanctities of religion. It is now notorious that men without any mental or moral qualifications become clergymen for the sole purpose of obtaining a living. These sons of mammon seek wages for work which they cannot perform, and indeed which they never intend to do. They vow that they are moved by the Holy Ghost to become the slaves of avarice. Some of them have several benefices, and give their curates hardly wages enough to find them decent bread. Did any of our tradesmen pay their journeymen as badly as many of the wretched journeymen priests are paid, we should have my lord Ashley calling upon the House to interfere: and the villain who thus robbed his workpeople would be held in universal contempt. I need not say that a *curate* is a journeyman parson, often a poor, miserable, crushed, spiritual operative, working for £50 a year to do the work for which his apostolical master receives his hundreds. I have somewhere seen even tablets in the church recording the stupendous fact that the individual named was distinguished in this life by a number of livings. The clergy send a great cry through the land about being robbed; but alas, the working clergy are plundered by none so much as by their own brethren. It is an old saying that there is honour among thieves, but we fear the adage must not be applied to these clerical vampires, for of all dishonesty and oppression, that which the wealthier priesthood exercise towards their poor brethren is the most glaring and disgusting. To accept of several livings without ability to attend to the duties of one, is an act of gross injustice to the country; and then to half starve the poor slaves that are hired to do the work of these idle or imbecile rectors or vicars is an infamous piece of dishonesty, which none but a person of the most corrupt principles would practice.

Of all offices which the caprice of tyrants have invented that of *bishop* is the most useless. These are the ecclesiastical despots of the hierarchy, raised up to enslave the clergy and the people. Where these exist the ministers work in fetters, and very appropriately confess that 'they are tied and bound with the chains of their sins.' No nation can be free that is burdened with a conclave of bishops. My lord of Exeter[1] is resolved that the world shall know this truth. Were this office abolished to morrow throughout the earth, instead of losing any thing, mankind

---

1 Henry Phillpotts (1778–1869), Bishop of Exeter.

would be infinitely benefited. But were the office good for any thing, no man but a lewd fellow of the baser sort would receive £10,000 or £20,000 a year from a church which is starving its curates. If the man really were a successor of the apostles, or had a grain of honesty or humanity in him he would refuse such enormous wages for doing nothing or worse than doing nothing. Dissenters do better without bishops than the church can with them. It is no use to say that it is the law of the land, or that our fathers left the money for this purpose. Our ancestors had no right to endow a nuisance or to bind their children in the swaddling bands of a dark and tyrannical age. What if they had bequeathed their property to a body of quacks and it was found that these empirics were poisoning the public health, should we be bound to continue the cruelty? As for church property it is all national property: – If not how came the Russell family with theirs? The nation has a right to adopt or confiscate any property that is employed for the injury of the realm. Let the church be fined for its vices, in enslaving the people, unmanning and pauperising the priesthood, and destroying so many millions of souls. This great national abuse must be summoned to give an account of its deeds. Far from enlightening and moralising the people, it has not even instructed or sanctified the clergy. The history of Oxford and Cambridge is too polluted to be written. The scandalous lives of numbers of the clergy could not be read. Their ignorance, follies, nonconformity, &c., &c., are proverbial. No sects contradict each other so much as the priests of the church of England. And shall these unworthy men have £10,000,000 a year to scourge the nation with irreligion, heresy, and formalism? But were the system as good as they say it is, yet who but a lewd fellow of the lowest description would receive wages for doing nothing? What shall we think of men who rob miserable Ireland of millions a year? Language cannot sufficiently denounce the plunderer who takes tithes from a poor people and makes them no return. Granted that the law allows it, then let the state alter the law. None but a villain will avail himself of a statute that allows him to be dishonest. If the hierarchy pleased it could abolish all its abuses to-morrow, and by conforming itself to the word of God become the bulwark of truth and the glory of the land. But we have said enough to shew that one of the most degraded specimens of mercenary lewdness is furnished by the hierarchy.

We have not exhibited a thousandth part of these enormities, and yet our space is nearly gone. We can only glance at a few other examples, or else the subject is a prolific one. – The master who obtains labour without giving ample remuneration to the labourer or operative: the merchant or tradesman who enriches himself by unjust means or dishonest gains: the landowner who extracts rent which requires that the poor man's loaf should be taxed to save the tenant from beggary: the servant who expects wages without a full quota of labour: – are one and all *lewd fellows of the baser sort.*' The God of heaven has said, 'thou shalt not be dishonest,' 'thou shalt not covet.' Indeed both the tables of the decalogue contain the purest religion and morality, and must be observed if we would be moral here or accepted in the world to come. The Saviour did not die to purchase for us an indulgence to be vile, lewd, and dishonest. 'Faith without works is dead.' 'Thieves, extortionate, and covetous' individuals cannot 'inherit the kingdom of God.' The Judge of all is no respecter of persons; he detests wickedness every where – riches afford no shield, poverty no plea, – all must be just, holy, benevolent, and consequently *truly noble*, or, perish. In this respect christianity stands preeminent among the religions of earth. It has but one law and that law is *love*. It has but one God and he is our universal Father. '*Our* Father who art in heaven' is as appropriate in the lips of a pauper as a prince. Christianity reveals but one Saviour, and he is our Brother, our Sacrifice, our Intercessor, and our King. It promises one Spirit to sanctify and teach us, by leading us into all truth. It gives us the hope of one heaven, from which all lewd mercenary characters will be excluded. In a word it is a noble religion, and proposes to enoble the whole human family. It is a leveller in the best sense of the word, because it demands that the noble and wealthy should come down from their pride, haughtiness, and tyranny, and that the poor should be raised from every kind of degradation. It knows nothing of worldly pomp or parade, but proposes to make all persons *great*, by making them truly, intrinsically, universally, and everlastingly GOOD. This divine nobility every peasant and operative may obtain, and thus be invested with a dignity compared with which crowns and coronets are mere baubles and toys.

It will perhaps be objected, to this tract and No. 12, that I have confined myself too exclusively to the crimes of the wealthy, and have not sufficiently brought forth the vices of the poor. My answer is ready. – Books on the faults of the labouring population, are not wanting: – every one is ready to talk or write fluently about these. The pulpit resounds with them; – newspapers, periodicals, and a large portion of our literature, not only publish, but frequently exaggerate them, and parliament has been so busy in talking about them that it has actually forgotten the ignorance and ungodliness of its own members. We have no persons who trample upon law, order, and religion so extensively and fearlessly as the legislators themselves. So many persons have addressed themselves with so much zeal and animus to pourtray the wickedness of the masses, that it is hardly necessary for me to write anything on that subject. Besides, history and fact have left on my mind a strong impression, that the 'Lewd fellows of the *baser* sort,' are not to be found among the fustian jackets and smock frocks. Many of the labouring classes have been sorely depraved, but truth forbids our writing them down as the MOST or the MORE lewd of the ungodly. Men who have had all the means of education at their command, who have had thousands spent on their schooling, who have rolled in wealth and have been under the pupilage, as they boast, of the only really sanctified and christian clergy upon the face of the earth, – can have no excuse for their offences, and if such persons with such advantages, are avaricious, dishonest, profane and obscene sensualists, gamblers and oppressors, they must be lewd fellows of the *baser* sort. Other criminals may be *base*, these are the *baser*. It is a notorious fact which could be statistically proved, that this empire is robbed to a far larger amount by its state paupers, &c., &c., then by all the more open felons that fill our jails or assize calendars. And further while religion and morality always work upward from the poor to the rich, wickedness of every description especially flows downward from the aristocracy and the wealthy. The nobility and clergy of this country have directly or indirectly contributed to the ignorance and corruption of the masses, more than any other agents amongst us, and therefore have the '*greater sin.*' We sanction, we excuse the vices of none, but when a comparison is instituted, we must conclude that the most debased are those who, notwithstanding all the advantages of wealth and education, not only degrade themselves, but corrupt their dependants and the people at large. A long chapter might be written on the obstructions that the majority of the aristocracy and state clergy have always thrown in the way of the commercial, civil, political, moral, and religious improvement of our peasants and operatives, and ten thousand thousand facts would prove that men of wealth and title, have been the lowest in principle, piety, and patriotism. But we add no more except to reiterate the axiom that, GOODNESS *is the only* GREATNESS.

No. 14.

TRACTS FOR THE FUSTIAN JACKETS AND SMOCK FROCKS.

REBEL RULERS
THE GRAND ORIGINATORS OF REVOLUTIONS;
A FEW WORDS FOR THE FRENCH.
BY THE REV. B. PARSONS,
OF EBLEY, STROUD, GLOUCESTERSHIRE.

'Yet once more I shake not the earth only but also heaven.' PAUL.[1]

It has been usual to lay the blame of all rebellions and revolutions at the door of the people, or the *mob*, as they are vulgarly called. But this charge is as unjust as it is untrue. The masses would not rebel if treated as they ought to be. The rulers must be guilty of rebellion against human nature and the great principles of universal rectitude before they can provoke their subjects to insubordination. There has rarely been any treason against princes until the princes themselves have set the example by committing treason against the king of kings. Historians, however partial to tyranny and despotism, have been compelled to admit, that the people when they have risen, have had great cause of complaint. Nothing more docile than the human mind; nothing more susceptible than the human heart. It can be led by instruction, and perfectly swayed by kindness and benevolence. The great principles of universal government and obedience are rational knowledge, equity, and love. Let these be recognized and practically illustrated by the example of the teachers and rulers and there will not be a rebel on the face of the earth. Not that we consider it to be the duty of governors to teach their subjects: their sole province is to frame and execute such laws as shall secure the lives and property of their people. When they proceed one step beyond this they are guilty of usurpation and despotism, by monopolizing the duties that belong to all, whether rich or poor. The surest way for a father or mother to have foolish and imbecile children is to do every thing for them. Keep them from the necessity of thinking and acting for themselves and they are sure to be degenerate. Ask the boy or the man what you will, and he refers you to his father, for he has not a single thought of his own. He is a six feet infant, wearing his swaddling bands long after he has passed his teens. That poor girl is little better than a lifeless doll.

1 Hebrews 12: 26.

Woe be to the luckless wight that takes her 'for better and worse!' Poor fellow, he will find it all WORSE, from the honey-moon to the grave. – And why? She once had bright eyes and a sharp intellect, and was born with as much mind as Hannah Moore[1] or Mrs Sommerville,[2] but alas! her mother did every thing, and never allowed her to think or act for herself, and as a consequence her whole soul has been doomed to mental and moral paralysis and rendered little better than a nuisance upon earth. The mischief that parents thus do on a small scale, governments effect to a larger extent. They wish to think and act for their subjects. Their greatest ambition has been to reign over an empire of infants, or rather of machines. – They must, forsooth, tell them when to lie down and when to rise up. At the sound of the curfew every fire must be put out and every light extinguished. Some parishes in England still sound this ancient knell of liberty, and the sympathies of the individuals who demand church-rates to perpetuate this precious example of despotism are more in harmony with William the conqueror than with the freedom and christianity of the nineteenth century. To please tyrants, every thing must be done by an act of legislation. The nation must be an assemblage of puppets, and the king, queen, emperor, president, or prime minister, the showman, who by the mere tug of a string or a wire can make their unmanned subjects perform all sorts of manouevres, pranks, or cruelties. Punch and Judy are beautiful fac-similes of what the tories, the Louis Philippes, the centralizing whigs, &c., &c., wish mankind to be: only they would hardly like for the disputes to be so bloodless. For how could our modern patrons of war bear the thought of settling a quarrel rationally, unless they could walk through the reeking gore of innocent victims, and decorate themselves with garlands dyed in blood? In the estimation of thousands the very acme of governmental skill is to render men a mass of living automata, who will buy where the lords wish them to buy, and sell where they tell them to sell; who will fight when they want them to fight, and kill whom they command them to kill; who will believe the state creed, say the state prayers, support state priests, rivet their own chains, pick their own pockets, and, in fact, do any thing and every thing to impoverish and stultify themselves and enrich the aristocracy. Such is the millennium after which modern despots sigh, and for which all those who encourage centralization, commissionerships, state religion, and state education, very effectively labour.

The immortal Burns has sung –

'A man's a man for a' that.'[3]

Yes, every man is naturally a man and every woman a woman, and tyranny on the one hand or sycophancy, flunkeyism, and obsequiousness on the other, are only accidents of humanity. Our duty is to 'honour all men,' for all are the offspring of God, and are corporeally and spiritually equal; and until treated as they ought to be will surely rebel. 'There is a spirit in man and the inspiration of the

---

1   Hannah More (1745–1833), religious writer and founder of the Religious Tract Society.
2   Mary Sommerville (1780–1872), scientific writer.
3   Robert Burns, 'Is There for Honest Poverty', l. 12.

Almighty giveth him understanding.' This spirit was made by eternal equity to recoil at injustice. 'Tread on a worm and it will turn:' even that reptile writhes under cruelty. There is perhaps not an animal, however weak or torpid, but in some form or other gives utterance to its protest against injustice. Yet rulers have been so besotted as to hope to render man, who is created in the image of God, such a phlegmatic lump of insensibility that he may be robbed, flayed, unmanned, barbarized, and massacred, without breathing a complaint; or, at best, to be only a dog, to lick his chain and fawn on the wretch that lacerates his sides with the thong. Never, never, while God is God – and justice is justice – and man is man, shall they effectually succeed. Tyrants may for a time lift their iron front against heaven, despise the claims of equity, and trample their fellow man in the dust, – but vengeance slumbereth not. Like the flood, it may meet with obstructions, or like the volcano, it may slumber for centuries, but the very delay shall render its outbreak the more terrific, irresistible, and destructive. Sleep does not paralyse, but nerve, the hand of a giant. The history of the world is the history of revolutions. From the days of Nimrod[1] the path of time has been strewn with the wrecks of empires. One cannot move a step backwards without stumbling over obsolete crowns, coronets, helmets, thrones, sceptres, and the almost infinite paraphernalia of despotism. The guilty actors in these dramas of injustice and blood have long since gone to their account and cursed the destiny that made them princes instead of peasants, and set them on thrones rather than at the plough, the shuttle, or the anvil. What slave that writhed under their lash would now exchange with them, though ten thousand thousand worlds were offered as a bribe?

Revolutions are the result of oppression, and kings and rulers by setting justice and humanity at nought, have been their authors. The day of retribution even in this world at length comes. 'Verily there is a God that judgeth in the earth.' He 'standeth in the assembly,' – the parliament, privy council or conclave, – 'of the mighty, he executeth judgment among these' earthly 'Gods.' The ruins of empires are the monuments of his justice, and afford a terrific commentary on his vengeance towards all who have trampled upon the rights of the poor. The nations of Canaan, Egypt, Nineveh, Babylon, Persia, Greece, Rome, &c., &c., are all at this day as perfect examples of the indignation of Jehovah against tyranny, as the uplifted mountains and broken rocks are of his omnipotence; and, when duly understood; physical, political, and moral revolutions shall universally extend his praise.

Perhaps there is hardly a national history more instructive than that of France. Here human nature has exhibited almost every phase. A people more blessed by nature or more cursed by despots can hardly be found on the face of the earth. Its skies are genial, its soil fertile, and its mines rich. Its union with the continent on the one hand, and by means of its rivers and the sea, with the whole world on the other, gives it advantages of no common value. Its people are capable of the profoundest thought and deepest feeling. For industry and politeness they have

---

1 Nimrod: Described in Genesis 10: 8–12 as the first 'mighty one on earth'.

few equals. And, strange to say, though their country has undergone so many revolutions, yet the long patience of the masses under the most galling oppression has been proverbial. Their masters have had hard work to provoke them to mutiny. Not a slave ever toiled harder at the galleys, than have the former rulers of France to cover themselves with infamy, and force their subjects to rebellion. Every natural right has been violated; every solemn oath and pledge perjured and broken; all the ties of consanguinity have been burst asunder, and every form of meanness, sensuality, imbecility, barbarian cruelty, and hypocritical sanctimoniousness practised by royal or noble personages. The court and aristocracy of France seem to have vied with each other to show the world how far below beasts and demons, men and women wearing crowns and coronets could sink. Some have called the people cruel and bloodthirsty; but if they had not been prodigies of patience and humanity, their governors would have seduced them far below any nation on the earth. Their princes and nobles have desired above all things to inure the masses to sensuality and slaughter. There is not an act of violence or inhumanity of which the people have been guilty, but was learnt from their rulers. Strange that governors who wish their citizens above all things to thirst for blood, should expect them after all to be humane and gentle. Whatever has been cruel in French revolutions has only been the natural result of the war spirit, with which monarchs, priests, and government journalists have laboured to indoctrinate the nation. Who invented and directed the saint Bartholomew massacre?[1] Who abrogated the edict of Nantes?[2] These deeds sprung not from the *canaille,* or the mob. If the people in any instance have made popular liberty a bye word, the court and the aristocracy have done far more to cast a reproach on crowns and the peerage. It will require ages of good government for the rulers of christendom to roll away the odium that French monarchs and their minions have brought upon all kinds of political and moral order, whether good, bad, or indifferent. It was high time that such a blot on social and civil government should be entirely obliterated. All the barbarity that has been charged on the populace, was taught them by their superiors. To make them cordially hate all other nations was the policy of their rulers, that they might have a pretext for standing armies, places, pensions, and enormous taxes. In the Bartholomew slaughter, they were instructed to murder their own fellow citizens in cold blood. The battle field also is not the worst exhibition of war. The previous training is the most barbarian part of the business. The military school is the grand gymnasium to render men heartless and value human life at a cipher. All martial glory is the price of blood. The aspirant to honor must wade through human gore to seize the crown. As there is no royal road to learning, so there is no humane path to the warrior's wreath. The purple of kings cannot exalt him, he must wear 'garments rolled in blood' or die without fame. Until he has slain crowds of his fellows he has no rep-

---

1 The Massacre of St Bartholomew (24 August 1572), which began the killing of some 50,000 French Protestants.

2 The Edict of Nantes (1598), extending religious liberty to French Protestants, was revoked in 1685.

utation. A warlike nation must be a bloodthirsty nation, and the exaggerated cruelties of the reviled '*sans culottes*' in France, are only a faint reflection of that inhumanity which the court and aristocracy always harboured in their bosoms. Never were men more bitterly outwitted. The spirit that they evoked hurled them from their power and made them a warning to the world. Princes will soon learn the danger of putting edge tools into the hands of the masses, and the folly of trusting to swords as a substitute for equitable laws and a righteous sceptre.

But as one object which I have in view is to show the *fustian jackets and smock frocks*, that their French brethren of the masses have had every provocation, I must refer to facts. It has been common to hold up the revolution of 92 to exe-cration, and we are not going to utter one word of extenuation respecting any of its faults, we only wish that the burden of its guilt may rest on the right shoul-ders. Whatever was cruel or barbarian the people had learnt from the kings, the princes and the nobles. They had been trained in a school of aggression, plunder and revenge. Mangled corpses, weeping widows, bereft mothers, orphan chil-dren, plundered houses and burning cities, had caused the temples and cathedrals to resound with '*Te Deums*' and '*Hallelujahs.*' Christianity was made especially to revel in carnage; the blessed virgin was transformed by the priest into an amazon or a fury, and her immaculate and merciful son who when on earth wept over human woe, was represented as far more pleased than Mars of old, with hecatombs, not of bullocks, but of men. Christianity was baptized with blood, and in its name and under its standard, cruelties were committed at which Vandals would have blushed. It is no wonder then that a nation writhing under every species of tyranny and oppression, should have felt atheistical concerning the divine origin of a religion which, as the priests asserted, sanctioned all these abominations; nor is it strange that they turned their arms against their taskmasters.

The following extracts from a traveller in 1796, will give some idea of the provocations which the French people received from the monarch, nobility, gen-try and clergy before the revolution. The passage especially refers to the sufferings of the farmers and peasantry, because in France the majority of the peo-ple were agriculturalists, and the husbandmen were the most burdened with taxation. The writer which we quote observes –

'Before the revolution, the king, the clergy, the nobility, and the gentry, possessed at least four fifths of all the lands in France; the farmers and peasantry were loaded with rents, taxes and tithes. The clergy everywhere knew very well how to take care of themselves; their lands paid no tax whatever and they had immense possessions; the gentry, who possessed all the offices of value, civil and military, were likewise exempt from taxes, and of course the whole burden of the state fell heavy upon the people, who were utterly despised as well as plundered by the other two orders. The inhabitants of the towns, by their trade and manufactures, were enabled in some degree to support the arbitrary impositions of the ancient government; but the condition of a French peasant before the revolution was most deplorable.

In the first place, he had his rent to pay to his landlord; that was the least and lightest of his burdens; he had the tithes to pay to the clergy, in which however he had one advantage, in that he paid them to a priest of his own religion; he was tormented with a swarm of begging friars, who, at every fresh crop, had fresh demands upon his charity, for meal, for wood, for meat, or for wine; he was obliged perhaps, in the middle of his little harvest, to set off, ten, fifteen, or twenty miles from his cottage, with his horse and cart, and work for a fortnight on the public roads, during which time he must support himself and his beast at his own expence, and for which he was not to receive one penny; this duty was called in France, the *corvee*; he was subject to the capitation tax, which was fixed by the law; he was subject to another tax called the *taille*, which was settled according to the good will and pleasure of the collector, who judged of his ability to pay according to the appearance he made, so that a peasant was afraid to be seen in a whole coat, or to have a good horse in his cart, for fear the collector seeing anything like ease or comfort about him, should make that an excuse for screwing up the tax still higher upon him; for as I have said, the only rule for the amount of the *taille* was the pleasure of the tax-gatherer. The peasant was subject go another tax, still more odious and unjust, I mean the tax upon industry. The tax-gatherer took upon him to decide how much a man might earn in the year, and rated him accordingly, at the price of so many day's labour. Another tax was the heavy excise upon tobacco.

Another, and a most unjust and iniquitous one, as it was managed, was the tax upon salt, called the *gabelle*. Every man was obliged to pay for so much as the collector supposed he might consume in a year, and this tax which was a very heavy one, he must pay, even though he did not consume a single grain; it was in vain for the peasant to say he had no occasion for, and had never used, perhaps, the tenth part of the salt he was rated at; he was forced to pay equally, and to such a length did they carry this abominable oppression under the old government, that if a peasant near the coast had two or three sheep, and one of them happening to have the scab, should follow the natural instinct which would lead it to wash itself in the salt water, the peasant was fined heavily for this indiscretion of his sheep and obliged to pay for having cheated the crown; nay, the very shell-fish which they picked up along the shore, they dared not boil in sea water: the element which God made for the use and convenience of man, was forbidden to the French peasant, and he must eat his fish raw, rather than the king should lose his revenue. If a man used salt which had not paid the duty, he was heavily fined; if he had not money to pay the fine, his little moveables were sold to make it good; if he were caught smuggling this indispensable necessary, he was sent to the galleys, and if with arms in his hands, he was banged up directly, without ceremony. All these heavy taxes and impositions went to the king; and as the French have a king no longer we may judge whether the peasants, at least, have any reason to regret his loss.

I have mentioned the rents which the tenants paid to the gentry, and where the land was let for its value that was but reasonable, but in most instances, the farms were let on short lease to the highest bidder, and at rack rents, and the tenant was in addition goaded with heavy *corvee*, or duties of various kinds; – he was bound to draw home his landlord's firing, to harvest his corn, to cart his hay, and was subject to numberless other impositions of a grievous and horrible character. But it was in the execution of the *game laws* that the tyranny of the French gentry was most remarkable; the crops of the peasants were actually laid waste by the immense quantity of hares, rabbits, partridges, and pheasants which seeming to know that they were protected by the law, devoured his property before his eyes; and if the unfortunate peasant, moved either by rage or hunger, killed one of these invaders, he was seized and condemned to the galleys for life, where he was kept, chained as a slave, to the oar, or in other cases compelled to work in prisons or on the fortifications, but always in irons, and without hope of pardon. To such an extent was this system carried, that when his crop of clover or lucern was ripe, the tenant dared not cut it down without the permission of the *head game keeper*, and if one of the under game keepers owed him a grudge, he had only to say that there was a partridge's nest in the field, and the unfortunate peasant must be content to see his hay rot, and waste away before his eyes, without daring to put a scythe in the grass; it was of little consequence that his fellow-labourer, the horse, or his cow, the support of his children, should starve through the winter for want of fodder, provided the *game* was preserved for his landlord. Such was the situation of the peasants in France before the revolution; – they were fleeced by the crown, oppressed by the gentry, plundered by the clergy, and despised by all.'

If, after reading these extracts, we take into consideration the ignorance in which the people were kept, and the little value which the example of the monarch, priests, and gentry, taught them to set upon the rights, the property, or the lives of others, we have a perfect explanation of all the irreligion, atheism, or inhumanity with which the French revolution of the last century is branded. The masses had been as perfectly trained by their superiors for all the outrages with which they are charged as any student in our universities to take his degree of batchelor of arts. There was not a thief that pined in the galleys, nor a murderer that hung on the gibbet, that had been such an adept in plunder and blood as the princes, the priesthood, and the peerage of France; and the revolution was nothing but the people acting over again a tragedy which the self-styled higher orders had been performing for centuries. We will not then allow it to remain uncontradicted that the furious rabble were the originators of that tremendous convulsion. The quotation which I have here given is bad enough, but does not record a thousandth part of the abominations. There were deeds of sensuality and villainy towards the peasantry which I must not stain these pages with recording. In fact, the people had every inducement to rebel. Their rulers were ruthlessly wanton, they revelled in injustice and oppression, and left not a single effort untried which was calculated to arouse the nation to vengeance; and to crown the whole they did every thing that precept and example could effect to demoralize and debase the masses and render them perfectly callous to every feeling of humanity. There was not a tie left to bind them to their princes, the laws, or religion; and the anarchy which followed was the natural effect of the treatment and tuition which they had received from their governors. The guilt of all that bloodshed and atheism which sent a thrill of horror through all Europe lies chiefly at the door of the wealthy and educated portion of the nation. It has been common for some years past to parade before the country, month after month, the most revolting tales of the French revolution, and the object sought, has been to impress the public mind with the thought that the people must not be trusted with their rights and liberties, or else confusion and bloodshed will overspread the land. But the insinuation is unfounded; for there is scarcely a single thing in which the English mechanics, operatives, and labourers of 1848 resemble the French populace of the last century. 'Tis true we have among the aristocracy many who are distinguished for sabbath breaking, gambling, and sensuality; – men who thirst for the glory of that slaughter-house, the battle field – who fill the army and navy with their sons – who covet sinecures and pensions – who uphold every abuse in church and state – and if left without restraint would over-turn the throne and ruin the nation. But then we have in the country a moral and enlightened people. Christianity, in its native dignity, has been among us and has taught its great lessons of equity, humanity, and love. We have also learnt the *impotence* as well as the cruelty of war, and the *omnipotence* of MORAL FORCE. Moral force carried the reform bill, burst the fetters of the slave, and repealed the corn laws. Hard was the struggle between aristocratical tyranny on the one hand, and right and common sense on the other – but truth and justice, as they always will, prevailed. Our Sunday schools, day schools, free press, public meetings, free discussions, conventicles, and barn preachers, have wrought wonders. We have among the masses, notwithstanding all their defects, the most enlightened and moral race of mechanics, operatives, and labourers upon the face of the earth. These know their power and how to use it. The late efforts to get up a physical force demonstration in England and Ireland, though probably originated by the minions of the great, and aided by their purses, have most signally failed. No! the people of these lands will not rebel. They will obtain *equitable* reforms by *rational* and *legal* means. They ask for nothing that would in one iota infringe on the nat-ural rights of any one. '*The rights of man*' are the rights of all mankind, and therefore include the just claims of the monarch and the nobility. The operatives have too much nobleness in their souls, to wish to rob the rich of a single farthing; all that they want is by a just representative body and wholesome laws to prevent the aristocracy from robbing them. Though in many instances the wealth of the nobles was obtained by dishonourable means, yet the present possessors need not fear that the masses have any desire to touch a penny of this ill-gotten treasure. To participate the spoil would be to countenance the plunder, and prove them-selves as dishonest as the persons who first committed the robbery.

There is then a most important difference between the feelings of the French and the English respecting the redress of grievances. The former have great faith in *physical* force, the latter little or none. The French have not as yet been allowed to exercise their *moral influence* and therefore may have but little confidence in its efficacy; but the English have been accustomed for ages, more or less to wield this mighty weapon, and have found it invincible and always victorious. Like the good old Jerusalem blade of John Bunyan's[1] pilgrim, it never fails. In France the man who flys to arms is a hero, in England he is a savage, a paltroon, and a traitor. Spies and state minions have been paid by former French governments to get up plots and insurrections, that popular liberty might terrify the middle classes and make them side with tyranny. But among us the masses are becoming too wise to be thus duped. On our last *tenth of April*, what zeal was there in certain quar-ters to produce a panic, but the result showed on what miserable data the alarm was trumpeted. It will soon be impossible to find fifty men in the country amongst the operatives or peasantry who will have the least faith in violence of

---

1 John Bunyan (1628–88), author of *Pilgrim's Progress* (1678).

any kind, and the tyrannical ministry who may want to excite sympathy by crying '*wolf*,' will have to parody the old ditty –

> 'Oh dear, what can the matter be!
> Oh dear, what shall I do!
> Nobody coming to murder me!
> Nobody coming! Oh no!'

In 'the tale of a tub,' Swift[1] introduces a simpleton who wanted to become
popular by persecution, and because no one thought him worth a horse whipping
or the pillory, ran his head against a post or something else that his wound might
excite sympathy. Modern despots follow this bright example. What a windfall it
is to whigs and tories to find a few hundred pikes, or pounce upon two or three
physical force orators. They can thence draw an argument to uphold a standing
army; to find offices, red coats and pensions, for the pauper nobility, and deprive
the people of their rights for the next twenty years. But as we have said, the
nation has opened its eyes and seen through this folly, and before long such a
thing as a firelock, except for the gentry to shoot hares and partridges, will not
be found from John O'Groat's to Land's end.

It is a glorious fact that the people of these realms have always been wiser,
more equitable, humane, and religious, than their rulers. John Bull has kept a
grand national school for centuries, in which he has laboured hard to educate the
nobility and gentry in common justice and common sense, and though his pupils
have been more than usually dull he has advanced them a stage in the right direction; and hence while the French governors have led the people into all kinds of
crime and cruelty, the English middle and working classes have, to some extent,
enlightened and humanized both the parliament and the aristocracy. In our sister
country vice has moved downwards from the throne to the workshop and the cottage. Among us virtue has moved upwards with such vigour that it has even
taught and reformed the priesthood. Not that the French people are more cruel
than we. A kinder hearted race the sun does not shine upon. But liberty has been
denied to this generous nation to express its opinion or become virtuous. The lessons taught have been lessons of oppression, injustice, and blood.

Of late years every thing has been done to render the populace savage. The
government of Louis Philippe was the climax of all injustice and despotism. It
was the political cess pool into which had flowed all the abominations of all the
tyrannies that have cursed the world. 'Tis true the crafty monarch had tried to
arch over this sink of iniquity, and plant the surface with evergreens, but the but-
tresses were continually giving way and exposing the infamous accumulation
below. His sceptre was an effort to restore all that was cruel and inhuman in
ancient despotisms, and to gloss them over with the varnish of modern civilization. His nine ministers were to do all things and render the nation an empire of
puppets. He had his '*Minister of Interior*,' – his '*Minister of Justice*,' – his '*Minister of
Public Worship*,' – his '*Minister of Instruction*,' – his '*Minister of Public Works*,' – his

---

1 Jonathan Swift (1667–1745), Irish satirist and cleric.

'*Minister of Trade*,' – his '*Minister of Finance*,' – his '*Minister of Foreign Affairs*,' – and his '*Minister of War*.' All these men had hosts of government minions, placemen, pensioners, and spies, under them; so that here was the most complete apparatus of oppression and slavery that the world ever saw. There were upwards of a *million* of public functionaries paid by the state, and only 180,000 electors to choose the representatives of the people! Liberty was a farce; the press was silenced, except to echo what the monarch approved; public meetings and public opinion were suppressed; the priesthood and the schoolmasters were state slaves to render the nation an obsequious mass of servility; the people were watched by spies and police and ground to the earth by taxation; and it was fondly hoped that all the world would soon follow in the rear of this archtyranny. Our Neros at home had the audacity to extol this crusade against liberty, and commissioners, placemen, a state priesthood and state school-masters, were to extinguish the last spark of British spirit in our own land. But the engine, we might say '*the infernal machine*,' has burst. The high pressure was carried so far as to bury its originators in confusion, and France was free! Some evils have been the consequence, but not a thousandth part of what might have been expected from a populace deprived of liberty to think and educated in blood. The civil war has been but the desolation of a few days, but the government of Louis Philippe was intended to be a perpetual scourge and pestilence to demoralize and destroy men's property, bodies, and souls, until the day of doom. Even the lives that have been sacrificed have exhibited to the lovers of war the natural result of their principles. – For if we must have carnage, that our Wellingtons may have garlands dipped in blood, then it is more noble and generous for any nation to slay its own citizens than to fall upon the inhabitants of other countries. After all, *civil wars* are ten thousand times more creditable than the murder of foreigners. If our aristocracy and priests advocate military glory and blood then let them slay their own brethren instead of satisfying their appetite with the massacre of strangers. We must say, notwithstanding all that has been uttered and written against the French people, that their revolutions and civil commotions have not lowered them one iota in our opinion. Their rulers have disciplined them in every crime they have committed, and done every thing to prevent them from being free and virtuous. Had they possessed our means of education they would very probably have surpassed us in the most generous exercise of every noble affection and principle. That some of them may feel an antipathy to us is natural; their rulers have fostered this feeling and we have deeply injured them by our unjust tariffs and iniquitous wars. But the breach may be healed; the French are forgiving, and that kindness which is the key to the human heart can destroy every vestige of jealousy in their bosom. Let us honour them with confidence, treat them as brethren and compatriots, and afford them every aid in their struggle to be free, virtuous, and happy; and then the union of English and French patriotism and liberty shall present a bulwark of freedom before which the tyrannies of the world shall tremble and against which they shall contend in vain.

It has been my happiness, while writing this tract, to visit Brussels as one of the delegates to the Convention of the *Friends of Universal Peace*, held in that city.

Nothing could have been more kind, generous, nor hospitable than our reception. At Ostend, the public authorities, accompanied with music, flags, and a large concourse of citizens, awaited our landing. We were the friends of universal brotherhood, and this one fact secured us a hearty welcome. The truth is, the nations and especially the masses, are nowhere bloodthirsty, unless they are made so by the princes, the nobles, or the priests. The common people have common sense enough to prefer a friend and a customer to an armed foe. It is only in palaces, mansions, and privy councils that you find the great projectors of massacres and desolation. And yet, with all their boasting, not a few of them would cease to advocate slaughter if they had to take the front of the battle, for although they may not shudder to shoot others, they have little disposition to be shot; hence, they make the ignorant masses their tools, and much as they despise them, yet thirst for the glory of wearing garlands dipped in their blood. Wellington's trophies are all dyed with plebeian gore. But for this they would have no dignity. And thus operatives and peasants are, after all, the artizans who elaborate the wealth and glory of the great. The rents they receive are earned by the sweat of the laborer's brow; the pay and pensions they grasp are chiefly wrung from the hard earnings of the swinish multitude; the poor man's loaf was taxed to enable the lords and landowners to give marriage portions to their daughters; and the veins of the rabble must be opened to supply the only dye that can give splendor to the victor. Neither the heavens above, the earth beneath, nor the waters under the earth can furnish another pigment that will satisfy his taste. Nothing else that God has created in the whole universe will do. Blood, the blood of the mean, vulgar, low-born serfs, is the only compound that can gratify his ambition. To be a man of blood, to wallow in blood, to receive the wages of blood, and wear wreaths stained with blood will alone satiate his savage soul. Well did a candid warrior of late assert at a public meeting that '*War is the most damnable profession under the skies.*' And yet to call forth this desolating fiend was the object of the late infamous proposition to increase our '*national defences.*' How dare we revile the French with being bloodthirsty when we have actually burdened ourselves with a tax of upwards of FORTY MILLIONS a YEAR to irritate them and teach them the art of war? Had we spent a thousandth part of this sum in distributing the blessings of peace and in propagating the great principles of justice, liberty, universal brotherhood, and love; our own country would have been a paradise without a criminal, a pauper, a poor house, or a prison; and not only France, but Europe and the world have been equally happy. It may suit our national vanity to declaim against the French, but our enormous debt testifies that we have spared no costs, that we have even brought our country to the verge of ruin, in our zeal to injure and enrage our neighbours. Talk of cruelty, what cruelty can equal the history of our wars with that country? Lions, bears and wolves, if they could read, would blush to peruse our doings in our Gallic expeditions, and the enumeration of the treasure and blood we have wasted on the plains of France in our efforts to do her every species of injury, might make demons turn pale. Let us then no longer blaspheme the French; let us cease to irritate them by military armaments and martial trophies; let our churches be no longer polluted and

paganized by banners and escutcheons; or our squares and cathedrals with barbarian monuments, columns, or statutes to our Pictons, Howes, Nelsons, or
Wellingtons; but instead of thus proclaiming our own shame and provoking our
neighbors, let us by every act of generosity and christian brotherhood practically
demonstrate to our brethren in France, that we repudiate the crimes of our
fathers and rulers, and desire nothing so ardently as 'peace on earth and good will
among men.' Were we only to act thus rationally, we should soon find in the
French a generous reciprocity of benevolence which would obliterate the past and
be pregnant with every hope for the future.

TRACTS FOR THE FUSTIAN JACKETS AND SMOCK FROCKS.

THE POTATOE BLIGHT,
AND HOW TO PREVENT IT.
BY THE REV. B. PARSONS,
OF EBLEY, STROUD, GLOUCESTERSHIRE.

'And there shall be no more curse.' *Revelation*.[1]

'The Potatoe Blight!' 'The Potatoe Blight!' For the last three years this has been the almost all-absorbing topic of conversation and discussion. If you embark in a steamer, even the sea does not make people forget '*les pommes de terre*', these '*apples of the earth*,' as the French say. On a coach, in a railway carriage, or an omnibus, still the very mention of a potatoe arouses the sleepers and elicits volumes of eloquence of all sorts and kinds. Go to the shop, the kitchen, the dining room, or the drawing room; the same subject awakens the attention of all. Whether seated in the first, second, or third class, the stranger who enters has hardly taken his seat, shown his ticket and adjusted himself for the whistle, ere he looks you in the face, and commences, 'You have been travelling I presume, Sir?' 'Yes Sir.' 'Travelled far, Sir?' 'For several hours past.' 'Indeed! How do the potatoes look?' Here you are fairly launched on a wide sea of conjecture. Taciturnity or silent meditation are at an end. But supposing that at length the subject is given up, and to pass away the time without appearing sullen, or proud, or silly, you take up a newspaper whether daily or weekly, metropolitan, or provincial, and it is a hundred to one but you will find, in prominent capitals, or italics, 'POTATOES,' or '*The Potatoe Blight*.'

Then again as to remedies, why we have enough to fill a volume, some theoretic, some practical; some professedly founded in science, and some on conjecture; but all hitherto distinguished for the one characteristic that they have singularly failed. It is no wonder that in an age of so much quackery, pills and ointment, a medicine for potatoes should at last be advertised. The only matter for astonishment is that the '*panacea*' has not been thought of earlier. '*A Pomme de Terre Morrison*,' might have made his fortune before this, without saving or curing a single root. It is a shame to call the English people '*infidels*.' A people more

---

1 Revelations 22: 3.

disposed to believe can hardly be found, especially if the thing is a hoax or an absurdity, or if there is some quackery or physic in the matter. Some have thought that there is more money spent in medicine in our little island than in all the world. We laugh at Catlin's Indians for attaching so much importance to their '*medicine bag*,' but really they might return the compliment with interest. Why you can hardly enter a church or chapel yard from one end of the country to the other without finding, and sometimes on two or three tombs,

> 'Pain was my portion!
> *Physic was my food!*
> Groans were my devotion!
> *Drugs did me no good!*'

Nothing could be more logical or natural, than that pain should be the portion of him that made *physic his food*, or that the chief result of copious drugging should be a still more abundant multiplication of groans. But even a dying testimony is too often unheeded, and therefore Abernethy[1] once said, 'Since my time doctors have increased *ten to one*; but, thank heaven! diseases have kept pace with them.' We physic everything and therefore it will not be surprising if the potatoes come in for a large share.

However if the observations made and the nostrums proposed provoke a smile, we are not disposed to treat so grave a subject with levity. The suffering that has resulted from the failure of this supposed necessary of life has been unutterable. The tale of '*Elihu Burritt's three days at Skibbereen*,'[2] has scarcely any parallel in the narrative of human woe. And yet this is not a thousandth part of what might be narrated. The loss to the country in the perishing of the root itself and then the further damage in so large an amount of wealth not being distributed through the land in barter, or the purchase of our importations or manufactures, are almost incalculable. Indeed, the visitation has been felt to the ends of the earth. It is evident that the Deity has here spoken in accents which the world, whether willing or not willing, has been compelled to hear. As of old, he has proclaimed if not in words, yet in more emphatic deeds, '*Be still and know that I am God*, I will be exalted among the nations, I will be exalted in the earth.'[3]

Courteous reader, whether you are a christian, or a sceptic, you will allow me to say that I am a believer in the bible, and after nearly forty years of close study, never a firmer one than at this day. But permit me to add that if I was a socialist, or an infidel of any class whatever, I should write the following tract, and use the same arguments; because, though they might not weigh with myself, yet they must speak to the conscience of every christian; and as so large a portion of the country, consists of believers in revelation, my sentiments drawn from a book so generally received as the infallible word of Jehovah, cannot fail to produce reverence, or to convict of hypocrisy. And further, the remarks will be of a practical

---

1 John Abernethy (1764–1831), physician.

2 Elihu Burritt (1810–79), American philanthropist. Between 20 and 24 February 1847, Burritt witnessed the effects of the Irish Famine at Skibbereen.

3 Psalms 46: 10.

tendency, which if followed must benefit every one and make us all better and happier. It is perfectly lawful to call upon every person to reduce his principles to practice, especially if he talks much of the utilitarian and benevolent character of his particular creed or profession. Now, there are no persons upon earth, who assert more confidently the advantages of their religion, than those who embrace the scriptures as their guide. They affirm that there is no justice, purity, benevolence, or mercy equal to that enjoined in their sacred writings; and that if these were cultivated, there would not be any oppression, slavery, violence, war, bloodshed, malice, envy, or uncharitableness among men: in a word that, 'Godliness is profitable for all things, having the promise of the life that now is, and of that which is to come.' Now it is quite fair that every sceptic should demand of the professed followers of the Son of God, a practical exhibition of these great principles, and I do hope that the infidels of the country will stand forth as one man, and insist that christianity shall be something more than a name and that those who profess it shall show their *consistency* by their lives. Their master, the Lord Jesus, has laid down as a rule, that his disciples are to be known by their 'works of faith' and 'labors of love.' His words are, 'by their fruits shall ye know them.' A christian in name and not in deed is sunk very far below fallen angels, for whatever may be the vices of the latter, they do not designate themselves the followers of the Son of God. If I was an infidel, how I would lash those hypocrites who call themselves 'members of Christ and children of God,' and yet set justice, purity, benevolence, and mercy at defiance. The prophets of old never spared a vice because it was committed by one of their own clan, or of a princely rank. Those sturdy moralists paid dear for their fidelity, but still nothing could deter them, and against a formal and hypocritical church, they especially 'cried aloud, spared not, and lifted up their voice like a trumpet.' Religious teachers are become so very polite in our time, that some of them do homage to vice when blessed with wealth or adorned with a mitre or a coronet; and the man, who with 'the sword of the spirit in his hand and the girdle of truth on his loins,' condemns the crimes of the christian world, is not unfrequently severely censured by the reputed respectables of the day. A thousand to one but his salary will be mulcted, and he may rest assured that his head will never be honored or dishonored with a mitre. And therefore to use the expressive, though ungraceful words, of that old man, Isaiah, we have so many '*dumb dogs,*' who never bark except at pure religion. We do hope that our unbelievers will take up the matter and demand that christians shall either 'show their faith by their works,' or else admit that he who by his wicked deeds denies his creed 'is worse than a infidel.'

But now to my subject. I will not take up any time in describing the nature of the potatoe disease, nor give any summary of the numerous physical remedies that have been devised. It is an old saying that 'prevention is better than cure,' and I beg humbly to suggest, that this dire calamity may be averted in future. I am, as I said before, a firm believer in the bible; but I am not an intolerant one, nor do I quarrel with any man whose creed is different from mine. Until we, as christians, can show others that there is more reason on our side than on theirs, they must of necessity follow their convictions. I have a deep impression that sceptics have been very unfairly dealt with by the religious world. We have too often refused the trouble of showing them that ours is an interesting, rational, and benevolent religion, and when we have said a little to prove that we are *theoretically right*, our lives have presented such an ocular demonstration that we are *practically wrong*, that we need not wonder if men who are philosophical enough to judge of 'a tree by its fruits' or of 'faith by its works,' should conclude that those principles which leave us to indulge so many vices can hardly claim to be from above. If the infidel asks after our christianity, we tell him that our creed is a just, a generous, and a merciful one; and we give him a proof of this by spending £20,000,000 a year on war, that we may destroy the bodies of our enemies, and according to our own belief send their souls unprepared into eternity! We show them a church with starving curates, over paid dignitaries, and a laity so ignorant that the civil power is called in to educate them, hang them, or transport them as may seem best to its wisdom. If they inquire for our vaunted 'members of Christ, children of God, and inheritors of the kingdom' we point them to hosts of generals wearing laurels dyed in blood, to steeple chasing, fox hunting, gambling, swearing, sabbath breaking, debauched, licentious lords and commons! If they demand specimens of piety, we exhibit all sorts of worldly mindedness, bribery, oppression, tyranny, and ungodliness! and the sceptic cannot understand how all this viciousness and villany can harmonise with heavenly religion. We call unbelievers unreasonable, but alas! the accusation may be retorted. We are the unreasonable people, for we expect men to believe, without first proving by our lives that our religion is worthy of their attention. Seeing then we have done so little to render the gospel inviting, and so much to make it scandalous, I cannot use any hard language respecting my erring brother who has been led into unbelief by the paganism and vandalism of professing christians. Scepticism is intended by the God that made us, to be a security against credulity. 'Prove all things, hold fast that which is good,' are injunctions that sanction unbelief until we have reached the foundations of faith. Indeed he who has never doubted can hardly be said to believe. His creed is rather the passive credence of the careless and superstitious, than the rational well grounded confidence of the disciple of truth. Without then the least intolerance to other persons, I again repeat my honest conviction that the Bible is the word of God, and that in its sacred pages, we have, strange as it may appear, a perfect protection not only from the potatoe blight, but from every other visitation that might injure the fruits of the earth. I know that in making this statement I run the risk of being laughed at, and by none so much, as by some who call themselves christians, still I must abide 'by the faith once delivered to the saints.'

Now in the sacred volume it is expressly declared that every visitation of blasting, mildew, locusts, caterpillars, palmerworms, or any other desolation, is an express punishment for the sins of mankind. The drought, or the deluge, plague, pestilence or famine, are all said to be scourges for the wickedness of the human family. On the other hand, all kinds of blessings are promised to individuals or nations that shall 'do justly, love mercy, and walk humbly with God.' It may be said that these sentiments are borrowed from the old testament, and are obsolete,

but to this objection it is sufficient to reply, that the providence of God still super-
intends all his creatures; that Jehovah is 'the same yesterday, to day, and for ever;'
that his aversion to sin, and reward to virtue, are unchangeable; that religion in
all ages is one; and thus the old testament and the new agree in spirit. The rites
and ceremonies of Moses were a typical christianity instituted to usher in the gospel by means of symbols suited to instruct and edify the Jews and through them
the world, and God's dealings with the sons of Abraham were intended to inform
mankind at large to the end of time, of what they have to expect at his hands.
Indeed we continually hear ministers quoting Moses and the prophets to show
that the *blessings* of the old testament are secured to believers of all nations. But
if the *benedictions*, why not also the *chastisements*? To represent the Almighty as
become indifferent to sin either through any change in his nature, or the atonement of Christ would lead to atheism; because he who can change cannot be
God. It may be pleasing to ungodly and careless professors to hear of nothing but
mercy; and hence evangelical preaching is more popular for its merciful than its
moral character. And this is so well understood that the moral part of the doctrine is too often merged in the mercy, or just comes in at the end of the sermon.
Indeed to preach the pure morals of the new Testament is not unfrequently
branded as legal and pharisaical, and its unpopularity has been too much for the
courage of many a modern preacher. But then this accommodation of religion to
human prejudice, or irreligiousness does not at all alter the case. Jehovah is the
same inflexible and invincible enemy to iniquity. Justice, purity, and benevolence,
are as immutable as the Eternal himself, and therefore the divine legislator and
judge will continue so to exercise his perfect control over the physical world as to
render his administration a scourge to vice and an incentive to virtue.

In the twenty eighth chapter of the book of Deuteronomy, we have a clear
exposition of the principles according to which our Creator governs mankind.
There all virtue or religion is said to consist in our attending to the voice of
Jehovah. This is perfectly rational and just, because he who made us is the only
person who knows how to govern us. The laws of God must be perfection itself.
The Almighty CANNOT give an unjust command. Nothing unholy, partial or
unkind can by any possibility proceed out of his mouth. To obey him therefore is
the highest virtue, piety, religion and worship. His physical laws, as far as we can
understand them are perfect, and his moral laws *must* be the same. And what our
reason infallibly dictates respecting the statutes of the king of kings, revelation
most satisfactorily demonstrates. Nothing can be more simple, comprehensive
and sublime, than the command, '*To love our maker with all our hearts, and our
neighbor as ourselves.*' Here in the one word 'LOVE,' and that word, – the sweetest,
the most thrilling and enchanting that can proceed from any lips, – we have comprehended everything that belongs to legislation, equity, or devotion. Nor can
this unchangeable rule and standard of right alter until the Eternal shall cease to
exist. Heaven and earth may pass away, but this first principle of rectitude
remains the same and must remain for ever and ever. To suppose the Creator
indifferent to its observance, is as absurd as to assert that he can be annihilated.
The text in Deuteronomy which we have quoted, merely directs us 'to hearken'

to this voice of 'LOVE,' and then assures us that if we obey, every blessing shall be ours, but if we disobey, we are justly threatened with the most unequivocal proofs of divine displeasure.

From verse the 1st to the 13th, of chap. 28th, Moses enlarges upon the temporal benefits of obedience, and assures us that those who thus honor Jehovah shall have all that heart can wish. They are 'to be blessed in the city, in the field, in their offspring, in the fertility of their field, their kine, and their flocks, in their basket and their store.' They are to be blessed 'in lying down, in rising up; in their storehouses and all that they set their hands unto;' Jehovah pledges himself by an oath to establish them. Their enemies are to be afraid and flee from them. They are to have plenteousness in every thing that can make them prosperous and happy. The 'good treasure of heaven' is to be opened to them; 'every work of their hands' is to be blessed; they are to be at the head of other nations, and to be so rich as to enable them 'to lend' to their neighbors, but never as long as they obey are they to be so poor as 'to borrow.' The reader of the sacred volume must be aware, that these promises uttered by Moses are echoed and re-echoed by the prophets and apostles to the end of the book of revelation. We are again and again told that they are not confined to the Jews or the Jewish dispensation, but that they shall be realized by all nations who reverence God's universal and immutable law of LOVE. In fact they are so constantly repeated that I might fill a volume with quotations.

On the contrary, if the laws of Jehovah were transgressed, he threatens them with the loss of all things that would conduce to their happiness and prosperity. They were to be '*cursed* in the city, in the field, in their basket and store, in their offspring, in the fruits of their field, their cattle and their flocks, in their coming in and going out;' they were to have 'rebuke and vexation in all that they set their hands unto because of the wickedness of their doings.' 'They were to be smitten with pestilence, consumption, fever, inflammation, with burning, with the sword, with blasting and mildew.' The 'heavens above were to be brass, and the earth beneath iron.' In a word, every kind of calamity was to be the consequence of rejecting and transgressing the benevolent laws of the God of heaven. From the 15th verse of the 28th of Deut. to the end we have threatenings of the most terrific character uttered for the purpose of showing us that Jehovah will not allow iniquity to go unpunished. It may be said that these judgments are very severe. But we reply that the Creator must show his displeasure at sin; and not to punish crime is to encourage it. Besides, iniquity is one of the bitterest of curses, and therefore were the Almighty to sanction it; he would countenance a scourge far more afflictive than any that he himself has ever inflicted. It is a grand mistake that sin owes its malignant influence to the existence of God. Were there no Creator, or heaven, or hell, yet iniquity, like the cholera or the plague, would be equally baneful. Tyranny, oppression, injustice, sensuality, intemperance, avarice, malice, envy, ambition, pride, and all uncharitableness embody in themselves an inseparable curse. As happiness is an essential attribute of innocence, so misery is an essential attribute of crime. It may be said that if sin thus naturally curses itself, what need is there for the Deity to interfere? We reply, that his benevolence demands it. What should we say of a father who expressed no concern about a disease or plague which was afflicting and destroying his off-spring, or who should utter no word of disapprobation respecting those who were robbing them of their rights and liberty? Now, if we expect that an affectionate parent must exercise his pity towards his children by showing his displeasure at what injures them, and if in such a case indubitable marks of indignation would be unquestionable proofs of love; then why not come to the same conclusion respecting the kindness of our indulgent Creator. His threatenings are undis-guised evidences of his benevolence, and the blight, the mildew, the caterpillar, and the locusts are only the messengers of his mercy. He afflicts us because he loves us, and the very curse that lights upon our substance is pregnant with divine compassion.

We may also here add, that the scriptures every where throw open the door of repentance. God is 'slow to anger, but plenteous in mercy.' However dire the vis-itation may have been, or however great the crimes which have evoked it, yet no sooner do the people turn from their iniquity than Jehovah restores his smile and benediction. The prayer of Solomon in the 8th chapter of the 1st book of Kings, and the answer of the Almighty in the 9th chapter is an abundant proof of this; and, in the last of the old testament prophets, we have a similar example of divine forgiveness. Indeed we might quote text after text for the correctness of this sen-timent, but we shall confine ourselves to the 3rd chapter of Malachi. There the Jews are informed that if they will return and obey the commands of the Eternal, he 'will rebuke the devourer for their sakes;' will make their 'land a delightsome land;' and 'open the windows of heaven and pour out a blessing that there shall not be room enough to receive it.' In the new testament the same promises are reiterated, mercy is to be proclaimed to every creature; and 'godliness' is said to be 'profitable for all things, having the promise of the life that now is and of that which is to come;' for if we 'seek first the kingdom of God and his righteousness, all these things,' our Lord declares, 'shall be added unto us.'

We might enlarge on this subject until we had filled volumes, but enough has been said to prove that providential visitations, whether in the form of a potatoe blight, or in any other mode, are proofs that God is justly and benevolently show-ing his displeasure at our sins and thus loudly calling upon us to repent. And further we have the assurance of the Eternal himself that if we renounce our iniquities he will remove his chastisements and pour upon us the choicest of his blessings. I have thus endeavored to show to the satisfaction of every believer in revelation that the late blight on potatoes, or any other production of the earth can be prevented. The calamity is a *physical* scourge for *moral* turpitude and con-sequently the remedy must be *moral*. For should not the punishment continue in this specific form, still if we refuse to obey the great principles of justice and benevolence, the Creator, from the love he bears to us, will convince us that no one can harden himself against the claims of virtue and be guiltless, and though Jehovah may spare long, yet he will not allow wickedness to escape the brand of his righteous displeasure.

Before I finish this tract, it may be necessary to advance a few facts to prove that our sins deserve the especial indignation of heaven. We are a very pharisaical people, and this spirit is no where more prevalent than among those who lay claim to evangelical piety. I grant the century we live in has been very remarkable for the noble institutions that have been originated and the good they have done. But in congratulating ourselves it is probable that we forget, that our very eminence arises from the indifference of other ages. Such institutions as the bible, missionary, tract, and anti-slavery societies, ought to have existed centuries ago. There was the same command to our fathers as to us, nor are we in a position to boast because we are attending to duties which our ancestors neglected; and especially not, if we consider the lukewarmness and avarice with which every benevolent enterprise in our day, has to contend. Take away a very small minority of the nation, and our great philanthropic undertakings would be abandoned. Institutions to degrade and destroy mankind are liberally supported. We spend £20,000,000 a year to rob and desolate the earth and massacre mankind. We waste £100,000,000 annually on poisons, and perhaps as much more on our other luxuries and vices, while a paltry *three* or *four* millions would cover all that we voluntary expend in philanthropy. Tithes and church-rates are not *voluntary* gifts and therefore are paid *reluctantly* and consequently against the wills and inclinations of churchmen themselves, for if they pay them *willingly* they pay them *voluntarily*, which would be to them a great abomination. No one laughs so loudly, or scowls so indignantly at *voluntariness* or *willingness* in religion as many of our modern episcopalians. We cannot then lay any flattering unction to our souls respecting the piety or generosity of the age in which we live, for whatever we may do for the elevation of man or the glory of God, we do a hundred times as much to uphold the cause of the prince of darkness. Aye, and while we are thus liberally and vigorously sustaining the works of iniquity, we positively have the audacity to call ourselves christians, and to boast that we have 'renounced the devil and *all* his works, the pomps and vanities of this wicked world and all the sinful lusts of the flesh!' and thus our religious profession involves us in deeper guilt than that which overthrew Sodom or Gomorrah. My own impression is, that considering our light and knowledge, our advantages and facilities for doing good, there never was a country more deeply culpable in the sight of God than England is at this present day. Tyre and Sidon, Sodom and Gomorrah, and probably the world before the flood might boast of their piety if they compared themselves with us.

We are told in Ezekiel xvi. 49 that the 'iniquity of Sodom' consisted in 'pride, fulness of bread, abundance of idleness,' and in neglecting to 'strengthen the hand of the poor and needy.' But each of these crimes is probably more rife among us than they were in the cities of the plain. It would be difficult to find a prouder race than the aristocracy, and not a few of the middle ranks of England. The pride of rank, ancestry, and wealth are carried to the most disgusting lengths. Persons whose ancestors were royal courtesans, minions, or sycophants and who were rewarded with titles as the price of their infamy, look in our day with supercilious contempt on the pure and honest blood of the useful artisan or peasant. We have men whose heads are become giddy with pride, because their brows are decorated with laurels dyed in human blood; or, because they are paid for being colonels without regiments, admirals without ships, and clergymen without duties. The honor of which thousands boast, is the foulest disgrace. Some also, who have not one spark of intelligence, or one virtuous trait to recommend them to notice, have the assurance to claim our homage because their fathers were renowned, never considering that it would be just as venerable to wear the old clothes of their progenitors and expect that we should bow down before them on that account, as to wish to be respected for paternal virtues which they have neither talent, courage, nor moral principle to imitate. Far more reason had the old fox when tarred and feathered, to be proud of the plumes which he had stolen. And then there is the pride of wealth, than which, nothing can be more irrational. Mammon is one of the meanest of the demons. 'The love of money is the root of all evil.' The basest of mortals have been affluent. Wealth has often been obtained by the vilest means; in many cases, the possessor has sacrificed every humane principle, every honorable feeling, and even his very soul, to grasp it. There are more minds unmanned and polluted by this vice than by any other passion. The highest authority in the universe has told us that 'it is easier for a camel to go through the eye of a needle than for a rich man to enter into the kingdom of God.' How strange then that the possession of wealth should provoke pride and make any persons imagine that they are better than the rest of the human family. And then as to civil rank, this has not usually been based on any rational foundation. Kings have not generally been kings because of any superior intelligence or piety. The peerage that is hereditary has no moral origin. There is no more dignity in being born a marquis than a peasant. My lord Thurlow told the house of lords that an hereditary duke or peer was *an accident of an accident.* Military rank is rarely the reward of merit, and if it were, the honor itself is a libel, not merely on christianity, but on humanity itself. A hero has lately declared, that *'his profession is the most damnable upon earth.'* Clerical promotion does not depend so much upon christian principle, as upon the politics or avarice of the patrons; and the priest who rises has not unfrequently to barter away every manly, patriotic and pious characteristic. He sells his soul for office and gold. Even the magistracy is subjected to political caprice, and members of parliament are notorious for almost every thing but the qualifications which their duties demand. Civil, ecclesiastical, military, or magisterial ranks, even if pride were lawful, can therefore be no matter of self gratulation. We may also observe that intellect and moral pre-eminence, instead of provoking pride, produce humility. The really learned and intelligent man knows how little he knows. True genius is always humble under the sense of its deficiencies, and lowliness and self abasement are the truest marks of evangelical virtue. There is a world of philosophy in the questions, 'Who maketh thee to differ from another? And what hast thou that thou didst not receive? Now if thou didst receive it, why dost thou glory as if thou hadst not received it?' The fact is pride is one of the most unseemly features of any human being, and a vice most hateful to the deity; and yet as a nation we are eaten up with it, and far more deserving of punishment than Sodom, or

Gomorrah. The pride of birth, rank, wealth or office has made us inhuman to our own species. It has destroyed the sense of universal brotherhood, and rendered millions deaf to the obligations which this relation involves. Ladies and gentlemen, whose talents, wealth, and rank might long ago have banished ignorance, poverty, and crime from our world, have lived and died in indolence. Pride has their own ruin and through them the ruin of multitudes in this world and the world to come. All God's children, whether rich or poor, are equally dear to him. We are all responsible to the eternal, not only for the sins we have committed, but for all the physical, mental, and moral, benefits we can confer upon mankind. Yonder lady, whose chief business on earth seems to be the toilet, the drawing room, and the levee, and who was created to be a seraph to drive want, ignorance, vice and woe from the locality in which she lived, will soon be arraigned at the bar of heaven to hear the doom of her negligence, and through eternity will curse the rank and wealth that generated the pride which has plunged her into perdition. We may talk sentimentally and piously of the vices of the poor, but too often are silent of the fact that they are, in ten thousand thousand cases, to be traced to the negligence, the injustice, the oppression, the haughtiness and pride of the wealthy. Yonder gambling, fox hunting, luxurious squire or nobleman, was born to be a missionary, was sent into this world to be an angel of mercy to mankind, but rank and pride have ruined him. His mental and moral powers have been blasted and withered by it. He neither 'fears God nor regards man.' If you judge from his life, you might suppose him the plenipotentiary of Beelzebub, and that his chief business on earth was to curse himself and scourge his species, that his behest is to crush the poor and needy; to exact from his brethren the largest amount of labor for the smallest possible degree of remuneration; to roll back the tide of liberty and knowledge; to brood, like an evil genius over his domain, lest human thought should burst forth into light, liberty and maturity, and man again be restored to the image of God. His boast is of savage sports, bloodthirsty wars, electionary corruption, successful gambling, iniquitous pensions and sinecures, or perhaps unblushing deeds of debauchery. He lives a moral pest, he dies impenitent, the clergyman calls him his 'dear brother' and buries him 'in sure and certain hope of a resurrection to eternal life.' Sodom presented no parallel of wickedness that might be classed with this. But I have not hinted at a thousandth part of the baneful influence of pride. In preventing fraternization, except with satan; in producing idleness and stoicism; in generating sycophancy to those above and haughtiness to those below; in crouching for honors without meaning or merit, for salaries without labor, for pensions without desert; in cultivating the very meanness which it professes to shun, and effectually excluding itself from the real dignity to which it pretends to aspire; in polluting and blighting the soul which has given it birth, in cursing all things within the range of its influence; in sympathy with hell and an insolence to heaven; we have in PRIDE a criminal passion which at the present day is one of the direst desolators of our land. We need not then wonder at the *potatoe blight*, even if we confined our attention to this vice alone. But I have not done. I have yet much to say respecting the other charges brought by the prophet against Sodom and Gomorrah, and to show that England is far more guilty than those polluted cities. I shall however reserve my remarks on these subjects for my next tract, and conclude by observing that to prevent our being still more severely punished there is no door open but that of repentance.

The old world had a hundred years given it to amend its ways and avert the deluge. Sodom and Gomorrah were warned by Lot. The Canaanites were spared three hundred years. The Jews had prophet after prophet to warn them. Jonah was sent to Nineveh, and that great city was saved in consequence of the penitence of the people. Our Creator is boundless in goodness, long suffering is one of his most renowned attributes. 'Who' says the prophet, 'is like unto thee, a God that delighteth in mercy.' Were his word obeyed there would 'be no more any curse.' Every one then who violates the laws of God, or rejects the gospel, is doing what he can to bring desolation on the land and destroy its fruits. Such is the faith of every believer in revelation, and therefore the duty to repent and save himself and his country is most imperative and obligatory.

No 16.

TRACTS FOR THE FUSTIAN JACKETS AND SMOCK FROCKS.

THE POTATOE BLIGHT, AND HOW TO PREVENT IT.
BY THE REV. B. PARSONS, OF EBLEY, STROUD, GLOUCESTERSHIRE.

> 'And all nations shall call you blessed,
> For ye shall be a delightsome land
> Saith the Lord of Hosts.' – *Malachi*.

In my last Tract on '*the potatoe blight*,' I showed that according to the sacred volume, all visitations, of *blasting, mildew, locusts, caterpillars*, &c., are scourges for sin, and that this arrangement of providence is not severe but benevolent. The Creator cannot smile upon iniquity. His divinity forbids it. He who approves of whatever can injure mankind cannot be God. Not to punish immorality would be to encourage it. Christians are not fatalists. The Jove of the ancients was himself subject to fate. His omnipotence was a farce. Often did he confess to his suppliants that decrees, over which he had no control, prevented his answering their requests. He had also not unfrequently to wage an unsuccessful warfare with his brother divinities. The caprices of the goddesses to aid their favorites gave him no little trouble. The God of Revelation sits on his own Imperial throne without a rival to thwart his purposes. He holds the reins of universal empire and 'doeth according to his will' in the armies of heaven and among the inhabitants of the earth and none can stay his hand or say unto him, 'What doest thou?' He wings the seraphs, not an archangel moves but at his command, nor a sparrow falls without his notice. He 'upholds all things by the word of his power.' He keeps the planets in their orbits, the stars and the sun in their centres, and yet he feeds the birds, clothes the lilies, and counts 'the hairs of our head.' It is at the direction of his benevolence that the former and latter rain fall in due season;' and the drought or the deluge obey his behest. He 'opens his hand and satisfies the wants of every living thing.' Under his guidance crosses and afflictions 'are blessings in disguise;' and his very wrath is the benevolence of a father who seeks the welfare and perfection of all his children. Such a sublime and sympathetic ruler is the Divinity for man; – 'the desire of all nations.' Sceptics long for his reign. The God that they reject is a tyrant who smiles on the rich and frowns on the poor. An aristocratical deity whose littleness is fascinated with such baubles as coronets, hereditary dignity, diplomas, titles, and heraldic fictions; and to support them sanctions the devastation of countries, the plunder of his poor children, hecatombs of victims and rivers of human blood. The atheism of Christendom is mainly to be attributed to the church. The priests have failed of their duty. They have clothed the godhead in terrors, or exhibited his mercy as a capricious thing pandering to the vices of favorites. Infidelity has demanded a reform and refused to acknowledge as the object of faith and worship a being who smiles on oppression, tyranny and cruelty. It is a refreshing thought that the government and destiny of our world is in the hands of God and that the dispensations of providence are intended to advance our welfare. The only thing that can injure man is wickedness, and there is nothing in the universe that Jehovah hates but *sin*. Even Lucifer is abhorred, not as a creature but as a *sinner*. Our country at the present time groans under the weight of its crimes. We are far more guilty than Tyre or Sidon, Sodom or Gomorrah. And what is worse, those sins which are most abominable in the sight of God are hardly thought of. Doubtless we have blasphemy, debauchery, drunkenness, and sabbath breaking among us to a fearful extent, but then, in most instances, these vices are traceable to others. They are the results of injustice or neglect. Had the ministers of religion, the lords and ladies of our day, the wealthy classes and the professed christians of the age, performed their duty, these evils would long ago have been banished from the land. The poor must be viewed and treated as God's '*offspring*' and our brethren. They must have better houses, and in a great many instances, more equitable wages. In many of their miserable dwellings, decency and morality are out of the question. The mockery of remuneration which many a landowner with his £50,000 or £100,000 a year pays the laborers that produce his wealth, is a libel on human nature. I condemn none but the guilty and none but the guilty therefore can be offended. But the truth must be spoken. The Judge of all the earth will do right: and looks not merely at transgressors but at those who in any way might have prevented their wickedness. The lady that lounged on a sofa when she ought to have been ministering physical, intellectual or spiritual benefit to her own sex, will stand at the bar of God deeply stained with the blood of souls. The nobleman, squire, farmer or manufacturer who spends his wealth and time in gambling, horses, hounds, strong drink, luxury of dress, equipage, or table, and leaves his poor brethren to languish in miserable hovels, in squalid ignorance, vicious and vulgar manners and morals, will soon be arraigned before the eternal for all the evil that he could have prevented and the good he might have done. The priest especially ought to have been the leading spirit of the age. Truths of the most thrilling import were committed to his trust. His stewardship is the most tremendous under the sun. Not only the temporal but the *eternal* destiny of multitudes was left in his hands. It was his charge to produce a good conscience in every heart. He had the word of Jehovah and the Holy Spirit placed at his disposal to regenerate the people. His commission from the skies was to produce universal justice, purity, sympathy and benevolence. His ministrations were to make angels of mercy of all his hearers, but especially of the wealthy and the aristocracy, and should he neglect his duty he will hereafter be deemed the most execrable of assassins. He poisoned, starved, withered and doomed to perdition the souls of his hearers, and when he dies, to use the words of Blair,[1] 'the common damned will shun his society.'[2]

> The king of heaven, is our universal father,
> 'His heart is made of tenderness, his bowels melt with love;'

And therefore not merely as a God of justice, but as a God of mercy he must 'visit for these things.' Why should we have fertile seasons or abundant crops? The chief use we should make of them would be to increase our pride, luxury, and indolence. Besides we have had these for years. The 'earth has brought forth by handfuls;' and has done so from time immemorial and yet we are told that our peasants and artizans are *untutored savages*,' and the church has the audacity to proclaim its own shame by asking the parliament to take the cause of education in hand! The clergy have vied with each other in showing to the country and the government how woefully they have neglected their duty. The best paid priests upon earth have at last awakened to activity, but it has been to publish the barbarism of their parishioners and thereby their own negligence and unfaithfulness. Never was there a people so completely duped as the English. Under the name of *Liberty and Christianity*, greater wickedness has been committed, greater tyranny practised, and more plunders effected in this country, than in any other nation upon earth, whatever may have been the despotism, or superstition under which it has groaned. In my former tract on this subject I quoted the statement of Ezekiel concerning the crying sins of Sodom. He classifies her iniquity under *four* heads. 1st 'Pride,' 2nd 'Fulness of bread,' 3rd 'Abundance of idleness in her and her daughters,' 4th She 'strengthened not the hands of the poor and needy.' In pages 9 and 10 of tract 15, I advanced a few facts to show, that as far as *pride* is concerned, we are more guilty than the cities of the plain and therefore need not wonder at any scourge that may come upon us. Whatever pride there was in Gomorrah, Babylon or Jerusalem, may be more than paralleled in our country at the present day. But enough of this already.

II. *'Fulness of bread'* was another crime charged upon the devoted cities. The Hebrew word rendered *'fulness'* means not merely *enough* but *more than enough*, and here it denotes *satiety, luxuriousness, and excess*. The verse also speaks of the 'poor and needy' and shows that while the wealthy had too much there were crowds who had too little. It is highly probable that Sodom had arrived at such a pitch of perfection in politics that it had but two classes, the *rich* and the *poor*. And can we boast of being superior in morals to those abandoned rebels? Have we not amongst us 'fulness of bread,' and half-fed poverty? The dogs and horses of our landowners are far better housed and fed than the peasants who give to the land all its value and procure for their lords thousands and tens of thousands a year. And yet in an age of true civilization, humanity and christian principle the food,

---

1 Hugh Blair (1718–1800), Scottish divine.
2 See *Sermons of Hugh Blair* (1837), sermon LVI.

clothing, and dwelling, of the laborer would be first attended to. If the cart horse must be well fed, if the hunter must have his full quota of corn, if the hound, the bull dog, and the poodle must have a daily supply; if we cry shame at the niggard who starves her cat, what epithets can sufficiently execrate the injustice which gathers immense wealth from the sweat of the laborer's brow, and then dooms him to all the miseries of coarse and scanty fare, insufficient clothing, and cold, comfortless dwellings? That old radical the apostle James has a striking text on this subject. 'Behold,' says he, 'the *hire* of the laborers who have reaped down your fields, which of you is kept back by fraud, crieth; and the cries of them which have reaped, have entered into the ears of the Lord of Sabaoth.' Had this text been more frequently preached from, we should have had upright masters and landowners, a moral and happy peasantry, and no potatoe blight. Ah, but then the words are legal and not evangelical! For the religion of our day rejects a considerable portion of God's word as not sufficiently spiritual for its transcendental piety. And yet these truths contain no small portion of the *gospel* of Messiah's kingdom. Once on a time when he entered the synagogue of Nazareth and they gave him the book to read, we are told that 'he found the place where it was written "The spirit of Jehovah is upon me, because he hath anointed me to *evangelize the poor*, he hath sent me to heal the broken hearted, to preach *emancipation to those in bondage*, the recovery of sight to the blind, to set at *liberty* them that are bruised, to proclaim the acceptable year of the Lord."' Here you have politics and spirituality blended. What a *radical*, Isaiah must have been to have uttered such words, and must not our hyper-evangelicals be shocked that the august person mentioned should have quoted them? The fact is, the *true gospel* includes temporal and spiritual salvation. The King of kings is the Father of all, and he expects that we shall show our spiritual preeminence by attending to the physical, social, intellectual and religious emancipation of all his creatures, but especially of his poor children. The doctrines of the Redeemer were *radical doctrines*, and the common people heard him gladly. As he read the text just alluded to, 'the eyes of all in the synagogue were fastened upon him, and all bare him witness and wondered at the gracious words that proceeded out of his lips.' How the masses – the fustian jackets and smock frocks, – the chartists, – 'the people who knew not the law and were cursed' for their ignorance by the very men who boasted that they had a commission from heaven to give them knowledge, – how all these despised operatives must have rejoiced as they heard these words of liberty and salvation from the lips of the Son of God. Here was *'the people's charter'* with a witness, and the Lord Jesus was not afraid to read it in public. He told the rich who were present that his mission was to *'evangelize the poor.'* This is something beyond merely 'preaching the gospel to them.' To christianize the masses is a great deal more than proclaiming christianity to them. The latter is essential to the former, but there must be more than mere preaching before any one can be a christian. So to *'evangelize the poor,'* means that they are thoroughly imbued with the political as well as the spiritual principles of the gospel, and consequently that they know their rights and how, in rational and peaceable manner, to gain and use them. Depend on it, that in our Lord's sense, we have had a comparatively small portion of evangelical preachers. We trust that our peasants and operatives will soon demand the *gospel*, the *whole gospel*, and *nothing but the gospel*.

The destruction of Sodom and Gomorrah was one of the most thrilling gospel sermons for the fustian jackets and smock frocks, that ever was preached. 'The cry of the city was great and reached to heaven, and Jehovah came down' to investigate the matter, and he found 'pride, fulness of bread,' &c. There was enough for all, but the aristocracy monopolized it, wasted it or gave it their doy and steeled their hearts against their indigent brethren. They had a rich country, 'the plains were well watered as the garden of the lord.' They lived in an earthly paradise. Perhaps there had been no blight for years. The granaries groaned with corn and the people sighed for bread! As we read these facts who can wonder that fire and brimstone descended, or that these cities became '*the Dead Sea!*' There was *enough*, there was *too much* and yet there was *want*. Perhaps the political economists wrote books on the subject and said it was a difficult point! There may have been a Malthus, or a Lord John Russell then, for 'there is nothing new under the sun.' There may also have been a state church, and the priests may have delivered homilies to the masses on the *advantages of poverty*, and have begged them to be resigned and not to meddle with politics. Probably they so far succeeded that no social reformer was left. A few moral force chartists and right hearted patriots would have rescued them. 'Ten righteous persons would have saved the cities.' Doubtless it was a difficult case for the politicians and state moralists. There is nothing so hard to tyrants as to do justice. There was a superfluity of bread on the one hand, and there was a starving people on the other, and the grand the insurmountable difficulty was to bring the redundant corn and the empty mouths together! The protectionists declared that the only way was to tax the poor man's loaf again!! The sir James, the sir Robert's and lord John's shook their heads; the clergy said it was an inextricable mystery of Providence that there should be so much bread and so many craving appetites! Their reverences could not understand how it was that the universal father had made provision for all! and so the corn rotted in the store houses and the people died of famine, until divine indignation put an end to the matter. Oh these Mystery-Mongers! Suppose in one of the countries of the moon there was a duke who rolls in wealth and has ten children, and that the eldest takes all and leaves the others without bread, would any one say that it is a mystery of providence that the younger branches are left to be state paupers and either starve or beg for sinecures, pensions, to be 'slaughter-men,' or engage in any dirty work that the prime minister of that satellite may desire to be done? Doubtless we should deem all these *lunar* politicians, sentimentalists, and moralists, *Lunatics*, and wish we could only send a Lord George Bentinck,[1] or Mr Fitzwilliam to tell them, that if one child eats up, or throws to the dogs, the dinners of the other, the poor souls who are thus robbed will have to subsist on short commons, or no commons at all. We too have, or can have bread enough and to spare, we have an industrious people who ask for labor and not alms; we have a bountiful providence waiting to bless the earth with exu-

1 George Bentinck (1802–48), MP for King's Lynn 1836–48.

berant fertility, but the world has bad laws, and heartless aristocrats, and the cry of gorged luxury on the one hand, and of skeleton pauperism on the other, ascends hourly to the God of justice, and the pestilence and potatoe blight are the evidences that he is not inattentive to the injuries of the poor and needy.

III. – There was in Sodom '*An abundance of idleness both in her and her daughters.*' The same charge may be brought against Britain at the present time. To have nothing to do seems the elysium after which thousands sigh. That father 'rises early and late takes rest, eats the bread of carefulness,' oppresses all with whom he deals and would rather part with his blood than his money for any benevolent object; and the climax of all his aspirations and toil, is that, 'his children may have nothing to do!' The result of all this, is a race of sentimental daughters sickly in body and imbecile in mind; and a generation of sons who drink champagne, pollute their bodies and God's air with cigar smoke, and end their days in dissipation or obscurity. As a righteous doom, the family becomes extinct, for the decree of Jehovah is that 'the name of the wicked shall rot.' No persons on earth have such facilities for being useful as our wealthy men and aristocracy. They could redress every political wrong, might bless the peasant's home with plenty, his mind with knowledge and his heart with religion and the hope of eternal felicity. They might more than realize the ancient fables concerning the beneficent visits of the gods. Every print of their steps should be marked by civilization and beauty. The corn, the olive, the rose and the lily would attest that men in the image of God had been there. The fine arts, learning, intelligence and philanthropy should be the indestructible monuments of their fame. That individual has lived to little purpose who needs a tablet or a statue. We cannot tell where the dust of some of the greatest men that have ever lived sleeps. There is no pillar of brass or marble to record the names of such individuals as Abraham, Moses, Isaiah, or the Apostle Paul, and yet we shed no tear. It is all well. God will take care of their ashes, their spirits are with the blessed, while their piety and philanthropy have left their names as household words to the end of time. Labor is the benevolent appointment of heaven. Wages are only the more sordid remuneration of toil. A healthy circulation, a blooming cheek, undisturbed digestion, sound repose, and spirits that never flag were intended to be among its nobler rewards. But its greatest joys were to arise from the '*mens conscia recti,*' 'the mind conscious of right.' The thought that something has been done to cultivate the earth, to minister to the wants of our species, to alleviate human woe, to advance the cause of liberty, truth, intelligence, and piety, and especially to answer the end for which Jehovah called us into being, and the Saviour bled on Calvary, – such reflections as these, – afford the soul an inward source of satisfaction and bliss second only to the happiness of heaven. The men and women of Sodom lived to no good purpose, and their appropriate monument is 'THE DEAD SEA.'

The paralysing hand of sloth also not only smote the men, but 'their daughters' were blighted with it. They had 'an abundance' of this accursed bane. Some tell us that the word '*daughters*' here refers to the other cities of the plain. Should we grant the correctness of the criticism, still we have facts enough to show that the influence of woman was last in these scenes of corruption and this must have been the result of their own negligence. Had woman done her duty, those grosser vices that sunk the males below beasts and demons, would never have stained their character. Woman was created to soften and refine the other sex, and where she fulfils her mission the men are chaste, intelligent, benevolent, and godlike. Her influence is all but omnipotent. But then she must be the principal agent in producing that elevated state of mind and morals which shall duly appreciate her deeds and adequately honor her worth. The daughters of Sodom were a race of slothful insipid dames, so that the men turned from them in disgust. Such was the natural fruit of their indolence. There is a guilty idleness in our country which must be just as offensive to the Creator as the sloth of the daughters of Gomorrah. Vices change their form. Civilization, as it advances, removes a portion of their grossness. We can have polished crime and exquisite wickedness. The robe, the coronet or the crown may decorate the tyrant, and the debauchee, and the most finished gentleman may be the most consummate villain. The *swell mob* are said to be so refined that the 'masters of assemblies,' might admit them to the queen's levee. They have sometimes passed for courtiers, and if we examine the pension list there are more senses than one in which the resemblance might elude the keenest observer. But though men and women may guild their offences, or clothe them in a religious garb, so as to palm them upon the public, yet 'the searcher of hearts' cannot be deceived. The polite and fashionable iniquities of christendom are infinitely more hateful to the God of heaven than any of the vulgar transgressions, and sensuality of dark ages, or savage times. We have among us the counter part of the wickedness which degraded the daughters of Sodom. The 'idleness' is the same, while its guilt because of our greater light and privileges, is of a deeper hue. Woman as we have before observed, was created to be the 'glory of man,' and to make our world a paradise. To neglect her high vocation is not only one of the greatest offences, but the source of almost every evil. Had the wealthy ladies of England attended to their duties, our own country and the world would long ago have been regenerated and happy. What little good has hitherto been affected, has been the work of a handful. Our Hannahs, Deborahs, Marys, Priscillas, Loises, and Eunices have been found only here and there. The great mass of female talent has been dormant, or given to 'the pomps and vanities of this wicked world.' Had it only been used as the Almighty intended it should, there would not have been at this day a vulgar, uneducated man, or a low, ignorant woman throughout the length and breadth of the land. But it has been *unladylike* to be a philanthropists, or imitate the Saviour in doing good! The following quotation is from a distinguished and noble spirited woman, Mrs Chapman,[1] of America.

If we are not enough grieved at the existence of slavery, to ask that it should be abolished in the ten miles square over which congress possesses exclusive jurisdiction, we may rest assured that we are slave-holders in heart and indeed under the endurance of the penalty which selfishness inflicts, – the slow but certain death of the soul. We sometimes hear it said, '*it is such an odd unladylike thing*'! we concede

---

1 Maria Weston Chapman (1806–85), abolitionist.

that the human soul in the full exercise of its most godlike power of self denial and exertion for the good of others is emphatically a very *'unladylike thing.'* We have never heard this objection but from that sort of woman who 'is dead while she liveth' or to be pitied as the victim of domestic tyranny. The woman who makes it, is generally one who has struggled from childhood up to womanhood through a process of spiritual suffocation. Her infancy was passed as a convenience for the display of elegant baby linen. Her youth for a more public exhibition of 'braiding the hair, and wearing of gold and putting on of apparel'; while 'the ornament of a meek and quiet spirit' – 'the hidden man of the heart,' is not deemed worthy the attainment. Her summers fly away in changes of air and water, her winters in changes of flimsy garments, in inhaling lamp smoke or perhaps in drinking champagne at midnight with the most dissipated men in the community. This is the woman, who tells us that it is *'unladylike'* to ask that children may no longer be sold away from their parents, or wives from their husbands, and adds, 'they ought to be mobbed who ask it.' O how painful is the contemplation of the ruins of a nature created a 'little lower than the angels.'[1]

The spirit that in America branded it as unbecoming for females to labour for the emancipation of the slave, has made it unfashionable in England for ladies to employ their powers for the glory of God and the good of man. We know that there are honorable exceptions, but still by far the greater part of female talent that ought to be engaged in the cause of social, intellectual and religious progress, is wrapt up in a napkin and as a consequence the creator is robbed of his service, and shows his displeasure by smiting the fruits of the earth. Why should we have fruitful seasons to nourish men and women who pass their life in luxury and indolence while the world around them is cursed with ignorance, tyranny and impiety?

IV. – In Sodom, *'the hand of the poor and needy was not strengthened.'* The word *'hand'* in scripture stands for *skill*, or *power*. The poor man's *'hand'* is his all. It is his property, his capital, his fortune. Encourage and 'strengthen' it, and he will provide for his household and secure for himself provision in old age, and in doing so will bless all around him. For after all, the reward which he will secure to himself by his labor will be small compared with the immense revenue he will pour into the laps of others. 'The hand of the poor and needy' is God's instrument to produce fruitful fields, comfortable dwellings, healthy clothing, crowded warehouses and well stored granaries for the rest of mankind. The hand of the peasant and operative is one of the most valuable of God's gifts. Our working men and women, the fustian jackets and smock frocks, are the royal and divine almoners of the King of kings. If Jehovah opens his hand to supply our wants, he employs the poor and the needy to gather up and distribute his bounty, just as the son of God gave 'the bread to his *disciples* and the *disciples* to the multitude.' The rich are often spoken of as the benefactors of the working classes, when the reverse is more especially the truth, for the working classes are the agents that provide food, clothing, dwellings and luxuries for the wealthy. All the revenues of the country are earned by the hand of the poor. But for the masses there would be no

---

1 See [Maria Weston Chapman], *Right and Wrong in Massachusetts* (1839), p. 12.

income, robes or palaces for the queen, no mansions or rents for the aristocracy, nor any wares or cargoes for the merchant. We should have neither ships, merchandise nor seamen. Our lords and ladies would have to light their fires, wash their linen, prepare their food, sweep their houses and make their garments and furniture. What tinkering cobbling &c. we should then have in Windsor castle, Claremont, and the duke of Devonshire's! The queen may grant the *patent*, but the despised *artisans, laborers, and domestic servants*, give the *wealth* and the *power* to our dukes and lords, to enjoy the conventional elegance and splendor of the peerage. But for our working people all would be operatives, cooks, washerwomen, &c., &c., &c., and where then would be rank, robes or revenues? Does not nature itself then dictate that '*the hand of the poor and needy* should be strengthened?' Both policy and piety demand it. Indeed, here as in everything, piety would be the highest policy, proving to a demonstration, that those who would separate politics from religion are the enemies of God and man, for while they would rob christianity of the glory of rendering our social institutions equitable, holy and benevolent, they would deprive politics of all stability and revenues which right principles would inevitably confer. The God of heaven honors working men and working women. In willingness and power to toil, providence has conferred on the *fustian jackets and smock frocks* a dignity compared with which crowns are toys and coronets baubles. The celebrated Jane Taylor[1] who was no leveller, tells us, that

> 'A lord and a lady went up in full sail
> When a bee chanced to light on the opposite scale.'[2]

And if an industrious insect possesses such a preeminence, what must be the value of the human laborer?

To give energy to the '*hand*' of the operative, we neither ask for charity bread, charity clothing, charity education, or a *soi disant* charity church. Let pensions, sinecures, and standing armies be abolished – let the aristocracy no longer demand wages for doing nothing – let them keep their hands from the Exchequer, and have nobility enough to abstain from dishonorable pelf extorted from the sweat of the poor man's brow – let taxation be direct, and as a consequence, let the duties on the necessaries, the comforts, the knowledge, or trade of the country be removed – let our intercourse with all other nations be as free as the air we breathe, and as benevolent as the gospel we profess – let the suffrage be extended and the legislature consist of men whose impartiality shall enact equal laws – let the rights and liberties of all be respected and guaranteed – let luxury be restrained, and labor equitably remunerated – let the wealthy classes descend from that inglorious eminence in pride, sloth and extravagance in which they have pinnacled themselves by monopoly, oppression or vanity – let them recognise the brotherhood of man, and imitate him who came from heaven to elevate the masses by his instruction, example and benevolence – let these things be

---

1 Jane Taylor (1783–1824), children's author.
2 See Ann and Jane Taylor, 'A Wasp and a Bee', *Rhymes for the Nursery* (1835), pp. 90–2.

done, and 'the hand of the poor and needy will be strengthened' and the '*potatoe*' and all other '*blights*' will cease for ever.

It may be objected respecting the destruction of Sodom, that it not only punished the proud, luxurious, indolent and oppressive aristocracy, but also lighted upon the poor who groaned under their haughtiness and injustice, and therefore that it violated the great law of universal equity. Our reply is easy. There were not 'ten righteous persons in the city,' and when Lot's house was besieged, 'the *people* came from every quarter.' The masses had sold themselves to the wealthy, had copied their vices and had been their minions and slaves. Probably they lent themselves to be government *spies, soldiers, police puppets* or *hangmen*. They riveted their own chains, and stood ready, like the Croats of Austria, or the abject and ferocious vassals of Russia, to betray and massacre any patriot who denounced tyranny or demanded right and liberty. They may have voluntarily sold themselves to the clergy for a bason of soup, an old blanket or a loaf of bread, and by them have been taught to eschew politics and justice and liberty. They may have neglected public meetings, or allowed themselves to be duped into violence by aristocratical *spies*, and thus have been persuaded by the wealthy to commit crimes which gave a designing government the opportunity of setting the middle and higher classes at variance, and of *hanging*, *drawing*, quartering, and presenting the monarch with the human limbs of the poor fellows whom that very administration had taught to rebel. All these or similar follies and vices, may, and probably did degrade the working classes, and therefore as they countenanced and participated the crimes of their '*betters!*' they very justly fell by the same doom. Physical violence whether employed to perpetrate or to redress a wrong, is hateful to the king of kings. 'He that taketh the sword shall perish with the sword.' Moral power armed with truth, equity, and benevolence is omnipotent, and by these alone can injustice be annihilated and the nations saved.

It will perhaps be said that the facts referred to in this tract ought to have been addressed to the wealthy and the aristocracy, but the author is of a different opinion. 1st, because it would be of little use. Besides as men of education, who call themselves apostolical christians more orthodox than any other persons upon the face of the earth, the rich are not, or ought not to be ignorant. 2d, we want the *fustian jackets and smock frocks* to consider that the evils under which they groan must be traced solely to wickedness and injustice, and that so long as men in high life will devise, and it the other circles will countenance an infraction or perversion of the rights of mankind, providence will employ its benevolent scourge. And 3rdly, until the working classes, men and women become reformers and demand firmly, but rationally and peaceably the correction of all abuses, civil, political and ecclesiastical corruption will scourge the land, and bring down the just indignation of heaven. Our Lord and the prophets always exposed the vices of rulers, priests and hypocrites in the presence of the masses, and experience has long taught, that to give publicity in the ears of the people generally, to aristocratical tyranny is one of the surest ways to terminate its sway. I have not written a single word in condemnation of any good action, or patriotic individual, and I offer no apology for condemning or offending those who 'neither fear God nor regard man.'

The evils we have mentioned are only a few of that '*legion*', which at present insults the Creator and embitters the condition of the poor. One of our most crying evils is 'the national church.' According to high episcopalian authority, out of upwards of TEN THOUSAND PRIESTS, we have more than SEVEN THOUSAND who are 'blind leaders of the blind.' These men are absorbing millions a year to conduct souls to perdition. Here the guilt of a *state hierarchy* throws into the shade all the evils of plague, pestilence, tyranny, and bloodshed put together. The thousands who are annually ruined for both worlds by ungodly ministers beggar description. A million tracts could not depict a millionth part of the abomination. My sentiments on this point must exactly accord with the views of every *evangelical* in the country who is sincere in his creed. Surely we need not be surprised at the potato blight.

On the use of intoxicating liquors I might also enlarge. Thousands upon thousands of bushels of wholesome grain are annually converted into POISONS which destroy the health, the moral character and the comfort of society. Here the *moderate drinkers* are the chief consumers and consequently the principal supporters of this waste of the bounties of providence. Is it any wonder that the Creator should display his indignation?

Of war I have spoken in tracts 6 & 7, – '*The Chief of the Slaughtermen*', and '*The Knife and not the Sword*,' and therefore only remarks here, that our past and present guilt in shedding human blood, or arming ourselves to do so, (and Jehovah takes the will for the deed,) costs us FORTY EIGHT MILLIONS A YEAR. After reading this item of 'the superfluity of naughtiness,' we have just reason to fear that unless we speedily reform, the corn and other fruits of the earth will be smitten.

TO PREVENT the reiteration of divine chastisements, we must repent. The remedy is simple, unique, easy, and in the power of every one. The Lord Jesus is 'exalted a prince and a Saviour to give repentance and remission of sins.' The words of Isaiah are to the point, 'wash you make you clean, put away the evil of your doings from before mine eyes, cease to do evil, learn to do well, *seek rectitude, give right* to the oppressed, *administer justice* to the fatherless, plead the cause of widow; come now,' (on these conditions) 'and let us reason together saith Jehovah, and though your sins be as scarlet they shall be as white as snow, and though they be red like crimson they shall be as wool.'

No. 17.

TRACTS FOR THE FUSTIAN JACKETS AND SMOCK FROCKS.

THE QUEEN,
THE ARISTOCRACY, AND THE PEOPLE.
BY THE REV. B. PARSONS,
OF EBLEY, STROUD, GLOUCESTERSHIRE.

'Take away the wicked from the King,
And his throne shall be established in righteousness,'
The Proverbs of King Solomon.

No people upon the face of the earth have been more constantly, systematically, or ruinously duped than the English, and especially the working classes. The christianity of which we have boasted has been a species of baptized paganism. Under the shout of '*no popery,*' designing politicians and ecclesiastics have concealed crimes and superstitions at which Romanists would blush. These walls of our country were often placarded with tirades against the abolition of the bread tax, intimating that if these ungodly statutes were repealed the *wages* of the laborer would be reduced. The landowners and aristocracy were not ashamed to tell the peasant that they taxed his loaf to enable them to pay his wages. That is, they picked his pocket of pounds and gave him back a few paltry shillings as a compensation! Under the name of education everything is to be done to paralyse the mental and moral faculties of the masses. The government will make the nation pay DOUBLE what it would cost if the people educated themselves, and then mislead them into the belief that the instruction is next to gratuitous! Commissioners hunting for pensions, and pupil teachers seeking for worse than parish pay and actually selling all the attributes of free-born citizens for pelf, are among a few of those blighting influences with which state education will scourge the land. These minions are willing to rivet on the minds of both sexes any fetters which may be forged in high places by the designing and despotic craftsmen of the day. That high church and tory publication, '*the Quarterly Review,*' not long since let the cat out of the bag. In advising Sir Robert Peel how to govern Ireland, it used these very significant words,

'Be to her faults a little blind,
Be to her virtues very kind,

> Let all her ways be unconfined
> And *clap the padlock on her mind.*'[1]

This clapping '*the padlock on the mind,*' is the grand object of governmental tuition; and you have not only the sons and daughters of paupers, but persons of property, and men who once to gain popularity, pretended to be radicals, running a race in this unholy undertaking to enslave the country. There is nothing that *the fustian jackets and smock frocks* have more cause to be alarmed at, than this deep laid scheme of national education. Should it succeed we may begin to toll the knell of liberty, patriotism, and morality. Of course, as in all ages, the state clergy will be the chief promoters of the intellectual and spiritual degradation of the people. The world has too long been priest-ridden and schoolmaster-ridden, and the perfection of this educational stratagem is such that even infidels are duped by it. These used to have their eyes a little open to the corruptions of the day and were not at all squeamish in publishing them, but even our sceptics are asking for *state* interference in public instruction, and thus are lending a hand to blight the dearest prospects of the nation. Nearly every thing among us in the form of politics is so nicely contrived to deceive, that one might imagine that Beelzebub has had to direct our affairs, for the last hundred and fifty years.

Our war tax at present is *forty eight millions*, and we have been taught that this expenditure has been incurred for the purpose of defending the rights and liberties of the nation and the world!! But the reverse is the fact. Not a sword has been drawn nor a ball fired in the cause of freedom. To enslave the operatives of Britain and the Continent, to enlarge the power of despots, or restore them to their thrones, and to provide pay and pensions for an avaricious aristocracy, have been the grand objects kept in view by our destructive wars and extravagant army and navy establishments. Were it not that tyrants universally sympathise with these base designs, we should be the laughing stock of the world. In addition to all our other bonds, our national debt is a chain which for years has fettered our energies and industry and ground the people to the dust. We have actually spent our money and poured out the blood of our brethren for worse than nothing. We have done it to enslave ourselves and others; aye, and have done it in the name of *liberty*! It was well known that patriotic Englishmen would not expend their treasure and their blood in the cause of despotism, and therefore to dupe them the flag of liberty was unfurled, and thus they were practised upon by deep laid deception. By our wars we have plundered, ruined, and murdered millions. There is hardly a land from which the voice of our brother's blood does not send a cry to heaven against us. We are without exception the guiltiest nation that has ever existed, because we have had the bible to teach us better, and yet have been bold enough to perpetrate all this wickedness against God and man in the name of christianity and liberty. Well, the cup has passed round to us, and the injuries we have inflicted upon others are few compared with the scourges we have brought upon ourselves. Our national debt and our standing army, are the just retribution

---

1 Matthew Prior, 'An English Padlock', ll. 77–80.

with which indignant heaven is punishing us for our iniquity and hypocrisy. The other nations, notwithstanding our attempts to enslave them, will rise to be free long before Britain, while the debt we have incurred in our efforts to rivet their chains, will probably remain to enslave our country and our children for many generations. O ye operatives of the land! Ye fustian jackets and smock frocks! when will you open your eyes and look with a clear vision on the delusions by which you are enthralled? Under the pretence of glory they invite you to sell yourselves for a FEW PENCE PER DAY to be the assassins of other nations, but their chief object is to render you a race of regimental puppets, to provide half-pay and pensions for the aristocracy and be ready at a word to massacre your own countrymen if they should demand their rights. Remember if this iniquity is put a stop to you must be the reformers. Many of the wealthy classes have a vested interest in these abominations, others are afraid to stir lest they should lose caste, and our pious people are too spiritual to engage in the purification of this Augean stable, and therefore the hope of the world is vested in you.

There are few greater exceptions than that which is practised under the name of conquest and enlarged empire. Our colonies are a loss, but then of course we must keep them to find places for the sons of our extravagant nobility and gentry. They are refuges for the destitute. The very reverend the dean of St Paul's, the late witty and clear sighted Sidney Smith,[1] has put this matter in a strong light. 'Not only,' he says, 'is economy not practised but it is despised, and the idea of it is connected with Jacobinism, disaffection and Joseph Hume.[2] Every rock in the ocean where a cormorant can be perched, is occupied by our troops, has a governor, a deputy governor, storekeeper, deputy storekeeper, and will soon have an archdeacon and a bishop, military colleges, with *thirty-four* professors educating *seventeen* ensigns per annum, being half an ensign for each professor, with every species of nonsense, athletic, sarterial, and plumigerous. A just and necessary war costs this country about £100 a minute, whip cord £15,000; red tape £7,000; lace for drummers and fifers £10,000; a pension for one man who has broken his head at the pole, to another who has shattered his leg at the equator; subsidies to Persia; secret money to Thibet; an annuity to lady Henry *Somebody* and her seven daughters, the husband being shot at some place where we never ought to have had any soldiers at all, and the elder brother returning four members to parliament: such a scene of extravagance, corruption, and expense must paralyse the industry and mar the fortunes of the most industrious spirited people that ever existed.'[3]

Our colonies according to the speech of Sir W. Molesworth,[4] cost us at least £4,000,000 a year, while our trade to them all, is not worth £9,000,000, so that for every *twenty shillings* received for merchandise, we pay back *nine* in taxes. Our

---

1 Sydney Smith (1771–1845), Canon of St Paul's, essayist and theologian.
2 Joseph Hume (1777–1855), radical MP.
3 *The Works of the Rev. Sidney Smith*, 3 vols (1848), vol. 3, p. 34.
4 Sir William Molesworth (1810–55), eighth Baronet, MP for Leeds 1837, and Southwark 1845.

profit here is a dead loss. Is it any wonder that we have thousands among us destitute of the necessaries of life, when we are thus robbed to find places and pensions for the pauper children and relatives of the aristocracy? It has been customary to bewail the defection of America. Why if our brethren had not declared themselves *independent* they would have been a burden to us to this day. We never had a greater *gain* than the loss of America. In 1844 our exports to the United States amounted to £8,000,000, while our whole consular system there, though infamously extravagant, costs us not more than £15,000. So that to trade with our colonies cost us nearly FIFTY per cent, while to traffic with the independent Americans does not stand us in more than about ONE per cent. We hear a great deal about the repeal of the Union with Ireland, as if some awful calamity would befal us when the real truth is that we should be immense gainers thereby. A nation's greatness does not consist in the extent of its empire, the number of its colonies or dependencies, but in the industry, the happiness, the intelligence and morality of its inhabitants. It is not in subjugating and ruling other lands that its glory consists; but in denying ourselves to give to them the blessings of knowledge, civilization, religion, and peace, that we exalt ourselves and the world at the same time; hence one missionary like Williams,[1] Cary, Moffatt,[2] or Morrison,[3] confers more honor on our country than all the Nelsons,[4] or Wellingtons that have ever lived or all the troops that have watered the earth with their blood. I refer to these facts to illustrate the sentiment with which I commenced this tract that the English people are continually duped with false notions about liberty, glory, &c., &c., and are thus practised upon for the purpose of inducing them to beggar themselves with taxation, and pension, a heartless aristocracy, who pour contempt on the middle and working classes, endanger the throne and trample the laws and the constitution under their feet.

Another fatal delusion is the attempt to persuade the people that the chief cause of our national suffering is the royal expenditure. I believe that any man who will endeavor to inflame the minds of the masses on this subject so as to induce them to rebel, may obtain from certain whigs and tories very ample wages. The spy system of all ages has been the work of the aristocracy. These as regularly as gadflies or any insect of that species live on corruption or the blood of others. If I am wrong in this assertion, I am misled by history and parliamentary documents furnished by the men themselves. Their principle falls very far short of the old pagan of whom Horace[5] speaks whose maxim was,

'Get money! get it honestly if you can,
But at any rate get money!'[6]

---

1 John Williams (1796–1839), of the London Missionary Society.
2 Robert Moffatt (1795–1883), of the London Missionary Society.
3 Robert Morrison (1782–1834), shoemaker, missionary in China.
4 Horatio Nelson (1758–1805), admiral.
5 Horacius Flaccus (65–8 BC), Roman poet.
6 See Horace, *Epistles*, I. i. 62.

There is nothing that these gentlemen think so vile and base and so much below their dignity as to obtain '*an honest penny*,' by honorable labor or trade. It is true they traffic, but then it is in gambling, or political or ecclesiastical corruption, and therefore the nation has to be misled to call that honorable which is dishonorable, and the operatives and peasantry must be goaded on by spies to use treasonable language or employ physical force that a few of them may be condemned to be hung, drawn and quartered, and have their limbs presented to the monarch, and as a consequence their brethren be frightened from demanding their rights, and thus the aristocracy may continue their places and their pensions. It is high time that the fustian jackets and smock frocks should resolve to be deceived no more. Let it be laid down as a maxim, that the man, whoever he may be who utters one word of treason or whispers a thought about physical force or any violation of the laws is a *spy* and a traitor. It is one of the glories of our constitution that every reform which equity, reason, or religion can demand, may be obtained by rational, humane and peaceable means; so that every believer, however pure his creed, or spiritual his frame, may advance his piety and heavenly mindedness by becoming a political and ecclesiastical reformer. Indeed the day is not far distant, when it shall be deemed an impeachment of his allegiance to the Son of God, for a christian to stand aloof from his social duties, and on the other hand, activity in the cause of right and liberty shall be required as an essential criterion of scriptural godliness.

Here, to use a plain phrase, it is only to discover the right scent. It was lately thought that when '*The Crown and Government Security Bill*' was passed, public meetings would be put down and patriots silenced; and we fear that some have actually been frightened by it out of their wits and zeal for liberty at the same time. But there is no danger from this law. It is one of the most harmless things the whigs and toried ever did. Let it only be considered that the *aristocracy* and not the queen, are the cause of all the political and ecclesiastical evils under which we groan, and let the real culprits be exposed and condemned, and then what has any one to fear from this crafty enactment? The English monarch 'can do no wrong.' There is not a ruler or chief on the face of the earth who has less power to injure his country than the sovereign of these realms. We have a deep impression that the President of America has far more power than the governor of Great Britain. Our noble forefathers availed themselves of every opportunity to curtail the royal prerogative and wonderfully succeeded. William the Conqueror was perfectly absolute but his successors have been compelled from various circumstances to yield to the rightful demands of the people. Many of our princes have been usurpers; others have been ambitious, and extravagant, and consequently indigent; while in later years, the title to the crown has been the gift of the nation. Henry the 1st,[1] Stephen, Henry the 4th,[2] Richard the 3rd,[3] &c., &c., had not a shadow of right to the throne, and therefore courted popularity by giving

1 Henry I (1069–1135), King of England 1100–35.
2 Henry IV (1367–1413), King of England 1399–1413.
3 Richard III (1452–85), King of England 1483–5.

up a portion of their prerogative. Richard the 1st,[1] Edward the 1st,[2] Edward the 3rd,[3] Henry the 5th,[4] &c., were ambitious and engaged in expensive wars which rendered it necessary that they should draw largely upon the purses of their subjects, and to obtain funds granted the redress of injuries and the enlargement of liberty. The Houses of Orange, Hanover, and Brunswick, owed their thrones to the popular voice. Now our ancestors were patriotic men and they granted their property, or gave the crown only on condition that the monarchs should limit their own power and enlarge the liberties of their subjects. As a consequence, there is perhaps, not a sceptre in the world so perfectly harmless as the British. Whatever mischief is done is the work of *the ministry* of the day. These are the responsible advisors of the sovereign, and can be impeached for any attempt to infringe the laws or the constitutional rights of the inhabitants. But the ministry depends upon the parliament, hence if we have a *whig* parliament we have a *whig* prime minister and if we have a *tory* House of Commons we then are blessed with a *tory* premier and a whole tail of *tory* dependents. And if we had a majority of *radical* representatives we should be sure to have a *radical* administration. The sovereign of England can do nothing to injure the country without the commons. For if the lords can prevent the commons from doing any good, the commons can prevent the lords from doing any mischief. Were Nero, or Nebuchadnezzar on the British throne his power would be impotent if the commons were really the representatives of the people. Consequently whatever ills we groan under must be attributed solely to the House of Commons. The queen has little more to do with them than the man in the moon. Were our sovereign a seraph she would be powerless to bless us, until she obtained the consent of parliament, and were she a Jezebel, or a Herodias, she could do no harm without the acquiescence of this same lower House. The aristocracy are well aware of this. They know, that they have most unconstitutionally taken possession of the House of Commons, and have done so to enrich themselves from the public treasury. In accomplishing this object they have set every law, human and divine, at defiance. They have used the most unblushing bribery, perjury, and corruption. They have no more right to the House of Commons than the emperor of Russia, or the nobility of Japan, nor could they have obtained their present pernicious influence but by the grossest violation of the statutes of the realm. By their avarice they have again and again put the crown in jeopardy, and now sway an absolute sceptre over the queen and the nation. To maintain these usurpations every trick is resorted to. Spies are sent through the country to use all kinds of violent language, to persuade the masses that the sovereign is the cause of all our grievances and that they ought to fly to physical force and overturn the throne. These miscreants are paid large wages to excite rebellion. By these means the aristocracy hope to frighten the middle classes, to involve the operatives in treason, to get some of them hanged or trans-

---

1 Richard I (1157–99), King of England 1189–99.
2 Edward I (1239–1307), King of England 1272–1307.
3 Edward III (1312–77), King of England 1327–77.
4 Henry V (1387–1422), King of England 1413–22.

ported, to deter the rest from demanding their rights, and thus preserve their own despotic power. They know that if the truth comes out, the blame of bad government rests at their door, and therefore they want to divert attention from themselves to the queen and thus wish her to be the scape goat for their own offences. The fustian jackets and smock frocks must open their eyes to this craft of tyrannical usurpers, and resolve to lay the blame of their wrongs on the guilty agents that inflict them, and these are the aristocracy.

As to the expense of royalty, this is not worth mentioning. Supposing it were a million a year, the cost would be little more than *eight pence* per annum to the whole population or hardly *half a farthing* per week. Surely we need not put our lives in jeopardy for such a trifle. Besides the salary of the monarch is granted by the Commons, and therefore can be curtailed to any extent. Let us not quarrel so much with the queen for receiving, as with parliament for voting exorbitant sums. Here again you have a wheel within a wheel. A great deal of what Mr Cobden has so felicitously named '*the barbaric pomp*' of royalty, is kept up to find places and pensions for the needy sons and daughters of our peers. A large amount of what is voted to the monarch is paid back again to the aristocracy. The court swarms with the scions of the nobility. The queen can hardly look on a disinterested friend at her table or in her drawing room. The noblemen's wives or daughters who dine with the monarch are paid for this hard labour some hundreds a year! Numerous lords about her majesty receive their thousands for *doing nothing* and some of them have *deputies* to help them, who also dip largely into the royal purse for their sinecures. A loyal, or patriotic attendant is hardly known at courts. The majority come for the loaves and the fishes, and would just as soon attend the Pope, the emperor of Russia, or Louis Napoleon, if they could obtain higher wages. These high spirited lords and ladies, look with contempt upon the peasantry and operatives who labor for their bread, and yet they themselves hire themselves out to eat dinners and drink champagne!! Their loyalty is a marketable article and the queen has to pay them very dearly for its exercise. When one looks at it a little closely there is nothing on earth so forlorn as majesty surrounded with a race of smiling sycophants – mere vampires in disguise. How many a king must have felt the force of Byron's words,

> 'And none did love him though to hall and bower
> He gathered assailers from far and near,
> He knew them flatterers of the festal hour
> The heartless parasites of present cheer.'[1]

The comfort of the sovereign, is not in the least increased by these selfish attendants. Indeed many of them must be a perfect nuisance. It may smack of loyalty to vote large sums to the monarch or prince Albert, but nothing was farther from the thoughts of the '*ayes*' who did it. The money was for themselves. They have surrounded the throne with greedy chamberlains, stewards, ushers, grooms, comptrollers, mistresses of the robes, &c., &c., all of them peers, peeresses, or in

---

1 George Gordon, Lord Byron, *Childe Harold's Pilgrimage* (1812–18), ll. 118–21.

some way connected with the aristocracy, and waiting to take as large a sum as possible from the revenues of their royal mistress. Is it any wonder that the nobility and gentry spend a million of money to corrupt the country at a general election? They expect when they have bought up a House of Commons to gain two or three thousand per cent by their bargain. How liberally, as soon as they are comfortably seated, they begin to vote money for the civil list, the army, the navy, the church; for annuities, pensions, salaries, &c., &c., seeing there is not one of these items, out of which they do not expect to obtain an enormous per centage. Let us not then blame the queen. The commons make the grants, and of course do so for the aristocracy who have procured for the majority their places as the *mis*-representatives of the interests of the nation. Give us the suffrage and the ballot and then we shall have a *people's house*, and public expenditure reduced to a rational and equitable standard. Those who now oppress the country are so loyal that they are delighted if they can by means of spies persuade us to lay all the blame upon the monarch. They hope to conceal their extravagance behind her majesty. They place the sovereign in the front of the battle and endeavour to make her their shield. When the fact is, that for every hundred that she receives they absorb thousands.

It may also be said that a better monarch than Victoria never sat on the British throne. We are no flatterers of kings, and the history of royalty in England is far from being the most honorable page of our records. Some of our princes have been a disgrace to humanity. But we believe there are few persons who have one evil thing to say of our present sovereign. The corruptions and errors of her reign, are not chargeable upon her, but upon her ministers. Young and inexperienced she came to the throne, and every '*Mentor*' has been carefully excluded from her presence. The aristocracy feared that she had a benevolent heart and would become popular by swaying a sceptre of righteousness, and have done all they could to render her unacceptable to the country. A monarch that sided with right and liberty would be the idol of the masses and the annihilation of oligarchical tyrants. As far as we can gather the feelings of her majesty from her private deeds, we believe that it may be said without exaggeration or fear of contradiction, that her desire is to be a constitutional sovereign and to rule the people for their good. Surely there is not a patriot in the country who would exchange Victoria, for Mr Polk,[1] General Taylor,[2] or Louis Napoleon. Tell us not that she is a *woman*. We look on this as a decided advantage. Women have as comprehensive minds as men, and far better hearts. A female stoic is a prodigy almost as rarely seen as Halley's comet. Besides the men of this age and especially the generality of the nondescripts that sit in the House of Lords or have places bought for them in the House of Commons are proverbially little minded. A thousand of such souls could dance on the apex of the smallest hair on a mite's back without discommoding one another. And this intellectual pigmyism is not to be wondered at. There is nothing so fatal to mental and moral developement as avarice. Men who

---

1 James Polk (1795–1849), eleventh President of the United States.
2 General Zachary Taylor (1784–1850), later twelfth President of the United States.

run after church livings, commissionerships, sinecures, or pensions have souls infinitesimally contracted. Persons who will sell themselves to shed blood are of a genus that has no type among beasts or demons. We feel confident that a parliament might be elected from the factory girls of England which, with Victoria at their head would govern our country far more equitably and rationally than ever has or ever will be done under the premiership of lord John Russell or sir Robert Peel. It is a blessing rather than otherwise that we have a female on the throne. Indeed there is no view of the subject which will not induce us from our inmost hearts to pray, '*God save the Queen!*' We have said enough to show that our monarch is not the cause of our grievances; that the expences of royalty are comparatively small and entirely under the control of the House of Commons, and that we have at present a Queen who has never yet evinced one desire to oppress her subjects. On the abstract question of a republic and a limited monarchy we have not time here to dwell, but if we had, it would be easy to show that England can be as free, as economical, and as democratic under a king or queen as France or America under a president. If our sovereign were dethroned to morrow, I query whether it would not take us months barring all the turmoil and uncertainty of a public election, to find a single individual who could or would sustain the office of chief magistrate more patriotically, usefully and majestically than queen Victoria. But granted that we could, yet the little advantage that would be derived from a change would be dearly bought by the confusion and bloodshed which would first ensue. It would take us years to recover from such a convulsion.

It has been well said that the English constitution is not 'a *manufacture* but a *growth.*' It has within itself all the elements of improvement, and without the least violence can be matured and perfected. This the aristocracy know, and they perceive further that the only persons who will bring it to perfection are *the middle and the working classes*, and hence their policy always has been to sow discord between these two most important branches of the community. There are not a few who believe that the panic created on the 10th of April, the barricading of the bank, the swearing in of special constables, the calling out of the military, &c., &c., was nothing but a political trick to frighten the bankers, tradesmen, and others, and prevent their amalgamating with the operatives in seeking the redress of our national wrongs. The spy system has revealed some striking facts on the other hand, and have shown what villains there are in the world and how low men in power can sink when they hire such miscreants for the purpose of preventing a great nation from obtaining that justice which the law and constitution guarantee. These things must not be forgotten by the fustian jackets and smock frocks. You can defeat your enemies by their own arms. Never say one word against the queen. Invite all spies and policemen to your public meetings. Beg them to take notes, and by your speeches let them know that you are far more loyal than the aristocracy, and that you have a far greater regard for the property, the peace and prosperity of the country. That you are *really* more loyal and patriotic every one knows. You do not wish to pick the pocket of the monarch or the nation. You only ask for those reforms which would establish the throne, render the sceptre majestic, and give right to all classes of the community. You do not want pensions and sinecures. The grand difference between you and the aristocracy is this. 'They cannot dig' but are *not* ashamed to beg: you are able and willing to dig, but are ashamed to beg, and therefore the patent of true nobility is yours. With these royal principles in your bosoms, why not make them known. Let them be proclaimed from John O'Groat's to Land's End. Publish it far and near that you have no wish to touch the property of any one however dishonorable may have been its source; that you ask for unrestricted liberty for your labor, that you may have a fair remuneration for your work. You are the children of the soil. England is the place of your father's sepulchres. To you it is indebted for its wealth and greatness. Your hard hands have administered to its necessities, and raised it to its present pinnacle of glory, and now you ask, you rationally ask, that you may be free to enjoy your just share of the resources of your fatherland. You who feed others have a right to be fed, you clothe others, even the nobles and the queen, and you have a right to ask that you may be permitted to clothe yourselves. You build mansions for the great and certainly ought to have dwellings in which health will not be sacrificed nor decency outraged. You above all persons in the country ought to be represented in parliament and protected by the ballot. Wealth can always defend itself and therefore has nothing to fear. Rich men who do their duty by their servants, workmen and dependants are sure to be respected. Justice and benevolence are both an impenetrable shield and a diadem of glory. 'For a good man, some will even dare to die.' But the 'poor is despised of his neighbour,' and therefore in every truly civilized and christian land the rights of the laborer would be first attended to and represented.

In demanding the suffrage you have religion and equity on your side; in protecting this right by the ballot, you are also supported by the sanction of revelation; in denouncing the avarice, the injustice and tyranny of the aristocracy, you have volumes of facts as your voucher; you have the outraged constitution of your country as your witness, and the prophets of the most high God as your examples. With these truths before you it would be absurd to utter treasonable language against the queen. She taxes you but a little comparatively and of that little a very great part is absorbed by the men who profess to have voted the money for the express service of her majesty. The monarch does not cost you *half a million* a year, but the aristocracy burden you to the amount of MILLIONS. Our national debt takes from us *twenty eight millions a year*; our army, navy, and ordnance, *twenty millions more*; the church, nearly *twelve millions*; making in all SIXTY MILLIONS per annum!!! Now by far the greater part of this is a tax for the aristocracy. They plunged us into our ruinous wars. By far the greater part of our national debt went into their pockets. We are now paying interest on the millions that have been grasped by them. Our fathers obtained money to enrich the nobility and they have left us to pay the interest on what they borrowed. Our present war establishment is kept up for the peers and their dependents. The church belongs to the lords and gentry. It is one of the greatest deceptions to call it '*the poor man's church*.' After having consecrated a number of drones who cannot pray without a book and cannot preach until they have bought a ready made sermon they tell the government and the nation that the people are becoming '*untutored savages.*' For three hundred years multitudes of these ungodly priests have been taking the public money for doing worse than nothing. Nearly all the ecclesiastical livings are in the hands of the aristocracy. Even those in the gift of the crown are at the disposal of the premier, and the premier though named by the sovereign is really made by the commons, and the majority of the commons are returned by the aristocracy. Here you have again a wheel within a wheel. The whigs and tories have lately found out the folly of keeping asunder, they have perceived that by doing so, they were destroying their own power and strengthening the cause of the people. Our elections prove that they are become one. The difference between whigs and tories is gone for ever and there is no longer any hope from either of these parties. Look at the pension list, the army, the navy, or the church and you will find each of these factions by swarms. By them the queen is reduced to a cypher. No one now asks, who is on the throne? The only question is, 'Who is the prime minister?' Whatever tyranny is practised the premier is at its head, and this personage is generally one of the aristocracy or if not, he has no power unless he surrounds himself by the nobility. By the laws of the constitution, *the minister* may be impeached, but who would undertake that task in our days? The majority of the commons are his aristocratical supporters who have bought their places by bribery, for the very purpose of supporting the premier and as a consequence be able to dip largely into the public purse.

Instead of crying, 'Down with the queen,' the watchword must be, '*Down with the corruption and despotism of the aristocracy.*' To accomplish this glorious consummation, there is no occasion for violence. No insult must be offered to their persons, or estates. But public meetings should be held, lectures delivered, and all the injustice of the lords and their minions be exposed. In emancipating the slaves, we drew not a sword, nor touched a lucifer match. We did far better, we published the enormities of the system, and it speedily fell. So here, we must bring forth in the light of day, the avarice, the meanness, the corruption, the tyranny, the treason, the rebellion of the aristocacy. The mouth of every man, woman, and child should be filled with these facts. It must be shown that there is no dignity or nobility in anything but justice and virtue, and that ducal or royal ancestry cannot enoble a man who robs the public treasury, burdens the nation with taxes or crushes the rights and liberties of the masses. To talk of the philanthropy of the vermin that waste our fields would be more rational than to extol the patriotism of a race of senators who sacrifice their country to their lust of gold. In publishing and condemning such baseness we violate no law human or divine, who injure no virtuous person, we trample no right in the dust. We only demand that the lords shall not rob us of our property, destroy the majesty of the laws or the monarch, nor impoverish and ruin the land of our fathers.

It is brought as an argument against the suffrage, that *property* would not be represented. But property is not represented under the present system. The only thing represented, is the *pauperism* of the nobility. Buckinghamshire has but half the population of Manchester, and yet Buckinghamshire sends *fourteen members* to parliament and Manchester but TWO! London, Liverpool, Manchester, Birmingham, and Leeds, have a population equal to Bedfordshire, Hants, Suffolk,

Sussex, Berks, Bucks, Herts, Cambridge, Dorset, Cumberland, Oxford, West-moreland, Hereford, Northampton, Rutland, north and east Yorkshire, and yet the towns mentioned above elect only *twenty four members*, while the counties and towns in the latter catalogue have ONE HUNDRED AND FORTY TWO!! Why not only the operatives but the middle classes are not represented. There are *forty two pocket boroughs* rated at less than £1,000,000 which have a represen-tation equal to all the great towns in the empire with a rental, exclusive of machinery, of £20,000,000 a year. 'The annual value of rateable property repre-sented by *three hundred and thirty members* is £6,200,000, while the amount represented by three hundred and twenty eight is £78,000,000!' So much for the representation of property!! Here again all is delusion. Property in this country is not represented. The PAUPERISM of the aristocracy is the chief thing attended to. If property was represented the people would have the suffrage, for the *peas-antry and operatives* are the *wealth* of the empire, and therefore that man contradicts himself who pleads for the representation of property and denies to the masses the franchise. But the corruption resorted to by the vaunting christian aristocracy of the empire. Is it any wonder that these men take the money from our pockets to pay *spies*, to persuade the masses to utter treason and fly to phys-ical force. They act thus basely for the purpose of bringing some of them to ruin and deterring others from seeking the redress of wrongs. Without the suffrage, the ballot, shortened parliaments, electoral districts, the payment of members and the abolition of the property qualification, these evils will not be annihilated. But to accomplish this, there must be constant agitation. Let all treasonable lan-guage be avoided, all physical force repudiated, and the middle and working classes unite, and then we shall possess a power which will sweep all these abom-inations from the land.

No. 18.

TRACTS FOR
THE FUSTIAN JACKETS AND FROCK
SMOCKS.

PHYSICAL FORCE AND MORAL FORCE.
BY THE REV. B. PARSONS,
OF EBLEY, STROUD, GLOUCESTERSHIRE.

> 'He shall give equitable laws to the nations
> And shall reason with the multitudes of peoples,
> And they shall beat their swords into ploughshares
> And their spears into pruning hooks,
> Nation shall not lift up sword against nation,
> Neither shall they learn war any more.'
>
> *Isaiah.*

We talk a great deal about *civilization* and *civilized* nations, and yet perhaps not one person in a hundred inquires into the meaning of these terms, and this is particularly the case with the learned, the gentry and nobility. Ask yonder deep read scholar or clergyman the signification, and he will pour forth an inundation of metaphysical circumlocute verbosity, so that a man must be supernaturally gifted in abstruseness to be able to detect any thing under this turbid stream of erudition, I have heard of a wise bishop who had opened his eyes to not a few of the follies of our schools and colleges and discovered that his learning had made him more of a barbarian to the masses, than the masses were to him, and being rather disposed to preach intelligibly, used to take his texts to an illiterate old woman of plain understanding and ask for her opinion of the words, and he generally found that this humble Priscilla was right in her interpretation. So here you may depend upon it that the reputedly ignorant *fustian jackets and smock frocks*, have a far clearer and more correct English idea of '*civil*' and '*civilization*' than the majority of your Oxford scholars. Ask yonder swineherd, weaver or washerwoman the meaning of these terms, and either of these unsophisticated Saxons will tell you, 'that a *civil* person is one who is not *rude* either in his words or actions, that he is distinguished by kindness and will harm nobody.' You might send a clown to college, but a thousand years of drilling in sophistry would be insufficient to rob him so far of the common sense he inherited from his mother, as to make him believe that a man who knocks another down, or shoots him with a pistol or a cannon, is a *civil* or *civilized* individual. The aristocracy, the kings of the earth and many of the ministers of religion, may be duped by such nonsense, but our peasants and factory girls are not so foolish. Poor Elihu Burritt, the learned blacksmith and 'Universal Brotherhood man', was terribly laughed at the other day. He and some of his associates who are so degraded and unchristian as to wish to put an end to bloodshed, had the misfortune to say in one of their publications 'that the *civilized* world was become tired of war.' To be sure what a hubbub there was! That any human being in his senses should ever have dreamt that '*civil*' or *civilized* nations would for the next thousand years become tired of war! Sure the Peace Congress is mad! St Luke's is of course the only appropriate place for such maniacs. O how the *Times*, 'the leading Journal of Europe,' flared up! What eloquence it summoned to the task of exposing such arrant folly and absurdity! The civilized world tired of war! No, not they indeed. Look at '*civil*' and *christian* England spending *twenty millions* a year on bayonets and slaughter-men, and grinding its poor operatives and tradesmen to the dust to obtain the money from their pockets! England knows nothing of peace. For when she cannot shoot the French, the Caffers, the Sikhs, or the Chinese, she keeps up a large peace establishment!! and ruins, beggars, starves, and dooms to premature death myriads of her poor children at home by the burdensome taxes that she extorts from them to support her military extravagance. Thus the work of destruction is always going on in this *highly polite and civil country*! 'War kills its thousands but peace its tens of thousands,' and yet what monster outside the walls of a lunatic asylum would dare insinuate that we are not highly *civilized*? Why not a few of the ministers of the gospel advocate slaughter and when they hear of a battle implore the universal Father and God of mercy to give courage to our soldiers that they may increase the glory of our christian land by sending some thousands of our fellow creatures unprepared into eternity! At the report of carnage, plunder, desolation and death, how sublimely our churches and cathedrals resound with '*Te Deums*!' How anxiously forsooth the angels hasten from their thrones to convey to heaven the souls reeking with revenge and gore who have just sent shoals of their brethren to perdition!! Verily we are civilized with a witness! And besides our own refined christianity, we have the highly civilized French, Prussians, Austrians, as well as the glorious Croats and Russians all delighting in war! and therefore what drivellers these Peace Society scribblers must be to intimate that the civilized world is tired of massacre! Such are in substance the opinions of a Journal which is the great favorite of the nobility, clergy, and many of the gentry. Ask a mill boy the reason why the *civilized* world is not tired of war, and his reply will be, '*because they are not civil or civilized*.' So far a head of the sophistry of the schools is the common sense of our factory girls and peasants. War is brute force and no man who advocates it is civilized. To level our neighbor or enemy to the earth, whether with fist, club, or firelock is not civil except in the Irish sense of the old ballad,

'He meets with a friend and for love knocks him down,
With his sprig of Shelelah and Shamrock so green.'

But very few people think such rough play a good sign either of love or civility. So long as the nations have a single soldier, bayonet, cannon, major, colonel, general, or commander in chief, they can lay little claim to civilization. For you may put all our politeness and gentleness into one scale, and weighed against the barbarism of war, they will appear as the small dust of the balance. Our humanity is the meekness of tamed lions, bears or wolves. Only let the French, the Indians or the Caffers do any thing to provoke us and we stand prepared, with more than a fiendish fury, to blow them to atoms and hurl them to perdition in a moment, and if our vengeance should succeed, are ready to insult heaven by appointing a day of national thanksgiving for the triumph of our cruelty! The world can never be said to be civilized until the words of the prophet shall be literally fulfilled, 'And they shall beat their swords into ploughshares and their spears into pruning hooks, nation shall not lift the sword against nation, neither shall they learn war any more.'

Here the pioneers of practical civilization must be our working men. The nobility will not take the lead. There is hardly a noble family in the country but has apprenticed several of its sons to learn the art of war. Many of the bishops and clergy are quite willing that their children should pollute their hands with blood provided they may at the same time dip them into the national purse. These successors of the apostles are worse than Judas. That arch traitor had sufficient conscience left to induce him to cast away the bag that contained the price of blood but these shed the blood and keep the money which was received as the wages of slaughter. Few men have been more cruel or depraved than the chief priests who hired the false apostle, and yet even these were afraid to keep in their possession 'the thirty pieces of silver' but our modern churchmen are quite in ecstacies when they learn that their families are enriched by this inhuman traffic in carnage. Not a few of our tradesmen, merchants, manufacturers and professional men keep a vulture's eye upon the army and navy. They do not like for their sons to obtain an honorable living by weaving cloth, spinning cotton, or dealing either wholesale or retail in such trash, and therefore they speculate in commissions, crouch to the prime minister, and to gain his smile, sell the dearest rights of their country, in the fond hope that their relatives may make their fortunes by shooting the poor Africans, the Hindoos, or the Chartists. And then they have the audacity to call this avarice of slaughter and pelf 'patriotism.' And the dandies who are dressed up like footmen or Wombwell's Menagerie attendants, and wear livery for which every poor woman that drinks a cup of tea has to subscribe, strut about our streets like bantam cocks, go to church and say prayers in regimentals, and in common conversation embellish almost every sentence with oaths and blasphemy. 'To swear like a trooper or a dragoon' is a proverb of long standing founded on a well known fact. Depend upon it, a time is coming when the dress of a sweep or scavenger, aye of a pauper or common beggar will be deemed far more honorable than the taudry trappings and blood stained paraphernalia of these desolators of their species. But you may be sure that period will never arrive until the fustian jackets and smock frocks shall take up the matter. You must resolve that your sons shall not sell themselves to shoot their brethren for *thirteen pence* a day. The patrons of war want your hard earnings and your precious lives. They demand your children to shoot or be shot, and your money to pay them. Never imagine when your boy is entrapped to be a soldier that you have freed yourself of a burden. The nation has not only to find him food and clothing, but to give enormous sums to the scions of nobility who profess to look after him, and these funds, be it remembered are chiefly taken from the hard earnings of the operatives. Set your faces then against physical force in every shape and form. War may be called courage but it is the courage of brutes. It would be far more rational to erect monuments in St Paul's or Westminster Abbey over the cocks that have died fighting in a cockpit, or the dogs that have been killed in a bull fight or bear garden, and to inscribe on the marble that 'THEY FELL GLORIOUSLY WHILE CONTENDING AGAINST THEIR FOES,' than to engrave such inhumanity over the tomb of an ambitious, paganized christian who died in the guilty effort to rob a fellow immortal of life, and entered eternity and appeared at the bar of heaven foaming with rage, thirsting for revenge, and covered with his own blood and that of a brother who had never done him any harm. If you set your face against arms, and teach your children to abhor war, there will be no troops, and our ministers instead of defying and provoking other nations, or misgoverning their own subjects, will act pacifically towards the French, Americans, &c., and will be compelled to proceed justly at home. As soon as you refuse to furnish simpletons to be corrupted in a barracks, converted into machines by military despotism, and slaughtered like beasts on the battle plain, all this cruelty and barbarity will come to an end. They cannot do without you. Tyranny cannot be tyranny, despotism cannot be despotism without you. You are the tools with which they work. And therefore as I have repeatedly said in my former Tracts, you must be the principal reformers. The hope of the country and the world is vested in you. The nobility will not reform abuses. They fatten upon them. Corruption is the food on which the majority of the aristocracy of all ages feast and live. Our merchants will not come forward as a body. Many of them hope soon to be numbered with the nobility whose vices they delight to ape. The majority of the ministers of religion are too *spiritual*, or too *worldly*, to seek the redress of our wrongs or lift their voices against war. The tradesmen in too many instances are afraid to speak out. They stifle their convictions to save their wealthy customers. There is nothing that our gentry, clergy, and nobility hate so cordially as an independent and conscientious man. All who obtain their smile must purchase it by being slaves. We boast of having emancipated 800,000 West Indian Negroes, but we have millions among the middle classes at home held in bondage by the church and aristocracy. And though their taskmasters cannot use the cartwhip or the stake, yet with more refined cruelty they would *starve* their victims to death if they dared to be *men* by daring to be free. You then, – you, – the fustian jackets and smock frocks, are the patriots that must perfect the reformation. None of the other classes can do without you. You furnish them with servants, operatives, mechanics, and laborers. You drive the shuttle and the plough; you dig the ground, excavate the tunnel and work the mine. The fields would be barren, machinery would rust, and capital be at a discount but for you. You are all in all to the prosperity of the land. Remember your dignity and act worthy of it. Put an end to war by refusing to fight and you will do more to *civilize* the nobility, gentry, clergy, and government than has ever been effected by our colleges or the priesthood. The aristocracy cannot slay and devour without you. You give the bear his talons and the lion his teeth. Deprive them of these instruments of death and they will become harmless as lambs and will be as distinguished for fawning as they have been for avarice.

But you must not only disdain to be the physical force tools of tyrants, you must resort to no violence yourselves. The beasts of the forests are distinguished for brute power. Many of them have muscle and nerve far beyond any of our race, and yet there is not one of them but has succumbed to man. We can harpoon the whale, rein the horse, tame the elephant, yoke the reindeer to our car, and bind the tiger, the wolf and lion. The eagle cannot fly too high, nor the shark dive too deep for our grasp. God has given us 'dominion over the fowls of the air, over the fish of the sea, and over every living thing that moveth on the earth.' 'Every kind of beasts and of birds and of serpents and of things in the sea is tamed and hath been tamed of man.' The very elements obey us, each human being may say, –

> 'I can command the lightning and am dust!
> A monarch and a slave! a worm, a god!'

And not only beasts, but men more savage than the brute creation, can be subdued by reason. In man we have all the ferocity and poison of the animal world, blended with the malignity of fiends; and yet man has not merely been tamed but rendered a seraphic and godlike being. Still this was never effected by physical force. The soul cannot be taken by bullets, nor regenerated by bayonets or brick bats. Here argument, reason, justice, and benevolence are the only successful arms.

> 'Lions and beasts of savage name
> Put on the nature of the lamb.'[1]

But this happy transformation has never been effected by violence or in the battle field. It would be as rational to seek the Graces in a Menagerie or pandemonium as in the field of war. There every vile passion revels, and the furies exult. Malice begets malice and rage enkindles rage, so that physical force is impotent for any purpose but that of engendering evil. If the foe that we injure lives, he lives to hate us more intensely, and if we slay him, he dies unreformed. But moral force appeals to justice and heaven, and thus with irresistible authority rebukes the wicked and not unfrequently extracts his malignity, saves the enemy and converts him into a friend. The following considerations should induce us at once and for ever to repudiate every appeal to force or arms.

I. – Physical force is barbarous and cruel. It consists entirely in inflicting injuries on the bodies or substance of our enemies. We belabor them with blows, pierce them with wounds, or commit some depredation on their property. In

---

1 Isaac Watts, 'The Power of the Gospel', l. 17.

acting thus we degrade ourselves to a level with brutes or savages. The elephant can use his trunk, the bull his horns, the lion his teeth, and the scorpion his sting, but neither of these can *reason*. The Vandals could lay countries waste, sack and burn cities, trample every right in the dust, and massacre the people. To achieve such mischief a human soul is hardly needed. The less of intelligence, feeling and conscience the better. Hence in our land, soldiers are never drawn from the moral and enlightened classes. Only the more hardened, thoughtless, dissipated and depraved enlist. The barracks are schools of every thing which is low, vulgar, sensual, and adapted to pollute the mind and brutalize the heart. If you want a specimen of the dark ages, go to the barracks, if you would have the most melancholy spectacles of the degradation of our species, go to the barracks. And this must be so, so long as we delight in war. Civilized and merciful men would not sell themselves to learn the art of murdering their fellows. The soldier is not sought to perform any thing humane or philanthropic. His whole work is desolation and death. He is the savage, the Goth, the Vandal, the Turk of a barbarous age in the midst of the schools and benevolent institutions of a more enlightened period. Learning and christianity have done little for him. Eighteen hundred years of gospel truth has passed over his head without eradicating his barbarism. When at rest he wallows in sloth and sensuality, and when in active service his noblest exploits consists of plunder, massacre and desolation. Whatever good follows the war is effected by negotiation, and this could much more easily have preceeded the carnage, and would have done so, had not the instigators and directors of these murders been as heartless as the poor dupes whom they have employed as the implements of their cruelty. And not only the soldier, but the professed patriot or reformer who flies to arms is an enemy to his species and a traitor to his own cause. To demand a right at the end of a pike or the mouth of a cannon is a demonstration that we are entirely disqualified for the work we have taken in hand.

II. – The employment of *physical force* proves that we are as cruel and unjust as the enemies with which we contend. It is supposed that they have done an evil on the one hand and we therefore commit an equal, or a worse piece of injustice on the other. The crimes are consequently the same, or if there is any preponderance it is on the side of those who avenge themselves. The chief difference is only that of priority. My enemy has knocked me down and I imitate his brutality and knock him down in return. He has set me a bad example and I follow it or perhaps exceed his violence. The French or Americans have offended us and we take the most tremendous vengeance. Their supposed delinquencies convert us into savages. The deeds of Nelson and Wellington during the last war might make Nero or Tamerlane[1] blush. Is it any wonder that God has forsaken the majority of our preachers or that christianity languishes among us, seeing so many of the ministers of the sanctuary approve of this carnage and slaughter roll back the tide of liberty and civilization? Say the aristocracy or any other oppressors have injured us and we resolve to wreck our malice on their persons or property, to set

---

1 Tamerlane (*c.* 1336–1405), Mongol leader.

fire to corn stacks, to burn mansions and manufactories, or thrust pikes into the hearts of our foes, by such rage and madness we prove that we are just as vile as our opponents, and were we placed in their stead should most probably have exceeded their injustice.

III. – Physical Force never has done any good. All the nations of antiquity depended on the sword and they all fell. Egypt again and again has been overrun and to day is among the basest of the kingdoms. Nineveh and Babylon, the empires of Alexander and the Cæsars are no more. Where is the dominion of Attila,[1] Tamerlane or other ambitious despots who built all their hopes on brute violence? What have the nations of Europe gained by their wars? The French revolutions have been characterised by nothing so strikingly as by the appeal to arms, and vengeance has fallen with seven-fold fury on the heads of the monarchs and nobles who taught their subjects to set little value on human life. As for ourselves, we are blessed with a debt of nearly EIGHT HUNDRED MILLIONS, with a degraded soldiery, a vicious and tyrannical aristocracy, a corrupt military House of Commons, and a cruel priesthood ready to invoke the dogs of war. Such is the result of our valor! Our liberties are in jeopardy, our trade and commerce incalculably injured, our poor people crushed to the ground with taxation and many of them actually dying of want! These are a few of the good things for which we are paying nearly FIFTY MILLIONS a year. What too, may we ask, has ever been gained by civil war? The man who is not more willing to suffer than to inflict an injury in the cause of liberty is unworthy of emancipation. Did the Newport riots gain any thing for the masses, or have any of the outbreaks since that time had any other effect than that of throwing back the cause of the people? With the history of the world before us we maintain that violence from the days of our Lord until now has never won a single advantage for the human family.

IV. – Physical Force cannot reform any one. All social and moral evil is in the soul and therefore cannot be eradicated by swords and staves. Bludgeons, blunderbusses, and artillery cannot teach. No heretic was ever convinced by being burnt, no insurgent was ever reformed by being hung, nor any aristocrat rendered humane by the incendiary. You may employ the sword to mow down one race of tyrants, but another will immediately spring up to take their places. How often Rome changed its Emperors. How many were dragged to the guillotine in France, and yet their successors were no better than those who had been executed. The Jews of old slew monarch after monarch, but the man who obtained the vacant throne almost invariably 'walked in the ways of Jereboam the son of Nebat who taught Israel to sin.' The fact is, it is not in the nature of physical violence to eradicate moral delinquencies. We may brutalise ourselves and others by such iniquities, but not a reform will ensue unless we employ nobler remedies than the match, the firebrand, the sabre, or the cannon.

V. – By *Physical Force* we treat men as if they were beasts, and seem to forget that in every human being there is a living soul, a divine principle, which can be appealed to, instructed and reformed, and that no one is too far gone in crime or

---

1 Attila (*c.* 406–53), King of the Huns 434–53.

injustice to be reached and reclaimed by the voice of reason and religion. The moderns have discovered that even brute animals can be governed far better by gentleness than by blows. Flogging is found out to be a sorry cure for rebellious soldiers or sailors. Prison discipline of late years has assumed a more humane form. We have fewer stripes and better tuition. And the age of reason has dawned upon maniacs and lunatics in consequence of a milder and more rational treatment. Physical force is only suited to brutes and even there the less the better. The advocates of war treat mankind as if they were dogs, asses, or wild beasts, and wish to thrash them or shoot them at pleasure. The thing is perfectly aristocratical. Our nobility have generally looked with disdain upon the masses and treated them as the lower orders of creation, created to bear burdens, pay taxes, and be bastinadoed or massacred at pleasure. And led by such august examples, we need not wonder if some of our operatives, especially when inflamed by government spies, should occasionally have resorted to physical force for the redress of their wrongs. But by whomsoever employed, violence is as unmanly and irrational as it is unjust and cruel. Mankind were created to be influenced, not by cartwhips, bludgeons, scimitars, pikes or cannon, but by reason and persuasion.

VI. – For the masses to employ *Physical Force* is to strengthen the hands of their enemies. Nothing would please the aristocracy so much as a thorough insurrection of the working classes. The late chartist trials have shown how anxious many of the patrons of bad government were for an outbreak. How delighted they would have been to have had the nation put under martial law, to have called out the troops to fire upon the men who asked for the constitutional redress of our wrongs. Parliament might then have been summoned, '*Habeas Corpus*' suspended, the Cobden agitation prohibited and large pensions awarded to the starving sons of the nobility. Remember that the man who utters one word about physical force is a Goth and a traitor, and most probably is in the pay of the aristocracy, and ought to be shunned as a tory minion or government spy. Physical outrage never has and never can effect any good for the people. 'They that take the sword shall fall by the sword.' One of the grand excuses for keeping police establishments and standing armies is the supposed disposition of the people to resort to violence. Let this charge be practically confuted by the pacific conduct of the masses, and let there be a full exposure of the injustice under which the nation groans, and a firm demand for constitutional right and equity, and all the jobbing of the gentry and nobility in the trade of war must come to an end.

But while *Physical Force* is brutal, barbarous, useless, and in the last degree impotent, and impolitic, *Moral Force* is humane, rational and omnipotent for all the purposes of reform. By Moral Force we appeal to reason and equity. Our sword is that of the Spirit and with it we pierce the inmost soul. Our enemies cannot stand against it. The apostles by moral force assailed the various existing superstitions of the day, and had their professed successors followed their example, the world would long ago have enjoyed a millennium of brotherhood, liberty and peace. The Son of God used nothing but the force of persuasion, equity, benevolence, and a holy life to establish his religion. The achievements of this mighty principle are so numerous and glorious that volumes would be insufficient to enumerate its triumphs. In our own day it has performed wonders and has failed in nothing that it has resolutely taken in hand. It abolished the Slave Trade and Slavery in our Colonies. It carried the Reform Bill, and Catholic Emancipation, repealed the Test and Corporation Acts, the East India Monopoly, and the Bread Tax. There is nothing that can stand before it. The voice of reason, justice, and benevolence is the voice of God, and it would be as easy for rulers to dethrone the Eternal as to prevent the final success of any principle founded in equity. Let the masses arm themselves with moral force and their cause is triumphant. It can obtain the Suffrage, the Ballot, Annual Parliaments, Equal Electoral Districts, the payment of Members, and the Abolition of the Property Qualification. It can separate the Church from the State, abolish our standing Army and Navy, and with them all Pensions and Sinecures. It can reduce the extravagant salaries of our Prime Ministers, Chancellors, &c., &c. In fact there is not an evil or abuse in the country but must fall before the people when armed with the majestic, irresistible and divine energy of *Moral Force*. And what is still more cheering, every man, woman, and child in the land can gird themselves with this omnipotent power. It is the wish of the God who made us, and the Saviour who died for us, that we should be thus equipped. Christianity is a radical religion intended by our Creator to eradicate every thing that wars with the rights of mankind, and had its own ministers faithfully proclaimed its doctrines and morality we should long ago have been delivered from every social wrong. As the priesthood has been unfaithful, let the Fustian Jackets and Smock Frocks lift their voices. It is one of the deepest stratagems of priestcraft to assert that only episcopally ordained ministers have any right to propagate the gospel. It was well known that these would be silent respecting the political and social corruption of the age and therefore if left to them that it would flourish unmolested. Away with this doctrine of devils. Assert your rights, call public meetings, expose the injustice of the state and the heresies of the church. Never utter one word of treason against the laws or the monarch. The Premier, the Aristocracy and the Commons are to blame for your wrongs. Meet often, meet in large numbers, invite the police and government spies to attend. By the peaceable and equitable character of your assemblies set your foes at defiance and by the irresistible energy of Moral Force you shall save your country and bless the world.

With this Tract I shall for the present close the series. Want of time and various pressing duties prevent, or I had intended to bring out in full relief the Radicalism of *Job, David, Solomon, Isaiah, Jeremiah, Ezekiel, Daniel,* and those other unflinching reformers, *the minor prophets*. The radicalism of the virgin Mary, and of all the New Testament writers would afford materials for volumes, and prove that the religion of the scriptures contains in the fullest sense of the word, 'the *People's charter.*' Perhaps at some future time I shall return to these subjects. Nothing has been more productive of infidelity and irreligion than the support which many professing christians have given to despotism, and the apathy with which others beheld its desolating influence. To show the working classes that God our Maker and Christ our Saviour sympathise with them in every struggle to obtain their rights was one object I had in view in writing these Tracts, and I am happy to know from the many communications and thanks which I have received from all parts of the country that I have not written in vain. I could fill pages with these flattering extracts, but I shall confine myself to the following from that distinguished clergyman, the Rev. Thomas Spencer,[1] late Perpetual Curate of Hinton Charter House, near Bath. The bold truths which this gentleman has enunciated in his very Popular Tracts, and especially in his last entitled, *'Justice for the industrious classes,'* and *'the Evils of undue Legislative interference,'* impart no common degree of weight to his commendation.

Ainslie's Belvidere, Bath, Dec. 30th, 1848.

My Dear Sir,

Mrs Spencer has just finished reading to me your Tract on *'The Queen, the Aristocracy, and the People.'* I thank you for it, I am delighted with it. Of all your Tracts this seems most adapted for extensive circulation throughout the kingdom. Your congregation ought to organize themselves and taking Ebley as a centre, each person according to his ability ought to procure from 100, 500, or a 1,000 and leave one in every house, village and town in the neighborhood extending as far as their energy and ability will enable them. You have to the greatest nicety expressed my views respecting our good Queen and bad Aristocracy. If you feel any difficulty in urging your congregation to second your noble efforts and circulate their pastor's christian sentiments send them this letter and let the request come from me a disinterested looker on.

I remain my dear Sir, yours faithfully,
THOMAS SPENCER.

The Rev. B. Parsons.

Ainslie's Belvidere, Bath, Jan. 9th, 1849.

My Dear Sir,

When I wrote last I had only read your Tract, 'The Queen, the Aristocracy and the People.' This morning, Mrs Spencer has read aloud to me *'The Potatoe Blight,'* part 2, with which I am extremely delighted. This is our mission to vindicate the Bible from false and fashionable protestantism and bring it forth as glad tidings for the industrious classes and as a comfort to men of toil and oppression and at the same time 'the two-edged sword' with which they may effectually contend and ultimately defeat their oppressors. Were the Church of England such as I could desire, I should be glad to see you occupying the pulpits of our large parochial churches and declaring the whole counsel of God, to a people who never hear more than a part, and that part only such as is favorable to the existing order of things. Clergymen whose brothers or sons are in the army will no more see the spirit of peace which pervades the gospel than the slave owning clergy of South Carolina will see the passages in their bibles which condemn their holding their fellow creatures in bondage. Men who live upon the taxes and get fat upon the National Debt will not only oppose our efforts to seek justice for the masses, but they would oppose even though one rose from the dead to contend on our side, and they would try to put to death this new champion of right as their predecessors tried to put to death Lazarus, not because they did not know of the miracle, but because they did know

1 Revd Thomas Spencer (1796–1853).

and hated him the more on account of the powerful testimony his very existence bore in behalf of the truth.

I am my dear Sir, yours very faithfully,
THOMAS SPENCER.

The Rev. B. Parsons.

I have quoted thus largely from Mr Spencer, because the judgment, patriotism, and piety of that gentleman render his testimony and approbation of more weight and value than that of ten thousand of the common clergy or aristocracy.